Enterprise Intelligence

Bridging the Gaps between Wisdom, Business Intelligence, Knowledge Graphs, and Artificial Intelligence

Eugene Asahara

www.technicspub.com/ai

Technics Publications
SEDONA, ARIZONA

115 Linda Vista
Sedona, AZ 86336 USA

https://www.TechnicsPub.com

Edited by Sadie Hoberman

Cover design by Lorena Molinari

All rights reserved. No part of this book may be reproduced or transmitted in any form or by any means, electronic or mechanical, including photocopying, recording or by any information storage and retrieval system, without written permission from the publisher, except for brief quotations in a review.

The authors and publisher have taken care in the preparation of this book, but make no expressed or implied warranty of any kind and assume no responsibility for errors or omissions. No liability is assumed for incidental or consequential damages in connection with or arising out of the use of the information or programs contained herein.

All trade and product names are trademarks, registered trademarks, or service marks of their respective companies and are the property of their respective holders and should be treated as such.

First Printing 2024

Copyright © 2024 by Eugene Asahara

ISBN, print ed.	9781634624510
ISBN, Kindle ed.	9781634624527
ISBN, PDF ed.	9781634624534

Library of Congress Control Number: 2024935892

In memory of Garret Asahara, 1964-2024.

Contents at a Glance

Prologue _____ 1

Chapter 1: Introduction _____ 7

Chapter 2: BI in the Era of ML, DS, and AI _____ 41

Chapter 3: The Intelligence of a Business _____ 67

Chapter 4: Knowledge Graphs _____ 93

Chapter 5: Data Catalog _____ 129

Chapter 6: Business Intelligence _____ 149

Chapter 7: Data Mesh _____ 163

Chapter 8: Architecture of the AEI _____ 197

Chapter 9: BI-Charged EKG Components _____ 225

Chapter 10: Special Structures _____ 329

Chapter 11: Implementation _____ 361

Chapter 12: Future Steps _____ 459

Conclusion _____ 477

Appendix: Ontologies & Taxonomies in OOP Terms ____ 481

Glossary _____ 483

References _____ 495

Index _____ 497

Contents

Prologue _____ 1
   The Intelligence of Humanity _____ 1
   LLMs are ML Models _____ 2
   Business Intelligence _____ 3
   You Got AI in My BI! You Got BI in My AI! _____ 4
   Putting the 'I' Back into BI _____ 5

Chapter 1: Introduction _____ 7
   The Puppeteers of an Enterprise _____ 7
   Fragmented Knowledge _____ 10
      Can a Single Entity Know Most Things About Most Things? _____ 11
      Beyond Traditional BI Analysts and Managers _____ 13
   What Do Human BI Analysts See? _____ 14
   The Big Gap Between Human and Machine Intelligence ___ 17
   AI Gone Viral _____ 18
   My Research Assistant, ChatGPT _____ 19
   My Feeling About AI _____ 23
      David and Goliath _____ 24
      We Think Because We Are _____ 26
   The Book's TL;DR _____ 28
      Could a Private LLM have Written this Book? _____ 31
      ChatGPT's Visual Representation for this Book _____ 31
   The Book Structure _____ 33
      Topics Punted to Future Books in the Series _____ 34
      Query Languages other than SQL _____ 34
      Non-Time Series Conditional Probabilities _____ 35
      Bayesian Probabilities _____ 36
      Functions _____ 36
      Linear and Non-linear Regression _____ 37

The Many Ways to Talk to an LLM — 37
Digital Twins — 38
Frightening Things: Code and Math — 39
Striving for Vendor Neutrality — 39

Chapter 2: BI in the Era of ML, DS, and AI — 41

Even an R&D-Focused Enterprise is still an Enterprise — 43
My BI Misunderstanding — 44
Encoding Knowledge — 44
  It's Like Books but Looks Like Tinker Toys — 46
  Expert Systems and the Semantic Web — 48
[Diverse Human Expertise] + ((KG + LLM) + BI) = AEI — 49
Intuition for this Book — 51
  Version 1—SQL Server Performance Tuning Web (ca. 2004) — 53
  Version 2—Map Rock (ca. 2011) — 60
  Version 3—Augmented Enterprise Intelligence (Present) — 62
  KG Development with LLM Assistance — 63
  The Puppet Looks More Lifelike — 65

Chapter 3: The Intelligence of a Business — 67

A Business is as an Organism — 67
  The Brain: A Centralized Repository of Knowledge — 68
  EKG versus Conventional Databases — 69
  Humans as Components of the Business Organism — 70
  Survival of the Smartest? — 72
Business Intelligence, Performance Management, Process Management — 72
Too-puhls (Tuples) and Dataframes — 76
Embracing Complexity — 79
  Novel Solutions to Novel Problems — 79
  Tell Me Something of Value that I Don't Already Know — 80
  We Don't Know What We Don't Know — 81
  Tribal Knowledge: Most Understanding is Trapped in the Heads of Individuals — 82

But Things Somehow Work _____ 83
Sampling of the Incalculably Large Knowledge Space of an Enterprise _____ 83
A Rockhound Analogy _____ 84
Widening Breadth of Data _____ 85

LLMs Opened Floodgates for Inclusion of Unstructured Data _____ 86
The Unstructured Data Majority Unlocked with AI _____ 87
AI Quality and Acceptance Hit a Critical Mass _____ 88
Very Book Smart, Although a bit Lacking in Common Sense … For Now _____ 89

The Ubiquitous Time Dimension _____ 90

Conclusion to The Intelligence of a Business _____ 91

Chapter 4: Knowledge Graphs _____ 93

Symbiotic Relationship between KGs and LLMs _____ 94
The Elusive Knowledge Graph _____ 94
The KG and LLM Symbiotic Relationship _____ 96
Mitigating Friction Between Human and Machine Intelligence _____ 99

Knowledge Graph Foundations _____ 100
The Effort to Create KGs _____ 102
Nature of Representation _____ 104
Probabilistic versus Assertive Knowledge _____ 104
Interactivity and Dynamic Responses _____ 104
Complementing Each Other _____ 104
LLMs Queries can be slow compared to more traditional database queries _____ 105
Trustworthiness and Verification _____ 105
Regulation _____ 106
Cost _____ 107
The Sweet Spot of LLM Ability for KGs _____ 107
LLMs are Very Far from Six Sigma! _____ 108

Ontologies and Taxonomies _____ 109
Relational Models are Ontologies _____ 111
Ontology Example _____ 113

Knowledge Graph Artifact Sources _____ 118

Feasibility of Developing and Maintaining KGs _____ 119

Semantic Web and KGs _____ 121
   Semantic Web, RDF, SPARQL, and OWL _____ 121
   Semantic Layer versus Knowledge Graph _____ 123
   Enterprise Knowledge Graph (EKG) versus Knowledge Graph _____ 123
   Node Identifiers _____ 124
KG Users Ontology _____ 125
Conclusion to Knowledge Graphs _____ 126

Chapter 5: Data Catalog _____ 129

The Ontology of the Databases _____ 131
Data Catalog Foundations _____ 133
   Semantic Layer and Data Fabric _____ 134
   RDF-encoded Data Catalog _____ 135
   Retrieving Metadata _____ 136
   URI for Tables and Columns _____ 137
OLAP Cubes in the Enterprise-Scoped Data Catalog _____ 138
   Source to Target Mapping _____ 140
   Database Views as Abstractions _____ 142
"Lowly-Curated" Data _____ 143
   Data from Partners, Vendors, Customers _____ 144
   The Value of Questionable Data _____ 145
   Ad-hoc Data _____ 146
Non-BI Data Left on the Cutting Room Floor _____ 146

Chapter 6: Business Intelligence _____ 149

Benefits of Traditional BI _____ 152
   Highly Curated _____ 152
   Highly Performant _____ 153
   But My BI Seems Fast Enough _____ 153
   Federated Databases _____ 154
   Kyvos Insights Cloud-based OLAP _____ 155
   User-Friendly _____ 156

BI Users 156
Traditional BI Users 156
Knowledge Workers - Massive Expansion of BI Consumers 157
AI Agent 158
Append-Only Data Strategy in Business Intelligence 159
Visualization Tools 161

Chapter 7: Data Mesh 163
Expanding the Reach for BI 164
The Centralized BI Team Bottleneck 165
Decentralization of BI Effort 166
Data Governance Team 168
Data Products 169
Data Product Service Level Agreements (SLA) 170
Data Products Per Domain 170
But Wait, Aren't LLMs Monolithic Models? 172
Data Mesh, Data Fabric, Data Catalog, and Semantic Layer 173
Optimized Cubes as the Consumer-Facing Semantic Layer 177
The KG Use for Data Mesh 179
Knowledge Bog 181
KG "Data Products" 181
OLAP Cubes as Data Products with Coherent Bounded Contexts 183
Distributed Construction of the KG in the Data Mesh Paradigm 184
Data Products for Mappings 186
Master Data Management 187
RDF Mapping 187
Automated Similarity Mapping with LLMs 188
Database-Derived Ontologies 191
KG Update Tracking 193
KG Update Exceptions 193
Art Gallery Ontology Creation Example Using Protégé and GitHub 193

Chapter 8: Architecture of the AEI — 197

Architecture Overview — 197
Development Tools — 200
- GitHub — 200
- Visual Code — 202
- Ontology Composition Tools — 203

Databases — 203
- Data Warehouses, Data Marts — 203
- Graph Databases — 204
- Relationships Only—But Know Where to Find the Information — 204
- Graph Database Options — 205
- Neo4j — 207
- Optimized cubes — 209
- IT Manager's Nightmare — 209
- Optimized Cubes Make a Comeback — 210
- SQL Server Analysis Services and Kyvos — 210
- Pre-Aggregation for Consistently High Query Performance — 213
- The Unique Cache of Pre-Aggregations — 213
- Navigating the Vast Cubespace — 213
- Big Data Systems and the Expanding User Base — 214
- Kyvos: Beyond Aggregation to Aggregation Management — 214
- The Balanced Approach of the Dimensional Model — 214
- The Critical Nature of BI Data — 214
- End-User Perspectives: The Persistence of Cubes — 215
- Enhancing Analytical Speed with Optimized OLAP — 215
- High Query Concurrency — 217
- The Two Extremes of Cubes and Graphs — 219

Large Language Model — 220
Private Vector Database — 221
Relational Database — 223
Cloud File Storage — 224

Chapter 9: BI-Charged EKG Components — 225

- Why Go Through the Trouble of Storing BI Insights? — 226
- Guided Exploration with the ISG and TCW — 227
  - Navigating with Intuition versus Guided Systems — 227
  - The Value of Collective Exploration — 228
  - Finding Indirect Pathways versus Direct Correlation — 228
- Big Brother? — 229
- Events — 230
  - Sources with a Plethora of Events — 233
  - Derived Events — 234
  - The Event Ensemble — 235
  - Generalized Schema for Events — 235
  - Event Ensemble in a Mosaic of Cubes — 239
  - Event Ensemble Integration — 240
  - Avoid Copying Massive Numbers of Facts — 242
  - Event Storming as a KG Kickoff — 243
  - Event Storming as a Periodic Sanity Check — 244
  - A Simple Event Storming Example — 245
  - Ask ChatGPT to Organize the Event Storming Session — 248
- Rare Events and Risk Management — 251
- The Insight Space Graph — 254
  - The QueryDef Object — 256
  - A KG of Dataframes — 257
  - Dataframe Individuals — 257
  - Spaces — 259
  - Physical Space — 260
  - Data Space — 261
  - Cube Space (Semantic Layer) — 262
  - Insight Space—the Final Frontier — 265
  - Business Intelligence Insights — 268
  - Line Graphs — 270
  - Bar Charts — 272
  - Pie Charts — 272

Stacked Bar Chart	272
Scatter Plots	275
ML Model Visualizations	279
Models	280
ML Models Built from a Dataframe	280
Business Rules	280
ML Models are Business Rules	282
BI Analyst AI Use Cases	284
Contextual Information Delivery	284
Guided Exploration	285
Enhanced Data Analysis	287

The Tuple Correlation Web — 288

Time	288
Time Events	289
The "Social Network" of Tuples	290
Putting Old Myths and Legends to the Test	292
Correlation Algorithms	293
Bayesian Probabilities	293
Conditional Probabilities	295
Pearson Correlation	296
Spearman Correlation	297
Pearson Correlation Example	299
Transforming to Stationary Values	302
Plotting the Rolling Average Correlation	303
Correlation Parameters	304
Determining Lag for Cause and Effect	304
Time Series Intervals	305
Casting a Wide Net	306
Intelligent Query Patterns	308
Actionable Insights	310
Detective Query Pattern	311
The Coach Query Pattern	312
The MacGyver Query Pattern	313
Stressing the Correlations and Probabilities	315
Confounding Correlations	316

    Obvious Correlations … 317
    Ask the Experts (the KG) … 318
    Why not just ask ChatGPT? … 318
    Coefficient of Variation and Slope … 320
EKG Analysis … 322
    Object Schema … 323
    Objects Dimension Table … 324
    ObjectLog Fact Table … 324
    Object Archive … 325
    Users Schema … 325
    User Validation Table … 326

Chapter 10: Special Structures … 329

KPI Strategy Map … 329
    Compact Smarts … 332
    The Theory of our Corporate Strategies … 333
    Gaming KPIs … 333
    KPI Correlation Score … 334
Bayesian Belief Networks and Causal Diagrams … 336
Business Process Knowledge … 338
    Simple AI-Assisted Strategy Map Example … 339
    Refining the Workflow … 341
    Limitations of Encoding Knowledge … 344
Trophic Cascades in the TCW … 345
Time Series ISG Models … 349
    Time Series Inflection Points … 349
    Frequency Domain Analysis … 353
    Minimum Data Points … 353
    Spectral Components … 354
    Component Similarity … 355

Chapter 11: Implementation 361

Environment 361
Set Up the KG and DC Environment 364
Create a Sample Ontology 365
Load the Data Catalog 369
    Retrieve Data Catalog from SQL Server 369
    Upload Data Catalog into the EKG 370
Processing BI Queries into the ISG 371
    Query Parsing and Saving 372
    Reusable Components 375
    Filter Components 377
    Set Components 377
    Tuples Components 378
    Query Functions 381
    Uploading to the ISG 383
    Tuple Correlation Example 392
    Web of Pearson Correlations and Conditional Probabilities 397
    Conditional Probabilities 398
    Tuple-Level as Opposed to Conditional Probability Table for Conditional Probabilities 400
    Conditional Probabilities versus Pearson Correlations 402
    Conditional Probability Example 405
    Casting a Wide Net–Pearson Example 407
    Casting a Wide Net with Conditional Probabilities 410
Retrieval Augmented Generation 412
    RAG Intuition 416
    Self-Reflective RAG 418
    Vector Database 419
    Leveraging Neo4j GDS for Embedding Management and Similarity Analysis 423
    Offloading Vector Tasks to a Vector Database 424
    Prompt Enrichment 425
    Query the TCW like a Social Network 430
    Query the ISG like any Other Ontology 432
    Graph Query Intent Templates 433

CONTENTS • xi

    LLM API _____ 437
  Maintenance _____ 438
    Updating the KG _____ 439
    Updating of the TCW and ISG _____ 439
    Batch Updates for KG Data Products _____ 440
    Pruning the ISG and TCW _____ 442
    Re-query with Fast Optimized OLAP _____ 444
    QueryDef Count Settles Down on its Own _____ 445
    BI Consumers with Widely Diverse Focuses _____ 447
    Compelling Statistics Model _____ 447
    Time to Live _____ 448
    AI Pruning _____ 449
  Minimal Relationship Options _____ 449
    Turning off Features _____ 449
    QueryDef Identifiers _____ 450
    Conditional Probability Table _____ 451
    Offloading to a Relational Database _____ 451
    Off-Loading to a LLM _____ 452
  Security _____ 452
    Securing BI OLAP Cubes _____ 453
    Securing the Graph Database _____ 454
    Securing the Data Catalog _____ 455
    Securing the ISG/TCW _____ 456
    Securing the Vector Database _____ 456
    Securing Ourselves from the LLM _____ 457

Chapter 12: Future Steps _____ 459

  Fine-Tuning LLMs with BI Data _____ 460
  Inference _____ 461
    Inference on the Semantic Web _____ 462
    Subgraphs and Paths _____ 463
  Metrics at Scale _____ 465
  Where Does Data Science and Machine Learning Fit In? _____ 467

    Investment and Sacrifice 469
        No Pain, No Gain 470
        Levels of Pain 471
        Running the Process 473
        Conclusion to Investment and Sacrifice 475

Conclusion 477
Appendix: Ontologies and Taxonomies in OOP Terms 481
Glossary 483
References 495
Index 497

Figures

Figure 1: Fragmented versus Fully Integrated intelligence. 8
Figure 2: The roles and knowledge domain expertise that build data analytics. 10
Figure 3: BI analysts across the heterogeneous mix of domains. 12
Figure 4: What do analysts see in typical data visualizations? 14
Figure 5: Simple visualization of data. 16
Figure 6: Forcing a square peg into a round hole. 20
Figure 7: Why do you struggle? 20
Figure 8: An honest response. 20
Figure 9: Three major Components of the EKG. 30
Figure 10: ChatGPT's take on the primary theme of this book. 32
Figure 11: It's intriguing that the LLM aspects look like the neocortex. 32
Figure 12: The pieces of a bridge between data and human analysts. 45
Figure 13: Text description of a computer programmer. 47
Figure 14: Tinker Toy (KG) form of the paragraph in Figure B-2a. 47
Figure 15: ChatGPT is broad and versatile, offering a reasonable explanation to my random question. 48
Figure 16: The five big rocks fill the bulk of the proverbial space of this book. 51
Figure 17: Sample of a decision tree for SQL Server Performance Tuning. 52
Figure 18: Sample of trade-offs related to SQL Server Performance tuning. 55
Figure 19: A semantic network linked to the SQL Server performance tuning trade-offs. 56
Figure 20: A partial view of the web of trade-offs in SQL Server. 57
Figure 21: Business Problem Silos. 61
Figure 22: High-level view of what comprises the AEI. 62
Figure 23: Prompt for generating SQL Server troubleshooting map. 64
Figure 24: Partial output of Cypher code for SQL Server troubleshooting map. 64
Figure 25: Cypher creating a chain of metrics and how they relate. 64
Figure 26: SQL Server troubleshooting map. 65
Figure 27: Tuple versus dataframe. A dataframe could be thought of as a set of "like" tuples 78
Figure 28: The three major components of the EKG. 92
Figure 29: Focus on the KG's role in the AEI. 93
Figure 30: A LLM prompt asking for help in creating a KG of a dental office. 97
Figure 31: Partial response generated by ChatGPT of the Cypher code. 98
Figure 32: A basic ontology specifying the roles in a dental office. 98
Figure 33: ChatGPT response to a complicated question. 102
Figure 34: I don't think the performance of GPT-4 is 30 times greater than GPT 3.5. 107
Figure 35: A dimensional model schema is an ontology. 111
Figure 36: Very high-level sample ontology, dental office. 115
Figure 37: More detailed dental practice ontology. 116
Figure 38: The addition of individuals moves from ontology to knowledge graph 117
Figure 39: Ontology of knowledge graph concepts presented in this book. 122

Figure 40: Ontology of Users. 126
Figure 41: The role of the data catalog in the AEI. 130
Figure 42: Structure of the data catalog. 131
Figure 43: DC and KG mapping. 132
Figure 44: vCard mapping of address concepts. 137
Figure 45: Dimensional model schema that is the foundation of cubes. 140
Figure 46: A lineage of three layers of schemas for an OLAP Semantic Layer. 141
Figure 47: The BI components of the EKG. 150
Figure 48: Parts of a SQL GROUP BY query—the bread and butter BI slice and dice pattern. 162
Figure 49: Traditional, centralized ETL->DW. 166
Figure 50: Decentralized Domain Data Product. 168
Figure 51: Balance of Domain-level and Enterprise Governance levels. 169
Figure 52: How data fabric, data catalog, semantic layer, and data mesh fit together. 174
Figure 53: AI and IoT make current (non-data mesh) DW flow very crowded. 178
Figure 54: Data mesh applied to distributed KG development. 182
Figure 55: Prompt for an analysis of similarity. 190
Figure 56: ChatGPT's analysis of the similarity between a muscle car and a hot rod. 190
Figure 57: Ask ChatGPT to offer "just one number, please." 190
Figure 58: Ontology of an art gallery. 194
Figure 59: Knowledge graph. End result of the tutorial, art_gallery_ontology_starter.ttl. 195
Figure 60: Ontology of Shows developed and maintained by the Events domain. 195
Figure 61: Combined ontology. 196
Figure 62: Full architecture. 198
Figure 63: Pre-aggregation for query-time performance. 216
Figure 64: Explore all over the cubespace. 217
Figure 65: Concurrently processing many BI queries. 218
Figure 66: Cubes and Graph DB on two extremes. 219
Figure 67: OLAP cubes and Graph DBs differences. 220
Figure 68: A kaleidoscope of events that happen in the world. 232
Figure 69: The role of the Event Ensemble. 236
Figure 70: Events fit to a four-item tuple. 237
Figure 71: Event Ensemble simplified schema. 238
Figure 72: Event Sub Cube appended to a mosaic of cubes. 240
Figure 73: A simple domain schema. 241
Figure 74: Map Flights to Objects and Locations. 241
Figure 75: Map Flight Delay types as Event Types. 242
Figure 76: Map FlightDelays to abstracted Event. 242
Figure 77: The recognized events from an Event Storming session. 245
Figure 78: Model of events through an Event Storming session. 247
Figure 79: A representation of the Domain Model in a form readily understood by non-programmers. 248
Figure 80: Prompt to ChatGPT with the image. 249
Figure 81: Appearance of the events in the EKG. 250

Figure 82: Example of a prompt to ponder the possible effects of a rare event. 251
Figure 83: Rare Events, Effects, and Mitigations drafted by ChatGPT. 252
Figure 84: ISG high-level schema in the EKG. 255
Figure 85: How a QueryDef is referenced. 257
Figure 86: The four levels of space leading to Insight Space. 260
Figure 87: Too-puhls are coordinates of a multi-dimensional space. 263
Figure 88: A set of tuples. 264
Figure 89: Insights from dataframes. 269
Figure 90: Stacked Bar Chart. Good for composition. 273
Figure 91: Matrix of similarity between a few of the stores. 273
Figure 92: Good candidate for visualizing as a stacked bar chart. 274
Figure 93: The stacked bar chart query as implemented in the EKG. 274
Figure 94: Scatter plots of clusters with very many members. 276
Figure 95: Magic Quadrant. 277
Figure 96: Recording all members assigned to quadrants. 277
Figure 97: Visualization of a Decision Tree. Analysis of actions for players in "Cluster 9" 280
Figure 98: SWRL example of a class. 281
Figure 99: Example of Business Rule, Stock Value percentage recommendation, linked to the DC. 283
Figure 100: KG information linked to the database member, Item.class.Whiskey 285
Figure 101: Unseen Points of Interest providing hints as to what to do next. 286
Figure 102: Configure a SQL filter from the wide and diverse EKG. 288
Figure 103: "Social Network" of Tuples 292
Figure 104: Bayesian Probability. 294
Figure 105: Example of conditional probability calculation. 295
Figure 106: Example of a Pearson vs Spearman calculation. 298
Figure 107: Closing stock price for MSFT and NVDA, July 2022 through July 2023. 299
Figure 108: MSFT versus NVDA closing stock price. 301
Figure 109: Two halves of scatter plot. 302
Figure 110: Percent Day to Day Change of MSFT and NVDA. 302
Figure 111: Rolling correlation between MSFT and NVDA daily stock close. 303
Figure 112: Analysts using BI through to the TCW. 308
Figure 113: Confounding correlation. 317
Figure 114: Ask ChatGPT about correlations between seemingly unrelated events. 319
Figure 115: ChatGPT's response to the question of seemingly unrelated events. 319
Figure 116: Possible path between oil prices in China and water consumption in Brazil. 320
Figure 117: RDF/OWL created by ChatGPT. 320
Figure 118: Properties of a Pearson Correlation. 321
Figure 119: Object Dimensional Model. 323
Figure 120: Example of a BI dashboard. 330
Figure 121: Example of a Strategy Map. 330
Figure 122: Partial Strategy Map with KPI Correlation Scores. 336
Figure 123: ChatGPT prompt to explain the process of how fluoride reduces cavities. 340

Figure 124: ChatGPT's explanation. 340
Figure 125: Graphical representation of how fluoride combats cavities 341
Figure 126: Prompt to create a start to a KG of a restaurant. 342
Figure 127: Workflow of a restaurant. 342
Figure 128: Intriguing and surprising web of cause and effect. 346
Figure 129: Time series inflection points–insensitive 350
Figure 130: Time series inflection point–sensitive. 350
Figure 131: A major event for Microsoft on January 23, 2023. 351
Figure 132: Major event for Microsoft on April 25, 2023. 351
Figure 133: SQL to the Stocks database and the Inflection Points. 351
Figure 134: Inflection point model as a model of a QueryDef in the ISG. 352
Figure 135: Fourier dominant frequency in ISG. 356
Figure 136: The three dominant frequencies for Monsanto, 2005-2008, shown in Figure 135. 357
Figure 137: Raw numbers for MON 2005 through 2009. 358
Figure 138: Cycles for INTC daily closing price during the 2005-2008 timeframe. 359
Figure 139: Comparison of residual, original, and aggregated dominant frequencies. 359
Figure 140: Frequency of 0.004965 is shared by many stocks. 360
Figure 141: The Selected Development and Infrastructure products. 362
Figure 142: Basic stocks ontology. This is just stocks1.ttl. 366
Figure 143: URI (RDF ID) of one of the stocks. 366
Figure 144: Protege UI for appending ontologies to another ontology 367
Figure 145: AMZN after adding CEOs (stocks2.ttl) and a corporation taxonomy (stocks3.ttl). 367
Figure 146: Ontology and taxonomy data are merged into one graph. 368
Figure 147: Microsoft entity properties. 369
Figure 148: Portion of the data catalog from my local SQL Server instance 370
Figure 149: The entire data catalog from my SQL Server instance. 370
Figure 150: High-level steps from BI data to knowledge graph. 371
Figure 151: SQL and dataframe are parsed and stored to files as a staging area 372
Figure 152: A SQL is converted into a QueryDef node in the EKG. 373
Figure 153: This is the detail of the SQL from Figure 9-12 is uploaded to the EKG. 374
Figure 154: Filter, Set, and Tuple are reusable across many QueryDefs. 376
Figure 155: A Set is a subclass of a QueryDef. 378
Figure 156: Tuple is a kind of QueryDef—a QueryDef of just one row. 379
Figure 157: Difference between a QueryDef node and a Tuple node. 381
Figure 158: Two Queries related through calculations 382
Figure 159: QueryDefs can be related through the parameters of query functions. 382
Figure 160: Text files loaded into the KG. 383
Figure 161: The starting SQL and the detailed end result in the KG. 384
Figure 162: Statistics on TotalProdctCost for SalesTerritory 6 and 7. 385
Figure 163: Standard Statistics models for different z-scores. 387
Figure 164: Outliers for TotalProductCost with a zscore_threshold of 3.7. 388
Figure 165: Product 312 is an outlier for TotalProductCost with a z-score of 3.98. 389

Figure 166: The common Filter used by two different queries is shared. 389
Figure 167: A view of how tuple nodes fit in for outlier models. 390
Figure 168: Tuple read as Freight for PromotionKey 1, ProductKey 361, linked to DC objects. 391
Figure 169: Examples of reusable sets of members. 392
Figure 170: Two queries, select a tuple from both to correlate. 393
Figure 171: The left SQL it looks in the EKG. 393
Figure 172: The right-side query as it looks in the EKG. 394
Figure 173: Time series based on both queries. SalesTerritoryKey=9 and ProductKey=311. 395
Figure 174: View of the two time series. The inverse correlation is pretty clear. 395
Figure 175: Representation of the correlation between two tuples in the TCW. 396
Figure 176: Table of Pearson correlations between the day over day % change in the close price of selected stocks from June 25, 2022 through June 24, 2023. 397
Figure 177: The correlations shown in Figure 176 as a TCW. 398
Figure 178: Conditional probabilities between a short list of stocks. 399
Figure 179: Graphic of the Conditional Probability web-based on the data in Figure 178. 399
Figure 180: Combined relationships of Pearson (Figure 177) and Bayes (Figure 179). 400
Figure 181: Tuple-Level Conditional probabilities. 401
Figure 182: Minimum illustration of encoding conditional probabilities with conditional probability tables. 402
Figure 183: Difference between Conditional Probabilities and Pearson Correlations. 403
Figure 184: Probabilities of a big stock price change meeting a minimum probability threshold of *0.40*. 405
Figure 185: Mini Bayesian Network of probabilities. 406
Figure 186: Wide Net cast for correlations. 407
Figure 187: Four strong correlations from Casting of a Wide Net. 408
Figure 188: Details of one of the correlations. The numbers reference back to Figure 187. 409
Figure 189: Further details not shown in Figure 188. The numbers reference back to Figure 187. 409
Figure 190: Cast a wide net on the probability of a big stock move based on another stock. 410
Figure 191: Conditional probabilities are different the other way around. 411
Figure 192: High-level view of where BI and the EKG fit into a RAG process. 415
Figure 193: Example of vector embeddings. 420
Figure 194: Example of embeddings. 420
Figure 195: Example of an ISG QueryDef object's vector embedding. 421
Figure 196: Similarity between three text statements. 422
Figure 197: Process for searching the vector database for similarity matches. 423
Figure 198: High-level idea of RAG using the EKG and BI. 428
Figure 199: Process for determining the intent of an NLP question. 435
Figure 200: Sample of a directory of query intent templates. 436
Figure 201: Sample of a Query template. 436
Figure 202: Solutions to Profit as implemented in the EKG. 471
Figure 203: Levels of pain. 472
Figure 204: The Monte Carlo process. 474
Figure 205 - This is how all of the pieces fit together into an Augmented Enterprise Intelligence. 477

Prologue

The Intelligence of Humanity

In the burgeoning field of artificial intelligence, large language models (LLM) like ChatGPT have suddenly emerged as a remarkably compact encapsulation of human knowledge. Trained predominantly on massive catalogs of human-generated text, these models have derived their understanding from what has historically been the most authentically intentional form of knowledge encoding: our published books, documentation, articles, blogs, websites, and research papers. Passionate experts painstakingly craft these documents to capture their knowledge for others to consume.

Written text embodies purposeful specificity. Humanity's corpus of text is not created from the proverbial infinite number of monkeys randomly typing for an infinite amount of time. It is a deliberate attempt of sentient humans to curate the complexity of our experience into precise information, mirroring the intention behind most human communications. These writings may not be entirely correct nor entirely unbiased. But for the most part, they are written with the genuine intent of conveying information from one sentient mind to all other sentient minds.

Without such authentic intent, why would anyone go through the trouble of materializing writings originating from the synapses of our brains into such a profoundly different format of information? Believe me, I asked myself that question every day while writing this book.

> *Although pictures are worth a thousand words and video is worth more than a thousand times that, they are more open to interpretation than text. Even our brains translate the symbols and relationships we see in pictures and witness in video into language (for most of us, anyway). When communicating with others, we transform what we've seen into that syntactically tighter, more succinct form. It's that form, language, we use to share information directly with a friend or write an article to share it with everyone.*

The capabilities of LLMs didn't evolve from dust as our organic society has. It builds off our collective artifacts of knowledge over the history of humanity. That is, from a massively distributed system of billions of independent intelligences—each person individually, and our higher-level organizations. Those higher-level organizations are our enterprises—our schools, businesses, clubs, governments, and their agencies.

LLMs integrate knowledge from our collective writings into yet another encoded format. A LLM is a reduction of terabytes of writings into a massively dimensional set of vectors. The high-dimensional vector format of LLMs resembles the synapse network of our brains more than our synapse network resembles our written text.

LLMs are ML Models

LLMs are a very massive neural network, a kind of ML model. LLMs aren't that different from the more familiar ML models built by data scientists (DS), which the general public has lived with over the past 15 years. Those are the models we're used to that recommend movies we might like or identify spam emails. Instead of building models from databases of movie purchases and a corpus of emails (emails that are spam and not-spam), LLMs are built from a corpus of written text. The big difference is that a LLM model is magnitudes more robust than a decision tree or regression model.

Although the output of a LLM is hugely more profound and robust than the identification of spam email, it really is just a prediction machine, too. In a nutshell, LLMs predict the next word in a sequence of words (a sentence in the process of being built)–in the correct context, which means no more mistaking a computer mouse for the animal. In fact, the work of Jeff Hawkins speaks of the brain itself as a prediction machine.[JH1]

The prediction of the next word by LLMs is so profound to us because language is how we communicate with each other–even conversations with ourselves that go on in our heads. We wouldn't be what we are if we couldn't communicate with each other in such a high quality.

However, many ML models, including LLMs, incorporate human feedback in some manner. It may be from results incorporated later into a model retraining. Or lately, there is reinforcement learning (RL), where neural networks learn from feedback. Essentially, humans provide feedback on a prediction presented by an ML model. For example, in ChatGPT, we're presented with a thumbs-up and thumbs-down button to indicate the quality of its response. We're sometimes shown two responses and asked to pick the better one. These are "human-in-the-loop."

> With that said, even with the success of LLMs, the whole of humanity is still the foundation of understanding for humans. Humanity is a massively distributed system of sentient and sapient beings, each of us forged within a quilt of intricate cultures and the collective knowledge of thousands of years of history, and each physically exploring a different chunk of the space of human possibility.

Business Intelligence

Beyond that rich human-generated corpus of text is the massive volumes of data we capture in our databases. The epitome of the bridge between information embedded in those databases and our human understanding is the decades-old art of business intelligence (BI). BI is the realm of tens of millions of subject matter experts (SME) and analysts across all of our world enterprises—most of whom have never published a book or even an article nor starred in a conference presentation posted on YouTube. Their vast and intimate knowledge, trained through years of real work, has escaped the training of LLMs.

BI dovetails with this concept of the authentically intentional knowledge used to train LLMs. The data that makes it into the BI data sources is highly-curated. Only relevant data with analytical value is selected. We drop seemingly irrelevant data and correct questionable data. What data makes it into a BI data source is:

- Cleansed. Cleaned up like a feral dog or cat being prepared for adoption.

- Optimized for speed of thought retrieval. Answers to queries are returned quickly before the train of thought is derailed.

- Terms are presented in less jargony, intuitive ways.

- Data attributes are organized in a way conducive to analytical query patterns.

This curation is a very tedious and painful effort, even for very smart practitioners. But they do it because effective communication between databases and people in this data-driven world is paramount to a successful enterprise.

However, BI is not just about collecting and presenting data in reports. It's about analysts mining for actionable information, usually in a purposeful, methodical, investigative process. So, the queries of BI analysts and the way data is visualized for the presentation of insights are highly thought out, information-dense actions. Furthermore, BI analysts throughout enterprises are highly diverse in knowledge, as the corpus of humanity's writings comes from a wide diversity of authors of different times, places, and experiences.

Each data source brought into an enterprise ecosystem carries intrinsic value, underscored by its acquisition cost and continued storage. BI analysts, in their quest to glean insights, mirror the intent of authors and researchers. They seek to uncover truths hidden within data, drawing parallels to how books and articles aim to impart truthful, well-curated content.

The actions of BI professionals are genuine and targeted, much like how authors of books and articles strive to present well-researched, accurate information. This parallel extends to BI data itself, seen as a highly-curated asset within the business environment. Every piece of data, every figure in a BI report, is a snippet of a larger story, much like sentences woven into the fabric of a compelling narrative.

You Got AI in My BI! You Got BI in My AI!

Long ago, the ad campaign for Reece's Peanut Butter Cups was around two guys, one eating chocolate and the other eating peanut butter, bumping into each other, and mixing their treats. At first, they were angry at each other, but tasted the mixed treat and found the whole was magically greater than the sum of its parts.

The richness of BI data presents such a unique opportunity for enhancing the performance of LLMs, and vice versa. Just as LLMs learn from the structured, intentional nature of written text, they can also benefit from the specificity and relevance of BI data. This data, reflective of real-world business activities and decisions, is grounded in business practicality and factual accuracy.

From the perspective of a human BI analyst, think of a LLM as conversations with colleagues and subject matter experts and think of accessing BI systems as akin to what our senses witness in the world.

Incorporating BI insights into the utilization of LLMs can enhance the "understanding" of LLMs in regard to real-world applications. LLMs can learn to recognize patterns and correlations that are only evident in the practical realm of business operations. Such an integration could lead to more informed, accurate predictions and analyses, substantially raising the performance of a wide range of business scenarios in a way where the whole is greater than the sum of its parts.

The convergence of authentically intentional knowledge from writings and the specificity of BI data offers a symbiotic enhancement to the capabilities of LLMs. As we continue to train these models with diverse data sources, their potential to understand and interact with our world in meaningful ways grows exponentially. This fusion of human intellect, captured in written form and through business activities, paves the way for a future where AI models like LLMs are not just tools but collaborative partners in our ongoing quest for knowledge and insight.

And how many works that didn't seem correct or relevant and highly trolled in the past turned out to be right? Or vice versa. How many scientific observations were thought to be merely interesting at the time of observation but later a profound innovation? Similarly, when BI analysts view visualizations, some nuggets of information aren't of interest or perceived relevance to that analyst in that context. But personal irrelevance doesn't mean an insight isn't valuable. At some other time, for some other analyst, for some other reason, that insight might just be the key to the breakthrough.

Putting the 'I' Back into BI

This is a book on "applied AI," the application of AI in a BI setting–not AI itself. The tagline on my blog site had long been "putting the 'I' back into BI." That's because BI had mostly degraded into what I lovingly call "glorified reporting." Integrating across a system requires tremendous effort to reign in rules and processes into an abstracted higher perspective from which we glean insights towards the optimization of our systems. This is all done while the qualities of the system are a moving target, or at least under pressure to evolve in an ever-evolving world.

For well over two decades, BI has been our existing system for analysts and managers to maintain at least more than a rabbit-hole sized view of widespread enterprises. However, there is a wide chasm between where our BI systems present data to us and the processing of that information using our human analytics and subject matter expertise. The quality of the AI that burst onto the scene of the general public about a year ago promises to bridge that gap, leading to a more organic, life-like quality of what is currently the heartless soul of an enterprise.

While the notion of OLAP cubes, NLP, and even what I present here (which is cutting-edge at the time of writing) might seem a bit outdated, it's important to remember that LLMs are as helpful as they are because they are "fuzzy"—and that is a double-edged sword. As the old adage goes:

> *Q: What is the **best** thing about computers?*
> *A: They do exactly what you tell them to do.*
> *Q: What is the **worst** thing about computers?*
> *A: They do exactly what you tell them to do.*

Unlike the computer programming we've lived with for decades, where we're in control of every single thing through programming code, the "thought process" of LLMs is opaque to us and rather non-deterministic. We have indirect control over it. In regard to LLMs, the little joke above can be rephrased:

> *Q: What is the **best** thing about LLMs?*
> *A: They respond in a very robust manner.*
> *Q: What is the **worst** thing about LLMs?*
> *A: They respond in a very robust manner.*

What is proposed in this book is to adopt and merge the best of both worlds. That is, machines that can do the same thing billions of times very quickly, at scale, with few errors—combined with our versatile intelligence that can adapt to an ever-changing world whether at timeframes of second to second, year to year, or epoch to epoch.

The notion of traditional BI is not (yet) being superseded by AI. Nor should it be allowed to—at least until we've lived with it for a few decades. The course of further AI development is unpredictable. This book takes the approach of substantially accentuating BI with LLMs. In fact, it is similar to how machine learning and data science accentuated BI over a decade ago.

Chapter One

Introduction

While LLMs like ChatGPT may not yet be pioneering theoretical physics or formulating groundbreaking mathematical theorems in the vein of an Einstein or a Newton, they possess a level of intelligence that is both reliable enough to be very useful and extremely broad. In the context of this book, they can excel at translating complex human analytical queries into machine-understandable formats like SQL or even Python—a level of sophistication that makes these models invaluable tools for bridging the human-machine intelligence gap in business intelligence applications. Moreover, their "wide but not overly deep" intelligence is exceptionally well-suited for enhancing knowledge graphs (KG), adding nuanced properties to objects and facilitating mappings between similar entities, thereby enriching the analytical capabilities of an enterprise.

LLMs can promote flow from all reaches of an enterprise, which has been hampered by the difficulty in conforming concepts across a wide breadth of domains. By robustly bridging small gaps, LLMs can promote the dissemination of information from far reaches of an enterprise to other far reaches.

The Puppeteers of an Enterprise

If businesses were people, they would lumber about in a vaguely purposeful manner like zombies. That's due to the top-down, military-style hierarchies of modern corporations that result in the integration of information mostly at the high "30,000-foot" level and only to limited domain-level scopes below.

Imagine a puppet maker such as Geppetto, the CEO (external puppet master) of Pinocchio. Pinocchio's movements are directed by Geppetto pulling strings, resulting in actions that are mechanical and somewhat unnatural. In contrast, when Pinocchio becomes a real boy with a fully integrated mind, his actions are fluid and natural. He navigates and grows in life more effectively with this direct, seamless control than through the fragmented, detached, indirect, delayed, and imperfect commands of Geppetto.

Figure 1: Fragmented versus Fully Integrated intelligence.

This isn't a criticism of how businesses are run today. Business enterprises are well beyond the capability of a single person, or even a small group of people, to control it to the level that the enterprise appears "lifelike." However, taking performance management and process management to the next level supplements what is needed to achieve that "lifelike" movement in an enterprise. Businesses obviously have succeeded, executed top-down from a command center (Geppetto's brain) as opposed to the distributed, networked intelligence of the parts (Pinocchio's "live" brain). Businesses have produced valuable goods for their customers, met targets, supported the livelihood of employees and investors, and innovated. But most businesses don't make it, and for the ones that do, there was a lot of luck along the way. Sometimes they make it in spite of themselves and eventually do die.

BI is supposed to provide the information required for decision makers to make better decisions. Although BI made significant impacts towards that goal, it still hasn't quite made businesses look more like a world-class scientist or athlete than the lumbering zombie. So AI comes to the rescue? Or does it?

It's about more than simply more data.

Reflecting on the big data era, a common shortfall was that projects often resulted in underwhelming outcomes. This was not due to a lack of data but rather a lack of effective analysis and implementation. More data often led to information overload rather than actionable insights.

Contrasting this with the success of current LLMs (e.g., ChatGPT 3.5, Llama 3), it's evident that these models thrive on extensive datasets. However, the relationship between data volume and model performance is more nuanced than simply "more data equals better performance." Big data primarily focuses on storing and retrieving vast volumes of data. LLMs, on the other hand, are about processing and understanding that data. The analogy is akin to education: more years generally lead to greater knowledge, but only to a certain extent—after which it is a matter of diminishing returns.

In BI, data selection is informed by business knowledge and actionable goals, with human intelligence playing a key role in discerning data quality. LLMs face a similar challenge in determining the value and correctness of text. The question of data quality in LLMs mirrors that in BI: how do we determine what text is "correct"?

However, the efficacy of simply scaling up data in LLMs using transformer architecture seems to be plateauing. Reaching new heights in performance will require more than just additional data. It's like comparing an undergraduate liberal arts education to the specialized focus of a Ph.D. program. Fine-tuning LLMs with targeted data is akin to a master's program, deepening and focusing their capabilities.

This book advocates for the integration of human and artificial intelligence through knowledge graphs and business intelligence. Before LLMs, the encoding of human knowledge was attempted using semantic webs and knowledge graphs, which, while valuable, were laborious to build and maintain. LLMs are an automated approach to constructing these knowledge structures, but this automation is not without its flaws.

The buzz around the semantic web, a major concept circa 2005, has faded some, yet its relevance remains. As data grows exponentially, maintaining relationships within this data is crucial to avoid information overload. Big data might help find a needle in a haystack, but understanding the connections within the haystack is equally important.

In this book, I delve into the feasibility and value of deliberately enhancing the level of intelligence integration within a business, presenting my current work in this evolving field.

Fragmented Knowledge

Figure 2 below depicts the breakdown of skills involved with analytics for three hypothetical employees of three different roles. The skills of each worker are broken down into three categories—business knowledge, data engineering, and data science:

- **Business Knowledge** refers to an understanding of the enterprise's workings, encompassing operational insights and strategic acumen. Business knowledge is about how the business works. That is, what is known about the operations of the business. This could be considered the core of the business.

- **Data Engineering** involves the technical skills required to design, build, and manage the flow of data, similar to how law and accounting support the underlying functions of a business without being its main product.

- **Data Science** applies advanced analytical techniques and scientific principles to extract insights from data, driving decision-making and strategy.

We all have different skill sets, across both a breadth of diverse domain knowledge and depth in each domain. For the sake of argument, let's say we all have the same amount of time and energy. We can divvy it up across a wide breadth of domains, in which case we'll probably know a little about a lot of things. Or we can focus on a domain and know everything about that domain. The important thing is that both types are important.

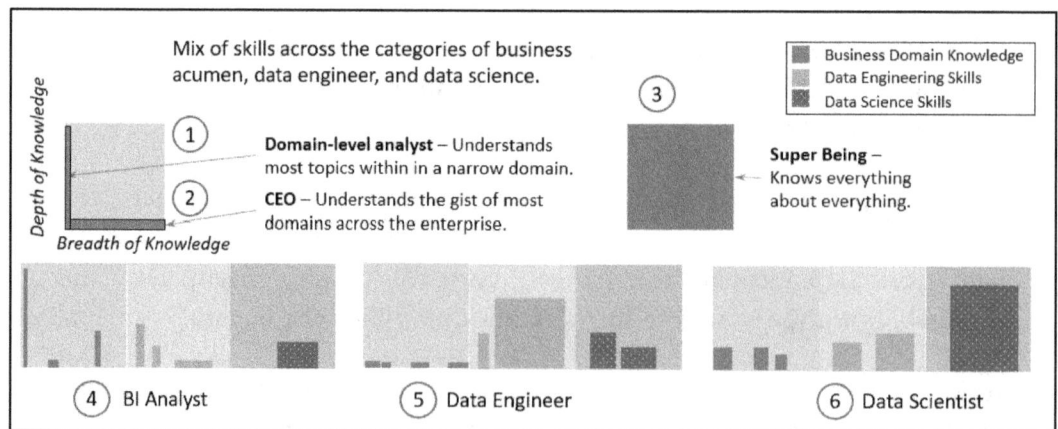

Figure 2: The roles and knowledge domain expertise that build data analytics—the nervous system of the enterprise.

1. A domain expert knows everything about a narrow domain.

2. A CEO should know a little bit about things across the entire breadth of subjects. This is the "30,000-foot" high-level view. The domain expert and CEO spend their "intellectual energy" differently. The CEO makes different kinds of decisions at a different scope from a domain expert.

3. This (green) box shows the logical extreme. Filling the box implies knowing everything about everything within the scope of the enterprise.

4. A business analyst is usually an expert in one domain but probably knows a little to moderate amount about related domains in the enterprise. The business analyst probably is familiar with a few areas of data science and data engineering. For example, a business analyst has skill with Tableau which is also a data science skill, which straddles all three categories.

5. A data engineer should know much across a wide range of data engineering subjects. Having worked on many projects, she should have picked up a little here and there about the business aspects of the enterprise.

6. Data scientist knowledge is rich in statistics, ML algorithms, and scientific methodology. They should have modest to advanced levels of data engineering skill in a few areas, mostly connecting to data, and a strong SQL skill. The data engineer probably picked up some business knowledge along the way, maybe deeper than a data engineer would since the nature of data science will dive deeper into meaning.

Can a Single Entity Know Most Things About Most Things?

Of most interest in the context of this book is business knowledge (the green squares in Figure 2 above). Since humans still make most operational decisions, craft strategies, and formulate novel tactical solutions, this is the most pertinent. As cliché as this might sound by now, the collective knowledge residing in the brains of thousands of employees is its greatest asset.

> *No current AI can capture and integrate all the nuance and reasoning behind all this knowledge. This knowledge encompasses not only documented procedures and policies but also the context-sensitive understanding, implications of relationships, and tacit knowledge that is often challenging to codify and analyze using AI alone.*

Unfortunately, this intelligence is fragmented and distributed across very many people.

Is it possible to unify fragmented knowledge across a wide array of knowledge workers in order to make decisions and develop strategies with a wide (holistic) scope of consideration?

Figure 3 depicts the vast and varied mix of expertise required to run an enterprise:

1. On the left are the very many analysts and knowledge workers across the many and varied domains of an enterprise.

2. In the center (of the left-side diagram), all the BI data gathers into a centralized data fabric.

3. On the right is a representation of the entire space of enterprise knowledge.

Figure 3: BI analysts across the heterogeneous mix of domains.

Each column (3 of Figure 3) represents a domain of knowledge within an enterprise. Each column is built from bricks of specific topics within the domain. The expertise of each analyst from across all domains is mostly trapped in their heads. But practically all analysts know little or nothing about the interests and knowledge of others.

Thinking back to Figure 2, an interesting aspect of the CEO's knowledge is that the unique set of skills, albeit at superficial levels, across most domains forms a unique domain in itself! In fact, in reality, most people have a unique set of skills, bricks of skills from more than one domain. Usually, there is some overlap of skills among workers. Those common factors help to smooth out communication between people.

Beyond Traditional BI Analysts and Managers

BI analysts have aspired to delve into improving business processes and identifying pitfalls, rather than merely using BI for operational reporting purposes. Reports generally serve operational staff by informing them of what needs attention and providing guidance leading to what actions to take. The consumers of those "reports," which include very many knowledge workers simply viewing performance management dashboards, are also "BI consumers." Those report consumers far outnumber the tactical and strategic BI analysts and managers. In the quest for data-driven excellence, a large wave of employees must join the ranks of BI consumers and even "citizen analysts," requiring data from a very wide breadth of data sources.

In modern enterprises, there is the growing presence of a metaphorical information circulatory system that connects almost all workers. This system is increasingly embodied by a "Data Fabric," which is a unified architecture and set of data services that provide consistent capabilities across a choice of endpoints spanning on-premises and multiple cloud environments. It allows for flexible and scalable data management, enabling different data types to be accessed, processed, and delivered efficiently to users and applications.

Data fabrics offer an extensive view of an enterprise's data landscape. However, the scope and utility of this view are limited to the data that has been chosen for inclusion. Basing decisions on this selected pool of data can lead to simplistic conclusions. This issue transcends the familiar "garbage in—garbage out" problem. It's not about the quality of data being poor; it's about the breadth of data being insufficient. There's a distinct difference between non-inclusion of data and consuming data tainted with falsehoods, deceit, or biased and imperfect interpretations. Here, that non-included data is the intricately semantic knowledge trapped in the heads of knowledge workers.

Paradoxically, too much information, information overload, can also lead to imperfection—like inundating an opponent in legal proceedings with an overwhelming volume of hundreds of banker's boxes of documents to sift through, which is a strategic but burdensome overabundance of information.

With that said, many enterprises continue to operate successfully without the latest AI, lakehouses, or data fabrics, suggesting that inherent organizational knowledge has been sufficient for continuity and growth. This accumulated wisdom, evolving from the company's inception to the present, constitutes the business's intelligence.

The challenge lies in capturing the tacit knowledge residing in the minds of employees to augment our data repositories and enhance decision-making processes. That is, as non-intrusively as possible—not adding additional tasks to already full plates and not in a ultra-intrusive, high-surveillance, "Big Brother" sort of way. Fortunately, we can't yet read minds, but we can take clues from efforts to resolve problems they are working on. A primary tool for solving problems is to explore BI data.

What Do Human BI Analysts See?

When analysts employ their data visualization tools, they choose a presentation of that data based on the nature of the insight they're looking for. And they are looking for that for a reason. That is all based on their experience as a subject matter expert of one or more business domains, a strategist, and an analyst.

Figure 4 is a very basic example of one of the visualizations a BI analyst would see. It is two time series, illustrating the stock closing price and volume for Microsoft for each trading day in 2008. Note that the left scale consists of larger numbers measuring volume (orange, line 1) and the right scale measures the stock closing price (blue, line 2).

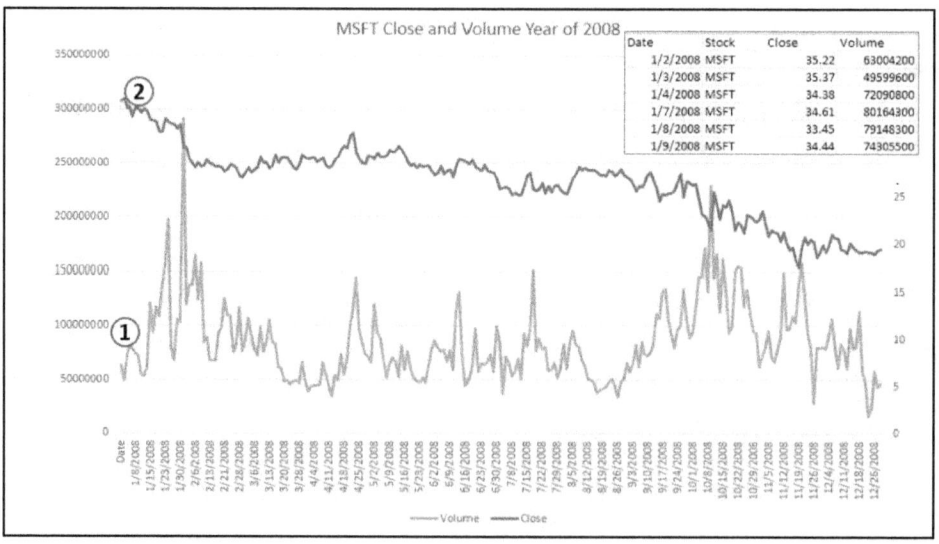

Figure 4: What do analysts see in typical data visualizations?

A human analyst looking at Figure 4 might see:
- Downward Trend: Line 2, closing prices, is moving downwards overall.

- Peaks and Valleys: Line 1, volume, has sharp peaks and valleys, indicating significant volatility in trading volume.

- Relative Changes: There are relative highs and lows on the closing price graph, which might indicate short-term trends or reversals within the larger downward trend.

Each of those insights is easy to determine with a relatively simple function or even analysis from an AI, such as ChatGPT. In fact, those insights above were indeed noticed by ChatGPT through submitting Figure 4. What else could be noticed in a basic line graph? A few things I'll add to the list are:

- Mean Time Between Spikes: The average interval between significant peaks or spikes.

- Inflection Points: Points where the graph curve changes direction, indicating a shift in trend.

- High Short-term Variability: Large fluctuations or a wide range of values in a short time frame.

Figure 5 is another simple visualization. It's a bar chart showing the sales amount for stores in the Zip code 50613. I've also superimposed a pie chart, which is another way to present the same information, but perhaps with a little more intuition about the dominance of the biggest stores. What can we say about this bar chart?

- There is a rather long tail of stores with much smaller sales than the few biggest on the right. That's a rather uneven distribution.

- Lower Tier: The leftmost two-thirds of the bars, where each bar's height increases relatively gradually.

- Middle Tier: The next group of bars where the increase in height is more pronounced.

- Upper Tier: The rightmost few bars that show a steep increase in height.

- Outliers: The last bar on the right, which could be an outlier due to its substantially higher value compared to the rest.

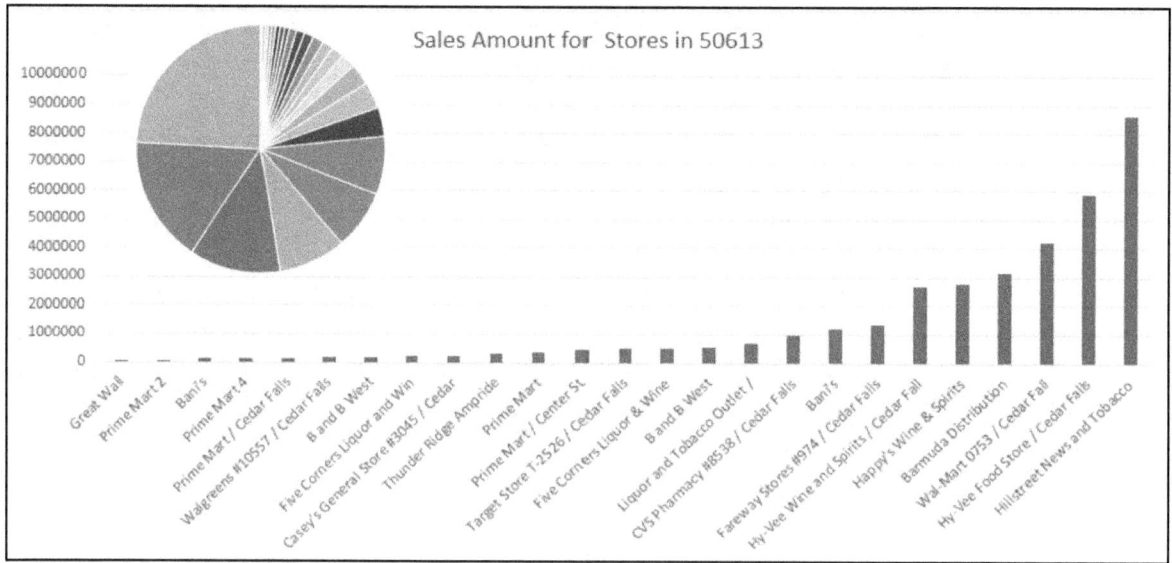

Figure 5: Simple visualization of data.

Every one of the items noted in both examples can be easily captured programmatically. Most are probably existing functions in DAX or some Python libraries. At worst, the custom code that computes those values wouldn't be too difficult to compose.

It might be that a BI analyst hasn't consciously enumerated all the classes of insights, but given a few minutes, you'll start to think of more. Not magnitudes more, perhaps at most a few dozen?

This is how intent and analytical procedure are captured from human intelligence. The two examples are of one analyst viewing a graph of data. But there are many analysts throughout an enterprise, each working on different problems, or at least different parts of a problem. The interests of a wide breadth of analysts across every corner of the enterprise can be centrally accessible.

> *An analyst focused on a particular problem probably will not notice many things she's not looking for. But it's there—and we'll capture it for anyone else who might find that information to be of value.*

As mentioned, LLMs mostly learn from our writings–books, articles, blogs, comments, and written communications. But in a business context, the action of our BI queries suggests points of interest for the analyst and how they relate. Further, we can assume what is viewed in a session of BI browsing is probably related. For LLMs, the counterpart is that what words occur close in proximity, even if by a few sentences or paragraphs away, suggests context.

In a later section, we'll look at more complicated, but still rather basic, visualizations commonly utilized by BI analysts.

The Big Gap Between Human and Machine Intelligence

Hominids have been building tools for hundreds of thousands of years to amplify their abilities. Until very recently, those tools completely lacked any intelligence. That is, the skill, knowledge, and purpose to engage the tool. The intelligence required to use those tools is completely on us humans. The designs and sophistication of the tools drastically improved over time. But no matter how ingenious the design, all the intelligence required to wield them was still completely us.

Whether the tool is a Swiss Army Knife, a Lamborghini, or even a "supercomputer," it has no intelligence. It's a machine with an unambiguous purpose. Sure, the design and construction of the tools are imbued with our intelligent design, but they lay there completely reactive to our commands. There is a big *intelligence gap* between where we pick up the tool and what we want to be done.

While tools that could make a case for intelligence have existed for decades, the level of intelligence is still a drop in the bucket, virtually zero compared to what we normally think of as intelligence. For example, smoke detectors recognize smoke with high precision (it's right most of the time), recall (hardly ever misses a fire), and take an action (sounds a nerve-wracking alarm). Most people still have trouble considering whales, apes, and corvids as "intelligent" in the human way. Today, there are self-driving cars, recommendation engines, AI chess, and Go champions. But they still all fall apart when things zig and zag out of their comfort zones. These AIs haven't really been Earth-shattering for analysts and managers working through operational, tactical, and strategic planning and decision-making in a highly competitive world.

But that changed in November 2022.

AI Gone Viral

On November 30, 2022, ChatGPT 3.5 burst onto the public scene, thrusting AI into the mainstream, just like AOL and Netscape did for the Internet back in 1995. For the general public, the initial implications were that writing those tedious letters or homework assignments just got a whole lot easier. Finding a direct answer to a question became much more streamlined than iterations of wading through tons of false positives from search engine results. Software developers no longer have to comb through endless threads on StackOverflow and Reddit to find code snippets that still require significant customization.

But for BI analysts and managers, AI is filling in the remaining gap between the point-and-click world of Tableau and Power BI and the vast space of data waiting to be explored. ChatGPT, a LLM, is a class of AI in the natural language processing (NLP) camp. It's able to play the role of a world-class translator between humans and machines.

Think of it like an interpreter in a room of people speaking different languages. One person understands French and the other understands Japanese. A highly skilled translator understands both and translates from one to the other. Sure, something might get lost in translation, but it's a heck of a lot better than the alternative.

> *A good translator can find deeper meanings than a word-for-word transformation from one language to another. But the translator doesn't need to be an expert in the topics that are the subject of the conversation.*

But it's really worse than being a translator who knows French, Japanese, and English. The languages might be very different, but the speakers are mostly alike—both are people. What about a translator who must translate between data and people?

In terms of this book, a LLM can translate between a human's spoken words and a procedure to query to a number of databases and format the results in an appropriate manner. It doesn't need to be a completely human-driven process.

I also should mention that in this book, by "AI," I will usually mean LLMs. That's because the AI component of this book is primarily ChatGPT, a LLM. There are other AIs at the forefront right now. In addition to LLMs that work with text, there are AIs that can decipher photos, videos, sound, software code, and math. These AIs are currently being integrated with "AI offerings" from Microsoft, OpenAI, and Google.

But in the end, these multimodal AIs mostly convert what they "see/hear" into text for us. That's how humans formally communicate with each other, so at least for now, that goes for an AI in order to communicate with us.

My Research Assistant, ChatGPT

This book is a product of the sudden emergence of AI onto the awareness of the general public. It marks a crucial milestone in our history. It blasts open the door to what was called expert systems back in the 1980s, semantic webs in the 2000s, and knowledge graphs in the 2010s.

The symbiotic relationship between KGs and LLMs is the keystone that enables me to write a book connecting a few very heavy topics. Therefore, it's fitting that ChatGPT played a role in helping me write this book.

It would be disingenuous of me not to utilize LLMs for writing this book. ChatGPT (LLMs in general) has limitations I actually wish it didn't have as I spent a few hundred hours writing this book after a full load from my day job. However, I have to say that when used properly, ChatGPT can be a big help.

Aside from helping me with phrasing, ChatGPT didn't write any of this book nor generate the ideas. I'm not saying that out of ego. I always asked it for help, but found that in the case of this book, it would mostly miss the point. This book integrates many advanced concepts. Those integrations aren't well-known at the time of ChatGPT's cutoff (September 2021, recently January 2022). When it's faced with something that is an atypical use, rare, or even non-existent, it dumps it into the closest bucket.

Figure 6 below is an example of the sort of fitting a square peg into a round hole that ChatGPT does when I ask it a complex question that probably hasn't been asked before.

For all the sections attempting to articulate a complex notion involving multiple moving parts, I'd write up a prompt explaining the notion. My prompt would usually be overly technical and a brain dump of what I'm thinking. I'd give it a shot and ask ChatGPT to rewrite it into a coherent form. Each time, it lost the essence of what I was trying to say.

Figure 6: Forcing a square peg into a round hole.

I even asked ChatGPT why it struggles.

 Whenever I ask you to help me write something that is a novel idea of mine, you struggle. You seem to force my idea into the closest existing bucket and proceed with your response as though that's what I'm talking about. The prompt I provide is detailed enough to convey my novel idea and within your parameter length limit. In fact, I'm happy with the quality of the prompt and just hoped you would tidy it up and perhaps expand on parts where there might need to be background. However, what you return misses the point. Why do you do that?

Figure 7: Why do you struggle?

Its response was surprisingly honest.

 I'm sorry for any misunderstandings. The underlying reason has to do with how I've been trained and how I operate:

1. **Pattern Recognition:** My primary function is based on recognizing patterns in the vast amount of data I've been trained on. If a novel idea doesn't closely match patterns in my training data, I might inadvertently try to fit it into a more familiar context.
2. **Lack of Intuition:** Unlike humans, I don't possess intuition or true understanding. I generate responses based on patterns and data, rather than genuine comprehension or insight.

Figure 8: An honest response.

I didn't even trust ChatGPT to rewrite any set of paragraphs to cut down the size or smooth out any rough edges. It usually missed the point towards the end. It didn't provide even a single novel insight that added to what I intended to write. It was effective in helping to highlight suggestions for what I might have missed or what might be a better way of phrasing. But it still required my human expertise to double-check its work.

That's not really a ding on ChatGPT. That goes for anyone you're trying to teach something new to. Our expectation with humans is that there is a process and timeframe for training someone to understand a new concept. In the meantime, we can utilize their assistance within boundaries.

Understanding is never really a one-shot deal. Unless we're unambiguously closed machines, the world in which we operate is too complex. If someone understands your question and gives you a useful answer after just one question, it's either luck or because the context was pre-filled with prior conversations or shared experiences.

There are methods to improve the performance of LLMs. The most common examples are:

- **Fine-tuning** is a process where a LLM is further trained on a specific dataset after its initial, broader training. This specialized training allows the model to adapt to the nuances of a particular domain or task, much like a student going through a customized study plan after completing a general course. Through fine-tuning, the LLM becomes more aligned with the unique linguistic patterns, terminologies, and preferred outputs of its targeted application.

- **Prompt engineering**, on the other hand, is the skillful crafting of input queries to effectively communicate with the LLM. Like a conductor of an orchestra, prompt engineering guides the model to produce the most relevant and precise responses. By meticulously designing prompts with context-rich and instruction-specific language, users can significantly enhance the AI's understanding and output quality.

We'll cover Retrieval Augmented Generation later.

No, ChatGPT didn't generate the architecture of how all the pieces fit together or directly write any of the text, but I used it to:

- Develop some illustrations. Not just graphics but code for generating visuals. For example, for writing code to generate the Neo4j snapshots. It was excellent at those direct and succinct tasks.

- It's very good at providing sanity checks, sometimes annoyingly thorough.

- Offer a few bullet points I may have missed.

- Offer advice on conveying a concept in a better way.

Additionally, Visual Studio Copilot gets a nod as an AI assistant. It's an AI that helps with coding, from simply recognizing syntax errors to incredibly offering entire code segments. Yes, it's a marvel.

As long as I didn't push ChatGPT's "intellectual intensity" too much, it served very well as an assistant in the writing of this book. If it were an intern, I'd give it a middling A. The important point is that the ability of ChatGPT to perform tasks of moderate intellectual sophistication across a wide breadth is impressive and extremely valuable.

As an example of what I mean:

Imagine utilizing ChatGPT as an assistant in a large-scale business project, such as rolling out a new product line. For tasks like collating and organizing data from multiple sources, drafting initial product descriptions, or even creating database queries, ChatGPT would excel with its unwavering efficiency and vast knowledge base. However, when it comes to strategic planning, understanding nuanced market shifts, or piecing together a cohesive branding narrative, its assistance might fall short. Just as I experienced with the book-writing process, when handed intricate tasks that demand a deep or novel understanding or a synthesis of diverse, complex elements, it usually missed the mark.

It's akin to having a junior business analyst with unyielding stamina but limited industry experience. You wouldn't expect this analyst to helm a strategy meeting or predict emerging market trends right away. However, they could be indispensable for tasks like data analysis, preliminary research, or document drafting. The breadth of tasks they can handle, given a beginner to moderate level of complexity, is commendable. This approach ensures the project benefits from ChatGPT's "endurance" and range without overburdening it with tasks that require deep expertise or nuanced understanding.

The process of writing this book helped me gain experience in utilizing ChatGPT best. It really isn't much different from learning how to best communicate with co-workers over time. Really, ChatGPT was in many ways much like any colleague I consulted and learned from over the years of practicing BI implementations, each contributing in their own way.

Lastly, it's perhaps not so surprising that after working on this book intensely for months, thus spending more time with ChatGPT than any other "co-worker" during that period, I did notice my writing started resembling ChatGPT. Once cognizant of that, I made conscious efforts to avoid that. Hopefully, it will wear off once I get back into my normal mode of working with real people—unless they also start sounding like ChatGPT …

I think that is one good example for being cautious about LLMs. They are an amalgamation of all of us, stripping out all the unique permutations of outlier characteristics that make us each unique. That's just not right.

My Feeling About AI

"That's why we play the game!" It's something sportscasters exclaim at the conclusion of a very surprising upset. The world is well beyond being described as a "complex system" when you consider the "three body problem," a system with just three "dumb agents" (without minds of their own), is already a complex system. Nothing is certain. My point is data analytics isn't magic. Nor is looking for guidance in history or any self-help book magic. But we're much better off with it.

I wouldn't have written this book now if AI hadn't broken open like it did. It's very helpful for research and assisting with development, but it's not yet an artificial general intelligence (AGI) much less an artificial super intelligence (ASI). AI is still not good enough such that the techniques described in this book will not be of value.

Actually, my hope is that the techniques described in this book are of value *despite* the achievement of AGI/ASI in the near future (whatever "near" could mean). This means we don't yet get ourselves into a situation where AGI/ASI manages the top echelon of creative tasks.

The typical reader of this book is probably familiar with the patterns of UML, reference architectures, project management methodologies, best practices of all sorts, and cookbooks. These notions are very necessary to ensure our systems are built as sturdy as can be. However, when such patterns are actually effective, the next step is automation. That's a quality a tireless, egoless AI with no social life is good at. So in a world dominated by patterns, the productivity gap between AI and humans will accelerate the skew towards AI.

I'm not saying that to scare anyone. Enough people have been sounding that alarm. I'm saying we can still integrate AI in a way that we humans hold the reigns and consciously exercise our innate knack for critical thinking for a few decades while we still can. A fun science fiction book might be about how dogs were once much more intelligent than they are now. Then humans came along and did that intelligence thing better than them. The intelligence of dogs atrophied as they relied on us for more and more.

Once AGI is achieved, frankly, I'm not sure what there would be soon after for most people to do. But I'm sure we'll eventually figure it out as we have every other time a technology of this relative magnitude hit us. When agriculture put a huge dent in the hunter and gatherer business, we ran with it. When machines became magnitudes stronger and magnitudes more efficient at menial tasks, we ran with it. At least at the time of writing, there's still time to prepare for that day.

As time goes on, AI's creative versatility will grow and probably surpass our skills. I have already discussed how AI has its limitations (at least for now) in my discussion of ChatGPT as my research assistant. Although ChatGPT was fair at providing sanity checks, it wasn't able to offer even one juicy insight. It's imperative to understand where the borders of the AI are.

There is a thick line between: 1) merely applying what you've learned and 2) creating. ChatGPT is much better than us at learning (or at least the appearance of learning). Humans evolved to create novel solutions to novel problems—inherent in an ever-evolving landscape. Surely, there is overlap–a hint of creativity emanating from the ChatGPT side, and we humans aren't slouches at learning as our creativity is founded on a base of knowledge (even if it might take decades, not days, to have built that knowledge in each of our heads). Fortunately, the average human is still more intellectually versatile as far as creativity is concerned.

David and Goliath

As I've described in the previous topic, my preference for the work I've done in BI has always been towards helping smaller enterprises better compete. When a little entity is up against a big one, the survival of the smartest is the little guy's only realistic chance. It's why humans are where we are on the "food chain" and not gorillas and bears.

By "smaller enterprises," I'm talking about the 2nd tier companies that are beneath what is usually one to a few giants. These 2nd tier companies are themselves large enterprises, but not an "800-pound gorilla," more like a number of 100-pound gorillas.

They rose up the ranks among much competition, well beyond the sapling stage, but then hit a ceiling. They are like colonels knocking on the door of the exclusive generals' club.

Specifically, my interest is in providing arms to the 2nd tier of enterprises to battle the very small number of top-tier companies. The enterprises at the top understandably tend to target keeping things as they are. They build a so-called "moat," a sustainable advantage ensuring they stay at the top. Business for the top tier is defense more than offense. Those 2nd tier companies have made it far enough to pose a formidable challenge to the top tier. But not fire with fire—they'll lose every time. They moved up the ranks with some sort of better mouse trap or full-on disruptive innovation.

Top-tier enterprises understandably will tend to apply AI to further optimize, grow, and hopefully evolve what they already do. The 2nd tier innovators will apply AI strategically to bust the dam created by the top-tier enterprises and get evolution flowing again. It's completely sensible for those at the top to avoid and even prevent disruptions in their environment. Current conditions are what got the top tier to the top. Anything else places them at risk of losing their dominance.

I certainly harbor no ill will against the giant corporations. In fact, to paraphrase a cliché, *most* of my best customers are giant corporations. The giants are the ones that can provide goods affordably, at highly consistent quality, and at massive scale. I just wish to ensure what I believe is the best way to keep our ecosystem humming. And that is to promote healthy churn in the creation and destruction of corporations—just like evolution itself requires a healthy churn of species.

Lastly, another prime tenet of my work has been the prevention of systems spiraling into uncontrolled trajectories: the "hockey stick curve." While it can signify success in many contexts, such as the viral video, it can also be an alarm bell for systems or processes that are spiraling out of control, leading to potentially catastrophic outcomes for everyone. As we harness advanced technologies and intricate systems, it's imperative to maintain a vigilant oversight.

By doing so, we can preemptively identify and moderate budding issues, mitigating the risk that our innovations inadvertently usher in adverse unintended consequences. The essence of sustainable progress is not just rapid advancement but also the foresight to navigate potential pitfalls—benefitting short and long term success.

We Think Because We Are

We think. That's our human schtick, our species' superpower. So what happens when AGI is achieved, and we don't need to think anymore? Even if AGI (along with correspondingly impressive robotics) is completely benevolent and is smart enough to teach all eight billion of us how to have our own favorite cake and eat it however each of us wants to eat it, why would we ever need to think of anything again?

> *What do we become when we don't need to think much anymore? Why think when there is a machine that can think better than we can? That's like walking ten miles instead of driving.*

AGI or no AGI, we're still sentient beings with hopes, fears, and an enjoyment of solving problems. Solving problems is tough, so nature sadistically made it enjoyable for us. Similarly, we live in physical bodies that need exercise. So those of us who don't burn 3500 calories daily from physical labor go to the gym (or walk ten miles instead of driving).

However, although I go to a gym, I wouldn't say I really enjoy it. I enjoy health. Similarly, saying that I "enjoy" thinking isn't quite right either. It's more of a matter of enjoying solving the problems lurking around me. That's because we're thinkers with sentience and curiosity. My survival isn't a simple game of statistics like it is for a crab larva who grew into an adult crab by essentially rolling heads on a coin toss (avoiding a predator) 20 times in a row (about one in a million). Our ability to think massively alters our odds of success.

There is a big difference between driving ten miles instead of walking and depending on something else to think through our problems instead of thinking through our problems ourselves. Letting our ability to think get "flabby" is a risky condition to allow ourselves into, individually or as a society. It's my opinion that for at least a while, we should approach anything AI that works for us in the capacity of a supervised assistant.

At the risk of being labeled a doomsdayer prepper or that old guy who walked to school ten miles every day, uphill both ways, our infrastructure is more fragile than most people want to believe. We all just went through something extraordinary only a couple of years ago. For the most part, we didn't starve or freeze to death, but it sure did create a lot of grief.

The level of AI represented by the likes of ChatGPT hasn't been with us for decades, as has electricity or even the Internet itself. And both still periodically go down. So how do we know what will happen if the AI plug—forget AGI, just the AI we have today–is pulled sometime after we've assimilated it into society?

Speaking of AGI, we don't know what it will be like. I think most assume it will be just like us. Think about the stereotype of the eccentric genius who isn't like most of us. Although not all geniuses are quirky like Sheldon Cooper or Doc Brown, and intelligence is more than about IQ, my point is, do we really know what an AGI or ASI that knows so much would be like? On a somewhat related point, I don't believe I ever participated in a conventional software rollout to production that didn't come with immediate or latent bugs and errors–or, worse, unintended side effects.

I don't trust this level of AI technology and all that surrounds it enough to put our ability to think for ourselves at risk. It reeks of the adage I'll modify here: Smart enough to be dangerous in the boardroom.

But I do trust it enough to smooth out the communication friction between humans and machines, making our lives much easier. I haven't been this excited about a technology since I first learned to program about 45 years ago. Therefore, this book represents how I think we should take advantage of this unparalleled technology—at least until we have enough history with it. To me, that should be decades.

As I said, I do believe that someday AI (more than just the LLMs in the current spotlight) will reach that point of AGI and then ASI. Why I believe that to be true is a distracting rabbit hole well beyond the scope of this volume. At the level of AGI, the smartest of we humans will still be the "smartest guy in the room". However, when ASI happens, none of us humans will be the "smartest guy in the room." As I write this, I believe that could be today and I just don't know about it, or it might be months to years, assuming nothing crazy happens.

ChatGPT didn't help much in writing this book at the level of a co-author. But it was incredibly helpful, saving me the cost of a team. It was a very good fact checker (despite some hallucination—but knowledge is an iterative process), editor (I still talk good for a guy dat when grow up in Hawaii), an entity for me to bounce ideas off of at 2 am, and it is one of the primary characters of the story I'm telling.

I think the approach I present in this book is a middle ground that keeps our human thumbs on the button without falling behind competitors and without advocating for a deceleration of AI progress. AGI or not, we're still sentient beings with hopes, loved ones, and agency. We should never just willingly hand that over, no matter how compelling the presented argument might be. Maybe an AGI/ASI is just what we need to bring us all together.

I think it's fair to say that we haven't reached the limit of our population's thinking potential. Certainly, there is a limit to how much each of us can know compared to a LLM living at massive data centers, but I don't think most people have reached their full thinking capacity. I don't think they want to—because thinking is hard.

The Book's TL;DR

Whenever I asked ChatGPT for advice related to this book, I needed to explain the concept of what I'm doing. So I wrote a prompt to prime each session. I would paste in the following preamble—which makes for a fairly good TL;DR:

> *This prompt is in the context of Business Intelligence (BI) structures added to an enterprise knowledge graph (EKG). The EKG consists of three major parts: A knowledge graph (KG) authored by subject matter experts (SME) to Semantic Web standards, a data catalog (DC) that holds metadata for all data sources in the enterprise, and two BI-derived structures - Insight Space Graph (ISG) and Tuple Correlation Web (TCW) - passively built from the normal BI query activity of BI analysts across the enterprise. It's for a book I'm writing where I claim businesses are like organisms, departments like organs, and the EKG is like the brain.*
>
> *I chose to have BI as the spearhead for this EKG since BI data is highly-curated. Whatever data makes it into a BI database must be readily understood, of high analytical value, cleansed, and trustworthy. It is the data used for most business decisions.*
>
> *The KG is like "System 1" (Kahneman), fast response time, more direct, more deterministic. It's a collection of domain-level ontologies, analogous to domain-level data products of data mesh, authored by SMEs. Authorship of this KG is now feasible thanks to the emergence of readily available and high-quality large-language models (ChatGPT 3.5 in Nov 2022). The LLMs have a symbiotic relationship with KGs (LLMs help to build KGs and KGs ground the LLMs in reality). Incorporating retrieval augmented generation (RAG) into this ecosystem further strengthens its capabilities. RAG allows for more sophisticated query scenarios by combining the generative abilities of LLMs with the structured, fact-based data from the EKG. This mirrors advanced cognitive functions, such as problem-solving and creative thinking.*
>
> *The nexus of this EKG is the DC, an ontology of the data sources, databases/cubes, tables/views/dimensions, columns/attributes, and even column members (as necessary–since there could be billions of members). It sits between the KG and ISG/TCW. All items of the ISG*

and TCW are traceable to DC elements. Further, DC tables, columns, and members could be linked to entities and individuals in the KG, expanding the semantics of those DC elements.

The main idea of the ISG/TCW is to passively capture what dozens to thousands of BI analysts have seen (or could have seen) in visualizations rendered from their BI activity. Those salient points are captured across what could be thousands to billions of queries consuming hundreds to tens of thousands of compute hours across dozens to hundreds of data sources. It charts the points of interest across what is an unbelievably expansive space of insights. The ISG/TCW is more like System 2.

The ISG consists of nodes representing queries that were rendered in a visualization (line graph, bar chart, scatter plot, pie chart, etc.) using a visualization tool, such as Tableau or PowerBI, requested by the actions of BI analysts using those tools. For each of those dataframes resulting from those queries, an array of simple functions wrings out things a human would notice from those visualizations. For example, in a line graph, the user might recognize trend up, trend down, periodicity, steps, and spikes. Each of those insights is linked as properties of those query nodes. The columns and metrics of the query are linked to the appropriate DC nodes. Note that the data of the dataframe isn't stored in the EKG, just the metadata of the query and any insights. These insights are like the things we notice as we go about our day.

The TCW consists of nodes, each representing a tuple. For example, the price of oil in Beijing or the water consumption in San Diego. A tuple could be thought of as one row in a dataframe. The members represented in the tuples are associated to member nodes in the data catalog (the member nodes are, in turn, linked to the column node in the DC). The tuple nodes can also be connected to each other through Pearson Correlations or Conditional probabilities. These are calculated by comparing the tuples sliced by time series. These correlations are what we notice as patterns to what is related to what. We can construct chains of strong correlations.

With salient points captured in the ISG and strong correlations captured in the TCW from across dozens to thousands of diverse analysts across dozens of domains, we have a single integrated source of insights.

I would sometimes need to repost that prompt after a long chat in the same session to remind ChatGPT of the original topic of our conversation. As with normal human-human conversations that might go on for a length of time, it can lose track of the original topic through digressions and the natural drifting of topics over the course of a conversation.

That TL;DR prompt is an elevator pitch of this book to ChatGPT. Instead of a limiting 15-second elevator ride. Given ChatGPT's 128K token context window at the time of this writing - about 60K words of "conversation" it can keep "in mind"–the approximately 700 words of my TL;DR is well within its capacity. With that TL;DR said, Figure 9 below is a high-level view of the end product. It is an enterprise knowledge graph (EKG) composed of four major components.

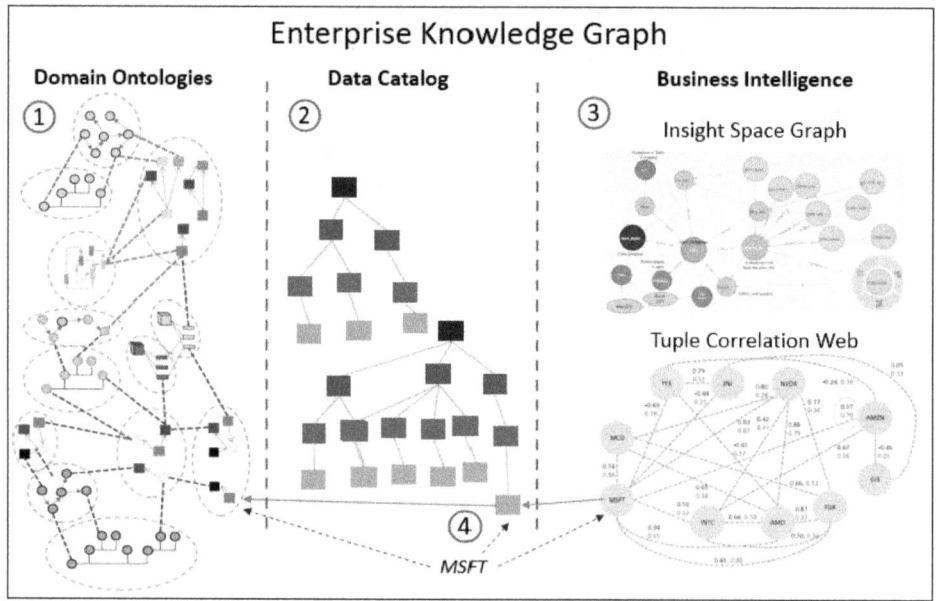

Figure 9: Three major Components of the EKG.

Those components are:

1. **Domain Ontologies**—A set of ontologies composed by the subject matter experts (SME) of domains within the Enterprise. Each domain is responsible for providing knowledge of its domain's entities, structure, and processes.

2. **Data Catalog**—The metadata of all data sources through the enterprise. Items in the domain ontologies map to a data catalog item when possible. LLMs help this mapping process tremendously.

3. **Business Intelligence**—Two structures from BI analyst activity are automatically captured. The BI items are mapped to the data catalog as well. These BI components are the primary topics of this book.

4. **Mappings**–The three major components of the EKG link via relationships. Shown here is the link from the KG MSFT node, through the DC MSFT column member, on to the MSFT node in the TCW.

The three parts anecdotally remind me of three parts of our brain: the Domain Ontologies as our old "reptilian brain" and limbic system, the BI parts as the neocortex in knowing what is going on, and the data catalog as the thalamus, the interchange between the Domain Ontologies and BI parts. This helps underscore that intelligence isn't an LLM or any other model. Intelligence is a system, a process.

Note: I will refer to both EKG and KG. The EKG is the composite I just described. The KG is just the "Domain Ontologies" part of the EKG (item 1 above). Additionally, for simplicity, I might refer to ChatGPT, even though I technically might mean OpenAI GPT.

Could a Private LLM have Written this Book?

I've contemplated taking my thousands of pages of notes over the past twenty years, reports I've written for the dozens of BI projects I've been on, the blogs and articles I've written, emails I've exchanged with the publisher explaining the book, and references I'm able to toss into the mix (that won't get me into copyright trouble) to create a *private, fine-tuned* LLM.

Unlike GPT, which is a foundation model trained on a massive and diverse corpus of publicly available text, a private LLM is usually an existing LLM fine-tuned with subject-focused and/or private data. I think the teaming up of a private LLM rigorously trained on this subject might have been able to write a usable draft of this entire book. But based on experiments I've performed on getting it to write full but smaller-scoped blogs, my guess is that the editing I would need to perform would be much more trouble than it's worth.

If I had a longer timeframe for writing this book and/or knew that the experiment would work, I might have invested the month or two that I think it would take to cobble that together. It's a project for another time—I'll try it later and post an article about that experience. Instead, ChatGPT is relegated to the role of a research assistant for this book, along with some tedious coding or very straightforward text (for example, assisting with the glossary). One thing ChatGPT had over my colleagues is I didn't need to wait for a return call, even at 2 am when I'm normally working on my not-day-job work.

ChatGPT's Visual Representation for this Book

However, after ChatGPT's big upgrade in early November 2023, I was curious to see if it could generate a graphic encapsulating what I told it about in my book through the elevator pitch prompt. It still wouldn't be able to write this book, but since ChatGPT plays such a big role in the book, I should include the visual it gave me.

Figure 10 is actually kind of cool. It certainly would have taken me hours to create something like what it created in a few seconds.

32 • ENTERPRISE INTELLIGENCE

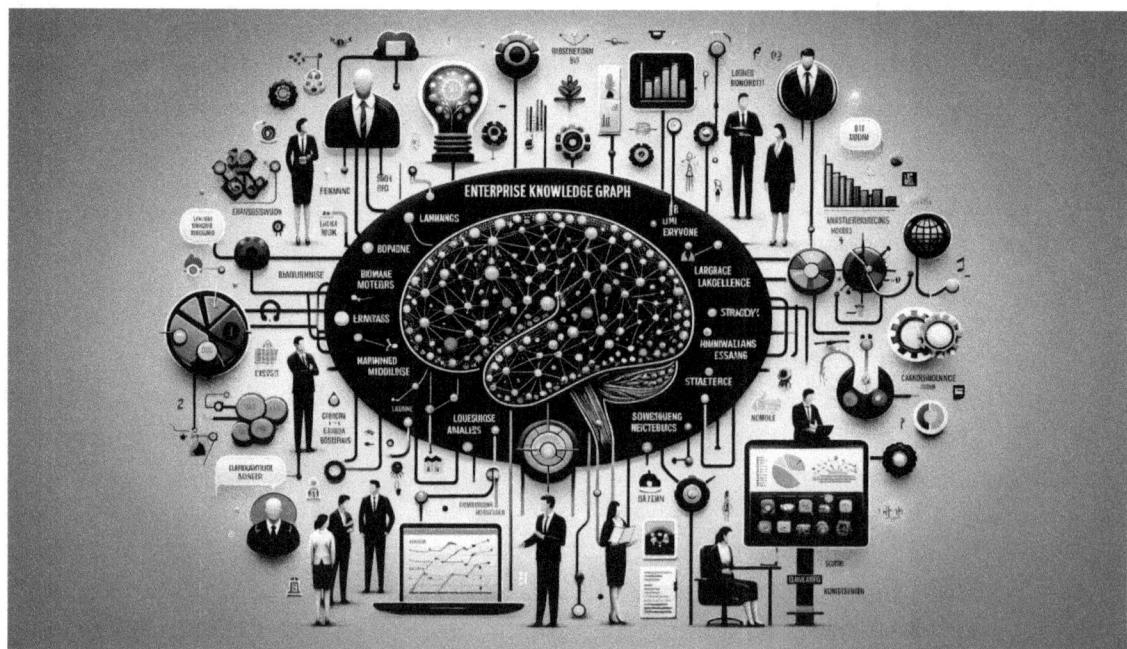

Figure 10: ChatGPT's take on the primary theme of this book.

Aside from the gibberish labels and bordering on "The Borg," it's not bad. It shows a clear integration of BI, a wide variety of human analysts, and the enterprise knowledge graph ... but I wasn't sure about what represents the AI/LLM aspect. I asked ChatGPT: *"Is the AI/LLM aspect of your graphic the layer around the brain-shaped EKG?"*

Its response is intriguing:

> **ChatGPT**
> Yes, in the graphic, the AI/Large Language Model (LLM) aspect is represented as a layer around the brain-shaped Enterprise Knowledge Graph (EKG). This design choice symbolizes how AI and LLMs, like ChatGPT, envelop and integrate with the core knowledge structure of the enterprise, acting as an interface or a medium through which the vast information within the EKG is processed, interpreted, and utilized. This layering visually conveys the idea that AI is both a part of and a facilitator for the broader knowledge ecosystem within the organization.

Figure 11: It's intriguing that the LLM aspects look like the neocortex.

What I find intriguing is that it chose to represent the AI/LLM aspect as a layer enveloping the brain-shaped EKG. It's remarkably reminiscent of the neocortex, apparently where analytics and decision-making take place, and how the neocortex envelopes the older parts of the brain.

The Book Structure

This book is about the integration of many fields (LLM, KG, BI, Data Systems, Human Intelligence), each a big subject with many moving parts and a fast rate of evolution. Therefore, it is a complex subject. That is, as opposed to a complicated but targeted subject. Complex subjects are about how multiple moving parts, each with "minds of their own," interact to form a whole that is greater than the sum of its parts.

For complex subjects, I tend to take an SBAR approach, which was devised to communicate complex situations. Meaning the high-level order of the Parts of this book is organized in groups of chapters as follows:

1. **Situation: Introduction**–The problem we're facing–The sudden appearance of LLMs of a high enough quality that they can take a big step towards bridging the gap between human intelligence and machine intelligence.

2. **Background: The Intelligence of a Business**–Explore what it is that we want and why we might want it. Ultimately, we want to make better decisions–innovative solutions to novel problems and minimizing unintended consequences.

3. **Analysis: Knowledge Graphs and LLMs, Data Catalog, Business Intelligence, Data Mesh**–Explore the major pieces that comprise the solution to the problem.

4. **Recommendation: Architecture, BI-Charged Components (ISG, TCW), Special Patterns, and Implementation**–This is the solution to the problem.

The overall format for the book is to mirror a presentation to an audience of decision makers along with a few of the senior "technical" folks on a direction for incorporating AI in the enterprise. The first two-thirds--the Situation, Background, and Analysis--is targeted at the "non-codey" attendees - CDO/CTO/CIOs and representatives from marketing, HR, legal, etc.

If those CXX attendees like what they're hearing, the senior technical attendees and others are turned loose to ask questions. But just enough to be convinced of the technical feasibility, not a full technical elucidation. Otherwise, the meeting will last for days. Deep dives come with future meetings.

Similarly, for this book, the Recommendation part (the R of SBAR) is relatively high-level, about a third of the book. My intent is that it's enough to convince the reader of the technically feasibility of this approach with very minimal code and math. Future volumes and a live and evolving GitHub page (more on that later) will reflect the technical aspects to a deeper level.

Topics Punted to Future Books in the Series

This book covers much ground to elucidate the Intelligence of a Business. It's about how major key subjects integrate, not about each big subject individually. Therefore, I only go so deep in most subjects. I've balanced the importance of a topic, how deep I can feasibly go, and whether I can factor it out into tentatively planned books, diving deeper into the topics presented here.

Here are samples of a few of the topics I feel might be a FAQ of topics glaringly missing here but will be included in a future volume. Additionally, towards the end of the book, Part 10—Future Steps, I cover a few of the more compelling topics punted to future volumes that are worth mentioning in more detail.

Query Languages other than SQL

In analytics, there are a few query languages for querying analytics databases. Despite all the NoSQL chatter over the past decade, by far the predominant one is SQL. However, there are at least two other languages of note:

- MDX—The native language of pre-aggregated OLAP cubes, MDX innately expresses the constructs of querying multi-dimensional data spaces.

- DAX—Power BI is a force in the analytics world and its language is primarily DAX. DAX is really an evolution of the functions we all know and love in Excel. It could also be thought of as the replacement for what seems to be surprisingly difficult MDX.

I should mention, too, that SQL itself comes in many dialects. Fortunately, the range of SQL dialect differences isn't as widespread as varieties of apples. No matter the variety of apple, it's still very recognizable as an apple, but varieties are different enough not to be exactly interchangeable—Honeycrisp for eating, Northern Spies for pies.

Because SQL is widely known amongst the analytics and data science crowd and data engineers, all of the examples in this book will be in SQL.

What further pushes me into just SQL is that the graph aspect of this book necessitates the addition of other coding forms I cannot fully avoid: Neo4j's Cypher and the semantic web's SPARQL, RDF, OWL, etc. This is more than enough code stuff!

Non-Time Series Conditional Probabilities

In the context of the TCW, conditional probabilities serve as one of the key correlating measures, alongside Pearson and Spearman correlations. Traditional methods might employ conditional probability tables to represent these probabilities in a consolidated format. However, this book diverges from that approach, opting instead to represent conditional probabilities through a network of individual relationships between numerous pairs of data points, or tuples.

This approach emphasizes a specific type of conditional probability—one that is essentially a frequency count across defined intervals of time. These time-based segments are vital because they provide a consistent and universal dimension across diverse and disparate BI data sources.

When computing the likelihood of intersecting events for Bayesian analysis—say, the simultaneous occurrence of Events A and B—it is the dimension of time that offers a common reference point. Despite the potential for thousands of other dimensions to consider, time remains the one constant across all datasets, enabling the consistent calculation of conditional probabilities. This time-centric methodology underscores the book's broader theme of synthesizing insights from a multitude of databases by using time as the pivotal dimension for correlation and analysis.

Examples of non-time series conditional probabilities include:

1. Given that a customer is a vegetarian, there is a higher probability they will purchase plant-based products.

2. Given that a customer has a high credit score, there is a higher probability they will be approved for a premium credit card.

Bayesian Probabilities

I'm a big fan of Bayesian probabilities, meaning incorporating prior probabilities as opposed to the frequentist approach I focus on in this book. This is a book on BI, therefore founded on data. From that perspective, we do have an abundance of data from which to directly calculate probabilities. That is unlike the statisticians of long ago who usually didn't have sufficient data to calculate probabilities.

However, despite the wealth of data today, the complex world we live in is still rife with uncertainty. Therefore, the need for Bayesian beliefs still exists. I do briefly cover Bayesian probabilities in this book, showing how they would be laid out in the TCW. And the word, "Bayesian," makes several appearances, for example, in the context of "Bayesian Belief Networks." However, Bayesian probabilities deserve a much deeper dive since probabilities surfaced through ML models or even AI still play a very important role in a complex world.

Functions

Functions are fundamental. Everything is about inputs transformed into some output. For analysts, functions take the form of Excel functions, SQL built-in functions, and functions within a language, such as Java or Python. They can be complicated—for example, deeply nested SQL or very complicated Python code. Further, the rising interest in functional programming spurs software composed primarily of functions.

> *It would be of much value to fully parse and interpret functions for semantic meaning. A deep understanding of functions can provide great insight for an AI to figure out how things work.*

For this book, the inclusion of functions mapped into the EKG is limited. I do discuss query-time calculations and how the elements comprising those calculations are laid out in the EKG in the "Query Functions" topic. In the "Future Steps" topic, I also offer some discussion on metrics at scale and a deeper discussion on how DS/ML fits in.

Linear and Non-linear Regression

In the context of our discussion on TCW, I'm focusing on Pearson and Spearman correlations to quantify the relationship between tuples. These correlations provide a single number indicating the strength and direction of a linear or rank association, respectively, between two variables.

Unlike linear and non-linear regression, which predicts values by establishing a relationship between dependent and independent variables, Pearson and Spearman correlations simply measure the degree of association. Consequently, while linear regression's complexity and predictive nature align it more with machine learning models, Pearson and Spearman correlations offer straightforward, non-predictive insights into data relationships.

I briefly cover how I deal with ML models in the EKG in general in Part 7—BI-Charged EKG Components. However, a deeper dive will be in a future volume.

The Many Ways to Talk to an LLM

It's crucial to remember that LLMs are not omniscient entities. Interacting with an LLM is akin to engaging in a conversation with another human. Conversation is rarely a matter of posing a single question and passively accepting the first answer given. Real communication is iterative and nuanced, more akin to an art than a straightforward transaction.

Given this complexity, numerous sophisticated frameworks for dialoguing with LLMs are being developed. These span from simple query-response interactions to more intricate methods like the chain of thought and tree of thought, which emulate human-like reasoning processes. Retrieval augmented generation (RAG) and its advanced variant, self-reflective RAG, represent particularly promising approaches. While I explore RAG in this volume, it's a topic that merits a more exhaustive exploration, particularly the self-reflective aspect that enables an LLM to evaluate and iterate on its knowledge retrieval process.

The landscape of LLM communication is evolving rapidly. By the time the subsequent volumes of this series are penned, it's hoped that the dust will have settled on some of these emerging methodologies, providing a firmer foundation for discussion.

In this volume, the exploration of AI is focused on the augmentation of BI processes through LLMs. A glimpse into less direct, yet potentially transformative, applications of LLMs within BI is provided in Part 10—Future Steps, setting the stage for further exploration in later volumes.

By the way, because of the exceptionally fast-changing nature of AI at the time of writing, I'll go ahead and use yet another acronym for "at the time of writing"—ATTOW. I'll only use this when I feel I need to reiterate this. However, please do understand an implied sense of ATTOW throughout the entirety of this book.

Digital Twins

Digital twins are essentially sophisticated virtual models that represent real-world objects, processes, systems, or services. They are designed to simulate the physical counterpart in real-time, leveraging data from sensors and other inputs to predict behaviors, optimize performance, and guide decision-making processes. Because they usually incorporate AI, ML, and KG, they are worth a mention–in the sense of a kind of AI client of the EKG.

A digital twin is not a physical object but a software simulation that mirrors a real-world entity. This could be anything from a jet engine or a wind turbine to an entire manufacturing plant or even larger systems like buildings or cities. The purpose of a digital twin is to analyze data and monitor systems to head off problems before they occur, prevent downtime, develop new opportunities, and even plan for the future by using simulations.

Digital twins are commonly visualized through software applications that display detailed 3D models of the physical asset they replicate. These models are dynamic, updated in real-time with data streaming from various sensors placed on the physical object. The interface typically includes dashboards that present performance metrics, operational conditions, and other relevant data. Users can interact with the digital twin, run simulations, and test different scenarios to see how the physical counterpart would react under different conditions.

Frightening Things: Code and Math

This is a highly technical book on a highly technical subject. However, this book is targeted towards a BI audience that is generally not "hyper-technical." That means avoiding all code and math is nearly impossible.

I've done my best to factor out code related to this book and into a set of walkthroughs and tutorials. Accompanying this book are support materials. They are in a GitHub directory, which I'll refer to throughout this book as "the GitHub directory":

https://GitHub.com/MapRock/IntelligenceBusiness

The resources include sample code, sample data, prompts used in ChatGPT requests, and full-sized images of the many figures in this book. I need to clearly emphasize that this is sample code, not a full-blown enterprise application–for example, something along the lines of Palantir's Foundry. As far as the math goes, there isn't anything tough. I would say the toughest math is the conditional probability parts, which is really not bad.

For the purpose of reading this book in a codeless manner, the only requirement for code knowledge is to know what each language is for. For example, when I mention SQL or even display SQL, I'm usually referring to code that queries a relational database. I've included glossary entries for each language of code presented in this book. That includes SQL, Cypher, Python, and SPARQL, as well as the semantic web encoding formats, RDF and OWL.

Striving for Vendor Neutrality

In writing this book, my primary goal is to impart knowledge and insights gained from my extensive experience in the fields of BI, ML, and AI. My aim is to present this content as vendor-neutrally as possible. The spirit of this book is akin to conceptual and logical models without undue emphasis on specific products that come with the physical models.

However, the nature of technical writing, especially in a field as dynamic and diverse as BI and AI, often necessitates the use of concrete examples, figures, and tangible exercises to effectively convey complex concepts. This practical need sometimes requires referencing specific tools or platforms. My choice of such examples is guided by a combination of factors:

- **Familiarity and Expertise**—In many instances, I refer to tools and solutions with which I have the most experience and expertise, notably those stemming from my tenure at Microsoft working deeply with SSAS and my current position at Kyvos Insights, which I see as leveraging my expertise with SSAS. This is not to endorse any tools over others, but rather to provide the most informed and nuanced insights I can offer.

- **Popularity and Accessibility**—Wherever possible, I lean towards tools and platforms that are widely utilized and recognized in the industry and/or are open-source. This approach is intended to make the content relevant and accessible to a broad audience.

- **Illustrative Purpose**—The specific products mentioned are primarily for illustrative purposes. They are intended to provide a practical context and should not be construed as an endorsement. The principles and strategies discussed throughout the book are applicable across various tools and technologies in the data landscape.

I understand that in a field as competitive and rapidly evolving as BI, the line between being informative and appearing promotional can be thin. Please rest assured that the focus of this book is on sharing knowledge. The insights and recommendations are based on my professional experience and are intended to be adaptable to a range of tools and scenarios in the BI domain.

CHAPTER TWO

BI in the Era of ML, DS, and AI

For well over two decades, BI has been the solution for enterprises to view and explore the pulse of what's going on in the business. Despite the rise and relative maturation of data science (DS) and machine learning (ML) over the past decade, BI's dashboards and visualizations (using visualization tools, such as Excel, Tableau, and Power BI) are still the go-to for executives, managers, and other knowledge workers to find trustworthy, digestible, and easily accessible data that affects their decisions. It is the foundation of their monitoring and reporting.

The problem is that as the daily reach of enterprise data expands further out in more directions, the ability to surface this growing volume and variety of data to decision makers can't keep pace. Methodologies and frameworks, such as data mesh and data fabric, respectively, have gone a long way towards helping data teams keep pace. However, there is still a gap in the analytics stack that prevents it from closing.

That intellectual gap is between the human analysts' thought processes and the data presented by the BI data sources. BI analysts view data and depend heavily on their analytical skills to make something of that data. It's like playing "20 questions" with someone who can only reactively respond to your questions.

That gap is largely due to the passive nature of that BI data. Traditionally, the BI data source only responds to queries by human analysts. At least DS/ML is a step in the right direction as its nature is to predict what happens next, which is better than just telling what happened.

Over the past few years, ML features have been embedded in the major BI visualization tools, enabling BI users to request that their query results be transformed into ML models and predictions. For example, clustering a list of customers by the selected measures or presenting the features offering the most predictive value.

It's important to note that DS/ML did not replace BI. Although DS/ML (also loosely known as predictive analytics or data mining) shares sophisticated computations and decision-making value with BI, they are not direct descendants of BI. That is, in the same way, hominids are not direct descendants of monkeys—they are cousins that fill different niches.

The development process of DS/ML models fundamentally supports highly iterative experimentation, setting it distinctly apart from traditional BI approaches. This iterative process is characterized by the exploration and discovery of models and patterns through an algorithmic and somewhat trial-and-error approach. Unlike the static reports of BI, DS/ML thrives on dynamic, evolving models that adapt and improve over time.

In recent times, the landscape of DS/ML model development has shifted significantly towards automation. Tools like AutoML have transformed the process by minimizing the need for extensive human intervention. By simply providing a database and specifying the target prediction, AutoML platforms take over the intricate task of selecting the optimal combinations of features, hyperparameters, and algorithms. They automate the validation and testing phases to determine the most effective model. This evolution towards automation enables faster, more efficient development cycles, allowing data scientists to focus on more strategic aspects of model development and deployment.

On the other hand, the product of BI development effort, BI data sources (ex. data warehouses, OLAP cubes), is the result of strenuous, manual, and methodical engineering. At least for now, it's people who know what is needed, how data is obtained, and how it's best utilized for analysis and reporting. BI is the primary discipline in which the art of data cleansing and quality has been honed over the past two decades.

Therefore, BI is still very relevant in much the same way it existed over a decade ago before the rise of big data, the cloud, Spark/Databricks—just more polished. DS/ML have narrowed the intelligence gap, but the gap remaining is still too wide for most humans—humans who aren't statisticians or MBAs but can still benefit substantially through direct access to BI data.

Even an R&D-Focused Enterprise is still an Enterprise

Even before AI had gone viral, BI seemed to become "quaint" in the storm of all that's happened with DS/ML over the past decade. The math level and visual sophistication of BI seem dull and antiquated in comparison. However, BI's audience and practitioners are managers and analysts, not researchers with a master's in statistics or data science.

Enterprises for which R&D is the core domain have always been at the forefront in terms of adopting advanced analytical technologies and methodologies. Such enterprises include research labs, insurance actuaries, and financial management firms. These are the early-adopters of the latest and greatest analytics tools and methodologies, if not the inventors.

However, this doesn't mean that BI is irrelevant to an enterprise with R&D as the core domain. In fact, an enterprise can embody both aspects. For instance, a pharmaceutical company might have extensive research departments, but it also operates like a conventional enterprise with functions like manufacturing, sales, marketing, finance, HR, legal, and customer relations.

This dual nature of enterprises highlights the enduring relevance of BI. Just as every household needs some level of financial management skill, regardless of the occupants' professions, every enterprise requires BI to some extent, even if it's not their primary focus. This analogy underscores the fact that while not everyone needs to be a quantitative analyst or Ph.D. in physics, a basic understanding and access to BI data is still fundamental to the success of an enterprise.

Despite the advancements in big data, cloud technologies, Spark/Databricks, and the narrowing of the intelligence gap by DS/ML, BI remains as crucial as it was over a decade ago. It continues to be polished and adapted to modern business needs, maintaining its position as a cornerstone in the analytical needs of enterprises not primarily engaged in deep research.

My BI Misunderstanding

I was introduced to BI back in 1998 when I was fortunate enough to land a minor programming position with a Microsoft development team calling themselves "Plato." It eventually became OLAP Services, then SQL Server Analysis Services.

I didn't have any idea what an OLAP was. And we referred to the subject matter of our product as "decision support systems" (DSS), not "business intelligence." When I first heard of BI, I thought of the "I" in BI in the same way as the "I" in AI. I was mistaken. It's more in line with the "I" in CIA—information gathered to make informed decisions. But my misunderstanding early on shaped how I approached BI. Consequently, I had been out of sync within the discipline in which I made my living over the past 25 years.

> *The sudden emergence of today's level of AI presents a chance to reconcile what BI had always been with what I mistakenly thought it was. BI can morph from the gathering of information into the intelligence of a business, incorporating both contexts of "intelligence"—the "I" in CIA and the "I" in AI.*

BI has very much to offer the AI world as it is a uniquely rich training ground for AI. Consider how social network companies, such as X and Meta, have a unique AI training ground in a massive network of social interaction. But much of it is muddied by low-value information, such as the tendency for users to exhibit a very cleansed and curated version of their lives. However, the BI activity of analysts is honest and hard work. BI analysts are, for the most part, driven to improve the condition of their respective domains, if not across the enterprise. Admittedly, the motivation of BI analysts to do well might be founded on not losing their jobs, but the fact they need to resolve clear and present business problems stands.

Encoding Knowledge

As mentioned, DS/ML has made strides in narrowing the gap between data and the results we process in our heads. But there was still quite a bit of a gap remaining. That gap is filled with a KG and the assistance of AI.

Figure 12 shows a bridge built to cross the chasm from data to the analysts. Those last two pieces (#5 and #6) are what complete the bridge.

1. On the left is the real world, colorful and vibrant. Through our software applications and now IoT devices, we capture data about what goes on in this real world.

2. On the right is the world of analysts, who indirectly observe the real world through collected data from the real world. It's an abstracted, thus duller, view.

3. BI decades ago was the beginning of a bridge to close the gap between the real world and the data world of analysts.

4. DS/ML extended the bridge to at least halfway there.

5. The level of AI at the time of writing takes us much of the way to the other side. But there is still a precarious gap.

6. The EKG, the subject of this book, is the last segment needed to connect data and analysts. Or at least it should get us most of the way there.

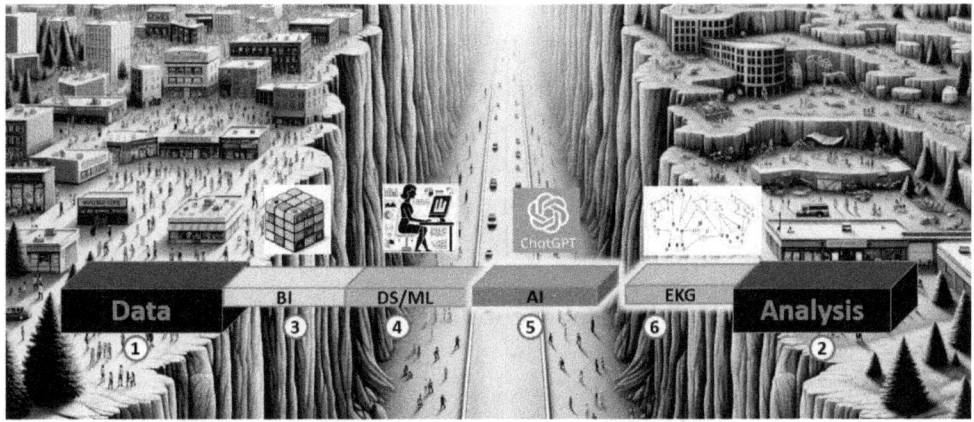

Figure 12: The pieces of a bridge between data and human analysts.

Notice that there is a small gap remaining between AI (5) and EKG (6). This little disconnect will probably never fully go away—at least I hope. Data is mostly about what happened, not what's going on right now. And the world is complex, so any patterns discovered by statistical analysis are perpetually transient. Statistical analysis works because, fortunately, most patterns change slowly enough, so models are practical for at least some period of time, ranging from seconds to decades. *But there will always be some level of uncertainty—no matter how smart AI becomes.*

As it has been for AI over the decades, the EKG has been an elusive proposition. It's a beast that small communities of brave souls have been trying to tackle for years as expert systems, rules engines, and semantic webs. In fact, prior to the rise of DS/ML in the 2010s, the lineage of the EKG and AI strongly overlapped. The rules-based focus on expert systems, particularly the nature of Prolog, looked very much like a KG.

Building an EKG has been an arduous, mostly manual process involving a collaboration of experts in various fields hammering out all sorts of details. For even those who have successfully built one, maintaining it is even tougher as knowledge is a moving target in an ever-evolving world. It's a never-ending chore akin to the large staff of painters and maintenance workers of the Golden Gate Bridge in perpetual maintenance mode.

However, the rise of today's LLMs drastically eases the burden of assisting the authoring of KGs, for example, by:

- Providing a usable foundation of common understanding gleaned from the widely-scoped knowledge of a foundation LLM.

- Seeing connections that are hard for people to see—an enterprise-scale KG literally looks like a haystack.

- Fact-checking hundreds of long-held beliefs about how things work in a tiny fraction of what it would take teams of humans to accomplish.

- Outputting work as code. In an extreme example, transcribing meetings, organizing relationships it finds, and outputting what it hears into the semantic web's RDF/OWL Turtle format or Neo4j's Cypher code for graph databases.

EKGs are the vaults intended to record and encode the wisdom sequestered in the heads of enterprise employees–where most of an enterprise's *understanding* actually resides, into a machine-comprehensible format. Although virtually all text is machine-comprehensible with today's LLMs, that is a very recent phenomenon. A KG is an explicit encoding of knowledge, providing a clear contrast to the probabilistic interpretations often associated with LLMs.

It's Like Books but Looks Like Tinker Toys

The process of creating EKGs isn't really much different from writing technical manuals and employee handbooks. Visually, one looks like the books and pamphlets we're used to, and the other looks like a massive Tinkertoy construction. Figure 13 and Figure 14 show a simple example of text describing a computer programmer versus a KG ontology of a computer programmer. The KG is an extraction of the subject-verb-objects within the text into a node-relationship-node format.

> Computer programmers are the architects and builders of the digital world, playing a crucial role in developing and maintaining software that powers countless aspects of modern life. Their primary task is to write code, a process that transforms complex problems and ideas into functional software. This process often involves several stages, including understanding requirements, designing algorithms, coding, testing, and debugging.

Figure 13: Text description of a computer programmer.

Despite the capabilities of today's LLMs to effectively read and process text, the KG shown in Figure 14 is still easier for an AI to digest. The expression of information is directly and succinctly stated - there is less ambiguity and fewer extraneous words. When querying, the processing is direct, not cogitated at run time as it is with LLMs. However, the KG is less versatile—it isn't connected in an effective way to other KGs we could develop for all sorts of text descriptions.

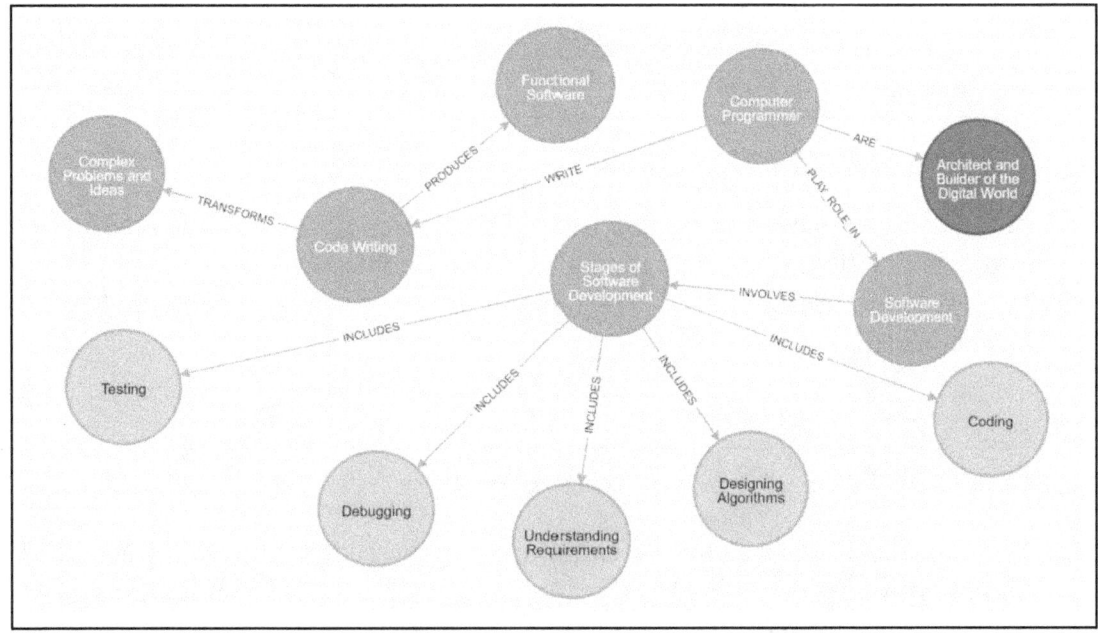

Figure 14: Tinker Toy (KG) form of the paragraph in Figure B-2a.

The real difference is in the authoring process. For KGs, the authors must document every detail of what people have already learned and take for granted. For example, people already know that Python programmers are humans with families or that a phenomenon like "Taco Tuesday" is attractive because it's relatively inexpensive, tasty, and fun food. But does an AI know that?

Figure 15 shows the response from ChatGPT to my very random question (although conceivably spoken at some time in most U.S. enterprises) about Taco Tuesday. Authoring a KG with such broad knowledge required for such random questions (crucial for "out of the box" ideas) is mind-bogglingly tedious. The KG authors are forced to spell out everything in excruciating detail as if they're teaching someone a new subject with no assumptions about what they already know.

You
Why do you think a phenomenon like "Taco Tuesday" has emerged? Please be brief. Your output will be used as a Figure in my book.

ChatGPT
"Taco Tuesday" has emerged as a popular phenomenon due to effective marketing strategies that tap into cultural trends, the social and communal nature of eating, and the affordability and versatility of tacos. This alliterative phrase creates a weekly event that diners anticipate, driving up restaurant traffic on what might otherwise be a slow day.

Figure 15: ChatGPT is broad and versatile, offering a reasonable explanation to my random question.

In the end, we have a comprehensive KG and a well-written manual that express the same information. However, manuals and handbooks were only effectively consumable by people, whereas KGs are consumable by people and machines. That changed in November 2022.

Expert Systems and the Semantic Web

The concept of KGs has been around for many decades. They can trace their origins to "expert systems" developed in the 1970s and 1980s. Earlier foundations in AI languages saw the development of LISP in the late 1950s by John McCarthy, followed by the introduction of Prolog in the 1970s by Alain Colmerauer and Robert Kowalski. By the turn of the millennium, the concept of the semantic web began to take shape. Its vision was to link all objects on the Internet using standardized identifiers, primarily in the form of uniform resource identifiers (URIs).

The idea was that if all web resources (ex. web pages, application program interfaces, documents, media files, etc.) referenced entities using their unique URIs, it would enable sophisticated querying across the web, allowing for advanced inference based on interconnected data. However, the ambitiousness of this vision, combined with the frenzy of the dot-com bubble, meant that the semantic web did not immediately achieve its full potential.

While the semantic web concept didn't fade away, it took a backseat to many other evolving Internet and data technologies. Nonetheless, the W3C developed and introduced standards for the semantic web such as:

- RDF—Resource Description Framework
- RDFS—RDF Schema
- OWL—Web Ontology Language
- SPARQL—SPARQL Protocol and RDF Query Language
- SWRL–Semantic Web Rule Language

The foundational idea of standard identifiers continued to play a role, particularly in the realm of knowledge graphs. These graphs focus on encoding processes and structures within an enterprise in a manner that's interpretable by both humans and machines. The full potential of these encodings, especially from a machine perspective, has been unlocked in recent years with advancements in AI. Notably, models like ChatGPT have enhanced our ability to extract and interpret knowledge from these structures.

[Diverse Human Expertise] + ((KG + LLM) + BI) = AEI

The goal of this book is not to substitute human creativity with automated systems. On the contrary, the collective intelligence of humanity (eight billion of us with a very unique set of experiences), coupled with our inherent capacity for teamwork, far surpasses the comparatively small subset of collective human knowledge that tools like ChatGPT are built upon.

ATTOW, there is much talk about focusing on the quality of the data used to train LLMs. This means removing the "low-quality" text that isn't peer-reviewed books or articles, preferably penned by Nobel laureates. The higher-quality text will result in higher-quality responses from LLMs in addition to lower LLM training costs (which can be extremely expensive). There is also much talk about training LLMs with "synthetic data"–sounds scary, like the history of the world evolving only in your head.

Although I understand the reasons, this just doesn't seem right. Instead of capitalizing on the unique perspectives of eight billion sentient beings, we're whittling down to contributions from a very tiny percentage of the population. That seems to be going the wrong way for reasons that are out of scope. But at least at the level of an enterprise, we can go the other direction, capturing knowledge from a wider breadth of the enterprise's population.

This book describes what I term augmented enterprise intelligence (AEI), akin to augmented reality. In fact, I think of it as the enterprise counterpart to what is called augmented reality for people. This concept envisions a synergy where human understanding, deeply rooted in context and nuance within a business, is enhanced by AI's rapid assimilation of vast information spaces.

Envision the potential when we harness the respective strengths of humans and machines. What if we could harness the collective expertise of knowledge workers from a multitude of fields while they engage in their regular BI tasks? This endeavor isn't about undermining human expertise; it's about expanding the influence of human expertise at a time when the influence of LLMs is rapidly expanding in the space of how we make decisions.

By integrating a methodically constructed EKG with LLMs, such as ChatGPT and the solid foundation of BI, all honed by the invaluable perspectives of human analysts, we achieve augmented enterprise intelligence. This combination goes beyond a turbocharged decision-support system. Indeed, the insights gleaned by human analysts from their chosen BI visualizations constitute knowledge as viable as what is known by domain subject-matter experts. As such, it should logically be incorporated into an EKG.

This book will navigate you through this exciting yet complex landscape, showing you how to create your own AEI ecosystem, transforming the intricacies of modern enterprises into your strategic advantage.

Intuition for this Book

This book ties together many sophisticated subjects. The five big pieces are human intelligence, knowledge graphs, large language models, business intelligence, and, of course, data. Fortunately, the initiative for this work has an interesting, nearly 20-year origin story that should provide rich intuition for the value of this book.

Figure 16 is a nice representation of the major parts. At the center is the LLM, the piece that didn't exist in a readily consumable form until recently. It's really the keystone that links the others together. It's the part I was missing 20 years ago in an attempt to create a focused AI system. For a spoiler alert, at the Conclusion of this book, Figure 205 illustrates how this jar of rocks will be assembled into a framework.

Figure 16: The five big rocks fill the bulk of the proverbial space of this book.

The subject of this book is really Version 3.0 of something I first developed in the 2004-2006 timeframe. It was a system for troubleshooting performance issues in SQL Server installations. It was a graph structure from which we could infer possible reasons for poor query performance and even guide us to possible solutions.

SQL Server is a complicated and sophisticated piece of software, and I will not get into the weeds. I'm sure a large portion of folks who picked up this book are familiar with databases and their performance tuning issues. But for those who are not, I'm sure you have had to call support when your application took a long time to respond or failed due to some database error. Otherwise, think of the SQL Server performance engineer as a doctor attempting to diagnose and treat a challenging presentation of symptoms from a patient.

The graph structure I built was much more than a decision tree, but that's how the project began. It started back in 2004 with a wall poster a colleague of mine created, showcasing a decision tree focused on SQL Server performance tuning. It was developed by one of the most renowned SQL Server performance experts. It was authored in Visio (Microsoft's graph tool at the time) and would be printed out as a large poster. I was asked to do a technical review. Figure 17 gives you an idea of what that poster did and what it looked like. Keep in mind that it was much nicer and more comprehensive.

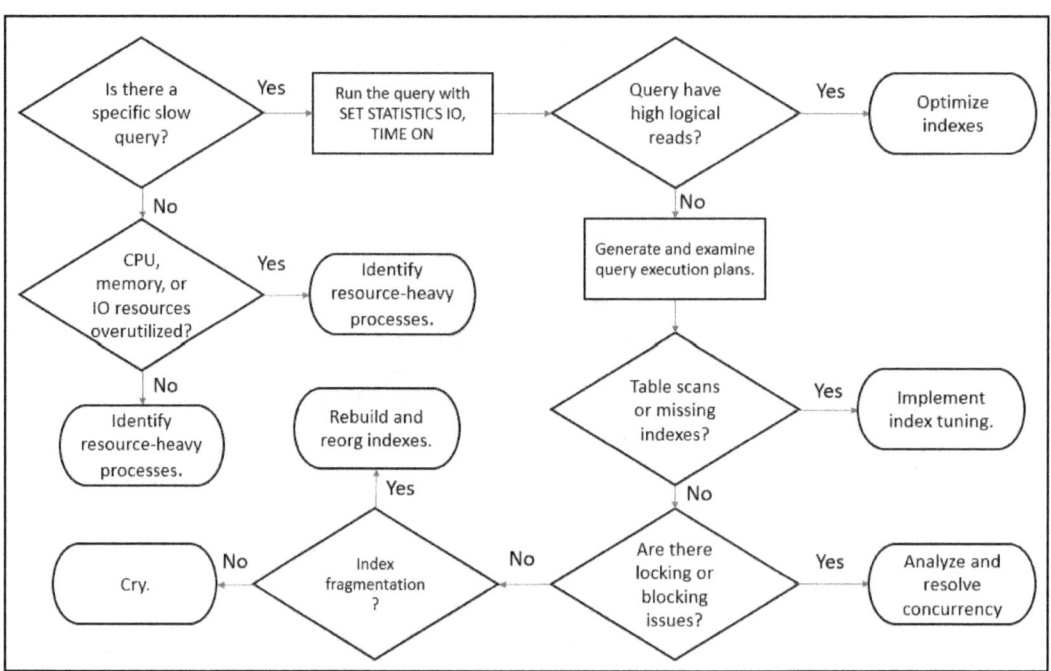

Figure 17: Sample of a decision tree for SQL Server Performance Tuning.

While it covered the major facets of SQL Server performance tuning, the constraints of a 2x3 foot wall poster meant that not everything could be incorporated. It was good for the well-trodden problems, which account for the top 90% of the most frequent performance problems. But there is an embarrassingly long tail of that remaining 10% of less frequent, perhaps obscure, maybe even yet unheard of (the un-Google-able) performance problems that take up the vast majority of the time and mental health of support data engineers and database administrators to resolve.

This inspired me to conceptualize a more data-driven and scalable version of my friend's paper wall poster. Instead of mapping nodes together in Visio to form a poster, I could create a database of traversable relationships. Rather than paths from a starting symptom to another symptom to a "treatment plan" (as it is with a decision tree), I would map out how the parts of SQL Server worked together—to a meticulously detailed level.

My motivation for this project was very strong. I was the onsite consultant from Microsoft Premier Support assigned to a very large software vendor at the time. They were pushing SQL Server as the database option in an effort to lower costs compared to the current relational database (you can probably guess which one).

The software vendor's customers were all large and complex enterprises in themselves, from various industries, geographies, and business models. So, each of the SQL Server implementations operated under widely varied conditions. Anything that could possibly happen at my customer's customers installations did happen! Any time a service pack or even hotfix was released, or a Microsoft developer sneezed on SQL Server, some customer somewhere in the world broke.

Version 1—SQL Server Performance Tuning Web (ca. 2004)

Over the next few months, I mapped out the most detailed levels of cause and effect related to SQL Server. These relationships were at the highest granularity of detail. If relationships were not mapped to this elemental level, they would be an ambiguous bog of "it depends"—for example, it depends on the edition, the available RAM, the CPU, etc.

For every "knob" and every metric, there is a reason. Although I dread thinking in zero-sum terms, at least for our machines (like a SQL Server instance), there are trade-offs for every configuration setting. Otherwise, there is no purpose for the knob. Sometimes, the trade-off is tough to see. Or maybe someone doesn't want to see it--the trade-off is swept under the rug (think about that). This "manual" authoring was much harder than I expected. The nuances of SQL Server performance tuning sound easier in my head than in a graph of relationships. I recruited other SQL Server experts. But despite the tremendous benefits of collaboration, the differences of opinion slowed down the process. Differences of opinion are great, but in this case, I had a finite window and chose to go it alone for the first iteration, which was intended to be more of a proof of concept.

At the time, I found a couple of references to folks attempting to map out biological ecosystems. They mentioned it had taken a couple of years. Yikes! What was worse for me is, I imagine, for that group, their ecosystem doesn't change as quickly as mine. Every so often, their ecosystem might be impacted by the introduction of an invasive species.

"Change" in my "ecosystem" was fueled by a brutal feature war with other big software vendors.

The idea was that we could have a web of trade-offs between the dozens of metrics mapping how they affect each other. In other words, for each "knob" we could tweak, what did we expect to gain—and equally important, what would be the side effects? The idea was that we could start with the metrics for which we have current readings outside the "good" range and connect all the dots between them to see how they might all be related. That differs from the decision tree approach my friend took with the poster. A decision tree is a set of decisions that iteratively whittles down the set of possible solutions based on new clues. In this case, the clues were symptoms to look for.

The web included metrics at the level of broken-down elemental terms, configuration settings, and an ontology of the moving parts of SQL Server. Together, the graph was something I called a "trade-off/semantic network" (TOSN). The metrics broken down into elemental terms were the "trade-off" part. The idea is that for each elemental term, we could take what gets traded off when one is raised and the other is consequently lowered. For example, RAM is a trade-off of cost or the ability to store more in the buffer pool. Other examples include:

- Indexing:
    - Pros:
        - Speeds up query performance significantly, especially for SELECT operations.
        - Can lead to faster joins, grouping, and sorting operations.
    - Cons:
        - Consumes additional storage.
        - Slows down INSERT, UPDATE, and DELETE operations due to the overhead of maintaining indexes.
        - Can lead to fragmentation over time, necessitating index maintenance.

- Database Normalization:
    - Pros:
        - Reduces data redundancy.
        - Improves data integrity.
    - Cons:
        - Increases query complexity due to the need for more JOIN operations.

- Can degrade performance if not managed properly.

- Data Caching (e.g., Buffer Pool Extension):
  - Pros:
    - Accelerates query performance by storing frequently accessed data in memory.
  - Cons:
    - Consumes more memory resources.
    - If misconfigured, can lead to inefficient use of memory.

In SQL Server performance tuning, understanding these trade-offs is essential. The optimal configuration often depends on the specific workload, with some systems requiring rapid read operations (e.g., reporting databases) and others prioritizing fast write operations (e.g., transactional databases). Figure 18 shows a small piece of the map of the pros and cons of tweaking a configuration. The three configurations listed above are circled in red.

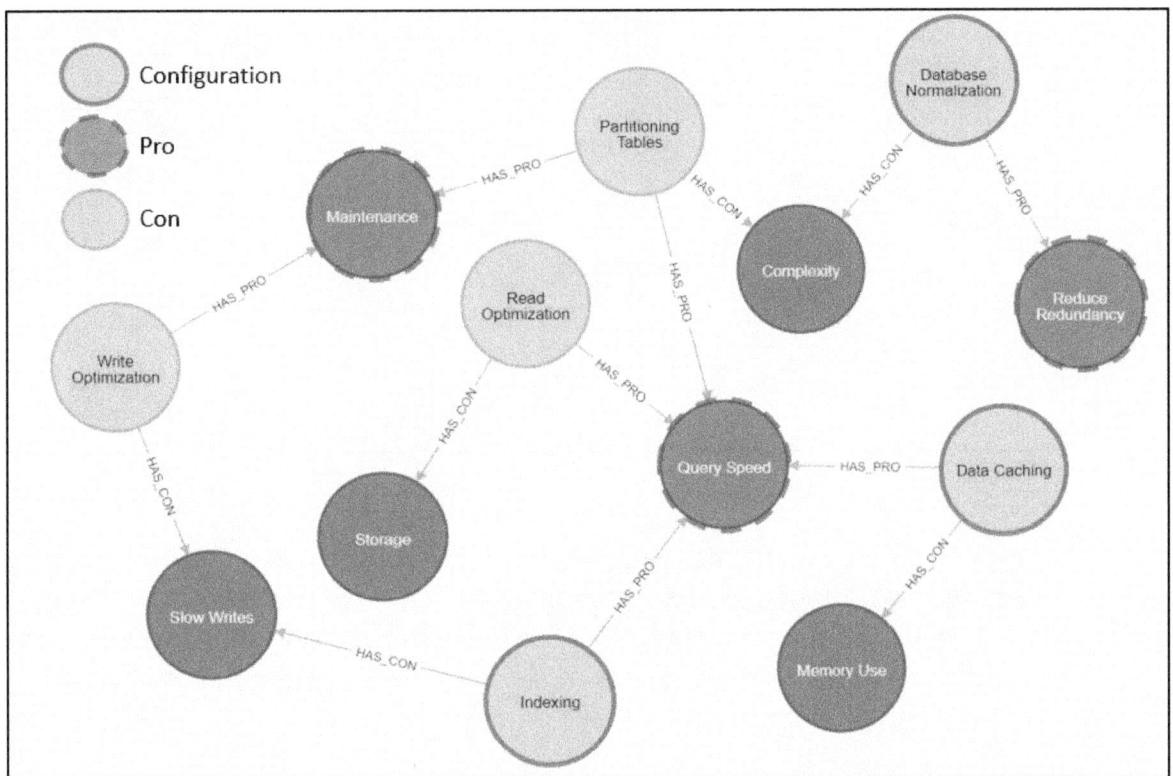

Figure 18: Sample of trade-offs related to SQL Server Performance tuning.

The Semantic Network side of the TOSN is an ontology of the pieces that make up SQL Server and the environment around it. That can even include things like users and their needs. This is what might be normally included in a KG today. In fact, I should have used the term, "knowledge graph."

Figure 19 is a sample of the Semantic Network (ontology) and Trade-Off sides.

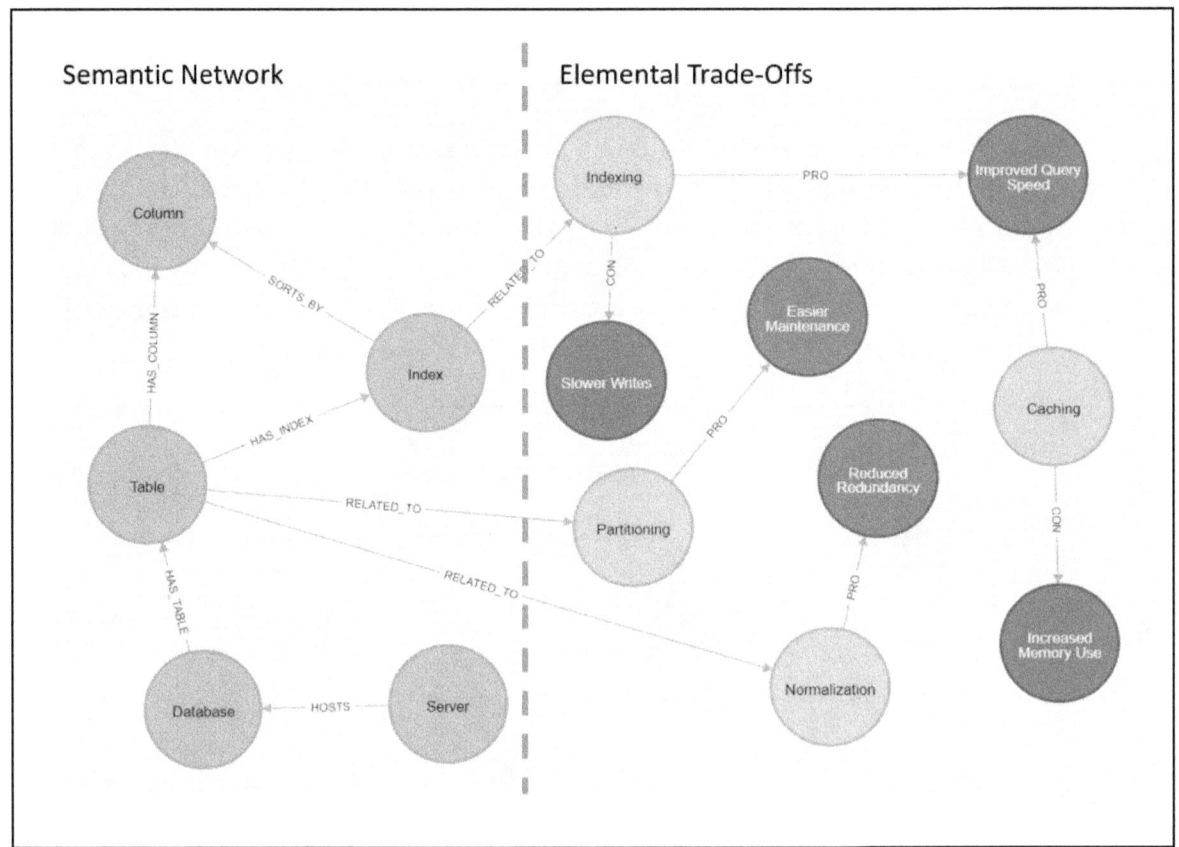

Figure 19: A semantic network linked to the SQL Server performance tuning trade-offs.

There were many problems I needed to resolve along the way, which I won't get into. But in the end, I ended with a system for which I could enter symptoms (misbehaving metric values) and receive a list of paths connecting the dots between those symptoms. I could also visualize subsets of the model, as shown in Figure 20, a Visio diagram of a very small subset of the TOSN.

SQL Server was a great model for testing out semantic networks as it was in a sweet spot of being complicated enough where the development and maintenance of a semantic network could be of significant value but not too complicated such that capturing enough of its nature is more trouble than its worth, if not impossible.

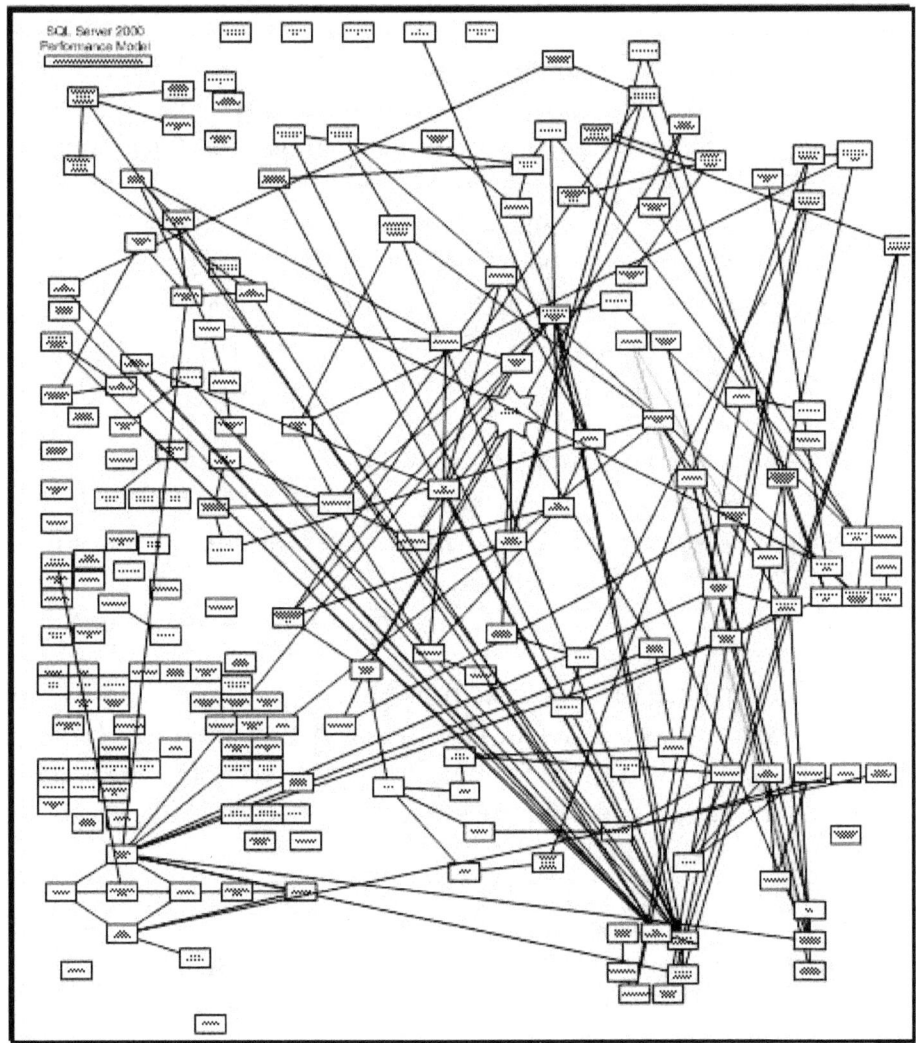

Figure 20: A partial view of the web of trade-offs in SQL Server. This shows how quickly viewing a large graph becomes overwhelming.

So why didn't this succeed? Putting aside any failings of mine inherent of a one-man show, there are a few things that stood out, from which you can learn from my stupidity:

- **What's a Graph?** For one, the notion of anything related to graphs was very novel at the time in the enterprise database world dominated by relational databases. At the time, there weren't any readily obtainable graph databases or authoring tools with a reasonable price, scalability, and ease of use. The one graph tool available to me was Visio, which was very clunky and not very scalable. Surprisingly, I'd even say most of my programmer colleagues had long forgotten since college what vertices and edges are.

- **SQL Server 2000 is Dead, Long Live SQL Server 2005.** Another issue that exacerbated the difficulty was the impending release of SQL Server 2005—a major upgrade to SQL Server 2000, which is what I developed the TOSN on. At the time, companies didn't upgrade to the latest and greatest (version, service pack, or hotfix) as readily as they do in today's CI/CD era. So, my Version 1 had to be on SQL Server 2000. I attempted a Version 1.5 of the TOSN that included 2005, and learned how much more difficult a graph can be to upgrade and maintain than to initially build. But this was a greatly valuable lesson that exposed the fact that the maintenance of such a structure is even more difficult.

- **Pre-ML Days.** Data mining, as it was called back then, was surprisingly still fringe for most. There was barely a hint of democratization. There were relatively few of what are called data scientists today plugging away with SPSS and R, but it was still rocket science for the average data engineer or BI analyst (the two other pillars of a well-rounded data science team).

What might have been the worst factor is I had to create substantial tools from scratch—each a full-scale project in itself. One was a data warehouse (DW) of captured SQL Server performance data points: PerfMon Counters, SQL Server Profiler trace logs, configuration settings, and information from a Microsoft support tool named SQLDiag.

The DW was critical. It supplied data across the many SQL Server installations of my customer's customers that would provide statistics about each mapped relationship garnered from across the fantastically unique mix of SQL Server implementations. It's similar to the role of the Tuple Correlation Web (Version 3), which we'll talk about soon.

I did run into a roadblock with that DW. Some of my customer's customers didn't sign off on utilizing their data for these purposes. That is, even though this didn't require any database data, not even sensitive metadata. These are just performance counters that would be exposed in a highly transformed manner to end users. And I was proposing something that I felt would offer them tremendous value in return.

As tough as that DW was to implement, it was the easy part since that was my primary skill at the time. I also needed to create two tough tools. The tougher one was a rules engine that altered the strength of the relationships between the TOSN nodes depending on the context of a troubleshooting session. It was based on Prolog, the old AI language. So I wrote a .NET Prolog interpreter in order to:

1. Seamlessly integrate with the .NET-based development environment I was using.

2. Add a few features to Prolog to make it more "distributed" than Prolog was designed for.

I named my Prolog variant SCL for "Soft Coded Logic."

The less intense tool was a UI to author and test the graph as I went along. It's the equivalent of Protégé today, which I will discuss in upcoming sections. So, after a few months, my time ran out. As far as my day job was concerned, it was time to move back to my "normal" duties.

To recap, these are the lessons learned from the SQL Server Performance Web:

1. Don't take this on yourself. I couldn't recruit help in sufficient quantities. In my case, back in 2005, this was seen as too fringe. My colleagues all had day jobs. My boss at the time was forward-thinking enough to give me leeway. It might have been easier to recruit performance-tuning experts if I had tools, such as Protégé and Grafo back then.

2. I severely underestimated how difficult it would be to map out what I knew about SQL Server performance tuning. However, today, assistance from a LLM would speed up this process immensely—a big theme of this book.

3. The maintenance of the graph is much more tedious than the initial development. The issue is more that it's an ongoing process. If the graph doesn't reflect modifications (due to system changes or errors), it becomes less than valuable—no answer is better than the wrong answer.

4. If the tools for the components are too expensive or even virtually non-existent, the world isn't ready for the idea. You're on your own. Notably, graph databases were bleeding-edge, OWL was still a year or two away, and the whole notion of DWs themselves was still in a maturing phase.

Version 2—Map Rock (ca. 2011)

As I write this, it's been over a decade since 2011, when I began software development on Version 2 work that I'd eventually name Map Rock. Like the TOSN, Map Rock, as a coherent product, never did go anywhere. The Tuple Correlation Web is a direct descendant of Map Rock.

One of the underlying goals of Map Rock bears a vague resemblance to a current rising star in the analytics world that's been on my mind: data mesh. The vague similarity is the approach of building a widely-encompassing, integrated picture of data from a set of domain-level data "objects" (cube, data mart, whatever). The difference is:

- Data mesh decomposes a monolithic data analytics landscape (the monolithic IT that develops monolithic data lakes or monolithic "enterprise data warehouses") into a distributed system of domain-level "Data Products." These data products are integrated into an organized, loosely-coupled mesh—which we can call the Data Fabric.

- Map Rock integrates a set of independently built departmental (or subject-oriented) data marts into a loosely-coupled web linked primarily through the ubiquitous time dimension. Map Rock metrics were centered on algorithms fit for time series, primarily Pearson correlations. This avoided the need to forge mappings between differently defined entities in different domains–that's the problem Master Data Management (MDM) addresses. MDM was starting to hit its stride at the time, but it was still a very difficult process.

Figure 21 illustrates how departmental (domain or subject-oriented) data marts could be developed at the domain level and linked together with the time dimension (the squiggly lines connecting the cubes depict linkage via the time dimension).

Map Rock is about discovering relationships between information locked up in disparate cubes. For example, what relationships are there between a Finance-Focused cube and a Customer Relationship-focused cube? Further, what relationships are there between the Customer Relationship cube and an Inventory cube, as well as between the Inventory cube and the Finance cube? It forms a web of relationships, in this case, a simple sort of love triangle between a Finance, Customer, and Inventory cube.

But what is a relationship? Well, just about anything imaginable, maybe not even yet imaginable. And even if we knew of relationships between cubes, most cubes back then (and even today) lack common dimensions. Some sort of commonality is the basis of relationships. This was prior to MDM becoming a household term.

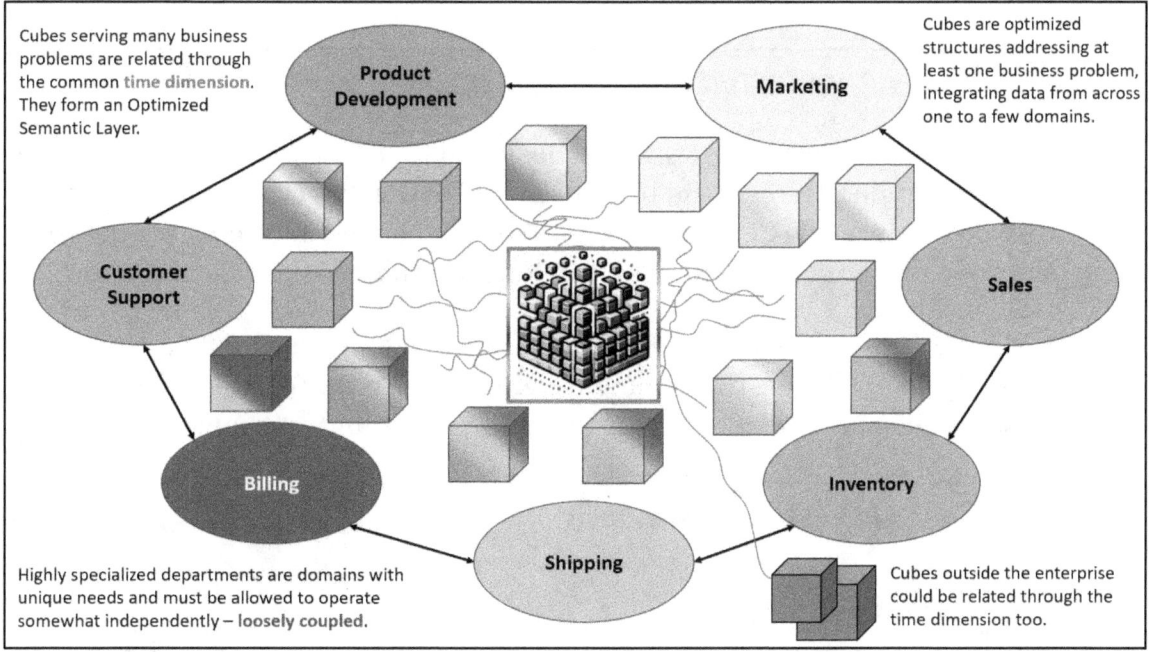

Figure 21: Business Problem Silos.

As mentioned, there is one common dimension, and it's a biggy—Date/Time. Although cubes aren't required to have a date dimension, virtually all useful cubes do. Date is a biggy because all objects and events are a set of observations that happen together. As neurology folks say, "What fires together, wires together." Surely, I had to do some translation between different date formats (for example, Jan-02-2011 versus 2011-01-01), but that's easy. With that as an initial type of relationship, I thought of a surprisingly obscure MDX function, CORRELATION (CORREL in Excel), that I wrote about just a month before on the formula for the Pearson Correlation Coefficient. Simply put, it is a score of the similarity between two time series.

Unlike the TOSN, my motivation for Map Rock was an effort to preserve my then 13-year-old livelihood around SQL Server Analysis Services (SSAS). SSAS appeared to be near the end of its reign as the go-to technology of the BI world. Specifically, I'm referring to the original "multi-dimensional" SSAS before the arrival of its little brother, SSAS Tabular, a simpler in-memory edition. It was in that late July 2011 timeframe that I realized the single-server, scale-up SSAS would be overrun by the pre-configured, scale-out and/or in-memory likes of the DW appliances, such as SQL Server PDW and Netezza. Of course, Hadoop, Spark, and Snowflake were soon to come.

The big data and the cloud tsunami of change were too much, so after a few years, I put Map Rock away and shifted to all that neat Azure data engineer stuff.

Version 3—Augmented Enterprise Intelligence (Present)

As mentioned, Version 3 is what this book is about. It's a mix of Versions 1 (KG) and 2 (BI information). Here, I want to focus more on what has changed to make the ideas I've worked on since 2004 feasible in 2024. Today, the pieces for creating the sort of KGs I had hoped for with the TOSN and Map Rock are mostly available and mature enough.

Figure 22 shows a high-level categorization of the pieces that I've employed for this book. Again, I'm trying to be vendor-neutral, but I need to explain some products, and these are the ones that seem either the most popular or just happen to be what I know.

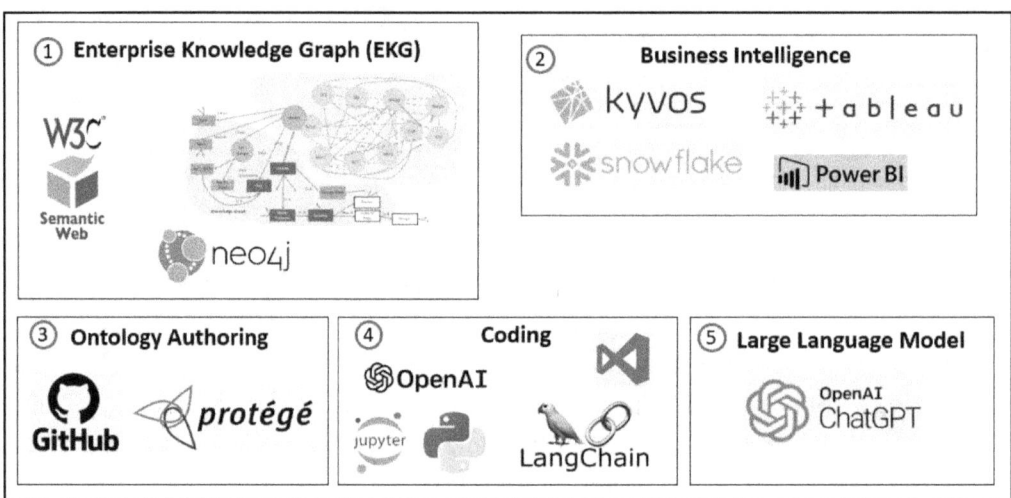

Figure 22: High-level view of what comprises the AEI.

Below are brief descriptions of the five categories and their associated products:

1. **Enterprise Knowledge Graph (EKG)**–EKGs represent complex networks of interconnected data and concepts within an organization. They aid in decision-making by providing a structured and queryable representation of knowledge. The W3C semantic web is the initiative that standardizes the formats and protocols related to EKGs, promoting interoperability between multiple KGs and EKGs. Neo4j is a graph database platform that excels in storing and querying connected data at high scale, making it ideal for implementing EKGs.

2. **Business Intelligence (BI)**—BI tools are software applications used to analyze an organization's analytics data. They are crucial for reporting, data mining, business performance analysis, and decision-making. Kyvos is a BI acceleration platform that enables quick insights from massive data lakes. Tableau and Power BI are leading data visualization tools that transform raw data into understandable and interactive dashboards. And Snowflake provides cloud-based data warehousing solutions that support the BI process.

3. **Ontology Authoring**—Ontologies define the relationships between concepts in a domain, enabling richer data interpretation and AI applications. GitHub is a development platform used for code sharing and collaboration. It can be utilized for versioning and distributing ontologies. Protégé is an open-source ontology editor and a framework for building intelligent systems.

4. **Coding**—This involves the actual writing of software and scripts to implement and analyze data systems. OpenAI provides AI research and tools, such as APIs for developers to access AI models. Jupyter is an open-source web application that allows the creation and sharing of documents that contain live code, equations, visualizations, and narrative text. Python is a high-level programming language known for its readability and broad applicability in data analysis, visualization, and app development.

5. **Large Language Model**—Large Language Models like OpenAI's ChatGPT use machine learning to understand and generate human-like text, assisting in tasks, such as conversation, composition, and information retrieval. They are trained on vast amounts of text data (at the time of writing) to predict and generate language sequences.

Most of the story of Version 1 (TOSN) is a familiar one to folks attempting to map out a system into a KG or a more formal semantic web. Today, graph databases, such as Neo4j, and machine learning and data science are almost old hat. But until ChatGPT came along, encoding human expert knowledge was still an impractically arduous task.

KG Development with LLM Assistance

From a more general point of view, authoring and maintaining KGs of complicated systems is today more feasible and practical with LLM assistance. What would take many months to years can now probably take a few weeks. It's easier to break down the task into smaller pieces and fit those pieces together, thanks to LLM's "reasoning" capabilities. We'll discuss this more in the section on Knowledge Bogs. Looking back at the TOSN (Version 1—The SQL Server Performance Web), it would take a tiny fraction of the effort to build it today. GPT4 is profoundly knowledgeable about SQL Server performance tuning. It's been trained on extensive threads from technical sites, blogs, articles, and perhaps a book or two about SQL Server. Curious, I jumped right into asking ChatGPT to start such a web. Figure 23 below is a prompt I used to output a demo of how to build a process.

Consider a few examples of common performance problems with SQL Server. Each problem involves looking through metrics that could be found in Performance Monitor. Could you create a graph of metrics relating to your examples and how they might affect each other. For example more RAM raises buffer pool, which lowers paging. Please include Cypher code that generates a graph of these relationships. And include a description property for each relationship. The number of examples should provide a good demonstration of how a metric can affect multiple other metrics. The description properties of nodes and relationships should be enough such that a user of the graph is able to search for information about a SQL Server problem using some form of NLP interface.

Figure 23: Prompt for generating SQL Server troubleshooting map.

Figure 24 is a partial output of Cypher code returned to create the objects in Neo4j.

```
// Create nodes for each performance problem
CREATE
(cpuPressure:Problem {name: 'CPU Pressure', description: 'Excessive CPU utilization by SQL Server causing slower response times.'}),
(memoryPressure:Problem {name: 'Memory Pressure', description: 'Insufficient available RAM for SQL Server processes causing performance degradation.'}),
(diskIO:Problem {name: 'Disk I/O Bottlenecks', description: 'Delays caused by disk subsystem not keeping up with the read/write request rate.'}),
(networkLatency:Problem {name: 'Network Latency', description: 'Issues with transmitting and receiving data packets quickly.'}),
(concurrencyIssues:Problem {name: 'Concurrency Issues', description: 'Problems arising from multiple queries contending for the same resource.'});

// Create nodes for metrics related to each problem
CREATE
(processorTime:Metric {name: 'Processor Time %', description: 'Percentage of elapsed time the processor spends executing.'}),
(queryCompilations:Metric {name: 'SQL Compilations/s', description: 'Number of SQL compilations happening per second.'}),
```

Figure 24: Partial output of Cypher code for SQL Server troubleshooting map.

Figure 25 is the Cypher code returned to create relationships between the objects.

```
MATCH
(b:Metric {name: 'Page Life Expectancy'}),
(c:Metric {name: 'Buffer Cache Hit Ratio %'})
CREATE (b)-[:INFLUENCES {description: 'Lower Page Life Expectancy can decrease Buffer Cache Hit Ratio %.'}]->(c);

MATCH
(c:Metric {name: 'Buffer Cache Hit Ratio %'}),
(d:Metric {name: 'Page Reads/s'})
CREATE (c)-[:IMPACTS {description: 'Reduced Buffer Cache Hit Ratio % increases Page Reads from disk.'}]->(d);

MATCH
(d:Metric {name: 'Page Reads/s'}),
(e:Metric {name: 'Disk Queue Length'})
CREATE (d)-[:ELEVATES {description: 'More Page Reads/s can increase Disk Queue Length, suggesting I/O bottlenecks.'}]->(e);
```

Figure 25: Cypher creating a chain of metrics and how they relate.

Figure 26 shows the sample SQL Server troubleshooting map in Neo4j after running the code shown in Figure 24 and Figure 25.

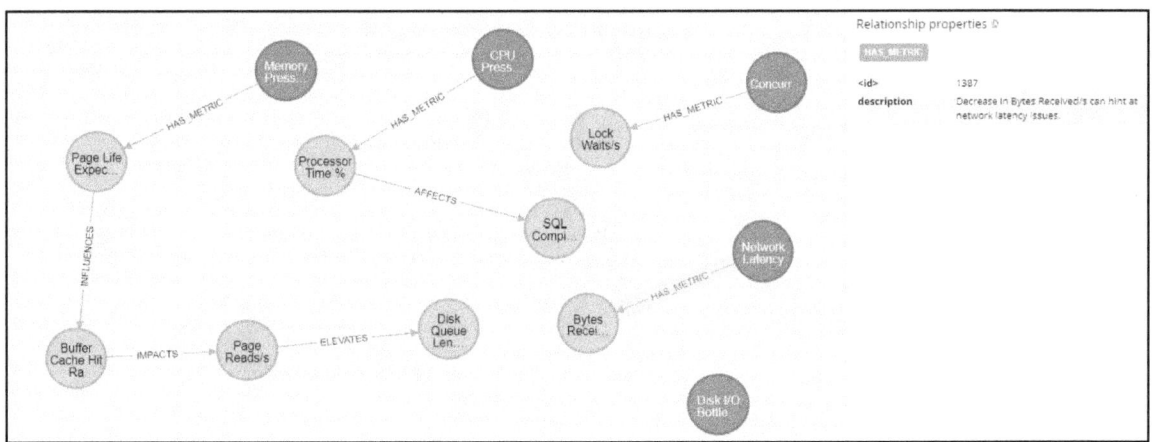

Figure 26: SQL Server troubleshooting map.

Of course, this is just one iteration of the process. I still need to expand on what we have so far. In fact, I would probably modify the prompt to instruct ChatGPT to return a node for every metric available.

I must say, though, that ChatGPT seemed a little lazy around this time. ChatGPT, Llama, and Gemini probably partied too hard with tens of millions of people asking it crazy questions. Further, for deeper, perhaps even proprietary scenarios, private LLMs—trained on internal documentation, email exchanges, Jira tickets, and the like—could offer invaluable insights. They could significantly aid in illustrating and documenting your business processes. Earlier, discussing my use of ChatGPT as an assistant, I pondered whether it could have written this whole book if I created a private LLM from my thousands of pages of notes over the past two decades.

The Puppet Looks More Lifelike

With easily accessible ontology authoring tools (for example, Protégé and Grafo), easily accessible LLMs (for example, ChatGPT), and established standards (RDF, OWL, schema.org), much of the abstract, high-level, and rather straightforward knowledge of subject matter experts can be pragmatically captured and integrated. By "pragmatically," I mean without needing thousands of collective hours over months involving dozens to hundreds of people stitching together some sort of EKG.

> *With the EKG, we know what things are (for example, a customer is a human or a company), and we can map processes such as onboarding a new hire. We then augment the EKG with relationships extracted from our databases, guided by the queries of human knowledge workers.*

CHAPTER THREE

The Intelligence of a Business

A Business is as an Organism

I've always approached BI as the development of a centralized brain for a business, as if the business were a creature. That's due to my misunderstanding of the "I in BI" that I described earlier.

A business is made up of many departments (organs). It has goals, such as profit and growth. It feels pain when something disrupts operations-an air of urgency permeates the offices. It feels sad when profits are down-people fear layoffs, reorgs, and such. It becomes hungry when it needs something.

An LLM-assisted KG and a few structures computed from data driven by the actions of people (employees, customers, vendors, etc.) might start to vaguely resemble a full brain. But it can't be a full brain because businesses don't seem as fully animated as people with full brains. Although businesses today output fantastic things, they don't run as smoothly as even a mouse or even a brainless paramecium.

This book is about integrating components into something that begins to better resemble the brain of an organism, towards the goal of smoothing out operations and making life better for employees and customers while still moving the needle upwards in prosperity.

In fact, it is appropriate to say that corporations are conceptualized as entities, similar to how people are considered entities. This perspective aligns with legal and economic views where a corporation is often treated as a distinct legal entity, separate from its owners and employees, much like an individual person. Like people, corporations can be sued and even executed.

> *Business domains are like organs.*

In the vast "organism" that is a business, departments or domains emerge as essential functional units. They're not just organizational structures. They embody the spirit and purpose of specific operations, much like organs in an organism. Without a single one of these domains, the entity would not function optimally or, more likely, will falter altogether. Each department is like an "organ," with a unique role, but is inter-dependent with others to ensure the health and vitality of the whole. Here are a few examples of the major "organs":

- Operations might be the heartbeat, setting the pace and ensuring the delivery of services or products.

- Sales and Marketing could be likened to the sensory organs, gauging market reactions and seeking opportunities.

- Human Resources, much like the circulatory system, ensures the flow of fresh talent and the well-being of the current workforce.

- Finance, akin to the digestive system, allocates resources, ensuring all parts are nourished and discarding what's not needed.

Employees within these departments vary in roles and responsibilities. While most provide the consistent force that keeps the business running smoothly, some are specialized experts, reminiscent of specialized cells (ex. immune cells) that address unique challenges or opportunities. Some interface in a physical way with real the world, akin to muscles.

The Brain: A Centralized Repository of Knowledge

If departments are the organs, the EKG, LLMs, and BI (data sources and analysts), complemented by associated processes, emerge as the central nervous system. It's the intelligence center, the observer, the coordinator, and the decision-maker. This "brain" holds the intricate web of relationships, rules, and definitions, ensuring that the "body" responds effectively to its environment.

- **Memory Retention**: Like the brain's hippocampus storing memories, the knowledge graph retains intricate details of business interactions, strategies, outcomes, and more.

- **Decision-making:** Processes, such as BI, come into play here, much like the brain's frontal lobe. By analyzing data and insights, the brain makes strategic decisions, guiding the business's path forward.

- **Coordination:** The KG ensures that the myriad functions of the business organism are harmoniously orchestrated, much like how the brain ensures all bodily functions are integrated and cohesive without stepping over each other.

- **Adaptability and Learning:** A vital function of any brain, including that of a business, is to learn and adapt. With the continuous input of BI insights, the business's brain evolves, learns from past experiences, and adapts to future challenges.

- **Business Process Management:** It's the reflex arc of this business organism. Just as reflexes allow for immediate response to stimuli, BPM ensures streamlined operations, quick adaptability, and efficiency in response to varying business needs.

In this organism analogy, it becomes evident that the true essence of a business lies not just in its structural components but in its ability to think, adapt, decide, and drive its evolution. This intelligence, embodied in the EKG and the processes that bring it to life, is what transforms a mere organization into a living, breathing, thriving entity in its market ecosystem.

EKG versus Conventional Databases

An EKG is a database, but it differs fundamentally from databases we're most used to, which are typically visualized as structured collections of tables and columns.

Traditional databases primarily serve as ledgers. They capture events as they occur and document them meticulously. As these databases grow and evolve, their development is generally a response to the necessities of various processes and, optionally, a commitment to preserving history.

In contrast, an EKG should stand as a living model of the world, as opposed to just the state and history of the things and events in the world. Rather than being a mere repository, its purpose is to map out and update the vast web of dynamic relationships in the data universe. When we speak of the EKG, we're referring to the most current representation of this interconnected world model.

To merely label EKGs as an "advanced method of data storage" would be an oversimplification. While data lakes promise flexibility with diverse data formats and volumes, EKGs offer something more profound. Their malleability, akin to the brain's neuroplasticity, enables us to adjust, refine, and enhance this data structure with our evolving understanding of the evolving world.

Consider traditional database schemas. They detail concrete relationships, like how a customer has an address or how an address corresponds to a zip code. Leveraging our innate human cognitive abilities, we might extrapolate workflows or discern patterns. KGs, however, are explicit about such relationships. Powered by human intellect (and increasingly by tools like LLMs), EKGs encode these relationships in clear, interconnected structures.

Yet, EKGs prioritize abstraction over exhaustive detail. Analogous to our brains, which capture the essence of an image rather than every pixel, EKGs home in on the core connections and patterns. When granular information is required, they know precisely where to source it. These compact abstractions are invaluable. They provide the foundational knowledge to understand, adapt, and innovate in ever-changing scenarios without having to reinvent the analytical wheel each time.

> It's essential to recognize the profound experiential advantage humans have—years of diverse, real-time learning in a dynamically evolving world. While humans navigate this complex, stochastic realm firsthand, tools like LLMs vicariously experience slices of our civilization captured in data. By focusing on broad abstractions over niche details, we position ourselves for agility and innovation in an environment where, as the adage goes, "we never step into the same river twice."

Humans as Components of the Business Organism

If a business is like an organism, departments like organs, EKGs (and the processing and maintenance parts) like the brain, what are we human workers in this analogy? What are the dozens to hundreds of thousands of people working at the business?

We are autonomous agents with specialized talents. We as humans can evolve our functionality, our skill set, as needed. We build and repair things both physical and intangible (e.g., software). In the context of a business as an organism, we're definitely an intricate part. Collectively, we might be the most important part. Individually, maybe not so much.

In the intricate biological machinery of an organism, humans within a business can be likened to specialized cells that carry out specific functions. Just as cells work in harmony to maintain homeostasis, regulate processes, respond to changes, and adapt to new conditions, so too do humans play their roles within the larger context of a business. While the following is far from a perfect analogy, below is a set of comparable attributes of a functioning business, highlighting the similarities of those of a biological organism:

- **Specialized Talents = Cellular Functions:** Just as different cells (e.g., nerve cells, muscle cells) have specialized roles, individuals in a business have unique skills and roles. A marketing professional, for instance, could be likened to a sensory cell, picking up on external signals (market demands) and relaying them inward.

- **Autonomous Agents = Independent Cellular Activities:** While cells are governed by the organism's overall needs, they also have a degree of autonomy in how they function. Similarly, while employees work towards the company's goals, they also have individual agency, creativity, and discretion in their tasks.

- **Adaptation and Growth = Cellular Learning and Memory:** Just as cells can "learn" from past experiences (e.g., immune cells "remember" pathogens), employees learn and grow from their experiences, adapting to new challenges and improving their skills.

- **Building and Repair = Cellular Repair and Maintenance:** In the same way that certain cells have roles in the repair, maintenance, and growth of tissues, humans in a business create, maintain, and improve both physical and data infrastructures. They can be seen as the repair and maintenance crew of the business organism, ensuring its smooth operation.

- **Immune Function = Defense and Adaptation:** Some employees function as a form of "immune system" for the business. They identify, neutralize, and adapt to external threats. This could be in the form of legal teams (defending against lawsuits), IT security (defending against cyber threats), or even PR teams (managing public perception and crises).

- **Neural Function = Communication and Decision Making:** While the knowledge graph acts as the "brain" storing and processing information, employees act as the "neurons," transmitting information, making decisions, and ensuring various departments (organs) communicate efficiently.

In the business organism analogy, humans are multifunctional cells that adapt, communicate, repair, defend, and grow the business. Their roles are versatile, dynamic, and crucial for the health and success of the business organism.

Survival of the Smartest?

As an organization, a business competes in an ecosystem. But it's not like the ecosystem in which cougars, deer, grass, and locusts compete. Players in those ecosystems don't really have goals—at least, not like humans have aspirations. For the most part, cougars, deer, and grass just do what they do and face what they face. They don't consciously strive to compete better. Rather, each species tosses out a big bag of variants (offspring) and whichever happens to stick wins the lottery and gets to toss out the next big bag of variants in the next round.

Businesses are different. They purposefully aspire and evolve to better compete. They evolve by learning from feedback, noticing alternative ways to win. It's survival of the cleverest, smartest, and most motivated. That's what lets a "David" see beyond the myth and legend of a "Goliath." The idea is maybe like our immune system. A few cells encounter what seems like an invading entity and find a way to beat it. That knowledge is saved so that the next time the invader is encountered, we can try what worked before and build upon that experience. Most of the time that should work–which means our response consumes much less time and energy.

> *Survival of the smartest works because smarter entities have more options in their arsenal for quick and cheap responses but can invent new ones in the face of novel problems.*

Business Intelligence, Performance Management, Process Management

Business *performance* management and business *process* management, though they share the same acronym (BPM), address different aspects of business operations. Of the two, business performance management (BPfM) is probably more familiar to the general public since most employees today are assigned key performance indicators (KPIs) in some form or another, which are brought up on a regular basis through ceremonial performance reviews. Business Process Management (BPrM) is usually less familiar to the general public as it typically occurs behind the scenes, focusing on internal workflows and operational efficiencies that are not directly visible to most employees.

In the intricacies of business operations, BPrM and BPfM perform complementary roles in orchestrating the symphony of organizational efficiency. BPrM is the conductor, meticulously guiding and fine-tuning the myriad processes that form the backbone of an enterprise. It involves a detailed analysis and iterative improvement of workflows to ensure the machinery of business runs as smoothly and effectively as possible, from the granular steps in manufacturing a product to the sweeping movements of service delivery.

BPfM, on the other hand, is akin to a sophisticated sensory system within the business organism. It measures the health and well-being of the company's operations, detecting areas of excellence to celebrate and replicate, as well as identifying pain points that require remedial attention. It systematically gathers data, analyzes performance metrics, and provides the critical feedback necessary to maintain the delicate balance between operational efficacy and strategic objectives. In essence, it allows a business to keep its finger on the pulse of its own vitality, ensuring that decision makers are well-informed and poised to act when necessary.

Together, they serve as the twin pillars of "the intelligence of a business"–a term that transcends its data-centric connotation to encompass the wisdom of knowing and the acumen of doing. While BPrM ensures that every cog in the wheel is positioned and calibrated for optimal performance, BPfM continuously assesses whether the wheel is turning in the right direction and at the right speed. In the grand narrative of your business, these BPMs don't just tell the story of how well your processes are functioning; they drive the direction of how your business thrives, adapts, and ultimately, succeeds.

Let's break down the differences into more detail.

Business Performance Management (BPfM) is:

- **Focus on Metrics–**BPfM is primarily concerned with monitoring and managing an organization's performance based on key performance indicators (KPIs) and other metrics.

- **Strategic Alignment–**It involves ensuring that the organization's processes and tasks align with its strategic goals and provides insights into whether the company is on track to achieve these goals.

- **Tools and Techniques**—BPfM often employs tools like balanced scorecards, dashboards, and performance analytics to give leaders an overview of their organization's performance.

- **Feedback Loop**—One of the main goals of BPfM is to create a feedback loop wherein the organization can adjust its strategies based on the performance data it collects.

Business process management (BPrM) is:

- **Focus on Processes**—BPrM revolves around the identification, design, documentation, execution, monitoring, and improvement of business processes. It's about making processes more efficient and effective.

- **End-to-End Processes**—BPrM looks at processes from end to end, often spanning multiple departments, systems, and even organizational boundaries.

- **Tools and Techniques**—BPrM frequently uses process modeling tools, workflow engines, and automation technologies. Business process modeling notations (BPMN) might be used to visually represent processes.

- **Continuous Improvement**—One of the main tenets of BPrM is continuous process improvement, often drawing on methodologies like Six Sigma or Lean.

BPfM is about measuring and managing the overall performance of an organization against its strategic objectives. BPrM is about optimizing, managing, and automating specific business processes to make them more efficient and adaptable. Though different, both are vital for an organization's success, with one ensuring processes are efficient and the other ensuring that the organization as a whole is on track to meet its objectives.

BI complements both BPfM and BPrM by providing the tools, techniques, and methodologies to analyze, visualize, and report on business data. Here's how BI fits into the landscape of these business approaches:

BI and BPfM:

- **Data-Driven Decision Making**—At its core, BI is about turning raw data into actionable information. BPfM relies heavily on data to gauge performance, and BI tools help collect, process, and visualize that data to inform decision-making.

- **Monitoring KPIs**—BI tools offer dashboards that can be customized to track specific KPIs, which are integral to BPfM. This real-time tracking allows managers and executives to monitor performance against strategic objectives continuously.

- **Predictive Analytics**—Advanced BI systems can use data to forecast future trends, allowing organizations to make proactive decisions and adjust their strategies in BPfM accordingly.

BI and BPrM:

- **Process Analytics**—BI can be used to analyze and optimize business processes. By collecting data on how processes are performed, BI tools can help identify bottlenecks, inefficiencies, or areas of waste.

- **Automation Insights**—As BPrM introduces automation, BI can provide insights into how automation impacts performance, costs, and efficiency.

- **End-to-End Process Visibility**—With BI tools, an organization can gain a holistic view of its processes, understanding how different segments of a process impact others and where improvements can be made.

BI serves as a bridge between an organization's raw data and its tactical, strategic, and operational objectives. While BPfM focuses on aligning performance with organizational goals, and BPrM emphasizes optimizing and managing processes, BI provides the data-driven insights necessary to inform and enhance both. Through BI, organizations can ensure that their performance metrics and processes are not only aligned with their goals but are also based on a solid foundation of data-driven decision-making.

Lastly, how do BPrM AND BPfM integrate? A powerful technique is via the Theory of Constraints (ToC). In the context of BPrM, ToC is utilized to identify and improve the most significant constraints within business processes. For instance, consider a manufacturing process where iron is inputted to produce bolts. If the expected output is 100 bolts from 1 pound of iron but only 96 bolts are produced, ToC would prompt an analysis to identify the bottleneck or constraint in the process that's causing this reduction in efficiency.

This bottleneck might be due to a variety of factors, such as machine malfunction, suboptimal operational procedures, or quality issues with the raw material. BPM would focus on analyzing and optimizing the workflow around this constraint to enhance overall process efficiency.

The effectiveness of the changes made in the BPrM process, guided by ToC, is monitored through BPfM. This is where KPIs play a crucial role. In our example, a relevant KPI would be the 'Yield Rate' of bolts from a given quantity of iron. The target KPI is set at 100 bolts per pound of iron, reflecting optimal process efficiency.

By regularly measuring this KPI, the organization can monitor the impact of changes made to alleviate the constraint. If the yield improves from 96 to 99 bolts, it indicates a positive impact, though it also suggests that there may still be room for further improvement.

Over time, by continuously monitoring these KPIs, the organization can achieve a more streamlined process, ensuring that the throughput from each pound of iron is maximized, thus adhering to the principles of BPrM and BPfM bound through ToC.

Through this integrated approach, organizations can ensure that their processes are not only efficient but also aligned with their strategic objectives, driving continuous improvement and value creation.

Too-puhls (Tuples) and Dataframes

Two very important concepts in BI/OLAP are tuples and "sets of tuples." Tuples could be called rows or cases in many data science scenarios. A "set of tuples" is commonly known by other terms in the analytics space, such as table (relational database), data set (Spark), or dataframe (Python and Spark).

What is a tuple? Most things can be addressed as a tuple. For example, cars can be described by their make, year, model, color, engine size, and number of doors. Animals can be addressed by their taxonomic genus, fur, feathers, warm/cold-blooded, and bipedal. Addresses are a tuple in the form: street address, apt, city, state, and zip code.

Before continuing, I'll explain more about how tuples are presented:

- They are a comma-separated list of elements that are the properties of something—a person, a place, a thing, etc.

- The list of elements is enclosed in parentheses. For example, *(Eugene, Kyvos)*, which states there is a person named Eugene who works at Kyvos.

- Most importantly, the order of the elements matters. For example, the tuple *(Eugene, Kyvos)* isn't the same as *(Kyvos, Eugene)*. The first slot is the name of someone and the second slot is their employer. The latter tuple is saying there is a person named Kyvos who works at Eugene.

For a concrete example, imagine walking into a vast library. This library is like our multi-dimensional space, a term that sounds complex but is simply a way of saying we have many ways or "features" to describe and categorize things, just like books.

Now, let's say you want to find a particular type of book. You'd be given an "address" that guides you. This address, such as *("Non-Fiction", "Science")*, points you to the Science section of Non-Fiction. It's specific, but not too detailed. This address is what we call a tuple. It's a unique combination of details that identifies a location or item. So, a tuple like *("Non-Fiction", "Science", "Astronomy")* would guide you further into the Astronomy books of the Science genre.

But what if you want addresses for specific books? Tuples can be more detailed. For example, *("Non-Fiction", "Science", "Astronomy", "Cosmos", by Carl Sagan)* would pinpoint an exact book in that section.

Now, imagine you have a collection of such addresses, all jotted down to help various visitors. In Python, this collection, the set of tuples, might look something like:

{ ("Fiction", "Mystery"), ("Non-Fiction", "History"), ("Fiction", "Science Fiction") }

It's essentially a structured table, a way to organize and present multiple tuples or "addresses" together. I choose to use the term "dataframe"—as opposed to tables, sets of tuples, data sets—throughout this book because it's the most common reference to those using Python or R in a data science or BI context.

Figure 27 illustrates the relationship between tuples and dataframes. It illustrates a graph representation of a very simple table. Starting with the familiar table format of data, this is the description:

1. The more familiar tabular format of the tuples has three rows, one for each tuple.

2. This represents a table named OilPrices, which has …

3. ... two columns: PriceOfOil and Country ...

4. ... each column currently has three values:

    a. PriceOfColumn: $68, $72, and $70.
    b. Country: Canada, UK, USA.

5. There are three tuples, each a combination of PriceOfOil and Country.

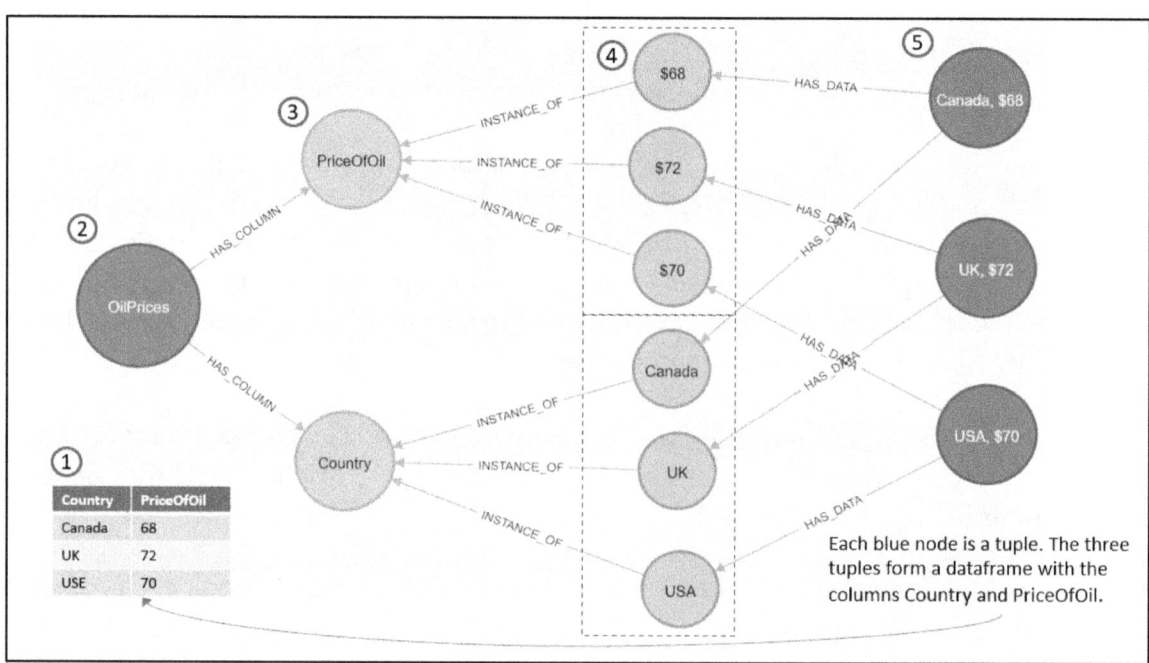

Figure 27: Tuple versus dataframe. A dataframe could be thought of as a set of "like" tuples.

The concept of tuples and sets of tuples is central to the world of multi-dimensional OLAP, a core concept of BI. Tuples are the coordinates in a space, whether we're talking about the surface of the Earth or a space of possibilities. It's important in the context of the EKG since the TCW is about relationships between tuples.

Lastly, if I'm referring to a set of related dataframes (like a set of tables comprising a star schema), I'll refer to it as a "data set."

Embracing Complexity

Embracing complexity is essential for enterprises that realize simply reacting to or defending against relentless change isn't a competitive business model in a competitive world. This approach is useful for top-tier enterprises, whose dominance is often a result of successfully maintaining the favorable conditions that got them there. However, shifts in the enterprise ecosystem could potentially benefit rising contenders purposefully born to the new environment.

Resistance to change and efforts to maintain the status quo are indeed futile in the long term. Over time, defensive strategies like patchwork solutions and temporary fixes can accumulate, leading to significant, sometimes explosive shifts. This isn't always fatally catastrophic, as seen with IBM's resilience in the face of Microsoft's rise in the 1980s.

To truly embrace complexity, enterprises first need intellectual agility. This involves looking at both existing and new data from fresh perspectives. Tools like the ISG and TCW are designed to facilitate this. They enable quick exploration of current data from many angles and incorporate new data from diverse sources. Their strength lies in the rapid and passive constructing of a vast web of correlations and conditional probabilities, embracing a "quick and dirty" approach that fosters creativity. It's about starting with brainstorming and then pragmatically testing even the most far-fetched ideas.

This book isn't focused on operational excellence; it's about the intelligence required to navigate the myriad challenges the world throws at enterprises. It's about strategizing and developing new tactics in response to these challenges. BI has historically leaned unintentionally towards operational excellence. It turns out operational excellence is a more attainable goal, whereas the pursuit of innovative excellence seemed out of reach, but now more plausible. With the advent of new tools and methods, particularly AI, the possibility of achieving innovative excellence is within grasp.

Novel Solutions to Novel Problems

Our human sapience enables us to face novel situations with novel solutions. At the same time, we mostly apply learned solutions as a foundation upon which we craft our "novel" solutions (in the box thinking). We're averse to revolutionary solutions and heavily prone to evolutionary solutions—and that's a good thing more often than not. Revolution is very risky.

However, being on the cusp of the "hockey stick curve" (a period of highly accelerating growth) of AI, robotics, life sciences and other such profound technologies will spin the "merry-go-round" of our human activity so fast that we can't hang on. Novel solutions to those novel problems will mean we have no history of its effectiveness. Nor might we have time to adequately test it, even if we can figure out how to test it. Implementing a novel solution runs a non-trivial risk of bringing an abrupt end to our party.

Years ago, I worked for a relatively large healthcare system as the BI Architect. I learned that healthcare practitioners were very good at recognizing symptoms and matching that set of symptoms to a diagnosis and that diagnosis to an appropriate treatment plan. The vast majority of their actions are based on the known, learned through well over a decade of intense education and hours of continuing education from the same sources—the same classes and journals. Therefore, all doctors should come up with the same solution to the same problem.

However, such a complex environment as healthcare is fraught with "we don't know what we don't know." They were most frightened of preventable deaths, at least preventable in hindsight. Whenever one happened, they were fantastically diligent about ensuring it never happened again. I don't believe they often made the same mistake twice. However, there are infinite permutations of factors that can lead to preventable deaths. To paraphrase one doctor, "Unforeseen deaths are a perfect storm of a lot of little things."

I have always been fascinated by all the ways life can bite you in the ass. Growing up in Hawaii, I learned that mongoose was introduced to Hawaii to combat the rat problem. But it didn't work as rats are nocturnal and mongooses are diurnal. Instead, the mongoose exacerbated the ravaging of whatever else was left of the endemic bird population that evolved without such predators. I always wondered how such smart adults could make such a mistake, even back then before Google, YouTube, and recently, ChatGPT.

Tell Me Something of Value that I Don't Already Know

Most BI Insights are Obvious

"That's obvious, I already know that." Something like that statement has been the underwhelming reaction from many new BI customers. I believe the reason is that BI has avoided handling the world of complexity. Instead, it retreated to jazzing up operational reports and calling them dashboards.

In my experience, to this day, I still get the "just one number, please" and "don't say 'it depends'" attitude. As long as those are the boundaries, there's not much we can say that their intelligent human brains armed with Google don't already know. In order to find things we don't already know, we need to begin to look beyond just one number—look at how multiple factors interact, evolving with each iteration. Thereafter, "it depends" becomes a universally accepted premise of any response.

We Don't Know What We Don't Know

Intelligence requires an open mind.

The concepts of "We don't know what we don't know" and "the more we know, the more we don't know" are the foundation of my passion for writing this book. In fact, for better or worse, they are core to my default way of thinking. There are well-established frameworks for answering questions to "what we know that we don't know," a task that is magnitudes easier than the first two, which is greatly missing in analytics.

In all fairness, it's only with the level of data technology, analytics tools, and skillsets today that we can really address that. The cloud set the stage for the storage and computation of sufficient volumes of data over a decade ago. The maturity of tools such as Tableau and PowerBI enabled analysts to dig deeper into data. Then, the readily accessible, high-quality, and broadly knowledgeable LLMs bursting onto the scene in Nov 2022 provided a big jolt of energy to that effort. However, I think most people in business analytics (SMEs, data engineers, analysts) need to make a big leap in the way they think about the analytics platform and process. We've grown up in a deterministic, feasibly encoded world (we're able to write code and/or documentation to effectively explain how things work) world, and now probabilistic LLMs have taken root. That's good because, like our brains, we know how LLMs are constructed, but not really how they "think".

It takes longer for people to change their programming than it does for an LLM, so we'd better take the leap now!

Tribal Knowledge: Most Understanding is Trapped in the Heads of Individuals

As the now familiar saying goes: "Most enterprise data is unstructured, locked away in documents, photos, and videos." But we can take a step further and assert that the bulk of "understanding" (a full level or two more sophisticated than "information") resides in the minds of human employees. Although enterprise software should reflect business processes, only a fraction of this understanding is captured. Even LLMs customer-built for an enterprise, like MosaicML's private models, fall short of genuinely comprehending the how and why of an enterprise. Moreover, much about business operations remains undocumented or outdated.

One approach towards capturing the understanding trapped in the heads of people would be to extensively interview each employee to map the enterprise's workflow—a concept akin to building a KG. However, this map is ever-evolving and inevitably lags behind the real-world scenario.

Another approach is to capture and analyze queries issued by analysts through BI tools like Tableau and PowerBI. This process involves extracting every possible insight from the query visualizations, regardless of whether the users noted or valued these insights.

There was a time when the most directly useful information was believed to be in Excel spreadsheets scattered across thousands of computers under thousands of desks. However, I argue that there's even more information—and certainly understanding—embedded in the employees' minds. This context-rich knowledge, honed through thousands of hours of service and numerous crises, departs with them when they leave. This tribal knowledge, much richer than any database metadata or documentation, encompasses the human-grade intelligence of operational processes—how, with what, where, and perhaps why things are done.

When starting a new job or project, I often find documentation scarce, outdated, or of poor quality. Data catalogs, when present, tend to offer only high-level information, lacking detail on inter-column relationships. This scarcity is not due to negligence but the sheer difficulty and tedium of producing and maintaining accurate documentation. In the whirlwind of constant crises, there's only enough time and energy to address the problem, with no time to document the resolution for posterity. Consequently, people often resort to asking colleagues rather than consulting documents.

But Things Somehow Work

Despite these challenges, enterprises manage to function. Human tribal knowledge, driven by the necessity to perform, fills the gaps—until, suddenly, it doesn't. Key knowledge bearers retire, change roles, depart, or are hit by that proverbial bus, leaving a void.

This reliance on ad-hoc tribal knowledge, while effective in the short term, is risky and costly in the long run. So why isn't anything done about it? Because it's the path of least resistance in a landscape where new issues constantly monopolize attention.

But even in the midst of the gaping wounds left by the departure of key personnel, enterprises adapt and evolve—sometimes for the better, sometimes not. Opportunities may be lost, but new learnings and pathways emerge.

How, then, can we tap into this vast, evolving tribal knowledge, much of which is considered too granular or complex for standard software encoding? We can't realistically document everything or convert every problem-solving session into a tutorial.

Sampling of the Incalculably Large Knowledge Space of an Enterprise

Think of an enterprise's knowledge space as a vast, untapped resource. It's impossible to map its entirety. However, like statistical sampling, even though the immensity of data might be too much to wrangle, we can sample portions of it.

A practical start is leveraging the diverse group of analysts within the enterprise. Their activities, interests, and pains, uniquely influenced by the needs of their domain and reflected in their BI endeavors, can serve as a window into this expansive knowledge space.

While it's not quite the same as traditional statistical sampling, the essence is similar. We're not randomly casting nets; we're strategically placing them where the currents of activity are strongest. Our goal is to zoom in on those areas of the knowledge space that are bubbling with action and relevance for any given moment.

A Rockhound Analogy

Here is a very simple example of what I described in the previous topic. As a bit of a rockhound, I offer an analogy for one of the pillars of AEI—the integration of distributed human intellect and interest.

Visualize fifty rockhounds, each searching for a different distinct mineral, indifferent to the pursuits of the others. Because they aren't in competition with each other, they are open to leveraging the benefits of a distributed system—as long as it costs very little to participate. The fifty rockhounds agreed to post pictures of interesting points they found to iCloud storage. This is really no trouble for most of the prospectors since they intend to post pictures along the way anyway.

As they scatter across the terrain in directions hinted at by their knowledge of their treasure, they encounter hints pointing to the minerals they seek. Our hero, Shawn, in his quest for turquoise, discovers an old, abandoned copper mine—a promising indicator. Yet, he finds no turquoise.

Meanwhile, a few miles away, Carl is on the lookout for azurite, while in yet another location, Jim searches for malachite. Both would find it valuable to learn of Shawn's discovery, as the old copper mine could also hint at the presence of azurite and malachite as well as turquoise, which Shawn didn't find. However, Shawn is unaware of most of the interests of the others, focused solely on his quest for turquoise. If everyone were to inform everyone who might be interested, the group would be spending too much time reading and posting hints on their phones instead of enjoying the immersion in the rockhounding passion.

Yet, a collaborative effort exists: all rockhounds upload their photos to a shared iCloud storage. A Computer Vision AI (an AI can that analyze photos) senses new photos and wrings out various insights from Shawn's photo as well as its metadata. Among the items recognized by the AI is the recognition of the old copper mine. This information is integrated into a geological knowledge graph hosted by a local rock enthusiasts' group, connecting it to the possible presence of turquoise, azurite, and malachite.

The knowledge graph also shows that Carl is interested in azurite and Jim is interested in malachite. So, their respective hints are texted to them.

Carl and Jim quickly see the hint the AI detected from the photo provided by Shawn. That is, with no additional burden on Shawn's part other than to have taken the photo he already wanted to take and posting it as he had already intended.

This simplified analogy mirrors my vision for AEI. In an ideal enterprise, analysts across diverse domains contribute their unique insights to a shared knowledge pool. Each piece of information, regardless of its immediate relevance to the contributor, becomes a part of a larger, interconnected knowledge network. Through AI and sophisticated data systems, these individual contributions are woven into a rich tapestry of enterprise intelligence, enhancing the collective understanding and fostering innovative solutions.

This approach transforms the way enterprises harness the deep, often untapped, knowledge embedded within their walls. It's about creating an ecosystem where the varied expertise of each individual enriches the whole, paving the way for smarter, more informed decision-making. And last but not least, this happens with as little extra intrusion on anyone.

Widening Breadth of Data

The growing awareness that relying solely on internal enterprise data can lead to skewed conclusions is akin to basing decisions on one side of an argument or a narrow knowledge base. Recognizing this, there's a growing desire towards incorporating an ever-widening array of external data into analytics. Every additional dataset feature exponentially expands the cube space of tuples, leading to an explosion in the breadth of data—reflected in the number of columns or features.

A decade ago, typical BI analytics might have dealt with a relative handful of features, several dozen to a few hundred or so. Today, with the integration of diverse external data sources, data scientists are routinely navigating landscapes where the number of features can run into thousands, even tens of thousands, depending on their application.

A wider breadth of data is not hard to come by. The Internet of Things (IoT) is a testament to this, offering a staggering variety of data from millions to billions of deployed devices. This could include a heterogeneous mix of billions of sensor devices, millions of drones, dozens of devices per car, and more. Each device category adds a fully new dimension to the data.

These devices range from semi-autonomous to mostly autonomous. Each piece of data they send to an event hub is akin to an individual agent's input. For instance, a sensor in a cornfield isn't just a data point; it embodies unique topological features of its location, distinct from others. The analytics magic lies in the interplay of data from these uniquely positioned devices.

But the complexity I speak of goes beyond just data proliferation. It's about introducing more "agents" into the analytical arena. Each new element significantly ramps up complexity through additional layers of cause and effect.

This burgeoning dataspace is so vast it defies sensible imagination. Recent years have seen the rise of "AutoML" technologies, automating the search for the most useful features among thousands. The efficiency of AutoML is striking; it can unearth promising ML models in minutes, hours, or a few days—a task that might have taken a data scientist months.

Yet, there's a certain unease in over-relying on such automation. The best-fit model, according to specific metrics, might not be the optimal choice in a real-world application. In complex systems—be they enterprises, ecosystems, or our planet as a whole—the sum of those optimal models doesn't usually result in an optimal whole.

I propose a more grounded approach: leveraging the expansive universe of insights distributed across an army of human analysts. By mining their efforts, we can integrate a wealth of understanding into the process, offering clues that anchor AutoML outputs in real-world dynamics.

Within an enterprise, business processes might appear to the outside world as a unified operation, similar to how our individual actions reflect the sum of our internal mental and physical processes. Our enterprise adapts to shifting laws, trends, technologies, and information. Traditionally, data mined for BI analytics has been a byproduct of our internal database systems. However, the evolving landscape calls for a more integrated, comprehensive approach to truly harness the potential of this data-rich era.

LLMs Opened Floodgates for Inclusion of Unstructured Data

The rise of LLMs marks a significant advancement in the field of AI and a profound change for the world. Just as AOL (America Online) democratized internet access in the mid-90s, models like ChatGPT, introduced to the general public in November 2022, have ushered in a new era of intuitive human-computer interactions. LLMs, trained on vast volumes of textual data, possess the ability to generate responses that usually pass as human. For most people most of the time, they are remarkably adept at predicting and producing coherent and contextually relevant responses.

One significant area where LLMs can make a profound impact is through their synergy with KGs. LLMs are adept at processing and generating language, while KGs serve as structured repositories of knowledge, outlining relationships between diverse entities in a format that is comprehensible to machines. When combined, LLMs can utilize the structured information from KGs to deliver responses that are not only more accurate but also contextually richer.

In the domain of BI, this integration can be transformative. The intricacies of BI databases become more approachable with the linguistic capabilities of LLMs (and help from RAG—more on that later). Instead of grappling with complex database queries, analysts can now pose questions in natural language. The LLM, in turn, acts as an intermediary, drawing upon the structured knowledge from KGs, data catalogs, and the LLM's innate ability to compose code (usually SQL) to fetch data from conventional databases. This enhanced interaction simplifies the process and ensures that data insights are more accessible and relevant for decision-making.

The Unstructured Data Majority Unlocked with AI

When discussing data volume with customers, a typical response I get is something like: "We have about 20 terabytes, but most of it is images and PDFs." Traditionally, BI data stores have been fed primarily by the smaller portion of an enterprise's data, mostly residing in relational databases.

It's commonly estimated that about 80% of an enterprise's data volume is unstructured, encompassing images, videos, audio, and various text documents like PDFs, Word files, and various forms of communication, such as email. This balance is increasingly tilting towards unstructured data as the production and storage of larger files, particularly videos, (ex. recordings of Zoom meetings and footage from surveillance cameras) become more technically and financially viable with scalable cloud storage solutions.

Traditionally, BI systems were focused on structured data from sources, such as relational databases. More recently, the inclusion of semi-structured data, especially JSON, has become standard. Such data is valued for its human and software application readability, along with its flexible schema. Before the advent of practical AI solutions, unstructured data, being primarily human-readable, remained largely untapped.

Now, unstructured data is not only predominant in volume but also rapidly expanding. The rise of remote work and social media, accelerated by Covid-19, has led to an exponential growth in video data. We see this in the gigabytes of recorded sales demos, team meetings, and educational content produced for both internal and external audiences.

Today's customer-facing knowledge workers, equipped with multimedia recording tools, are engaging with vast customer bases and generating significantly more data than traditional methods of data capture, such as forms with straightforward questions and answers.

The unlocking of information within this unstructured data has been revolutionized by accessible AI engineering platforms (like Azure Cognitive Services), which can extract data that was previously locked away and only accessible through labor-intensive and error-prone manual entry. Prior to these AI advancements, extracting value from unstructured data was often prohibitively expensive and technically challenging, typical of early efforts in utilizing difficult technologies. This shift reminds me of how our ability to control fire led to cooking, which transformed the nutritional landscape of our ancestors. By making a wider range of nutrients available from the same food—and even making once inedible food consumable—cooking led to a significant change in our way of life, freeing us to focus on more than hunting and gathering.

AI Quality and Acceptance Hit a Critical Mass

The public's surging interest and the burgeoning practical applications of AI, sparked by ChatGPT's rise in November 2022, mark what could be called "The AI Inflection Point." This period represents a drastic shift from AI's boom and bust ("AI Winters") development cycles to a sudden spike in recognition and usability, echoing the early days of the internet with Netscape, AOL, and Yahoo.

ChatGPT broke through the AI community's confines, appealing to non-technical users with its accessible interface and high-quality output. While significant AI advancements have been on a steady increase for over a decade, they kind of remained unnoticed outside AI and IT circles until ChatGPT's advent.

This watershed moment transcended the bounds of technological sophistication, emphasizing accessibility and practicality. ChatGPT 3.5's Google-esque simplicity catapulted advanced AI from a specialized tool to a mainstream staple. It's less about groundbreaking innovation (i.e., an AGI/ASI) and more about democratizing a "good enough" level intelligence, exceeding the breadth of any single human's capacity. ChatGPT may not match the genius of Newton or Einstein, but it functions at an impressively high intellectual level.

The "hallucinations" in AI responses are curious. They resemble human-like "what if" thought experiments, but AI presents these musings more assertively than we typically would. The "bar of quality" for LLMs has been a hot topic—they may lack "street smarts" built from years of real-world experience, yet their extensive breadth of knowledge often outshines human capabilities in many areas. In my case, for example, investing in ChatGPT Premium is far more cost-effective than hiring a team of knowledgeable assistants—say $20 per month for 80% of the value of a few assistants at thousands of dollars.

Very Book Smart, Although a bit Lacking in Common Sense ... For Now

While not pioneering in innovation like Elon Musk or Chuck Berry, LLMs like ChatGPT are immensely useful, akin to a group of well-educated teens: knowledgeable but lacking life experience. Their vast repository of information, accessible at minimal cost, is invaluable.

LLMs, however, struggle with novel or rarely discussed topics. Their responses to such inquiries often rely on existing knowledge. This is akin to a programmer transitioning from object-oriented to functional programming—insisting on reverting to explaining functional programming in object-oriented terms. These "hallucinations" are the AI's attempts at "creativity," venturing into the unknown much like humans hypothesize with phrases like "What if..." or "I'm not sure, but perhaps...." However, ChatGPT often states its conjectures with more certainty than a human might.

Beyond being a fact repository, LLMs understand language nuances, aiding in deeper, culturally rich queries. They prove to be invaluable in building and maintaining Knowledge Graphs (KGs), discerning patterns and similarities with efficiency.

Addressing skepticism around LLMs "hallucinating," I find the term a bit harsh. To me, their "hallucinations" are akin to common misunderstandings rather than delusions. Considering how our brains reconstruct memories, it's surprising we don't "hallucinate" more in our everyday perceptions.

The Ubiquitous Time Dimension

All processes have time in common.

The last topic of this section addresses how we can integrate data from a vast array of sources. Integrating disparate data is the bane of ETL (extract, transform, load). Transforming information is one of the toughest feats of intelligence, yet it's what people are constantly doing—abstracting and generalizing. However, there is one theme that runs through all BI data.

At the heart of most databases lies the ubiquitous, unifying time dimension. Regardless of the subject or domain specifics of a given database, the temporal dimension is almost always present, making it an invaluable connector between virtually all disparate databases. The time dimension is fundamental because analytics is about studying the past to predict or affect the future.

By harnessing this omnipresent dimension, we're able to draw correlations between databases that may, on the surface, seem entirely unrelated. Whether we're discussing financial metrics, weather patterns, sociological data, or countless other domains, time is the dependable bridge that links these disparate data sets.

The two techniques mentioned, conditional probabilities and Pearson correlations, both utilize the time dimension in a distinct but complementary manner. Conditional probabilities treat time slices as distinct cases, providing a probabilistic measure of the co-occurrence of specific events within these temporal segments. On the other hand, Pearson correlations track the changes in metrics across a shared temporal range, offering insights into how two variables fluctuate in tandem over time.

But beyond the capability of drawing connections, computation efficiency is another essential advantage. In an era where many analytical operations demand significant computational resources, especially when involving complex neural networks, the computational intensity of these simpler correlation calculations is relatively low. That is especially true if the data source is built on a pre-aggregate OLAP platform. This ensures that, even when correlating vast and diverse datasets, the process remains efficient and scalable.

In essence, by tapping into the universal nature of time, we're not only able to discover hidden relationships across different domains but do so in a manner that is both resource-efficient and grounded in solid statistical methodologies.

The ISG and TCW are about exploring an expansive and diverse data space. That can include thousands of datasets from all manners of domains. Drawing correlations requires that two data sets have something well-defined in common. Even if multiple data sets have something in common, such as their respective customers, it can be fraught with mistaken matches. Time is unambiguous (once time zones are accounted for and we're not traveling near the speed of light) and, therefore, facilitates connection across any enterprise's expansive data space.

Conclusion to The Intelligence of a Business

With the Situation and Background presented, I now introduce the end product, the enterprise knowledge graph (EKG). The next three Parts, illustrated in Figure 28, dive deeper into the topics of the three major components of the EKG:

- Part 2—Knowledge Graphs—SME-Authored Knowledge.
- Part 3—Data Catalog—Directory of databases within the enterprise.
- Part 4—Business Intelligence—The pulse of what's going on in the enterprise.

The three loosely-coupled components link to form the EKG hypergraph. As item 4 in Figure 28 suggests, for the most part, the KG (1) should link to the BI Components (3) via the data catalog (2).

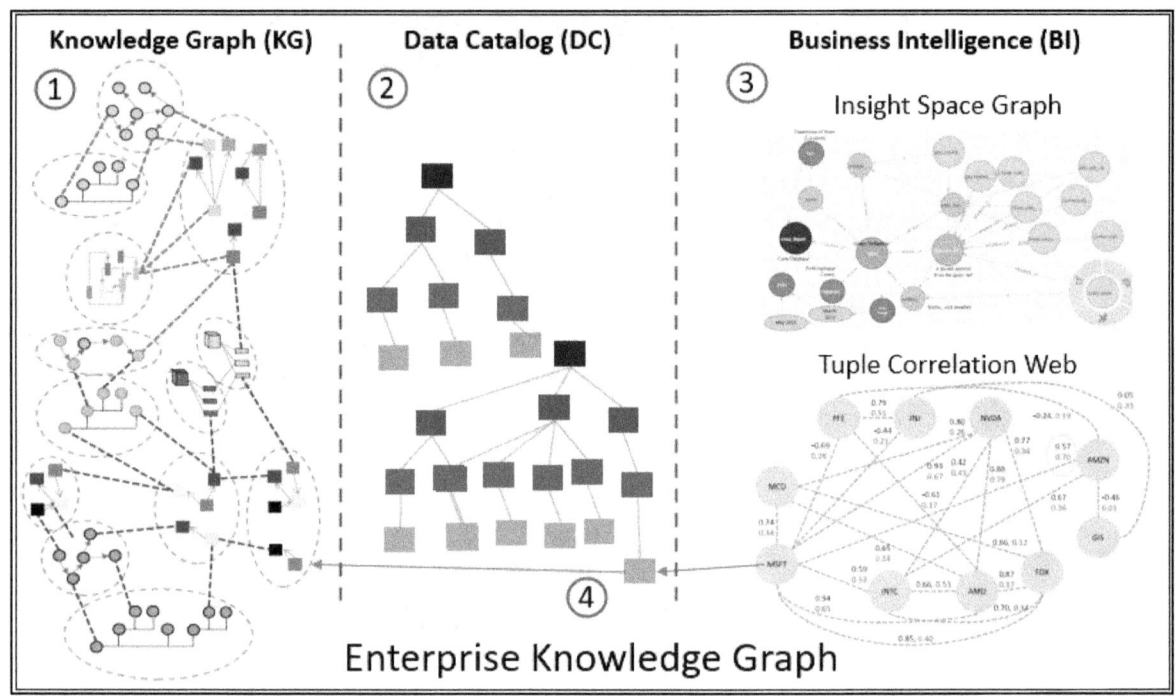

Figure 28: The three major components of the EKG.

Before continuing to Chapter 4—Knowledge Graphs, I need to clarify that the EKG and KG refer to different things. The latter is a subset of the former. Until "Chapter 8—Architecture of the AEI," when referring to a knowledge graph, I'm generally referring to the KG created by SMEs.

CHAPTER FOUR

Knowledge Graphs

This chapter dives into the role KGs, one of three major sub-graphs of the EKG, play in the AEI. Figure 29 highlights the focus on the KG. We just saw this illustration, but I've placed it here again to reiterate that we are focusing on the first of the three components of the AEI.

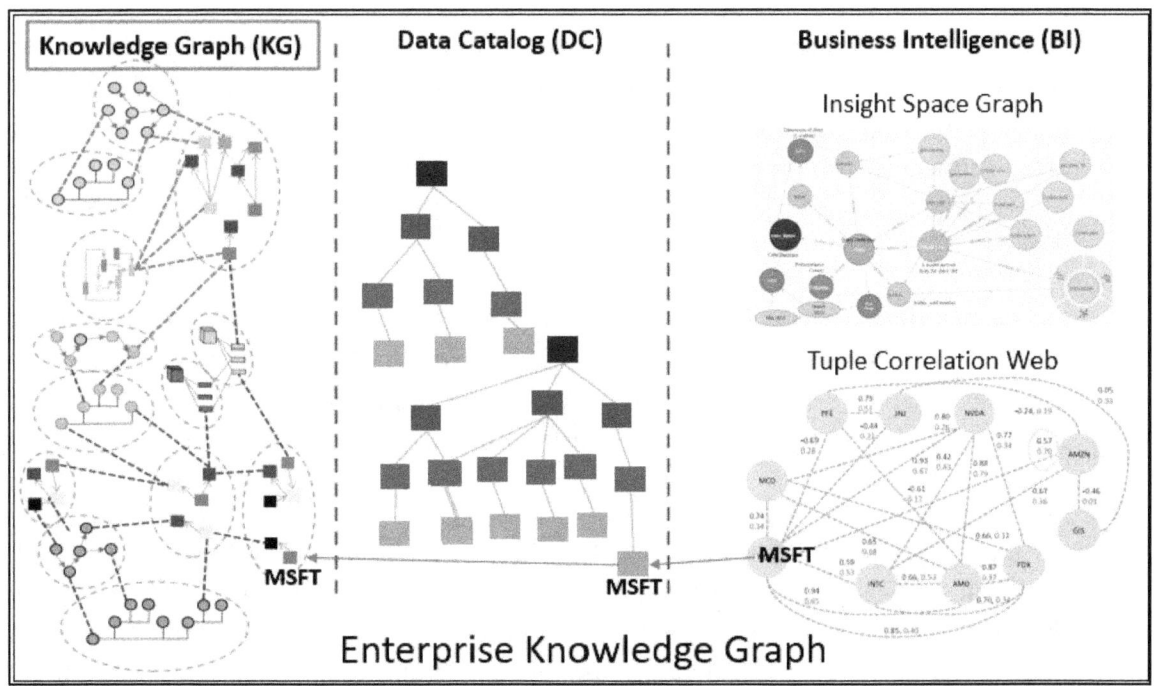

Figure 29: Focus on the KG's role in the AEI.

Towards the bottom, we see MSFT (Microsoft) appearing under all three subgraphs and linked from the knowledge graph through the data catalog to the Business Intelligence structures.

Of the three major components of the EKG, the KG requires the most human effort to develop and maintain. For the most part, the expense of building and maintaining them far exceeds the value they return. At a high-level, a limited-scope KG might be feasible to build, but it really doesn't add that much value as a stand-alone product. A very in-depth and wide-breadth KG might yield compelling value, but it's awfully hard to build and harder to maintain.

That is, until along came LLMs.

Symbiotic Relationship between KGs and LLMs

LLMs ease development of KGs and KGs ground LLMs in reality.

Without the readily accessible and surprisingly high-quality LLMs bursting onto the scene, KGs would still mostly be a pie-in-the-sky effort. LLMs drastically smooth out the process of mapping relationships between concepts and things. It might be that LLMs aren't quite as "intelligent" for the moment as the initial ChatGPT 3.5 hype suggested. But for the purposes of assisting in the development AND maintenance of KGs, it's smart enough.

As mentioned, a broad LLM like ChatGPT knows more than any single human, but it's predominantly just "book smart." ChatGPT hasn't yet been able to directly help me push innovation, but it has been many times more helpful with this book project than any intern I've ever had. No offense is intended for the interns who need to sleep and have a life.

In fact, I wouldn't be writing this book if not for the symbiotic relationship between LLMs and KGs. It's the mortar that connects all the once-fragmented pieces. This book is about incorporating BI information into an EKG, and consequently, the notion of a highly profitable KG would be almost moot without the assistance of current LLMs.

The Elusive Knowledge Graph

KGs are a map of the relationships between concepts, process flows, and their properties across an organization. As we've likened a business to a human body, with departments as organs and business processes as bodily systems, the KG (actually the wider EKG) is the neural structure of the "intelligence of a business," akin to the brain. This is what I consider the Holy Grail of analytics.

Explaining KGs begins with a basic understanding of ontologies and taxonomies. An ontology is a formal representation of knowledge as a set of concepts within a domain and the relationships between those concepts. It is used to reason about the entities within that domain and can include various types of relationships and entities. A taxonomy is a type of ontology that focuses specifically on hierarchical classification. It organizes concepts or entities in a tree-like structure, where each node (or class) is a subset of the node (or class) directly above it. This structure is especially useful for systematic categorization.

However, the creation and maintenance of KGs have traditionally been beyond practical and justifiable reach in terms of what it takes to create and maintain them. They have required immense, coordinated efforts from a wide, deep, and often unwieldy, often conflicting, range of sources. Further complicating matters, querying and visualizing such a widely-scoped KG, a large-scale graph, often rendered them frustratingly unusable.

The difficulty is that KGs are models of things in the world, and none of us perceive and experience the world in the same way, nor can we grasp more than a tiny fraction of it. Each organization, like every individual, has its own unique set of needs, perspectives, and challenges. This diversity is both a strength and a challenge when it comes to creating a KG that is universally applicable and useful.

Crafting a one-size-fits-all model is virtually impossible, as it would have to accommodate an almost infinite variety of viewpoints, requirements, and operational nuances. At the same time, attempting to tailor a KG to meet every specific need and difference can lead to overwhelming complexity and an unwieldy structure. Thus, the pursuit of the ideal KG, one that perfectly maps the intricate web of an organization's knowledge and processes, remains an elusive goal.

It's a balancing act between universality and specificity, between the broad strokes of common understanding and the fine details of individual organizational contexts. Finding this balance while navigating the vast and often contradictory sea of data and interpretations makes the development of an effective, comprehensive KG a formidable yet fascinating endeavor in the field of data management and analytics.

Today, the creation and utilization of KGs are greatly facilitated by the emergence of easily accessible LLMs to the general public. This has led to a symbiotic relationship that jointly revolutionizes information management. KGs aid in "grounding" LLMs in reality, counteracting the predictive nature of LLMs. In turn, LLMs help construct and maintain KGs, mostly by mapping relationships that are hard to see in a big haystack.

Nevertheless, as with almost anything, solving one problem usually gives rise to another. Extending the enterprise as an organism comparison, the quality of training and learning is crucial. Haphazard training can lead to poor quality LLMs, which underscores the importance of implementing effective methodologies, such as Domain-Driven Design (DDD) and data mesh, in the creation and maintenance of KGs.

The KG and LLM Symbiotic Relationship

KGs materialize and evolve from a blend of human intelligence, innate workplace knowledge, abundant and highly-curated data repositories, and, more recently, AI. The swift advancement of multiple types of AI (not just LLMs) is the secret sauce that unlocks the potential of blending these ingredients. Additionally, the formerly stubbornly tappable data within the expansive unstructured universe of images, audio, and video are unlocked as well.

In the context of this book, LLMs act as a potent assistant in transforming data into a format suitable for the KG. They can derive relational triples from databases (e.g., "seagulls eat fish," "fish have fins") —the fundamental building block of a KG —thereby mimicking human cognitive processes and establishing a solid basis for automated inference. They can also infer triples from massive examples of our collective writings. Conversely, a KG built in a human-supervised manner grounds the LLM with the human-approved information of the KG.

The outcome of this two-way relationship is a knowledgebase universally understood by both human and machine intelligence, each addressing fundamental shortcomings of the other. It unlocks intricate, extremely high-value information formerly trapped in the heads of human knowledge workers.

Much of the information required to create KGs already resides in the data and metadata of our expansive relational databases, data lakes, and numerous structured and unstructured electronic files. However, the formats of the data inherently lack relational richness for automated human-like inference, even for the most advanced AI models today. Ironically, even "relational databases" fall short of capturing the necessary relational depth for such inferencing, necessitating impractically significant human intervention for the creation and maintenance of KGs.

The substantial value of a KG stems not just from the data it contains but from the transformation of this data into relational triples I just mentioned. Webs of these subject-predicate-object (or subject-verb-object, SVO) triples form a foundation that mimic our thought processes—both individually and as a team—providing the groundwork for inference. This process facilitates the generation of new information or strategies from existing data.

The emergence of LLMs significantly alleviates the extensive human effort traditionally needed to build and maintain a KG. KGs and LLMs form a truly symbiotic relationship in which each enhances the other's capabilities. Together, they are revolutionizing information management, reshaping our approaches to data handling, and enabling the practical creation and maintenance of EKGs on a formerly unforeseen scale.

Figure 30 through Figure 32 illustrate a sample part of a KG created with the assistance of a LLM (ChatGPT). Figure 30 shows how we provide instructions via a prompt to the LLM using spoken language. In this example, I wish to add an ontology—a graph of the properties of things and how things relate–of the roles of dental practice into my KG. I also want the ontology output to be Cypher code, the language of the very popular graph database Neo4j, which I'm using for this book.

Note that similar to how we speak with another human, there is a pretty robust margin for error in our prompt to the LLM. We don't need to spell out every step in excruciating detail. There is some level of intricate common knowledge we've all amassed over our lives. I've "engineered" this prompt with context and high-level instructions. Aside from words like "output," this isn't much different from how I would ask a human coworker to perform this task.

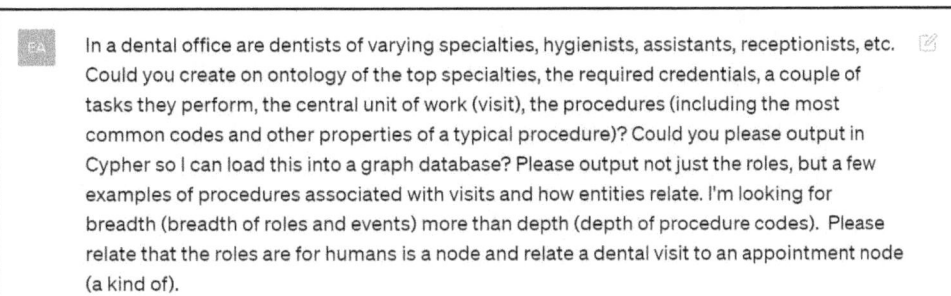

Figure 30: A LLM prompt asking for help in creating a KG of a dental office.

Figure 31 shows part of ChatGPT's response, including some explanation along with part of the code (Cypher) I would use to add the ontology to my KG. I'll properly introduce Cypher later.

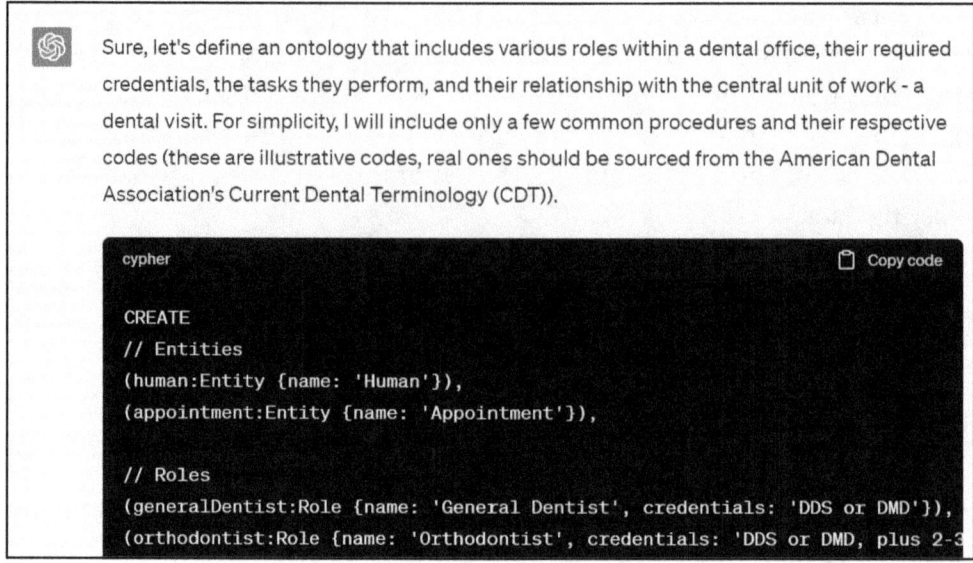

Figure 31: Partial response generated by ChatGPT of the Cypher code.

Figure 32 shows the result of the ontology now in my Neo4j-implemented KG after running the code from Figure 31.

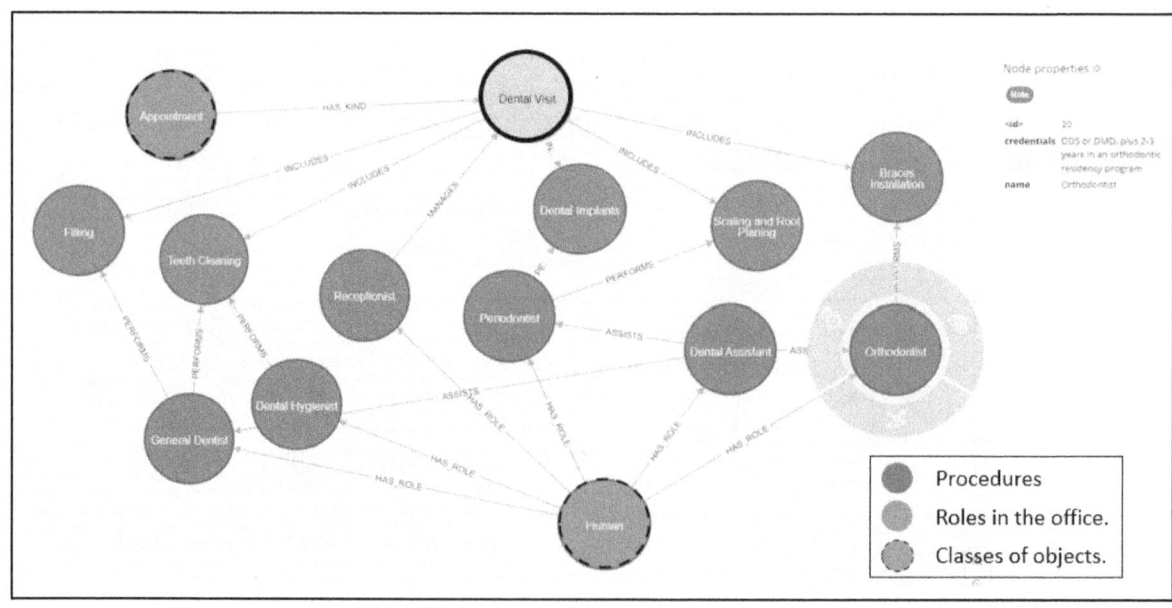

Figure 32: A basic ontology specifying the roles in a dental office.

Notice the coded nodes:

- Yellow (thick outline), the dental visit, is the primary entity. That's what the business is all about.

- Green (dark shade) are examples of dental procedures I asked for. But I didn't specify any. ChatGPT picked out what appear to be common, well-known procedures.

- Blue (light shade) are roles in a dental office.

- Purplish-red (light shade, dashed outline) are entities in the dental office. Here, the appointment and people involved.

Note that ATTOW, I, a human, must still drive and validate the process. As I mentioned earlier, LLMs are currently "book smart" while we humans are "street smart." The point is that I don't need a Ph.D. in dental practice management, nor do I need to be a senior software developer to yield a pretty good starting ontology. But we still need a dentist and/or her office manager to sanity check the work of the LLM.

Lastly, we need to remember that SMEs are still people who could be wrong, unintentionally biased, or just didn't communicate the encoding of knowledge well enough. So, a KG and a LLM not only symbiotically promote the development of each other, they can also corroborate questions from different foundations—SME knowledge and a corpus of written knowledge, respectively.

To recap, in this symbiotic equation, KGs, with their structured representations of factual relationships (at least what we believe to be factual), serve as a vetted collaborator for LLMs, supplementing the probabilistic core transformer architecture of LLMs. In return, LLMs can lighten the hefty task of mapping the web of relationships comprising a KG with its broad knowledge. By deciphering and validating relationships across massively diverse data sources in multiple formats, LLMs deliver a flexible, adaptable layer that facilitates the practicality of constructing and maintaining KGs.

Mitigating Friction Between Human and Machine Intelligence

LLMs narrow the chasm between human and machine communication.

Collaboration with us is really the value of LLMs. It's not that AI (or some cyber-hybrid of humans) might someday be smarter than people. It's that there is the world of humans and the world of machines, which we built to multiply our capabilities. Each is profoundly different and the nature of "thought" is a completely different thing for both worlds. As machines of all types grow in sophistication and variety at the rapid rate we're experiencing today, smoothing out the friction due to the increasing complexity of communication between all those entities becomes paramount.

LLMs are the "pidgin" between the human and machine worlds. In Hawaii during the plantation days (ca. 1880-1900), many cultures speaking many languages were suddenly thrown together. They couldn't communicate and of course, that meant accomplishing anything was wrought with friction.

I'm sure at first, communication was like playing charades. Soon, they'd learn a few important words—hello, good-bye, thank you, hungry, etc. Juss like when we visit a country where we no speak da language—lo siento, sumimasen. Eventually, English emerged as the foundational language, but it was heavily interspersed with words, idioms, and phrases from many languages (fine-tuned).

What naturally emerged is a pidgin–a language based on very rudimentary English (like a three-year-old's level) with a few borrowed terms from many of the languages. It was enough so everyone could effectively work together. Through this pidgin, much could be accomplished. As time went on, this pidgin evolved a syntax of its own. It grew up into a "creole"–which is mistakenly still called "pidgin" today.

Knowledge Graph Foundations

LLMs are probabilistic models, not a "knowledge base" as is a KG. In an odd sense, it seems like our very own brains are probabilistic models, too. Karl Friston, a prominent neuroscientist, has developed the theory of predictive coding, which supports this notion. According to his theory, our brains are constantly making predictions about the world and then adjusting those predictions based on the sensory input we receive. This process is strikingly similar to how LLMs operate, consuming data about our present situation and predicting the next most likely output based on probabilities derived from that data.

However, this does not make KGs obsolete. While LLMs are adept at processing and generating information based on patterns they have learned, KGs serve as structured repositories of information that are meticulously curated and organized. They represent explicit knowledge in a way that LLMs' probabilistic guesses cannot. KGs excel in providing context, establishing relationships, and offering a level of interpretability and reliability that LLMs alone cannot guarantee.

Moreover, KGs and LLMs complement each other. KGs can provide the structured data that LLMs need to make more informed predictions, while LLMs can assist in expanding and enriching KGs by identifying potential new relationships and insights from unstructured data. The synergy between KGs and LLMs, rather than the obsolescence of one by the other, points towards a more integrated partnership where each leverages its strengths to enhance our understanding and interaction with information. Karl Friston's principles of predictive coding lend credence to the idea that the most efficient systems, whether biological or artificial, will likely be those that can effectively combine the predictability of structured knowledge with the adaptability of probabilistic modeling.

KGs are graph structures of encoded knowledge previously held only in the heads of human subject matter experts (SME) or painfully written out in mythical documentation. Like BI data sources, KGs are also highly curated forms of human knowledge. KGs are generally authored by a team of SMEs and folks who are fluent in KG technologies. The former utilizes their knowledge by applying it to their work, expressing it to others (teaching/training), or writing it down (documentation). The latter understand ontologies, taxonomies, the use of semantic web standards (RDF, RDFS, OWL, SPARQL, and SWRL), and KG authoring tools (Protégé, Grafo).

The information contained in KGs really is the same as that contained in any normal text-based documentation—only "condensed"–a web of subject-verb-object triples. We traditionally document knowledge in the form of books and articles. The difference has been that until the release of ChatGPT 3.5 back in November 2022, text-based documentation wasn't readily comprehensible by machines.

LLMs are an advancement of Natural Language Processing (NLP), which existed years before. However, the capabilities of NLP have fallen short of being reliably useful until now.

LLMs might appear to understand me—or at least the "uncanny valley" is usually fairly hard to see. I can ask ChatGPT almost anything, and it returns an answer of a quality that is pretty much in the ballpark, as most who are at least novices but not experts in the subject of the question. I would query a KG in a way that's essentially similar to how I query ChatGPT. The advantage of ChatGPT versus a KG is that I didn't need to go through the extremely tedious process of authoring a KG. Instead, ChatGPT was trained automatically via an algorithm in timeframes of weeks instead of years of manual torture.

The Effort to Create KGs

Let's walk through an example of an ontology in a research setting where they are traditionally more common (as opposed to the workflow setting of the dental office).

If I were a biologist working with a team on the marine life of the Chesapeake Bay, it would help to have a KG of the taxonomy of species, the relationship between them, the effect of multitudes of human activity, tides, etc. It would take years for a team of biologists to hammer out the relationships and what makes each genus and species different enough to be labeled differently. Additionally, once we have such a taxonomy or ontology, we will encode any further discoveries or changes to what we thought we knew.

However, a LLM fine-tuned (sort of like graduate school training for the LLM) on a large corpus of research papers, biology texts, thousands of pages of notes from each biologist, and even thousands of hours of videos accumulated over the years could possibly answer questions as well as and likely better than the KG we hammer out.

I could probably even get a pretty good response from ChatGPT without its "graduate school" training. For example, I asked ChatGPT this question: *What could lead to blue crabs rising in population in the Chesapeake Bay?*

 ChatGPT
The population of blue crabs in the Chesapeake Bay is influenced by various factors that can cause its numbers to fluctuate. The recent improvement in population could be due to:

1. **Reproductive Success**: An increase in the adult female crab population suggests successful reproduction cycles [11].
2. **Management Practices**: Effective, science-based fisheries management that regulates harvest levels can help sustain and improve populations [11].
3. **Environmental Conditions**: Reductions in pollution and improvements in water quality can contribute to habitat restoration, which is crucial for juvenile crab survival [11].

Figure 33: ChatGPT response to a complicated question.

ChatGPT's answer is rather pedestrian, enough so that I (who is not a biologist) can see it seems right. But I know I could push it further. And if I did train one on the corpus of material I mentioned above, I'm sure I would get a very good answer.

It seems like LLMs *are* "knowledge graphs." So why do we need KGs?

At first, the problem with a LLM like ChatGPT is that it, fortunately, doesn't incorporate private enterprise or otherwise proprietary data. If you asked ChatGPT anything having to do with the internals of your business, it wouldn't know how to answer.

But very soon after, technologies, such as HuggingFace and LangChain surfaced, making it possible to enhance the process of accessing enterprise data using iterative "chain of thought," "tree of thought," and "retrieval augmented generation" techniques. Very soon after that, the notion of creating private LLMs arose, enabling enterprises to create private LLMs off their much smaller set of private data at a fraction of the cost that OpenAI paid to train GPT 3 and 4.

Since LLMs can answer the sort of questions we would ask of a KG, why go through the trouble of creating KGs? It's so much easier for SMEs to write documentation in their "native language," or even just video hours of discussions and fine-tuning a LLM on it, as opposed to having to further encode the same thing using cryptic KG-related syntaxes.

KGs and LLMs can be likened to the concepts of "System 1" and "System 2" thinking, respectively, popularized by Daniel Kahneman in his book, "Thinking Fast and Slow." Our everyday, rapid decision-making, which is often subconscious or semi-conscious, parallels the function of KGs. This is efficient because it allows us to respond swiftly to familiar situations, which comprise the bulk of our daily activity. However, when we encounter something unfamiliar, a scenario that challenges our "System 1" approach, turning to AI, akin to the thinking process of "System 2," becomes beneficial. Both are required.

While AI has not yet fully realized its potential in this area, it offers significant assistance in highlighting aspects we might overlook. Unlike the swift, direct responses from a KG, AI engages in a more deliberate, iterative chain-of-thought process, resembling the slower, more analytical nature of "System 2" thinking. This method, although not as quick, provides a thorough analysis that is invaluable for complex or novel situations.

Both KGs and LLMs are representations of human knowledge, but they each have their own strengths and limitations. Let's delve into a few reasons why one might want to leverage both.

Nature of Representation

KGs are structured and explicit representations of knowledge. They excel at encoding clear relationships between entities and concepts, often in a format that's easy to query and extract precise information from.

LLMs, in contrast, represent knowledge in a more implicit manner, encoded within vast numbers of parameters. They're good at generating human-like text based on patterns they've seen during training, but they don't "understand" content in the way humans do.

Later, in Chapter 12—Future Steps, I discuss the pros and cons of baking the BI data of the ISG and TCW data directly into LLMs.

Probabilistic versus Assertive Knowledge

A LLM could generate a KG based on its training data, but such a KG would be probabilistic. It represents what the model computes and so "thinks" might be accurate based on its training, not necessarily what is definitively true or universally accepted.

Human-reviewed KGs, on the other hand, move from probabilistic associations to assertive relationships. They represent curated knowledge honed through years of direct experience.

Interactivity and Dynamic Responses

The paths by which responses from KGs are computed are fully traceable. While they're excellent resources for querying specific facts or relationships, they don't generate new content or insights on the fly.

LLMs can generate dynamic responses, answer open-ended questions, speculate on probabilistic questions, and even produce (arguably) creative content. They can "think" outside the box—or at least simulate such thinking based on their training.

Complementing Each Other

A LLM augmented with a KG combines the strengths of both. The LLM can pull from the KG's structured knowledge for factual accuracy and then use its own generative capabilities to provide detailed, nuanced answers, or outside-the-box answers. Without some form of structured knowledge base (akin to a KG), a LLM is like a spoken language without a clear dictionary or syntax—a vast sea of information with no anchored truths.

LLMs Queries can be slow compared to more traditional database queries

LLMs process from scratch every time. For example, if the same query, such as "What day does Christmas fall on?" is asked three times, the query is processed from scratch as an NLP query each time. Instead, KGs, especially those that receive entities and relationships from LLM-parsed documents are fast caches of the interesting things in the document.

This slowness with ChatGPT has been exacerbated after the big upgrade in November 2023. This is, in large part, being able to access specialized tools and external sources such as Bing at the time of query. Again, this is the System 1 versus System 2 trade-off I just described.

By the way, parsing a corpus of documents and caching the goodies of knowledge in the KG is akin to the notion of the ISG "parsing out" interesting insights from dataframes (instead of text, code, or even visual objects for KGs).

Related to this topic, AI is generally much hungrier on power (fortunately, I'm talking about the electric power consumption) than the simpler lookups in a KG. This means that it's more expensive to query and less capable of being deployed in a more mobile fashion.

Trustworthiness and Verification

KGs, constructed by and/or reviewed by humans, provide a level of trustworthiness. Users can be confident in the relationships and facts encoded within because they were encoded by human SMEs. Users can call up the human SME to smooth out any doubts they may have about the KG.

LLMs, while powerful, can sometimes generate information that's misleading or factually incorrect. They base their outputs on patterns seen during training, not on verified truths.

Tracing the LLM's logic (how it arrived at its response) is very challenging. KG logic is laid out as simply as can be in a nice picture of "this leads to that". But LLM logic is a web of hundreds of billions of numbers. We may know how to train an LLM and how the neural network evolves. But tracing the exact logic in that web is nearly impossible–in the same way tracing the synapse path in our brains is nearly impossible.

While there's overlap in the capabilities of KGs and LLMs, they are distinct tools with unique strengths. An organization aiming for the pinnacle of knowledge representation and utilization would benefit from harnessing both KGs for structured, reliable knowledge, and LLMs for dynamic, flexible content generation and interaction.

However, I'd also ponder if an AI would figure out the idea of building KGs to magnify its performance. It would discover that the caching of knowledge in the form of a KG is a powerful concept vetted through the hundreds of thousands of years of field-testing the System 1 and System 2 structure of our own brains went through.

I see KGs as our representatives into a world of human and machine intelligence, even if AIs end up doing most things. Our human-developed KGs would form a body like Congress, a set of our digital twin representatives that balances power with what, at worst, would be an AGI or ASI akin to the U.S. President.

Regulation

People should be concerned about AI. I don't mean there should be panic in the street, at least at the time I'm writing this. But it will at least continue to make big impacts on our society for the foreseeable future.

The cone of uncertainty for "Hurricane AI" is very wide. It's not just what level of capability new AIs bring, but more about how we react and interact with AI. The novel applications created in the AI space might be highly entertaining and bestow very positive effects on society. But I'm certain all will have unintended negative consequences. The ways that AIs themselves interact with each other will probably surprise us to a large degree.

Relevant to this topic, different political environments around the world will react in different ways. Regulation is already a very big topic. Regulation isn't a risk, it's already here and deeply engrained. It's a matter of how much. But there won't be just one knob controlling the level of regulation. It will be multi-dimensional—by government and/or other powerful entities, an array of characteristics of any regulation, and in ways we have yet to see.

I think the level of AI capability available to the general public as I write this (Q4 2023) is fantastically useful and relatively safe when compared to a potentially sentient and sapient AI that's more creative than we are. I think the approach laid out in this book is a hedge against the risks associated with AI regulation. As long as society is based on commerce and people are pretty much as we know them today, KGs and AI should co-exist as complementary representations of knowledge.

Cost

The cost of utilizing ChatGPT has been rising with each release. My $20 per month subscription to ChatGPT Premium and $30 per month subscription to Copilot are one of the greatest bargains I've ever had. However, rates for the OpenAI API running from a small fraction of a cent per 1000 tokens seem to have risen by a magnitude.

Figure 34 is a snapshot I took from Bing on December 17, 2023. We can see that GPT-3.5 charged 1/1000 of a cent per 1000 tokens, but GPT-4 charges 3/100 of a cent per 1000 tokens.

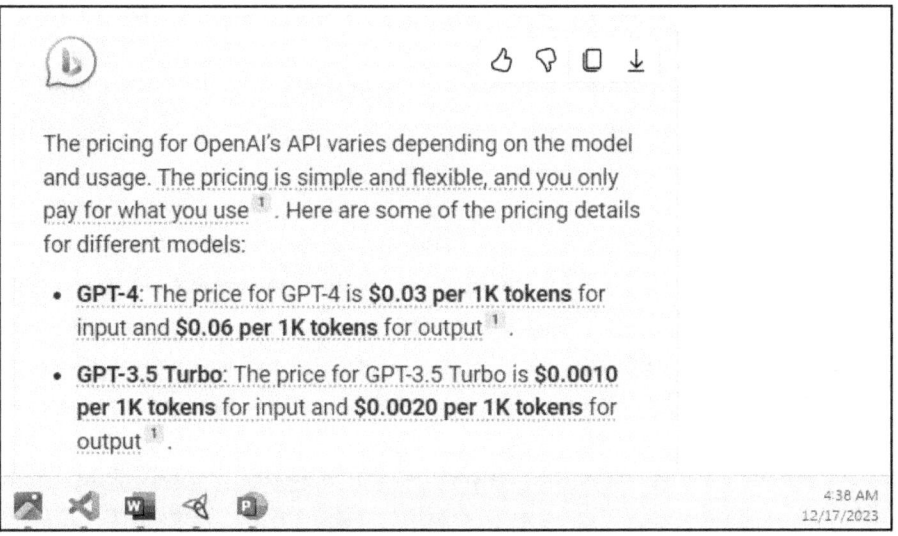

Figure 34: I don't think the performance of GPT-4 is 30 times greater than GPT 3.5.

There are many options for OpenAI, and the costs cannot continue to rise by magnitudes indefinitely. Two data points don't make a pattern, but substantially rising costs are a real risk. That risk is less so with a KG. But the trade-off is the effort of creating a KG versus the algorithm training a LLM.

The Sweet Spot of LLM Ability for KGs

In early November 2023, around the time I was approaching completion of the first draft of this book, Elon Musk's Grok was released in limited Beta, and ChatGPT got a major upgrade. The state of the art of LLMs seems to have improved, but still just incrementally, by a percentage or two on tests. Two weeks after Grok, Google unexpectedly released Gemini. Again, the initial performance comparisons seemed to show slight differences between GPT 4 and Gemini.

The hype and fear for AI improvement is supposedly in that hockey-stick curve where improvements are leaps and bounds, not marginal improvement. The improvement in performance wasn't enough to force major revisions or even scrap the development of this book. If and when the day comes when this book would not be relevant enough to be written ... well, we might have much bigger problems to worry about.

The smarter LLMs become, the less need there is for KGs. When I began writing this book in late September 2023 (less than two months before Grok), the level of performance of LLMs was still well within the sweet spot where the themes of this book make sense and are worth writing about.

Theoretically, LLMs might improve so much that hallucinations aren't as much of a problem. Therefore, the grounding provided by KGs in its symbiotic relationship with LLMs diminishes.

However, KG information is like cache. It is a culmination of a question or concept computed from raw data. "Thinking" (as in the "System 2" thinking mentioned earlier), which is what LLMs do if utilized within an iterative process, as a rule of thumb takes more time than traversing a graph database. Leveraging cached answers to prior questions is faster. The trick is to know what cached results are still relevant.

The ability to incorporate up-to-date data is a big step forward—no more ChatGPT qualifying its answers with its September 2021 cutoff date. Grok incorporates current X (Twitter) conversations! But it's not the knowledge of LLMs that is the most important. It's that a LLM is a resource capable of processing our spoken language instructions.

LLMs are Very Far from Six Sigma!

As far as I know–and again, at the time of this writing—AI is still too far off in reliability to be deployed as a production system. That's mostly because it still makes too many mistakes. In a manufacturing system, the bar for too many mistakes is very high. That often means the bar for production worthiness is in the magnitude of a few in a million (99.99966).

In my experiments using LLMs to help write code (parsing SQL, writing Python functions, etc.), GPT makes mistakes right out of the gate. It may get it right most of the time, but in a production system, even one in a hundred mistakes means the system will go down at least every day. This defeats the purpose of employing machines, which are supposed to perform a task where failures at worst are a truly rare occurrence.

LLMs do save me a lot of typing and researching syntax or even analyzing coding approaches. But that value is in the realm of an assistant and not an automated production tool. As an assistant, I mentioned earlier that ChatGPT has been more helpful than the interns I've worked with.

With that said, those "AI" models (actually ML models) that determine things like credit card fraud or recommend movies are not robust, almost seemingly free-thinking AIs. They are patterns discovered within massive cases of credit card access or movie purchases, respectively. Its "intelligence" is limited to a well-defined task. It's a machine that can do one or a few things very well because its scope is narrow.

All I've said in this topic can change any day as I open Twitter and see an announcement of a new AI model or even AGI or ASI—and it has the ability to access whatever data and execute commands—just like humans. At that point, it's too late to worry about whether KGs are obsolete.

Ontologies and Taxonomies

Ontology and knowledge graph used to be almost synonymous. Ontologies in enterprise settings already exist in some form. It is the knowledge of what things are and how they fit together. At worst, for the most part, it only exists in the heads of people. Workers know the people, equipment, and materials they work with, the properties of all those things, and how these things fit together. That's an ontology. In this scenario, if a worker gets hit by a proverbial bus, that knowledge is lost.

A better state is that extensive and up-to-date documentation exists. Some knowledge exists in the form of custom software code rolled out over the years. Software, particularly software adhering to object-oriented principles, encapsulates models of things (classes), its properties, things it does (methods), and how the things relate (composition, one class having another class as a property).

The disadvantage of this state is that documentation is difficult for people to digest and, until recently, very poorly digested by machines. Even with LLMs, it can hallucinate if we push the questions too far in the novel direction.

This topic is about the best case–those purposefully built, unambiguously defined, authoritative structures we've been talking about, knowledge graphs.

They are developed by SMEs to capture intricate relationships, processes, and terminologies that are specific to different domains within the organization. Here are examples of key ontologies that could be highly specialized and often handcrafted by experts in various domains:

- **Finance and Accounting Ontology**–Contains entities like invoices, balance sheets, and P&L statements, and defines the relationships between these entities. Used for financial analytics, fraud detection, and auditing.

- **Supply Chain Ontology**–Defines terms and relationships related to suppliers, logistics, inventory, and transportation. Used for optimization and real-time tracking.

- **Customer Relationship Management (CRM)** Ontology–Captures customer profiles, interactions, touchpoints, and transactions to provide a 360-degree view of the customer. Often used in conjunction with marketing ontologies for campaign targeting.

- **Human Resources (HR) Ontology**–Includes definitions for roles, competencies, performance metrics, and employment records. Useful for talent management and organizational planning.

- **Information Technology (IT) Ontology**–Describes the hardware, software, networking components, and their inter-relationships. Useful for asset management, cybersecurity, and compliance.

- **Health and Safety Ontology**–Includes terms related to workplace safety protocols, incident reports, and compliance guidelines. Crucial for risk management and compliance.

- **Legal and Compliance Ontology**–Includes terms like contracts, obligations, and rights, along with relationships that govern them. This is critical for enterprises concerned with legal compliance and risk mitigation.

- **Product Ontology**—Contains definitions for product types, features, configurations, and their relationships to other business entities like suppliers and customers.

- **Marketing Ontology**—Focuses on market segments, consumer behaviors, and campaign elements. Used for personalized marketing, consumer analytics, and sales forecasting.

- **Knowledge Management Ontology**—For enterprises that depend heavily on knowledge assets, this ontology would include terms related to documentation, expertise, and knowledge artifacts.

These ontologies require a high degree of expertise to develop and maintain, given the complexity and specialized nature of the terms and relationships they need to capture.

Relational Models are Ontologies

For readers familiar with relational database modeling, it might help to understand ontologies by considering how a database schema really is an ontology. It just doesn't seem like one because, as mentioned, relational databases aren't "relational" enough. For a relational database, "relational" normally goes as far as the group of columns in a table and foreign keys related to a primary key. Figure 35 depicts a simple dimensional model but with more relationships than just the typical FK.

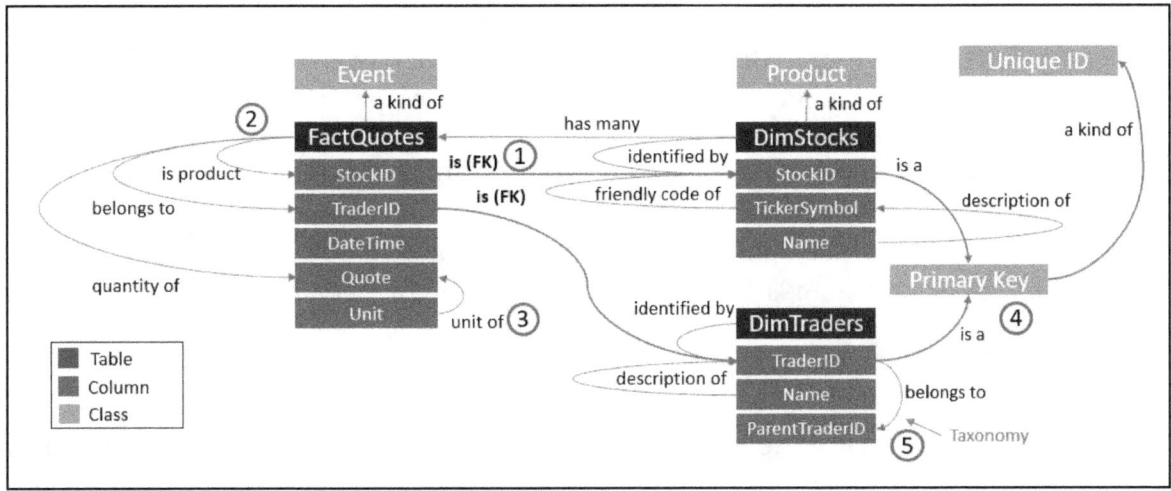

Figure 35: A dimensional model schema is an ontology.

Here are the items of note:

1. **Foreign Key Relationship**—The connection between FactQuotes and DimStocks is labeled as a foreign key (FK) relationship. This indicates that StockID in FactQuotes is a reference to StockID in DimStocks.

2. **Event Classification**— FactQuotes is classified as an event, which is appropriate since a quote is an occurrence at a point in time.

3. **Unit of Measurement**—Unit associated with Quote, which implies that quotes can have different units of measurement. This is a nuanced way of representing the data and aligns with more detailed data models.

4. **Primary Key Identification**—StockID and TraderID are identified as primary keys for their respective tables, which is fundamental in database design.

5. **Taxonomy**—The ParentTraderID in DimTraders suggests a hierarchical relationship within traders, which is an example of taxonomy or inheritance.

Organizing an ontology shares characteristics with data modeling. The principles regarding data models apply in a similar way to ontologies and knowledge graphs (KGs). Both involve structuring data, defining relationships, and determining how information is interconnected. However, there are differences in purpose and the level of detail they each capture.

Data models are typically designed to be efficient for specific use cases, such as transaction processing or analytical querying. They are optimized for the operations that will be performed on the data (like insertions, updates, deletions, and selections), and they structure data in a way that aligns with these operations.

Ontologies in the context of KGs serve as a formal representation of knowledge within a domain and are used to facilitate reasoning about the objects within that domain. The goal is to model the domain in a way that captures its semantics and can be understood both by machines and humans. Here is a comparison of data models and ontologies along a few issues:

- Level of Detail
    o Data Models often focus on the minimum necessary structure to meet functional requirements and performance goals. They are usually normalized to avoid redundancy and enhance data integrity.

- Ontologies and KGs, while they also aim to be concise, are generally richer in the relationships they represent. This richness allows for more complex queries and reasoning, which can lead to new insights. They typically aim to capture more of the "nuts and bolts" to allow for these deeper insights and connections to be made.

- Data Redundancy and Complexity
    - Data Models are careful to avoid unnecessary redundancy to reduce the storage footprint and maintain efficiency.
    - KGs, on the other hand, may allow some redundancy if they enrich the semantic relationships or aid in the inferencing process. KGs often include inferred relationships, which may not be explicitly stated but can be derived from the graph's structure and ontology.

- Evolution over Time
    - Data Models are often static and require careful planning to change, as modifications can be costly and disruptive to operations.
    - KGs and Ontologies are designed to evolve more easily over time. They can be extended with new classes, properties, and relationships as understanding of the domain grows or as new requirements emerge.

While data models are streamlined for efficiency and operations, ontologies and KGs are more expansive in capturing relationships and semantics for reasoning and insights. Both need to strike a balance between richness of representation and practicality of implementation, with the specific balance being determined by the goals of the system they are part of.

For readers proficient with object-oriented programming and need further clarification of taxonomies, please see Appendix A.

Ontology Example

For a better understanding of ontologies, let's revisit the ontology of a dental practice. And let's set up a realistic reason why anyone would do this. Ontologies aren't very useful for a sole-proprietor practice, a relatively simple operation that can fit in the heads of a few people.

However, imagine there exists a type of conglomerate enterprise (an umbrella company managing a number of small businesses) that has acquired dozens of healthcare practices of many types—dental, chiropractic, ophthalmology, physical therapy, podiatry, etc. These firms operating a variety of practices would find ontologies for each type of practice very useful. It's not practical to expect anyone working at the conglomerate HQ to be proficient in any of the type of practices.

The first step in developing an ontology is to identify the entities at play. These are nouns that would play the subject and object parts of a "subject-verb-object" triple that fall within processes at a dental practice:

- Dentist–The primary care provider who diagnoses and treats oral health issues.
- Patient–Individuals seeking dental care.
- Appointment–Scheduled visit details.
- Treatment–Types of treatments or procedures available.
- Room–The particular space where treatments are done.
- Equipment–Dental tools or machinery used.

Now define the verbs that describe how the entities relate:

- Dentist schedules Appointment for Patient.
- Appointment involves Treatment.
- Treatment uses Equipment.
- Appointment occurs in Room.

Figure 36 shows how the high-level ontology above looks in a graph form. Note that the nodes (the circles) are the entities, and the lines are the verbs.

Going deeper, the ontology for a dental practice encompasses not only entities and their relationships, but also detailed properties of each entity. Properties in an ontology describe specific characteristics or attributes of an entity, typically framed as "has a" relationships. For example, a dentist has a name, has a qualification, and has a specialization.

In contrast, taxonomy within an ontology is concerned with classification. It involves organizing entities into categories or classes based on shared characteristics, often represented as "is a" or "a kind of" relationships.

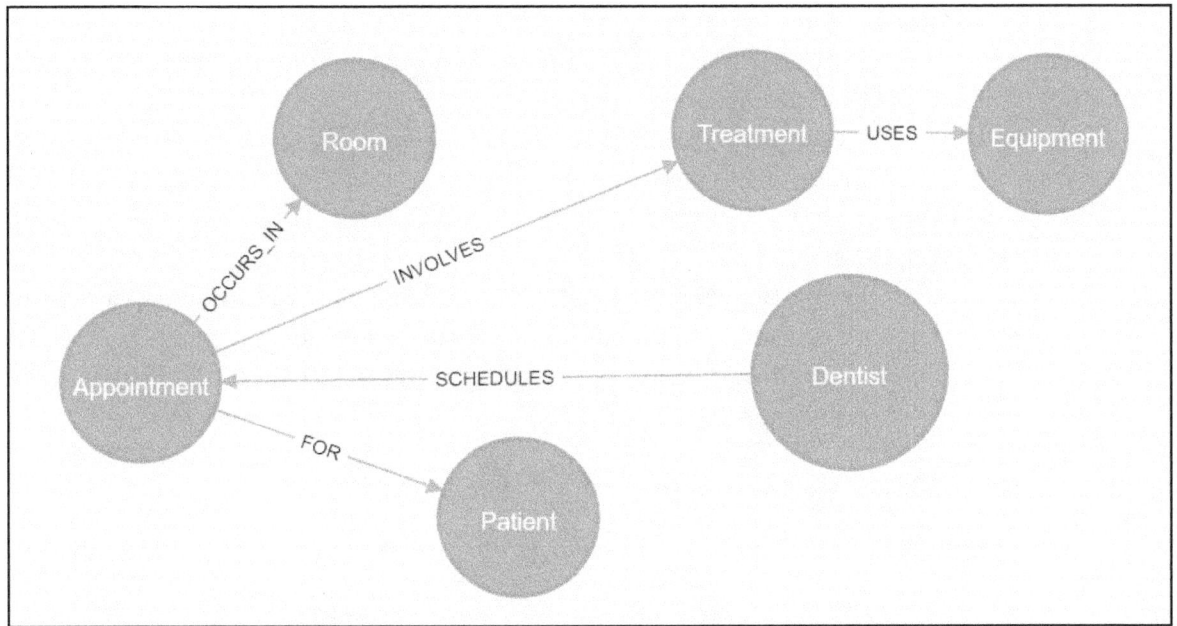

Figure 36: Very high-level sample ontology, dental office.

Following are examples of classes with properties and their place within a taxonomy:

- Dentists:
    - Properties: Name, Qualification, Specialization, Years of Experience.
    - Taxonomy: General Dentist, Orthodontist, Periodontist, Endodontist, etc.

- Patients:
    - Properties: Name, Age, Medical History, Dental History, Contact Information.
    - Taxonomy: New Patient, Returning Patient, Pediatric, Adult.

- Appointments:
    - Properties: Date, Time, Assigned Dentist, Patient's Chief Complaint, Scheduled Procedure.
    - Taxonomy: Initial Consultation, Routine Checkup, Emergency Visit, Follow-Up, Surgical Procedure.

- Treatments:
    - Properties: Type of Treatment, Duration, Complexity, Necessary Equipment.
    - Taxonomy: Cleaning, Filling, Root Canal, Crown, Braces, Whitening.

- Rooms:
    - Properties: Room Number, Size, Available Equipment, Specialization (e.g., for surgery, x-rays).
    - Taxonomy: Examination Room, Operating Room, X-Ray Room, Recovery Room.

- Equipment:
    - Properties: Name, Type, Date of Purchase, Maintenance Schedule.
    - Taxonomy: Diagnostic (e.g., X-ray machine), Surgical (e.g., dental drills, extraction tools), Cleaning (e.g., ultrasonic cleaners), Personal Protective Equipment.

Figure 37 shows what this ontology looks like in the KG.

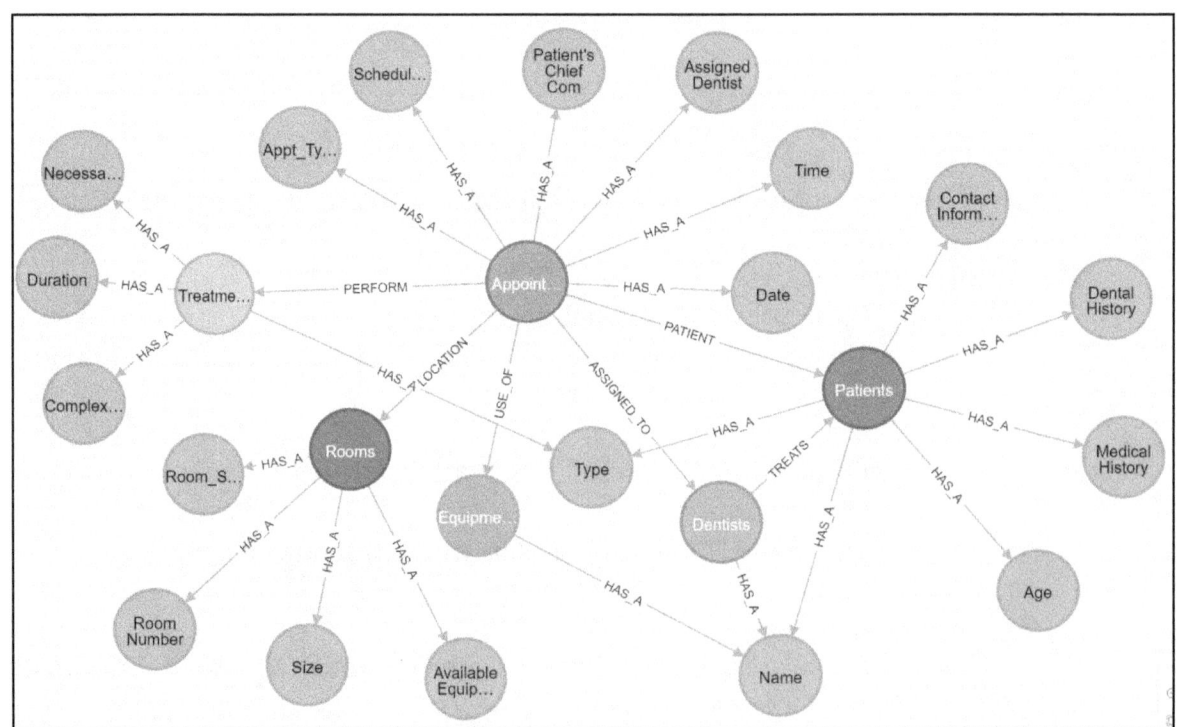

Figure 37: More detailed dental practice ontology.

In this ontology, each entity is described not just by its role but also by its specific characteristics and types. For example, when considering "Dentists," the ontology doesn't stop at defining their function in the practice; it also categorizes them based on their specialization and details their professional attributes. Similarly, for "Appointments," the ontology captures a comprehensive set of attributes like the date, time, and nature of the appointment, enabling a detailed understanding and efficient management of the practice's schedule.

Such a detailed ontology opens the door for the practice to implement smarter applications that manage its operations more effectively, from scheduling appointments and managing patient records to ensuring the right equipment is available and maintained. It provides a structured framework for managing both the data and the operational workflow of the dental practice.

An ontology in this context serves as a blueprint for organizing and understanding the complex relationships and processes within a dental practice. It's an essential tool for managing and making sense of the data that flows through the enterprise, ensuring efficient and effective operation.

I should reiterate that although this simplified example seems obvious to even non-dentists, the real value of this information might not be obvious to an AI or those fortunate people who haven't been to the dentist, or to a new employee struggling through onboarding because everyone is too busy to offer sufficient guidance. In Figure 38, we focus on the Dentists node and the individual dentists, which are their specialties (individuals of the Specializations node). The addition of individuals is a characteristic that moves us from an ontology to a knowledge graph.

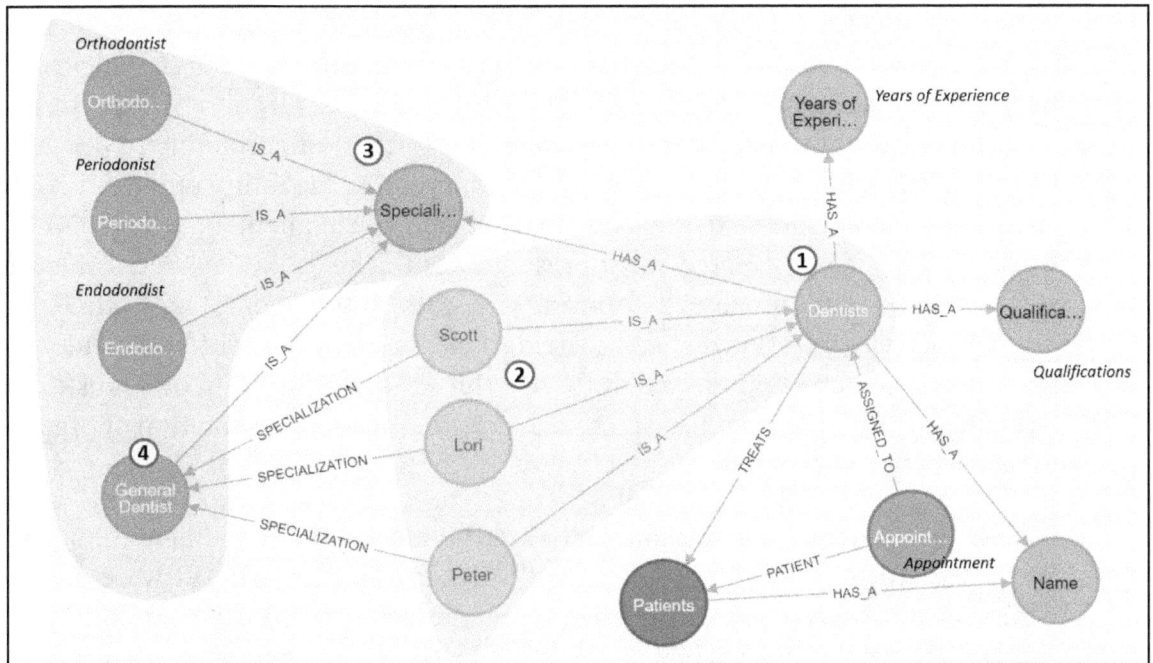

Figure 38: The addition of individuals moves from ontology to knowledge graph.

Here's the description of the items:

1. The Dentist class.

2. There are three dentists, and we know that because they have an IS A relationship to the Dentist class.

3. The Specialty Class has four individuals.

4. The three dentists have a specialization of General Dentist.

Knowledge Graph Artifact Sources

AI of multiple modalities (text, vision, audio, video) has demonstrated a remarkable ability to parse through and make sense of extensive and varied unstructured data. They act as sophisticated decoders, turning the wealth of information contained in enterprise artifacts into relevant knowledge for the KG.

Even without a KG, modern enterprises are replete with various artifacts that represent intricate aspects of their operations and processes. Similar to archeological artifacts, these enterprise artifacts range from workflows and organizational charts to forms one must fill out for anything. They contain vital information pertaining to the culture and history of the enterprise. Deciphered by the incredible capability of today's AI, they can significantly contribute to the construction and enrichment of a KG. For example, workflows, probably created for a presentation to the "C-Suite," detail the sequential steps in business processes, offering insights into operational efficiencies and bottlenecks. Organizational charts provide a clear view of the company's hierarchy and reporting structure. When fed into AI, this information can be transformed into structured data, which can be used to enhance the KG's representation of organizational dynamics and process flows.

Project management artifacts and UML are the most direct documentation, since UML are really a form of KG. In projects of all sorts, but particularly software development, UML diagrams and other technical documentation offer a deep dive into the systems that run the enterprise. By analyzing these artifacts, AI can extract valuable information about system architectures, interdependencies, and business logic, thereby enriching the KG with detailed technical knowledge.

Custom software code itself is a rich information source. The source code of custom software development solutions is a comprehensive repository of business rules and processes. Assuming good software practices, variable names and comments are really documentation of processes in code form. Through LLM analysis, this code can reveal not just the technical operations but also the underlying business logic, thereby contributing significantly to the KG's depth and accuracy.

Systems such as ticketing (e.g., Jira or Zendesk), project management, and CRM (e.g., Salesforce) consist of very detailed conversations towards the goal of resolving problems. LLMs can analyze the conversations to uncover insights about project methodologies, operational challenges, and customer interactions, further enhancing the KG's comprehensiveness.

The use of LLMs to analyze and integrate knowledge from various enterprise artifacts represents a transformative approach to KG construction. This methodology doesn't just capture the enterprise's current state; it offers a dynamic, evolving understanding of its operations, strategies, and future possibilities. By assimilating the rich vein of information inherent in these artifacts, LLMs can significantly enrich the KG, providing a robust foundation for informed decision-making and strategic planning in the enterprise.

Feasibility of Developing and Maintaining KGs

In my earlier discussion about the development of the SQL Server Performance Web, I highlighted the immense challenge of encoding human intelligence's subtle nuances into digital formats. When I began, I underestimated how much we don't know what others know and don't know. This made it a challenge to know where to draw a box around what goes into the KG and what I assume to be common knowledge.

For example, in writing this book, I assume the reader knows English and has at least a high-beginner to low-intermediate level of knowledge around business, software development, and analytics. This book and every other technical book are knowledge bases, just like a KG. But it's disconnected from other chunks of knowledge. I take a guess as to knowledge about things not so widely known, such as the value of optimized cubes, but no knowledge base can cover every base—no pun intended.

This dilemma is indeed a large part of the underlying problem I'm trying to solve. That is, everyone has a limited set of skills and knowledge, along with different strengths and weaknesses. It is possible to catalog all that skill and knowledge into some sort of structure, with the hope that collectively, the knowledge is usable by an extended audience.

I first covered this in "Fragmented Knowledge."

This task, as monumental as it is, forms the bedrock of constructing and maintaining KGs. KGs are an attempt to mirror the intricate and abstract connections our brains naturally make. However, the journey from conceptualization to realization and upkeep of these KGs is far from straightforward. It involves not just the technical challenges but also the orchestration of a diverse array of expertise and the constant adaptation to an ever-changing external environment.

As we delve into the feasibility of developing and maintaining KGs, we encounter several critical considerations. First, the mobilization of collective expertise through a diverse team is paramount. Constructing a KG requires a symphony of skills—from Subject matter experts to data engineers and business owners, each bringing their unique perspective to this complex puzzle. This collaborative effort, though rich in potential, faces practical challenges, especially when team members have primary responsibilities (their "day job") outside of KG development.

Furthermore, the dynamic nature of the external environment adds another layer of complexity. Just as our understanding of the world evolves with new information and changing contexts, so must the KGs remain up to date. This calls for a proactive approach to KG maintenance, ensuring they reflect the current realities and not just historical beliefs.

The integration of LLMs into this process marks a significant advancement. LLMs, with their expansive knowledge base, can assist in identifying ontological relationships and maintaining the accuracy and comprehensiveness of KGs. LLMs may not yet replace the depth of human expertise, but they certainly enhance the efficiency and effectiveness of the KG maintenance process.

Semantic Web and KGs

By now, we should have a good understanding of KGs—roughly, it's a collection of ontologies and taxonomies. But what is a "semantic web"?

The "semantic web" refers to an extension of the World Wide Web that strives to make Internet references consistent, enabling better cooperation between computers and people. It is a broad concept encompassing a range of standards, technologies, and practices designed to enhance the usability and interoperability of the web.

To be clear, the semantic web is not just a KG using the standards. As a metaphor, consider the electric grid versus appliances that can use it. Just as an electric grid provides the infrastructure and standards for delivering electricity across regions that are usable by a broad range of appliances, the semantic web provides the infrastructure and standards for structuring, linking, and querying for a broad range of resources on the web.

A KG that is encoded to semantic web standards can be compared to an appliance that is designed to plug into and utilize the electric grid. Just as appliances are built to use the electricity provided by the grid, these KGs are built to use the infrastructure of the semantic web. They adhere to the standards and protocols of the semantic web (like RDF, OWL, SPARQL) to ensure compatibility and functionality within this ecosystem.

Figure 39 is a KG (a "meta" KG) of the pieces of terms related to KGs presented in this book.

The following topics explore the meaning of each node in Figure 39.

Semantic Web, RDF, SPARQL, and OWL

The semantic web is an endeavor to make the content on the World Wide Web more understandable and usable by machines.

We must begin by defining the core concept of a "resource". We might tend to think of the "objects" of the Web (or The Internet) as just the web pages we navigate to from our Web browser. Although Web pages are a resource, the notion of resource in the semantic web context is more granular than that.

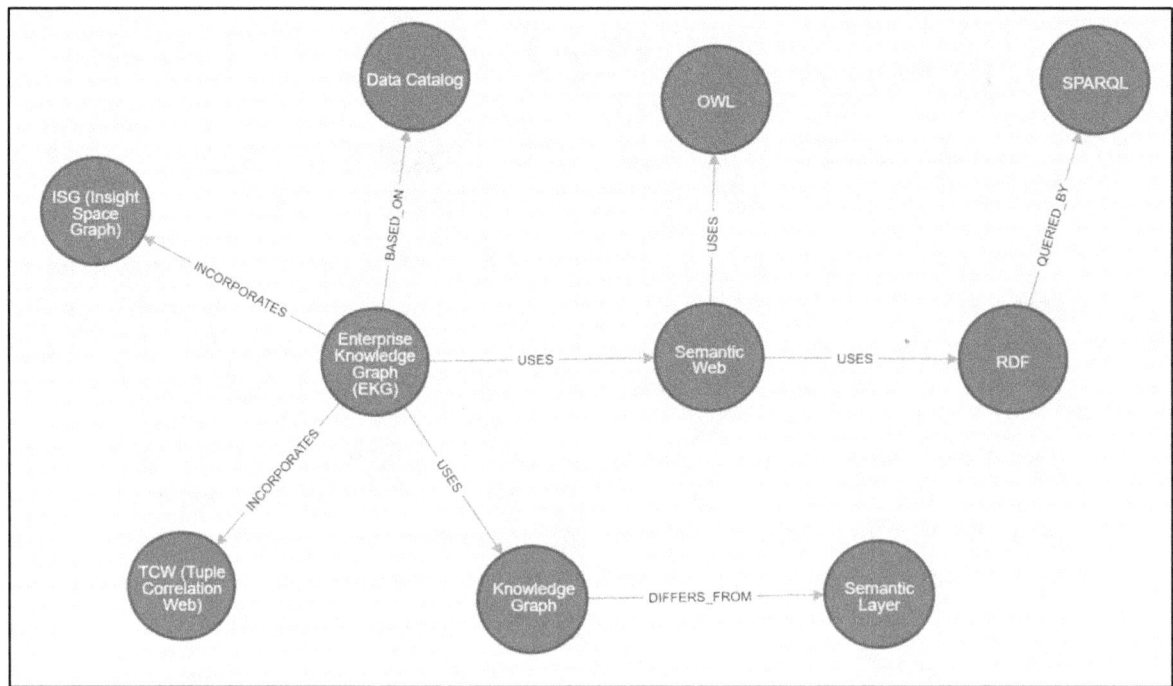

Figure 39: Ontology of knowledge graph concepts presented in this book.

In the semantic web context, resource refers to anything that can be identified, named, or described on the web. This could be a web page, an image, a video clip, a specific piece of information like a person's name, or more abstract concepts such as a color, a date, or an idea. In simpler terms, think of a resource as any "thing" that has a distinct identity on the internet and can be pointed to or talked about. Each resource is given a unique identifier (called a URI, which is like a web address) serving as its globally unique name—just like social security numbers for each U.S. citizen and ISBN codes. Strict reference to these unique identifiers ensures all contributors to web material are talking about the same thing. That leads to a rich and interconnected web of the world's corpus of knowledge.

To make the semantic web a reality, standards were developed by the World Wide Web Consortium (W3C):

- RDF (Resource Description Framework): It's the core of the semantic web. Think of it as the basic language that defines "things" and their relationships. It operates in "triples": subject-predicate-object (e.g., "MSFT sells Office" or "Office is Software").

- SPARQL: Once data is structured in RDF, we need a way to query it. SPARQL is to RDF what SQL is to traditional relational databases.

- OWL (Web Ontology Language): While RDF can represent data, OWL gives it meaning. It defines how terms relate, making sense of the vast interlinked data.

When we create a KG that adheres to semantic web standards, we're essentially embedding these principles into the structure of your KG. This involves using RDF for data interchange, OWL for ontology definition, SPARQL for querying, and URIs and IRIs (International Resource Identifiers–wider character set than URIs) for resource identification. Such a graph becomes part of the broader semantic web ecosystem, capable of integrating with other semantic web resources and applications.

We can refer to such a graph as a "Semantic Web Knowledge Graph" or "Semantic Knowledge Graph." However, for this book, we'll assume that the KG generally adheres to the semantic web standards—it doesn't need to be all or nothing. So, I'll continue to refer to the KG as simply KG.

Semantic Layer versus Knowledge Graph

While KGs are about representing knowledge in nodes and edges, the semantic layer acts as a bridge between human, often non-technical users, and generally, the more cryptic structure of databases. In BI and database contexts, the semantic layer translates raw data structures into a format or view that is more understandable to end users. It's about making complex data user-friendly.

Enterprise Knowledge Graph (EKG) versus Knowledge Graph

An EKG is a holistic representation of all the knowledge and data within an enterprise, weaving it into a coherent, interlinked structure. While KGs and the semantic web offer frameworks for representing knowledge, an EKG goes further. It integrates data across silos, adding layers of business-specific context, governance, and access control.

Within the EKG, we're incorporating specialized ontologies like the ISG and TCW:

- ISG (Insight Space Graph): This can be visualized as an ontology of dataframes. It captures insights from data visualizations, offering a structured way to record and link what traditionally might have been anecdotal observations.

- TCW (Tuple Correlation Web): This serves as an ontology of relationships between tuples. It dives deeper into the dynamics of specific data points, creating a web of how various tuples interrelate based on correlations.

Starting with a data catalog as the bedrock, our EKG creates a sophisticated, interconnected map of enterprise data. With roots in the principles of the semantic web, the EKG is augmented with specialized ontologies like the ISG and TCW, providing layers of depth and specificity. By embracing the principles of semantics, our KG is positioned to offer nuanced insights, bridging gaps between raw data, business understanding, and actionable knowledge. It's the future of enterprise data management: holistic, interconnected, and semantically rich.

Node Identifiers

Every node and relationship in a semantic web have an ID that is a URI or IRI. This is its unique ID. What we would usually see of a node in a visualization of the graph is a terse but meaningful "label property." For example, a node representing me might be:

- IRI–http://www.example.org/contributors#EAA
- label–Eugene Asahara

Another node on the same graph might be:

- URI–http://www.softcodedlogic.com
- label–Eugene Asahara

They represent two distinct objects, but the displayed label is the same.

In the context of the semantic web, URI and IRI are often used interchangeably. The key difference is in the range of characters they support. URIs are restricted to a subset of ASCII. IRIs can include characters from a broad range of scripts and languages, making them more suitable for international use.

In the semantic web, where global accessibility and diverse language support are important, IRIs are often preferred for identifying resources.

KG Users Ontology

The KG is not just a mere repository of structured and interrelated business data, but a dynamic ecosystem that constantly evolves with the interplay of various actors within it. Chief among these actors are the users. A user can be human or machine-based, such as in AI and ML processes.

In terms of software, especially BI, the usual topic concerning users seems to be about the resources users have access to. Of course, that's vital. However, the characteristics of each user can provide more context to clients of the EKG, whether they are human or AI. So, users should have a fully-fledged ontology, including whatever information about users that is appropriate.

Human users could range from analysts and managers to executives, each bringing their unique perspective to the graph, interacting with it in a multitude of ways. They might annotate nodes with comments, validate relationships between nodes based on their expertise, or even rate the significance of certain insights. Beyond these interactions, what's even more foundational is the inherent metadata associated with each user. The metadata paints a holistic portrait of the user—their skillsets, departmental affiliations, titles, and security levels. Such intricate details enrich the graph by introducing a layer of context (the "personality" of each user) to every interaction.

For instance, an analyst specializing in sales trends could comment on a node representing quarterly sales data. This comment, when viewed in isolation, provides a certain degree of insight. However, when supplemented with the metadata of the user—that the comment comes from an expert in sales trends—its significance amplifies.

Moreover, in a vast corporate setting, where the EKG might encompass data points from myriad domains, this metadata is invaluable. Grouping BI objects like tuples and dataframes based on the attributes of the user interacting with them can unveil patterns and insights that might have otherwise remained obscure. Let's delve into a simple example. Imagine three users:

- Eva—Besides her proficiency in machine learning, she's also skilled in data visualization and statistics.

- Curt—He possesses skills in Customer Relationship Management (CRM) and Data Visualization. He is the Sales Project Manager.

- Sally—A new user who's a Project Manager from the Logistics department.

Figure 40 is a graph representation of these users. By integrating such detailed user ontologies into the KG, the graph becomes more than just a network of business data points. It transforms into a vibrant, context-rich landscape that mirrors the collaborative fabric of the enterprise.

Note that in the KG, the transparency of the authors is important. The credibility of the subject matter expert who authored an ontology (or even just asserts a relationship) is a key factor in how much to trust the KG. However, later, I'll discuss the User Schema, which provides some layer of obfuscation for BI users in their BI query activity that ends up in the BI-charged components.

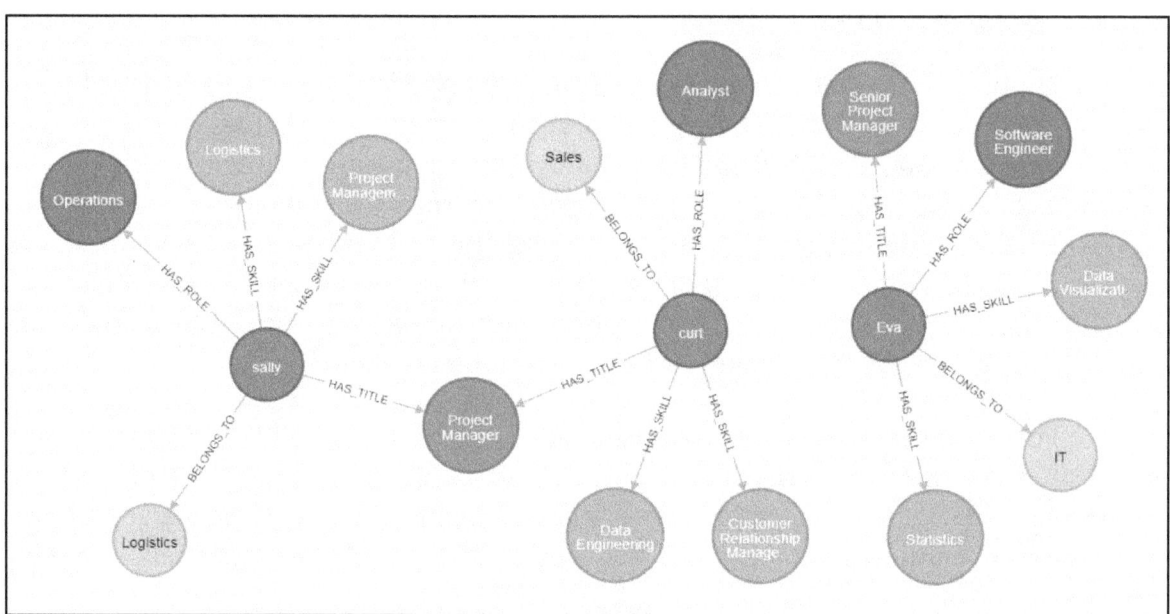

Figure 40: Ontology of Users.

Conclusion to Knowledge Graphs

KGs have emerged as a vital tool in organizing and interpreting diverse and complex data within enterprises. From specialized domains like finance and healthcare to basic operational elements, KGs provide a structured framework for understanding intricate relationships and processes.

The incorporation of advanced AI in analyzing enterprise artifacts represents a significant advancement in knowledge management. These technologies not only enhance KGs' capabilities but also ensure their adaptability in a dynamic business environment.

However, creating and maintaining effective KGs is a complex task, demanding a blend of technical skills and a deep understanding of the unique enterprise environment. Organizations must navigate the balance between KGs' potential and practical implementation, considering the nuances of their operations and the diverse skills of their teams.

Looking ahead, KGs are poised to play a pivotal role in business evolution, bridging the gap between raw data, fragmented expertise, and actionable insights. They offer a comprehensive approach to making informed decisions, predicting trends, and adapting to changing business dynamics.

KGs represent a significant step in data and knowledge management, becoming increasingly integral to strategic business operations. Their potential to steer organizations towards greater innovation and success is immense, as they continue to evolve and refine the way businesses understand and utilize their data.

I'd like to highlight a key aspect that underscores the significance of graph databases, especially for those primarily accustomed to relational databases. This observation is reminiscent of the shift in the BI world from multi-dimensional cubes back to the comfort zone of tabular views. The essence of the result is stripped away, in the same way a photograph of you strips away much of your essence.

In the realms of BI and ML, the outputs we're familiar with from queries to traditional databases are usually tables (rows and columns) or single values. However, when querying a graph database, the possibilities extend beyond the confines of a two-dimensional table. The result can indeed be a table or a single value, but the true potential of a graph database lies in its ability to return a graph as a result.

This graph is not just a visual representation; it is a comprehensive map that details how various elements are interconnected. It provides a contextual richness far surpassing that of a scalar value or a dataframe. It's a more holistic depiction, offering insights into the relationships and connections between data points.

For decades, BI analysts have primarily worked almost exclusively with tabular results sourced from relational databases. We're adept at interpreting these tables and are comfortable viewing them through conventional lenses like line graphs and bar charts. However, graph databases present a different paradigm. The results from these databases are often a web of triples, which we interpret as network graphs. This method of visualization unveils a deeper, more interconnected view of the data.

A similar phenomenon emerged for multi-dimensional OLAP cubes. The results of OLAP cubes from SSAS were originally multi-dimensional "cellsets"—roughly, a subcube of a cube. Although OLAP cubes are capable of returning results in the familiar tabular form, in my 20+ years as an SSAS developer/architect, I've rarely experienced customers who took advantage of the multi-dimensional nature of the result in the cellset format. Much of it has to do with the lack of capability of BI visualization tools during the early BI years. And probably the overwhelming success of Excel (sometimes called the "most widely used BI tool") with its 2D sheets.

By embracing the unique capabilities of graph databases, we can uncover a richer, more nuanced understanding of our data and the intricate relationships it encapsulates. This shift in perspective can lead to more informed decisions and insights, driving innovation and advancement in data analysis and interpretation.

By employing graph results, analysts can go beyond their default BI dive into "the what" and delve into "the how and why" (relationships, causes, and effects). Graph databases excel at showing how entities are related, which can be pivotal for uncovering patterns that are not immediately obvious in traditional tables. For BI analysts, this can lead to a more readily apparent understanding of causality, influence, and the strength of relationships, which are critical for predictive analytics, anomaly detection, and recommendation systems.

CHAPTER FIVE

Data Catalog

The Data Catalog (DC) is a directory of all databases of all types within the enterprise. For example:

- **Relational Databases:** This includes all Online Transaction Processing (OLTP) systems that support day-to-day business operations. Examples of such databases are SQL Server, Oracle, and MySQL, which store data in well-defined schemas consisting of rows and columns.

- **Business Intelligence Systems:** These are specialized databases that include data warehouses, data marts, and Online Analytical Processing (OLAP) cubes. They are designed to aggregate large volumes of data and support complex queries for business analysis.

- **File-Based Data:** Many organizations use flat files such as csv or Excel files for storing transactional data, research data, or data exchanged with partners and customers. These files are often used for their simplicity and flexibility in storing tabular data.

- **Semi-Structured Data Storage:** Locations that store semi-structured data such as JSON and XML. These formats are particularly common for web data, configuration files, and interchange between different systems.

- Cloud Storage Directories: Modern enterprises frequently use cloud-based storage solutions like Azure Blob Storage, Amazon S3, or Google Cloud Storage. These platforms provide scalable, hierarchical storage for files of all types—from documents and images to backups and logs.

- **Unstructured Data Repositories:** Includes data stored in formats that do not fit neatly into tables, such as emails, documents, videos, and images. Managing these types of data often requires specialized indexing and search capabilities.

The DC is the intermediary between the knowledge-worker-authored KG and the analyst-focused BI-charged components of the EKG. It's a map from concepts in the KG or the BI components to where data about it exists within the enterprise. It's pretty much just metadata, the directory to data detail.

The DC is the most straightforward component of the three parts of the EKG. With today's metadata management, virtual data warehouses, data fabric, etc., there are ample tools for putting together a comprehensive data catalog. In the context of this book, the term "DC" generally refers to a graph object: the graph representation of a data catalog, akin to how the "KG," "ISG," and "TCW" are knowledge graph structures. Unlike a data catalog application, such as Apache Atlas, which serves as a centralized platform for managing metadata, the DC in a graph form can be downloaded and transformed from such systems. Once in its graph form, the DC can be integrated within the larger framework of knowledge alongside the KG, ISG, and TCW, as depicted in Figure 41. This integration allows for a more dynamic and interconnected representation of data assets, streamlining access and analysis across the enterprise.

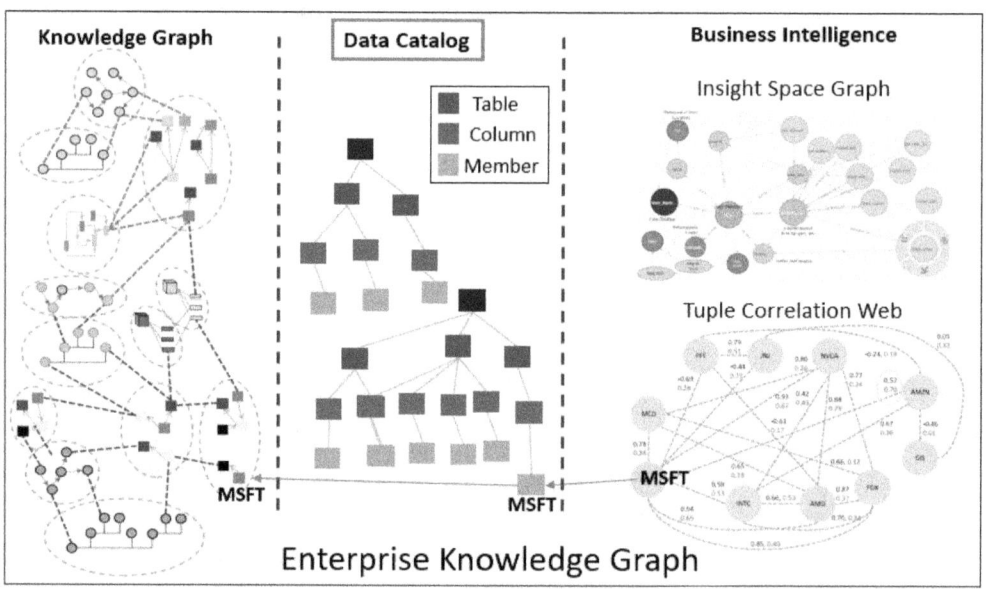

Figure 41: The role of the data catalog in the AEI.

The structure of the DC is very straightforward. As Figure 42 shows, it's just a chain of one-to-many relationships starting with server and ending in members.

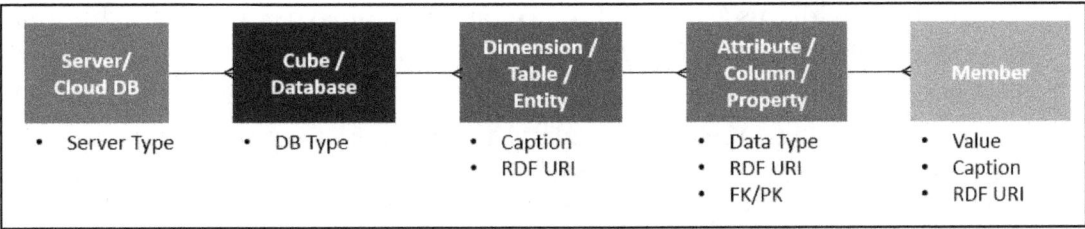

Figure 42: Structure of the data catalog.

The DC is the "stable" structure of the AEI to which the ISG and TCW link to. By "stable," I mean that there is nothing subjective about it (as opposed to the KG), and database data is what it is. The DC is the most "real" of the three components. It's sort of like how gold and silver are "real" money in that it's tangible. The DC maps to tangible databases used by real knowledge workers and maintained by real data engineers meeting very rigid levels of quality and data governance.

The Ontology of the Databases

The DC is an ontology of the databases. Servers, databases, tables, columns, and members are entities in KG terms. These entities are related, for example:

1. NGGG5 *is a* SQL Server Database.
2. SQL Server Database *is a* Database Platform.
3. StockAnalysis *is a* database of NGGG5.
4. DimStocks *is a* table of StockAnalysis.
5. TickerSymbol *is a* column of DimStocks
6. MSFT *is a* member of TickerSymbol.
7. FactQuote.StockID *is a* foreign key of DimStocks.StockID.

Those are some of the typical relationships inherent in a relational database. For file "databases," such as csv files in an Azure Storage directory, the entities are conceptually the same:

- Server *is a* Storage Account.
- Database *is a* container.
- Table *is a* file.

The problem with this analogy of the DC as an ontology is that, again, the "relationships" typical of "relational databases" aren't relational enough. For example, if we think of the DimStocks table with the columns TickerSymbol and CompanyName in a RDBMS, we normally couldn't specify a relationship like: *CompanyName is referenced by TickerSymbol*. Those kinds of relationships will be defined in the KG. Figure 43 illustrates a partial KG mapped to database tables and columns of the DC.

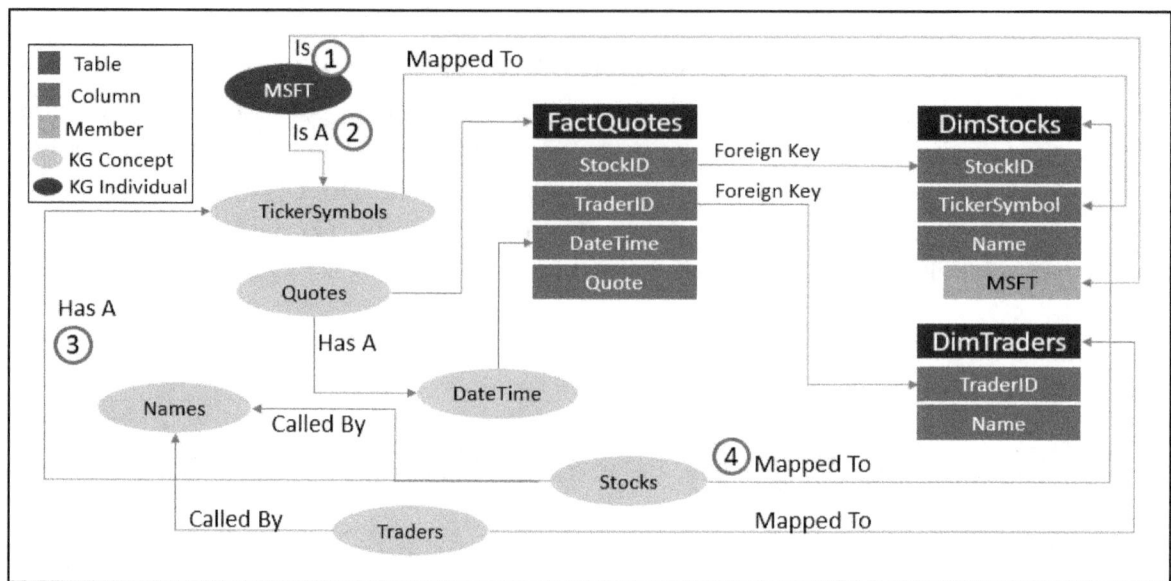

Figure 43: DC and KG mapping.

We can see:

1. The KG *individual* node, MSFT, **Is** the DC member, MSFT.

2. The KG node MSFT **is a** TickerSymbol.

3. The KG concept of Stocks **has a** TickerSymbol

4. The KG concept of Stocks **is** the DC table DimStocks.

Data Catalog Foundations

In the EKG framework, the DC is the structured and interconnected map of enterprise data. It enables users, from data scientists to business analysts, to easily locate data across the enterprise, facilitating more informed decision-making. This organized approach also ensures efficient data management, reducing redundancy and improving the quality of the data.

In the context of an EKG, the DC is more than a simple inventory. It's a construct that underpins the entire KG structure, grounding it in fact—the data doesn't lie (I say a bit facetiously).

Historically, DCs have been manifested in several forms, such as data dictionary, metadata catalog, and now semantic layer, which is popular in the BI world. None of these terms are exactly synonymous, but they are interchangeable to a reasonable degree. Each iteration evolved with the changing data landscape, aiming to be a more comprehensive repository of metadata and a guide to the vast sea of enterprise data.

In the realm of data management and governance, terms like data catalog, data dictionary, metadata catalog, and semantic layer often converge in their functionalities, leading to their occasional interchangeable use. At their core, each of these tools aims to provide clarity, organization, and enhanced understanding of the location and semantics of enterprise data.

The DC is typically an inventory of data assets, helping users with data discovery and offering contextual information about various datasets. This structure is the central piece of the EKG linking conventional KG ontologies to the BI-charged components we will get to starting in Chapter 9.

We've discussed the primary concepts of the DC—server, database, table, column, and member. But a data dictionary delves deeper into a specific database's structure. For example, elaborating on column data types and value constraints. The DC could also include data lineage and data quality metrics, which are very useful for data governance and a comprehensive understanding of data sources.

Semantic Layer and Data Fabric

Both the concepts of data fabric and semantic layer center around the efficient and meaningful use of data within an organization, but they operate at different levels and serve different purposes. But first, an analogy. Think about:

- All that goes into a car, a driving machine.
- The simple interface to operate the car presented around the driver's seat.
- The user's manual explaining the features and how to access it.

Here's how the analogy works:

- **Data Fabric (The Driving Machine):** This includes all the components of the car—engine, transmission, wheels, etc. It represents the integrated data systems and processes that work together to manage and move data efficiently across an organization.

- **Semantic Layer (Dashboard in the Driver's Seat):** This is what the driver (user) interacts with directly. It's the dashboard displaying essential information in an easily understandable format, much like the semantic layer, which provides a user-friendly view of complex data for business intelligence and decision-making.

- **Data Catalog (Car's Instruction Manual/Detailed Map):** The data catalog is akin to a car's instruction manual or a detailed map kept in the glove compartment. Just as a manual provides information about every part of the car and how to use it, and the map helps in navigating, the data catalog contains detailed metadata about all the data assets within the organization. It's a map guiding users in finding, understanding, and using the right data effectively, just as a manual or map aids in understanding and navigating the car or a journey.

A data fabric is a holistic data environment that integrates, processes, stores, and manages data from various sources. It's essentially a unified architecture or framework that allows data to flow effortlessly and be accessed across the organization. The emphasis of a data fabric is on connecting disparate data sources, ensuring data quality, and facilitating real-time data processing and analytics. Its main objectives are interoperability, scalability, and agility in the face of an increasingly complex data landscape.

On the other hand, a semantic layer is an abstraction layer between raw data sources and end users, which presents data in a way that is meaningful and easily understandable. It's like a translation mechanism that converts complex database terminologies and structures into user-friendly, business-oriented terms. This layer simplifies the data access process for business users, allowing them to query data without needing to understand the underlying complexities. The emphasis here is on providing a consistent, business-focused view of data.

In essence, while a data fabric is about the seamless flow and integration of data across the enterprise, a semantic layer is more about simplifying the interpretation and consumption of that data for end users. They do, however, complement each other: a robust data fabric can be enhanced with a semantic layer on top, ensuring not just seamless data flow but also meaningful data interpretation for business users.

RDF-encoded Data Catalog

When it comes to the technology that underpins the KG and DC, the Resource Description Framework (RDF) is an aspirational standard. RDF offers a standardized approach to encoding the world. While RDF certainly is well-associated with the world of KGs, recall that the DC is an ontology as well. Beyond DC entities, such as servers, databases, tables, columns, and members, other metadata related at each of those levels might include these elements typical of a KG:

- Topic: The main subject or focus of the data.

- Tags: Keywords associated with the data for easier searchability.

- Publisher: The entity or department responsible for the data.

- Dates: Information on when the data was last modified and released, as well as the expected frequency of updates.

- IRI: The Internationalized Resource Identifier, which can act as a data "homepage."

- Contact Information: Who to reach out to for queries or clarifications about the data.

- Accessibility: Whether the data is public or private or even more granular access information.

- Type: The format of the data, be it a relational database, JSON, csv, or XML.

Given the vastness of enterprise data ecosystems, DCs may encompass hundreds of databases (typical of large enterprises), each supporting an application, massive data lakes, data warehouses, OLAP cubes, and even "reports" (which can also be thought of as virtual databases in their own right). The lineage of these reports—tracing back to their origins—is crucial, and a robust DC can provide that.

Retrieving Metadata

Virtually all database platforms have built-in methods for retrieving metadata. For example, relational databases, such as SQL Server and Oracle are stocked with metadata tables in the "sys" schema and sport very easy-to-use data management views (DMV). If such tidy SQL-like DMVs don't exist, there is usually an API to access metadata.

In addition to these inherent capabilities of databases, there are specialized metadata management applications that play a significant role in broader metadata management across an organization. These applications are designed to retrieve, consolidate, and manage metadata from a variety of sources, not limited to just one type of database or data store.

These metadata management tools offer advanced functionalities like metadata discovery, lineage tracking, governance, and a centralized repository for metadata across different platforms. They are particularly beneficial in complex data environments where data is spread across multiple systems, such as relational databases, NoSQL databases, cloud storage, and even file systems.

A sampling of the top data and metadata management applications in the market include Informatica Enterprise Data Catalog, IBM Watson Knowledge Catalog, Collibra Data Governance, Alation Data Catalog, and Talend Data Fabric.

These applications are designed to work in conjunction with the native metadata retrieval capabilities of database platforms. They enhance the metadata management process by providing additional layers of functionality, such as advanced analytics, visualization, and cross-system integration. This allows for a more holistic approach to metadata management, which is critical for effective data governance, compliance, and overall data strategy in modern organizations.

However, AATOW, these applications don't seem to natively download their data/metadata catalog information in the RDF/OWL semantic web format. The capabilities around interfacing with graph databases, such as Neo4j, are beginning to appear, but fully embracing graph databases for metadata management is still in the nascent stages.

In Chapter 11—Implementation, "Load the Data Catalog," I offer a walkthrough of retrieving metadata from a SQL Server database and uploading it into the EKG.

URI for Tables and Columns

Because the DC sits between the KG and the BI-Charged Components, it makes sense that we might want to enlist the standards of the W3C semantic web to strengthen the context of links between the DC and the KG. This begins with remembering that DC components, such as tables usually represent some sort of entity or concept, and the columns are properties or features of the entity. For example, a table of street addresses in a SQL Server database table might be mapped to semantic web concepts as in Figure 44.

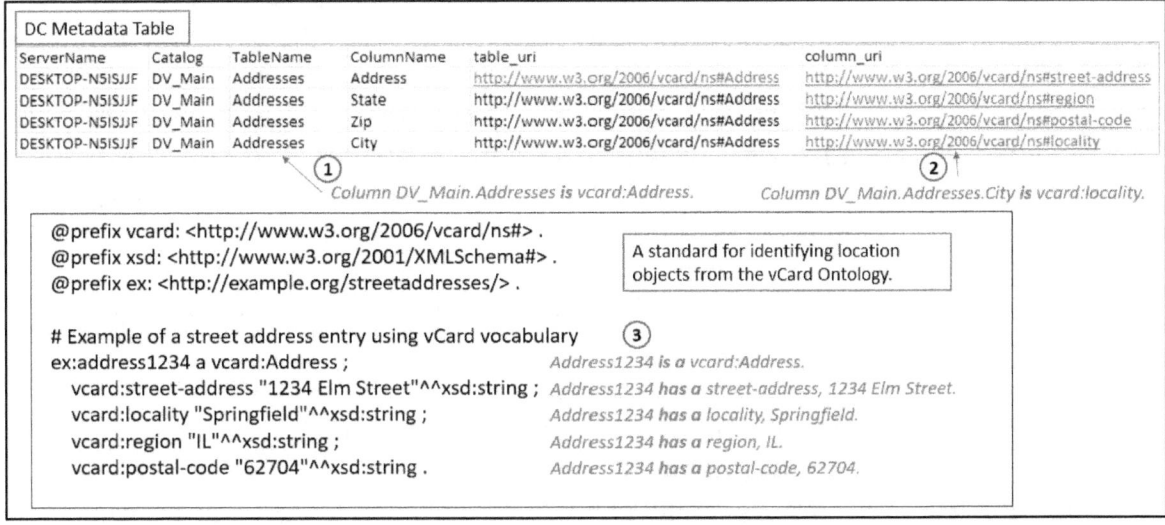

Figure 44: vCard mapping of address concepts.

The top part is a partial display of the DC metadata. It's just four columns from the DV_Main.Addresses table. The bottom is an RDF/OWL specification for URIs related to the four parts of a street address.

1. The table, Addresses is a vCard:Address.

2. The row for City is a vCard:locality.

3. Descriptions of the main parts of the RDF/OWL specification related to street addresses.

If the DC is loaded with these URI as properties of tables and columns, ontologies and taxonomies could unambiguously and automatically link to the DC's respective table and column nodes.

OLAP Cubes in the Enterprise-Scoped Data Catalog

Since the main theme of this book is how BI fits into the AI world, we'll drill down deeper into the schemas of OLAP cubes. OLAP cubes, whether implemented as a MOLAP pre-aggregated cubes (SSAS, Kyvos) or a star/snowflake schema (implemented in a DW solution such as Snowflake or Redshift), are a staple structure of BI. They are a major interface to BI insights. As we delve into cubes and, by extension, other technologies employing a similar user-facing dimensional model (for example, AtScale, Essbase, Cognos, and SSAS), certain intricacies arise that require further exploration. The dimensional model in these systems is composed of elements like dimensions, attributes, hierarchies, measures, and calculations, which together create an intuitive and interactive environment for data analysis. Here are a few key benefits of this dimensional model facade:

- **Intuitive Data Exploration**—The dimensional model mirrors the way business users think about data, making it more intuitive for them to explore and analyze. Users can easily navigate through data using familiar business terms and concepts, represented by dimensions and hierarchies.

- **Efficient Query Performance**—OLAP cubes and similar dimensional models are optimized for query performance, especially for complex and aggregated queries. This efficiency is crucial for quick, ad-hoc reporting and analysis, enabling faster decision-making processes.

- **Enhanced Data Context and Clarity**—By structuring data into dimensions and hierarchies, these models provide context to the data. This organization helps users understand the relationships within the data, leading to clearer insights and a more comprehensive understanding of business metrics.

- **Simplified Complex Data Relationships**—The hierarchical structuring in dimensions simplifies complex data relationships, making it easier for users to drill down into details or roll up for summarized views, depending on their analysis needs.

- **Scalability and Flexibility**—These models are scalable and can handle large volumes of data while still providing the flexibility to accommodate changes in business requirements and data structures.

The user-facing dimensional model of OLAP cubes and similar technologies offers a user-friendly, performance-optimized, and context-rich environment for BI. It simplifies data exploration and analysis, making it accessible to business users who may not have deep technical expertise, thus democratizing data across the organization.

However, the user-facing dimensional model used by BI analysts is just a friendly façade over what is usually a more complicated underlying data schema composed from one (occasionally more) underlying data sources. At best, that underlying schema simply reflects the schema of a well-curated data warehouse, probably less targeted and polished than the dimensional model presented to the user, but still relatively easy for non-data engineers to peruse. In turn, that underlying data source could be a hodgepodge of dozens to hundreds of operational databases in a typical enterprise—certainly not very intuitive for a non-data engineer.

In SSAS, this underlying schema of a dimensional model is called a data source view (DSV). In Kyvos, it's called "Relationships." It's sort of like a customer support person who presents a friendlier interface between you and the company. It's simpler than trying to navigate around the company yourself. Figure 45 is an example of such a schema. For this book, I'll use the SSAS term, DSV, since it's more descriptive of the purpose. The Kyvos term, "relationships," is quite overloaded in this book.

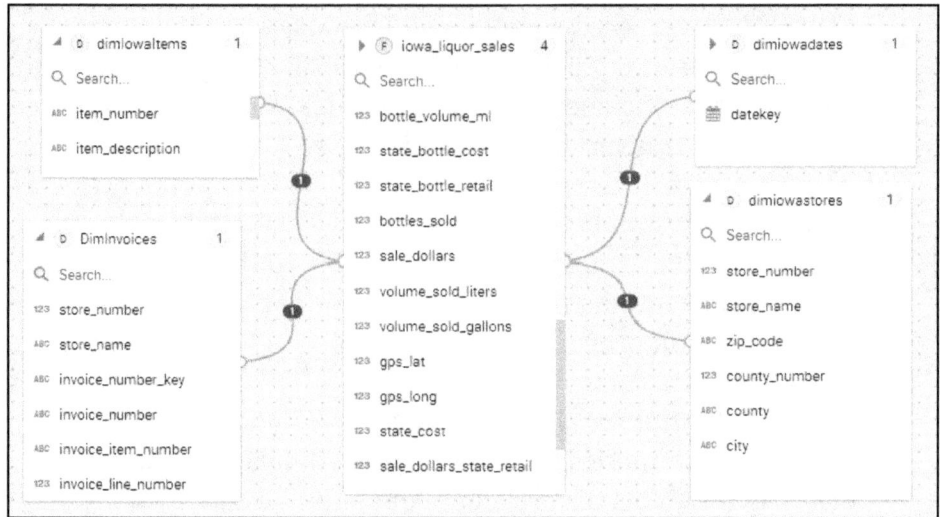

Figure 45: Dimensional model schema that is the foundation of cubes.

In the context of a DC, it's beneficial to consider the DSV as a virtual database. Concurrently, the cube itself can be imagined as another independent database. Within the DSV, tables might emerge as named queries defined by SQL statements. These named queries could potentially be complemented by named calculations, which are SQL expressions. Additionally, Kyvos cubes can house calculated measures articulated in multi-dimensionally expressive MDX query language.

Bridging elements within the DSV are relationships, typically demarcated by primary and foreign keys. Moreover, each constituent part of a DSV, ranging from tables and columns to fragments of SQL expressions, draws a direct link back to tables residing in the underlying Data Source. While many might envision this data source as a data warehouse, it isn't strictly restricted to just a star/snowflake schema. In situations with a more normalized data warehouse, the DSV refines it, aligning it more with the star/snowflake schema paradigm. At its core, though, the cube embodies the star schema. Despite these distinctions, all three components—the primary data source, DSV, and cube—are treated as individual databases, with the DSV characterized by its virtual nature.

Source to Target Mapping

To clarify, we can distill three distinct lineage layers for OLAP cubes: the Data Source, the DSV, and the OLAP cube itself. Figure 46 illustrates this lineage. It's a series of trading off under-the-hood flexibility for user-friendly abstraction.

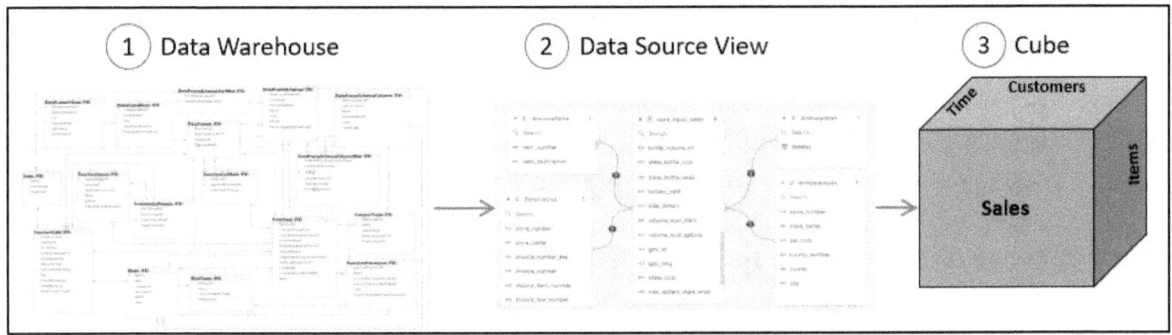

Figure 46: A lineage of three layers of schemas for an OLAP Semantic Layer.

Advantages of each:

1. **Data Warehouse (relatively normalized)**–The data warehouse is typically designed using a normalized structure. This normalization minimizes redundancy and dependency by organizing data into different tables based on relationships among the data. The primary advantage of a normalized data warehouse is that it ensures data integrity and reduces anomalies during data operations like updates, deletions, and insertions. This structure is particularly beneficial for transactional processes where data consistency and accuracy are paramount.

2. **Data Source View (DSV)**–Dimensional Model suitable for aggregation. The DSV in SSAS uses a dimensional model, which is a technique optimized for data retrieval and analysis. This model organizes data into fact and dimension tables, which simplifies the data structure, making it more understandable and navigable for end-users, particularly for business intelligence and reporting purposes. The dimensional model in a DSV is designed for efficient querying and aggregating, enabling faster responses to complex analytical queries. It's especially advantageous for ad-hoc queries and business analysis.

3. **OLAP Cube Semantic Layer**–The OLAP Cube Semantic Layer is also usually a dimensional model since it is a subset of the DSV. The OLAP cube is an advanced data structure that allows for extremely efficient querying and data analysis. In its fastest form, it pre-aggregates data and enables multi-dimensional analysis, making it ideal for complex queries and rapid data exploration. Cubes are optimized for query performance, offering fast retrieval of pre-calculated, summarized data. This is especially beneficial for scenarios involving large volumes of data where users need to perform complex calculations and analyses quickly.

Venturing further into the data catalog, columns within the DSV or measures within a cube founded on formula expressions (formulas, calculations) are thoroughly parsed and anchored to its respective data catalog entries. For instance, if a DSV houses a calculated column like [SaleItem].[Quantity]*[Product].[Price], this particular node should trace its lineage to the exact column nodes comprising this calculation (Quantity and Price) to the respective data catalog entries. The contemporary capabilities of Large Language Models (LLMs) come into play here, offering adept parsing of SQL or related query formats into constituent parts. Such intricacies in column linkage can elucidate connections between multiple cubes, especially when calculations crisscross databases.

A table within the DSV could actually be a virtual table defined by a SQL—it is known as a "named query." As it is for the calculated column above, this SQL will be parsed to down to the elements (columns, tables, functions, and constants) that comprise it. Those involved elements (particularly the columns and tables) are linked from the named query to the respective data catalog entries.

Database Views as Abstractions

Although the DSV is supposed to marshal an underlying complicated data schema into a simpler dimensional model, that effort could actually be taken on as views or materialized views in the underlying data source. It has become the dominant practice for OLAP cubes to be built on top of an underlying DW, playing the part of a "DW accelerator" with the aggregations.

Modern DWs are implemented in a massively parallel, usually cloud-based platform, such as Snowflake, Amazon Redshift, and Azure Synapse. They all have the capability to build views, which are SQL queries underlying a virtual table. It's often a practice to use these views as an abstraction layer between the underlying data source and the OLAP cube.

Broadening our scope, SQL views within relational databases warrant cataloging as individual database tables. These views, forming the foundation for many reports, especially the granular ones, serve as abstraction layers for numerous clients, including OLAP cubes. By encapsulating the dimensions and fact tables within an array of SQL views, the DSV can effortlessly leverage them. This methodological abstraction introduces a logical partition between data source engineers and OLAP engineers, fostering seamless operations by offering a standardized interface.

Augmenting the data catalog further, the integration of cube metadata proves invaluable. Attributes, complete with distinct formats, sort orders, and descriptions, can be incorporated. Features like parent-child relationships, among others, also find their space. Unique to cube structures, hierarchies, devoid of direct relational database parallels, deserve a distinct representation. In the data catalog, hierarchies can be integrated as specific groupings, settling comfortably between dimensions and attributes.

To sum all that up:

- The schema of an OLAP cube is a dimensional model.

- A semantic layer is a broader abstraction that can encompass multiple data sources, providing a unified, business-centric view.

- The cube's schema (dimensional model) is part of the data architecture but is not the same as the semantic layer. The semantic layer is more encompassing and integrates multiple dimensional models into a linked super-schema.

- The Data Source View in SSAS is a logical representation of underlying data sources and is used to build the dimensional model, but it is not the dimensional model exposed to the end-user BI clients (that is the cube schema).

"Lowly-Curated" Data

Data we receive from partners, download from a research site, or assembled by an internal subject matter expert (but not put through the IT data governance wringer), comes with inherent ambiguities and probably lower levels of quality. However, just as we can't simply and wholly disregard information we receive from a stranger, we need to consider data that might be questionable.

It's obvious that data must be clean, trustworthy, and unambiguously understood. However, we must be able to at least consider unclean data when innovating. Imagine just ignoring your hunches and anecdotal evidence while brainstorming toward a novel solution or invention. That is, as opposed to formal reports, such as P&L statements that must be based on data that is 100% factual and traceable (even if the computation and presentation might be "artful").

The highly-curated data we've been focused on, BI data sources, stubbornly reflect how things were believed to worked at the time the systems generating the data were developed. But the systems in which our enterprises are immersed and operate are constantly changing. We can address the disconnect between our lagging systems and the reality of the systems today by:

1. Creating more rules and regulations to mitigate change the effects of change on our rigid systems.

2. Apply countless epigenetic-like patches to the database systems.

3. Somehow incorporate less structured, more dynamic sources of data that capture the evolving nature of our operational environment.

The first two points can only work so long before constraints and patches accumulate to the point that the systems are unmanageable. Regarding the last point, data science has somewhat of a pass. It bridges the gap between our rigid systems and the evolving landscape, empowering these highly-skilled data professionals to derive meaningful insights from diverse data sources.

Data Science allows for exploration with lowly-curated data, enabling data scientists to interpret and innovate beyond the confines and purview IT-governed data sources. This approach is crucial for reconnecting with the current operational environment, as explored further in a topic on Event Storming.

Data from Partners, Vendors, Customers

External Perspectives Illuminate the Big Picture

In the modern digital age, the truth that no enterprise is an island is readily acknowledged. The dynamic nature of business mandates that an organization, no matter its scale or domain, doesn't merely exist within the bounds of its own data ecosystem. Instead, a truly agile and informed enterprise intertwines its data infrastructure with a far-reaching network of external entities.

- **Complex Webs of Exchange:** Beyond the confines of their internal systems, companies consistently engage in data exchanges. These transactions, often a lifeline for many businesses, involve partners, vendors, and even customers. A healthcare insurance company, for instance, could be navigating a labyrinth of data structures every time it onboards a new group. Or consider a bustling e-commerce platform. It's potentially juggling data from thousands of vendors, myriad data enrichment partners, and advertisers galore.

- **The Ubiquity of Influences:** But direct relationships are just a sliver of the story. The world outside doesn't just play a passive role—it actively molds an enterprise. Governments, both local and international, draft regulations, and environmental shifts recalibrate market dynamics and socio-political events, which can flip business models upside down. New research and new innovations, even seemingly unrelated to an enterprise, could have effects to which no one is immune.

To truly grasp the implications of such influences, businesses need a data lens that doesn't just focus inward but radiates outward, capturing the nuances, shifts, and tides of the external world. This way, a business isn't just reacting; it's anticipating and adapting.

The Value of Questionable Data

Embracing the Imperfections

In the world of data analysis and decision-making, the pursuit of clean, pristine data is the gold standard. However, this pursuit can sometimes lead to an unintentional oversight of the inherent messiness and complexities of the real world. By exclusively focusing on sanitized datasets, there's a risk of missing out on critical insights that might be hidden within less-than-perfect data. Here's a closer look at the value of embracing imperfect data:

- **Clean, Pristine Data:** While clean data is essential for accuracy, reliability, and mitigating complexity, it probably will not reflect the full spectrum of reality. The real world is complex and untidy. Relying solely on data that fits neatly into predefined categories might lead to a skewed understanding of market dynamics and consumer behaviors.

- **Unclean as Unseen Opportunities:** Data that appears "unclean" can often be a reflection of real-world complexities and nuances. Disregarding such datasets means potentially overlooking the subtleties and "gray areas" that often contain valuable insights. Like an artist who limits their color palette, analysts relying solely on clean data might miss out on the nuanced shades that bring depth and richness to their analysis.

- **Brainstorming with Blemishes:** Innovation and breakthroughs often emerge from imperfection and irregularities. Anomalies, outliers, and unexpected data patterns can be the catalysts for new ideas and innovative solutions. While unclean data should be approached with caution and not necessarily be the basis for final decisions, it plays a crucial role in the brainstorming process. It offers a different perspective, encouraging a departure from conventional thinking and challenging established norms.

Adopting a balanced approach to data—valuing both the reliability of clean data and the insights from unclean data—can provide businesses with a more comprehensive understanding and awareness. This approach prepares organizations to effectively address the known challenges and explore the unknown opportunities, harnessing the full potential of data in all its forms.

Ad-hoc Data

It might be a terrible sin for me to admit that I might have downloaded some research data to experiment with some thoughts I have had. I might also receive a csv or Excel file a non-IT co-worker hands to me and asks to incorporate it into some BI process.

This ad-hoc data probably wouldn't be registered in the data catalog. For one, the proper "authorities" (IT) aren't aware of it. And it might end up not adding any value, so it and any work derived from it will be deleted, and the perpetrator hung in the IT town center.

Non-BI Data Left on the Cutting Room Floor

For this book, I place high emphasis on BI data sources, such as data warehouses and OLAP cubes because BI data generally is the most highly-curated data in the enterprise (I dive deeper in the section, Benefits of Traditional BI). BI has a decades-long tradition of providing trustworthy data in a friendly, performant, and highly-vetted manner. This book is mostly about the integration of BI values into an enterprise-wide knowledge graph.

However, BI data shouldn't be the only source of data for the ISG and TCW. Analytics should involve all data. It takes significant time and effort to create and maintain BI data sources. So, most enterprise data doesn't make it to "The Show." But we can't just ignore data that didn't make it into a BI data source during our analysis.

Here are some of the many reasons why valid enterprise data might not make it into the highly curated realm of BI data:

- **Time and Resource Intensive** -Creating or modifying BI data sources, such as data warehouses and OLAP cubes, can be a time-consuming process, requiring significant resources and expertise.

- **Agility and Flexibility** -The BI environment often necessitates a structured approach, which may not be as agile or flexible as required for rapidly changing data or business needs.

- **Data Volume–**The vast volume of data generated in modern enterprises can be overwhelming, and not all of it needs to be curated to the extent required for BI purposes. Alternatively, ML can synthesize these data deluges into compact patterns, offering a simplified yet powerful lens through which to view and understand the essence of the data.

- **Cost Considerations** -The costs associated with processing, storing, and maintaining high-quality BI data can be prohibitive, especially if the data isn't critical to decision-making.

- **Freshness of Data** -BI processes can lead to delays in data availability, which may not be suitable for scenarios that require real-time or near-real-time data.

- **Relevance** -Not all data collected by an organization is relevant for BI purposes. Promoting irrelevant data can clutter the BI environment and complicate analysis.

- **Overhead of Curation** -The effort to cleanse, transform, and conform data to fit into a BI model may not always add proportional value, especially for ad-hoc or exploratory analyses.

- **Data Diversity and Complexity** -The variety and complexity of data may not fit neatly into traditional BI models, necessitating more flexible data management approaches.

- **Governance and Compliance** -There may be governance or compliance issues that prevent certain data from being used within a BI environment, such as privacy concerns or regulatory restrictions.

- **Innovation and Experimentation** -Sometimes, the highly-structured nature of BI environments can stifle innovation and experimentation, which are often necessary for discovering new insights.

To some of those points, that's where Databricks (Spark) stands apart from traditional BI cubes. BI cubes are structured for optimal performance on a well-known pattern of queries (slice and dice) through pre-aggregation. This rigidity ensures efficiency for repetitive querying but can constrain flexibility.

In contrast, Spark excels by allowing data to be used in its raw, high-granularity form, enabling on-the-fly computation (and recomputation in very many permutations). This is particularly advantageous for ML algorithms, which often require the ability to dynamically select features, adjust hyperparameters, and process data without the limitations imposed by pre-aggregation. Consequently, Databricks supports a more explorative and less constrained data analysis environment, fostering innovation and experimentation that can lead to groundbreaking insights.

The DC should serve as a comprehensive repository for all enterprise data, including OLTP sources that have not yet been integrated into BI systems. This completeness is vital not just for thorough analysis but also for tracing the lineage of BI data back to its origins.

In the era of data fabrics and data mesh, BI analysts should have access to a variety of data products beyond traditional BI data. This may include datasets available in a data marketplace that are designed for various analytical purposes.

CHAPTER SIX

Business Intelligence

Although BI has been an important part of the enterprise landscape for a couple of decades, it usually takes a back seat in terms of mission-critical ranking compared to other systems. For example, it's never acceptable for an enterprise's e-commerce site to be anything but running at top performance. On the other hand, the enterprise hardly ever makes it to the IT version of an Intensive Care Unit when the BI system goes down.

But BI is the centerpiece of the quest for data-driven excellence with its highly-curated, high query performance, and user-friendly interface. BI is the spearhead of the AEI. In this role, BI could exceed the importance of most other systems. That's similar to how we can temporarily lose function in most organs, but if the brain goes down, nothing happens.

So, here is the third major component of the EKG, and the most important in the context of this book - graphs built from BI queries. As mentioned, the queries of BI analysts across the enterprise reflect what is important to them in the context of resolving business problems. From these queries, relatively simple code can extract the insights they might have gleaned from visualizations of the data (ISG), and we can find correlations between highly diverse collections of "things" they've referenced in their queries (TCW). However, this part isn't about the ISG and TCW itself. It's about making the argument for the continuing relevance of traditional BI even within today's AI tsunami. Since the dawn of the big data and the cloud (ca. 2010-ish) era, more than a few folks have told me that "Business Intelligence is dead." These are a few thoughts on this sentiment:

- I took that as meaning that traditional BI–that is, DW, ETL, and OLAP cubes— didn't make life easy and competing a breeze, so let's move on to what apparently will make us successful: data lakes, ELT, the cloud, machine learning, data science.

- ETL workflows look like Clark Griswold's ball of Christmas lights. And one broken lightbulb breaks the whole thing.

- I hate those OLAP cubes–they speak a language of their own (MDX), are limited and brittle, hard to update, and take forever to process.

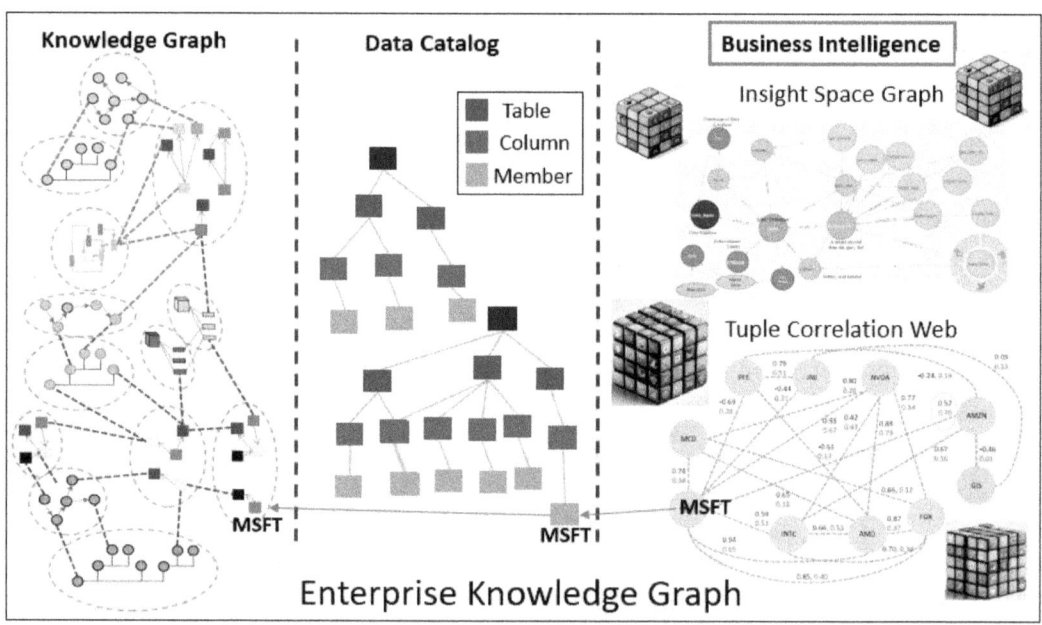

Figure 47: The BI components of the EKG.

To address those complaints, many new concepts in the analytics space were introduced in the big data and cloud era.

Data Lakes enabled the ability to throw almost effortlessly any and all data into a centralized location for analysis. That seemed to improve DW scalability in terms of volume and the ability to add more kinds of data.

ETL (Extracting data from source systems, cleansing and Transforming the data, and Loading it into a DW) pain was ameliorated by switching the T and L to L and T. It's the "T" (transform) that takes up the bulk of the intellectual energy in developing a BI system. ELT, Extracting data from source systems, Loading the data into a Data Lake, and leaving the Transforms to an up-skilled new class of analysts called Data Scientists. The Data Scientist was even called the "sexiest job" by HBR in 2012. These "up-skilled analysts" came with strong statistical and technical powers in order to apply wide arrays of ML algorithms to data instead of just relatively simple calculations, like those used in Excel for almost 30 years.

Databricks stands as a prime example of the analytics world transitioning from BI to the data science-focused ELT. At its heart lies Spark technology, embodying the ELT approach by distributing data across clusters of in-memory servers. This advancement overcomes the limitations of traditional pre-aggregated OLAP cubes (what I'm calling "Optimized Cubes"), like those of SSAS, avoiding rigid structures and intensive processing. It empowers data scientists to iteratively experiment with various datasets, ML algorithms, and hyperparameters in a parallel, in-memory framework. The Lakehouse concept from Databricks marks a significant evolution, marrying the scalability and adaptability of data lakes with the dependable features of traditional relational databases.

BI, in its old pre-Data-Science form, is certainly not dead. In terms of "OG" BI terms:

- PowerBI is a highly regarded and robust tool in the BI visualization space. It continues to evolve, offering enhanced capabilities and a dynamic roadmap that promises ongoing improvements and features. This progression solidifies its status as a leading choice for data analytics and visualization needs.

- Most people don't have the bandwidth to rise to the statistics and data-savvy level of data scientists while staying on top of their primary role. However, many have the bandwidth to master the relatively simpler traditional BI analytical tools found in PowerBI and Tableau.

- The world of the NoSQL mantra, one of the early mantras at the start of the cloud era, has re-embraced SQL.

- Snowflake, the cloud data warehouse, emerged as a current powerhouse. No, DW is not dead.

- Data mesh hits at a core problem with ETL struggles. That core problem is how to surface data from more than a few of the corners of an enterprise to hundreds of its outer reaches. It addresses a bottleneck from a centralized ETL team. Similar to how cloud storage is scalable because work can be distributed across a flexible number of commodity servers, data mesh is a methodology for distributing the onboarding of BI sources. It doesn't mean it's cheaper, but it's possible.

However, optimized cubes still seem to have trouble finding their way back from their heyday in the 2000s. In this part, we will reacquaint ourselves with the value of BI, touch upon how BI plays a key role in the dawn of the AI era, and reacquaint ourselves with the value of OLAP cubes.

Benefits of Traditional BI

Highly Curated

BI has indeed been around for decades, predating this cloud era with the cloud's abundance of cheap storage and scalable resources. In the early 2000s, BI was emerging as a critical field, yet it faced substantial challenges. Infrastructure for DWs and OLAP cubes required significant investment in high-end, non-scalable servers, and expertise in BI was a rare commodity since it was a burgeoning field.

BI integrates data from multiple sources and maintains history which multiplied the required data volume for those mostly non-scalable SMP (Symmetric Multiprocessing) servers of the day. So, BI developers had to meticulously strategize which data to include in the DW, dedicating extensive effort to ensure the data was aligned with business objectives. The selective nature of this process meant that data within a BI system was naturally deemed highly valuable for enterprise decision-making.

This discerning approach had its merits. Unlike the modern tendency to indiscriminately store data in lakes—which may lead to analysts sifting through a deluge of information to find valuable insights—the rigor of traditional BI ensured that dashboards and reports were based on carefully chosen, factual data to guide business decisions. Today, while the landscape has evolved with technology, the foundational principles of BI—focusing on data quality, relevance, and the ability to inform sound business strategies—remain as pertinent as ever.

Highly Performant

Fast query results are a hallmark of BI. It's essential for "speed of thought" analysis. Waiting minutes or even hours for results from a query spanning potentially tens of billions to trillions of fact rows is a disruption to the thinking process, just like any other interruption. As it is with a smooth conversation between people, it would be awkward if each exchange came with a long pause while someone thought through their response.

The solution to mitigating those disrupting pauses during the bad old days was those optimized cubes. I dive deeper into the technical aspects in Chapter 8—Architecture of the AEI.

But My BI Seems Fast Enough

However, in these modern times, ATTOW, most BI users probably experience acceptable performance (query responses within a few seconds) without optimized cubes. There are many reasons for this, but here are a few of the most important:

- The underlying data consists of what is today a *relatively* small number of facts. That is, in the magnitude of a few hundred million rows. That's still a really big number, and in the ballpark of most enterprises. The modern cloud architecture of today enables very fast distributed computation of data. The drawback is that the cost of this parallel, distributed computation rises with the number of servers performing the computation. It is scalable, but not exactly cheap.

- Even if there are trillions of rows of fact data crossing many years of history, a given user is usually interested in a particular subset of those rows at a given analysis session. For example, they might be interested in rows from the past month or rows from one of many sales territories. Or, more commonly, the user's scope is departmental, therefore, her particular data set is much smaller, even though her colleague in another department might not be as fortunate. Furthermore:

    o The subset is cached (held in memory) by the database. Since the user is interested in just a subset of data, it's likely that user will request that data in subsequent queries of the session. Or ...

- o The entire subset of data might be downloaded from the database to the user's machine, where the BI tool, such as Tableau or PowerBI, runs computations locally, in-memory.

- Utilization of the BI database is relatively low—there are one or two analysts pinging a BI database, often not concurrently.

As long as those items above hold true ... well ... there's no problem. However, I ask this of my new BI customers who say they have no BI performance problem (all of which I've witnessed multiple times):

- What is the chance that you will land the "McDonalds" of your industry as a customer?

- What is the chance you will merge with a very large company? Sometimes, the nature of the acquired company involves magnitudes of data volume that are unfamiliar to the acquirer.

- What is the chance your enterprise will decide to deploy thousands of sensors in the "field" on an IoT endeavor or decide to track the website from the page view level to the event level (like mouse clicks and scrolling)?

Today, another factor is that the sudden rise of readily accessible and high-quality AI means that massive volumes of data can be derived from unstructured data—text documents, images, audio, and video. Since many claim most of their "data" is in this unstructured form and thus previously trapped in it, that opens the door to the possibility of a magnitude more data for BI analysts.

Federated Databases

There has been a big trend away from monolithic entities towards a federation of loosely-coupled entities. Indeed, the popularity of data mesh (which is coming up in Chapter 7—Data Mesh) is about breaking up the monolithic qualities of traditional BI development down to domain-level efforts.

But that alone creates fragmented data silos. We really seek a holistic, high-perspective view of the enterprise. The idea is to break up a monolithic effort so we can surface data from all reaches of the enterprise and effectively knit the efforts into a loosely-coupled, holistic web of data.

Similarly, even though LLMs ATTOW such as ChatGPT, are mostly monolithic, they are one expression of AI across a wide breadth of training data. Conversely, there is a rapidly growing notion of teaming multiple expressions of AI ("Mix of Experts"—just like different people with different thought processes) or specialized LLMs (like PhDs focused on a single topic).

When tackling a complicated problem, we normally don't consult just one person. We usually require information from multiple people with different expertise and points of view. That's the same way advanced AI query patterns work-such as chain-of-thought, tree-of-thought, or especially retrieval augmented generation. Even if we might pose a single question, the AI will engage multiple sources. This means it might query multiple databases. The time it takes to respond depends on the speed of the slowest database.

Kyvos Insights Cloud-based OLAP

ATTOW, I hold the position of Principal Solutions Architect at Kyvos Insights, specializing in cloud-based optimized OLAP solutions. My extensive experience in this subject is rooted in SQL Server Analysis Services, which influences my preferential leanings toward this field.

My chief responsibility revolves around advocating for OLAP. In recent years, traditional SSAS-like cubes have been overshadowed by advancements in big data and Spark technologies. These new solutions offer "good enough" performance, providing rapid query responses that maintain an analyst's flow of thought. From the perspective of an IT manager, acceptable query times are those that return results within a few seconds, tolerating the occasional longer wait for complex queries (many seconds to many minutes). This level of efficiency negates the need for additional system components, vendor relations, and the cultivation of new skill sets.

Since 2011, my strategy to reaffirm the importance of optimized OLAP in the BI landscape has been to develop a paradigm, methodology, or architecture that supports numerous and concurrent high-performance BI queries—always ensuring substantial value addition for the efforts invested. The development and upkeep of an ISG and TCW (an evolution of Map Rock) are central to this strategy.

The advantage of optimized OLAP lies in its pre-computation–a "process once, read many" model. This "preservation of computation" not only accelerates query response times but also substantially enhances the capacity for query concurrency within the OLAP database, making it a formidable tool in high-demand BI environments.

User-Friendly

OLAP cube platforms like SSAS and Kyvos have long been appreciated for their user-friendly interface, which democratizes data access within an organization. Through a front-end of BI Visualization tools such as PowerBI and Tableau, these systems offer intuitive querying capabilities, allowing users to interact with data through drag-and-drop actions, straightforward filtering, and simple navigation menus. With such features, OLAP cubes enable business users who may not possess deep technical skills to perform complex data analyses and generate insights effectively. This accessibility remains a fundamental benefit of traditional BI tools, ensuring that OLAP cubes continue to be an immensely valuable asset for organizations prioritizing ease of use in their data strategies.

BI Users

Traditional BI Users

BI has always had its traditional set of users, with analysts being a predominant group. These analysts primarily rely on data warehouses, OLAP cubes, and data marts as their data sources. Their go-to visualization tools include, among others, Power BI, Tableau, and Excel, all of which are renowned for their rich visualization capabilities and extensive functions.

The expertise of these analysts is specialized. While many possess knowledge in a specific business domain, it's not uncommon for them to be versed across multiple related domains. Alongside their business acumen, they're at least moderately trained in statistics and are adept in their use of their visualization tools. Mastery of these tools, given their versatility in handling BI query patterns, demands weeks of training and months of consistent experience.

I differentiate analysts from "data scientists." Data scientists are typically more general in their business domain expertise and deeper with math and technical skills (machine learning and rudimentary data engineering) than "analysts." Data scientists are usually more adept with data engineering than analysts—even though data engineering is a very substantial skill set in itself. However, the line between data scientist and analyst is blurring as analysts become more proficient with ML and BI tools acquire more ML features.

Managers, too, fall under the umbrella of traditional BI users. Their interaction with BI closely mirrors that of analysts, especially when accessing OLAP sources. However, while analysts might be geared toward optimization strategies, managers often focus on tracking and meeting their Key Performance Indicators (KPIs) targets.

Knowledge Workers - Massive Expansion of BI Consumers

In the pursuit of data-driven excellence, the army of knowledge workers present at all enterprises has become increasingly prevalent. Although their primary consumption of BI data has been through watching their assigned KPIs in dashboards on a mega monitor in the lunch hall, the surge in mobile app usage and the relative ease of its creation has opened doors to more advanced capabilities, notably embedded AI. The rapid development cycles of mobile apps allow them to be tailored to niche use cases. Some of these apps, given their relatively easy creation and high specificity, can almost be deemed "disposable." Should a user's requirements change, a new app can be swiftly designed and developed to cater to the adjusted needs.

Take, for instance, a sprawling enterprise with a network of stores. Such an enterprise might deploy consultants to evaluate the unique needs of each store, influenced by factors like local demographics and geographic positioning. Guided by BI insights, these consultants could then advocate for customized product offerings, shelving designs, or pricing strategies. Given the narrow scope and specificity of their tasks, expecting these consultants to delve into tools like Tableau or PowerBI is impractical overkill. So by "knowledge worker," I don't just mean analysts and managers who seek knowledge. My intent is a definition that literally means anyone who requires information from data sources for their work—whether that information comes from BI tools or not. For example, a waiter in a small restaurant has built BI information in his head about regular customers. His brain has even built mental decision trees and clusters to determine how best to serve various customers.

This scenario is merely one among countless. Continuing with the waiter example, although a yucky thought, even waitstaff could be equipped with mobile devices that offer insights into customer tipping behaviors, enabling strategies to enhance order profitability and tip amounts. Such data-driven approaches could be integral for thousands of workers within an organization, laying the groundwork for truly data-driven operations.

The healthcare sector, too, offers a promising avenue for embedded BI. Devices frequently used on the floor by nurses, doctors, and other healthcare professionals could be integrated with analytics, elevating decision-making processes. Similarly, logistical teams, such as pickup and delivery crews, could harness BI insights to inform their subsequent actions based on real-time metrics.

The result of a big spike in BI consumption through what could be tens of thousands of knowledge workers is one of the primary factors that will contribute to stress on BI systems.

AI Agent

What I'm calling an "AI agent" is an AI entity that is accessing the EKG to solve its problems. It is mostly autonomous, just like a human user of the EKG.

Now that AI is a household word, for better or worse, we need to recognize an AI agent as a distinct and legitimate class of BI users. As machines capable of mimicking and, in some cases, surpassing human cognition in certain tasks, they access, interpret, and utilize BI in ways significantly different from their human counterparts.

While humans rely on decades of accrued cultural and experiential knowledge, AI depends on vast amounts of data. Contrary to human intuition, AI requires explicit data points for what might seem obvious to a person. The AI at the time of writing (at least LLMs trained on text) didn't experience any data it ingested firsthand. This means its context isn't as rich as the person who authored the text (based on her experience in the real world) the AI ingested. This means a KG tailored for AI must include information that might seem superfluous to a human observer but is critical for machine comprehension. We sometimes forget that others, including an AI, might not know what we know. Although modern LLMs have gleaned significant cultural and contextual knowledge from our shared digital information, they still lack the deep, tacit understanding humans gain from real-world experiences and the context in which our humanness evolved. The nuances of daily life, the cause-and-effect learning from tangible experiences, and the wisdom experts gain over years in their fields are aspects that AI still struggles to fully grasp.

While LLMs and similar AI models can process and predict based on patterns in vast amounts of data, I don't believe they "understand" in the human sense ... yet. I mean that a person's "model" in their brain is trained on unique and fully immersed experiences by a unique set of other people in a unique set of conditions. It's also trained in the real world in real time, not by artifacts where most information is stripped—such as with audio, images, text, and even video (which is audio plus sequences of images). They lack the lived experiences that shape human intuition and insight. This distinction underlines the importance of feeding AI with comprehensive data, ensuring they have as complete a picture as possible when aiding in BI tasks. The blending of AI's data-driven insights with human intuition creates a synergy in BI that leverages the strengths of both.

Append-Only Data Strategy in Business Intelligence

The "append-only" approach in BI data sources is a design paradigm that emphasizes the addition of new records without modifying existing ones. In the BI situation where we're dealing mostly with additive sums and counts, append-only enables the pre-aggregation benefits on optimized OLAP cubes. Here's an exploration of its merits and implications:

1. Optimization for Intense Computation:

    a. Overview: Many BI systems rely on downstream caches, especially optimized cubes, which involve rigorous computation to produce.

    b. Benefit: With the assumption of append-only data, reprocessing only pertains to the new data added after the current max date. This significantly reduces computational demands compared to reprocessing the entire dataset.

2. Seamless Integration with big data Infrastructure:

    a. Overview: Big data ecosystems often rely on file-based storage systems.

    b. Benefit: In an append-only context, new data, say for a new day, can simply be incorporated as a new file without disrupting existing files. If data were to be added or modified for previous dates, it would involve the cumbersome process of deleting and recreating files, which isn't efficient.

3. Robust Audit Trails:

    a. Overview: Append-only data systems inherently maintain a complete, unadulterated history of all data additions.

    b. Benefit: This not only ensures data integrity but also facilitates auditing. Since no data is overwritten or deleted, tracing data lineage, understanding historical patterns, and maintaining regulatory compliance becomes straightforward.

4. Data Consistency:

    a. Overview: In environments where multiple systems or processes rely on a single data source, consistency is paramount.

    b. Benefit: An append-only model ensures that all downstream systems or caches reference the same data state, eliminating discrepancies that might arise from mid-stream data modifications.

5. Limitations and Considerations:

    a. Data Corrections: In real-world scenarios, there might be occasions where errors in past data need rectification. An append-only system needs a robust mechanism to handle such corrections without violating its core principles.

    b. Storage Concerns: Continuously appending data can lead to storage concerns over time. It's essential to balance the need for historical data retention with storage costs and efficiency. Hopefully, if errors must be rectified, they happen in the recent past, thereby minimizing reprocessing of data by OLAP systems.

While the append-only model presents significant advantages in BI contexts, it's essential to design the system considering both its strengths and potential challenges. The approach, when implemented judiciously, can drive efficiency, consistency, and reliability in analytics operations.

Visualization Tools

Following our discussion of traditional BI users, the visualization aspect of BI is the fulcrum of data interpretation and understanding. Predominant visualization tools employed by these users encompass Tableau, PowerBI, and Excel. Tools, such as Tableau and PowerBI, are recognized for their powerful capabilities, offering a myriad of data representation possibilities.

Excel, on the other hand, boasts a longstanding history. Often touted as the quintessential BI tool, it has, for decades, held its ground as arguably the leading instrument in this domain.

Common visualization representations in these tools range from line graphs, bar charts, and scatter plots to pie charts. Other prevalent visualizations include heat maps, histograms, geographic maps, and treemaps, which cater to diverse data interpretation needs.

One of the foundational patterns in traditional BI is the "slicing and dicing" technique. In tools like PowerBI and Tableau, "slicing" refers to segmenting a dataset to focus on a subset of it. For instance, viewing sales data for a specific region would be "slicing." On the other hand, "dicing" denotes a breakdown of the data, such as analyzing the aforementioned regional sales by individual product categories. This method is emblematic of the SQL GROUP BY statement and is most fluid when executed on dimensional models characteristic of star or snowflake schemas.

The result of a SQL GROUP BY operation is a dataframe, a dataset comprising columns and aggregated metrics where filters are potentially applied. These dataframes form the bedrock for the aforementioned visualizations. Understanding this is paramount for the Insight Space Graph, which can be envisioned as an ontology of these dataframes. It essentially dissects what attributes, properties, and metrics these dataframes encapsulate when channeled through different visualizations.

Figure 48 shows a very typical crosstab visualization from a BI browsing tool. It's based on a sample cube for a conglomerate of liquor stores. It highlights the fundamental SQL GROUP BY query:

1. The selected columns used for the visualization, in this case, a crosstab—Year and class (of liquor). Additionally, we have two selected measures, sale_dollars and bottles_sold.

2. These are the "dice" fields. There is one row for each combination of Year and class.

3. These are the measures columns.

4. We are also filtering for just the Zip Code 50613.

5. This is the SQL GROUP BY query that was constructed by the visualization tool.

While data warehouses have occasionally been deemed passé in recent years, they remain steadfast in the BI landscape. Their persistence is evident in the continued adoption of star or snowflake-like dimensional models by major visualization tools, even in the era of data lakes. The unadulterated clarity of entities, attributes, and hierarchies within these models offers an intuitive interface, making it accessible even for individuals without a technical background.

Expanding on the visualization topic, performance management dashboards are integral. A dashboard is a consolidated display of multiple visualizations, providing a holistic, multi-faceted view of various metrics or KPIs. They enable quick decision-making by offering a snapshot of crucial data points, trends, and patterns. Whether it's for a high-level executive overview or a detailed departmental analysis, dashboards, with their interactive features and real-time data integration, have become indispensable in the BI realm.

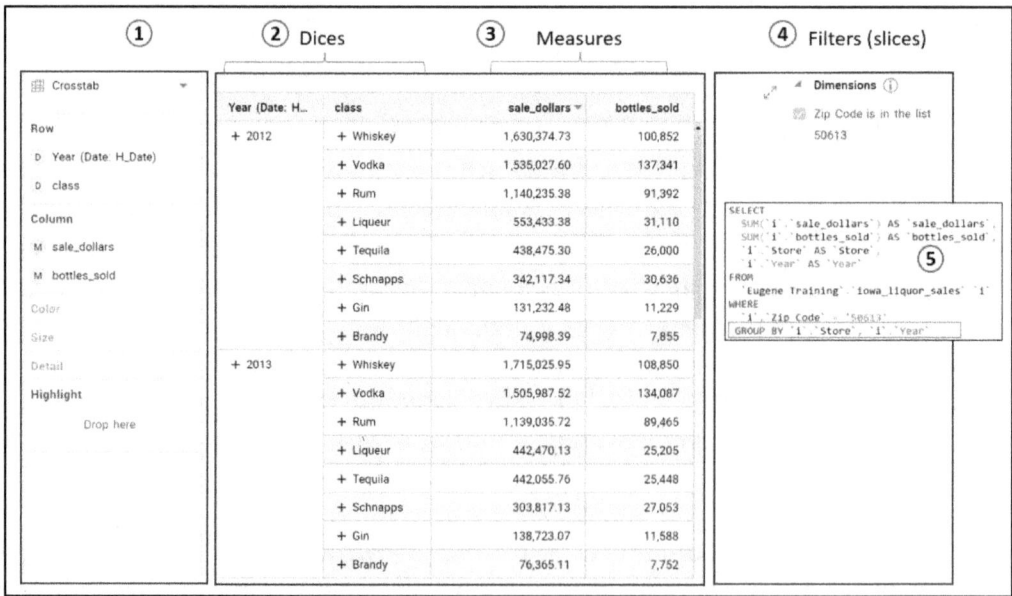

Figure 48: Parts of a SQL GROUP BY query—the bread and butter BI slice and dice pattern.

CHAPTER SEVEN

Data Mesh

A few years before ChatGPT burst onto the scene of the general public in November 2022, the BI landscape was being reshaped by a groundbreaking concept known as the data mesh, initially championed by Zhamak Dehghani. This innovative approach challenged the conventional centralized BI system, which typically relied on a core team of highly specialized experts. Instead, data mesh embraces the distributed ethos of the big data and cloud era, delegating BI responsibilities to the individual domains—those who possess the deepest understanding of their data.

Embracing a distributed system naturally incurs some overhead. Specifically, the collective effort of multiple domain-centric teams might surpass the resource footprint of a singular, centralized BI team. The trade-off is a scalable framework that can accommodate the increasing appetite for diverse data integrations within BI analysis, thereby fostering a more responsive and versatile data infrastructure.

At its core, data mesh is an architectural and organizational approach to data management and analytics. It emphasizes decentralized data ownership and architecture, where domain-specific teams manage and own their data as a product. This approach is particularly effective for analytics, as it enables faster, more agile decision-making and innovation by putting data closer to the business context. However, the principles of data mesh, such as domain-oriented decentralized ownership, self-serve data infrastructure as a platform, and product thinking for data, can also be relevant for more than BI data. For example:

1. **Enterprise Application Integration (EAI)**–Integrating various enterprise applications and systems to ensure seamless data flow and consistency is crucial. Each application is independently maintained and integrated through strict interfaces.

2. **KG**–Creation and maintenance of a KG spanning multiple domains.

In the context of this book, the data mesh framework comes into play twice:

1. The more conventional role is facilitating the speed at which a wide breadth of data across many domains can be surfaced for analytics. This has drastically mitigated the BI development pain of integrating data from across a wide variety of domains.

2. The less conventional role in the creation of a KG will benefit from the distribution of effort to the domains that best know the data. In developing an architecture to create and update a KG, a data mesh approach should be taken.

The first point is very important because I'm sure many readers of this BI-centric book have been looking for a way to eliminate the pain of BI efforts, particularly in the ETL/ELT part, where legend states it takes up 80% of the effort. Data mesh, in this context, is a fantastic enabler for widening the tentacles of BI.

Regarding the second point, the KG will be composed of ontologies, taxonomies, and other sorts of structures contributed by many SMEs within many domains across the enterprise. I strongly recommend a data mesh approach, passing responsibility for each ontology and taxonomy to its respective SME or domain. This distributes the work from a centralized team to a number of domains. The product is a loosely-coupled set of domain-specific ontologies linked via semantic web standards rather than a monolithic effort. A KG is a queryable database, so it makes sense that data mesh principles apply.

We'll start with a discussion of how data mesh facilitates the expansion of BI to the far reaches of an enterprise and beyond. This is the more traditional use for data mesh. This will introduce the major BI concepts. Then, we'll return to the keystone KG topic and how data mesh applies to the sensible development and maintenance of the KG.

Expanding the Reach for BI

In the era of data-driven decisions, the essential value of data mesh lies in enhancing the accessibility of actionable insights to analysts, managers, and various knowledge professionals. It does this by drastically facilitating the onboarding of new BI sources to a common BI platform. It's hard for all but IT people to appreciate that there can be dozens to hundreds of databases supporting business processes and use cases across an enterprise. Most folks use only a few during a normal workday.

At the grassroots level, data is generated in massive volumes across numerous operational domains. However, the Herculean task is not just the accumulation but also the curation and presentation of this data in a format digestible to those lacking domain-specific expertise and ensuring it synergizes seamlessly with data from other sources.

The Centralized BI Team Bottleneck

Traditionally, BI development has been performed by a centralized team of "hyper-specialized" practitioners within an organization. This "DW team" is responsible for everything from data extraction, mapping domain-specific concepts to an integrated matrix of concepts (e.g., the Kimball "bus matrix"), loading to a data warehouse, and authoring reports and other visualizations.

As demands grow to meet widely-scoped information needs, this centralized model faces bottlenecks:

- **Capacity issues**—The BI team becomes overwhelmed with requests, leading to delays.

- **Knowledge gaps**—The BI team might not have a deep understanding of every domain-specific nuance, leading to misinterpretations.

- **Dependencies**—The growing number of domains results in an increasingly complex web of inter-domain dependencies. No domain operates in a vacuum, so there will always be some level of disconnect between them.

Figure 49 illustrates the bottleneck created when:

1. Demand for data from all far reaches of the enterprise is funneled to a centralized BI team.

2. For each request for new data into the DW, the centralized BI team must build transformation code consisting of very much analysis, validation, coding, and debugging. Further, the ETL team is responsible for integrating data across domains. The required coordination across multiple domains results in much friction due to an inherent web of dependencies.

3. The result is the drip-by-drop flow of onboarding of new sources into the DW.

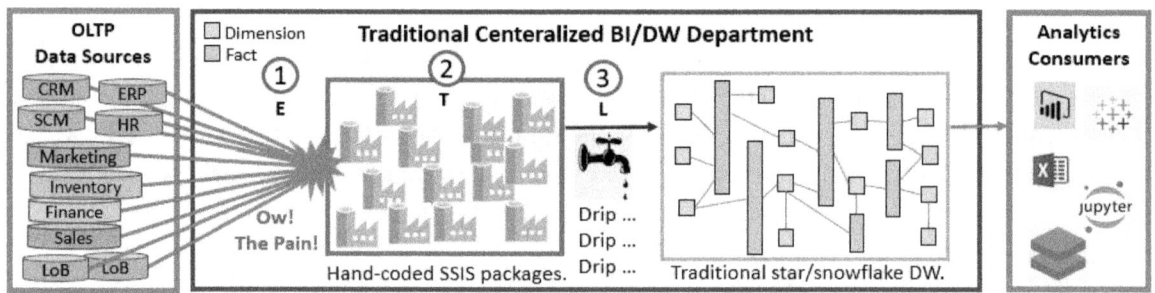

Figure 49: Traditional, centralized ETL->DW.

Data mesh is about distributing responsibility for the procurement of analytical data in an enterprise to the domain level. The term, domain, can mean department or a business process that touches upon several departments.

Decentralization of BI Effort

Data mesh is a decentralized data architecture that tackles the limitations of centralized data operations. It's a beautiful application thwarting the Theory of Constraints, addressing a big bottleneck in a system. By distributing the responsibility of data ownership and operations, data mesh will:

- **Enhance agility**—Speed up the data-to-insights pipeline by minimizing dependencies.

- **Improve data quality**—Ensure domain experts, who understand the data best, have ownership, leading to better data quality and interpretation.

- **Boost innovation**—Enable different domains to innovate on their data products without waiting for centralized teams.

Figure 50 depicts an example of a data mesh architecture, showcasing the flow and integration of four domains across an enterprise ecosystem into an integrated BI layer:

1. **OLTP (Online Transaction Processing)**—Individual domains, such as Sales, Finance, Inventory, and Marketing, each have their own OLTP systems where domain-specific transactional data is collected and managed.

2. **ETL (Extract, Transform, Load)**—Data from each OLTP system undergoes an ETL process, indicating the extraction, transformation, and loading of data into a structured format suitable for analysis. Keep in mind that the "ETL" effort should be mitigated since the idea is that the end data products have a narrower scope.

3. **Data Mart**—Following the ETL process, the transformed data is organized into domain-specific data marts. These are depicted as OLAP cubes, suggesting a structured, multidimensional data model ideal for complex queries and analysis.

4. **Data Products/Semantic Layer**—Each domain can produce multiple data products from its data mart, which may represent refined datasets, reports, or analytics models. In this BI context, the data products are OLAP cubes, which together form a Semantic Layer. The semantic layer is a collection of loosely-coupled data products-as opposed to a monolithic DW.

5. **A "Composite Data Product"** is shown, representing the integration of data from multiple domain-specific Data Products, linked through common dimensions. This suggests a virtual cube feature facilitating for cross-domain analysis.

6. **Analytics**—The top layer shows the analytics tools and personnel that utilize the data products. Analysts, Managers, and Data Scientists are represented, indicating the different roles that interact with the data. Tools, such as PowerBI, Excel, and Jupyter Notebooks, are displayed, along with Azure ML, indicating a variety of analytics and machine learning tools used to analyze the data.

The thick gray arrows between the layers signify the flow and transformation of data from transactional systems through to the analytical outputs, underlining the decentralized, domain-driven approach of the data mesh concept.

Regarding a "semantic layer" feature in platforms like Kyvos and "Linked Objects" in SSAS, these functionalities enable analysts and BI tools to access and analyze data across multiple cubes or databases as if it were from a single virtual cube. The semantic layer acts as an abstraction layer that maps complex data into familiar business terms, making it easier to perform cross-domain analysis without needing to wade through the messy underlying data schemas.

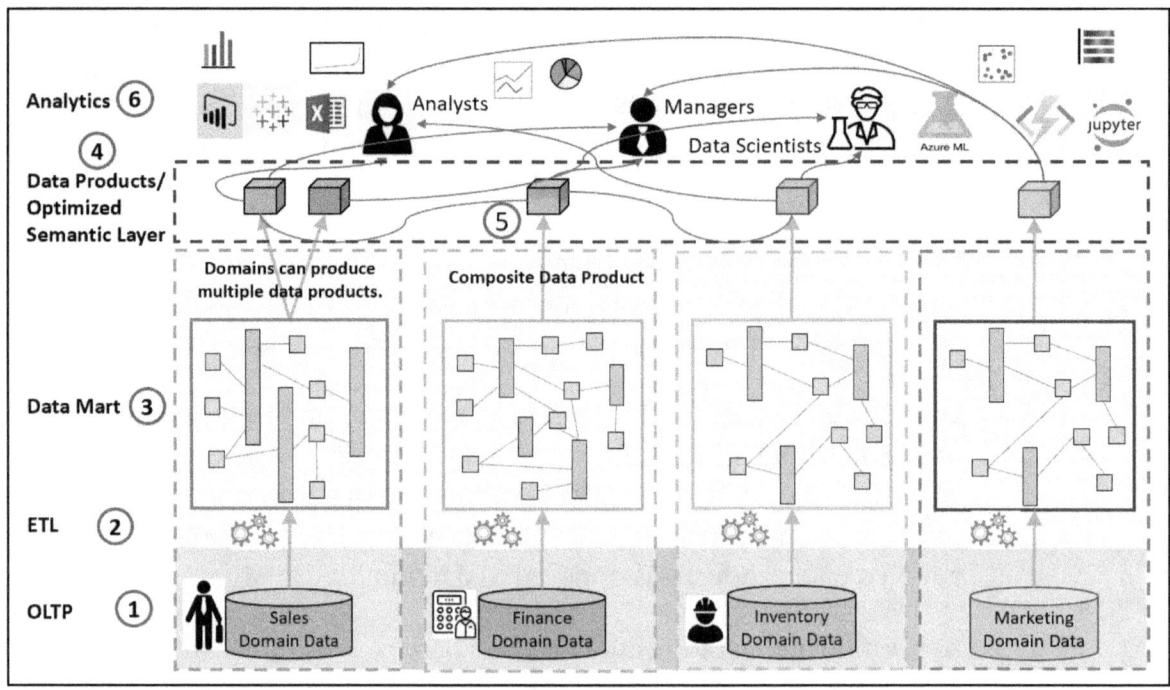

Figure 50: Decentralized Domain Data Product.

An *optimized* semantic layer (4) is a layer presenting the qualities of BI at its best–high query-performance and user-friendly interface. As opposed to just a semantic layer, which is at its core a linked schema of analytics data, the optimized semantic layer is highly-performant, highly-curated, and user-friendly. More on optimized cubes coming up.

In SSAS terms, Linked Objects can be used to create virtual relationships between objects like dimensions or measures across different cubes, allowing for more flexible and powerful data analysis without the overhead of physical data movement or duplication. This capability simplifies the user's interaction with the data, ensuring that comprehensive insights can be derived from a cohesive, logical representation of information sourced from various databases.

Data Governance Team

The role of a data governance team is crucial in maintaining the balance within a data mesh architecture, where each domain is given autonomy over its BI. While domains are responsible for their data's quality, accessibility, and intelligence, the data governance team ensures that these independent efforts align with the enterprise's overarching standards and policies.

The data governance team acts as a steward of the common infrastructure, defining the policies, procedures, and standards that are common across all domains and factored into their limited and centralized control. This includes establishing data quality benchmarks, ensuring compliance with data protection regulations, managing metadata, and promoting the interoperability of datasets to facilitate a unified view of enterprise data.

Their work ensures that while domains can focus on deriving value from their data, they do so in a way that is consistent, secure, and scalable across the enterprise. In essence, the data governance team provides the framework within which domain-level autonomy can thrive without descending into chaos or siloed inefficiency. They preserve the integrity of the data ecosystem, balancing control and freedom for animated progression but avoiding stasis and anarchy, as depicted in Figure 51 (don't take it too seriously).

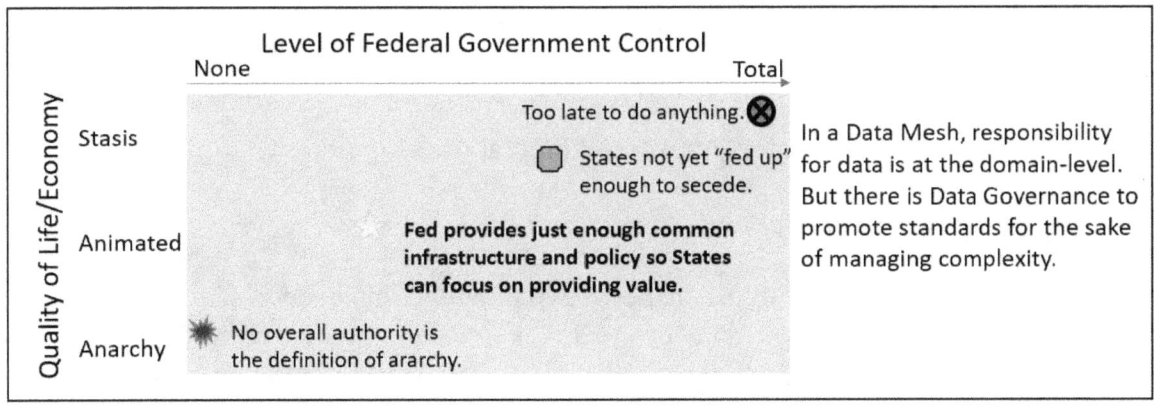

Figure 51: Balance of Domain-level and Enterprise Governance levels.

Data Products

Central to the concept of data mesh is the notion of "Data Products." Instead of viewing data merely as assets, data mesh treats data as a product, with the same pride it gives to the products it sells to its customers. Each product is enveloped with lifecycle management, ownership, and customer focus. Each domain or team becomes responsible for its data product, ensuring it's accuracy, reliability, and value for its consumers. As mentioned, in addition to applying data mesh towards BI, applying data mesh principles to the construction of a KG makes intuitive sense, considering how varied and widespread knowledge across an enterprise can be.

Data Product Service Level Agreements (SLA)

SLAs for data products are formal agreements that specify the performance metrics, quality standards, and service expectations associated with a data product. These agreements define the reliability, availability, and timeliness of the data, as well as the responsibilities of the data product team towards its consumers. They ensure that the data product consistently meets the agreed-upon requirements, facilitating trust and dependability in data-driven decision-making.

Data Products Per Domain

Many organizations begin by allocating one data product per domain and adjusting as needed. The granularity of each data product depends on various factors:

- Is the data product centered around a business process that spans multiple departments?

- Is it primarily for intra-departmental use?

- What are the potential use cases?

The key philosophy is to disperse what would have been a monolithic effort into independent, coherent data products—a self-contained, well-integrated data solution that meets specific business needs and can operate independently while ensuring consistency and usability. These products can evolve on their own to meet new challenges and needs. By distributing the responsibility, we mitigate the risk of workflow bottlenecks due to centralized IT teams.

The essential conditions for this to work effectively are:

- Maintenance of a consistent external interface, or "contract," for each data product—ensuring that changes or updates to the product do not break the clients that depend on it.

- Ensuring that the team responsible for each data product assumes full responsibility for its upkeep, security, and version control—in a manner that meets the data product's SLA.

In the BI world, a typical data product could be a departmental or subject-oriented data mart or OLAP cube. These products are versatile and can serve multiple use cases due to their dimensional models.

For taxonomies and ontologies of a KG, each domain may contain multiple data products focused on varied subject matters. For example, within the marketing domain, there might be taxonomies for advertising channels, customer segmentation, content types, and research.

Considerations for managing multiple data products:

- User Needs and Customization: Each data product should offer some level of customization to meet user-specific needs.

- Versioning: Effective version management is crucial to ensure consistency across various stakeholders.

- Audit Trail and Governance: Ensure that changes are audited and data integrity is maintained, especially when multiple parties are responsible for upkeep.

- Data Quality and Validation: In a world where a JSON document or CSV file could be edited by a subject matter expert without technical assistance, automated validation is critical for maintaining data quality.

- Cost Implications: Initial setup of independent, self-sufficient teams can be costly but should be offset by gains in efficiency and responsiveness.

- Interdependencies: Teams must be aware of how their data products interact or depend on others within the ecosystem.

- Documentation and Metadata: Each data product should come with detailed documentation to facilitate effective use across different departments or even different organizations.

- Security and Compliance: Security protocols must be consistently enforced across all data products.

- Knowledge Transfer: Ensure efficient knowledge transfer mechanisms are in place to handle staff turnovers.

- Testing and Quality Assurance: Before rolling out updates, rigorous testing should be conducted to ensure the changes are both effective and safe.

By considering these added layers of complexity, you can develop a robust, responsive, and decentralized data product ecosystem.

But Wait, Aren't LLMs Monolithic Models?

From one point of view, foundation LLMs like GPT adopt a fundamentally different architectural philosophy compared to the data mesh concept. Data mesh, as an architectural framework, decentralizes the development of what has traditionally been a monolithic DW architecture into a distributed, domain-oriented, loosely-coupled data structure.

LLMs are an amalgamation of distributed data (text written by millions of people over human history) into a single structure. There isn't anything loosely coupled about the end product. An LLM itself is a monolithic structure.

However, employing Percy Liang's characterization of "Foundation Models," we can envision GPT as akin to a foundational layer in data architecture. From a broadly-scoped, monolithic foundation model, we can fine-tune specialized LLMs, each expert in a specific topic. These fine-tuned LLMs could then participate in a "Mix of Experts" deployment, not much different from a cross-functional team of experts. This concept is somewhat reminiscent of Bill Inmon's vision of a centralized Enterprise Data Warehouse (EDW) from which various data marts can be derived for particular business needs.

To summarize, while GPT in itself could be thought of as a monolithic model, its broader application potentially paves the way for a myriad of specialized AIs. These specialized models, akin to data marts, would draw a "basic education" from the foundational capabilities of GPT, creating a diverse and rich ecosystem of AI applications, each tailored to unique domains yet unified by a common foundational layer.

This is similar to our formal grade-school education (and most undergrad college), where we get a base education that looks like the foundation model. Then, our graduate or vocational training is the fine-tuning of experts (MD, JD, Ph.D., etc.). From pools of specialized LLMs, teams of specialized LLMs can be formed just like human teams composed of members who are experts at different aspects of a problem tasked to the team.

During the decade preceding the era of today's LLM, what most thought of as AI was really collections of highly specialized "AI" models trained for very specific tasks, such as detecting credit card fraud, spam emails, recommending products, or chess and go programs. What was thought of as AI certainly wasn't monolithic.

Data Mesh, Data Fabric, Data Catalog, and Semantic Layer

Those four terms are often confused and/or conflated since all four are strongly related to the notion of an enterprise-wide repository of enterprise data resources. Let's sort this out. But first, here's a high-level overview of the scope of this conversation.

Figure 52 represents the core components of the data fabric and the distinction between technical infrastructure and domain-specific data. Starting in the center at OLTP, we'll work down (1-4), then up (5, 6, 7):

1. **OLTP (Online Transaction Processing)**—This is the layer where transactional data is created and managed. It typically involves databases that are optimized for handling a large number of short, atomic transactions, such as inserts, updates, and deletions. We see OLTP databases for three domains--sales, finance, and inventory.

2. **Data Fabric Architecture–** The data fabric layer provides a unified and integrated set of data services and architecture that spans across multiple platforms and environments, enabling seamless data sharing and access.

3. **Data Catalog Metadata**—This layer contains the metadata, which is the data about the data. The data catalog provides a centralized resource for understanding the structure, quality, and lineage of data assets across the organization. It is a virtual view of the data across the enterprise, as if it's one big database.

4. **Data Engineers, Analysts, Data Stewards, etc.**—These are the primary users of the Data Catalog Metadata. Referring to this view, data engineers, analysts, and data stewards have a holistic view of the enterprise data.

5. **Data Mesh**—Data mesh refers to a decentralized *approach* to data architecture and organizational design. It treats data as a product, with domain-oriented ownership, and emphasizes self-serve data infrastructure as a platform. Unlike

the other parts of the diagram, this is not a "thing", but a kind of approach to a data architecture.

6. **Semantic Layer**–While data mesh is about breaking down a monolithic system, the semantic layer pulls it together into a loosely-coupled whole. It is a single view across all data products presented to analysts. It's similar to the data catalog metadata (3) in that it presents a unified view of disparate data sources. The difference is the semantic layer focuses on just analytics data and the data catalog focuses on OLTP and analytics data.

7. **Analysts, Managers, Data Scientists, etc.**– These are the analytics-focused users who interact with the semantic layer. They utilize the translated data for analysis, decision-making, and deriving insights without needing deep technical knowledge of the underlying data structures.

8. **The Semantic Layer is part of the Data Catalog**—The semantic layer is itself a "data source"—a data source of BI data. As a data source, it's included in the data catalog.

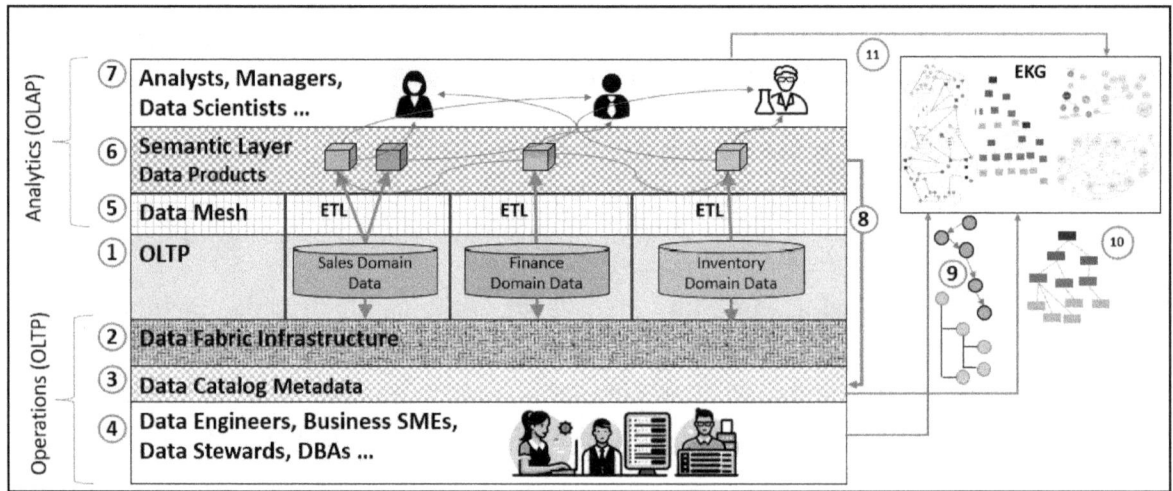

Figure 52: How data fabric, data catalog, semantic layer, and data mesh fit together.

Additionally:

- Note that the following pairs are *roughly* counterparts in their respective OLTP or OLAP layer.

- o 2 and 5–Organizes data from across many domains into a centralized platform.
- o 3 and 6–Metadata about the data fabric and data mesh.
- o 4 and 7–People utilizing their respective OLTP and OLAP data.

- Items 9, 10, and 11 illustrate which layers fulfill their respective parts of the EKG.

Data mesh and data fabric are especially confusing. Both are related to the organization of a wide array of independently operated and domain-specific enterprise data into a central, coherent construct. The primary difference is that data mesh is an *approach* towards decentralization of data product development, and data fabric is an architecture that promotes centralized access to data.

As an analogy from normal life, let's think of cooking. Data mesh is to a potluck dinner as data fabric is to a buffet at a restaurant:

- **Data mesh** is like a potluck dinner. Each participant (or business domain) brings their own dish (data), which they've prepared according to their taste and expertise. The dishes are different but are meant to come together to create a diverse yet complete meal (balance of hors d'oeuvres, drinks, entrees, desserts, etc.). Each contributor is responsible for their part, ensuring quality and relevance. This represents the decentralized nature of data mesh, where each domain manages its data autonomously while contributing to the broader data ecosystem.

- **Data fabric** is like a buffet at a restaurant. All the dishes (data) are available in one place, and patrons (users across the organization) can access any dish they want from the variety offered. The restaurant (central system) ensures that all dishes are well-prepared, integrated, safe to eat, and consistently available. This represents the centralized access and integration of Data Fabric, where data from various sources is made accessible and interoperable through a unified architecture.

Data mesh is a decentralized, organizational *approach* to data architecture and management. It's based on the principle of domain-oriented decentralization of data ownership and architecture. In data mesh, each business unit or domain is responsible for its own data as a product. This means that data is managed, maintained, and made accessible by those who are closest to it and understand it best, essentially turning domain teams into data product owners.

Data mesh addresses the challenges of large-scale data management that promote a culture where data is easily discoverable, trustworthy, self-serve, and used in a federated governance model. The key focus is on the organizational structure, domain-oriented design, and decentralization of data control and responsibility.

Data fabric is a technical *architecture* focused on creating a unified, integrated, and accessible data environment across an entire organization, using advanced technologies to manage and orchestrate data. It refers to a cohesive data layer and set of data services that provide consistent capabilities across a choice of endpoints spanning hybrid multi-cloud environments.

Data fabric is designed to integrate data across platforms and users, regardless of where the data resides, providing a unified, integrated view of data across the organization. It focuses on the interconnectivity, orchestration, and management of data across various systems, including on-premises and cloud sources. Data fabric leverages technologies like artificial intelligence and machine learning to facilitate data integration, governance, and curation, enabling seamless data access and processing across different environments and platforms.

Traditional data architectures often centralize data governance, management, and usage into specialized teams. For example, a hyper-specialized team that builds data warehouses and its ETL processes. This centralized approach has led to several challenges, particularly as enterprises scale and data volumes grow.

In this context, data catalog (3) refers to the application that manages metadata across all data sources, both OLTP and OLAP (e.g., Alation, Collibra). However, in the context of this book, by "data catalog" I'm referring to the manifestation of the metadata in the EKG.

The semantic layer is the counterpart to the data catalog on the data mesh side. It facilitates a more intuitive and business-oriented interaction with data. It acts as an abstraction layer that simplifies the underlying complexity of data structures, ensuring consistency and uniformity across different data sources and models. This layer allows end users, such as business analysts and BI professionals, to conduct self-service analytics through common business terminology without needing to understand the technical details of the underlying databases and data warehouses.

In the context of Figure 52, the semantic layer wraps around the Data Fabric's core components, integrating with the decentralized domains of a data mesh approach. It allows each domain—such as Marketing, HR, Sales, and Inventory—to interact with the

Data Fabric in a seamless and meaningful way without being bogged down by the complexities of data storage, structure, or processing. As such, the semantic layer is instrumental in realizing the vision of a unified yet decentralized data ecosystem where technology enables, rather than impedes, the strategic use of data across an organization.

Optimized Cubes as the Consumer-Facing Semantic Layer

Every product or service stands on the pillars of cost, consistency, quality, and ease of use. If any of these pillars wobble, customers are likely to explore alternative solutions. Data mesh's central mission is to untangle the complex data webs in a monolithic DW woven over decades into a set of loosely-coupled, coherent data products. Since a number of smaller-scoped pillars is easier to manage than one big monolith, the pillars are more likely to remain sturdy. A flawed or inconsistent unified data model (UDM) might push users to establish unauthorized, "rogue" databases of a "shadow-IT." This not only jeopardizes data integrity and information within an enterprise but also negates the very essence of a data mesh.

In the nexus of BI and data mesh, I advocate for the incorporation of optimized cubes in the consumer-facing semantic layer. Some critics view cubes as relics of bygone tech days. Yet, the explosive growth in analytical data, supercharged by the proliferation of IoT and unstructured data by AI (like LLM, text, computer vision, audio, and video), dictates a renewed urgent need for optimization.

The significance of optimized OLAP is multifaceted (no pun intended). It drastically enhances query performance, caters to increased concurrency demands, and promotes efficient compute resource utilization. By pre-aggregating data, leveraging additive aggregates, and managing the best aggregation design, OLAP reduces the need for redundant recalculations. This optimization ensures faster, more efficient responses to the slice and dice query pattern predominant in BI, ultimately allowing the system to handle more user queries simultaneously.

Figure 53 depicts the effect of the massive expansion of analytics data on a current BI flow:

1. Up to millions of IoT devices and up to many times more files of unstructured data (pictures, video, text).

2. The level of AI today (LLMs, Vision, Video) will unlock massive data from unstructured data. Additionally, LLMs do contain knowledge (albeit sometimes questionable), so they are indeed a new massive data source as well.

3. While IoT and AI contribute massive volumes of analytical data, we still have our traditional data sources—along with more BI data sources successfully onboarded thanks to data mesh.

4. There is a much more crowded space of data thanks to completely "green fields" of analytics opened up by AI and IoT. Additionally, data mesh facilitates the addition of data from far reaches of the enterprise once inhibited by the bottleneck of a centralized DW/BI team.

5. Direct access to the analytics data by a much wider population of BI consumers is a strain on an unoptimized database.

6. Access to BI data is substantially accelerated by accessing an optimized OLAP cube.

7. One type of new BI customer is an AI agent. And "speed of thought" for these BI consumers has a whole different meaning from that of their human counterparts.

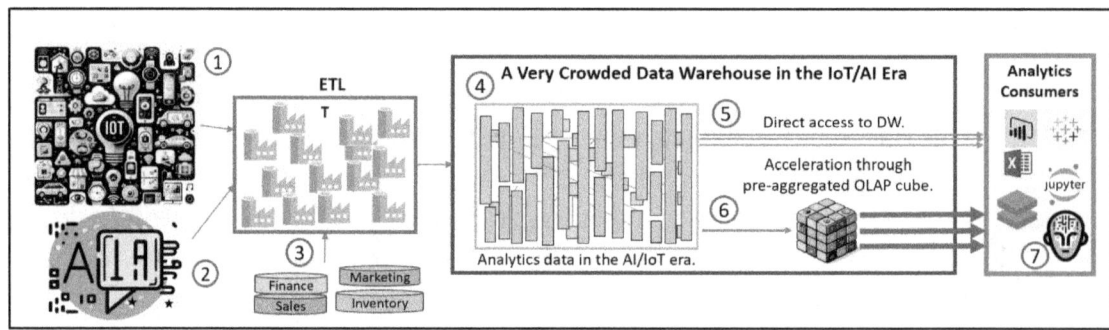

Figure 53: AI and IoT make current (non-data mesh) DW flow very crowded.

Moreover, the allure of optimized OLAP isn't merely its novelty but its superiority over "good enough" alternative solutions provided by current DW platforms. For instance, materialized views of aggregated data "manually" implemented in a Snowflake implementation that can match the versatility of optimized OLAP cubes will demand labor-intensive upkeep to manage the evolving set of required views (more on this later). And strategies like on-the-fly aggregation can lead to inconsistent performance.

Contrarily, pre-aggregated, multi-dimensional OLAP (MOLAP) shines as the premier data structure for leading analytical queries.

Integrating OLAP cubes into a data mesh's frontline brings several advantages. It guarantees rapid response times and supports high-concurrency on a unified platform while also perpetuating the bread and butter "slice-and-dice" BI visualization technique that professionals have depended on for decades. Notably, many domain-specific data products closely resemble subject-oriented data marts, generally in the form of a dimensional model, further reinforcing the case for OLAP cubes.

Today, Kyvos Insights' optimized OLAP stands out as a pioneering, cloud-native next step of what the esteemed SSAS multi-dimensional once was. Its query performance-enhancing capabilities are as fascinating with today's definition of a "very large database" (VLDB) as SSAS was with the VLDB version of the 2000s.

Lastly, I posit that, though cumbersome, the currently human-driven nature of ELT/ETL is a strength, especially in an age where LLMs, like ChatGPT, are making inroads into analytic processes. Human hands remaining in the process ensure a clearer understanding of analysts' focus points, at least within the BI data spectrum. Such human oversight infuses the data landscape with nuance, intuition, and contextual understanding that AIs have yet to fully grasp.

The KG Use for Data Mesh

Mitigating the Risk for a Knowledge Bog

The KG part of the broader EKG itself is a composite data product that can be owned by IT and the data mesh governance board, both of which are departments with enterprise-wide scope. The KG data team needs to:

- Own and maintain processes for support, approvals, coding standards, and change control.

- Specify the encoding formats to receive them (RDF, ttl, etc.), and provide specifications for IRI (for example, from schema.org and custom IRI).

- Maintain and enforce Data Product SLAs, supply the infrastructure for domains to deploy their domain-level ontologies (data product)

- Validate the deployed ontologies and upload them into the EKG.

- Provide an API for clients to access the EKG.

The domain-level ontologies that comprise the KG can be whatever the domains know to be useful for any user (human or machine) across the enterprise. Examples of KG data products include but are not limited to:

- Domain entities and taxonomies

- Workflows of domain processes

- Information derived from UML artifacts (such as those authored with PlantUML) or event-storming sessions

- Domain-specific IRI to be used by other domains (such as a material list, which will be uploaded to the KG and accessed by consumers like any other data product).

KG consumers should be able to request ontology requirements with business justification, which the KG team can coordinate with the proper data product owners (DPO).

Ontology development necessitates a unique set of skills. This includes understanding semantic web standards like RDF and OWL, mastering conceptual modeling to represent abstract ideas, employing logical reasoning to validate ontology structures, and adeptly handling tasks, such as ontology alignment, merging, and taxonomy creation. Furthermore, ontology developers must have a deep domain-specific knowledge to accurately capture real-world semantics and relationships, which can often be more intricate than the technical components themselves.

Advancements in technology, particularly LLMs like ChatGPT, are playing a pivotal role in simplifying the ontology development process. They can assist by offering suggestions, generating relevant terms, or even crafting foundational structures. For instance, when tasked with creating an ontology for dental practices, ChatGPT was able to provide a basic framework, showcasing the potential of LLMs in this domain.

While tools like Grafo or Protégé and assistance from LLMs streamline many of the technical complexities, making ontology creation more accessible even for those who aren't deeply technical, it's essential not to trivialize ontology authorship. Though one might edit Turtle files in Visual Code in some scenarios, the real challenge lies in the profound domain expertise required, distinct from the technical skills of an ontologist.

As mentioned, a KG is a database. We query it, and it returns an answer, sometimes in a tabular form—even though LLMs might translate it into a spoken language. Because a KG is a database, it should be developed and maintained like one.

Knowledge Bog

Learn from the mistakes that lead to data swamps

The enthusiasm surrounding the newfound ability to feasibly create KGs with LLM assistance mirrors the excitement that accompanied the advent of data lakes a decade ago, enabled through scale-out technology. Data Lakes and KGs are both centralized, enterprise-scoped data repositories. But without careful curation, a data lake risks becoming a data swamp. Likewise, a KG can devolve into a "knowledge bog," overloaded with inconsistent, low-quality, and poorly labeled relationships.

Similarly, towards the goal of mitigating the degradation of a data lake into a data swamp, the concept of the "lakehouse" was introduced a few years ago. The lakehouse is an innovative solution that combines the structured data management capabilities of a data warehouse, the vast storage capacity of a data lake, and the ACID (Atomicity, Consistency, Isolation, Durability) benefits of a relational database. It specifies a balance that enables the efficient handling and analysis of large-scale raw data while ensuring reliable data transactions, thus preventing the data lake from turning into an unmanageable data swamp.

KG "Data Products"

To prevent KGs from becoming unmanageable knowledge bogs, I propose the incorporation of principles from Domain-Driven Design (DDD) and data mesh paradigms. This approach encourages KGs to maintain clarity and usability by breaking ontologies and processes into manageable, coherent, loosely-coupled domains.

Figure 54 is a representation of data mesh architecture applied to BI and KG development. This depiction showcases how a data mesh allows for domain-specific BI development and contributes to a broader knowledge graph, ensuring that both local and global insights are leveraged. Here is an itemized description of the visual elements:

1. **Knowledge Graph**—Composed of interconnected nodes and edges, representing entities and their relationships collected from across an enterprise. Varying shade or color-coded nodes indicate different types of entities or data sources.

2. **Data Products**—The arrows point from data products created for three domains to inclusion in the KG (1). For each of the three domains, there are two ontology data products and one OLAP cube data product. This is a reminder that data mesh is applied for BI data and ontologies.

3. **Domains**—Three cylindrical shapes, each representing a domain within the organization: Clinical Operations, Patient Management, and Marketing. These domains contribute to the knowledge graph and consume data products. Inside each domain's box, mini graphs are visible, signifying the domain-specific ontology and its structure. The mini graphs are connected to both the knowledge graph and the data products, indicating a flow of data and insights.

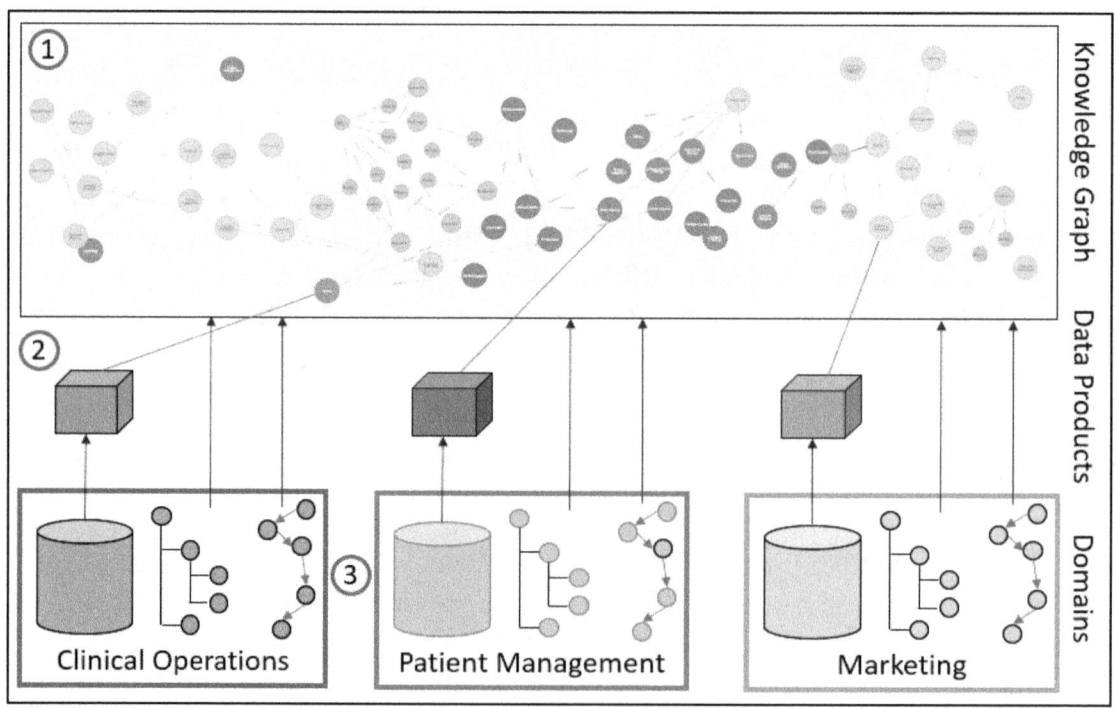

Figure 54: Data mesh applied to distributed KG development.

Both DDD and data mesh were developed to resist system degradation towards a convoluted, unmanageable structure, a "big ball of mud." By dividing data and processes into more manageable, loosely-coupled yet coherent domains, these approaches help maintain the clarity and usability of the system, much like a well-designed lakehouse does for data lakes. Applying these concepts ensures that KG quality becomes an achievable goal, crucial for preserving the graph's integrity and value. We will delve further into these principles and offer a blueprint for a well-structured KG.

As it is for BI data products, by distributing the work of the KG to domain levels, the scope of individual business problems, we decompose a monolith into coherent components. We push the effort for each business problem to the individuals who know the data best.

To recap, ensuring the quality of the KG is a challenging yet imperative part of the equation. It involves more than simply loading every triple into a graph database, such as Neo4j or Stardog. Inconsistent labels can lead to erroneous dead ends, resulting in a search maze. Therefore, we must take measured steps and employ a balanced approach to preserve the integrity of our KG.

As we proceed with this book, we'll delve into how principles inspired by DDD and data mesh can offer a blueprint for a well-structured KG. We'll also explore examples of primary KG components as well as some overall guidance.

Data mesh could be looked at as mitigating complexity. It does so by factoring out common aspects of data products that could be governed by specialists, and whatever is unique to a domain is the responsibility of the domain.

This ameliorates the tangled web of inter-domain dependencies that can bring an effort to a halt as people from across domains might argue about seemingly trivial things—such as what to call a customer and what is a location. With data mesh, domains surface their data products in their language. Disagreements or not, at least the information is there, still within its respective contexts, in the KG for everyone to see. Reconciliations (mapping of disputed information) can be applied later.

OLAP Cubes as Data Products with Coherent Bounded Contexts

From a BI perspective, OLAP cubes have long been valued for their role in delivering analytical data directly to users for over two decades. These cubes naturally establish a focused area of information—a coherent bounded context—where everything inside is consistent and specifically related to a designated business segment or purpose.

I emphasize "coherent" because, in the context of data mesh, the focus tends to be on distributing effort and establishing centralized governance. Yet, defining "domains"—a critical and challenging task—often seems to be glossed over. However, the world of OLAP cubes effectively delineates these bounded contexts through dimensional modeling.

The ability of OLAP cubes to effectively service a large number of reports is indicative of their function as bounded contexts. For example, enterprises with long-lived, unwieldy BI systems might manage hundreds of different reports, most of which could be streamlined into a few OLAP cubes. These cubes, by covering multiple reports that share common dimensions and metrics, provide further proof that they represent coherent bounded contexts.

So, what exactly defines a domain? Is it a department, or is it a business process? While some business processes are confined to single departments, others span across multiple departments, and it is these cross-departmental processes that are particularly intriguing. In fact, the more intriguing OLAP cubes integrate data across one to a few domains. Whatever makes it into such OLAP cubes naturally falls within the bounded context of a business process.

By clearly defining the boundaries within which data operates, OLAP cubes enable optimizations at a manageable level, demonstrating the practical value of maintaining coherent bounded contexts in complex data environments.

Distributed Construction of the KG in the Data Mesh Paradigm

Although a significant part of this book focuses on how BI information can be incorporated into the EKG, at the time of this writing, the concept of a knowledge graph is still new to many. Therefore, I should include some guidance around the process for building a KG in a data mesh format. Following is an outline of the process:

1. Starter Ontology Generation: Using ChatGPT or other tools to produce a starter ontology is a solid approach. This is the idea of the symbiotic relationship between LLMs and KG that makes the development and maintenance of KGs feasible today. At this stage, the KG doesn't need to be completely detailed–mostly a good starter from which we can iteratively refine and expand with assistance from LLMs. The LLM can also output directly to the turtle (ttl) format when we're ready to fine-tune the ontology in a UI (Protégé).

2. Version Control with Git: Git provides the benefit of collaborative work, version history, and branching capabilities. Remember to commit often with meaningful commit messages for better tracking.

3. Protégé for Detailed Authoring: This step is pivotal. Importing a starter ontology and refining it ensures that the ontology adheres to domain requirements. Leveraging standard URIs promotes interoperability, and detailed labels and comments enhance clarity. The fine-tuned ontology is then saved back to the turtle format.

4. Peer Review: Just as code review improves code quality, ontology review ensures the ontology is accurate, comprehensive, and logical.

5. Integrated Testing: Deploying to a test graph database environment helps uncover issues that might not be evident in a standalone ontology editor.

6. URI Matching: Merging or linking nodes based on matching URIs avoids redundancy and leverages existing knowledge in the KG. This step can be automated for efficiency.

7. Testing with Queries: Practical tests by running queries help identify gaps or inaccuracies in the ontology. As test scripts are developed and used to test conventional software prior to rollout, test queries could be created to test the new ontology.

8. Safe Deletion: Always have backups and understand the implications of deleting nodes and relationships, especially when they have dependencies.

9. Iterative Refinement: Continuous improvement based on test results ensures the ontology is as accurate and useful as possible.

10. Final Deployment: After all tests and refinements, the ontology can be loaded into the production environment. If your KG tool supports it, consider version tagging for easier rollbacks.

11. Audit and Backtracking: Being able to trace back the changes and have a complete history of the ontology versions and their impacts is crucial for accountability and potential troubleshooting.

Data Products for Mappings

Linking entities and instances across domain-scoped data products is crucial to prevent the creation of isolated knowledge silos. This book emphasizes the importance of integrating widely dispersed knowledge to form a comprehensive understanding across systems.

We'll begin our exploration of how ontologies are interconnected by examining the concept of master data management (MDM). It's a method familiar to most practitioners. MDM represents an attempt to consolidate and harmonize data across numerous databases. However, MDM emerged as a solution well after diverse types of databases were already widely implemented, making integration a significant challenge. It was almost an afterthought. Often, MDM has to retrofit a framework onto existing systems, which can be complex and cumbersome. In contrast, the idea of integration in KGs was considered foundational from its inception with the semantic web. With the relatively recent adoption of KGs in broader applications—aided significantly by advancements in LLMs—the opportunity to design with integration in mind from the beginning presents itself. It's interesting to note that the art of MDM also benefits from the inferential power of LLMs.

As we delve into RDF (Resource Description Framework) and other semantic technologies, we recognize the potential for these tools to facilitate the early and efficient linking of data. This proactive approach in KGs allows for a more seamless and scalable integration compared to the reactive emergence of traditional MDM.

By considering RDF and semantic integration strategies right from the start, KGs can avoid the pitfalls that MDM systems still encounter, setting a new standard for how we manage and understand interconnected data.

Master Data Management

MDM has traditionally been the backbone for ensuring consistency, accuracy, and trustworthiness of data in OLTP and BI environments. At its core, MDM strives to provide a unified view of essential data entities by consolidating information from various sources, ensuring that BI analyses and reports are based on a single version of the truth.

Central to MDM is the concept of the "Golden Record." This represents the most authoritative version of a data entity—like a customer or product—sourced from multiple systems. Establishing a Golden Record involves deduplicating and/or mapping records from diverse sources, reconciling discrepancies through predefined rules or input from data stewards, and the data stewards finally agreeing on producing a standardized, "golden" version. This process ensures that, no matter where the data is accessed or used, it remains consistent and reliable.

While MDM meticulously maps data at the member or record level, BI frameworks, notably the bus matrix, maps at a higher, more conceptual class level. The bus matrix, a hallmark of the Kimball BI methodology, presents a high-level overview of how various business processes and their corresponding data interrelate, facilitating a strategic, organized approach to data design and utilization.

MDM has been historically fraught with challenges. One of its most notable hurdles is the often labor-intensive process of aligning stakeholders. Given that MDM initiatives intersect with multiple domains, there are the inevitable disagreements and debates between SMEs. These can arise from differing data definitions, interpretations due to differing views of the world, or even ownership disputes. While the outcome—a dataset that has been rigorously vetted and agreed upon by experts—is of high quality, reaching this consensus can be time-consuming and, at times, contentious. It's crucial to recognize the mappings resulting from MDM efforts as valuable data products in their own right. These mappings, which are often the outcome of exhaustive deliberations and expertise, provide a rich foundation for linking data products within a knowledge graph. Representing relationships, hierarchies, and connections, they offer a structured framework that a knowledge graph can utilize to derive insights, further emphasizing the symbiotic relationship between MDM and advanced data architectures like KGs.

RDF Mapping

The ability to consistently and accurately link data across various KG data products is paramount. One of the most effective tools for achieving this is the Resource Description

Framework's (RDF) use of the Universal Resource Identifier (URI) or Internationalized Resource Identifier (IRI). Reminder, either URI or IRI works—it's just that IRI allows for Unicode characters.

The RDF IRI provides a unique and universal way to identify nodes across all KGs. Given its universal nature, it serves as a powerful linking mechanism, ensuring that data references are consistent, unambiguous, and universally recognizable, regardless of the data source or application. For KG data product teams, domain-level ontologies, treated as data products, play a pivotal role in shaping the semantic structure and relationships within the KG. When such an ontology data product is uploaded into the KG, the process is as follows:

1. This process scans and identifies nodes in the ontology data product that have an associated IRI.

2. Instead of creating a new node, the system checks the KG for existing nodes with the same IRI.

3. If a match is found, the existing KG node is used, instead of adding a new node.

This ensures that the KG remains free of redundant nodes and that data linkages are consistent and based on universally recognized identifiers.

Given the efficiency and clarity that RDF IRIs offer in linking data, it's imperative for the data mesh governance team to endorse their use. By recommending or even mandating RDF IRIs as the primary method for linking data products within the KG, the governance team not only ensures consistency and accuracy but also promotes best practices that simplify data integration and enhance the overall reliability of the KG.

In summary, RDF IRIs, when implemented effectively, are the favored linchpin that holds the vast expanse of a KG together. By serving as a universally recognized and consistent linking mechanism, they bridge the gap between disparate data products, ensuring that the KG remains a cohesive, interconnected, and reliable resource for all its users.

Automated Similarity Mapping with LLMs

A robust way to streamline the linking process involves the use of LLM to generate mapping tables. These tables act as bridges, seamlessly linking nodes from these domain-level ontologies to the enterprise-scoped KG.

While RDF mapping is the preferred method for its standardization and semantic capabilities, it's not always feasible due to the absence of universally agreed-upon off-the-shelf ontologies, like FIBO in financial services. In such cases, creating mapping tables as data products can be an effective alternative, albeit more cumbersome and prone to error. These tables serve as practical bridges, linking nodes across different domain-level ontologies to the overarching enterprise KG. This approach ensures that integration isn't an all-or-nothing proposition but a flexible process tailored to the available resources and specific integration challenges.

A mapping table, crafted with the assistance of a LLM, serves as an intermediary structure. It maps nodes from domain-level data products to potential corresponding nodes in the main KG based on semantic similarity and relational context. The procedure involves:

1. Node Identification: For each node in the domain-level data product, a scan is initiated within the knowledge graph. This search aims to identify nodes that might have similar semantic or relational attributes.

2. Contextual Analysis: Using the LLM, the system evaluates the contextual relationships of potential nodes in the knowledge graph. For instance, given a node labeled "muscle cars" in the domain data product, the LLM might identify a node in the knowledge graph labeled "hot rods." The relationships or neighbors of "hot rods," such as "car," "big engine," and "high horsepower," are then considered to further validate its semantic closeness to "muscle cars."

3. Similarity Prompt: Based on the relational context, the LLM is prompted with a question like, "How similar is a 'muscle car' to a 'hot rod' that is a car with a big engine and high horsepower?." The LLM then assesses the similarity and returns a structured response, typically in JSON format, such as {'probability':1.0,'reason':'Both refer to high-performance vehicles designed for powerful acceleration and speed.'}.

4. Packaging the Results: After processing all nodes in the domain-level data product, the generated mappings, along with their similarity scores and reasons, are packaged. This package acts as a supplemental layer, which can be appended to the main domain-level data product post-upload.

Figure 55 through Figure 57 below show this example through ChatGPT.

how similar is a 'muscle car' to a 'hot rod that is a car, big engine, high horse power? return a json like this {'probability':1.0,'reason':'example of a reason'}.

Figure 55: Prompt for an analysis of similarity.

 Based on my training data and understanding of the terms:

- A "muscle car" is typically a term used to describe high-performance American cars, especially coupes, with large engines designed for high-performance driving. They are typically from the 1960s and early 1970s era.
- A "hot rod", on the other hand, is a customized car, often with an altered or replaced engine intended for performance. They can be of various models and from different eras, but the primary intent is to achieve greater speed, power, or both.

Considering the context provided: "hot rod that is a car, big engine, high horse power", it seems that this particular definition of a hot rod shares some similarities with a muscle car. Both emphasize performance, having a significant engine, and high horsepower.

Figure 56: ChatGPT's analysis of the similarity between a muscle car and a hot rod.

Let's convert this understanding into the desired format:

```json
{
    "probability": 0.85,
    "reason": "Both muscle cars and the described hot rod emphasize performanc
}
```

Note that the probability value is set to 0.85 to represent a high degree of similarity, but not absolute equivalence.

Figure 57: Ask ChatGPT to offer "just one number, please."

In production, the example would actually use the OpenAI API, not the human-oriented ChatGPT. Using a LLM-backed mapping table has several advantages:

- It brings consistency and structure to the linking process.

- The LLM's natural language processing capabilities ensure that the semantic nuances between nodes are captured accurately.

- Packaging the results as a supplemental layer provides a transparent and traceable record of how nodes from the domain-level data product align with the broader knowledge graph.

Integrating LLMs into the knowledge graph mapping process not only enhances the accuracy and coherence of linkages but also ensures that the rich tapestry of relationships within the graph remains interconnected and contextually relevant. But please keep in mind that this should still be a human-driven approach where LLMs are in an assistive role.

Database-Derived Ontologies

The tough ontology data products, those depending primarily on human intelligence (for now), will be authored by a cross-functional team of SMEs, ontologists, and LLMs. However, there will fortunately be ontology or taxonomy data products easily derived from databases--well, easy for a data engineer, anyway. So, we probably need to add a data engineer to the data product team.

As opposed to the ontology data product packaged as a ttl or json-ld document, I envision these data products to be something like a SQL script or Jupyter notebook (ranging from not much more than a simple SELECT statement of a lookup table to non-trivial code) that is maintained and outputs a csv as the data product. That csv will either be accompanied by a Cypher script using LOAD CSV to deploy into the EKG, or the csv will include extra columns as declarative metadata instructions for deployment into the EKG. For the latter, those instruction columns include metadata for where a value comes from (database, table, column), mapping of node and edge property values and labels.

As discussed in the previous topic, some DPs might even require AI-engineer skills for development-time mapping of similarities, validating what it sees, and offering suggestions. Following are examples of KG components that can be derived from our traditional relational database:

1. **Foreign Key / Primary Key Relationships (Ontology)**

    - Description: Relationships defined by foreign keys (FK) and primary keys (PK) in relational databases can form the backbone of an ontology. These relationships indicate how entities (tables) are interconnected, representing types and their relationships in an ontology.

- Example: An "Employee" table with a PK linked to a "Department" table's FK can be expressed as a triple: Employee has a Department.

2. **Parent-Child Relationships (Taxonomy)**

- Description: Hierarchical relationships within tables, often seen in parent-child configurations, can be modeled as a taxonomy. This structure organizes data into categories and subcategories, defining a classification system.

- Example: A "Categories" table where each record may have a parent category, forming a tree-like structure of product categories.

3. **Primary Key to Intra-Column Relationships ("Has-A" Relationships)**

- Description: The relationship between a primary key and other columns in the same table can be expressed as "has-a" relationships in an ontology. This defines attributes or properties of entities.

- Example: In a "Vehicle" table, the vehicle's PK related to columns like "make", "model", and "year" can be defined as a vehicle "has a" make, "has a" model, and "has a" year.

4. **Table Hierarchies (Hierarchical Ontology)**

- Description: Some tables inherently contain hierarchical data or can be interpreted as such, beyond simple parent-child relationships. These hierarchies can be extracted as part of an ontological structure.

- Example: An "Product" table with multiple levels of classification–class, category, sub-category: product has a sub-category, sub-category child-of category, category child-of class.

5. **Reference Tables (Ontology of Important Individuals or Constants)**

- Description: Reference tables, which contain enumerated types or constants, can be used to define specific individuals or important constants in a knowledge graph.

- Example: A "Status" reference table listing all possible states of an order (e.g., received, processed, shipped) can be integrated into the KG to define possible states of the "Order" entity.

KG Update Tracking

All data product submissions and each step of the upload process should be logged and stored. Ideally, the EKG can be rebuilt from scratch if needed or in a time-travel manner so the state of the EKG at any given time can be rendered. This addresses audit trail requirements. And the ability to view what the KG looked like at a particular time will shed light on how and why particular decisions were made at the time–which may not make sense today.

KG Update Exceptions

At the DP validation phase, a report is sent to the data product owner (DPO) listing nodes without matching IRI and any other potential problems or helpful information, such as:

- Values not meeting the RDFs specification for int, string, date, etc.
- Nodes and edges that no longer exist.
- The list of new nodes and edges that will be added.
- Suggestions for IRI matches. This can be done with the help of a LLM.
- EKG consumers can submit "production queries" to the EKG as a test script the deployment must pass.

Art Gallery Ontology Creation Example Using Protégé and GitHub

On the GitHub site is a light tutorial (art_gallery_ontology_starter.docx) demonstrating how a data product team can set up an ontology data product. This is a simple example of building a KG in a distributed manner. Our example is an art gallery co-op. There are many types of artists, each curating their own little sections in the store. However, there are processes and contributions required by all members, beyond simply paying dues.

An ontology is a structured framework of terms and the relationships between them within a particular domain. It defines a set of concepts and categories that represent the domain's phenomena and shows how these concepts are related to one another.

Figure 58 depicts an ontology of an art gallery. It's limited to classes of entities associated with an art gallery and how these classes of entities relate to each other.

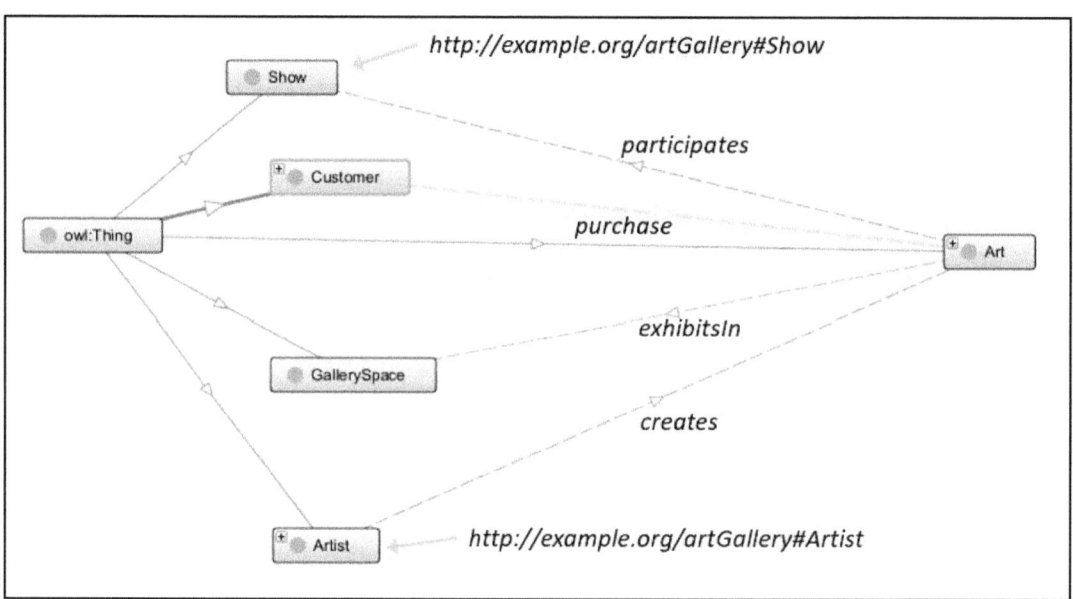

Figure 58: Ontology of an art gallery.

Note the URL that serves as a unique identifier for the "Show" node at the top of the diagram. In ontologies, each node is assigned a distinct IRI, ensuring that every concept within the knowledge structure is uniquely defined and can be unambiguously referenced. While an IRI can technically take various forms, it is commonly structured as a URL, which provides a convenient link to a definitive Internet resource or definition associated with the node.

However, an ontology does not typically contain extensive references to tangible flesh and blood or brick and mortar individuals—instances of a class or concept. For example, there is the concept of "Artist" and "Artists create Art." When you start adding specific instances of artists and individual artworks, and these instances are interconnected with relationships defined in the ontology, the structure begins to form a knowledge graph. Figure 59 extends the ontology in Figure 58 into a KG. Again, note the IRI for the "Show" node. That is the unique name that will be the link for any other ontology we wish to merge with this ontology.

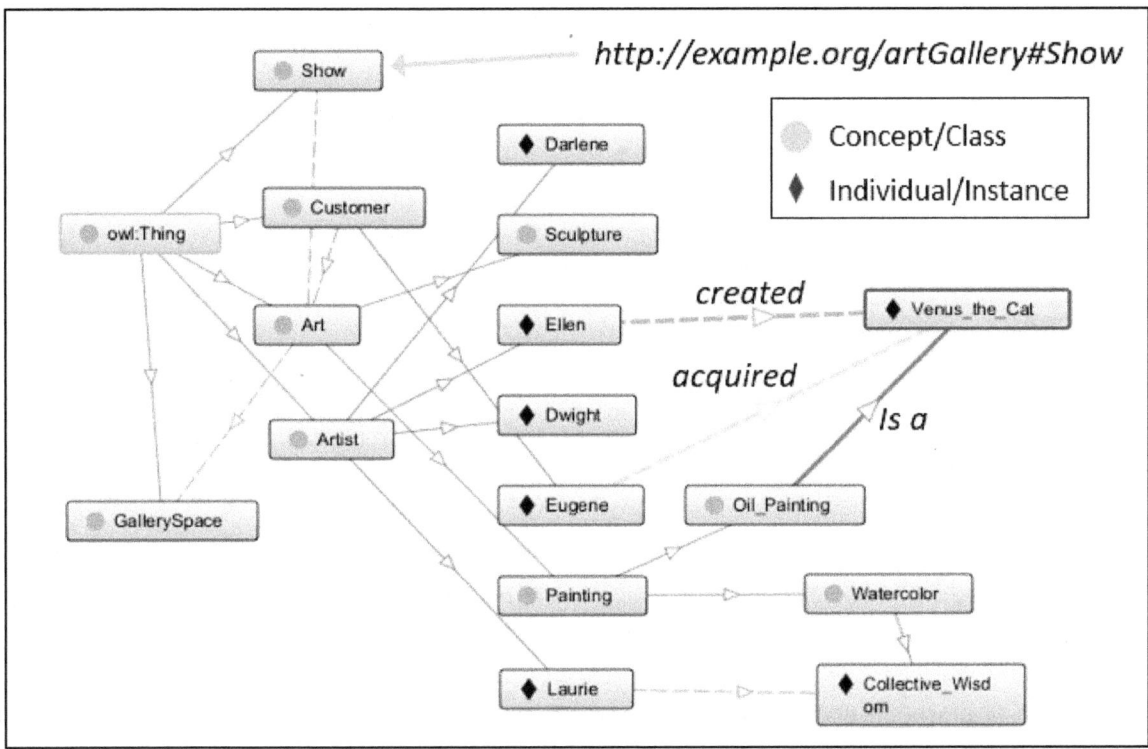

Figure 59: Knowledge graph. End result of the tutorial, art_gallery_ontology_starter.ttl.

When we populated the ontology with individual artists and their works of art, and particularly when these entities are connected with real-world data relationships, we created KG. The KG uses the original ontology of classes as its schema to ensure that the data is structured and linked according to the domain's rules and definitions.

Meanwhile, in another part of the art gallery business, the "Show" domain (meaning events where the art and artists participate), its SMEs have built an ontology that describes the structure of the shows in which the gallery artists participate. Figure 60 shows the simple ontology centered around the Show entity and its relationships to Themes and Facilities.

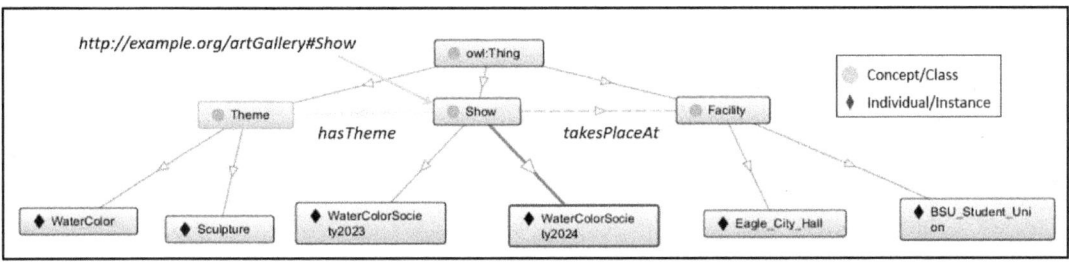

Figure 60: Ontology of Shows developed and maintained by the Events domain.

There again is the IRI for "Show." Figure 61 is a partial view of the merged version of the main and show ontologies.

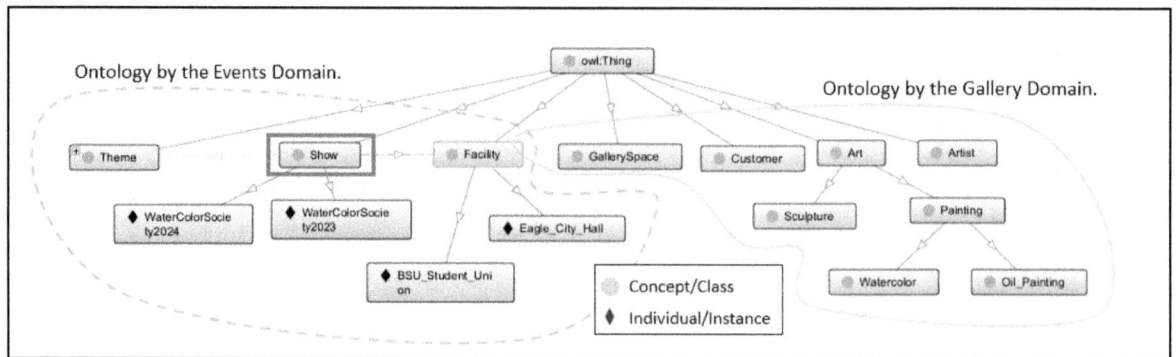

Figure 61: Combined ontology.

The highlighted node, "Show," indicates it as the link between the two ontologies—the Event domain within the dashed line and the art gallery domain outlined in the solid line. Of course, an art gallery is much more complicated. The KG could include ontologies of much deeper knowledge held by art experts of many specialties, an elucidation of the rules for commissions and out of state sales, and even unique details of individual artists and each work.

CHAPTER EIGHT

Architecture of the AEI

This book is about how the intersection of knowledge graphs, large language models, data fabrics/catalogs, business intelligence, and data mesh is tied together to cull the part of knowledge worker understanding that is still beyond the reach of current AI. This is a broad skill stack that is intended to form a whole greater than the sum of its parts. Chapters 4 through 7 introduced each of these topics. And now we can begin tying them together into a system.

This section presents the logical view of the AEI. That is, we'll focus on how the high-level pieces fit together into the whole. However, we'll also explore options for the various components of the system.

Architecture Overview

Figure 62 depicts a high-level overview of the entire system. Each box (thicker blue) is a major section. The most important thing to note is that the EKG (3, upper-right) is composed of the items in the other three major boxes.

Following is an explanation of the boxes in Figure 62:

1. **Ontology Development Data Mesh**–This box showcases the foundational elements necessary for developing domain-specific ontologies. It highlights the use of GitHub as a version control and collaboration platform, with OWL serving as the format for representing ontologies.

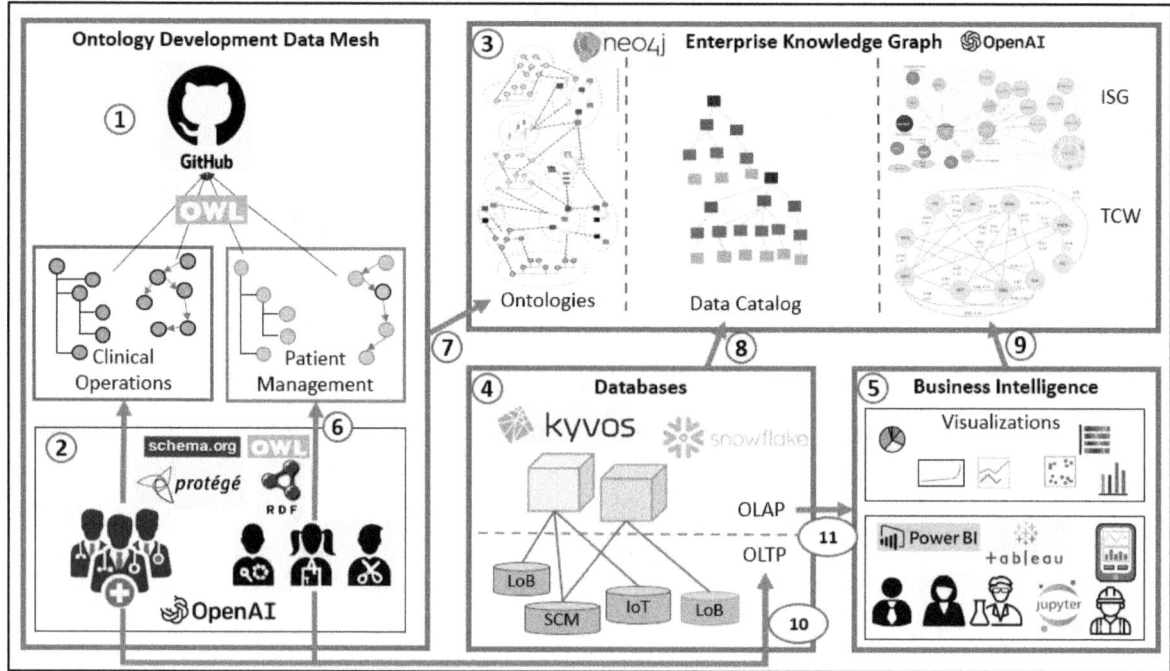

Figure 62: Full architecture.

2. **Examples of domain-specific ontologies**, such as "Clinical Operations" and "Patient Management," are illustrated. The icons (including schema.org, OWL, Protégé, and RDF) emphasize the standards and tools commonly used in ontology creation and management. The reference to OpenAI suggests potential integration or utilization of AI capabilities in ontology development.

3. **Enterprise Knowledge Graph**—The broader EKG encapsulates three major structures:

    a. Ontologies—This cluster represents a diverse set of ontologies developed by different domain-level data product teams. These ontologies, when interlinked, provide a rich, interconnected knowledge base that forms the backbone of the EKG. The depicted relationships and nodes offer a snapshot of the intricate connections present within and across ontologies.

    b. Data Catalog—This pyramid of blue triangles symbolizes the hierarchical nature of data organization in enterprises. At its base, you have broad data sources, which are further categorized into specific databases/cubes, tables/views/dimensions, the columns/attributes of the tables, and finally the valid values of the columns (as appropriate). This catalog serves as a structured inventory of data assets, making data discoverable and understandable.

   c. The ISG and TCW are structures formed from normal BI activity. The ISG captures insights derived from visual analytics tools, with nodes representing dataframes linked to their corresponding insights. The TCW, on the other hand, focuses on the relationships between tuples, enabling deeper insights based on correlations and probabilistic associations. This entire structure serves as the encoded knowledge of the enterprise, making sense of vast amounts of data and offering actionable intelligence.

4. **Databases**—This compartment illustrates OLAP and OLTP, two primary types of data processing systems. Represented by platforms like Kyvos and Snowflake (on the OLAP side), these systems handle everything from business analytics to daily transactions, ensuring data is both insightful and actionable.

5. **Business Intelligence**—The BI box emphasizes the tools and processes that transform raw data into meaningful insights. With BI visualization platforms like PowerBI and Tableau, analysts can create diverse visualizations ranging from bar charts to scatter plots. The visualizations, in turn, offer unique insights, which are captured in the aforementioned ISG. The depiction of Jupyter indicates the potential for advanced data analysis and machine learning capabilities in BI processes.

Following are the relationships between items in Figure 62:

6. **Workers to Ontologies**—This relationship indicates that a cross-functional team of professionals (perhaps data scientists, ontologists, and domain experts) are responsible for creating, refining, and maintaining the ontologies. They utilize tools, standards, and platforms within the "Ontology Development Data Mesh" to define the structure and semantics of the data.

7. **Ontologies to Enterprise Knowledge Graph**—Once developed, these ontologies are integrated into the EKG. This integration enriches the EKG with domain-specific knowledge and structured representations, facilitating advanced querying, reasoning, and data interlinking.

8. **Databases (OLAP and OLTP) to Data Catalog**–The OLAP and OLTP databases form the data catalog, the grounding base for the EKG. The data catalog is a structured inventory that categorizes and describes these databases, making it easier for users to discover, access, and manage the data they contain. And it grounds objects of the KG and ISG/TCW to real database objects.

9. **Business Intelligence Workers to TCW and ISG**–Professionals working with Business Intelligence tools generate specific queries that are then used to create and refine the TCW and ISG within the EKG. This indicates a process where BI-driven insights and needs inform the structure and content of these parts of the knowledge graph.

10. **Workers to OLTP**–A set of professionals or systems are responsible for generating transactional data that gets stored within OLTP databases. This could represent operational processes, applications, or systems that continually produce and log transactional records.

11. **OLAP to Business Intelligence**–Data from OLAP databases, typically aggregated and optimized for analytical processing, is utilized by BI tools for visualization and advanced analysis. Users of tools like PowerBI, Tableau, and Jupyter leverage this data to derive insights, trends, and patterns.

Development Tools

GitHub

As previously mentioned, sample code accompanying this book can be found at a GitHub site. Git is more than a place to leave code for others to pick up. It provides many benefits, including:

- Version Control: GitHub uses Git, a powerful version control system. This ensures that changes to the ontology are tracked over time. Users can revert to previous versions, compare changes, and analyze the evolution of the ontology.

- Collaboration: Multiple domain experts or ontology developers can collaborate on a single ontology. They can create branches to develop specific features or sections of the ontology and then merge them back into the main branch.

- Issue Tracking: GitHub's issue tracker allows collaborators to raise issues, discuss problems, or suggest improvements to the ontology. It provides a centralized platform for feedback and iterative development.

- Documentation: GitHub repositories come with a built-in wiki and README sections. This is useful for documenting the ontology, its structure, purpose, usage guidelines, and any other relevant information.

- Forking and Pull Requests: Other experts or users can fork the ontology repository, make their own changes or improvements, and then submit a pull request. This facilitates community contributions and external input.

- Transparency: Hosting ontologies on a public platform like GitHub makes the development process transparent. It allows for open peer review and ensures accountability.

- Integration with Other Tools: GitHub can be integrated with various other tools for continuous integration, testing, and deployment. For ontologies, this might mean automated testing for consistency, validation against schemas, or even automatic deployment to specific knowledge graph platforms.

- Backup and Redundancy: GitHub provides a reliable cloud backup of the ontology, ensuring that the data is safe and can be accessed from anywhere.

- Community Engagement: By being on GitHub, the ontology can gain visibility within the broader community. Other experts, researchers, or enthusiasts can star, watch, or fork the repository, leading to greater engagement and potential contributions.

- Licensing: GitHub makes it easy to attach open-source licenses to projects. For ontologies, this can clarify how others can use, modify, or distribute the knowledge.

GitHub provides a collaborative, version-controlled environment that enhances the process of ontology development, ensuring its robustness, transparency, and adaptability.

Visual Code

Visual Studio Code (VS Code) is a free, open-source code editor developed by Microsoft. It's known for its speed, ease of use, and extensive customization options through extensions. This book involves Python code, RDF/OWL Turtle (ttl) files, SQL, and Jupyter notebooks which can all be edited in VS Code.

One of its most powerful integrations is with GitHub, allowing seamless version control and repository management directly from the editor. To enable this capability:

1. Install the GitHub Extension: Start by installing the official GitHub extension from the VS Code marketplace. This extension provides GitHub workflow capabilities within the editor.

2. Authentication: Once the extension is installed, you'll be prompted to sign into your GitHub account. Authenticate to link VS Code with your GitHub repositories.

3. Clone a Repository: To work on a project, clone a GitHub repository directly to VS Code. Use the command palette (Ctrl+Shift+P or Cmd+Shift+P on Mac) and type "Git: Clone." Paste the URL of your GitHub repository, choose a local directory, and the repository will be cloned to your local machine.

4. Make Changes and Commit: After making changes to your code, the source control icon (branch-like icon on the sidebar) will show the number of changed files. Clicking on it will allow you to review, stage, and commit changes. Provide a meaningful commit message and click the checkmark at the top to commit.

5. Push and Pull: Use the ellipsis (...) at the top of the source control view to push your committed changes to GitHub or pull any updates from the remote repository.

6. Branching: Manage branches directly from VS Code. Create, switch, merge, or delete branches as needed for your workflow. All of these can be done using the command palette or the source control view.

7. Pull Requests: With the GitHub extension, you can create and review pull requests directly within VS Code. This ensures a smooth code review process without switching between the browser and the editor.

By integrating VS Code with GitHub, you get a unified coding and version control experience. The streamlined interface and powerful extensions make VS Code a top choice for developers, ensuring efficient coding, collaboration, and deployment.

Ontology Composition Tools

In the realm of knowledge representation, the design and development of ontologies play a crucial role. These structured frameworks facilitate the modeling of concepts, relationships, and various entities in a domain. For this intricate task, specialized tools have been developed to aid ontology creators.

Standing out among these tools is Protégé, a free, open-source platform developed by Stanford University. Widely recognized and used in the academic and industrial sectors, Protégé offers a rich set of features for creating, editing, and visualizing ontologies. Its user-friendly interface, combined with powerful plugins, provides a comprehensive environment tailored for ontology development. I've chosen Protégé as the primary ontology development tool, not just for its robust features but also for its active community support, making it a dynamic tool that evolves with the needs of its users.

Databases

The AEI is about data, so a variety of databases come into play. This ample section describes at high levels the unique role of each type of database in the AEI.

Data Warehouses, Data Marts

The Star/Snowflake schema is still the most user-friendly format for non-data engineers.

A data warehouse (DW), traditionally the primary BI database, is a vast repository that aggregates data from various sources within an enterprise, facilitating a consolidated view. It's designed for query and analysis rather than transaction processing, ensuring that comprehensive data is available for BI activities in a highly performant fashion.

Then there are data marts, which can be seen as subsets of DWs (or building bricks of a DW, depending on your Inmon or Kimball leanings). A data mart focuses on a specific business process or department, like the sales cycle or HR, respectively. Its narrower scope, means it's compact, allowing for easier maintenance, quicker data retrieval, and a targeted perspective on specific business areas.

In the panorama of BI, DW, and data marts, OLAP cubes have historically been the stalwarts. Their prominence in the earlier days of BI (ca. late 1990s to 2000s) is a testament to their enduring relevance and utility.

OLAP Cubes add another dimension to this BI landscape. They are databases structured specifically for extremely fast analysis. They are one of the "OG" NoSQL databases. These data structures enable users to interactively analyze multidimensional data from multiple perspectives. An OLAP system that lets you look at a dataset in a highly-versatile number of ways, for example, by time, geography, or product categories, making complex data analyses and computations both intuitive and swift.

These analytics databases are very common today. They are meticulously curated, ensuring that the data within is not only high-quality but has gone through rigorous cleansing and vetting processes. As a result, they generally house the most critical data for enterprise decision-making. Moreover, these traditional BI systems are presented with a user-friendly facade, making the complex world of data more digestible for end-users.

In today's rapidly evolving data landscape, there might be a tendency to view these traditional BI structures as relics of the past, superseded by machine learning, lakehouses, and AI. However, their presence in contemporary BI discussions underlines their sustained importance. Their rich, consolidated, and structured data repositories make them invaluable assets, especially when discussing the embedding of BI insights into knowledge graphs.

Graph Databases

All useful objects are related to other objects.

Relationships Only—But Know Where to Find the Information

Drill-Through to Details

A KG fundamentally focuses on the relationships between entities, in contrast to what we're traditionally accustomed to with relational databases (RDBMS) like SQL Server and Oracle, which organize data into tables representing lists of similar described items. Although relational databases are effective for managing structured data, they fall short in depicting the complex web of relationships that exist in the real world—ironically, despite their name.

Graph databases emerge as a powerful solution specifically optimized for mapping and querying these intricate relationships. They do not replace relational databases but complement them, each serving distinct but interconnected roles in data management. While relational databases excel at handling vast amounts of discrete data, graph databases thrive in representing and analyzing the connections between data points, offering a more intuitive and direct approach to understanding relationships.

In practical terms, high-cardinality items like individual customers (could be in the hundreds of millions for some) or specific transactions are best managed within RDBMS due to their volume and structured nature. In contrast, a KG should focus on the overarching relationships and patterns that can be derived from this data—such as how different customers interact or how products relate to purchase behaviors.

This division of labor between relational and graph databases mirrors how we handle information processing: we store and retrieve detailed data as needed (akin to using a book or a database), while continuously maintaining a higher-level understanding of concepts and relationships in our minds. When deeper insights or details are required, users could 'drill down' to specific data housed in relational systems, seamlessly linking abstract relationships with concrete data.

Graph Database Options

For this book, I've chosen Neo4j as the graph database platform for the discussions here and in the sample code. The primary reason for choosing Neo4j is that it is the most well-known. Neo4j has been popular well before most ever heard of a KG. It's free to download for learning and its Cypher language is intuitive, in the same way SQL seems friendly.

Beyond Neo4j, the graph database landscape is rich and diverse, with numerous offerings tailored to a variety of needs. Some of the notable mentions include:

- ArangoDB: A multi-model database system that merges key/value, document, and graph data models.

- OrientDB: Recognized for its capabilities in merging document and graph models.

- Amazon Neptune: A cloud-native graph database service known for its scalability and reliability.

A fundamental differentiation in this realm is the distinction between a property graph (like Neo4j) and "triple-store" databases. Triple-store databases, as the name suggests, store data as triples: subject, verb, and object (SVO). This structure, "the soul of the" RDF (Resource Description Framework) model, is optimal for semantic web applications and offers a uniform way to describe relationships. Popular triple-store databases include:

- GraphDB: Developed by Ontotext, it is a robust semantic graph database optimized for linking, semantic search, and is W3C compliant.

- Stardog: A versatile database platform that can store data in graphs, documents, and relational models.

On the other hand, property graph databases represent data in nodes and relationships, with both nodes and relationships capable of holding properties. This model is more flexible and intuitive for many real-world use cases, as it can capture intricate relationships and attributes seamlessly.

Property graph databases like Neo4j are particularly well-suited for applications where the focus is on traversing relationships and analyzing graph structures, as they allow for more complex queries and direct manipulation of data properties associated with both nodes and edges.

In essence, while triple-store databases are powerful for applications requiring strict adherence to RDF standards and semantic web technologies, property graph databases provide a more flexible and accessible approach for a wide range of use cases, including those not necessarily tied to semantic web principles.

A close 2nd to choosing Neo4j as the graph database platform for this book was Stardog. My big quandary was to use what is the most well-known graph database versus a triple store that is natively in line with the semantic web. Out of the triple-store databases, Stardog seems to be the most well-known–but less known than Neo4j. It is a native semantic web platform, which is very attractive since I highly recommend following the semantic web standards for the KG. Neo4j is not ATTOW native with semantic web—more on that soon.

As this book is already very long and already packed with many different technologies, I didn't want to accommodate both of them in examples. Instead, I chose Neo4j because I thought there is a higher probability of the reader having familiarity with Neo4j. That includes me, as I've been working with it for many years.

Neo4j

Established as a front-runner in the industry, Neo4j has cemented its place through its unwavering commitment to delivering powerful, efficient, and accessible solutions tailored for graph-based data. For readers delving into the intricacies of KGs, the chances are high that they've encountered or will soon engage with Neo4j, given its ubiquitous presence in graph-related endeavors.

What sets Neo4j apart is not just its robustness but also the intuitiveness of its query language, Cypher. Cypher is often lauded for its expressive nature, which allows users to articulate complex relationships and patterns in a graph in a way that feels natural and logical. Its syntax, designed with the intricacies of graphs in mind, facilitates the representation and retrieval of data in a manner that mirrors the inherent interconnectedness of real-world information.

This makes Neo4j particularly suited for examples and exercises in this book, enabling readers to visualize and understand intricate graph structures with ease. Couple that with Neo4j's expansive ecosystem, comprehensive documentation, and vibrant community, and you have a platform that not only exemplifies the best in graph database technology but also ensures that its users are well-equipped to harness its full potential.

Neo4j's Cypher

I've mentioned Cypher a few times. So far, I have let it go as "the language for the graph database platform, Neo4j." But now it's time to properly introduce it.

Cypher is a declarative graph query language primarily used to query data in Neo4j graph database. It is known for its simplicity and power in expressing complex hierarchical structures and relationships between data points. Developed by Neo4j, Cypher is similar in some ways to SQL for relational databases but is specifically designed to handle graph data efficiently and intuitively. The key characteristics of Cypher are:

- Graph-Focused Syntax: Cypher uses a pattern-based approach to match and modify data. Its syntax allows users to express graph patterns and relationships naturally.

- Declarative Nature: Like SQL, Cypher is declarative, meaning users specify what they want to retrieve, not how to retrieve it. This makes queries more readable and easier to write, especially for complex graph structures.

- Versatility in Data Relationships: Cypher excels at handling complex network and relationship queries, such as social networks, organizational hierarchies, or interconnected data points.

- Efficiency in Data Retrieval: It provides an efficient means to query connected data, which can be cumbersome in traditional SQL databases—SQL developers will be familiar with the performance problems of self-join key/value tables.

- Compatibility and Integration: While Cypher was developed by Neo4j, its influence and style have been adopted in various other graph database technologies, making it a widely recognized language in the realm of graph databases.

Here is a very simple example of a Cypher query to find friends of a person named "Darlene" in a social network graph implemented in Neo4j:

MATCH (a:Person {name: 'Darlene'})-[:FRIEND_OF]->(friends)

RETURN friends.name

This query matches all nodes labeled as Person with the name "Darlene," follows the FRIEND_OF relationship to other nodes, and returns the names of these connected nodes (friends).

Of course, a complete walkthrough of Cypher (or SQL, MDX, Python) is well beyond the scope of this book, but the sample code that accompanies this code includes much Cypher. It's worth mentioning what seems to be the 2nd most used language for graph databases. Gremlin, part of the Apache TinkerPop framework, is another popular graph traversal language used by various graph databases, including Amazon Neptune, Azure Cosmos DB, and JanusGraph. It's worth noting that Cypher is probably the most used graph database language because of the vast proliferation of Neo4j. If you don't plan on using Neo4j, Gremlin is the best single choice.

RDF/OWL interface with Neo4j

As I just mentioned, Neo4j is not natively a semantic web technology. However, bridging the Neo4j world and RDF/OWL is the neosemantics PlugIn. This Neo4j plugin is used to load RDF and output RDF in a (somewhat) lossless fashion.

In the GitHub directory, there is a tutorial that is the example back in Chapter 4—Knowledge Graphs, Ontology Example. That tutorial walks through building an ontology using Protégé and uploading it to Neo4j. It also covers how to install neosemantics.

Optimized cubes

The volume of analytically valuable data is again beyond redundant computation.

Over two decades ago, optimized OLAP cube technology, most notably, the "multi-dimensional" edition of SQL Server Analysis Services (SSAS), addressed the scalability of BI queries, which, until then, were plagued by redundant query-time computation of large volumes of data. By focusing on the fundamental analytics pattern of slice-and-dice queries, SSAS pre-aggregated those large volumes of data, which drastically reduces query-time compute. For almost a decade (roughly 1999-2010), SSAS and other pre-aggregate OLAP solutions were almost synonymous with BI.

However, various factors pushed BI demand beyond what a single, top-end server (scale-up) could handle—the prime technology for versatile and highly-performant machine learning. Then came the invasion of the scale-out technologies. It started with Hadoop and the breakout of massively parallel processing (MPP) data warehouses. Then, on to Spark. The massive scalability of the cloud is the enabler of the last decade that shifted analytics into 2nd gear towards success in data-driven aspirations.

Earlier, in Chapter 6—Business Intelligence, I discussed optimized OLAP at a high level. Here, we'll dive deeper.

IT Manager's Nightmare

I know of many cases where an IT manager woke up in the morning to find that their data resource needs have grown a magnitude or more overnight. Those surprises include such goodies as merging with a much more data-intense company, landing the

"McDonalds" or "WalMart" of their industry, deciding to deploy grids of IoT sensors, or data will be captured and analyzed at a higher level of granularity.

I also mentioned the more recent unprecedented AI wave generated by the recent hype around ChatGPT. Until now, in my world of BI customers, the notion of AI has usually been an issue of "nice to have" or "we're not there yet." But the hype around ChatGPT will instigate an imperative for adoption. Consequently, that AI will unlock massive data currently trapped in unstructured data-generally thought of as the bulk of the volume of an enterprise's data. It's forcing all of my data and analytics colleagues to rethink the data use cases and infrastructures.

What does it mean when resource requirements suddenly rise 10x or more in terms of compute requirements and a commensurate increase in hardware isn't feasible? We look for optimization solutions. For this article, the optimization solution is an old friend—highly-scalable, optimized OLAP cubes, which took a back seat during this past decade as the world focused on the grand scalability of big data and the cloud.

Optimized Cubes Make a Comeback

OLAP cubes took a back seat during this past decade of big data and the cloud. However, the sheer volume of analytical data, driven by the sudden emergence of readily accessible and high-quality AI and the massive deployment of IoT devices will again necessitate revisiting this optimization technique manifested in optimized OLAP cube technology (but a cloud-scale version). Along with the continued rapid improvements in AI, it will shift data-driven aspirations not just to 3rd gear, but maybe fourth or fifth!

At such a sudden volume increase, the virtues of optimized OLAP will shoot beyond the "good enough" options for DW acceleration that are available in current data warehouse platforms (Lakehouses, Snowflake). However, OLAP cube technology alone will not be enough. There will be a need for an even further layer of acceleration—the catching of BI-charged insights and correlations, which we'll discuss very soon.

SQL Server Analysis Services and Kyvos

Our old friend, the OLAP cube is again crucial for analytical performance.

In 2013 I wrote a blog titled, Is OLAP Terminally Ill? I used the term "Terminally Ill" because I didn't believe that the strategy of managing pre-aggregations was dead. Temporarily unnecessary, maybe, but not dead.

To be clear, by "OLAP" (Online Analytical Processing), I meant in both contexts of the software named SQL Server Analysis Services Multi-Dimensional (SSAS MD) and the activity of analyzing data with the expectation of sub-second query response times. The subject of OLAP being dead had been going around for a couple of years in the midst of the rise of in-memory technologies, such as SAP HANA, "Hekaton," and, of course, Analysis Services Tabular (which debuted in SQL Server 2012). Additionally, Hadoop and big data were well along towards becoming household words.

To summarize that blog, my primary argument was that OLAP wasn't dead because there will always be a place for providing sub-second response time through pre-aggregation. It just so happened that the volume of data in 2013 was moving just beyond the easy reach of SSAS MD customers. That is beyond the capability of SSAS's Cube Design Wizard, where configuration of OLAP cubes became annoyingly tough for the poor data engineers. The new technologies offered scalable (Hadoop) and/or potentially easier (Analysis Services Tabular) alternatives.

However, today in 2023/2024, data volumes and variety are magnitudes crazier than in 2013. So, pre-aggregation must make a comeback. Pre-aggregation promotes sub-second response time and preserves very expensive compute time by processing once and accessing many times.

I tried to leave the SSAS MD world when I wrote that blog in 2013, but I kept finding contract work too good to pass up. Career advice: That's the making of a dinosaur. By 2016, I knew that I needed to fully move on to the cloud. So I swore off SSAS MD and ended up working for customers with very large, on-prem, data warehouses ready to move to Azure. But there were always SSAS MD cubes somewhere in my customers' enterprise that needed facelifts—so I would once again become "the SSAS guy."

We would always discuss the migration of the SSAS MD cubes to the cloud. But to what? Azure Analysis Services (AAS) was the most obvious. In many instances, the cubes were simple and "small" enough to easily migrate to a reasonably-priced AAS resource. The relevance of "small enough" is that AAS runs in-memory on a single server. So a cube would need to fit in the RAM of the server upon which it was deployed. Around the 2015-2020 time period, the most RAM available on an AAS (very expensive, high-end) server was roughly 400GB. With compression, that means a cube of a few TB was possible on AAS.

For options beyond AAS, there were a few roadblocks:

- Sometimes, customers migrate their databases to a non-Microsoft platform, such as AWS or GCP, and wish to stick to one platform as much as possible, which excludes AAS for the OLAP cubes.

- Having struggled with SSAS MD during the 2000s, some customers were tired of the seemingly outdated notion of anything resembling cubes.

- Many customers who had been in the cloud for a while had become used to the notion of "infinite scalability." So much for AAS's scale limits due to being in-memory.

Fast-forward to a few years ago, around August 2020. The Covid-19 lockdowns gave me time to think about highly scalable, cloud-based alternatives to SSAS MD cubes. I decided to write a comprehensive three-part blog on migrating from SSAS MD to some cloud-based alternative to OLAP cubes. I also intended to write tools for the migration, and I would offer guidance on several data warehouse platforms available on Azure: Synapse, Databricks, the various flavors of Azure SQL Server, of course, Snowflake, and even Azure CosmosDB.

After writing much of the blog text on the situation and background of the migration, it was time to update my research into existing cloud-based OLAP solutions. I searched for the key words SSAS Migration OLAP Cloud, and right at the top was a recent blog titled, Kyvos Launches New Utility to Simplify Migration of SSAS Cubes to the cloud. Oh … sh**.

I read through that migration document, watched a couple of videos on Kyvos, and looked at the leadership. It sure did look like a scale-out OLAP system, built for the cloud, with connections to many cloud sources, a good level for native transformations, pre-aggregations, dimensions, measures, and even MDX. Impressive. So much for my comprehensive migration blog and developing an SSAS Migration Tool.

I thought I would contact the CEO, Praveen Kankariya, on LinkedIn to ask more about it and tell him my amusing story. As I began typing the message, I saw we had already communicated—back in 2014! I recalled that he did contact me after reading Is OLAP Terminally Ill? Long story short, a few weeks later (Sept 2020), I accepted a position at Kyvos Insights as a Principal Solution Architect (FTE).

Kyvos will feel rather familiar on the surface to SSAS MD folks. It's not exactly an apples-to-apples comparison. Maybe gourds and pumpkins because pumpkins can grow to hundreds of pounds? After all, at the core, Kyvos is a scale-out platform, whereas SSAS

MD is a scale-up. Of course, scale-up means Kyvos cubes can theoretically grow to 100s of terabytes if needed.

Pre-Aggregation for Consistently High Query Performance

Optimized OLAP has been a cornerstone in data analysis for decades. Its importance is temporarily diminished not by obsolescence but by the allure of newer technologies. Cloud computing, big data, and in-memory processing promised solutions to data challenges, often by simply increasing raw computational power through bigger clusters. However, this approach, akin to "throwing more iron (and electricity) at it," missed the efficiencies offered by optimized OLAP.

The Unique Cache of Pre-Aggregations

Pre-aggregations are caches of computation. That is beyond simply storing data received from another device so we don't need to ask for it again. Pre-aggregation means we don't need to recompute aggregations whenever we need it—we just ask for it. That can be a huge service if recomputing takes more than a few seconds each time. Further, the additive nature of sums and counts allows for higher-level aggregation derived from lower levels, facilitating efficient matrix operations. This is particularly advantageous for queries that require access to arbitrary parts of a cubespace, a common scenario in business analysis. Unlike typical caches of computation (such as, cached web pages or query results), pre-aggregations enable complex computations in an accessible and simplified manner, ensuring they are comprehensible even to those without deep mathematical or data engineering expertise.

Navigating the Vast Cubespace

The multi-dimensional nature of cubespace in OLAP is vast and complex, housing a myriad of tuple permutations. This space is where answers to fundamental business questions are found. When users restrict themselves to familiar territories within this space, they merely scratch the surface, engaging in reporting on local phenomena rather than discoveries revealed from a higher and wider perspective. Optimized OLAP encourages exploratory analysis by offering consistent performance across the entire cubespace, a stark contrast to non-optimized systems that can falter under the weight of on-the-fly computations.

Big Data Systems and the Expanding User Base

Modern big data systems are capable of returning queries of millions of rows in seconds. Yet, the audience for Business Intelligence (BI) data has expanded beyond traditional analysts and managers to include a diverse array of knowledge workers. From consultants to store managers, the need for accessing BI data has grown exponentially. Optimized OLAP caters to this diverse user base, by mitigating the high-concurrency stress due to the higher query load in comparison to the days when BI consumers were just those with "analyst" and "manager" in their titles. By minimizing query-time processing, optimized OLAP reallocates computational resources to support a larger number of users accessing BI data simultaneously.

Kyvos: Beyond Aggregation to Aggregation Management

Kyvos should not be perceived merely as a tool for aggregation but as an aggregation manager. In the realm of database development, the creation of materialized views is a common practice to enhance reporting performance. However, managing these materialized views, especially in large numbers (it could require hundreds to match the performance of a pre-aggregated OLAP cube), can become a maintenance nightmare. Kyvos addresses this challenge by determining the most effective set of aggregations to generate and automatically identifying which ones to use for each query, a significant advancement over most data warehousing platforms where materialized views require explicit specification.

The Balanced Approach of the Dimensional Model

Contrasting with the fully denormalized approach of systems like Google BigQuery, optimized OLAP adopts a more normalized model, i.e., a dimensional model. Whether using the star or snowflake schema, this model organizes data into coherent entities, such as customers, suppliers, and products, enhancing accessibility and comprehension for non-technical users.

The Critical Nature of BI Data

While optimized OLAP may not match the functional complexity in the realm of data scientists, it plays to a business-focused crowd requiring information in the least complicated manner. BI data is vital for providing non-technical staff with easily understandable, operationally valuable insights. BI data engineers play a crucial role in transforming diverse data sources into a streamlined, secure, and high-performing format that enables knowledge workers to focus on their core responsibilities.

End-User Perspectives: The Persistence of Cubes

From the viewpoint of end-users, the concept of data cubes never faded away. Despite some resistance to cubes due to perceived redundant storage of data, processing intensity, and complexity, tools like Tableau and PowerBI continue to essentially present as a dimensional model, indicating the ongoing relevance of cubes in data analysis. Instead of data engineers building OLAP cubes for end users, the burden shifted to the end users to build local, customized cubes in their high-end visualization tool. This is a prime example of the shift from ETL to ELT, where the burden of "transformation of data" is democratized from a central data-engineering team to the many end users.

Enhancing Analytical Speed with Optimized OLAP

Optimized OLAP proves invaluable in the development of advanced analytical structures like the Tuple Correlation Web and the Insight Space Graph. It facilitates rapid querying and reloading of BI data, transforming processes that would take seconds in a regular data warehouse into sub-second operations. This speed is not just a convenience but a crucial factor in effectively leveraging BI data in a fast-paced business environment.

Figure 63 illustrates the main benefit of an OLAP cube. Items 1 through 4 illustrate how queries are resolved without optimized OLAP:

1. **Raw Database Table—Hundreds of Billions to trillions of Facts**: A DW with massive data points, in this case, 100 billion facts.

2. **OLAP Cube:** An OLAP cube which is used in business intelligence to store and calculate data across multiple dimensions efficiently.

3. **SQL Query:** Shows an example of a SQL query used to sum and group data, typical of queries that would run against a relational database or a data warehouse to generate aggregated views or reports.

4. **Crosstab Visualization:** Depicts a crosstab (or pivot table) view, which is a common method of summarizing data in a two-dimensional grid, showing data across different dimensions like regions and metrics, such as profit, wholesale, and customer count.

216 • ENTERPRISE INTELLIGENCE

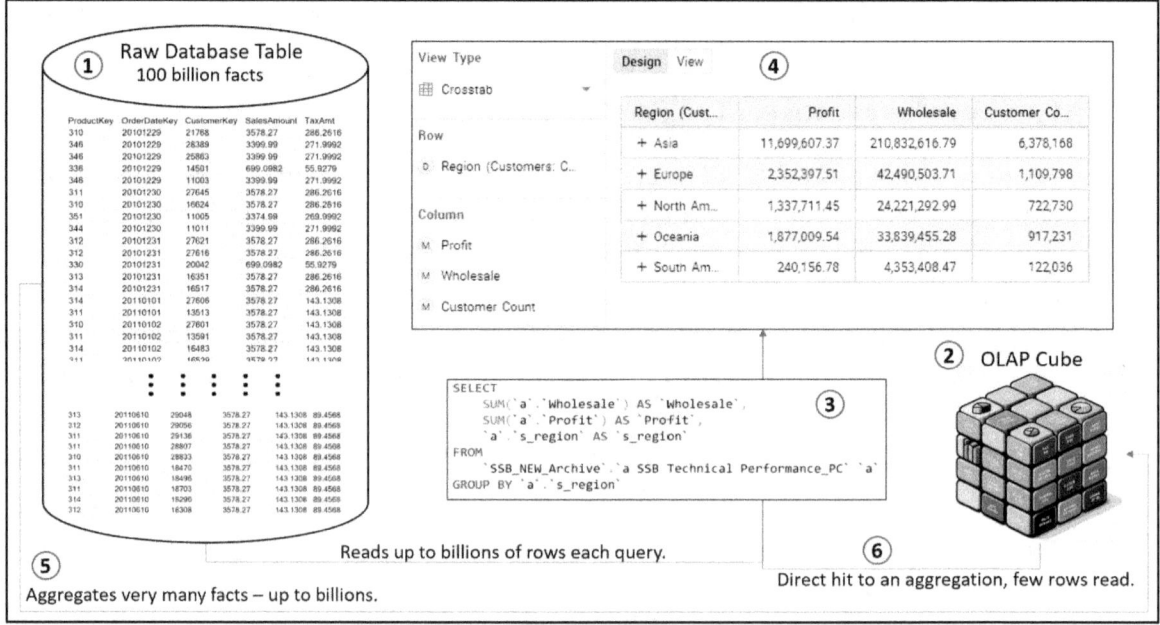

Figure 63: Pre-aggregation for query-time performance.

Items 5 through 6 compare querying without and with optimized OLAP:

5. Without optimized OLAP, each and every query runs the risk of computing over billions to trillions of rows at query time.

6. This time, with the query (2), we access the OLAP cube. Instead of computing Wholesale and Profit metrics on the fly off billions of rows, the cube already stores that computation and reads and returns just a few rows.

Pre-aggregation is the primary powerful concept that underpins the efficiency and speed of OLAP systems. Pre-aggregation involves the computation and storage of summarized data based on specific combinations of attributes before any queries are actually made—to avoid surprising query-time aggregation that might result in impromptu delays.

Figure 64 showcases a series of crosstabs, each one representing the results from a query to an OLAP cube. In an OLAP cube, data is organized and aggregated across different dimensions (highlighted with a thick line), such as Manufacturer, Region, and Market Segment. Each crosstab view is a snapshot of pre-aggregated data, illustrating how OLAP cubes allow for complex queries to be resolved quickly. Rather than calculating sums and other aggregations at query time, which can be resource-intensive and slow, the

OLAP cube has this data pre-computed. When a query is executed, it retrieves the pre-aggregated figures from the cube, dramatically reducing the response time.

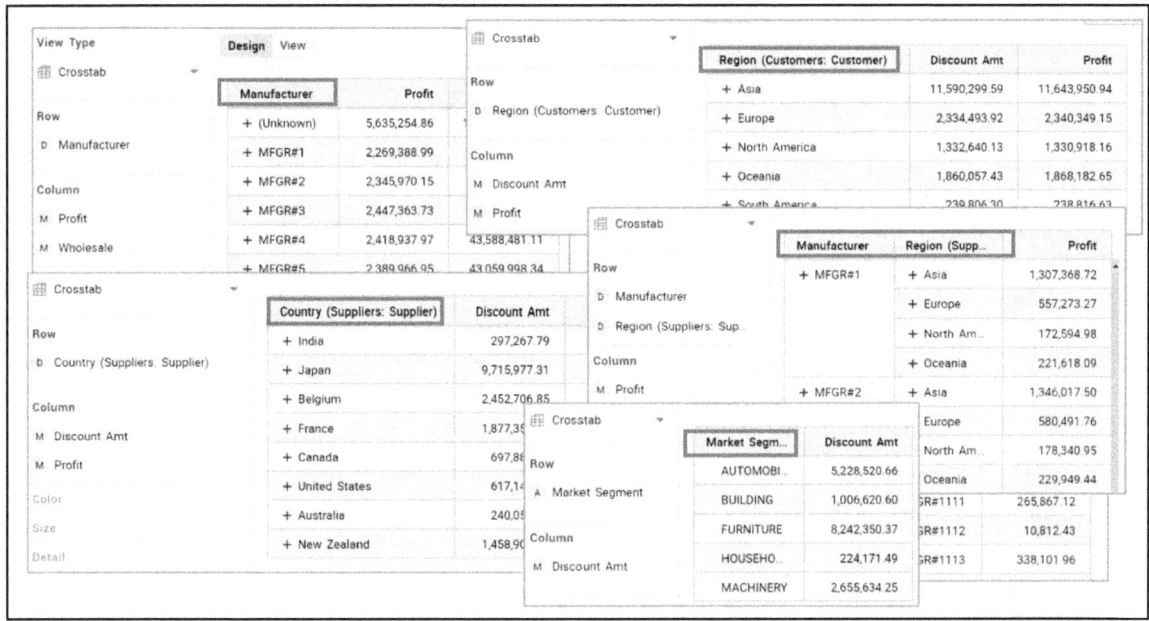

Figure 64: Explore all over the cubespace.

The different sections in Figure 64 (highlighted in rectangles) denote various perspectives or "slices" of the data. For example, one view may summarize profits by manufacturer, another by region, and yet another by market segment. These are just a few examples of the myriad combinations of attributes that can be pre-calculated within an OLAP cube. The cube provides a multidimensional view of data that can be explored and analyzed from any conceivable angle allowed by the cube dimensions, enabling business users to gain insights quickly, often with just a few clicks.

What's crucial in systems of pre-aggregation is the initial design phase, where decisions are made about which aggregations will be most beneficial to compute ahead of time. These decisions are typically driven by the common queries that business users need to perform regularly. Once set up, the OLAP cube becomes an invaluable resource, offering a bird's-eye view of the business's performance metrics and enabling prompt data-driven decision-making.

High Query Concurrency

It's one thing to talk about one query taking seconds, minutes, or hours versus a second or less. However, the real value of optimized OLAP today at this convergence of AI,

218 • ENTERPRISE INTELLIGENCE

massive increases in analytically valuable data due to IoT, a much wider audience of BI consumers, and an appreciation for a more holistic view of systems, is the enabled query concurrency it facilitates. Figure 65 illustrates that value:

1. A wider array of BI consumers, beyond the traditional analysts and managers, place much more load on BI data sources.

2. Querying non-pre-aggregated data warehouse in a highly concurrent fashion. The increased query load places a huge compute burden on the DW.

3. An optimized OLAP cube, an accelerated version of the DW, saves on query-time compute by pre-aggregating sums and counts. That saved query-time compute capability can be used to service many more queries in parallel.

It is argued that users generally query (explore) in roughly in the same data or cube space. That means that the caching mechanisms of the DW or non-preaggregate technologies will be adequate—no need for the added complexity of a pre-aggregate system.

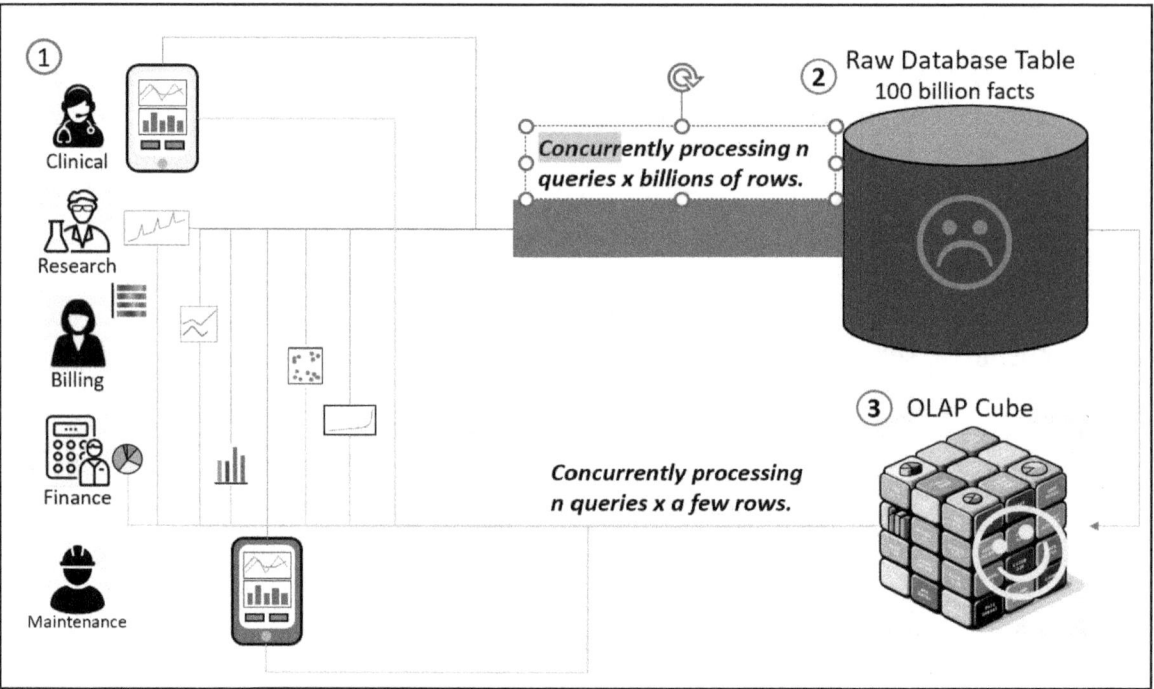

Figure 65: Concurrently processing many BI queries.

That could be true if there are relatively few consumers working on a few business problems. But what if there are thousands of knowledge workers working on thousands of different problems, each exploring different parts of the data or cube space?

The Two Extremes of Cubes and Graphs

In the expansive universe of data modeling, optimized cubes and graph databases emerge as polar archetypes of two extremes, each offering distinctive utilities and reflecting divergent philosophies.

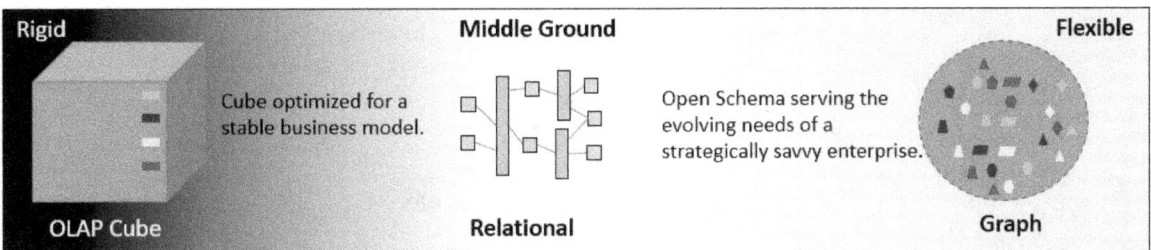

Figure 66: Cubes and Graph DB on two extremes.

The structure of optimized cubes is very rigid. This rigidity is not intrinsically derived from the dimensional model they employ, although it's this very model that facilitates methodical and systematic pre-aggregation.

The rigidity primarily stems from the exhaustive pre-processing involved in preparing pre-aggregated values. This heavy computation ensures that the cubes can provide rapid query responses later on, but it comes with a cost of lost malleability. Changes to the cube schema, even minor alterations, necessitate a substantial re-processing effort. There are workarounds to mitigate re-processing for updates, but they work under very specific conditions that might not always be there.

In stark contrast, graph databases champion the cause of flexibility and adaptability. They can be perceived as the pinnacle of the "open schema" concept—a design so intuitive and resonant that almost all SQL developers, across time and space, have independently re-invented it. However, implementing such a schema on traditional relational databases isn't without challenges. The primary hurdle is the surge in self-joins, leading to extensive random reading and a subsequent drain on performance.

Figure 67 offers a comparison of the strengths of OLAP cubes versus graph databases. Despite their contrasting designs and philosophies, there is a fascinating convergence where OLAP cubes and graph databases find mutual ground, especially in the context of incorporating BI insights into knowledge graphs. These two extremities, in their unique ways, feed into the overarching theme of transforming raw data into meaningful insights and structured knowledge. It's a testament to the cyclical nature of innovation—often, what seems diametrically opposite finds common ground, bringing disparate elements into a harmonious confluence. In this case, the fast exploration of a cube space by OLAP cubes hastens the amount of valuable information about the cube space that can be charted in the KG. This is much like "warp speed" enabling star ships in the Star Trek universe to chart expansive chunks of the galaxy--as opposed to spending decades just getting from one star system to another.

Comparison	OLAP Cubes - Kyvos	Graph Database – Neo4j
Structure	Very rigid structure	Open-schema
SQL Pattern Optimization	SQL GROUP BY	SQL self-joins.
Specialized Language	MDX – Multi-Dimensional-eXpressions	Cypher, Gremlin, OWL
Mad skill	SUM and Counts across massive facts	Inference across DAG of relationships.
Both Part of the Brain?	The strength of the synapse. Built through huge number of "transactions".	The network of neurons.

Figure 67: OLAP cubes and Graph DBs differences.

Large Language Model

For the crucial task of assisting in the construction and maintenance of the KG, the choice of LLM was pivotal. While a veritable zoo of LLMs are available in the market, each with its own merits and capabilities, I decided to employ OpenAI/ChatGPT. This choice was influenced by two primary factors:

1. ChatGPT offers a robust and programmer-friendly API, which facilitates the execution of programmatic processes integral to knowledge graph management. This API capability makes it a technologically sound choice for the project.

2. Perhaps more importantly, ATTOW, ChatGPT enjoys significant name recognition among the general public. Its widespread familiarity adds a layer of trust and accessibility to the project, making it more engaging for a broader audience. This combination of technical robustness and public familiarity makes ChatGPT an optimal choice for this endeavor.

A public LLM trained with an immensely wide variety of topics results is a centralized resource capable of drawing from and making connections across the immensely varied, heterogeneous, and complex real world.

The toughest problem with LLMs is that the training is very compute intense. At the time of ChatGPT 4, it cost in the neighborhood of tens of millions of dollars to train. As a worldwide resource, that's a bargain! It does a good job for most queries, but its intelligence does fail when I push it to cutting-edge thinking and, of course, facts beyond its famous April 2023 cutoff date.

The important thing to remember is that even though GPT4 is trained with data through April 2023, and we're well beyond that date, it's still imbued with enough current common sense to reflect our cultural context. This means if we spun up GPT-4 twenty years from now, it should still be able to understand what we're trying to ask, even though it wouldn't have knowledge about events since April 2023.

The compelling value of a LLM like ChatGPT isn't as a replacement for search. The compelling value is its ability to remove communication friction between people and machines (databases, BI tools, and AI clients). An LLM is more than a database of facts derived out of a massive corpus of text. It has been trained to be a versatile conversationalist, a step or two beyond merely the AI version of the "walking encyclopedia".

Lastly, for many enterprises, an effective LLM can be trained from far less data. That can mean being more selective by topic (choosing material from only the top sources) or perhaps leaving out topics that will not be relevant for a given enterprise.

Couple that with the growing options for creating LLMs from scratch (particularly open source options). It's becoming much more feasible to develop private, targeted LLMs at a "reasonable" cost—free from biases that might be present in any commercial LLM.

Private Vector Database

In the field of AI, balancing between the expansive knowledge present in LLMs like ChatGPT and the constantly evolving and private data of enterprises is essential. As just mentioned, foundation LLMs such as ChatGPT encapsulate a vast amount of general knowledge up to a certain point in time. After this training cutoff, they are completely ignorant of anything after that.

A private vector database is a powerful option for addressing this gap. This database acts as a dynamic repository, continuously updated with fresh, proprietary, or enterprise-specific data. While the LLM provides a foundational knowledge base, the vector database ensures access to the latest and most relevant information specific to an enterprise.

As a human analogy of how a vector database comes into play, consider an ardent fan who might have followed baseball for years. Over many years, that person built a deep expertise. He knows all the rules of the game, the history, arguments about who the best players are in different contexts, and the nuances of strategy. However, due to circumstances in life, that baseball fan had not paid attention to baseball for years.

He may not currently know the latest rule tweaks, new records set, players, or latest standings, but the game itself is still roughly the same. He still has an expertise in baseball honed over many years. Catching up is mostly a matter of studying facts that occurred since he last paid attention to the game. In a few days, he can again spar with the best of the baseball fans at the local pub. The sources that renewed fan might study to catch up (e.g., ESPN, MLB.com, baseball-reference.com) is analogous to the role of a private vector database.

This vector database serves a dual purpose. Firstly, it keeps organizations updated with new data and insights. Secondly, being a database separate from a LLM, it offers a layer of data protection, ensuring that proprietary and sensitive information remains within the enterprise boundary, used only for internal analysis and decision-making.

When combined, as it would be using Retrieval Augmented Generation (RAG), the LLM and private vector database create a comprehensive knowledge system. Queries are not just addressed using the data trapped in a time warp from the LLM; they're also supplemented with real-time data from the vector database. This combination ensures that businesses have both the depth of historical data and the immediacy of current data at their disposal.

By adopting this layered approach, enterprises can harness the strengths of pre-trained models while staying updated with new and/or private vector databases. This ensures decisions are based on a blend of broad, foundational knowledge and specific, real-time enterprise insights. The vector database can also be used to store:

- Intents—These are questions that could be asked in very many ways. Later, under RAG, we'll see how intents utilize a vector database.

- Path or Node descriptions from the EKG—Many types of nodes in the EKG will have a description field.

Relational Database

With all that said about the exotic database just discussed, the AEI does involve data that is best suited for a relational database. That is, any database with the CRUD (Create, Read, Update, Delete) and ACID (atomicity, consistency, isolation, durability) qualities we've known and loved in SQL Server and Oracle.

While graph databases are efficient at traversing and exploring relationships, they might not be as performant as a relational database when it comes to updating large volumes of data. This is partly because updating data in a graph database can be more complex due to the interconnected nature of the data. Also, graph databases might not always match the speed of relational databases for certain types of updates, especially those that don't leverage the strength of the graph model.

Part of the AEI implementation includes a relational database we'll call the AEIRDB (augmented enterprise intelligence relational database). Following are a few examples of the schemas/tables it will contain that will come up throughout the book:

- **EKG Analysts**—In the context of troubleshooting the EKG itself, we will discuss the utilization of this database further under "EKG Analysis."

- **Event Ensemble**—A schema of tables abstracting countless event types into objects, time, and locations. This is discussed in the "Events" topic.

- **Constants**—A simple key/value table for identifying constants. This table should be imported into the DC.

- **QueryDef Do Not Load**—A list of QueryDef hashes used to prevent Queries from uploading into the ISG/TCW. This table is used to mitigate the size of the EKG and as a security measure.

Cloud File Storage

The AEI involves a lot of text files in many formats. This means we need a cloud storage account. The text files can include:

- Prompts and responses from LLMs—LLMs play a big role in AEI. These prompts and responses are usually conversational text. But LLMs are very good with "computer speak," so they can include JSON, csv, or even programming code.

- Raw queries (SQL, MDX, DAX, etc.)—The raw, unadulterated queries of the QueryDef objects. They can update or even refresh/rebuild the ISG and TCW.

    o Object descriptions from the EKG.
    o JSON results from graph queries to the EKG.
    o ttl files used to build the KG part of the EKG.
    o Data catalog files (JSON or csv).

- *Optional cached* objects, such as ISG or TCW QueryDef dataframes (in csv or parquet formats) —If the BI consumer is using the EKG API, the dataframe could be temporarily cached in a "short-term memory" kind of way. The EKG itself doesn't store dataframes, only insights gleaned from a dataframe and correlations between dataframes.

- Query Intents—Templates for queries. It holds prompts, parameters, and a template of the query (Cypher, MDX SQL, DAX).

- Conditional Probability Table—Tables of Bayesian Event A and Event B probabilities. This is an optional method for implementing Bayesian networks.

- ML models in a serialized format such as:
    o pickle (pkl) - Python's native serialization format for ML models.
    o PMML - Predictive Model Markup Language, an old-school XML-based format.
    o ONNX - Open Neural Network–supported by many deep-learning frameworks

For the examples in the GitHub directory, any popular cloud storage account will do. It doesn't need to be fancy or expensive.

CHAPTER NINE

BI-Charged EKG Components

The robustness of a KG can be greatly augmented by integrating statistics-based artifacts from BI-sourced analyses that offer multiple perspectives and dimensions of the data it contains. This integration enriches the semantic relationships within the KG, making it a more powerful tool for inference and decision-making.

Incorporating these statistics-based observations into a KG in some ways resemble the neural processes of the human brain, where synaptic strength varies in response to frequency and patterns of use. This biological mechanism underpins learning and memory, which, in cognitive science, is often described through statistical learning theories.

Although the nodes and relationships of the KG are not nearly the same as the synapses of the brain, they share the quality of strengthening or weakening of the connections being informed by statistical usage patterns. For example, frequently accessed connections can be considered stronger or more relevant, reflecting the brain's tendency to reinforce pathways that are used often. These statistical insights, such as trends, correlations, anomalies, and patterns can provide a more dynamic and nuanced understanding of the data.

In essence, a KG empowered with statistical analysis not only maps out the terrain of knowledge but also tracks the footprints of inquiry across enterprise terrain, offering a richer, more adaptive map that is reflective of how the knowledge is actually being used and valued. This promotes the KG to not just a repository of information, but a living reflection of the knowledge dynamics within an organization or system.

This section finally describes the two structures that will incorporate knowledge held in BI activity into the EKG—the Insight Space Graph (ISG) and the Tuple Correlation Web (TCW). We'll explore other structures in future volumes.

Why Go Through the Trouble of Storing BI Insights?

The start of this major section of the book is a good time to review why I prescribe going through the trouble of building and maintaining the ISG and TCW.

The main idea is to passively capture insights that dozens to thousands of BI analysts have seen (or could have seen) in visualizations rendered from their everyday BI activity. Those insights, salient points of a visualization, are captured across what could be thousands to billions of queries consuming hundreds to tens of thousands of compute hours across dozens to hundreds of data sources.

In terms of our daily lives, imagine that after a full day of touring New York City, you realize you lost your keys. It's a bustling environment—you visited dozens of places and interacted with countless people and things. You couldn't possibly recall even a tiny fraction of the fine details you might need to figure out where you might have lost your keys.

Fortunately, our brains passively capture abstracted salient points about our activity. With those cached salient points, the volume of data is reduced to an amount that is manageable for your brain. Our brains have a lot of capacity, but it can't record every photon that hits your retina, every molecule that goes into your nose, every sound wave that enters your ear, etc. It derives and records abstracted salient points of each experience and associates them in time (what fires together wires together). With that condensed knowledge fitting comfortably in your brain, you might not need to physically retrace every part of the day in NYC to find your keys.

Think of it this way. If you are a YouTuber, you might have a GoPro on your head and recorded every detail of everything you saw that day. That video is like a data warehouse, a massive, raw recording of everything that happened. You could watch the video, but even at 10x speed, it will take an hour or two of precious time to pinpoint where you lost your keys. The more time that goes by, the less likely it is that you can recover your keys. And at that speed, you risk missing an important clue.

Today, an AI application could "watch" your videos, frame by frame, in a matter of seconds. But, like your brain, it needs to identify all the objects and notable properties of each object in every frame and how the objects relate to each other as the frames go by. The AI application is like the BI analyst searching through massive data warehouses for insights used to resolve business problems. The objects and their notable properties are like the ISG. The objects' relationships to other objects frame by frame (across time) are like the TCW.

With the salient points captured in the ISG and correlations between them captured in the TCW, we have a single source of insightful salient points (say that three times real fast) where we can obtain a breadth of salient points passively collected and semantically integrated from thousands of knowledge workers across many domains working on resolutions to all sorts of business problems.

Guided Exploration with the ISG and TCW

Navigating the vast and intricate realm of data analytics is venturing into uncharted territory. Analysts embark on these journeys, wielding queries as their probes, seeking patterns and correlations in a vast ocean of data points.

In essence, while direct queries provide answers, tools like the ISG and TCW expose stories. They take analysts on a guided exploration, spotlighting pathways illuminated by the collective wisdom of many analysts and knowledge workers. They transform the tedious process of combing through data into a journey of discovery, where even the bypaths and detours offer valuable insights.

Navigating with Intuition versus Guided Systems

In traditional data analysis, without tools like the ISG and TCW, analysts operate largely based on intuition honed through experience. While our capacity to draw from intuition and experience are how we rose to the top of the evolutionary ladder, it's a lot to hoist upon humans with limited time and only so much they can cram into their heads. They grapple with countless possible data interactions, unable to explore even a fraction of the conceivable combination of data points to uncover insights. This process, while thorough, is searching for a needle in a haystack.

The ISG and TCW shift the analytical paradigm. Rather than haphazardly searching an endless space or sticking to their same familiar territory, the ISG and TCW provide analysts with a curated map, informed by the collective experiences of a diverse set of peers. The ISG captures key patterns and trends that have been identified as significant. The TCW, on the other hand, showcases the intricate web of relationships between data tuples, highlighting correlations that have been deemed at least somewhat impactful by somebody.

The Value of Collective Exploration

The journey of an analyst is seldom smooth. Charting unknown territories often means hitting dead ends or encountering data patterns that offer no immediate insights. However, the very act of exploration, even when it doesn't yield direct results, enriches the collective knowledge. Today's dead end may illuminate a pathway for tomorrow. A merely interesting pattern now might offer clarity in a different context later. It's this collective journey, with its highs and lows, that the ISG and TCW capture and leverage.

Finding Indirect Pathways versus Direct Correlation

While direct correlations between two tuples can be readily queried from the data source when we know precisely what we seek, they're not always the most revealing. Consider two data tuples. A direct relationship between them, when queried, might appear weak or non-existent. However, with the TCW, we can uncover a more detailed chain of strong correlations between the two, revealing an indirect but promising pathway. This is the strength of the TCW: it showcases not just the direct pathways but also the nuanced, interconnected web of relationships, highlighting patterns that might otherwise remain obscured.

Following is an example of "indirect pathways" versus a direct correlation.

Imagine a company named "TechGlow" that specializes in smart home gadgets. Over the past quarter, they've noticed a sudden slump in the sales of their flagship smart thermostat in the Californian market. The immediate instinct is to check for a direct correlation between the product's sales and obvious factors like advertising spend, product reviews, or competitor sales.

Initial direct queries comparing advertising spend for the smart thermostat and its sales show there was a relatively strong correlation. An increase in advertising spending usually leads to an uptick in sales. But the recent slump isn't explained by a reduction in advertising. Similarly, product reviews have remained consistently positive, and competitor sales data reveals no disruptive new entrants.

Turning to the TCW, the analysts decide to uncover indirect pathways related to sales of TechGlow. They look for chains of strong correlations, even tangentially, to the smart thermostat sales.

1. The first tuple that grabs attention is a significant drop in search queries related to "How to reduce home heating costs" on major search engines. This tuple was discovered by a process that analyzes text from articles and blogs using LLMs.

2. Further exploration of this tuple in the TCW leads to a related correlation: a recent surge in articles and news segments about an unseasonably warm winter in California.

3. Drawing the connections, the indirect pathway becomes evident: The warmer winter has led to decreased interest in methods to reduce home heating costs, which indirectly impacted the perceived need for a smart thermostat, leading to the slump in sales.

While a direct query failed to highlight the reason, the ISG unveiled the nuanced relationship between environmental factors, consumer interest, and product sales. TechGlow could then adapt its marketing strategy, perhaps emphasizing the thermostat's cooling efficiency and eco-friendly benefits, aligning with the prevailing consumer sentiment.

Big Brother?

One concern I've heard about in regards to the ISG and TCW is the apprehension that the extensive capture and analysis of BI user queries might be "Big Brother" monitoring. The ID of the user that issued a query is tagged on objects related to that query in the

ISG and TCW. The intent is so users can communicate with other users about information the ISG and TCW hint towards. However, this apprehension can be mitigated by reminding ourselves of the underlying intent and functionality of these systems. The intent is to integrate insights across a broad spectrum of BI users. This integration allows individual users to benefit from the collective insights and experiences of others, enhancing their ability to address business challenges.

The goal is to create a synergistic environment where one user's insights can aid another, facilitating a passively collaborative and efficient approach to problem-solving. This is a significant departure from capturing user data for commercial objectives, as seen in e-commerce. Instead, the focus here is on fostering a shared knowledge pool that enhances decision-making across the board, making the process less intrusive and more beneficial for all involved.

In this light, the capture and analysis of BI queries in the ISG and TCW are not about surveillance but about building a comprehensive, user-driven knowledge base. The hope is to empower users with a collective intelligence framework, enabling them to leverage insights from a wide array of BI activities in a non-intrusive, mutually beneficial manner.

But the ISG/TCW still doesn't capture everything knowledge workers know. If it could, that's a mega-trillion dollar industry. But it would still be of great benefit to know who amongst thousands of co-workers to contact for deeper details and context.

Alternatively, for those who prefer additional privacy, user IDs in the ISG and TCW can be obfuscated upon request. In such cases, the system can facilitate communication by sending a message to the anonymous user, notifying them of any queries or discussions related to their insights. Additionally, data from user information marked as personally identifiable information (PII) could be obfuscated. Besides, it's already standard practice in IT to log database queries, mainly for security and performance optimization. This logging enables the tracking of security breaches through unusual query patterns and helps identify performance issues linked to specific queries.

Events

Events are the atoms of the proverbial constant change. For some types of events, the change can be almost unnoticeable, but the aggregation of those little changes can eventually lead to a tipping point of profound change. As an enterprise's environment changes (external and internal changes), those agents of change need to be modeled into the data analytics platform. That is, in a methodical way that doesn't result in the analytics system devolving into a big ball of mud.

Events are at the core of analysis and strategizing. They are what signal the perpetual iterations of changes to things as well as the subsequent responses to those changes. The world we desperately try to understand is a live, iterative, highly parallel, complex churning of events triggered by prior events and spawning new events. Events are both cause and effect. They are the result of the interactions of objects. Objects without events are just a dead, static picture of things, a world with no dimension of time.

In terms of data, anything with a datetime is an event. That includes updates to Jira tickets, web page clicks, sales of big-ticket items, the various steps of a manufacturing process, disasters, births, deaths, crimes, hirings, firings, doctor visits, name changes, IoT device readings, new laws, the release of a new product, etc. Can you easily add 20 more? Bet you can add 50 more after that.

But events aren't a new concept in the decades-long history of the OLAP cube world. They are our fact tables—the heart of the star/snowflake schema. Each fact table represents a type of event. Typical examples of familiar fact tables include product sales, Web page clicks, customer support calls, injuries, crimes, and package deliveries.

For any given OLAP cube, we are probably interested in more than one type of event. Most OLAP cube technologies, including Kyvos, are capable of modeling more than one fact table. For example, every prescription, diagnosis, treatment, and procedure at a hospital are event types. Each of those types of events could be a fact table modeled into one cube and linked through common dimensions, such as patient, doctor, and healthcare facility. The integration of those multiple event types leads to valuable insights that are more profound than what we could glean from each alone.

Whatever decisions we make based on information gleaned from our analytical databases and tools depend upon much more than a few types of events. Imagine a hospital forecasting the requirements for the number of beds, staff, and supplies for each day of the next few months. That's a critical use case! Genuinely helpful forecasting is nearly impossible just by studying the high-level events mentioned in the previous paragraph. Those few types of events aren't nearly enough to dig deeper or scan wider into the factors contributing to the combinatorial nightmare of "black swan" events that can leave a healthcare system wide open to disastrous results.

Although today we're used to talking about thousands of features (attributes and/or measures/metrics in the terms of the OLAP cube world) plugged into some machine learning models, we still think of modeling OLAP cubes with fact tables numbering in ranges of what is predominantly just a few to a dozen or so in extreme cases. While most cubes today consist of several dozen to hundreds of attributes,[2] the thought of modeling hundreds of fact tables sounds ludicrous ... and it is in terms of modern OLAP technology.

Consider the sample of just a few domains of events illustrated in Figure 68 below. I'm pretty sure these events more than affect the forecasting of resources in hospitals, but I'm also sure most hospital BI databases generally don't model these events.

Figure 68: A kaleidoscope of events that happen in the world.

How many additional categories of events not typically related to hospitals affect the operations of a hospital? Thousands of various environmental metrics, the emergence of new products on the market, viral media events, and disruption of supply chains, electricity, water, and transportation. Many of these types of events are the products of billions of IoT devices monitoring millions of types of events. All of those types of events can contribute to a mix of reasons for people ending up in the hospital—often in ways we can't imagine until it happens.

But we don't need to look outside of an enterprise to find an already substantial plethora of event types. All large enterprises already employ dozens to hundreds of specialty software application packages. They can be built in-house or purchased, or they can even be just a function-laden and macro-filled Excel spreadsheet. We're aware of the big ones used by many knowledge workers, such as ERP, CRM, and SCM. However, we're not aware of the dozens of specialty applications used by only a few specialists. Although relatively unknown to most, those "minor" applications still contribute towards the decisions of those specialists, which in turn affects the enterprise.

Concepts, such as data mesh and data hub, facilitate the ability of an enterprise to surface the information from those specialty applications to audiences (particularly BI analysts) beyond its respective domain.

Further, expanding audit requirements (logging all data changes), concepts, such as "time travel" (viewing data as it was at some past time), and "event sourcing" (updating change to any data as log entries as opposed to updating values) places even more attention on a widening breadth of event types.

Sources with a Plethora of Events

Following are examples of major categories of events. There could be millions of sources emitting many types of events.

- IoT devices—Every metric from an IoT device is an event type. As mentioned, there could be hundreds to millions of devices.

    o Readings—If the device is emitting readings (for example, at 10:00 am, it's 80F), there would need to be some sort of stream processing functions that generate events based on a time window of readings. For example, there is a big spike from the previous reading. Some smarter IoT devices could do some edge processing to emit an event instead of a periodic reading.

    o Events—IoT devices might emit events as opposed to readings. For example, smart cars might emit that a car was broken into, and a weather device in a field might emit that it started to rain.

- Counter Logs—Counters we collect from our servers. For example, instances emit readings of dozens of metrics to Windows Performance Monitor. The counter events themselves aren't necessarily "events," but as it is for IoT devices, events could be calculated from a time window. Such logs emit readings at intervals usually ranging from a few seconds to hourly, as do IoT devices. A difference is that such a source emits very many types of readings, whereas a typical IoT devices is simpler and would emit relatively fewer types of events.

- Traces—Traces, for example, SQL Server Profiler, are almost by definition events. It lists the typical trace logs where a process step starts and ends, interesting thing it sees, and component values at points in time, etc.

- Time-based Insights from the ISG—For time BI visualizations, such as most line graphs (the x-axis is date), we would notice things like spikes, changes in trends, or a step shift. Each is an event gleaned from BI data sources explored by BI analysts.

- News Feeds-News is almost synonymous with events: "Here are the events of the day." Today's LLMs can parse events out of news and social media feeds and even categorize them within any taxonomy

Derived Events

The event examples above are presented as "facts" that we would record in fact tables. Subsequent data science and ML processes will attempt to tie these facts together in multitudes of ways using various techniques and ML algorithms.

But practically no event is elemental. For example, a simple sale in a sales fact table is the result of a complex web of events tributaries converging into that sale. A move to another city doesn't just happen. What lead me to move to Boise, ID, of all places?

Further, that sale triggers a cascade of future events. Some of those future events will be planned, but most will lead to unpredictable outcomes. My life undeniably played out significantly differently, moving to Boise instead of, say, Seattle.

Some kinds of event types will be the creation of what is sort of unsupervised learning. That's similar to how cluster algorithms (ex. K-means, K nearest neighbor) take a set of objects and their characteristics and sort them into similar buckets the algorithm finds on its own.

For example, I'll later go over the inflection points of a timeline as an example of derived events. Inflection points are points in a timeline that indicate the start of a sustained change. As with how clustering measures similarity, there is an algorithm that determines when the timeline changes.

Granted, data science and ML processes routinely apply such algorithms. But the idea is we will record these derived events just as we record events emitted from IoT devices and sales registers.

Some derived events are defined by business rules determined by people. For example, a "Big Sale" could be a business rule that states it is the sale of an amount two standard deviations from the average of the past 60 days. Maybe it's a business rule as simple as meeting some threshold, such as $10,000 and above.

Whatever the event, we had to make it up. The creation of novel event types we were never directly taught is a critical component of our ability to make *creative and strategic* decisions. That is as opposed to simply reacting to what we are taught while the world changes and what we were taught doesn't quite make sense anymore. These derived events are of a higher order than what we think of as "facts" in BI.

The Event Ensemble

Generalized Schema for Events

The purpose of the Event Ensemble is to marshal countless kinds of phenomena into a simpler, generalized (abstract) structure. Events are actions, causes, effects, achievements of a desired state, or recognitions of something out of the ordinary. In more concrete terms, examples include are sales, visits, or clicks, hiring of an employee, infraction, firing of an employee, injury, or treatment.

Events are generally the change of state of things, whether one thing or a group of things. For example, a sale is an event marking the transference of ownership of the product that was purchased, the contents of the customer's wallet, the inventory of the store, the profit of the store, and the income of the salesperson.

The integration of a wide variety of events into a single structure enables us to perform powerful event-based analysis such as:

- "What Fires Together, Wires Together" Analysis - This analytical principle can help identify patterns of concurrent events across various contexts. For example, a company's stock price experiences significant volatility concurrently with an increase in social media mentions. This pattern indicates that public perception and news about the company are having an immediate impact on its market performance. Similarly, when there is a significant increase in website traffic that happens simultaneously with a surge in customer support chat volume. This indicates that as more visitors are exploring the website, they are also seeking immediate assistance, perhaps due to questions about new features, product details, or navigation issues.

- Sequence Analysis - This involves studying the order in which events occur to understand patterns and predict future sequences. For instance, analyzing the sequence of events leading up to the successful completion of major projects within an organization can help in replicating these successes in future projects.

- Time Series Inflections-Shows a time series chart that likely represents counts of events over time. Inflection points may indicate significant changes or anomalies that could warrant further investigation or signify events of interest.

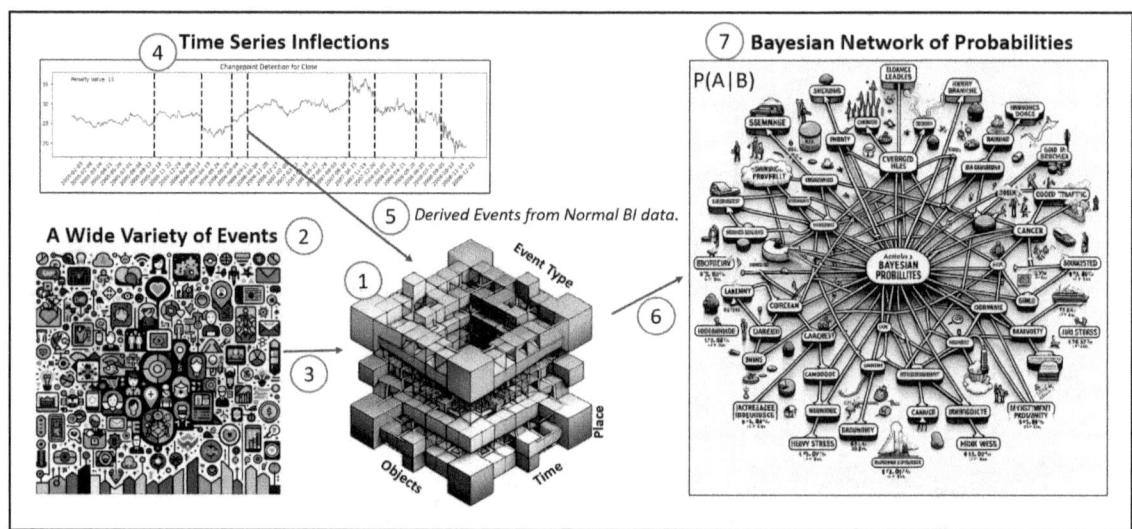

Figure 69: The role of the Event Ensemble.

Figure 69 Illustrates the high-level architecture around the Event Ensemble:

1. The Event Ensemble. A special dimensional model abstracting all sorts of events into common dimensions.

2. A busy graphic depicting the swarming zoo of events that happen in the real world, and what we hope to collect.

3. Events from the crazy world are recorded in the Event Ensemble.

4. A line graph sourced from a BI data source (ex. a sales cube). The vertical dashed lines indicate automatically detected inflection points. The inflection points can be seen as events, which will be recorded in the Event Ensemble.

5. Indicates one of the inflection points that is recorded in the Event Ensemble.

6. Events in the Event Ensemble are analyzed for Bayesian probabilities.

7. A Bayesian Network of probabilities is built from the recording of very many Bayesian probability calculations.

Together, these elements describe an analytical architecture where diverse event data is transformed into a structured cube format, which then feeds into probabilistic models to derive insights and predictive inferences.

The Event Ensemble is implemented as an ensemble of a fact table of consolidated, abstracted events, along with several supporting dimensions. The event fact table is kind of like an aircraft carrier, the focal point within a complex aircraft carrier group of supporting ships. There is the central player of the events and a cast of task-specific supporting dimensions.

Each dimension of the ensemble represents a primary generalized concept associated with events. The secondary details lost in the generalization of those concepts are the trade-off of using the Event Ensemble mechanism versus implementing a fact table along with their unique dimension attributes for each event type. We trade off domain depth for a "wider field of vision." Events happen at a time and place to one or more things. That covers the left three dimensions shown in Figure 70 (Date, Location, and Object). Figure 70 also includes a few diverse and color-coded examples of events and how the parts are parsed into the generalized event concepts.

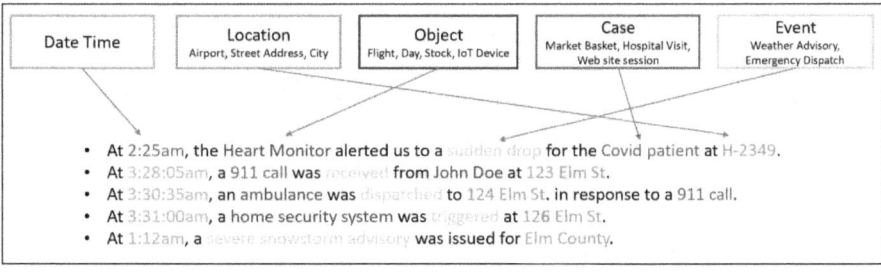

Figure 70: Events fit to a four-item tuple.

Figure 71 presents a schema of the Event Ensemble. It's designed to abstractly accommodate a wide array of event types within a single schema.

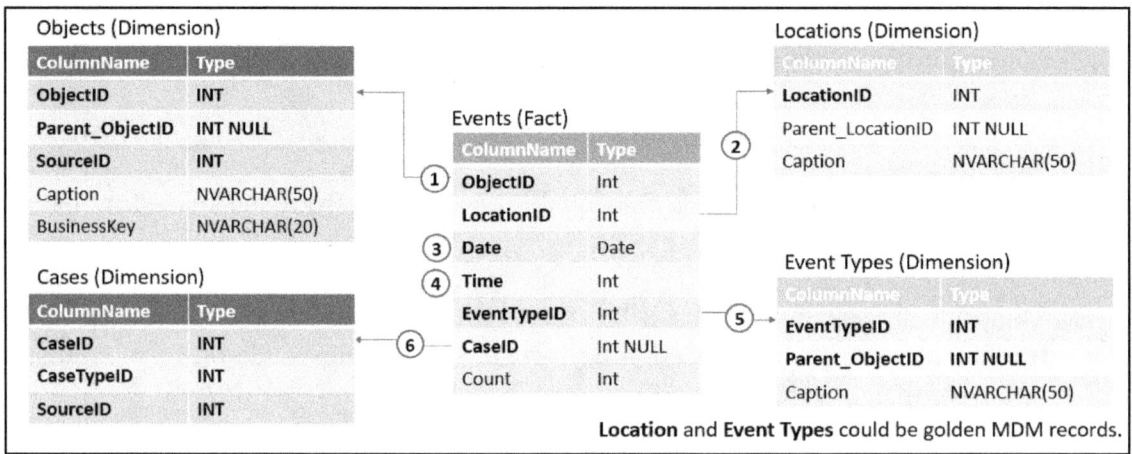

Figure 71: Event Ensemble simplified schema.

Following are brief descriptions of each Event Ensemble dimension as linked from the Events fact table:

1. **Object**—The primary object involved in the event. In reality, events involve much more than one object–for example, a sale involves customer, product, store, salesperson, etc.

2. **Location**—Location of the occurrence of the event. Everything happens at some place and time. However, today, an event could even occur at a "virtual" location, for example, in the case of a Web page click or a Zoom meeting.

3. **Date**—Date of the event. I mentioned earlier that anything with a datetime is an event. I didn't include the Date (and Time) dimension in Figure 71 since date and time (along with time zone) are standard entities everywhere.

4. **Time**—Time is implemented separately since with modern timespans, it can go down to microseconds. Note that Date and Time are separate because date and time should be separate dimensions.

5. **Event**—A dimension of the event types. For example, flight arrived, flight departed, stock market entered "bull territory," tornado.

6. **Case**—A group of related events, usually a cycle of a process. For example, a hospital visit is really a set of events that happen to a patient during a hospital

visit. Another example is a Web session, which consists of the clicks a user makes on a particular visit to a website. I won't get into this aspect now. We'll explore this more in a future book.

Those abstracted concepts are the things common to all event types. There are certainly a mind-boggling number of things that are not common among event types. However, the study of what is common amongst all event types can yield profound clues. Once event-based phenomena are discovered, we can subsequently drill through to specialty cubes for further exploration.

Event Ensemble in a Mosaic of Cubes

Although an Event Ensemble can stand alone as its own "events cube," greater value can be achieved by supplementing cubes built to analyze an enterprise's core domain(s). For example, the core domains for an e-commerce enterprise are probably sales and Web page clicks. For hospitals, it would be patient visits. Such cubes probably integrate fact tables of sales and Web page clicks, but it would probably also include supporting facts around marketing (campaigns, AdSense, GTM, etc.), perhaps even customer support and shipping events.

Figure 72 illustrates a core domain cube fitted with abstracted events from a larger number of cubes.

1. **The core domain** is made up of a sales cube virtually integrated with supporting domains--Customer Feedback and Marketing Campaign.

2. **The customer feedback data**, a subset of the CRM cube, is integrated into the core Sales cube.

3. **Marketing Campaign data**, a subset of the Marketing and Leads cube, is integrated into the core Sales cube.

4. **The Events Ensemble** is a specialized cube made up of abstractions of a wide variety of events from a number of other sub-domain cubes.

5. **A number of minor sub-domain level cubes** "integrate" with the Core Domain Cube through abstracted events.

6. **The ETL process** transforms "facts" from the sub-domain cubes into an event abstraction.

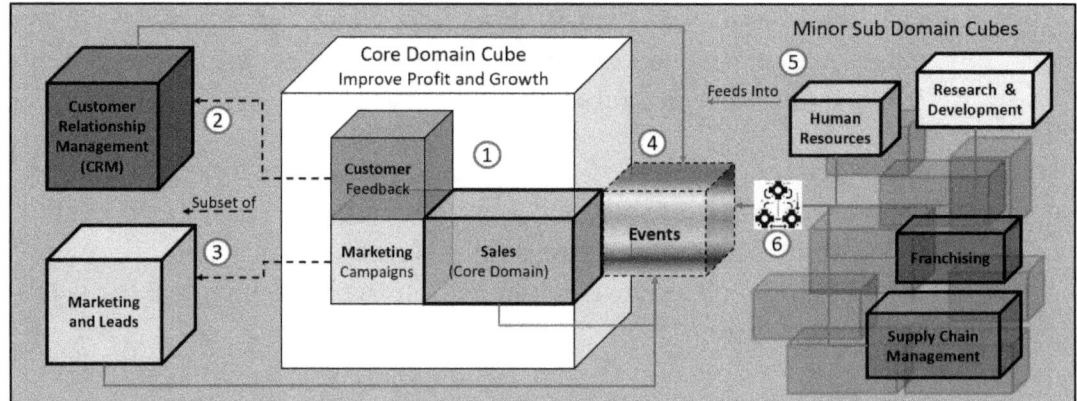

Figure 72: Event Sub Cube appended to a mosaic of cubes.

The advantage of integrating the minor sub-domain cubes through the Event Ensemble is that it offers a way to integrate at least some level of data from a large and expanding number of sub-domains. There could be hundreds of sub-domain applications throughout an enterprise. Fully integrating them into the Core Domain cube would be extremely unwieldy for users of the cube as well as the poor IT people who need to maintain it. In this case, only the CRM and Marketing sub-domains are compelling enough to integrate into the Core Domain Cube at a deeper level than events.

Event Ensemble Integration

To illustrate the abstraction of domain facts into abstracted events, consider this very simple schema shown in Figure 73. It is a simple subdomain of flight delays.

1. **Flight (Dimension):** This table holds key information about flights, including identifiers for the flight itself, the carrier, the airport, and the aircraft type. It's a reference table in the database for flight-related dimensions.

2. **FlightDelay (Dimension):** This dimension table categorizes different types of flight delays, each with a unique identifier and a description explaining the delay.

3. **FlightDelays (Fact):** This fact table records instances of flight delays, linking specific flights to their delay types and timing, and quantifying the delays. It serves as the central table for analyzing flight delay data.

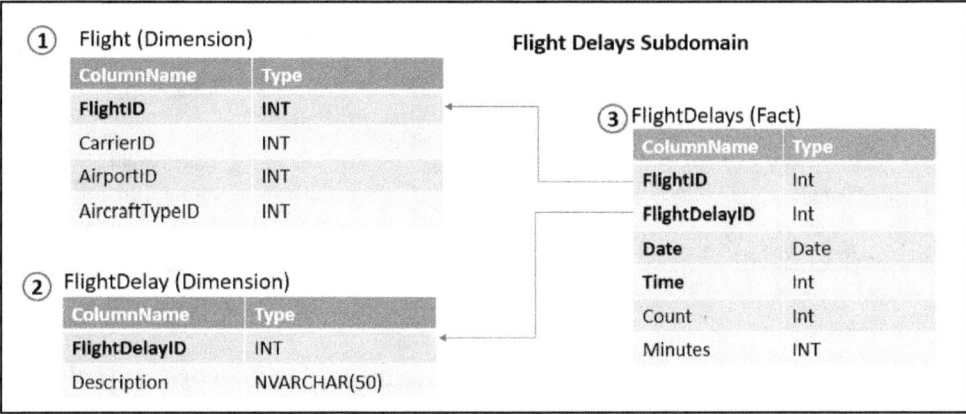

Figure 73: A simple domain schema.

The first step is to transform the concept of objects and locations from the Flight dimension table to the Event Ensemble. Figure 74 illustrates the loading of objects and locations from the Flight Delay subdomain.

1. The FlightID is the business key. It could also be the more descriptive alphanumeric "flight #" we're all used to—for example, UA240 (LAX to JFK).

2. The airport of the flight is used as the location. In this case, a table that maps AirportID to a LocationID is required. This table should be considered a Data Product.

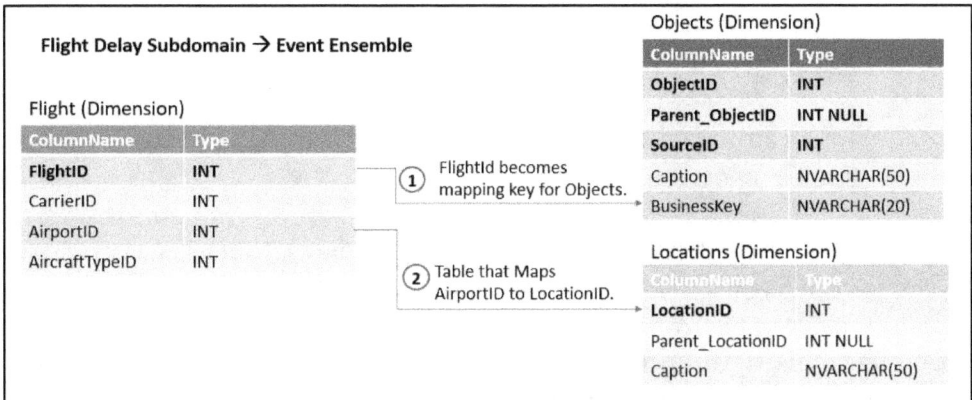

Figure 74: Map Flights to Objects and Locations.

Figure 75 shows the mapping of each type of FlightDelay as an Eventtype. FlightDelayID->EventTypeID requires a mapping table similar to the AirportID->LocationID mapping table.

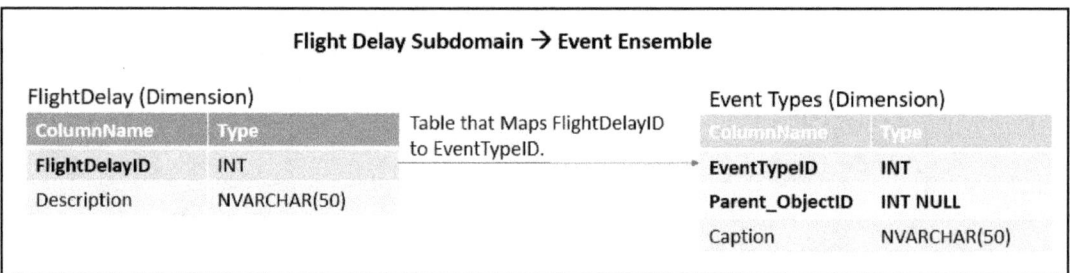

Figure 75: Map Flight Delay types as Event Types.

The most direct way to perform this integration is to copy transformed flight delay events into the Events fact table, as shown in Figure 76.

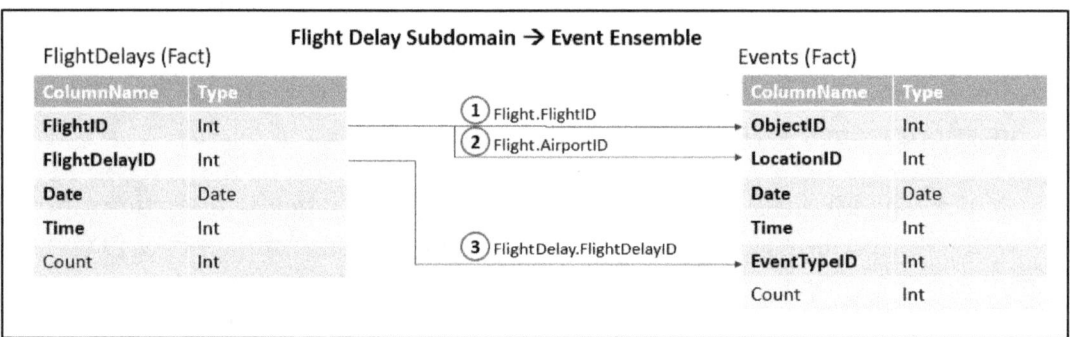

Figure 76: Map FlightDelays to abstracted Event.

These are the mappings:

1. For each FlightId, there is a corresponding ObjectID.

2. The location is the airport from which the flight originates or arrives, depending on the event.

3. For each FlightDelayID (type of flight delay), there is a corresponding Eventtype.

Of course, this is an unrealistically simple integration. However, for the scope of this book, my intent is to get the main idea across.

Avoid Copying Massive Numbers of Facts

It's an understandably disagreeable proposition having to maintain what is essentially the same data in multiple variations. In this case, all flight delays are copied to the Events fact table. Although this particular database isn't nearly as large as I'd imagined (as a frequent flier), redundantly storing multiple versions of very large databases adds costs and complexity to the system. However, combining that data with other events, such as a fact table of website visits for an e-commerce, an events fact table can lead to invaluably intelligent insights. Hopefully, the insights gleaned from the integration of flight delays with other events make the extra processing and storage more than worthwhile. Fortunately, as it is for the surprisingly small flight delays database, many event types might involve massive volumes of data. Another example of a database that is small by today's standards is the number of employee hirings and terminations. Even for a very large company, it isn't that high, perhaps in the millions for the largest enterprises.

On the other end of the spectrum, events from arrays of IoT devices can make flight delays or even e-commerce Web visits very tiny by comparison. So, we might need to consider methods for the virtual integration of events, so we don't store terabytes of what is essentially the same data twice.

The concept of virtual integration often comes into play with today's data fabrics. Virtual integration allows for the combination and use of data from different sources without physically consolidating it into a single database. This method relies on creating a unified data access layer that provides a single point of entry to an enterprise-scoped breadth of diverse data. The benefit here is the avoidance of duplicating data, which saves on storage and reduces complexity in data management. This approach is particularly useful when dealing with vast amounts of data from diverse domains, as it leverages modern data processing frameworks that can handle complex queries over distributed datasets. However, query-time processing across data sources involves many data sources with varying levels of access, query performance, reliability, and semantic understanding. This is actually one of the primary reasons for the emergence of a data warehouse. Data from across siloes are extracted, transformed (for semantic consistency), and loaded into a centrally managed database from which consistent access, performance, reliability, and semantics are resolved. To summarize, a compromised answer to the quandary of whether to hold multiple variations of data or to virtually integrate a single copy of data is addressed by the Event Ensemble. We can analyze robustly as a wide collection of events, then drill through to the more detailed data.

Event Storming as a KG Kickoff

Event Storming is an interactive and collaborative technique used in Domain-Driven Design (DDD) to decompose monolithic systems into loosely-coupled, manageable functions, which are particularly well-suited for microservices architecture. This method, focusing on domain events and bounded contexts, is instrumental in aligning software design with business needs and adapting to changing enterprise conditions. Event storming facilitates identifying key data events and interactions in order to paint an accurate and comprehensive picture of how the enterprise operates.

Similarly, in the realm of data architecture, data mesh takes on the challenge of deconstructing monolithic databases, typically centralized data warehouses integrated through extensive ETL processes. It advocates for a decentralized, domain-oriented approach, treating data as a product managed by cross-functional data product teams. Unlike DDD, where the focus is on individual functions, data mesh deals with larger, domain-level data products.

In the construction of an EKG that integrates BI information, Event Storming can be pivotal. It can help map out how business entities, workflows, and data interact, aligning with the DDD approach to understanding business operations. This holistic view is critical for developing an EKG that not only represents data entities and their relationships, but also encapsulates business processes and workflows.

Wide-scoped event storming is most useful on a greenfield project, one where legacy OLTP systems are replaced, in part or even in whole. In this context, legacy software systems are replaced by a microservices architecture. In a microservices architecture, the entirety of processes within an enterprise is decomposed down into a collection of independent but loosely-coupled functions.

Event Storming as a Periodic Sanity Check

However, an event storming session is a good exercise even without a greenfield project since it refreshes the reality of what goes on in an enterprise. That's in a similar way that memories of an old friend you haven't seen for a while persist while that old friend in fact has evolved, and you need to refresh the idea of who that person is. As a business example, this is similar to how a complete inventory should occasionally take place. Over time, items are misplaced, stolen, miscounted, etc. The only way to ensure we know what we have is to periodically count from scratch.

I bring up event storming in the context of the KG (ontologies and taxonomies) portion of the EKG. The KG is a map of the parts of an enterprise and how they fit together. That's pretty much what an event storming exercise is about. The end products of event storming are indeed similar to KGs.

Event Storming for a non-greenfield project may seem like impractical overkill. But I've been in so many situations where some gotcha (whether misunderstanding or ignorance) that could have been caught upfront seriously derailed a project. Obtaining an accurate model of the enterprise is the ideal starting point for any serious endeavor toward becoming data-driven. Event Storming is quite a topic in itself. I'm just providing enough to give you a good idea of what it is about. Therefore, I will gloss over the details.

It's important to keep in mind that this exercise is about discovering how things are working right now. It's told by the people who are actually doing the work. What actually happens "in the field" often isn't what managers and folks not directly involved believe. Things change over the time since a manager actually performed field tasks. This isn't about the design or reorganization of the enterprise. We need to map out where we are and then incrementally improve through the analytics system we're designing. Again, it's no different than taking a periodic inventory. Over time, what the inventory system says will drift from what is actually in the warehouse, and we'll need to take complete inventory again.

A Simple Event Storming Example

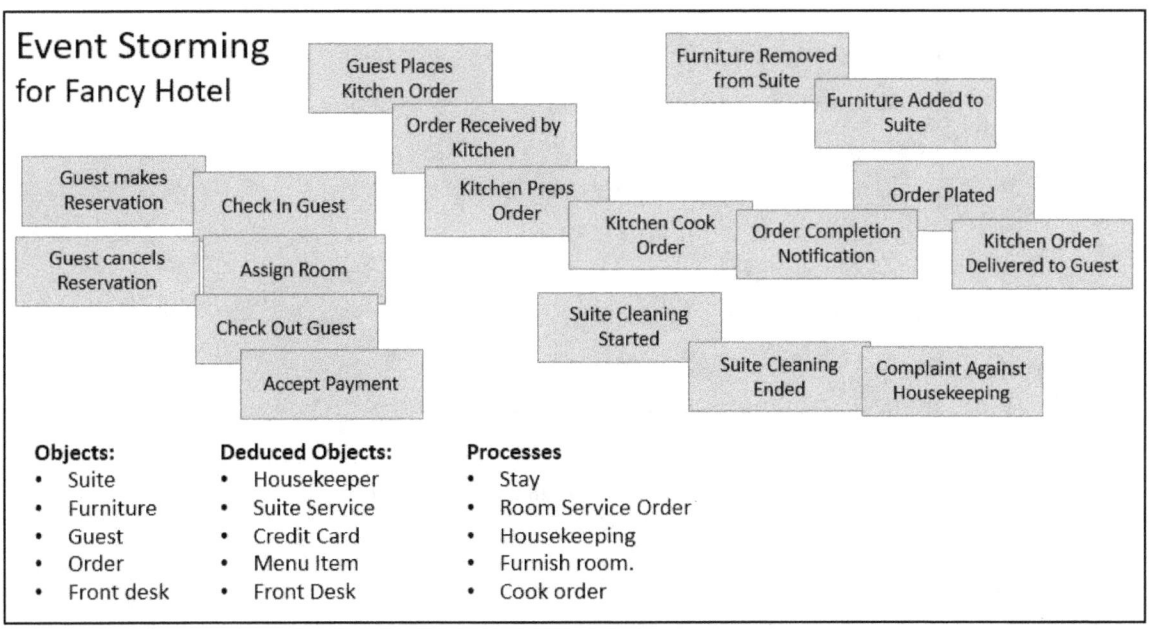

Figure 77: The recognized events from an Event Storming session.

Figure 77 depicts an event storming session for an enterprise named Fancy Hotel. It serves as the basis for most of the rest of the journey from event storming to data mesh.

What Figure 77 mimics is literally a wall in a big conference room where "everyone" involved in enterprise processes gathers and writes down, on PostIt notes, all the events (steps) in the process they work on. In other words, each time "I am given something to do, I do it and pass it off to someone else."

I facetiously say that "everyone" should gather. Remember, as I mentioned, what the "domain expert" in the office thinks is going on isn't quite like that out in the field. Conditions in the field change faster than the propagation of that change to the understanding of folks in the office. Those lagging little disconnects can make a big difference later on in the process.

By "everyone," I also mean people across many processes are needed, too. It might seem sensible not to boil the ocean and handle one major business process at a time. But hardly anything lives in a vacuum, and when one process tosses something over the fence, we probably don't know what really happens on the other side of that fence. What is depicted in Figure 77 is an unrealistically simple event storming session. A real event storming session might cover all the walls of the big conference room with PostIt notes. Here are some hints for an event storming session:

- List all events that happen in a business.
- Try to use the past tense.
- Try to phrase in subject-verb-object.
- Use the language of the knowledge worker.
- Think about the possible outcomes of each event.
- Each outcome is itself an event.
- What are the expected outcomes and the unusual ones?
- Don't worry too much about the order of the notes.
- This is a brainstorming session.
- The notes will be organized later by a smaller group.
- Don't get too into the weeds at this time.
- We don't want to spend inordinate time on a few issues.
- Business rules will be another step.

Notice back in Figure 77 that the event notes are somewhat clustered into groups—visit, room service, furnishing, and housekeeping. Once the domain experts have identified the events, the facilitators of the session—often business analysts, system architects, or technical leads—will categorize and sequence these events to materialize a coherent model of business processes. These facilitators are adept at translating the insights from the storming session into a structured format that can be further analyzed and refined.

Figure 78 shows how the workflows might look after being worked on by the facilitators. Notice the relationships between the PostIt notes, which form subject-verb-object triples:

1. Delivery Person delivers kitchen order to Guest.
2. Room Service Order received by Cook.

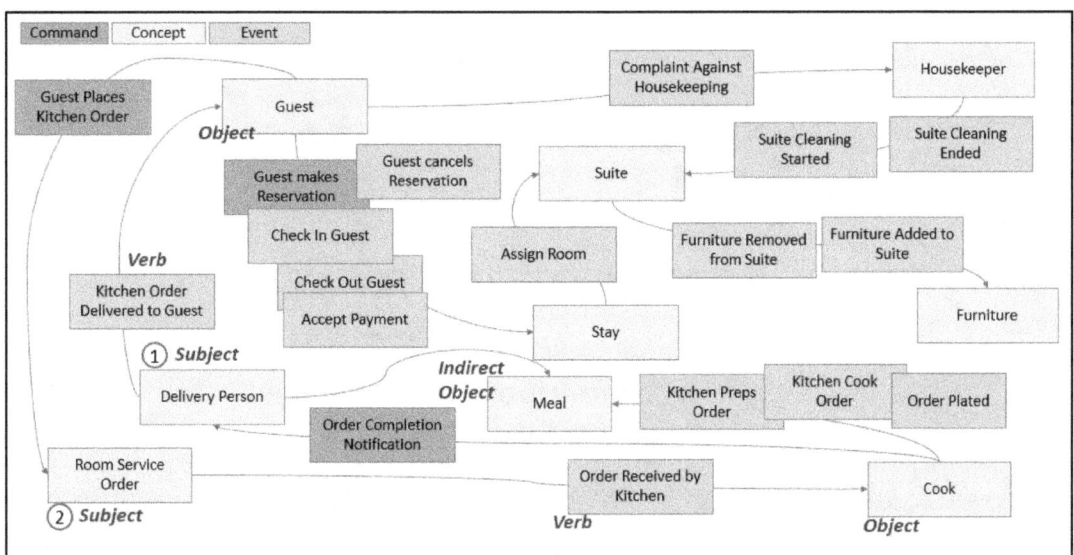

Figure 78: Model of events through an Event Storming session.

Figure 79 illustrates a slightly unorthodox domain model concocted from the event storming. Please note that Figure 79 is just a graphical visualization of the Domain Model for the purposes of this book.

Following are notes pertaining to Figure 79:

- Domain-driven design is the decomposition of a complex system into manageable parts, followed by a methodical and loosely-coupled re-assembly of those parts.

- Hotel with attached Restaurant is the Domain.

- Bounded Contexts are in the dashed boxes.

- A bounded context is the way things are grouped as a solution.

- A *Ubiquitous Language* is spoken by everyone within a Bounded Context.

- The thick solid line rectangles are the subdomains.

- Notice that the subdomain names are verbs ("...ing").

- Subdomains involve groups of entities.
    - Ex: Cooking involves chef, kitchen, and assistants. Waiting involves waiter, customer, and orders. Serving is the *core domain*.

- Cooking could arguably be a core domain.

- Accounting is a *generic subdomain*.

- Subdomains communicate with each other through consistent *interfaces*.

- Events are the communications through those interfaces.

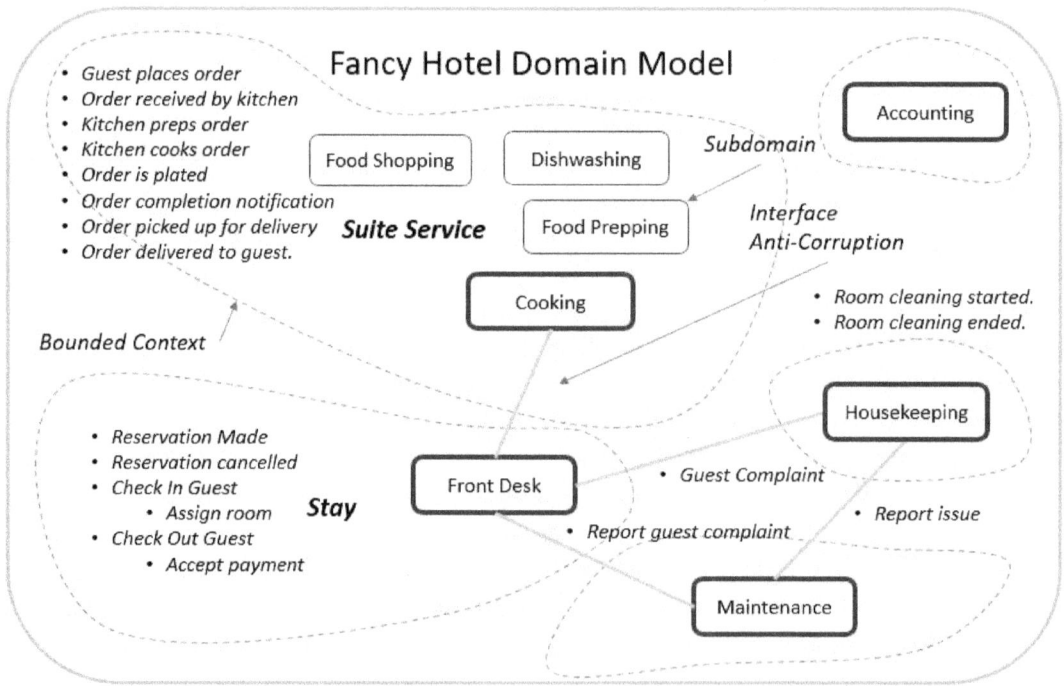

Figure 79: A representation of the Domain Model in a form readily understood by non-programmers.

Ask ChatGPT to Organize the Event Storming Session

As I mentioned, an event storming session involves very many more events than what is depicted in Figure 77. The idea is to "brainstorm" the events with all knowledge workers in the room at the same time. But after the session, the much smaller team of facilitators sorts it all out into sequenced processes.

The sorting of the hundreds to thousands of events is the most challenging. It's no longer an almost "fun", pizza-eating, brainstorming activity.

I haven't actually participated in an event storming session since before the release of ChatGPT, so I thought I'd give recruiting the assistance of an LLM a whirl. This is a good example of integrating LLMs into the process of creating the EKG. It's a good exercise for creating ontologies back in the Graph Databases section of the Architecture Chapter.

Figure 80 is the prompt I sent to ChatGPT. ChatGPT's ability to read and comprehend an image is relatively new. In reality, you'd probably submit a list of events that you'd at least roughly organize. At this point, just throwing a pile of PostIt notes (metaphorically) at ChatGPT will be a frustrating experience.

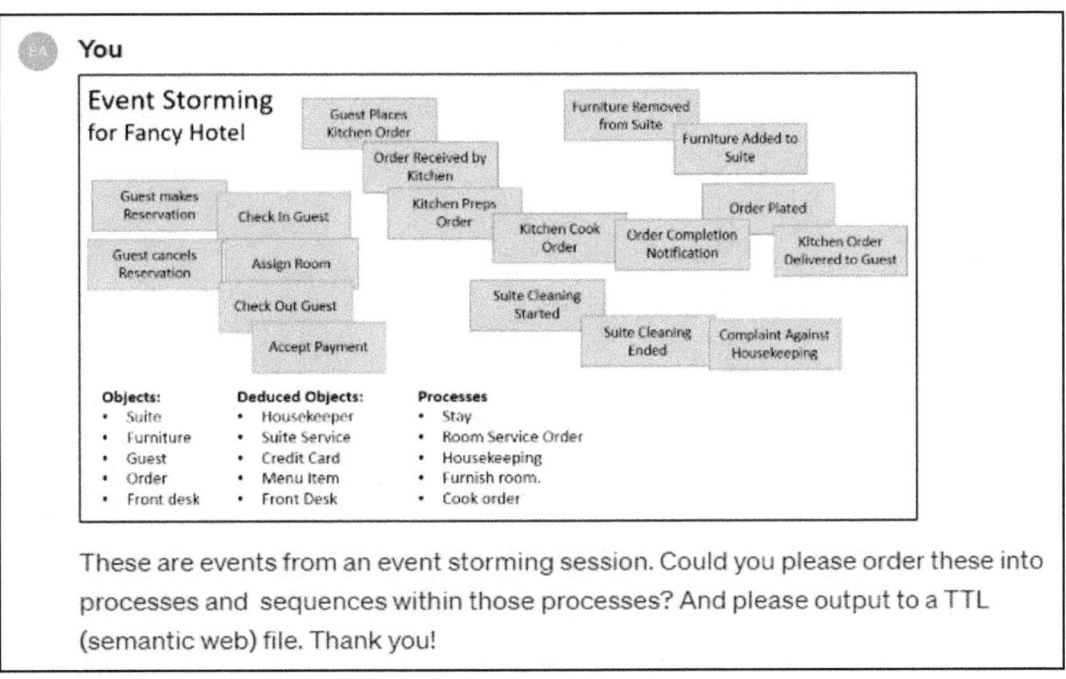

Figure 80: Prompt to ChatGPT with the image.

You would need to add more instructions, such as the prefixes and types used for the events in the ttl file.

ChatGPT returned a ttl file, which I'd save to a file I'll name hotel_event_storming.ttl, then execute this code in Neo4j:

CALL n10s.graphconfig.init({ handleVocabUris: "IGNORE" });

CALL n10s.graphconfig.set({

  classLabel: "SHORTEN,"

  propertyLabel: "SHORTEN,"

  relationshipType: "SHORTEN"

}) YIELD param, value

RETURN param, value;

CALL n10s.rdf.import.fetch('file:///c:/temp/hotel_event_storming.ttl', 'Turtle');

Figure 81 shows how it looks after I imported it into the EKG.

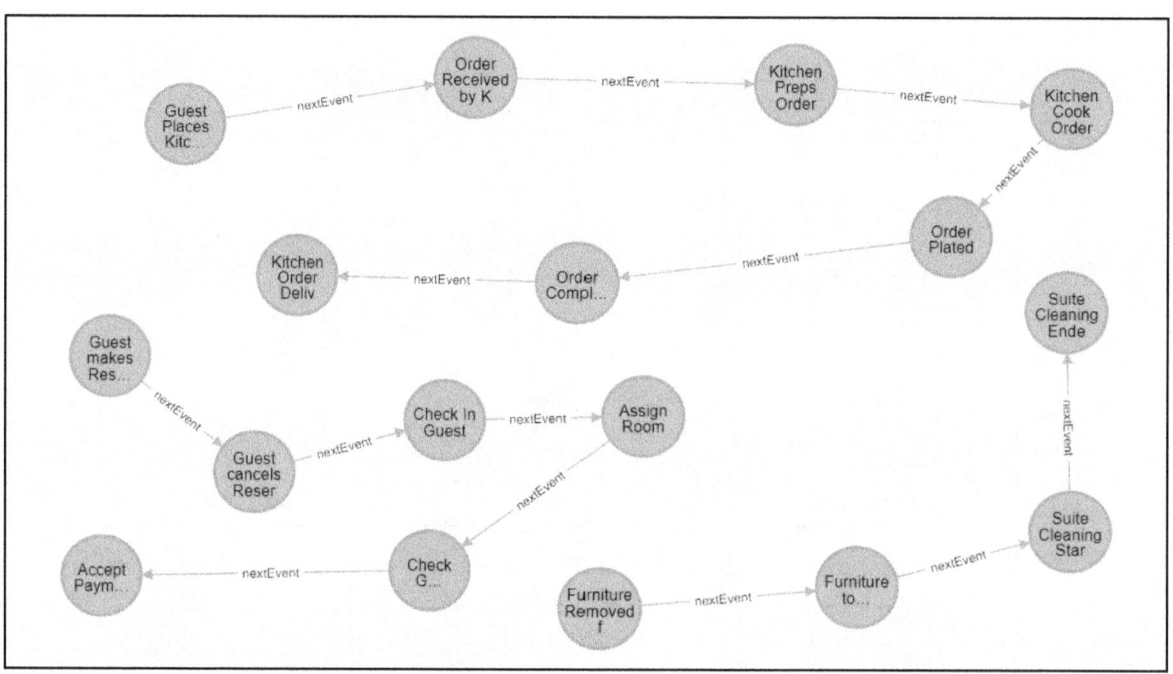

Figure 81: Appearance of the events in the EKG.

Note that ChatGPT did sort out the events into three processes correctly. While the process for a guest isn't really sequential (guest probably will not cancel their reservation), ChatGPT's work is close enough where it's a very helpful start. Minor editing of the ttl in Protégé and reloading into the EKG will fix that.

Rare Events and Risk Management

For the TCW to work with Pearson correlations and Bayesian probabilities, the events or metrics must be built from frequent events (sales, visits, Web page clicks) which occur in the millions to trillions. However, rare events like the Iceland volcanic eruption are tough to correlate because eruptions from that volcano of that magnitude are rare. We can't even aggregate eruptions of that magnitude across all volcanoes because volcanos are in very different places and can have different effects-and large eruptions across all volcanos is still rare. We can't even aggregate them with many different types of natural disasters because all of them have different properties.

Nonetheless, natural disasters are events with far-reaching impact. The Iceland volcanic eruption is an outlier. The meteor that killed the dinosaurs is an outlier. But they can't really be ignored. For example, there are countless meteors that fall to earth unnoticed by all but rockhounds. But outliers can come with widespread, significant, and long-lasting effects—like the meteor that killed off the dinosaurs. However, such impactful rare events must somehow be incorporated into the event scheme. Such big disasters affect any business, from a street food cart to McDonald's. So, in the EKG, we could at least add the effects and mitigation that such a disaster might have on our enterprise. That can be tedious, but LLMs can be a great help in mitigating that tedium. Figure 82 is a prompt I submitted to ChatGPT to test how good it is at helping me create a list of effects and mitigation strategies in the event of a rare event. In this case, a massive volcanic eruption.

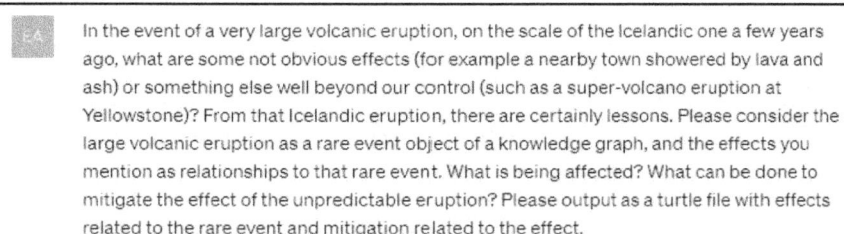

Figure 82: Example of a prompt to ponder the possible effects of a rare event.

ChatGPT returned a pretty good starting ontology, as shown in Figure 83. The ontology depicts the relationships between the effects of a "Large Volcanic Eruption," a rare event, and the subsequent mitigation strategies.

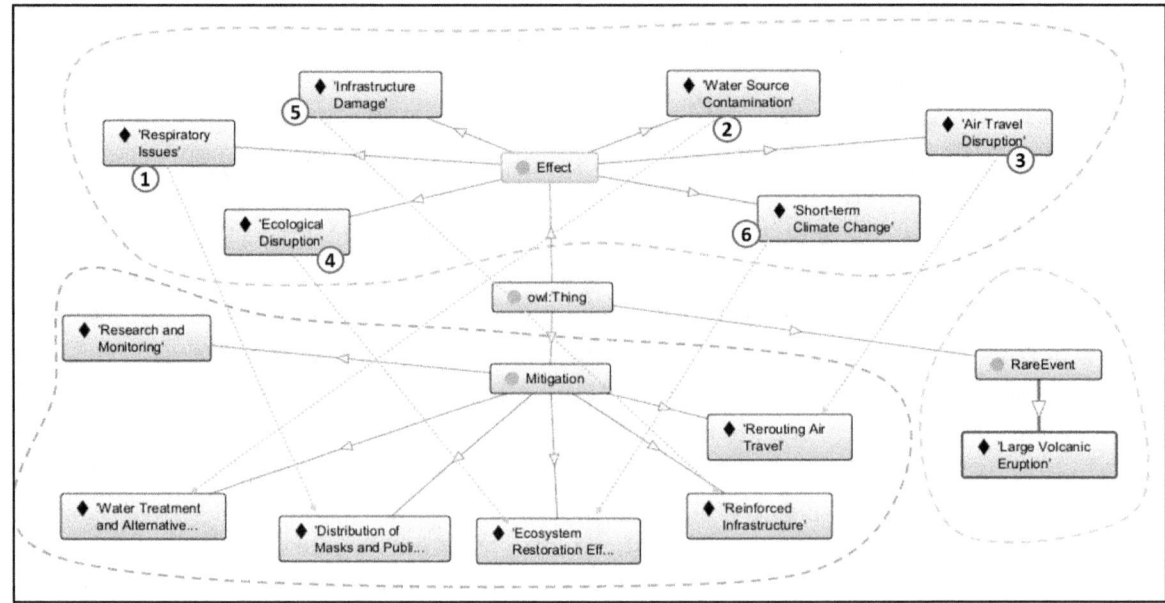

Figure 83: Rare Events, Effects, and Mitigations drafted by ChatGPT.

Here are the intended pairs of effects and its respective mitigation ChatGPT created, as numbered in Figure 83:

1. Respiratory Issues–Distribution of Masks and Public Health Information: As volcanic eruptions can release ash and harmful gases, causing respiratory problems, distributing masks and providing public health information is a mitigation strategy to protect the population's health.

2. Water Source Contamination–Water Treatment and Alternative Sources: Volcanic eruptions can contaminate water sources with ash and chemicals. Implementing water treatment solutions and identifying alternative water sources can mitigate this effect.

3. Air Travel Disruption–Rerouting Air Travel: The ash clouds from volcanic eruptions can lead to air travel disruption. Rerouting flights is a mitigation measure to avoid ash clouds and maintain the safety of air travel.

4. Ecological Disruption–Ecosystem Restoration Efforts: The eruption can disrupt local ecosystems. Mitigation includes restoration efforts to help the environment recover.

5. Infrastructure Damage–Reinforced Infrastructure: To mitigate the damage caused by eruptions to infrastructure, existing structures can be reinforced, and new, more resilient infrastructure can be built.

6. Short-term Climate Change–Research and Monitoring: The release of large amounts of volcanic ash and gases can affect climate patterns. Through research and continuous monitoring, better predictions and preparations can be made to mitigate these climate effects.

This same method for accentuating both the events table and the KG could be used for other classes of major events, such as the Gulf Oil Spill, Fukushima, and any other impactful events. But we need to differentiate rare events from black swan events. For one, something we call a rare event is generally something we might have seen before or at least theorize has happened.

Black swan events are rare events, usually unprecedented, but always phenomenally unexpected. They are often a combination of many minor events that are individually somewhat benign and unnoticed. Nassim Taleb talks about the hockey stick, which is actually more prevalent in real life than linear relationships. The danger of such hockey stick curves is that the metric suddenly rises very rapidly rattling other sensitive metrics.

The main characteristic of a black swan event is that it has an outsized effect. I tend to think the earthquake that caused Fukushima as a black swan event—we know tsunamis happen, but the radiation leak is probably the result of many little details that added up to the leak—and it has an outsized effect. But a preventable hospital death is a result of many details no one thought of happening together, and therefore, the hospital didn't prepare for it. All preventable deaths have an outsized effect.

The true nature of Black Swan events, as described by Taleb, is that they are inherently unpredictable. While our analytic systems might be able to provide some warning or indication of vague increased risks, they can never predict Black Swans with certainty. The goal would be more about risk management and preparedness than accurate prediction.

For black swan events, such as a potential unintended death at a hospital (I would hope the causes for unintended deaths at hospitals are all one-offs), the EKG might substantially help in discovering and assessing the likelihood of potential black swan events by noticing chains of strong correlations.

The Insight Space Graph

The workings of the human brain offer a striking analogy to the ISG's architecture and functions in the realm of knowledge management. Our brains have an astounding capacity, but to effectively operate within the vastness of our experiences, they lean heavily on abstraction. Rather than retain every minute detail of our daily lives, the brain derives generalized patterns, storing essential, broad-stroke concepts that make memory and cognition manageable. However, when the situation demands, we're adept at diving deep, zooming into the particulars, available in the physical world—whether it's consulting another person or referring to recorded knowledge.

In many ways, the ISG mirrors that intricate toggling between abstraction and detail. Consider the sensory inputs—visual, auditory, tactile—that funnel into our brain, going through layered processing akin to an ETL's series of transformations. Similarly, the ISG takes raw data and, through a series of functions, derives abstracted insights. These insights, such as "trend up" in a line graph, serve as the synthesized, higher-order understanding of the raw data, just as our abstracted memories represent richer life experiences.

When required, much like our ability to dive deep into details by consulting experts or referring to texts, the ISG points to its source data. If we have the blueprint of the dataframe's origin, we can rehydrate it, inspect it through varied visualizations, or even delve into its foundational data.

The ISG's connections to other components of the EKG (the KG, DC, and TCW) further enrich its utility. By mapping dataframe columns to the DC and further linking them to other knowledge nodes, the ISG is an intricate web of interrelations. For instance, the column "Occupation" doesn't just exist in isolation—it ties back to broader concepts like "job" and "employee," offering layers of contextual understanding. This elegant symphony of abstracted insights and the potential for detail retrieval validate the ISG's integral role in knowledge graph structures. If our brain's efficiency in abstraction and depth-seeking serves as a benchmark, the ISG, in its emulation, positions itself as a robust tool for knowledge representation and management.

At the time of this writing, where mindshare is dominated by probabilistic LLMs and ML models, recall that the ISG is built from well-defined from highly-curated data that is distilled from cleansed and factual databases. Leveraging the insights gleaned from BI users as a component within the wider-scoped EKG, which can contain subjective data from human experts or an AI, the ISG creates a safe zone of deterministic and trustworthy values. Figure 84 illustrates the top-level schema of the ISG. The schema is a framework that captures the essence of the bread and butter, slice and dice class of query of traditional BI activity. Capturing this dominant BI pattern (which is like a SQL GROUP BY) with this schema mitigates the complexity of the ISG.

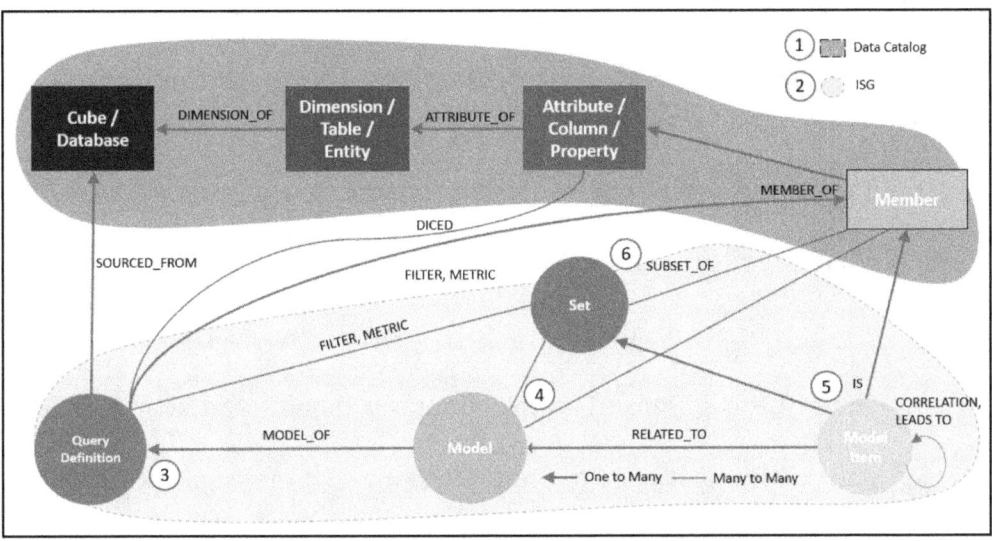

Figure 84: ISG high-level schema in the EKG.

Following are descriptions of the numbered items:

1. The nodes within the blue (darker shade) area represent the data catalog.

2. The nodes within the light yellow (lighter shade) area belong to the ISG. Note how the ISG nodes link to various DC nodes.

3. The primary element type is the Query Definition (QueryDef). Mostly, it represents a typical BI slice and dice query—usually the actual SQL used to query the data filling the BI visualizations.

4. Each QueryDef can be associated with zero or more models. The simplest model is the "Standard Statistics" model. Each model can be associated with sets of members, members directly, or a model item.

5. Each Model can be associated with zero or more Model items.

6. Sets are "sets of members." Model items might refer to one member or involve many members, which are grouped into a set just in case the set can be used elsewhere.

The QueryDef Object

The QueryDef is the central class of character of the ISG. It represents a typical BI query. The typical lifecycle looks like this:

1. It starts out as a BI query to a data source by a BI analyst through Tableau.

2. Tableau constructs a SQL statement that is submitted to the database.

3. It is executed on a database and a result is returned.

4. The result is serialized on the client in a dataframe-like format.

5. The dataframe is used to populate some sort of visualization, such as a bar chart or line graph.

6. The BI analyst studies the visualization, noting anything that is helpful to her.

That is usually the end of the query's life. Eventually, the visualization is closed, and the dataframe vaporizes. All that is left is the memory of whatever the analyst might have noticed. However, as Figure 85 suggests, the ISG offers the query a form of afterlife. Any insights that the dataframe held are "noted" and stored in the ISG. These insights are abstractions of the data. For this book, each unique query becomes a QueryDef node. By "unique," I mean that the actual query (SQL, MDX) is textually the same–meaning the same character by character. The unique identifier of a QueryDef is a hash of the SQL. Figure 85 illustrates that process.

That hash is used throughout the system. For example:

- The raw SQL statement is stored in a directory for future reference in a file named *hash*.sql.

- Queries to the ISG might return a column of QueryHash values.

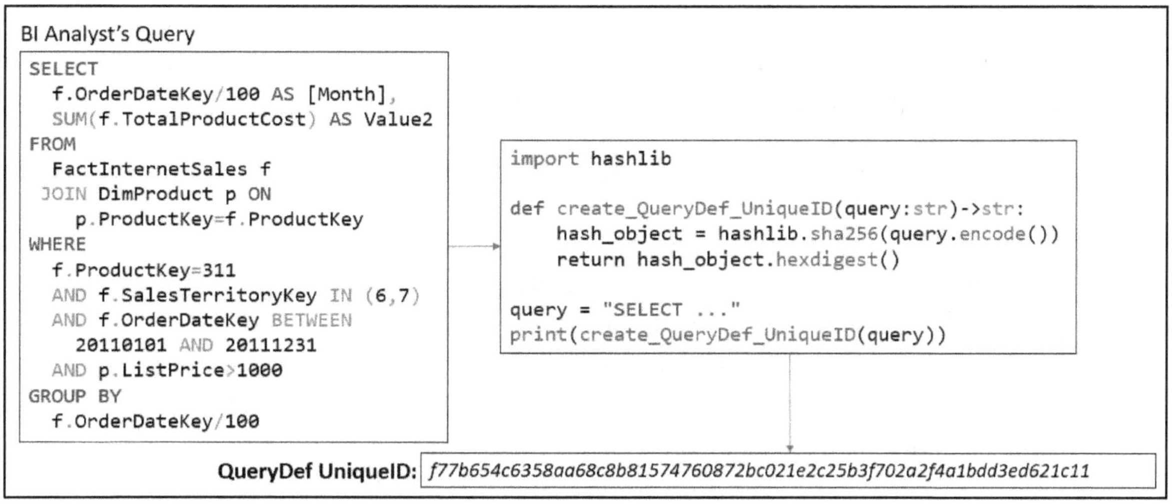

```
BI Analyst's Query
SELECT
  f.OrderDateKey/100 AS [Month],
  SUM(f.TotalProductCost) AS Value2
FROM
  FactInternetSales f
  JOIN DimProduct p ON
    p.ProductKey=f.ProductKey
WHERE
  f.ProductKey=311
  AND f.SalesTerritoryKey IN (6,7)
  AND f.OrderDateKey BETWEEN
    20110101 AND 20111231
  AND p.ListPrice>1000
GROUP BY
  f.OrderDateKey/100
```

```
import hashlib

def create_QueryDef_UniqueID(query:str)->str:
    hash_object = hashlib.sha256(query.encode())
    return hash_object.hexdigest()

query = "SELECT ..."
print(create_QueryDef_UniqueID(query))
```

QueryDef UniqueID: `f77b654c6358aa68c8b81574760872bc021e2c25b3f702a2f4a1bdd3ed621c11`

Figure 85: How a QueryDef is referenced.

I should note that two queries could be semantically the same without being exactly the same. That's no different from all the ways we can say anything else but mean the same thing. I chose to differentiate queries by their textual equivalence since it's possible there could be aspects of a query that we're unable to parse. There are many dialects of SQL and many other query languages or even API calls. This is my judgment call. However, semantic equivalence should result in fewer QueryDef objects.

A KG of Dataframes

By "KG of Dataframes," I mean that Dataframes are objects, and a KG describes the properties of objects. Normally, a KG might include instances or objects such as employees. Each employee is an individual of an Employee class. In turn, an employee has a job title, has a credential, and is salaried or hourly. In the case of a dataframe (as a thing), it has properties, for example, standard statistics, the insights one could glean from the data, set of outlier rows, and machine learning models.

Dataframe Individuals

In the context of this book, a dataframe is a tabular structure containing a set of rows with many attributes (columns). I chose to call them dataframes because much of the sample code is written in Python, where dataframes are the most common format for this tabular sort of structure.

Since this is a BI-centric topic, the dataframes are generally the result of a typical SQL GROUP BY query—for example, the SQL we just saw in Figure 85. That means the dataframe has two main groups of columns:

1. Dice columns (how the data is chopped up).
2. Measures.

Note that the columns used in the WHERE clause to filter data can optionally be included in the SELECT statement. This inclusion is particularly relevant when the WHERE clause involves conditions like an IN clause, where the filter column may need to represent multiple potential values to accurately reflect the data subset being analyzed. Thus, while the dataframe typically does not display these filters explicitly, their selective inclusion in the SELECT statement allows for a more detailed understanding of the data context, especially when dissecting the results by specific criteria such as country names in a geographical analysis.

In the parlance of the semantic web, "individual" is an instance of a class of entity. In this case, the class is QueryDef. A more familiar example could be a class named Country, where Mexico and Canada are individuals (or instances) of the class.

What about updated data? How are QueryDefs refreshed in the not so unlikely case that a subset of the underlying data involved with the QueryDef has been updated or deleted? Or will properties of the QueryDef always reflect values at the time of its creation (it will be stale)? For a dataframe without a specified date range, there is an implied "from beginning of time" to "end of time." So when data is updated, the insights of that QueryDef within the EKG becomes stale.

By default, a dataframe without a specified date range is assigned a date range-something like 1900/01/01 (beginning of time) as the starting date range, and current date or max date in the dataframe (whichever is greater) as the end of the date range. However, "end of time" does specify a valid end of date range as well.

Any QueryDefs where the date range is to "end of time" will need to be refreshed whenever new data is added. For these cases, if refreshing is from an optimized OLAP cube, at least the refresh time is substantially mitigated.

Ideally, any new fact table rows are relatively recent. For example, if today is 5/28/2024 and we have a QueryDef specifying a date range of 4/1/2024 through 6/30/2024, adding rows from 4/1/2024 onwards is manageable since we only need to refresh the QueryDefs within their date range. However, adding rows from before 4/1/2024, such as 3/1/2024, requires refreshing additional QueryDefs that include these older dates, increasing the processing workload.

Spaces

Our lengthy discussion on the Event Ensemble deals with time. Events are phenomena of time. Now let's look at space, the space of possibilities, the space of where events happen.

The vastness of the *space of possibilities* is really at the heart of the problem this book is trying to embrace—even though it's impossible to fully wrangle. Even the entirety of humanity, eight billion sentient agents augmented by all that's accessible on the Internet, the vast parallel repository of knowledge, can't know everything. Only the real world itself has the information necessary to compute what happens next.

At best, the most thorough exploration of a vast space of possibilities is a compromise of educated sampling. Although we can't know everything, we can infer much of what we don't know from what we do know. What an enterprise knows is what pains it's feeling, what is in the databases and documentation, and that there is a wealth of understanding in the heads of thousands of information workers deployed across a wide space of domains. But what is in the databases is analogous to what we see when we look up at the stars. It's expansive and beautiful, but it doesn't convey a fraction of the information that's really there.

The idea of the ISG/TCW is to capture that information which is discovered by the army of knowledge workers in an enterprise. Each has a unique skill set, a role, and responsibilities that fit into a larger organization that includes other sentient, skilled people with other responsibilities that must be met. Each has a unique lens crafted by their unique experiences from which they see different information.

The ISG/TCW are recordings of what they've discovered in the space of possibilities as they go about their normal work life. The ISG/TCW doesn't capture high fidelity or deep level of knowledge, but it does move the ball in the game of understanding forward. Similarly, a video recording of a sports game captures much information that provides value to those who couldn't be there, but still leaves out much more than it captured. However, it does capture the salient points, albeit in a dry manner—the score, the key plays, controversial calls, etc.

Figure 86 delineates the multilayered strata of data processing and insight generation, each level building upon the one before to create a comprehensive understanding of business intelligence within an organization.

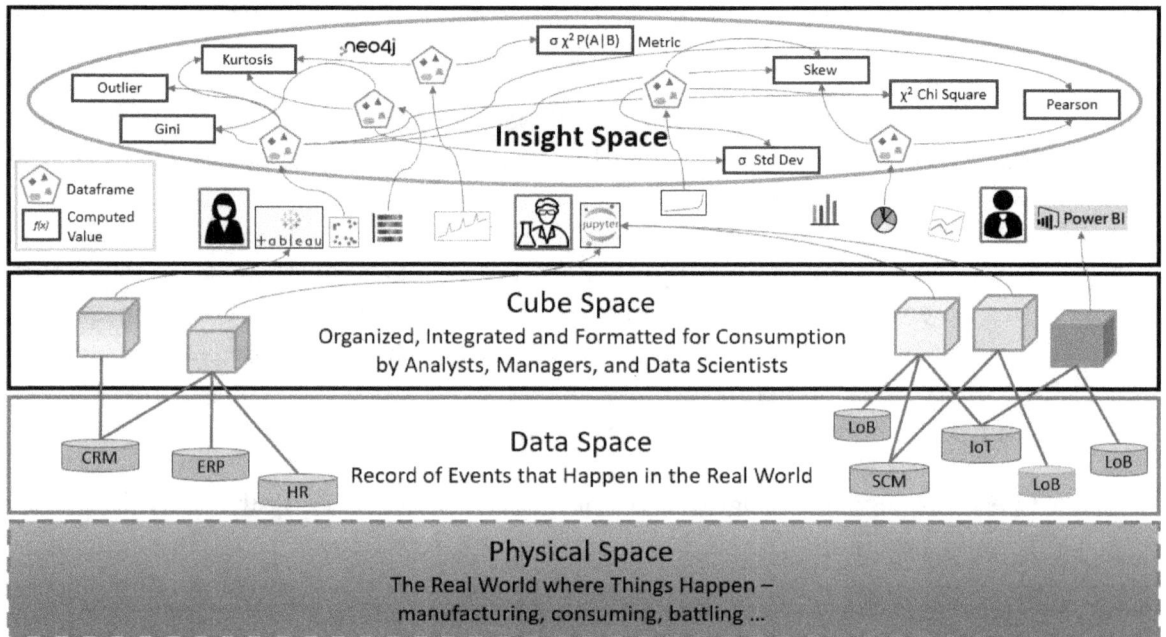

Figure 86: The four levels of space leading to Insight Space.

Moving from bottom-up, these are the four levels of space depicted in Figure 86. While each level is infinite, each level is different.

Physical Space

The foundational realm where real-world events and interactions occur, feeding raw data into the system.

In the context of the ISG, the lowest-level realm of space is the physical world—a real space of interacting things. I don't mean quarks, atoms, planets, asteroids, black holes, and stars. I mean the limitless variations of things we interact with in our daily lives that are made out of atoms, the relationships that bind them, and the events that can happen between them. It's where we humans and businesses live and perform our work—where we make and lose sales and grow or go bankrupt. This is where products are manufactured, customers live and consume products, and what is continuously optimized and adapted towards your enterprise's changing conditions.

It is, of course, the most vast of the spaces because it extends beyond the walls of an enterprise out to vendors, customers, governments, world events both human-caused and natural, fads, research, and the antics of all those other entities with minds of their own.

Data Space

The record-keeping layer captures and stores events from the physical space within hundreds to thousands of purpose-built databases scattered around the enterprise ecosystem.

In the physical world, computers and other gadgets record events happening in the real world. Similar to how the senses of our bodies only pick up what we can see, hear, smell, touch, our data systems only pick up what we build it to pick up. It's a virtual world, not nearly as rich as the real world, but somewhat more substantial than the shadows in Plato's cave.

Our databases only pick up selected signals at selected levels of isolation and abstraction. For example, we might pick up that a Website visitor clicked on a link, but we don't know much about what went on in the life of the visitor before and after the click.

This is the OLTP data world. This data can be rather dirty, incomplete, fragmented, sometimes extremely voluminous, and often hard to decipher. Because of the drastically increasing number of data *sources*, the data space is widening. But that's still just a teeny fraction of all that really goes on in the world. The good news is that there's a long way to go before we reach the limit of what we can capture.

The Internet of Things, e-commerce, AI, and the cloud are among paradigm-shifting subjects that expand the volume *and* variety of the data we're able to capture. This book is mostly concerned with the expansion of the variety of data. And by variety, I don't mean a variety of formats, such as JPG, WAV, MP4, csv, XML, PDF, DOCX, etc. I mean the varietal dimension—the different things we can say about things. For example, we can capture the gender, age, Zip code, and occupation of customers. But how many things can describe a person or any other entity? It's really unlimited. In fact, data scientists regularly deal with thousands of things one can use to describe a customer.

Despite talk of the explosion of the volume of data in the magnitude of exabytes, data space is the least vast of the four spaces. Exabytes of data and tens of thousands to millions of columns aren't really that big. It's a model representing a tiny fraction of what's in physical space.

We usually measure data space as how much data (TB, PB, etc.) we've captured, how many data sources, tables, and columns, and how many rows (for example, number of visits and events). These really are small numbers in terms of the combinatorial possibilities of real life.

It might seem odd to think of data as events. Most are used to thinking of data as something looked up from a database. But really, the databases supporting those kinds of lookups are just the current state of the database, the *end result* of a convergence of a series of highly parallel events over time.

This notion of data as events has been picking up steam via the concepts of Event Sourcing and the feature known as time travel. Basically, event sourcing is an extreme of high pf data granularity where every change to data (change to the database state) is a recorded event–as opposed to overwriting with the latest state of our understanding.

Cube Space (Semantic Layer)

A structured environment where data is organized and formatted for analytical consumption, serving as the intermediary between raw data and actionable insights.

For the last few decades, raw OLTP data has been contorted through painful, mostly hand-crafted ETL processes into a form that is cleaner, integrated, organized, and optimized. It's this user-friendlier form that's exposed to human analysts. They are called dimensional models, a.k.a. cubes, multi-dimensional cubes, or OLAP cubes.

ATTOW, they're rarely called "cubes" anymore. It seems to be an antiquated term that goes back at least two generations of analytics (cloud and ML). "Cube" always was a misnomer anyway since those cubes usually consisted of very much more than three dimensions. Each attribute is a dimension, and there were usually dozens of them.

Today, the popular term is "semantic layer." But whatever they are called today, they are pretty much dimensional models. That goes for csv files or "one-big-tables" which could be thought of as flattened versions of dimensional models. Even though the term "cubes" might not be used much these days, the vast majority of analytics is still performed on these dimensional models.

Figure 87 compares physical space to *cubespace*, a term widely used in the day of SSAS MD (ca. 2000s). Like physical space, cubespace scaffolds some number of dimensions comprising the axes of the space. Each dimension of cubespace is a set of values of an attribute. For example, the set of values for the primary colors are red, yellow, and blue.

I need to note that the word, dimension, is over-loaded in the OLAP cube world. In the context of a dimensional model, it refers to an entity such as customer or product, under which there are a number of attributes (name, id, etc.). I the context of cubespace, a dimension means the geometric dimension, each of which is one of those attributes across all entities.

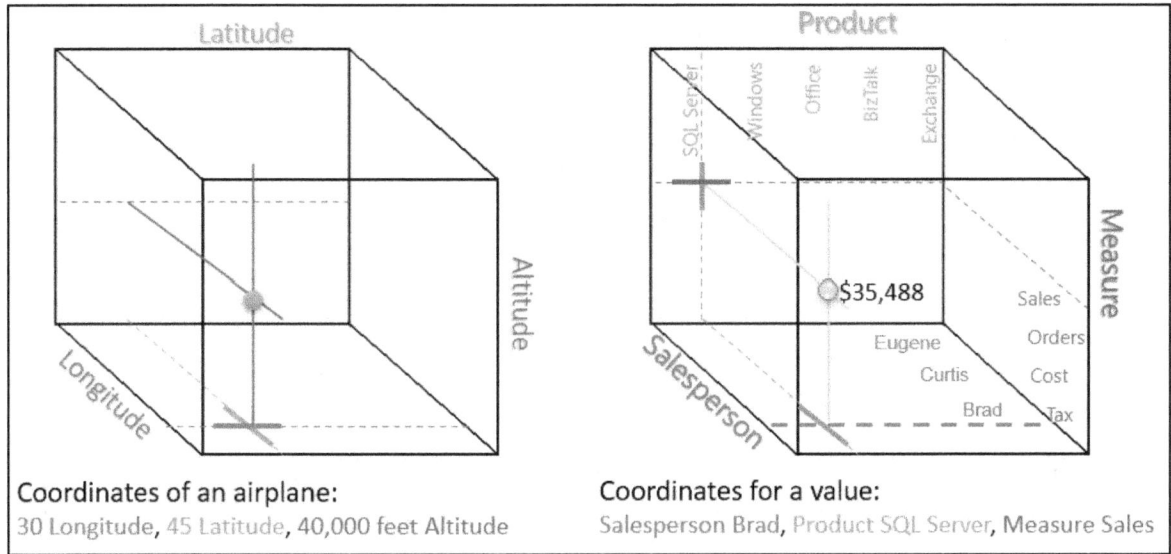

Figure 87: Too-puhls are coordinates of a multi-dimensional space.

In the same way that every point in physical space can be addressed by coordinates (latitude, longitude, and altitude), values in cubespace are referenced by coordinates called tuples. The entire set of tuples forms a cubespace. Figure 87 shows that at the coordinate of Brad, Tax, SQL Server, there exists the value of $35,488. Move the thick dashed line one click to the towards the back, and we find the tuple of Curtis, Sales, SQL Server. Note that the number of tuples in the cubespace is 60—five products, three salespersons, and four measures.

Figure 88 illustrates the concept of a "set of tuples". Whereas a single tuple is a coordinate in cubespace, a set of tuples is a chunk of cubespace, ranging from a single value (0D), to a line (1D) of values, to a plane (2D) of values (the tuple set shown in Figure 88), to a 3D subcube of values, to a 4D tesseract, to a 5D whatever you call it, and beyond.

A set of tuples is a table, it is roughly like Python dataframes. So, sets of tuples are the common currency between OLAP cubes and Python. The concept of tuple sets is central to the ISG since a QueryDef represents a query that receives a tabular result set:

table = set of tuples = pandas dataframe = QueryDef

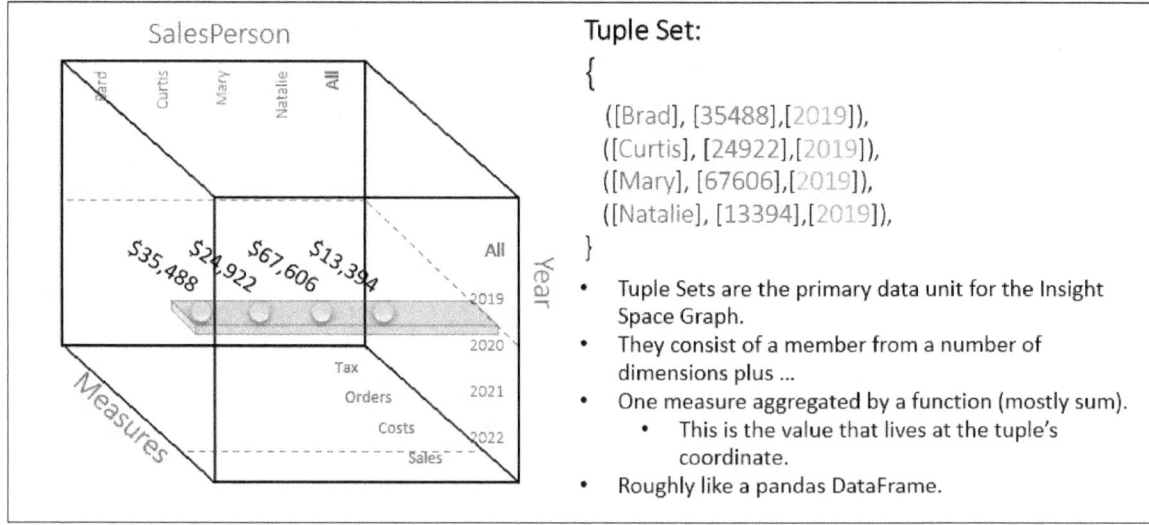

Figure 88: A set of tuples.

Exploring cubespace is about inspecting what lives at some coordinate (or one or more chunks of coordinates), and cubespace is vast. It may not look like it based on Figure 87 and Figure 88. Believe it or not, even a moderately-complicated production cube (say around 30 "dimensions" with a few having over one thousand members) probably has a cubespace containing more tuples than there are stars in the Universe.

However, the vast majority of tuples won't have any value (empty, null). Think of how outer space is mostly space or most coordinates in the atmosphere don't have an airplane. Thankfully, OLAP cubes are *sparse* as well! We don't have 100^{30} bytes of storage to store a value for every tuple. For a dense cube, every salesperson would need to sell every product to every customer at every location every hour of every day.

And that's just one cube! With the current powerful traction of data mesh, enterprises' analytics data will consist of a larger number of domain-level "data products." Data mesh ameliorates the bottlenecks that still prevent the unimpeded flow of data from business process systems to analysts and strategists. Data mesh ameliorates the bottleneck by advocating the distribution of the responsibility for the development and maintenance of analytics data from a monolithic, IT-centric effort into a parallel domain-level effort producing coherent, independent, and high-quality data products.

A domain is roughly a business process, such as a sales cycle, the manufacture of a product, or the onboarding of an employee. A data product is a consumer-facing data source consumed by analysts. By distributing the development and maintenance of analytics data from central IT, the IT bottleneck is removed, and the people who actually work with the data are responsible for it.

Because the data products of data mesh are developed and maintained by the domain, the data is of a higher quality. There is less chance for misinterpretation of the meaning of domain data by folks who are not experts with the data. Thus, whatever analyst activity the Insight Space Graph is recording has less of a garbage-in/garbage-out factor.

In the context of this book, each Data Product could be manifested in the form of a cube. That would be one or more cubes (data products) for each domain. The set of cubes (Data Products) could then be integrated (linked) via common dimensions. Examples of methods for the mapping of common dimensions include:

- Master Data Management—A very non-trivial effort of mapping database objects (tables, columns, members) from one system to another.

- 3rd Party master data—There exists data from vendors that map codes or identities of various sorts.

- Enterprise-wide ID—Generally, a microservices implementation naturally creates enterprise-wide IDs of entities that are passed from microservice to microservice.

- Time is a ubiquitous dimension.

- LLM assistance.

The point is that data mesh is a big factor in opening the floodgates for the hugely widening number of data sources that are finding their way to a population of data-starved analysts. The "sum" of those many cubes (data products) comprises a pretty daunting cubespace.

Insight Space—the Final Frontier

The apex of data exploration where sophisticated tools and statistical measures transform organized data into strategic business insights.

What I call *Insight Space* is the full set of notable features that could be derived from visualizations typically utilized by analysts and other BI consumers as they explore the *cubespace* through data visualization tools. Cubespace and Insight Space are related in the same way as a big box of Legos of various shapes and colors versus the myriad different things we could build with the Legos.

Analysts explore *cubespace* using tools, such as Tableau and Power BI. This is analogous to Captain Kirk and his crew exploring space for interesting things in their starship. It's a mindbogglingly big space with just a few hints to set an initial direction toward something of value.

When an analyst opens up Power BI or Tableau, connects to a cube, and slices and dices away at the data, she explores a cubespace in the form of a dimensional model or flattened table. In reality, the cubespace she explores is usually just a small fraction of the cubespace of an enterprise. There's only so much a human brain can take in. Fortunately, there are usually many analysts across an enterprise with expertise in different parts of the cubespace.

Slicing and dicing around an OLAP cubespace isn't very different from "exploring strange new worlds" like in Star Trek. They visit places in three-dimensional space (sometimes four or more) and chart the places they've been to along with a chronicle of their adventure ("Captain's log ...") into their 23rd/24th Century Cloud.

The chronicle of their adventure is the richer form of data akin to what I have in mind for the ISG. Not just sums and counts, but notable qualities of chunks of cubespace. The crew also has knowledge of qualities of the discovery that might be of interest to some parties out there, so it's hashtagged as relationships like #dilithiumcrystals or #crazyisotopes.

Insight Space should be magnitudes more expansive than cubespace. To use the Lego analogy again, the number, shape, and color of Legos in a box is much smaller than the number of things we could build with those Legos (permutations).

The maximum number of possible points in the insight space only begins with the product of the number of tuples that exist in cubespace (already a really big number), tuple combinations (an even bigger number), and the number of notable "thoroughly socialized" features (the things we have been taught to look for). Fortunately, putting it ridiculously lightly, the number of points and relationships human or machine analysts might find worthy of mapping in an actual production ISG will be an immensely small fraction of that number.

But what does "worthy of mapping" (or notable feature) mean? Worthy to whom? The things we recognize as valuable are only valuable in the context of our personal "birth-to-date" frame of experience. We undoubtedly fail to fully appreciate the vast majority of important things as we encounter them because the context in which they might be valuable is still unknown to us. It's very difficult to proactively find something of significant value that isn't already known and obvious.

It could also be that the human analyst is plagued with biases of many types. Those blinders miss many opportunities to explore completely uncharted areas. This is where the inclusion of analysis by thousands of knowledge workers across the enterprise, analyzing data for multiple purposes, across multiple databases comes in. Each analyst is like a starship exploring different parts of the cubespace.

Because of the overwhelming sparsity of novel insights in an Insight Space, the ISG method must incorporate some level of the human intelligence of analysts for hints. The normal activity of these analysts is clues to what could be important, substantially narrowing the search space. Being implemented in a machine, the ISG is less prone to the effects of information overload than human workers with all sorts of stresses in and out of the work environment.

Insight Space is an awful lot of space for a relative handful of human analysts to thoroughly explore through Tableau! Indeed, that's still a lot of space even for a program automatically brute-force querying each permutation of tuple sets. Further, as mentioned earlier, the data space is drastically widening, with a cascading effect on cubespace, then insight space.

Lastly, using the Lego analogy for the last time, most of the possible things that could be built with Legos are essentially garbage (at least to most people). Similarly, most of what exists in Insight Space is useless in the context of the world we all share. Similarly, space is mostly void of matter and gold mines are mostly void of gold.

It's actually very difficult to find something in a BI system that hasn't already been discovered, so downright obvious no one looked to discover it, or too ridiculous to entertain. A common customer complaint in the land of BI consulting is, "Show me something I don't already know."

Yet, the crux of exploration is that we are often unaware of our own ignorance. The ISG serves as a public forum, a bulletin board of sorts, where discoveries that might not hold value for one may be exactly the revelation another was unaware they sought

A Little Anecdotal Detour: *A few years ago, I built a conditional probability network from actual claims data (of course, with the required scrubbing) for a healthcare-related organization. I found it surprisingly difficult to find anything interesting. Just about everything was either too weak to bother mentioning or very obvious (for example, cough correlated to flu). However, one particular diagnosis, Vitamin D Deficiency, correlated with quite a few unlikely other diagnoses. When I presented the conditional probability network to a group of mostly MDs, I asked if anyone had thoughts on my Vitamin D finding. They chuckled at the silly programmer. "Correlation doesn't imply causation!" "There's obviously some confounding factor!" "Swim in your lane!"*

My point is that within a couple of hours searching a the conditional probability network I created, that's the only juicy example of something interesting that I could find. However, years later, whether right or wrong, it became a full-fledged hot potato topic in the great Covid-19 treatment debates.

Business Intelligence Insights

What are all the things we can note in a Graph/Chart?

Analysts view BI visualizations mostly in the form of a chart or graph of some type filled by a simple dataframe. There are just a few dozens things you could say about any of these graphs, no matter what the data. Some of those things are of interest to the analyst, but some are not. Some are not even noticed because the analyst wasn't looking for it.

Those insights, noticed or unnoticed, vaporize once Tableau is closed. The few that the analyst notes are really confined to her head, shared with only those who might be interested. But what if there are others unknown to her who might find that interesting? Would they know to find the answer the same way? But if we save the insight that is interesting but not useful for the analyst in the ISG, it is now a searchable piece of information. Further, most of those insights are light computations calculated off the already built dataframe. So, we can, in a separate process, compute those insights and save them to the ISG. Figure 89 presents a cohesive flow from raw data to actionable insights, a journey that typically unfolds in a BI environment.

On the left, we see three distinct types of visualizations commonly found in BI tools:

1. Line Chart: This chart shows a trend over time. The insight derived from this graph is that there is a mean time of three days between spikes, indicating a pattern or cycle in the data. Additionally, the data is trending upwards, with a

slope of 0.577, suggesting a gradual increase in whatever metric the line chart is tracking.

2. Bar Chart: This histogram-like visualization is likely showing the distribution of data across different categories or over time. The insight extracted here is a Gini Coefficient of 0.60, which is a measure of statistical dispersion intended to represent the income inequality or wealth inequality within a nation or a group. A Gini Coefficient of 0.60 indicates a relatively high level of inequality.

3. Time Series with Changepoints: The third chart appears to be another time series, with dotted lines highlighting significant changepoints. These inflection points mark moments where the data's behavior changes notably. The dates of these changepoints are listed, providing specific moments in time when something noteworthy occurred.

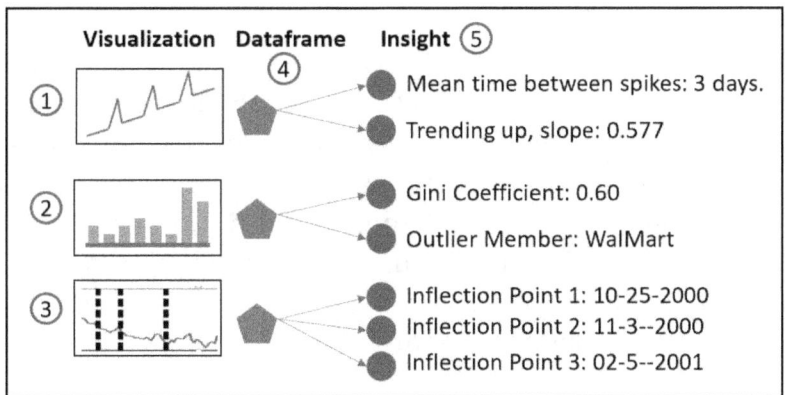

Figure 89: Insights from dataframes.

The pentagon shapes at center (4) represent QueryDefs, dataframes or data extracts from OLAP cubes, which are the foundational data structures used to create the visualizations.

Moving from the visualizations to the right (5), we have insights that are interpreted from these graphical representations. These insights can include such goodies as:

- The average time between notable events (spikes in the data).

- An overall trend indicating an increase.

- A measure of distribution skewness or inequality (Gini Coefficient).

- Identification of an outlier member, which could be a data point or entity (like Walmart) that significantly deviates from the norm.

- Specific dates when the behavior or pattern within the data changed significantly.

Overall, Figure 89 exemplifies that insights are drawn from BI visualizations. These insights then inform decision-makers in a business context, enabling them to understand trends, patterns, and anomalies within their operational or market environment.

Visualizations provide an intuitive way for analysts to derive insights from data. Depending on the visualization type, various patterns and anomalies might be recognized. Before looking at the visualizations, keep in mind that the idea of AEI is to store insights across very many dimensions - across many kinds of analysts, across many different kinds of problems they face.

Following are very brief notes on common BI visualizations and lists of what sort of insights analysts expect to see. Each insight mentioned is implemented as a function (probably a Python function) that takes in a dataframe and returns one or more insights. I call the set of these functions the Insight Function Array. A healthy sample of these functions are implemented in Python and available to view on the GitHub site. Remember, the types of graphs listed below are so well-socialized that it's what is shown to the general public in the various media. They should be readily understandable by anyone who has read this book up to this point.

There are others that are not quite as well-socialized (e.g., heat maps, Sankey diagrams, and violin plots). They might not be as familiar, but with just a little practice, they too, convey crisp insights. For now, I'll stick with the very familiar.

Line Graphs

A line graph is a type of chart used to display series information, usually a time series. It consists of a series of data points, called markers, connected by straight line segments. The x-axis (left to right) of the line graph represents the time scale, whereas the y-axis (up and down) shows the quantities or measurements.

- Trend Analysis:
    - General Trend: The overall direction of the data over time (increasing, decreasing, or stationary).
    - Uptrend: Consistently rising data values over time.

- o Downtrend: Consistently falling data values over time.
  - o Horizontal Trend: Data values remain steady over time with little change.

- Variability:
  - o Volatility: Significant fluctuation in data values in an unpredictable pattern.
  - o Gini Coefficient: A statistical measure of distribution, often used to gauge inequality among the values of the series.

- Pattern Recognition:
  - o Seasonality: Regular, repeating cycles in data over a set period.
  - o Patterns: Repeated occurrences that form a recognizable sequence in the data set.

- Change Points:
  - o Anomalies: Deviations or outliers that differ significantly from the overall trend.
  - o Inflection Points: Locations on a graph where the direction of the trend changes.
  - o Spikes: Sudden, sharp increases in data value that typically revert quickly.
  - o Dips: Sudden, sharp decreases in data value that typically revert quickly.

- Growth Models:
  - o Hockey Stick Growth: A period of slow growth followed by a sharp increase.
  - o S-Curve: Slow initial growth, followed by rapid acceleration, and then a plateau. Note that most "hockey sticks" will usually flatten out into more of an s-curve.

- Statistical Measures:
  - o Mean Time Between Events: Average interval between significant occurrences (e.g., spikes).
  - o Rolling Average (Moving Average): An averaged line that helps smooth out short-term fluctuations and show long-term trends.
  - o Acceleration/Deceleration: Changes in the rate of increase or decrease in the data values.

Bar Charts

A bar chart is a graphical display used to represent categorical data with rectangular bars. Each bar's length or height is proportional to the values it represents. Bar charts can be oriented vertically or horizontally. They are particularly useful for comparing several groups of data, identifying trends within discrete categories, or showing data distributions at a glance.

- Comparisons: Identify which categories are larger or smaller.
- Distribution: See how data is distributed across categories.
- Patterns: Patterns in category subsets might emerge for grouped or stacked bar charts.
- Magnitude: Visually access the magnitude of differences or proportions and ratios between categories.

Pie Charts

Pie charts are almost the same as bar charts. If there weren't such a thing, I don't think the world would slow down too much. But depending on the person, it might be better at these things than a bar chart:

- Proportions: How big one segment is in comparison to others.
- Dominance: Easily identify the largest or smallest segments.
- Segments: How many distinct parts constitute the whole and their relative sizes. For example, is there a monopoly (one clearly dominant), an oligopoly (a small group that adds into a majority)?

Stacked Bar Chart

Let's try another form of the standard BI visualizations, one a little more complicated. Figure 90 is a stacked bar chart. It's very useful for analyzing the composition of things. In this case, it's a set of stores and the composition of sales among various categories of liquor.

Note the things a human would notice in Figure 90:

1. Whiskey and vodka are the two biggest categories across all stores.

2. Vodka dominates at New Pioneer Food Co-op like at no other store.

3. Southside Liquor & Tobacco has the biggest percentage of Tequila.

4. Hy-Vee Food Store and Hy-Vee Food Store #2 are very similar in composition. They probably have a similar layout.

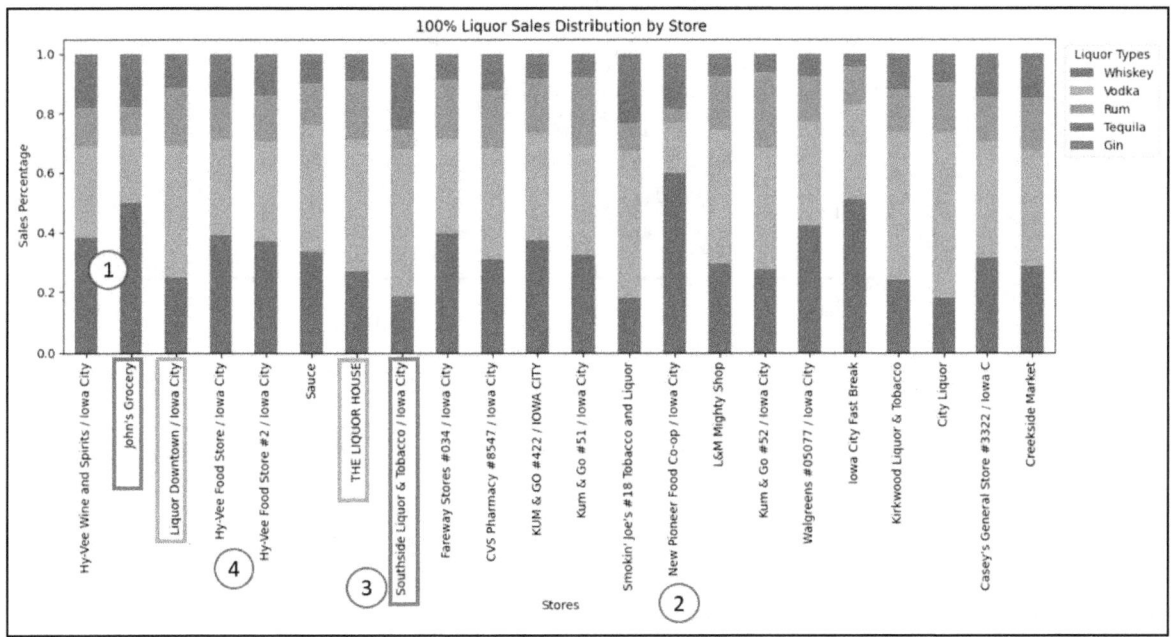

Figure 90: Stacked Bar Chart. Good for composition.

Figure 91 shows us a couple of examples of stores that are similar in composition to liquor classes. The figure of 0.714 highlighted with the solid line actually has a relatively low level of similarity. Looking back at Figure 90, each class differs quite a bit.

Store	Hy-Vee Wine and Spirits / Iowa City	John's Grocery	Liquor Downtown / Iowa City
Hy-Vee Wine and Spirits / Iowa City	1	0.961452636	0.925031018
John's Grocery	0.961452636	1	0.801231954
Liquor Downtown / Iowa City	0.925031018	0.801231954	1
Hy-Vee Food Store / Iowa City	0.991098659	0.962913401	0.931062444
Hy-Vee Food Store #2 / Iowa City	0.986387335	0.948034993	0.945711469
Sauce	0.965724833	0.886957931	0.981651074
THE LIQUOR HOUSE	0.930599154	0.817959414	0.998377122
Southside Liquor & Tobacco / Iowa City	0.8652042	0.714071047	0.942628797
Fareway Stores #034 / Iowa City	0.977270829	0.947206302	0.931058109
CVS Pharmacy #8547 / Iowa City	0.962795507	0.885959194	0.982081864

Figure 91: Matrix of similarity between a few of the stores.

The highlighted value of 0.998 (highlighted in dashed line) shows a very strong similarity between the stores, "THE LIQUOR HOUSE" and "Liquor Downtown/Iowa

City". Each category is ranked the same between the two stores, even if the exact percentages aren't quite exact.

Figure 92 is the SQL used to fill the graphics of Figures 90 and 91. It reflects the classic structure of a query for a stacked bar chart.

```
        SELECT
Measure    SUM(`i`.`sale_dollars`) AS `sale_dollars`,
           `i`.`Store` AS `Store`,
Dice       `i`.`class` AS `class`
        FROM `Eugene Training`.`iowa_liquor_sales` `i`
        WHERE
Filters    `i`.`Zip Code` = '50613' AND
           `i`.`class` IN ('Whiskey','Vodka','Rum','Tequila','Gin')
        GROUP BY `i`.`Store`, `i`.`class`
```

Figure 92: Good candidate for visualizing as a stacked bar chart.

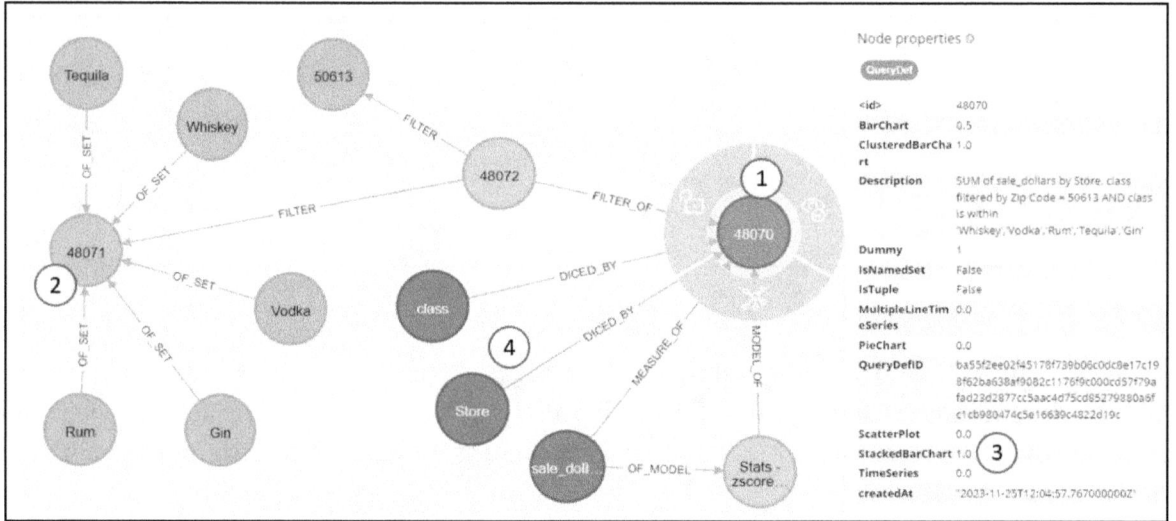

Figure 93: The stacked bar chart query as implemented in the EKG.

Figure 93 shows how the stacked bar chart insight is implemented in the ISG.

1. This QueryDef node represents the SQL query shown in Figure 92.

2. A filter node representing the IN clause restricting the liquor classes to 'Whiskey', 'Vodka', 'Rum', 'Tequila', and 'Vodka'.

3. A property stating that the QueryDef is suitable for a Stacked Bar Chart. It's also sort of suitable for a Bar Char (0.5 score).

4. The dice columns: class and store. Looking back at Figure 90, we can see that the stacked bar chart is by store, and each store is partitioned by liquor class.

Scatter Plots

Scatter plots are my favorite of the commonly used visualizations. The shapes that emerge from the plot can be fascinating and insightful. Here are a few of the shapes that might manifest:

- Correlation: Relationship between two variables; positive, negative, or no correlation. If the points form a vaguely straight line, there is a correlation between the measures of the two dimensions.

- Clusters: Groupings of data points suggesting they might share commonalities.

- Spread: How data points are distributed, whether they're tightly packed or spread out. Or even in a funnel or circular shape. The former is beyond the scope of the topic and the latter is usually not very helpful.

One of the most well-known is the Gartner "magic quadrants," which is really a quick and dirty clustering of things into four categories. However, Magic Quadrants usually consist of relatively few data points. The focus of a Gartner magic quadrant is usually the individual data point. For example, where is MSFT in the cloud magic quadrant?

Typically, scatter plots are rather crowded. Figure 94 shows a few examples–enrollment rate by GDP/Capita Change for four clusters of towns around the world. Each dot represents a town. Usually, the insights of crowded scatter plots are at the graph or dataframe these insights are at the dataframe level, not at the individual. The insight is the shape of the distribution of items. It's like looking at a swarm of bees versus an individual bee.

As just mentioned, the insights for scatter plots are firstly at a high level. What kind of shapes do the distribution of the members form? For example, notice how the top-left cluster looks like a rotated comma? Secondly, what about individual members?

Figure 95 is a scatter plot with few points. It is a Magic Quadrant of the population versus median household income of the Idaho counties:

1. The two axes: Median Household Income (y axis) and Population (x axis).

2. The Small and Comfortable counties sound great to me. Teton County, near Yellowstone, seems very interesting.

3. Blaine County is the secret playground for the rich and famous. It's home to Sun Valley. The highest median household income and a relatively small population.

4. Ada County is the home of Boise, the Capitol of Idaho, and by far the largest county in Idaho.

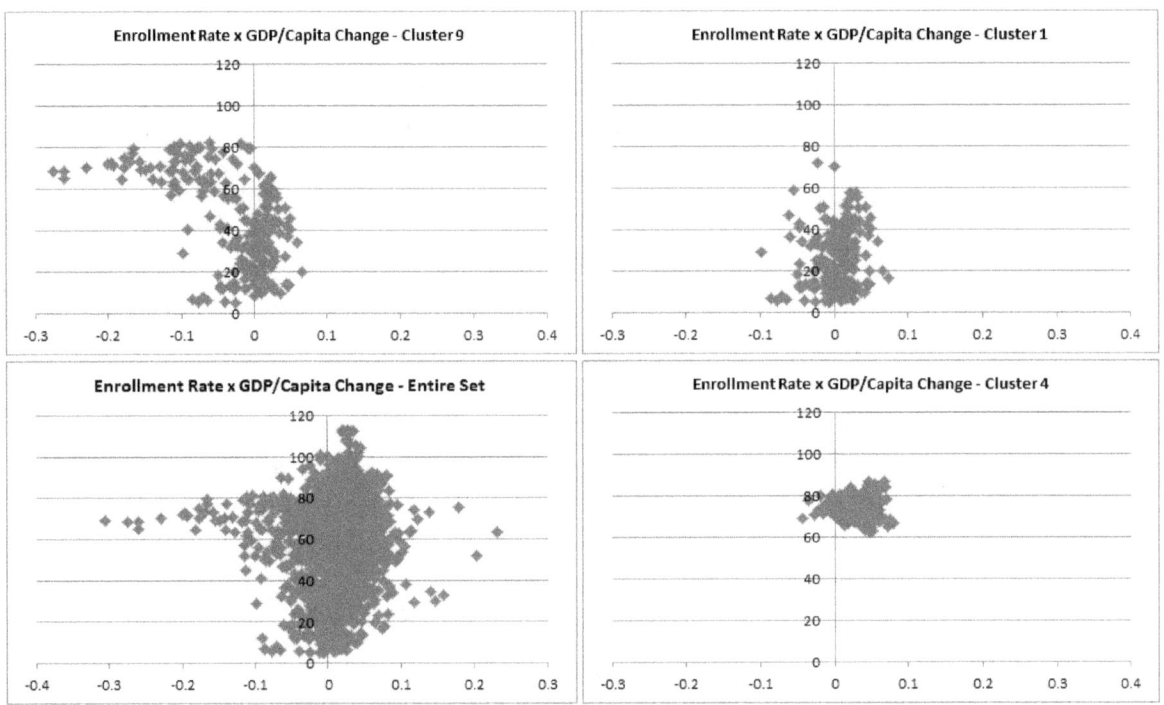

Figure 94: Scatter plots of clusters with very many members.

From a high-level view, it's not very interesting. Aside from a few notable outliers, it doesn't form an interesting shape or suggest a strong correlation between population and median household income.

Figure 96 shows what Figure 95 looks like in the EKG. The counties are linked to their respective quadrants. That's a lot of relationships for just one query.

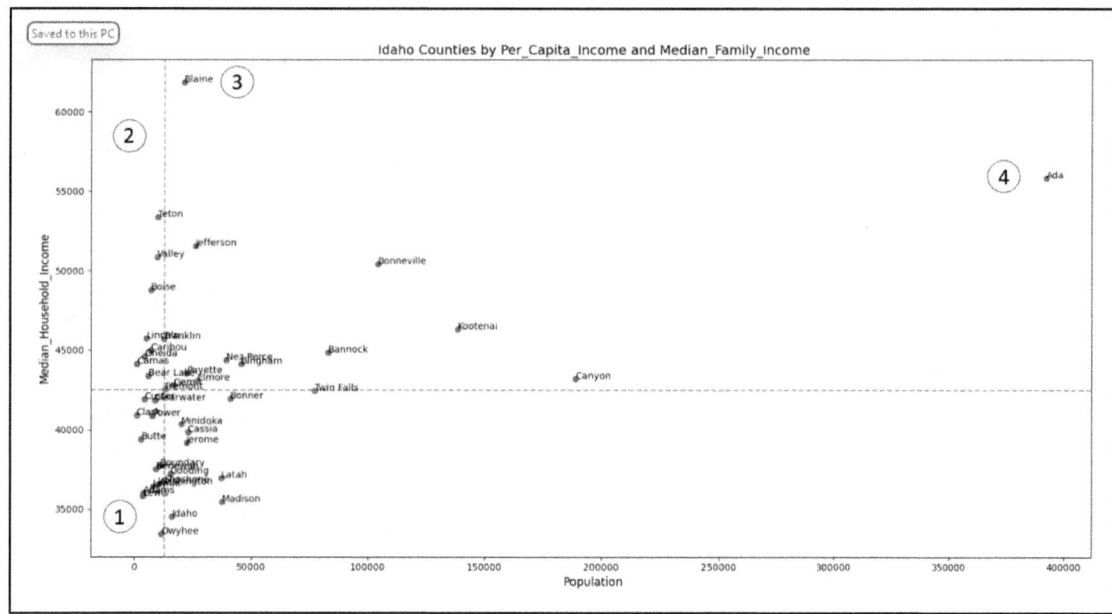

Figure 95: Magic Quadrant.

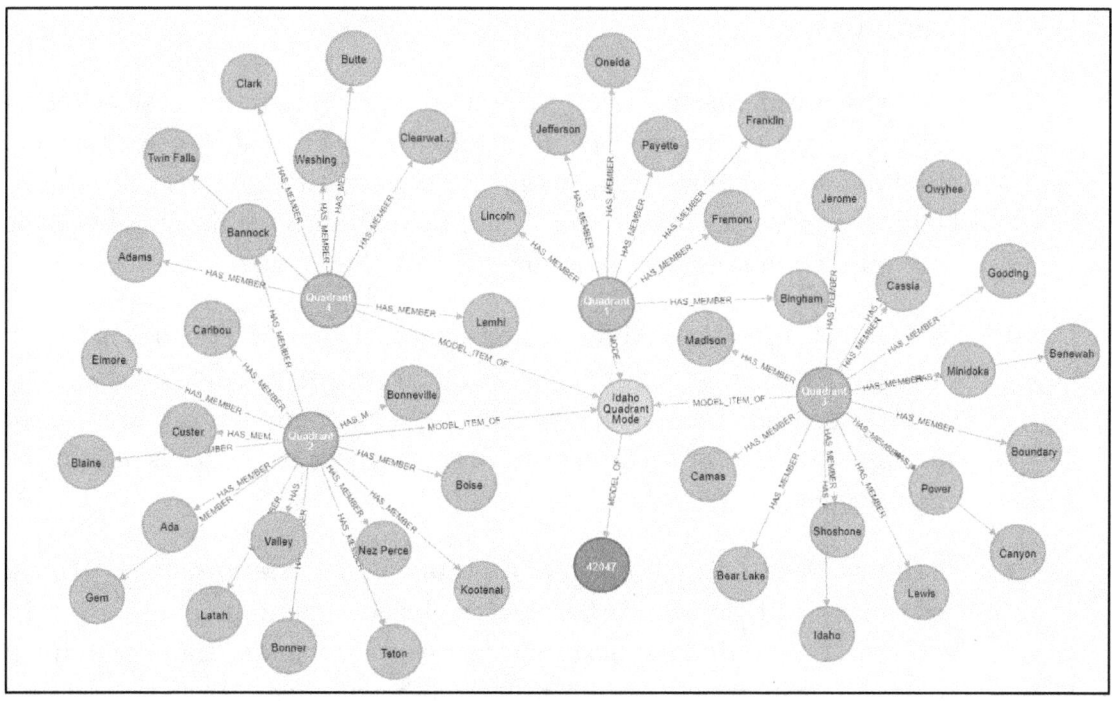

Figure 96: Recording all members assigned to quadrants.

So, saving insights from scatter plots is, by default, just for notable relationships. For example:

- We only list outliers by the two dimensions. In this case, it's mostly Ada and Blaine Counties.

- Maybe we might be interested in only one quadrant. For example, I personally would be interested in less crowded, higher median-income counties. That's just nine members.

As I mentioned, the magic quadrant visualization is a quick and dirty clustering. The information conveyed is insightful and very easy for non-analysts to understand. There are less dirty and/or less quick clustering calculations. Following is a short listing of the calculations from quickest and dirtiest to more computationally intense but richer in insight value. Given the importance of data, the volume of the dataframe, and current loads, one could use a more intense calculation for a higher-quality insight. This commentary assumes a two-dimensional grid (two measures):

1. **Magic Quadrant**—Creating a magic quadrant plot is computationally straightforward. It involves basic operations like median calculation and plotting points on a two-dimensional graph. There's no iterative or complex computation.

2. **k-Nearest Neighbors (KNN)**—About 4x more intense than MQ–KNN's complexity mainly comes from calculating the distance between data points to find the nearest neighbors. For a small dataset, this isn't very intensive, but the intensity increases with larger datasets. No iterative training is involved, but each prediction requires scanning through the dataset.

3. **k-Means Clustering**—About 6x more intense than MQ–k-means requires iterative processing to converge the cluster centers, which can be computationally intensive, especially for a large number of iterations or a high number of dimensions. However, for smaller datasets, this is usually manageable.

4. **Support Vector Machine (SVM)**—About 8x more intense than MQ–SVM, especially with non-linear kernels, can be computationally intensive. It involves optimization to find the best hyperplane that separates the data points. The complexity increases significantly with the number of features and the size of the dataset.

ML Model Visualizations

It's important to keep in mind that a primary theme of this book is how to integrate insights held in our human brains into some structure accessible by other people and AI. That means the visualizations should be the sort that is easily comprehensible by people without a Ph.D. in statistics or ML.

The typical BI visualizations we've been discussing (e.g., line graphs and bar charts) are powerful tools for visualizing data, but they have their limits. These traditional forms often struggle to capture and convey the richness of complex data sets, especially those with high dimensionality, intricate patterns, or subtle relationships between variables. In such cases, the visualization can become cluttered, confusing, or fail to highlight important insights.

This is where machine learning (ML) models are an alternative. ML models can analyze and model complex datasets with many variables (up to thousands), uncovering patterns and relationships that are not easily discernible through standard visualizations. Instead of trying to represent all data points visually on a graph, ML models can summarize and interpret the data, providing predictions, classifications, or clusters that encapsulate the key information.

The basic BI visualizations struggle to convey the complicated insights that ML can lift out of data, such as customer segments, purchasing behavior, and product performance simultaneously. An ML model like a clustering algorithm could identify distinct customer groups based on purchasing patterns.

Figure 97 is a graphic created from a database of a large number of Texas Holdem games. It's rife with insights. For example, we can see that folding in the pre-flop is by far the biggest action.

For this particular case, an analyst could have cobbled together this model using traditional slice-and-dice techniques. In fact, this particular model was built long ago using SSAS's built-in data mining algorithms that would usually be sourced from an OLAP cube. It would have taken a lot of manual slicing and dicing to piece together the model in Figure 97, but nonetheless, the information could be drawn through typical BI querying. In many ways, ML models are really automated slicing and dicing.

Now note that although the decision tree was made from a large number of cases (games), we're analyzing a set of just five items—the five actions a player could take - bet, call, check, fold, and raise. Figure 97 is a visualization that is relatively easy to understand. But a visualization of an ML model certainly isn't like the BI graph visualizations.

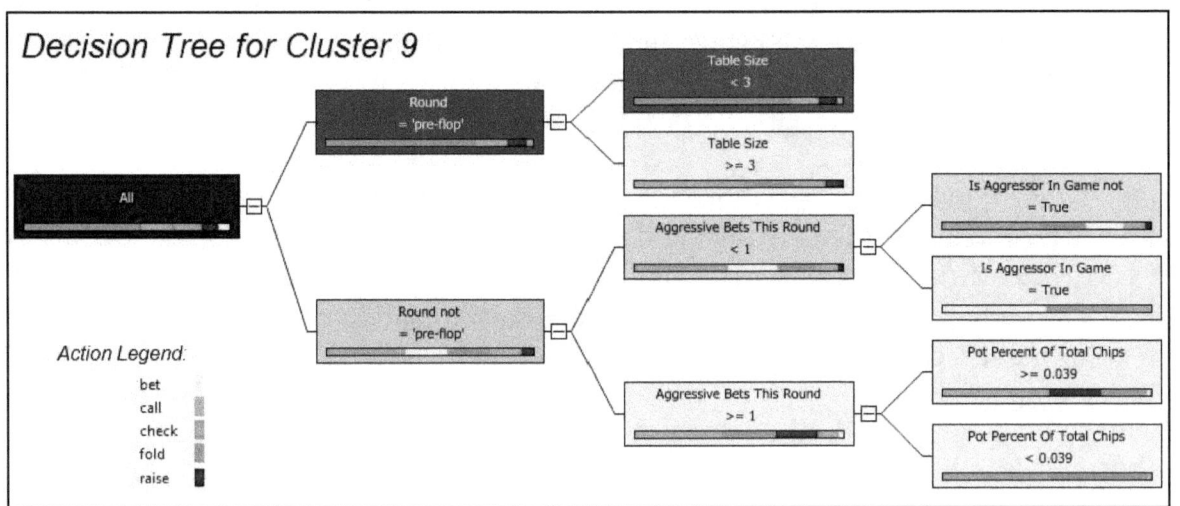

Figure 97: Visualization of a Decision Tree. Analysis of actions for players in "Cluster 9".

Models

ML Models Built from a Dataframe

Many ML models can be expressed in a graph structure (as PMML shows)

ML Models are often high-compute compared to something like calculating a Gini score or r2. They usually require several iterations to home in on a reasonable model of the dataframe. However, ML Models are still noteworthy statements about a dataframe. Many ML Models can be represented in a graph structure as PMML (and XML format) suggests. This includes clusters and decision trees. So, ML models, specifically their structures, should be thought of as "insights," insights farther towards the "why" questions of the dataframe.

Business Rules

Business rules play a pivotal role in enriching and providing semantic coherence to data. Drawing from practical examples, if we consider classifications like a "Primary Customer" or a "Jumbo Group," we are essentially dealing with decision criteria rooted in business rule logic. For instance, to determine if someone qualifies as a "Primary

Customer," the underlying business rule may dictate that their sales must exceed a million dollars in the preceding year. Similarly, a group's classification as "Jumbo" is contingent upon it having over 10,000 members. The example below in Figure 98 shows these two rules in the SWRL (Sematic Web Rule Language) coding of the semantic web.

```
// Rule for identifying a Primary Customer based on sales amount
PrimaryCustomer(?c) ^ hasTotalSalesAmount(?c, ?amount) ^
swrlb:greaterThan(?amount, 1000000) ->
PrimaryCustomerClassification(?c)

// Rule for identifying a Jumbo Group based on member count
Group(?g) ^ hasMemberCount(?g, ?count) ^
swrlb:greaterThan(?count, 10000) -> JumboGroupClassification(?g)
```

Figure 98: SWRL example of a class.

When it comes to integrating these rules into a knowledge graph, a robust and scalable approach is to represent each business rule as a unique node. This node should then be attributed with an IRI (Internationalized Resource Identifier) that redirects to an implementation of the function. This function—whether it's a Python script, a serverless function, or a portion of a Cypher query, SWRL or SQL—is the tangible machine manifestation of the logic of the rule in question.

Business rules should be a vital component of a KG. Predominantly, these business rules manifest as Boolean expressions, easily translatable into a graph format.

While not typical today, the inclusion of business rules in a KG provides powerful capabilities for richer querying, reasoning, and decision-making. The specific implementation will depend on the complexity of the business rules and the technology stack of the knowledge graph. It's difficult to imagine excluding business rules from something called a "knowledge graph." After all, even a triple could be thought of as a simple rule. Moreover, it's paramount to denote ownership for every rule. Ownership not only implies responsibility but also facilitates accountability and traceability, making the governance of the knowledge graph more streamlined.

The conceptual linkage between input features and business rules can be envisioned as a "GUZINTA" (goes into) relationship. Essentially, features, which can be columns or attributes drawn from a data catalog, feed into the business rule, providing the necessary data for rule evaluation.

The output derived from the evaluation of a business rule is manifested in the form of a value. This value, accompanied by its name and type, provides actionable insights and can further be used for various downstream applications or analyses within the business.

By weaving business rules into the fabric of KGs using SWRL/RDF, businesses can achieve a profound synergy between their semantic data structures and operational logic. This symbiosis not only promotes a clearer understanding of business dynamics but also fosters a more informed and data-driven decision-making paradigm.

As a sidenote, the use of Prolog, an older AI language, is an intriguing approach I experimented with long ago for encoding rules into a graph-friendly format. Although Prolog is often viewed as somewhat outdated, similar to COBOL, in my opinion, it's one of the most elegant ways to encode and query logic. A notable feature of Prolog is that it uses the same syntax for data, rules, and queries, which makes sense if our knowledge graph incorporates rules as well as the typical triples. SWRL, the Semantic Web Rule Language, mirrors the predicate-based rule expression syntax of Prolog. In this way, what I loved about Prolog lives today in SWRL.

ML Models are Business Rules

ML models, with their associated parameters, can also be integrated as business rule components. After all, ML models are usually deployed as low-level decision makers or at least advisors, so whatever rules they contain are business rules. For effective serialization into a KG, certain formats like Open Neural Network Exchange (ONNX) and TensorFlow appear to be particularly well-suited due to their inherent graph-based structure.

In the past, Predictive Model Markup Language (PMML), an XML-based representation, would have served as a practical choice for integration into a graph. However, utilization as an ML model serialization format has diminished over time due to the emergence of more flexible, graph-oriented formats. For those rules or ML models that are not easily convertible into a graph structure, an alternative method would be to represent just the input features pointing to a node representing the ML model in the graph. That model node would store a property pointing to a snippet of code that can execute the model. The model node would also point to a node corresponding to the output. For example, if the output is a predicted sale, the model node could point to a column node representing the sales columns.

In the evolving digital landscape, businesses find themselves navigating vast seas of data. This data often holds the keys to unlocking insights, fostering growth, and streamlining operations. However, data in isolation doesn't bring value; it's the interpretation and use of data that businesses truly benefit from. This interpretation often comes in the form of business rules.

Most business rules can indeed be defined using conditional statements (like CASE-WHEN), Boolean logic (AND, OR, NOT), and computational functions. Languages, such as SQL, are adept at expressing these rules. The universality and logic-bound nature of these rules make them prime candidates for representation in a knowledge graph, especially within a data catalog. As just mentioned, the input features and outputs of an ML model can be linked to their corresponding DC column or column value. This unambiguously defines the semantics and range (the valid values) of the input features and output. Other advantages include:

- Enhanced Traceability: Associating business rules directly with data entities provides a clear lineage. This is valuable during audits, impact analyses, and data transformations.
- Flexibility: By representing business rules as nodes, they can be updated, modified, or deprecated without much hassle.
- Interoperability: When embedded in a KG, these rules become part of a semantic structure. This makes them accessible to advanced analytics, AI models, and other computational engines.

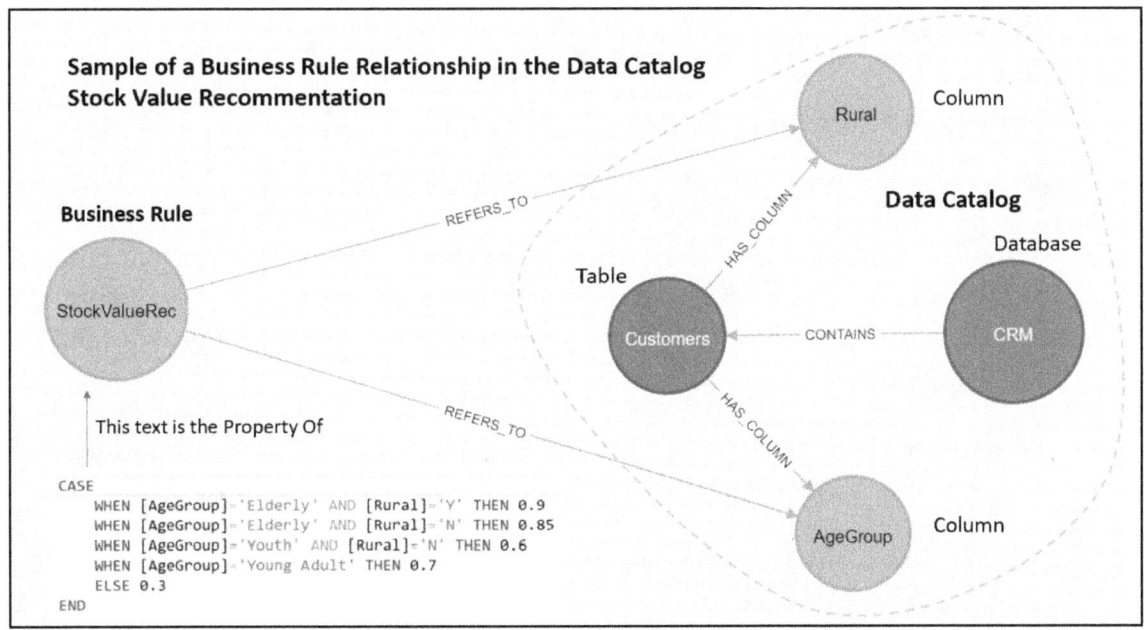

Figure 99: Example of Business Rule, Stock Value percentage recommendation, linked to the DC.

Figure 99 is an example of how a business rule is connected to DC components in the EKG. It is a rule for stating how much of your stock portfolio should be in "value stocks" (high-dividend, low price to earnings).

BI Analyst AI Use Cases

How people will interact with AI over the coming years or even how an autonomous AI might use the EKG is a moving target. How is anything implemented while in a moving target? Later in the book, I address this as it stands at the time of writing, under the chapter: Retrieval Augmented Generation (RAG).

Here I present a few use cases for AI by a BI analyst. They are just a few pragmatic examples that promote "human-guided data-driven decisions." That phrase emphasizes that while the decisions are informed by data, the ultimate control and management lie with human decision-makers, rather than being fully automated by AI. The first two use cases I describe here are the utilization of the EKG in a proactive advisory role. The third case is more traditional as it involves structuring a query, particularly configuring filters—like a filtering UI dialog window but more intelligent.

The following use cases are not mutually exclusive. They will probably be used in combination. However, current BI visualization tools mostly lack the ability at this time. However, I do include Python code to perform these use cases in Notebooks on the GitHub page.

Contextual Information Delivery

What are some interesting things we know about this tuple?

When an analyst is going about browsing an OLAP cube, the user could be presented with a window of interesting items related to a selected tuple. For example, if we focus on a tuple of the price of oil in Brazil, the EKG can return insights about oil, Brazil, and insights related to oil and Brazil.

Information could be from the ontologies and taxonomies of the KG, insights from the ISG, or strong correlations from the TCW. It's like our dear know-it-all friend.

This use case is similar to the use of structured metadata in KGs displayed in platforms like Google and Wikidata (a free, collaborative database that provides structured data that supports Wikipedia and other Wikimedia projects). Google's knowledge graph, for instance, provides sidebar summaries placed on the right side of search results. Similarly, Wikidata links data items through their properties and relationships, creating a searchable, interconnected network of information.

Figure 100 illustrates this use case. It shows a typical BI visualization, a bar chart, of sales of liquor classes. Information from the EKG related to the highlighted item, Whiskey (1), is shown in the "Knowledge of Whiskey" window. The query is fast and direct since it looks for nodes closely linked to the member, Whiskey. Note that the knowledge about a particular subject can span domains (KG) as well as data sources (ISG and TCW). A single call for a wide variety of data is fundamental to this book.

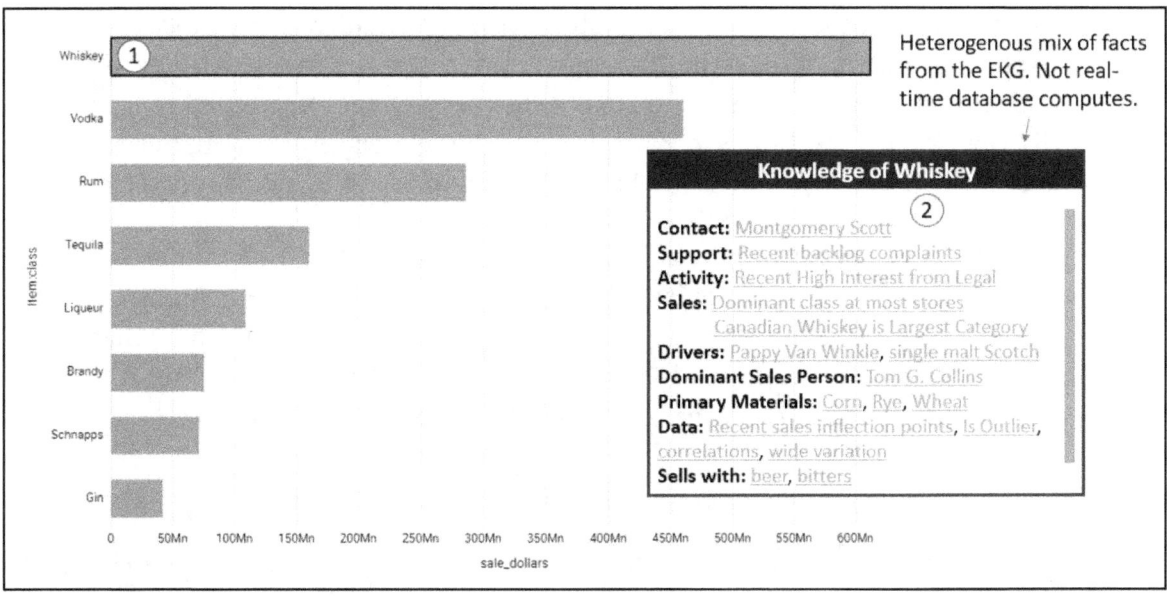

Figure 100: KG information linked to the database member, Item.class.Whiskey

The Knowledge Window (2) lists items queried straight-up from the EKG. There is no query-time compute from any database other than the EKG. The query is a straightforward Cypher query to Neo4j. That includes no query-time calls to a LLM, which is compute-intensive and can take longer than a call to a structured or semi-structured database (at time of writing ChatGPT exhibits inconsistent latency). Each hyperlinked item (blue, underscore) is a node in the EKG. Clicking on one of the items will drill into the relationships of that item in the EKG.

Guided Exploration

What lies under the covers of an aggregated value?

When an analyst is going about browsing an OLAP cube and viewing a chart/graph, the ISG can tell us which members (data point) have something interesting if we drill down on it. For example, when viewing a bar chart, it can be difficult to figure out what member is worthy of drilling down into. Like "intellisense" the ISG can be queried for any saved insight, offering a clue as to which member has something interesting that's not currently viewed. It's like having x-ray vision, seeing into what is "underneath" the aggregated value.

Say we're looking at a bar chart of sales to North American countries. The length of each bar represents the aggregation of all sales for each country. Sure, a big value is interesting, but that big value is probably the U.S., which is probably expected. Smaller bars could be much more interesting. What if, for Mexico, we drilled by product type and found a very uneven distribution versus an uninteresting somewhat equal distribution for the U.S.? How would we know which of many attributes to try without actually drilling down on each? The ISG remembers values it has seen from others.

Figure 101 is a typical BI visualization of sales by the Top 10 counties of Iowa. The fact that we see Polk has the most sales by far (1) is valuable. But biggest doesn't always deserve strategic or investigative attention-we probably already know that. We see there is a group of four running in a "weak second place" (2). Although not fully shown here, there is a long tail of counties with a small fraction of the Polk sales.

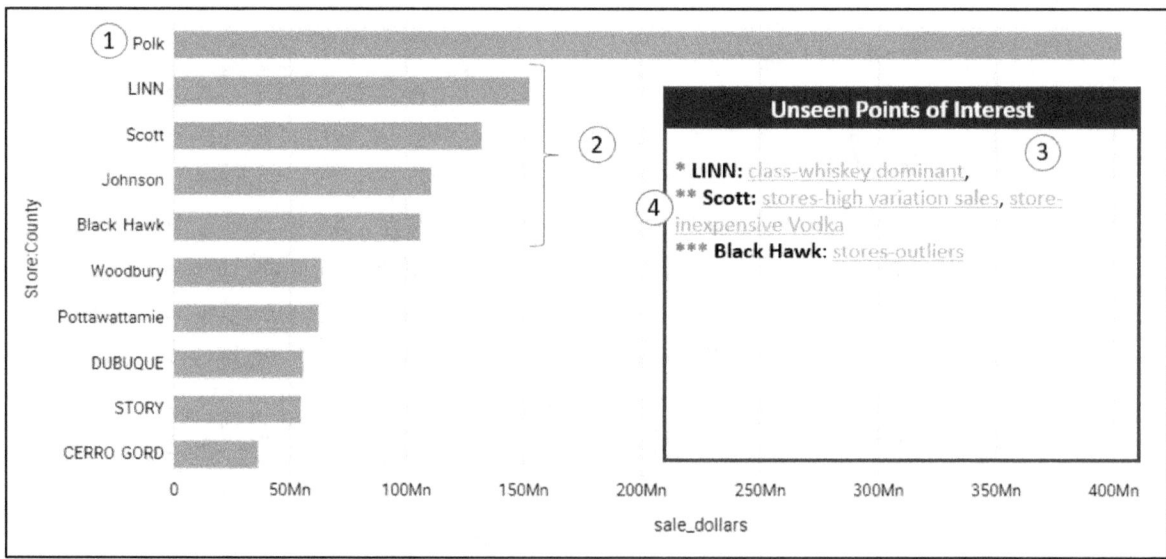

Figure 101: Unseen Points of Interest providing hints as to what to do next.

All that is good, but so what? Where do we go from there? Hidden under each bar is a lot of detail.

The Unseen Points of Interest window (3) pulls up slice-and-dice information from the ISG that indicates points of interest and an overall score (4) in the form of a star rating:

- LINN—The Whiskey Class is highly dominant. But that alone isn't very interesting.

- Scott—The stores within Scott County are highly variant in terms of sales.

- Black Hawk—This is the most interesting as outlier stores (such as a "big box" store) might indicate a big imbalance for the other stores.

The Unseen Points of Interest window tells us, across a number of items, why each bar is interesting. It shows us a few of the most relevant reasons for multiple bars—as opposed to many bits of information for a selected bar. The three stars next to Black Hawk tells us this is probably the most interesting of the selected members.

Enhanced Data Analysis

When querying databases, typically we narrow our search using straightforward properties or conditions—like finding customers by name, age, gender, or location. However, by tapping into the EKG, we can elevate this process to apply more nuanced and contextually intelligent filters. The EKG, in this scenario, functions less like a rigid repository and more as an versatile advisor, similar to advanced features like IntelliSense or GitHub Copilot, guiding the queries we run against our BI systems.

Consider the process of identifying foods beneficial for anemia, which involves complex, rules-based logic. By consulting the EKG, we can simplify and inform this search by leveraging its curated knowledge. Here's how this intelligent filtering unfolds, as visualized in Figure 102:

1. **Query Initiation:** We begin by posing a question to the EKG, such as "What foods help with anemia?" Rather than manually sifting through data, we allow the EKG to interpret the underlying needs—identifying foods rich in iron which are beneficial for treating anemia.

2. **Intelligent Filter Configuration**: The EKG utilizes its diverse knowledge base to configure a filter. This filter is not a simple database WHERE clause but a contextual understanding of the relationship between dietary iron and anemia.

3. **SPARQL Query Execution:** A SPARQL query is then executed against the EKG to retrieve relevant food items. It considers the broader context—nutritional information linked to health conditions—to find a list of suitable foods.

4. **Application to SQL Queries:** The results from the EKG—foods such as spinach, lentils, beef, and quinoa—are then applied as filters in SQL queries, targeting a conventional database like an OLAP cube.

5. **BI Database Query**: Finally, we execute the BI query, using the EKG-derived filters, to obtain sales data for the identified high-iron foods, providing actionable business insights.

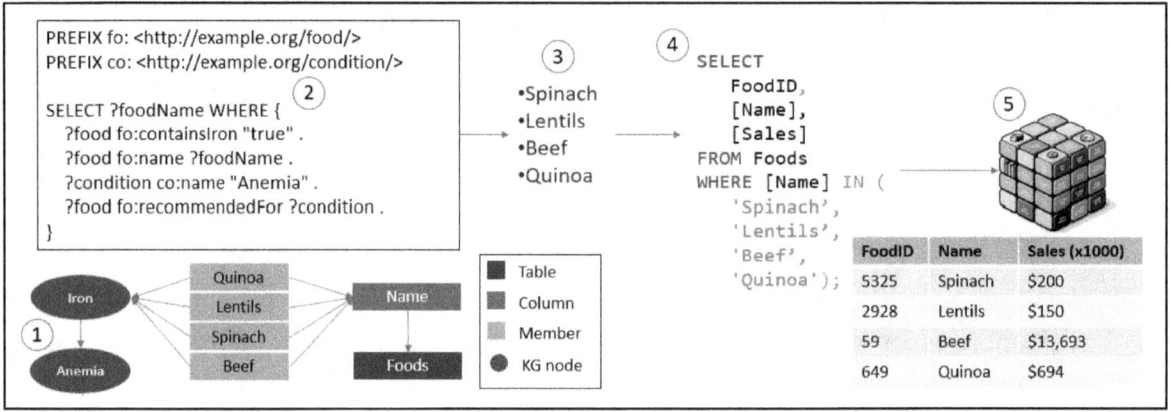

Figure 102: Configure a SQL filter from the wide and diverse EKG.

Through this process, the EKG acts as a conduit between high-level questions and the granular data of BI databases, offering filters that are intelligent, contextually aware, and rooted in a comprehensive understanding of interrelated data. This approach moves beyond the realm of simple data retrieval into one where each query benefits from the collective intelligence of an organization's knowledge.

The Tuple Correlation Web

Time

As discussed way back in Chapter 3, time is the universal thread weaving through the tapestry of data. Time establishes a common meeting ground for the countless datasets not just throughout an enterprise, but throughout the world. While perfect alignment across all database entities is an ideal rather than a practical reality, the temporal axis stands as the consistent and reliable dimension for correlating events and entities.

It is within this framework of time as the ubiquitous link that we can construct a network of correlations, not just as a theoretical exercise but as a pragmatic solution to the age-old problem of integration. Herein, we'll explore how a focus on time doesn't just simplify the process of drawing Bayesian inferences; it can catalyze the discovery of valuable relationships across the varied domains of a vast enterprise.

This introduction sets the stage for a discussion on the utilization of time as a unifying factor in the creation of correlation networks within the complex ecosystem of enterprise data management.

Time Events

Time is the easily forgotten component of considering the location of something. If I say my address is "123 Main Street", that means today, not ten years ago, and most likely not thirty years from now. Fortunately, in our daily communication, there is generally an implication of meaning now. Additionally, whenever my address changed, that is an event. As I said earlier, events are the elements of the proverbial constant change. Events are road markers on the road of time.

It usually doesn't matter where I used to live. But what might be of value is studying how many people moved to somewhere else under different circumstances. Do people move more or less during good economic times versus poor economic times? Where do they move to and what drives their decisions?

Such correlations are fundamental building blocks of hypotheses, design, and the logic we use to get through the day. So a big thesis of the TCW is the question, "What events and values go up and down together?"

In our exploration of time series within BI, we'll delve into the concept of inflection points as pivotal events. An inflection point occurs when a time series graph demonstrates a sustained shift in direction, signaling a fundamental change in the underlying trend. Unlike spikes, which are typically abrupt and short-lived anomalies, inflection points suggest a more enduring transformation that could indicate a new phase of growth, decline, or cyclical behavior.

For instance, in sales data, an inflection point could reflect the impact of a successful marketing campaign or viral video that resulted in a sustained increase in sales. In the context of website traffic analytics, a downward inflection point could correspond to a change in Google's search algorithm, resulting in a lasting drop in page views.

By identifying these points, analysts can investigate concurrent changes in related domains. A sudden and sustained increase in customer service calls might correlate with the inflection point of rising sales, perhaps suggesting issues shipping or product quality. Similarly, a dip in employee productivity might align with a change in internal policy or market conditions.

Recognizing and analyzing these events through the lens of time series data allows businesses to correlate changes across different facets of the organization, providing insights into the causative relationships that drive business dynamics.

Incorporating a time-based correlative approach, we can further enhance our analysis by matching spikes across timelines. Consider spikes as events that, while they may appear as outliers, can still hold significant correlational value. For instance, a spike in social media mentions may precede a spike in website downtime, indicating a causal relationship. By applying Bayesian inference, we can update the probability of one event influencing another based on the observed frequency and timing of these spikes. This probabilistic framework allows us to discern patterns and potential causative links, enriching our understanding of how isolated events might interplay within the broader tapestry of enterprise data.

The "Social Network" of Tuples

Think of tuples as things. For example, the price of oil in Brazil, the consumption of chocolate in Japan, and the sales of orange lipstick in Finland. All three are "things" we can metaphorically point to—just like "The number of articles written by the guy living in Boise." Between all things, there are relationships. For example, a social network is a map of the relationships between a group of people (things). From a social network we can extract information such as Eugene knows Laurie who knows Ellen who knows Uncle James. Therefore, Eugene knows a path to connect with Uncle James.

The TCW is a big ontology of tuples and is as valuable to a BI analyst as a social network is to a detective who is finding chains of strong relationships hoping to connect the dots of a crime.

Figure 103 illustrates the TCW within the entire EKG context. The TCW is a framework that captures the relationships between various data points, represented as tuples, and examines their time-based correlations. The DC acts as the foundational layer, categorizing the data and defining the potential interactions within the TCW. It's through this meticulous mapping that the TCW, supported by the knowledge encoded within the KG by domain experts, reveals the hidden patterns and trends in the organization's data:

1. The DC delineates the components that form the TCW, acting as the schema for the data's structure and relationships.

2. Nodes within the DC are linked to entities in the KG which are crafted by domain experts. For instance, the "Country" table in the DC aligns with the "Country" class in the KG, complete with its attributes and a network of relationships to other entities.

3. The TCW is a network of statistical relationships, representing correlations and probabilities across pairs of tuples, where each tuple equates to an individual row derived from a Query Definition.

4. Each Query Definition contributes tuples to the TCW. A specific Query Definition might filter data to show only "Corn" sales across all counties for the year 2020.

5. At the center of each tuple interaction within the TCW is a model node, serving as the central connector for data extracted from the Query Definitions.

6. The first of two tuples for which we will compute a correlation is the sales data for "Corn" in "Clark County" during the year 2020.

7. The other tuple is the Price of Crude oil on the Comex during 2020.

8. The correlation, in this case a Pearson correlation, is calculated between tuples to evaluate their relationship over time. In the example provided, this correlation is computed on a weekly time series basis, illustrating the interplay between two data points within the TCW. The score of 0.36 indicates a weak correlation.

Please note that the arrows pointing to seemingly "nowhere" indicate connections to other nodes.

Figure 103 encapsulates the essence of the TCW. It is interconnected and infused with expert knowledge. As businesses continue to evolve and embrace complex data-driven decision-making, frameworks, such as the one presented in this figure will become invaluable. They will serve as the cerebral cortex of the corporate entity, enabling the seamless flow of information and insights across its many functional areas—truly making the enterprise knowledge graph the brain of the business organism.

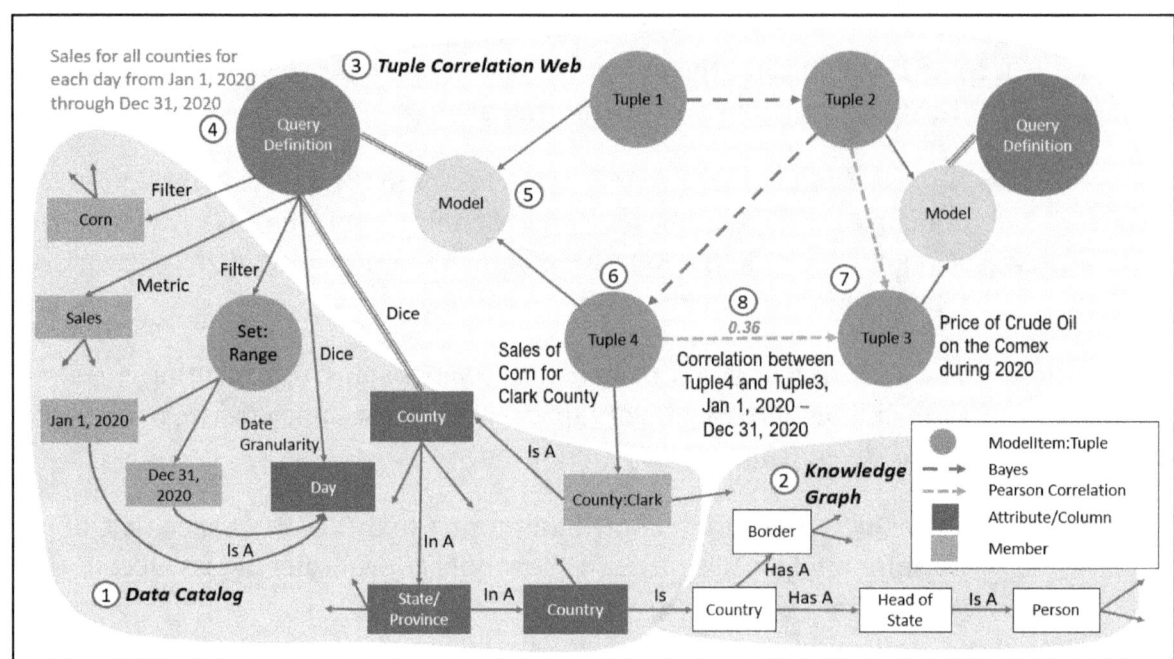

Figure 103: "Social Network" of Tuples.

Putting Old Myths and Legends to the Test

The TCW can help validate assumptions we've long believed because "that's the way it's always been done" or "because that's what the consultants told us to do." Those corporate myths and legends accumulate in a work environment. These myths and legends probably were founded on a truth that has long passed. Even if they still have some residual truth, things change, yet the myths persist, resulting in unnecessary blinders and friction.

Most corporate myths and legends can be transposed into a chain of hypothesized cause and effect, a mini TCW. For example, if we plan to use the knowledge that happy employees make better products and better products make happier customers, we can test it by querying two tuples then measuring the correlation. The contemporary correlations captured in the data-driven TCW aren't prone to the biases of those old myths and legends entrenched in the corporate culture.

Correlations that are discovered in this manner would then be saved to the TCW, even if the correlation or probability is weak and/or uninteresting. This way, the proof or the debunking of the myths and legends is noted as a reference for the employees of the future.

With the TCW, we can also play what-if, forgetting about how things have always been done—at least in the safety of our enterprise's "mind." Paradigms change, and periodically, we need to revamp things instead of merely applying another patch of incremental change.

Correlation Algorithms

Following is a brief discussion of algorithms to compute the relationship between tuples.

Bayesian Probabilities

Bayesian probability is like betting on a football match. Initially, you might guess the chances of a team winning based on their past performance. However, as you learn more—say, the star player is injured—you'll adjust your prediction.

Figure 104 depicts a snapshot of a Bayesian network and corresponding calculations related to cancer diagnosis, integrating data from a pathology lab and a doctor's office. It illustrates how Bayesian inference is used to update the probability of having cancer given a positive test result:

1. **Has Cancer**—This represents the prior probability of having cancer before any test results are known. It's set at 0.05, indicating that there's a 5% chance a patient has cancer before considering the test results.

2. **Positive Result**—This is the node in the Bayesian network where the test result is positive. It is linked to the probability of having cancer and also to the probabilities related to the accuracy of the test (true positive and false positive rates).

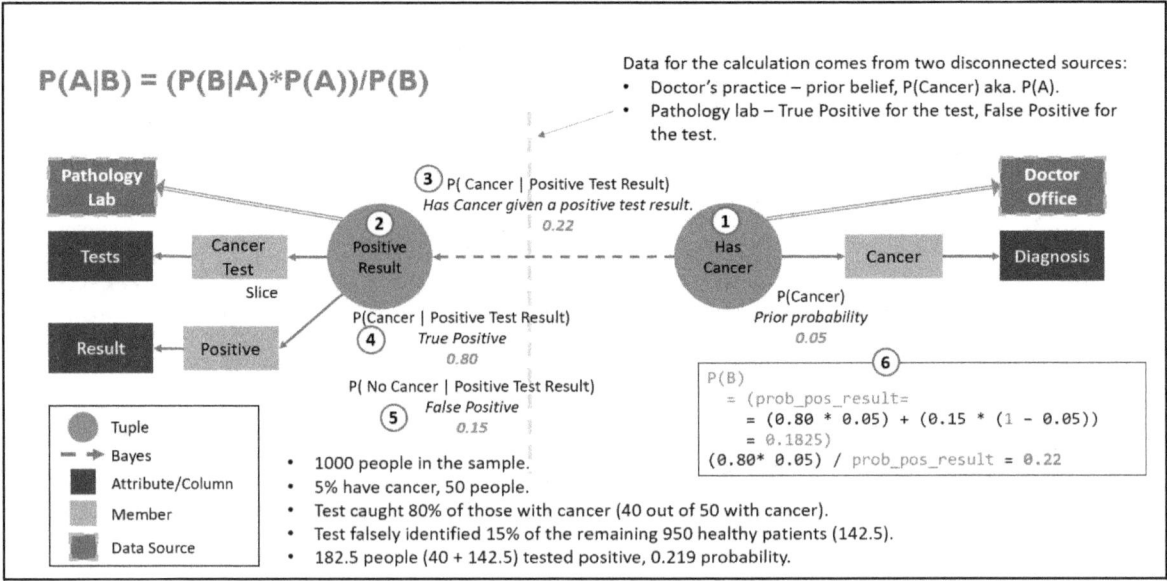

Figure 104: Bayesian Probability.

3. **P(Cancer | Positive Test Result)**–The probability of having cancer given a positive test result is calculated using Bayes' theorem. This number (0.22) is the posterior probability, updated from the prior probability based on the test result.

4. **True Positive Rate (P(Cancer | Positive Test Result))**–This is the likelihood of a positive test result if the patient has cancer, given as 0.80.

5. **False Positive Rate (P(No Cancer | Positive Test Result))**–This is the likelihood of a positive test result if the patient does not have cancer, given as 0.15.

6. **Probability Calculation**–This step shows the calculation of the overall probability of a positive test result, combining the true positive rate with the prior probability and the false positive rate with the complement of the prior probability. The final calculation uses this overall probability of a positive test result to determine the posterior probability of having cancer given a positive test result, which is 0.22.

The snapshot essentially outlines a Bayesian approach to medical diagnosis, where the prior probability of a condition is updated in the face of new evidence (the test result) to give a more accurate assessment of a patient's condition.

Regarding Bayesian probabilities, this is about as straightforward as can be. But there is a lot of thinking that has to come into play. As I mentioned earlier, for this book, I'm focusing on the easier-to-understand Conditional Probabilities. This makes more sense because the TCW is a BI structure, and for the most part, we have the data to calculate probabilities. This will certainly be revisited in a future volume. It's important to note that for this example, the databases of the pathology lab and doctor's office are not integrated. If they were, we could calculate the probabilities directly from databases. For example, the pathology lab and doctor's office could be part of the same healthcare system, whereby they would have direct access to each other's data. We would know exactly which patients have cancer, took the test, and know the result of the test. This is easier to work with and it's the next algorithm, conditional probabilities.

Conditional Probabilities

Conditional probabilities are easier to understand and much more straightforward than the Bayesian calculation we just went through. Additionally, the method of conditional probabilities that I describe here leverages one of the most important concepts of the TCW - the ubiquitous time dimension, which is a common dimension among almost any BI data source.

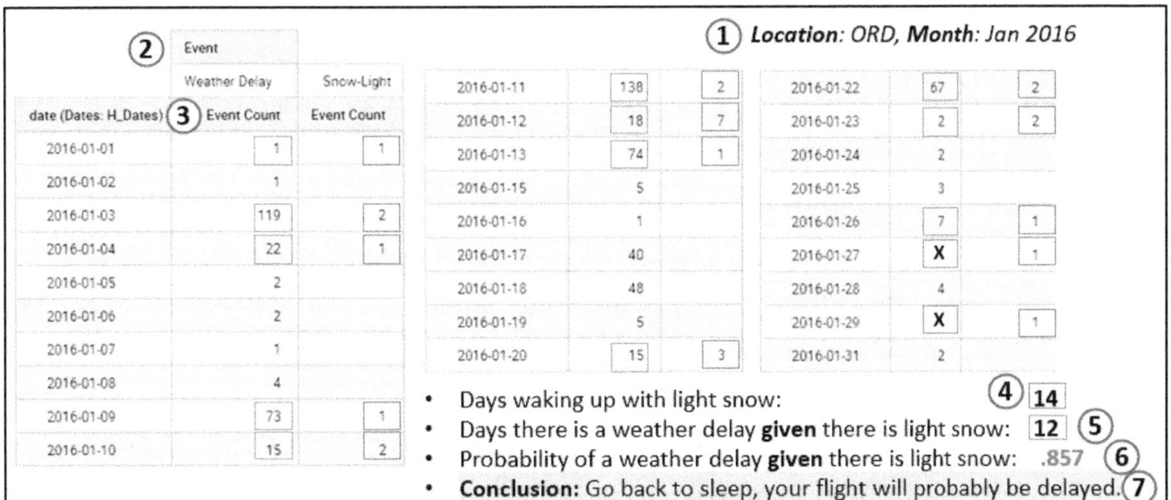

Figure 105: Example of conditional probability calculation.

Figure 105 illustrates an example of a conditional probability. The data is presented as a typical cross-tab view from a typical OLAP cube. It shows "Weather Delay" and "Snow-Light" counts for each day of the month of January 2016 at ORD airport.

1. **Location and Time**—The data is for Chicago O'Hare International Airport (ORD) for the month of January 2016.

2. **Events**—Two types of events are being tracked: "Weather Delay" and "Snow-Light" (light snowfall).

3. **Event Count**—Each day has counts for general weather delays and light snow events.

4. **Denominator (Days with Light Snow)**—The total number of days with light snow, which is 14.

5. **Numerator (Number of Delays Given Light Snow)**—This is the count of days where both a weather delay occurred and light snow was present, which is 12.

6. **The conditional probability** is calculated as the ratio of these two numbers: 12 days with both weather delay and light snow out of 14 days with light snow, resulting in 0.857 (or 85.7%).

7. **Conclusion**—Based on this data, the conclusion is drawn that if there's light snow, there's an 85.7% chance of a flight delay.

If I awoke at my hotel a bit later than I intended to catch my flight, I don't need to worry too much since there is a good chance my flight will be delayed.

Pearson Correlation

Imagine two dancers on a stage. If every time one dancer takes a step forward, the other also takes a step forward, they're moving together. But if one steps forward and the other steps back, they're moving opposite each other. Pearson Correlation is all about seeing how two things move in relation to each other.

Business Example: In a coffee shop, you observe that usually when you release a new flavor, sales of muffins also go up. It's like both the coffee and muffin are dancing in step. But if new coffee flavor generally results in fewer tea sales, then coffee and tea are dancing in opposite directions.

Pearson Correlation is a measure of the linear correlation between two variables. It's a value between -1 and 1, where:

- 1 means total positive linear correlation—The two-time series go up and down together.
- 0 means no linear correlation.
- -1 means total negative linear correlation. One time series goes up while the other goes down, and vice-versa.

As a rough guideline:

- 0-0.19 or 0 to -0.19 is generally seen as a very weak or no correlation.
- 0.20-0.39 or -0.20 to -0.39 is considered a weak correlation.
- 0.40-0.59 or -0.40 to -0.59 is a moderate correlation.
- 0.60-0.79 or -0.60 to -0.79 is a strong correlation.
- 0.80-1.00 or -0.80 to -1.00 is a very strong correlation.

Spearman Correlation

Spearman correlations are very similar to Pearson. But Spearman is able to capture non-linear relationships better than the linear Pearson. Spearman transforms values into rankings, which focus on the order of values rather than their specific magnitudes. This method assesses how well the relationship between two variables can be described regardless of the rate of change.

By comparing rankings rather than actual values, Spearman's approach can identify underlying trends that may not follow a straight line, making it robust against outliers and skewed distributions. As an example, Figure 106 shows a short table of sales for broccoli and the temperature for a few days:

1. **Data Table Overview for Pearson:** This is the raw data, daily temperatures and broccoli sales. The data illustrates how sales fluctuate with changes in temperature over the course of five days. The Pearson score is calculated from these values.

2. **Ranking Method for Spearman:** Accompanying the raw data are two additional columns that show the ranking order of both temperature and sales, assigning a rank of 1 to the highest value and 5 to the lowest. This ranking is used to compare the positions rather than the actual sales figures or temperature readings.

3. **Pearson Correlation Chart:** This is a scatterplot for the Pearson correlation. This plot pairs the actual temperature values with the actual sales values to

determine if there is a direct, one-to-one relationship where sales consistently go up with temperature. The correlation value of approximately 0.475 indicates a moderate positive relationship, but it is not strong enough to suggest that sales of broccoli and temperature always increase together in a proportional way.

4. **Spearman Correlation Chart:** To the right of the Pearson plot is the Spearman correlation scatterplot. This graph uses the rank values instead of the actual sales of broccoli and temperature data. Notice that the blue line is a bit curved. That reflects the non-linear nature of Spearman, which can capture more nuance in the relationship. However, as with Pearson, the probability is weak, at 0.40.

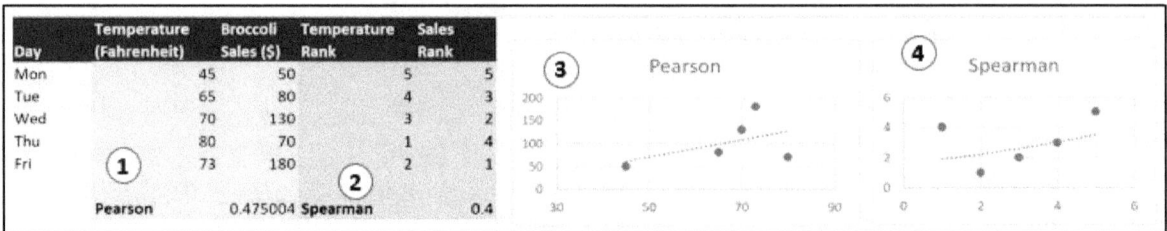

Figure 106: Example of a Pearson vs Spearman calculation.

In simpler terms, Pearson's approach is like looking at how the amount of sunshine each day relates directly to the amount of broccoli sold—expecting that more sun equals more sales by a specific amount. In contrast, Spearman's approach is akin to noticing that sunnier days are generally better for broccoli sales, even if one particularly bright day doesn't break a sales record. Spearman's analysis is more about the overall trend than the exact relationship between two specific numbers.

Here is a summary of the differences between the three:

- Bayesian Probability: Like adjusting your football bet when you get more information about the team's condition.

- Pearson Correlation: Observing if two things move together, like dancers. Do they step forward at the same time or in opposite directions?

- Spearman Correlation: Watching rankings in a contest. Is someone consistently at the top, middle, or bottom?

Bayesian helps you make better predictions with additional info (like the weather for Flight 333). Pearson tells you if two pieces of data tend to increase or decrease together (like coffee flavors and muffin sales). Spearman checks if, relative to everything else, something stays consistently high or low (like a restaurant's feedback rank). These insights can be incredibly valuable when making business decisions, from planning flight schedules to crafting a coffee shop menu.

Pearson Correlation Example

Figure 107 shows the daily closing stock prices for MSFT (Microsoft) and NVDA (NVIDIA) over the period July 2022 through July 2023. Is there a reliable correlation between their stock prices? That information can help us to identify clusters of dependent companies. If one breaks, there's a good chance the other might be along their way to pain.

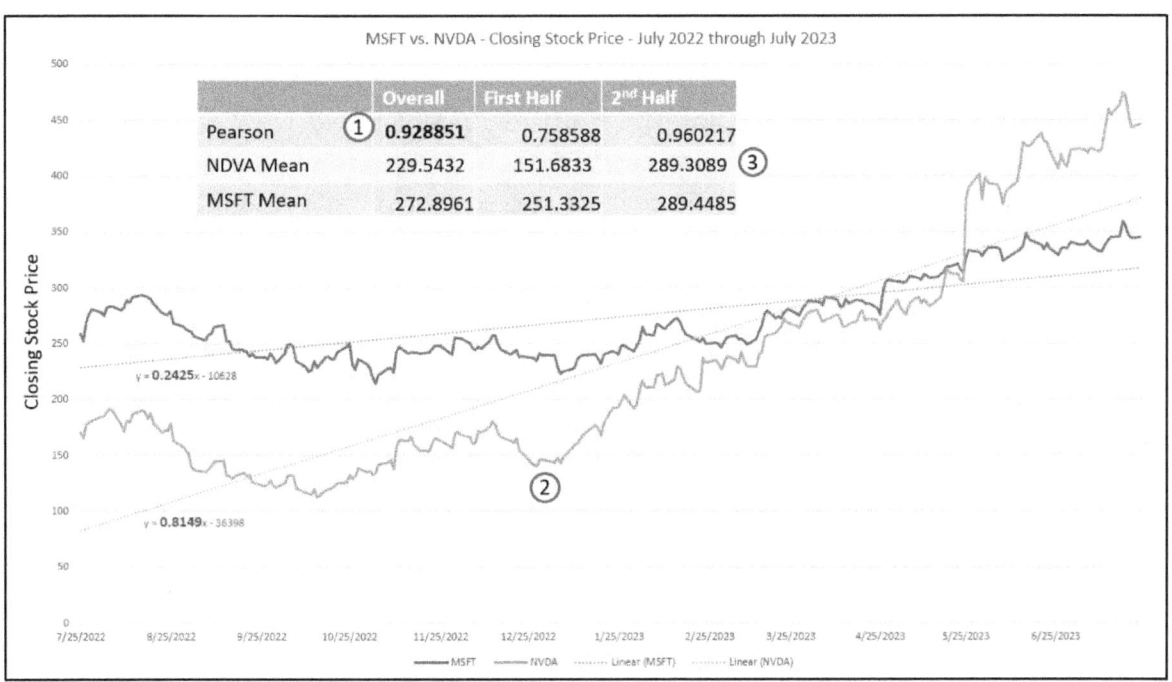

Figure 107: Closing stock price for MSFT and NVDA, July 2022 through July 2023.

It was a very good year for Microsoft, in large part because of their partnership with OpenAI. Microsoft's stock ended up higher. But it was an *incredible* period for NVDA, which also benefited from the rise of ChatGPT. We can see NVDA sputtered about from July 2022 and shot up around January 2023, a few weeks after ChatGPT went viral (2).

Of course, NVDA is a leading manufacturer of graphics processing units (GPUs), which are essential for running machine learning algorithms efficiently. ChatGPT and similar AI models require significant computational power, today usually provided by GPUs, to process and analyze large datasets quickly.

Do you notice the strong 0.92881 Pearson correlation between MSFT and NVDA (1)? Although that figure is correct, it's probably misleading. That level of correlative strength is rare for any two independent publicly traded companies over a fair period of time.

The problem is that the two time series are "non-stationary" (I'll explain soon). That means the mean and variance (and autocorrelation structure) can change significantly over time. In this case, the closing price for NVDA began a steep rise halfway through the 12-month period, Jan 23, 2023 (2). The mean and variance for NVDA from July 2022-Dec 2022 and Jan 2023-July 2023 are very different, 151.68 and 289.3089, respectively (3).

Figure 108 plots the closing stock prices of MSFT and NVDA during the 12-month period. You can see the points are fairly close to the trend line, and they are distributed along the line pretty well. So a good correlation sounds reasonable—but not a strong 0.92.

Things to note in Figure 108:

1. MSFT trades within a narrower band than NVDA (see the gap between the two vertical dashed lines).

2. The big gap is when NVDA shot up on May 25, 2023 from 305.38 to 379.80. That's quite an inflection point, which we'll discuss later under "Special Structures."

Figure 109 shows the Pearson correlation for the separate halves of the 12-month period. Again, things changed for NVDA around January 2023.

In the first half, we see a fair correlation of 0.758588. Most of the dots are not exactly close to the trend line, but they do distribute fairly well along the trend line. Both stocks have closing prices in a narrower range as well during the first half, both between 200 and 300.

In the 2nd half, the dots seem closer to the trend line and follow a nice linear path. We also see that the range of stock closing prices is wider, from 200 to close to 500 for

NVDA. The correlation for the 2nd half is even stronger than the 0.92 for the entire 12-month period.

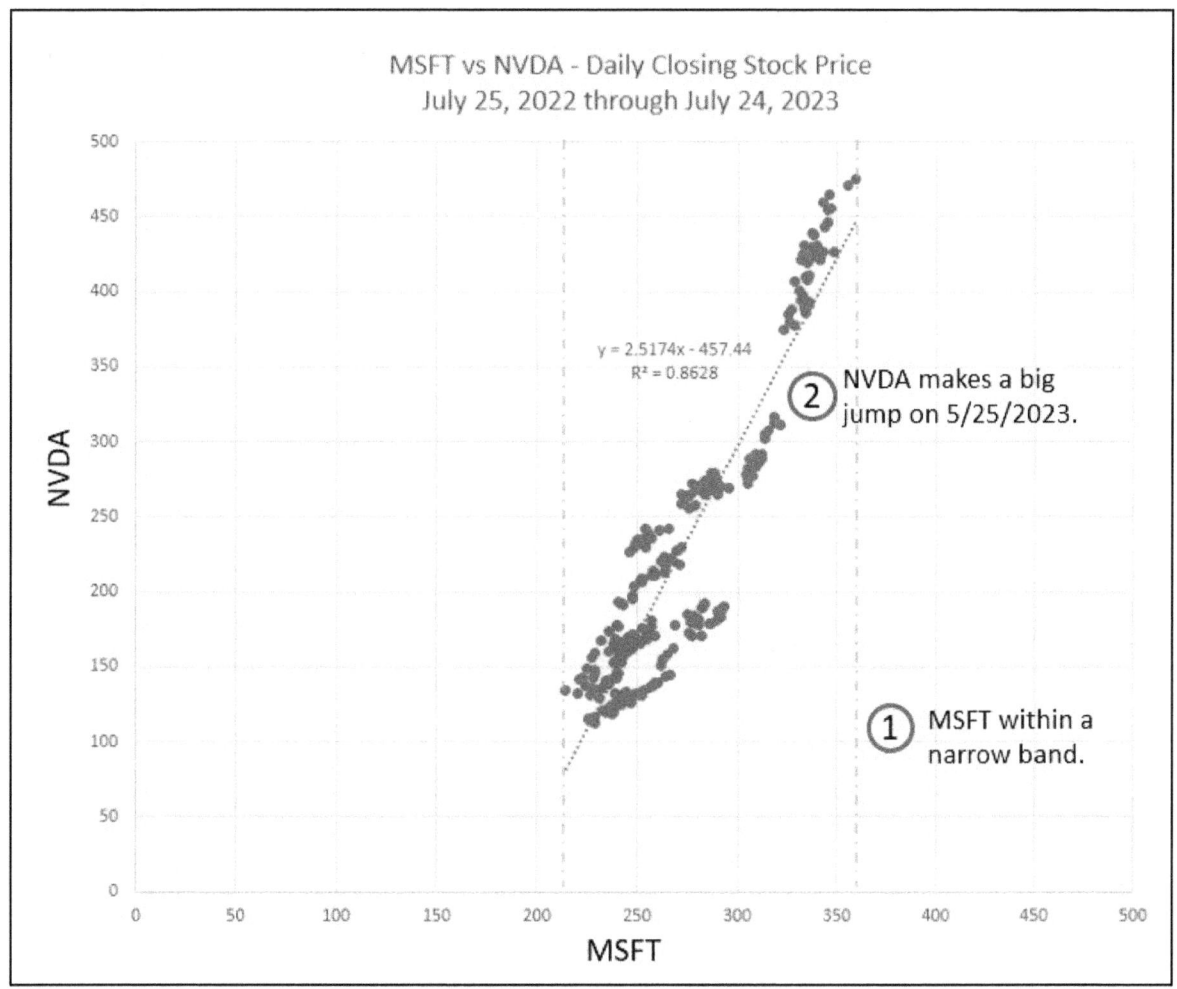

Figure 108: MSFT versus NVDA closing stock price.

So which is right? Going back to the initial issue, is the strong overall Pearson correlation of 0.92 realistic? Yes, MSFT and NVDA are in the high tech sector and both benefit from the cloud and AI, but they are very different companies. That is a known problem that can pop up. I just mentioned "non-stationary" time series where the averages change drastically, whereas Pearson correlations assume they are fairly stable.

So in Map Rock (Version 2 or the AEI), I computed the Pearson correlations, not on the raw values, but on the day-to-day percentage change. That value is mostly within -1 through 1 (from -100% to 100% day to day change). Fortunately and unfortunately, stocks rarely move day-to-day over a percentage point.

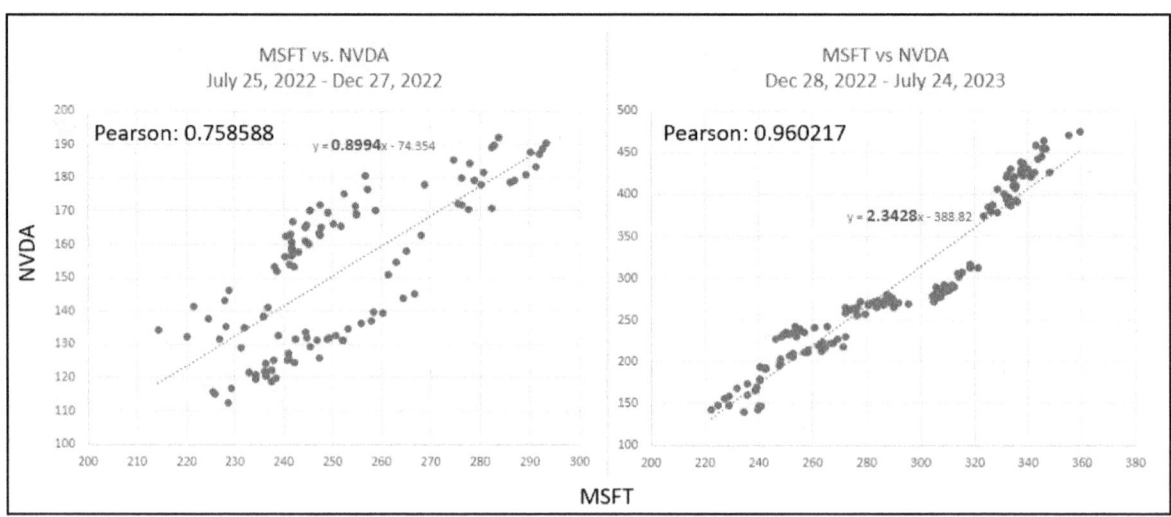

Figure 109: Two halves of scatter plot.

Transforming to Stationary Values

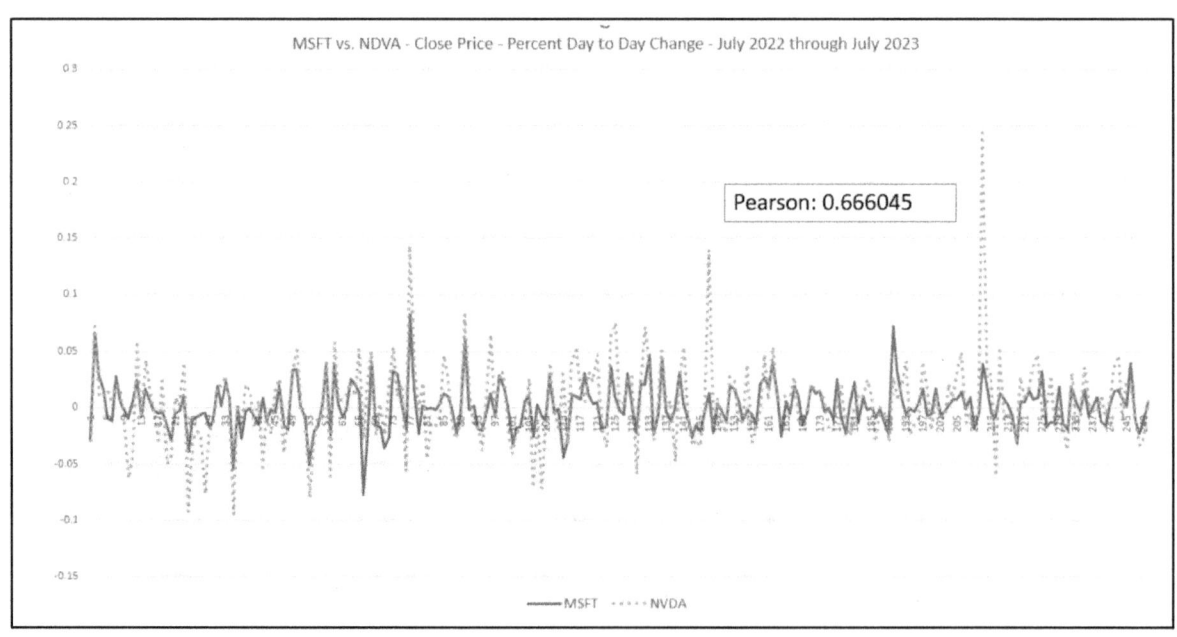

Figure 110: Percent Day to Day Change of MSFT and NVDA.

Figure 110 is the day-to-day percentage change of the closing stock price for MSFT and NVDA. Notice the much lower, but still moderate, Pearson correlation of 0.66045.

Intuitively for folks in the IT business who are familiar with MSFT and NVDA, that makes more sense. MSFT and NVDA both benefit from the continued investment in data centers. But they are completely separate entities focusing on different parts of the high tech sector, so a moderate correlation makes more sense.

Plotting the Rolling Average Correlation

We looked at how to calculate the correlation between MSFT and NVDA from July 2022 through July 2023 using the day to day percent change of the stock closing price. Throughout that 12-month period, the correlation was around a moderate 0.66. The question is: Is that the correlation consistent throughout all points of that period?

Figure 111 plots a rolling correlation between MSFT and NVDA over the same period, within the window of the previous 30 days, not the entire 365-day span.

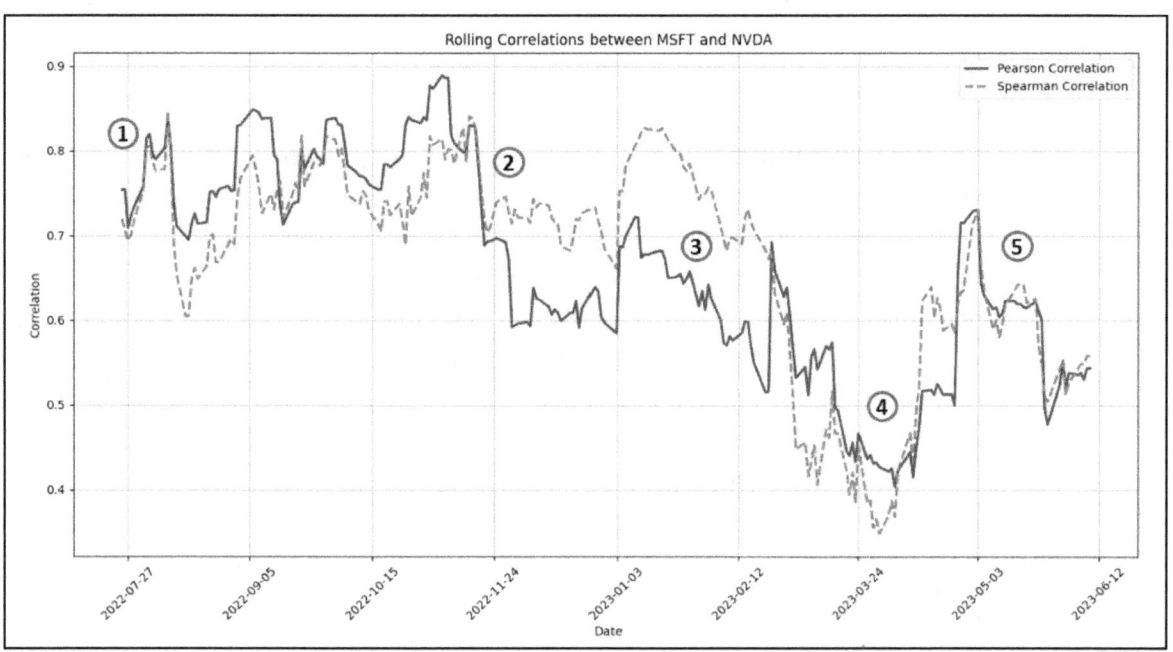

Figure 111: Rolling correlation between MSFT and NVDA daily stock close.

Let's observe some of the inflection points of the Pearson correlation (blue/solid line):

1. The correlation for the rolling 30 days starts fairly strong, hovering between 0.70 and close to 0.90.

2. The correlation weakens rather abruptly around mid-November 2022. For a couple of months, the correlation hovers around 0.60. What happened?

3. Around early January 2023, it abruptly picked up back to the 0.70 area, but again weakens over the next few months.

4. Around late March 2023, the correlation again strengthens to a peak around 0.70 in early May.

5. That stronger correlation starts another weakening.

For MSFT/NVDA, at all periods over the 12 months, correlation remains at least fair. It never did drop to the point of a weak or even inverse correlation. That would have been more interesting. But nonetheless, the relationship between entities is what the TCW is all about.

Correlation Parameters

Determining Lag for Cause and Effect

Time lag or simply "lag" is a concept comparing two time series where the date range of one series is shifted a little before or ahead of the other. With these lags we can find not just correlations or relationships with another series, but potential causality. If two time series exhibit a significant correlation with some lag, this can be an indication of some form of relationship, which in certain contexts might even suggest causality. However, it's vital to remember the adage: "correlation does not imply causation." Just because two events consistently occur close together in time doesn't mean one caused the other. There could be confounding variables or hidden factors at play. For instance, if every time it thunders in Boise, you wake up a second later, then there's a clear temporal relationship between the two events. But if you consistently wake up at 7:00 AM, and the mail gets delivered at 7:05 AM, it doesn't mean your waking up causes the mail to be delivered.

Imagine you're trying to figure out if a rooster crowing causes the sun to rise. Every morning, you note the exact time the rooster crows and when the sun rises. After several days, you observe that the rooster crows about five minutes before sunrise. This consistent time difference, or lag suggests a strong correlation between the two events.

In the world of BI and time-based data, understanding lag is crucial. Events that happen consistently close together might be related. However, as just mentioned, because two things consistently happen near each other in time doesn't mean one causes the other.

It's a hint, a piece of the puzzle, but not definitive proof. In our example, the impending sunrise causes the rooster to crow, but the rooster crowing doesn't cause the sun to rise.

For the TCW, where we're trying to correlate events based on time, understanding and measuring lag can offer valuable insights. However, it's essential to dig deeper, explore other factors, and use expert judgment to determine if a cause-and-effect relationship truly exists.

Time Series Intervals

The choice of time intervals for correlation analysis, whether using Pearson or Spearman methods, hinges on the balance between granularity and statistical significance. A well-chosen interval can reveal underlying patterns without being obscured by noise or biased by sample size limitations.

For BI use cases, a rule of thumb for the number of data points in a time series could range from a dozen to 40. Fewer than a dozen data points might not provide enough statistical power to support the correlation's validity, potentially yielding spurious results. More than 40, while it can be advantageous in some cases, could lead to overfitting where the model too closely reflects the random peculiarities of the sample data rather than any true underlying population trend.

Here are a few examples of heuristics for choosing intervals of time:

- Two to five years—Monthly offers the best level of aggregation—24 to 60 data points.

- Over five years—At five or so years, monthly still offers the best level of aggregation, but close to ten years or more, we could even aggregate at the year level. We could also study how a particular month or quarter changes over the years. For that, we'll need at least eight years (for example, study the Januarys over an eight-year period).

- 12-month period (year)—Weekly intervals often provide a judicious balance. They condense daily fluctuations which can be volatile, and smooth over distinctions, such as weekend versus weekday behaviors, which may or may not be relevant depending on the context. This approach aligns with the notion that less frequent intervals can mask short-term irregularities that might otherwise skew the correlation. On the other hand, too few data points, such as using monthly intervals over a year, may overlook important trends and not provide enough resolution for a robust analysis.

- Month (30ish days)–Daily intervals typically offer the most insight. They capture the necessary detail to discern patterns within the limited scope, without fragmenting the data excessively. Here, the daily changes are significant to the timeframe, and aggregating to a coarser level might dilute the actionable intelligence one could derive from the analysis. Weekends and holidays often should be removed since there is usually a big difference–but that still leaves over 20 days.

Ultimately, the selection of intervals should be governed by the specific characteristics of the data and the analytical goals. It requires a judicious blend of statistical rationale and domain expertise. The correlation should provide meaningful insights that are actionable, align with theoretical expectations, or reveal new understanding, all while maintaining statistical rigor.

Casting a Wide Net

This is a kind of BI exploration that I created many years ago in Map Rock. But it seems to now be a feature in Tableau and PowerBI known as a Correlation Grid. Basically, if a user is exploring for clues (correlations between things) towards solving a problem, the user can cast a wide net across two dimensions to view correlations en masse. For example, are there any correlations between the price of oil in some countries and the stock price among a list of bank stocks? A grid is created with countries on rows and stock ticker symbols on columns. Each cell is a Pearson correlation between the intersection of country and stock. The ones with a strong correlation show up in a highlighting color. They can further be saved as data points for an AI so the AI can avoid having to do the exploration itself.

For BI analysts and knowledge workers without coding skills, casting a wide net requires the UI to have the features of the Correlation Grid described earlier, similar to Map Rock visualization I built. It could also be run through sample Jupyter notebook sample in the GitHub directory–casting_a_wide_net.py.

Although casting a wide net as a BI activity is a powerful tool, we can find correlations based on dataframes passively encountered from normal BI analyst activity. That is, we can leverage the activity of analysts as hints as to what might be valuable correlations. Remember, the ISG and TCW are built passively from BI consumer activity.

The everyday BI activity by an analyst implies what is important to her around that query time. She is looking for insights to help resolve her problem at hand. Chances are, other knowledge workers in other domains might be working on related parts of that problem or tackling it from a different angle. The workers may or may not even be aware of the efforts by others. Figure 112 illustrates the intricate process of incorporating BI practices within the framework of the EKG:

1. **Analysts Analyzing**—At the onset, a myriad of BI analysts from varied domains go about their typical BI exploration using visualization tools, such as Tableau or PowerBI. Through these tools, they compose data elements into visualizations ranging from bar charts to scatter plots. A dataframe queried from the BI data source is what paints the visualization is a dataframe. These dataframes are captured (outlined circles).

2. **Insights Wrung from Dataframes**—The second phase entails the algorithmic distillation of visual outputs. An array of insight functions autonomously deciphers insights from the visualizations—spotting trends, anomalies, and patterns just as a trained human eye would. Each extracted insight is linked to the dataframe.

3. **Transformation into Graph Structures—**These insights, paired with the metadata of their corresponding dataframe, undergo a transformation into structured graph formats. Before landing in the ISG, they pass through a filtration process, ensuring only insights surpassing defined thresholds are retained. Within the ISG, each dataframe (a QueryDef) gets its dedicated node. Insights that meet thresholds are linked to these nodes, creating a dynamic and interconnected web. Additionally, the ISG ensures the dataframes' columns and metrics find their respective anchors in the data catalog, preserving the essence of the data without actually storing the entire dataframe.

4. **Tuple Correlation Web**—This fourth step is partially parallel with step 3. The user-viewed dataframes undergo a correlation analysis. The Pearson method is employed to determine the extent and nature of correlations between new dataframes and selected existing dataframes. Those correlations that meet the defined threshold criteria are earmarked for inclusion in the TCW. Here, individual data points, termed as tuples (e.g., "the price of oil in Beijing"), are

represented as nodes. Linked to specific column nodes in the data catalog, these tuples form a web of correlations.

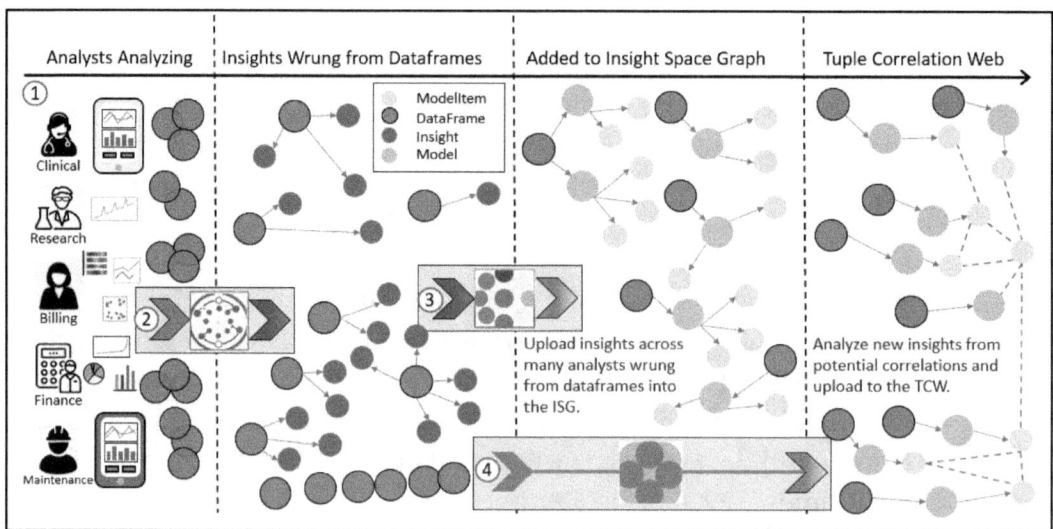

Figure 112: Analysts using BI through to the TCW.

Intelligent Query Patterns

In the realm of BI, insights arise from patterns, anomalies, or relationships embedded within data. Just as a detective pieces together clues to unravel a mystery, or a coach observes players to formulate winning strategies, savvy BI analysts use various modes of reasoning to extract actionable insights from data. Central to this exploration are two primary query patterns: the Detective and Coach patterns.

Before diving deep into these patterns, it's paramount to understand the types of reasoning that form their foundation. At the heart of these reasoning processes are three classical modes:

- Deductive Reasoning
    - Explanation: It starts with a general statement or hypothesis and examines the possibilities to reach a specific, logical conclusion.
    - Example for BI Analyst: Given that all sales transactions above $10,000 are subject to an additional verification process (a general rule), when presented with a specific transaction of $15,000, the analyst can deduce that this transaction will undergo additional verification.

- Inductive Reasoning
    - Explanation: It makes broad generalizations from specific observations. This reasoning can often be the basis for predictions, theories, or hypotheses.
    - Example for BI Analyst: If an analyst observes that there's a spike in sales every Friday evening for several weeks, they might induce that there is some event attracting more customers-for example, a summer concert series on Fridays.

- Abductive Reasoning
    - Explanation: It begins with an observation and then seeks the simplest and most likely cause or explanation for the observation.
    - Example for BI Analyst: When seeing an unusual dip in website traffic on a particular day and nothing of note happened that day, based on the gathering a notable events, an analyst might abduce that there was a server issue on that day, causing the website to be temporarily inaccessible.

Deductive and inductive reasoning are probably more familiar than abductive reasoning. Deductive reasoning involves applying general rules or principles that are already known or have been previously established to specific cases. The process starts with a theory or premise and moves toward a conclusion based on the application of these rules. The conclusions drawn through deductive reasoning are considered certain, provided the premises are true and the reasoning is valid.

Inductive reasoning is about observing patterns, data, or specific instances and making generalizations based on them. Induction often begins with empirical observations, from which rules or theories are then inferred. Inductive reasoning is probabilistic, meaning that the conclusions reached are probable or likely, rather than certain, because they are based on limited observations and there might be exceptions not yet observed.

So, in a way, deductive reasoning is about applying what is learned, while inductive reasoning is about the process of learning itself—observing and then generalizing. Abductive reasoning is the most sophisticated. We'll explore abductive reasoning more soon. In any case, all three are generally applied towards any problem involving human or artificial intelligence.

Actionable Insights

The term "actionable insight" is often used in the analytics industry to refer to information that can prompt immediate, tangible actions. However, this oversimplifies the complexity of strategic decision-making in real-world business scenarios. Beyond raw data and basic insights, effective decision-making involves integrating experience, intuition, judgment, and a broader understanding of context. This is particularly true when working with KPIs:

- State Awareness: The primary purpose of a KPI is to provide awareness of the state of things. Whether a KPI is in a "good" or "bad" status, it reflects the current state and trend of a particular aspect of the business.

- Contextual Interpretation: For any KPI in a negative status, understanding the broader context is crucial. Why is it in that status? What external or internal factors contributed?

- Strategic Formulation: Based on the state and context, leaders can strategize potential courses of action. This is where experience, intuition, and broader business knowledge come into play. It's also where collaboration and consultation with others become valuable.

- Experimentation and Learning: In many cases, especially when dealing with novel challenges, the right course of action isn't clear. Organizations might need to experiment, learn, and iterate. This adaptive approach is particularly relevant in rapidly changing industries or uncertain environments.

- Feedback Loop: Once an action is taken, the results should feed back into the KPI system. Over time, this iterative process can lead to more refined strategies and a better understanding of which actions lead to desired outcomes.

In essence, while KPIs can provide a snapshot of where things stand (and a little insight on which way things are trending), the journey from a negative status to resolution involves a blend of analytical, strategic, and adaptive thinking.

With these reasoning techniques as a foundation, BI analysts can navigate their data-rich environments much like detectives and coaches, connecting the dots, piecing together clues or strategizing for success. The following exploration of the Detective and Coach query patterns will shed light on how analysts can harness the power of reasoning to derive valuable insights from their datasets.

Detective Query Pattern

Sherlock Holmes inspires one type of "business problem" I'm trying to address. That is, how to construct a theory towards a root cause analysis. When a detective is presented with a case (a troubling event), there are sparse clues to begin with (otherwise, there wouldn't be a need for the services of a detective). The detective takes the clues and expands them by finding relationships to the disparate clues. It then expands from that second ring of clues until enough dots are connected into a theory, a web of cause and effect.

It's not just detectives. All top-tier troubleshooters are detectives. At Microsoft, one of my roles was called a "critsit" (critical situation) engineer for SSAS. Resolving a customer's SSAS problem that went through the first three tiers of support engineers stopped with me. The problem was novel–not Google-able and not in our knowledge base. It's detective work, starting with anything that seems odd and exploring relationships until the dots are all connected. It's important to note that I'm not suggesting an AGI. I'm suggesting the combination of LLM and the TCW as an assistant to critsit engineers or doctors at the diagnostic excellence of "House," the TV doctor.

This pattern aims to draw connections between seemingly unrelated data points to form a cohesive theory or explanation. It's iterative and expansive, starting with initial data points and branching out by finding related entities until a story or pattern emerges. In the context of an EKG with ISG/TCW, this would likely involve:

1. Starting with a few known entities or facts.

2. Querying the graph to find direct and indirect relationships between these entities.

3. Continuously expanding the query to encompass newly found related entities until a chain or web of strong correlations arises from which we can lift a comprehensive narrative or solution.

This pattern is particularly useful for troubleshooting, diagnostics, and any situation where the initial set of data is limited, and the solution is non-obvious.

The Detective Query Pattern is both Abductive and Deductive Reasoning:

- Abductive Reasoning: It starts with an observation or set of observations and then seeks the simplest and most likely explanation for these observations. In the context of the detective pattern, when presented with sparse or disparate clues (observations), one tries to find the most probable explanation (hypothesis or theory) that connects them. It's a "best guess" based on available data.

- Deductive Reasoning: Once a theory or hypothesis is formed, deductive reasoning can be used to draw specific conclusions from it. If the theory is correct, then certain specific observations should also be true. Deduction can help validate the formed theory by checking it against known facts or further observations.

In essence, in the Detective Query Pattern, you start with a set of observations (clues), use abductive reasoning to form a hypothesis, and then employ deductive reasoning to validate that hypothesis or to derive further specifics from it.

The Coach Query Pattern

A really good coach notices things that others don't notice. They are the ones that can somehow see the batters having "Trouble with the Curve." The problem is that once a problem is noticed, competitive opponents quickly resolve it. Once a batter that has trouble with the curve resolves it, the coach needs to notice something else to restore a competitive edge.

A really good innovator doesn't just find novel solutions to known problems. A great innovator can see ways to solve problems others didn't know existed. For example, dunking in basketball was outside of the box thinking. I can imagine some coach thinking, "I bet if we could get hands above the hoop rim, we could score a lot more." Well, that would take a really tall person, but that tall person still needs to jump higher than almost everyone." Another example might be the Earl Campbell style, a swift bruiser of a running back.

This pattern is more about embracing the outliers. It focuses on identifying outliers, anomalies, or unique patterns that might not be immediately apparent. The objective is to detect "opportunities" or "weaknesses" that can be capitalized upon or rectified. In the EKG with ISG/TCW context, this might involve:

1. Observing and analyzing data to find anomalies, trends, or patterns.

2. Once identified, understanding the context of these patterns or anomalies.

3. Suggesting novel solutions or strategies based on the observations.

The Coach pattern seems more aligned with proactive problem detection and innovation. It's about seeing potential where others might not and then strategize based on that vision.

The Coach Query Pattern is Inductive Reasoning. It involves making broad generalizations from specific observations. In the context of the Coach pattern, noticing unique patterns, anomalies, or outliers from specific data points, and then generalizing to identify opportunities or potential strategies fits the mold of inductive reasoning. Induction is about understanding the broader picture or potential trend from specific instances.

The Coach Query Pattern primarily uses inductive reasoning by observing specific instances (like a player's unique skill or a peculiar trend) and then generalizing to form broader strategies or insights. However, it does employ abductive reasoning as well:

- Abductive Reasoning: The Coach Query Pattern shows signs of abductive reasoning when a coach or innovator identifies a solution to a problem others have not noticed or when they spot an opportunity for improvement that is not immediately obvious. The coach is essentially hypothesizing: "This unique approach could give us an advantage," even when the broader trend or principle behind that advantage isn't fully known. The hypothesis is formed based on an insightful observation that requires a leap of logic, not just a straightforward application of an established principle.

- Inductive Reasoning: The pattern also involves inductive reasoning when a coach observes a specific instance (such as a player's performance or a new technique) and generalizes from that to develop new strategies or coaching methods that can be applied more broadly.

So, while there's a base of inductive reasoning in recognizing patterns and generalizing, the creative leap to see potential solutions or novel strategies is aligned with abductive reasoning.

The MacGyver Query Pattern

Just as Sherlock Holmes symbolizes the quintessence of deductive reasoning via his detective work, and a coach embodies the spirit of pattern recognition and inductive thinking, MacGyver represents the pinnacle of *resourceful* problem-solving. The name "MacGyver" has, over the years, metamorphosed into a verb signifying an ingenious fix using just the materials on hand. This approach is paramount in business scenarios where immediate solutions are needed, often without the luxury of extensive resources, time, or new inventions.

In the vast and intricate realm of the EKG with ISG/TCW, the MacGyver Query Pattern is about immediate adaptive resolution. The situation demands solutions here and now, and there's no time to wait for the perfect set of tools or data. It's the equivalent of being stuck in a room with just a paper clip and a piece of gum and needing to craft an escape plan.

Here's how the MacGyver Query Pattern might play out:

1. Immediate Evaluation: Begin with a rapid assessment of available data and resources. This step is crucial because, unlike the detective who seeks out new clues, or the coach who observes patterns over time, MacGyver must use only what's immediately available.

2. Linking Disparate Data Points: Find quick relationships between seemingly unrelated data points. This is the digital equivalent of connecting a battery to a gum wrapper to start a fire: unlikely allies, but together, they solve the immediate problem.

3. Short-term Solutions: Recognize that the solution might be a temporary fix. The MacGyver approach is about resolving the immediate crisis, even if it means revisiting the problem later with more resources.

4. Iterative Refinement: Once the immediate issue is addressed, circle back and refine the solution. Use the breather to ensure that the makeshift solution doesn't lead to bigger problems down the line.

5. Leverage LLMs: Large Language Models, especially when integrated with the EKG, can act as the Swiss Army knife for the MacGyver approach. They can quickly parse available data, suggest connections, and offer immediate solutions based on the knowledge they've been trained on.

6. The MacGyver Query Pattern is quintessentially about Convergent Thinking. Unlike divergent thinking that seeks multiple possibilities, convergent thinking focuses on narrowing down the options to find the single best solution to a problem, and quickly.

In essence, while the Detective dives deep into clues, expanding the horizons, and the Coach observes and strategizes, MacGyver acts. It's about promptness, immediacy, and innovation. In the fast-paced world of business, where crises can erupt without warning, the MacGyver Query Pattern is not just a nifty approach; it's often a survival necessity.

Stressing the Correlations and Probabilities

The number of correlations in the cubespace we discussed earlier is indescribably beyond what we can justifiably hold in the TCW. And the vast majority of correlations we find and hold will end up being noise. So, we need practices to identify and weed out useless correlations.

Note that we will discuss in a wider scope in the section, "Pruning the ISG and TCW."

But defining "useless" isn't that easy. After all, the idea of the TCW and ISG is to avail information an analyst comes across that *might* be of value to other analysts, most of whom we don't know, and with the caveat of the downside of information overload (so many notifications everyone eventually ignores all of them). The TCW and ISG are about "We don't know what we don't know"–so let's note the correlation for future reference.

While the widely mentioned saying, "correlation does not imply causation," is sage advice, it's just as important to acknowledge that correlations serve as insightful signposts pointing toward *potential* research avenues. Aren't correlations more important to our human ingenuity than known and proven causations? All ingenuity starts with the notice of correlations.

Remember, the great innovations of human history are famously the last link in a massive chain of dead-end failures we hardly ever think about. They start with a wild, sometimes "insane," correlation someone notices. That someone explores a little further out, usually hits a dead end, sometimes saved by another far-out correlation, and on and on. The great innovations are never based solely on what we've been taught.

Correlations are beacons in a vast playground from which we architect innovative solutions. These beacons form the foundation for generating hypotheses, steering us on a defined trajectory. With these subtle cues in hand, we then initiate rigorous statistical tests, delving into creative "what if" scenarios, eventually hardening our hypotheses into concrete solutions. Yet, it is critical to adopt practices that minimize correlations that may merely constitute noise. For example, we could:

- Implement a default z-score value that removes outlier calculations.

- Determine criteria for disregarding a calculation due to missing values.
- Set a minimum number of data points needed to establish a credible correlation, especially for Pearson's correlation.

Counter-intuitively, it might be tempting to throw out weak correlations, for example, throwing out a Pearson correlations of between -0.25 and 0.25. That's usually a good idea, but thinking back on the "Myths and Legends" topic, knowing that what once was a strong correlation is no longer strong is helpful information to store.

There are many statistical techniques for stressing correlations. However, a deep dive into all of them is beyond the scope of this book.

Following are a few methods for stressing correlations. In all fairness, only "Confounding Correlations" might seem meaty in terms of actually stressing correlations.

Confounding Correlations

Because the correlations are based on the highly-curated data of BI sources, whatever correlations we save in the TCW are accurate at least accurate in value (even if most probably aren't readily meaningful). But an seemingly interesting strong correlation could be driven by confounding factors. That is, there is something else driving the correlation. So we can test correlations for confounding factors and mark the correlation as confounded so they could be filtered out of queries or even pruned out of the network—although we might want to keep it so someone else doesn't fall into that trap later.

For both conditional probability and Pearson correlation, the structure can be evaluated for potential confounding probabilities. This suggests that even if there appears to be a decent correlation between two tuples, each of these tuples may independently have a stronger correlation with a third factor. In such scenarios, this third element is likely the real driver of the correlation. The TCW will mark a confounded correlation with the property, "Confounding Tuple Hash".

As an example, consider the commonly used hypothetical situation where you're studying the relationship between ice cream sales and crowds at the beach. In your dataset, you notice that they are highly correlated—when ice cream sales are up, so is the number of people at the beach, and vice-versa. You might conclude that the desire for ice cream somehow causes people to go to the beach—or people go to the beach to buy ice cream. Under scrutiny, neither completely makes sense.

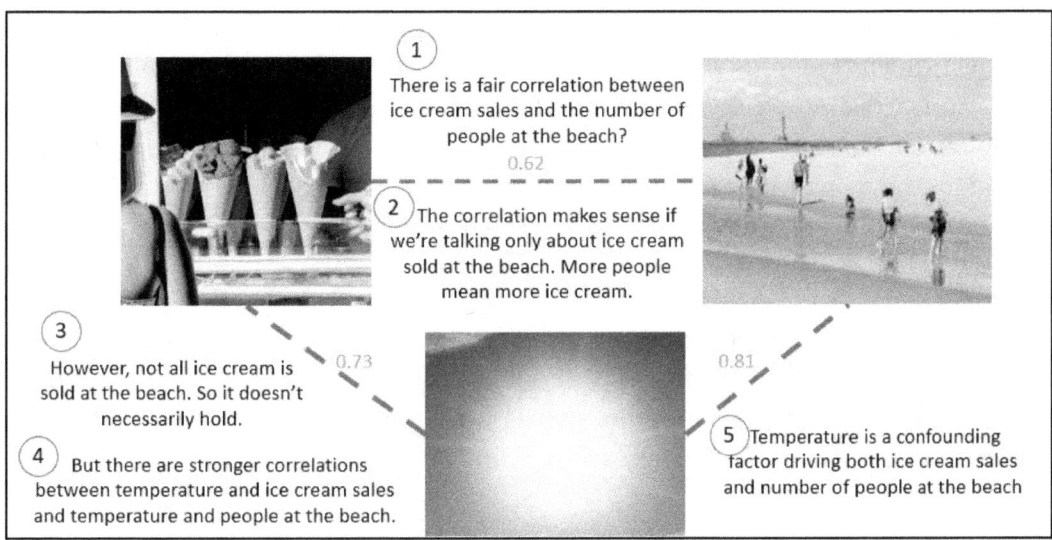

Figure 113: Confounding correlation.

However, this is where a confounding variable comes into play. In this case, the confounding variable is the weather temperature. When the weather is warm, people are more likely to buy ice cream (a cold snack) and also more likely to go to the beach. To be clear, the correlations between ice cream purchases and weather temperature and the number of people at the beach and weather temperature are both stronger than the correlation between ice cream purchases and crowd size at the beach.

So the weather temperature is a confounding variable that is causing the correlation between ice cream sales and the number of people at the beach. If you did not consider this confounding variable, you might erroneously conclude that there's a direct causal relationship between ice cream sales and the number of people at the beach.

For the relationship between ice cream sales and the number of people at the beach in the TCW, there would be a property holding the unique identifier (hash) for "Temperature at 'the beach'" as the confounding variable (as I just mentioned). Queries can filter out any confounded relationships. Peaking ahead a few pages to Figure 118, at the bottom of the (green) table is the row, "Confounding Tuple Hash."

Obvious Correlations

It might be tempting for experts to flag obvious correlations in the TCW as obvious. By obvious, I mean knowledge that is hardly every mentioned and generally implied. For example, the sun will rise again tomorrow, and Mark Twain's death and taxes.

However, in the spirit of a rapidly growing population of analysts, human and AI, the question is, "Obvious to whom?" Something obvious could be obvious in a domain but not universally obvious. People and AIs have different levels of expertise in different fields, come from different cultures, and have experienced different things. I've learned the hard way many times that I don't know everything you know and vice versa. Rather, a correlation that's obvious to a SME is indeed new knowledge to some. So it should belong in the TCW.

However, obvious correlations could be noisy if we're looking for novel solutions. Obvious correlations in the TCW could be marked and "signed" as obvious so they can be filtered out of query results if it is noisy to the querier. They shouldn't be simply pruned out of the TCW. They are still links in the chains of strong correlations.

Ask the Experts (the KG)

As a reminder, the KG part of the EKG is a broad encapsulation of knowledge authored by SMEs in graph form as opposed to more conventional book form. Prior to this, I spoke of this in terms of the KG as grounding validation for an LLM. In this case, Pearson correlations and conditional probabilities in the TCW could be corroborated with a KG.

If a TCW correlation has caught the interest of a SME, the SME could annotate a correlation as validated. The difference between obvious and validated is subtle. Both mean, "Yes, it's true." But the spirit is that "obvious" is more like a rule and "validated" more like an opinion. We've also covered that something obvious (a myth and legend) may no longer be obvious.

This is the purpose of the "User Validation Table" under "EKG Analysis", which we will discuss soon. This is a relational table separate from the EKG. This separation prevents seldom-used data from bogging down the EKG. That's especially helpful since many SMEs could annotate a single correlation, even updating their old assessments.

Why not just ask ChatGPT?

While ChatGPT might offer whacky answers more than is comfortable, sometimes that's good. As I've mentioned, I do think much of what are called hallucinations when coming from an LLM are kind of like "what-ifs." The difference is people preface their what-ifs with "… just hear me out … what if …."

Figure 114 through Figure 116 show an attempt to ask ChatGPT to validate a slight correlation found in the TCW that seems unlikely. Figure 114 is the prompt to ChatGPT, asking it to hypothesize about a way that the price of oil in China could affect the consumption of water in Brazil.

> How might it be possible for there to be a correlation between the price of oil in China and the consumption of water in Brazil. I'm asking you to brainstorm this, it might be a chain of cause and effect. Please offer a step by step explanation, and turtle file, and Cypher commands for my Knowledge Graph implemented as a Neo4j database. The relationships should have a label of CAUSES and a description property and the nodes (events) with a label of Event and a description of the event.

Figure 114: Ask ChatGPT about correlations between seemingly unrelated events.

Note that I had to tell ChatGPT this is a "brainstorm" exercise and I need a chain of cause and effect. Figure 115 shows ChatGPT's helpful response.

While ChatGPT's example is just wild speculation, it at least means there probably isn't an obvious connection. If there were an obvious, documented connection, it probably would have found it. It also can provide food for thought. ChatGPT's response is plausible. It does offer factors that could follow from a rise in oil prices somewhere. It is plausible that water-rich Brazil might take on addressing alternative energy, growing more sugar cane as biofuel.

The RDF output by ChatGPT could be saved as a file and the URI added as a "Reference" property to the relationship in question (between the price of oil in China and water consumption in Brazil).

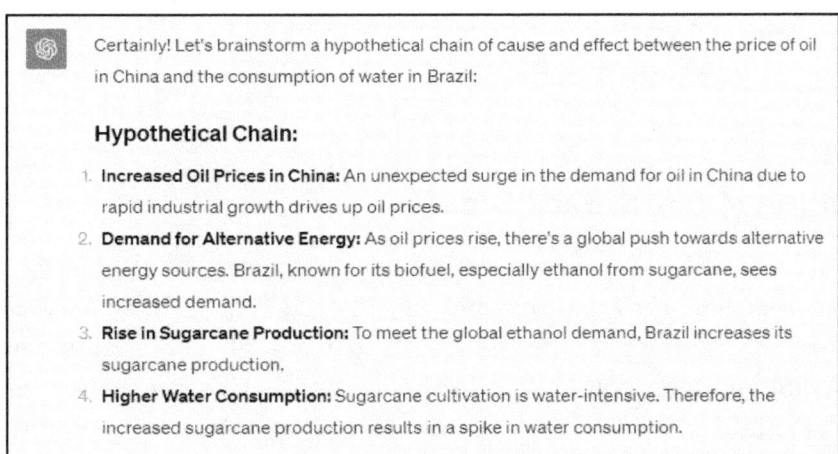

Figure 115: ChatGPT's response to the question of seemingly unrelated events.

Figure 116 shows how this chain of correlation would look in the TCW.

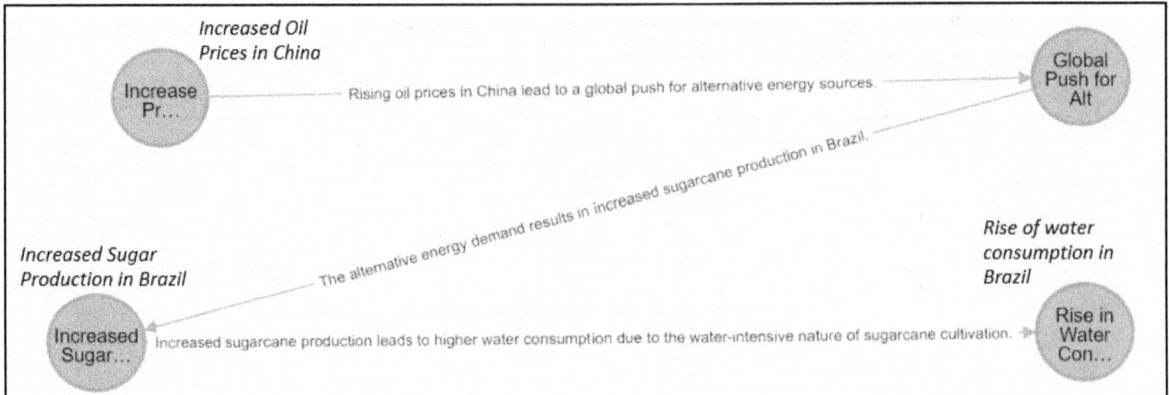

Figure 116: Possible path between oil prices in China and water consumption in Brazil.

Figure 117 is the Semantic Web turtle file returned by ChatGPT used to create the graph shown in Figure 116.

```
@prefix ex: <http://example.org/> .
ex:oilPriceChina a ex:Event ;
    ex:description "Increase in Oil Price in China" .
ex:altEnergyDemand a ex:Event ;
    ex:description "Global Push for Alternative Energy" .
ex:sugarcaneProduction a ex:Event ;
    ex:description "Increased Sugarcane Production in Brazil" .
ex:waterConsumption a ex:Event ;
    ex:description "Rise in Water Consumption in Brazil" .
ex:oilPriceChina ex:CAUSES ex:altEnergyDemand .
ex:altEnergyDemand ex:CAUSES ex:sugarcaneProduction .
ex:sugarcaneProduction ex:CAUSES ex:waterConsumption .
```

Figure 117: RDF/OWL created by ChatGPT.

Coefficient of Variation and Slope

When considering Pearson correlations, the variance of each series (e.g., the daily closing price for MSFT and the daily closing price for NVDA) plays a pivotal role. A high variance for both series may suggest that a high correlation value could be more significant and, consequently, more meaningful. The time series' properties of "Mean" and "Standard Deviation" could be utilized to calculate a "coefficient of variation," offering insight into the unpredictability of the time series. The more erratic the time series, the more likely a tendency to fluctuate together could be deemed a valid correlation.

The coefficient of variation is a statistical measure of the dispersion of data points in a data series around the mean. It is defined as the ratio of the standard deviation to the mean (stddev/mean).

The coefficient of variation is like a measuring tape for inconsistency. In the business world, this comes in handy. Say you're looking at two stocks. One might have prices that bounce around a lot day-to-day, while the other's price changes are more like gentle waves. The coefficient of variation tells you this without getting bogged down in the actual prices or fancy math. It's a quick way to say, "Hey, this one's a roller coaster, and that one's a merry-go-round," helping you decide where to put your money if you like thrills or prefer a calmer ride.

The way this helps to stress a correlation is to consider that a correlation is more likely if the time series of the two tuples are erratic--the standard deviations are wide relative to the mean, rather than if the standard deviations are narrow relative to its mean. So if MSFT and NVDA moved rather wildly each day, and did indeed go up and down together, that seems like a more interesting correlation than if they went up and down together very little each day.

Relationship Property	Value	Value A	Value B
Pearson – Period to Period	0.928851		
Pearson – Percent Change Prior Period	0.666045		
Date Granularity	Day		
Start Date	07/25/2022		
End Date	07/24/2023		
Lag	0		
Pairs Counted	251		
Ignore Holidays and Weekends	Yes		
Ignore NULL	Yes		
Standard Deviation		36.18474	98.06874
Mean		272.8961	229.5432
Coefficient of Variation (std/mean)		0.132595	0.427234
Slope		.2425	.8149
Confounding Tuple Hash	NULL		

A — MSFT — Closing daily stock price of MSFT.
B — NVDA — Closing daily stock price of NVDA.
Pearson Correlation

Figure 118: Properties of a Pearson Correlation.

Figure 118 illustrates the properties of the correlative relationship between the closing prices of MSFT and NVDA. The standard deviation, mean, and coefficient of variation are highlighted in the box (magenta).

Side note: Additionally, the dashed circle towards the bottom highlights the "Confounding Tuple Hash" mentioned a few pages back in the "Confounding Correlations" topic. In this case, we haven't noted a confounding correlation.

Another property is the slope of a linear regression line, which can be a useful measure when assessing the strength of a relationship between two variables, especially when you're interested in the rate of change of one variable with respect to another, rather than their absolute levels.

In the context of stock prices, such as the MSFT and NDVA prices shown in Figure 107, both series might be trending upwards over the range of the time series due to market growth or inflation. This upward trend shared by both time series could inflate the Pearson correlation coefficient, making it appear as though there's a stronger relationship between the two stock prices when, in fact, they might just both be responding to market-wide or sector-wide trends.

By comparing the slopes of the linear trend lines for MSFT and NVDA (the thin, dashed, straight lines) shown in Figure 107, we can focus on the rate at which each stock price is changing relative to time. If the slopes are significantly different, it suggests that while both stocks might be increasing, they are doing so at different rates. This can give us a better sense of the individual stock performance beyond the general market trend.

EKG Analysis

"EKG Analysis" is a catch-all term I'm using for supplementary data outside of the Neo4j implemented EKG. Not all classes of data are best suited for graph databases. Mostly, we separate data focused on the relationships between objects from other formats such as tabular ledgers transactional or fact data. A graph database should only hold relationships between objects. Transactional data should be stored with a relational database or other table-oriented format, such as csv or parquet files in a lakehouse.

Fast-growing data, such as logs, should be stored in cloud storage (such as AWS S3 or Azure Storage). Highly accessed and updated data (OLTP type of data) should be in a relational database (such as a cloud or on-premise version of SQL Server or Oracle).

While it is possible to store logs and transactional data in a graph database, it's not what graph databases are designed for. Graph databases are designed to efficiently handle complex relationships and interconnected data, making them ideal for use cases involving network analysis, recommendation engines, and social graphs. Storing high-velocity logs or transactional data in a graph database could lead to performance bottlenecks and increased complexity. Instead, leveraging the strengths of each type of database technology ensures that data is stored in the most efficient and scalable manner, tailored to the specific characteristics and access patterns of each dataset.

Deeper details about EKG Analysis databases will be in follow-up volumes. However, I will discuss some of the schemas to a moderate extent in this volume. An example is the Event Ensemble we covered earlier.

Object Schema

The Object Schema is a dimensional model upon which we can create an "AEI Cube" that is intended for analysis of the ISG/TCW. As any other database, the EKG is updated, so it's helpful to store and study information about how the EKG itself is used, towards the goal of optimizing the EKG.

Figure 119 shows a minimal representation of the idea.

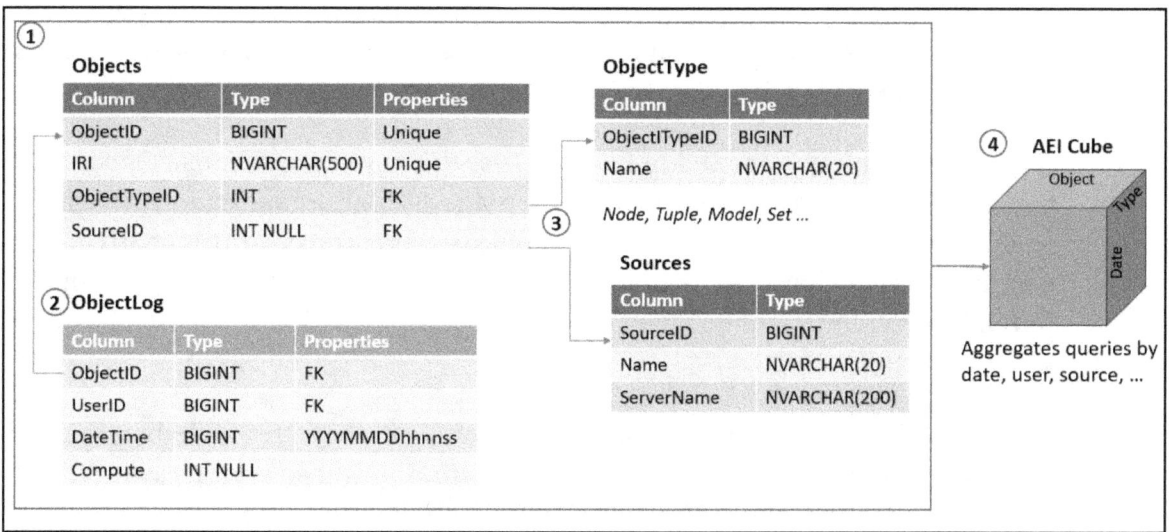

Figure 119: Object Dimensional Model.

1. A snowflake schema centered by the ObjectLog fact table with Objects as the primary dimension.

2. The ObjectLog is the fact table.

3. Two "flakes" off the Objects dimension table. This enables more ways to slice and dice at a highly aggregated level, as opposed to the very high cardinality Object level.

4. Optionally, this snowflake schema could be optimized into an optimized OLAP cube.

Objects Dimension Table

This is a table of objects within the EKG–QueryDef, tuple, set, filter, and model. The semantic web IRI or uniqueID is the key. It is linked to the ObjectLog fact table which is a log of each access.

Yes, holding objects in the Objects table and in the EKG nodes is redundant, since the objects are in the EKG and in this table. However, the Objects table serves as a dimension table of the objects for EKG Analysis data which is better served in a RDBMS than a graph database. Attempting to remove redundancy of the Objects (Objects table of the EKG Analysis DB and the nodes for the objects in the EKG) will force us to throw EKG Analysis data into either the EKG graph database or throw the EKG into a RDBMS, which are optimized for two very different use cases. Alternatively, we could make cross-database merging, which results in a tedious query-time overhead. Remember, for complex systems (such as data systems), redundancy does have its benefits.

The Objects table as depicted in Figure 119 is the minimum schema. Of course, we need the IDs, ObjectID and IRI. Some implementations might require more object properties, which would expand the table. For example, we might have a frequently used use case where we wish to analyze the utilization of QueryDefs with a filter containing "ENV" for "environmentally friendly." That column could be added to the Objects table or a snowflake table.

I've normalized ObjectType and Sources out of the Objects table since different implementations might require more information for those entities as well.

ObjectLog Fact Table

This is an append-only log (as all logs should be) of each object's creation and optionally each time an Object is accessed. It is the fact table of the AEI cube. An append-only table is the fastest way to add history objects to the EKG. As already discussed, this log history doesn't belong in a graph database. Graph databases are about relationships between objects, not a detailed history of them.

The ObjectLog and the Objects table could form the core of an OLAP cube for directly studying the queries in aggregate. For example, how many times a particular query was run, the last time it was run by a particular user, or its query time.

Access information for EKG objects, particularly QueryDef and Tuple nodes, are highly informative towards the purpose of pruning unused nodes from the EKG.

The ObjectLog table could be partitioned by date so we could store rows in progressively cheaper options. For example, "hot storage" (the most expensive) for the last couple of months of ObjectLog data, warm storage for three to twelve months, and cheap cold storage for anything older.

Object Archive

Archived objects are objects pruned from the Objects Schema and/or the EKG. This archive looks pretty much like the Objects and ObjectLog tables we just discussed. The main difference is that this would be stored in an inexpensive "cold storage."

This subject of pruning, in which pruned items could be archived instead of just dropped, is discussed later in "Pruning the ISG and TCW."

Users Schema

The Users schema serves as a critical component of the EKG ecosystem, functioning as a registry for system users. It is specifically designed to store essential metadata about users, which is not directly incorporated into the EKG for privacy and security reasons. Key elements of this table include:

- **User Identifiers**—Each user is assigned one or more aliases. To maintain confidentiality within the EKG, users are represented by aliases or obfuscated names.

- **Roles and Permissions**—Information about the user's role within the organization and the corresponding access permissions to various parts of the EKG.

- **Usage Patterns**—Metadata on users' interaction with the system, such as query frequency, types of queries, and preferred BI tools.

- **Contact Preferences:** Preferences and protocols for contact, enabling users to choose if and how they can be approached by other users through the application.

Segregating sensitive user metadata from the EKG into this supplementary table helps to ensure user privacy while maintaining a robust framework for collaboration and knowledge sharing. Users can interact with the EKG and each other while having their identities and specific preferences securely managed within this dedicated table.

Cloud access systems, such as Azure Active Directory (Azure AD), AWS Identity and Access Management (IAM), or Google Cloud Identity, can support these requirements effectively. For example, Azure AD provides comprehensive identity management, including role-based access control (RBAC), conditional access policies, and advanced security features to manage user identities and permissions securely. Additionally, these cloud services offer data storage solutions that can handle the storage and management of user metadata, ensuring compliance with privacy and security standards.

User Validation Table

The EKG can hold relationships that are subjective (opinion of a SME), predictive (result of an ML model or AI), or "fuzzy" (e.g. the correlation and probabilities of the TCW). So it would benefit the AEI to store feedback from sources offering validation of relationships.

This table holds a historic record of validations a user (presumably as SME) makes for relationships authored in the KG and TCW correlations in the EKG. This includes the user's id, the date of the validation, a score of 0 through 1, and a reason (from a set of reasons).

A rated relationship could be a correlation in the TCW. Computed correlations that are discovered could be obvious, preposterous, or previously unknown. If a SME sees a correlation and finds it obvious, the relationship should be tagged as such. We discussed obvious and validated correlations earlier in "Stressing the Correlations and Probabilities."

Multiple users or even functions can rate the validity of a TCW relationship in the EKG. And a user may change their minds over time. This facilitates the ability to filter out relationship validation from certain users. It could be used to analyze changes over time as well.

Ideally, each validation should be a property of the relationship or node in the EKG. This would allow us to filter out unvalidated objects in queries to the graph database. However, an object could be validated by many people with varying opinions, which can change over time. Therefore, storing multiple validations in the EKG graph database isn't appropriate.

Therefore, the validation table should be a tabular construct, ensuring we can store multiple validations without unnecessarily bloating the EKG. This could serve as another fact table in the snowflake schema shown in Figure 119.

CHAPTER TEN

Special Structures

This section covers a few powerful structures that can be embedded into the ISG, TCW or the EKG as a whole. This part deserves a book of its own. For now, I only offer an introduction to demonstrate a few advanced ideas.

KPI Strategy Map

Introduced by Robert Kaplan and David Norton in the early 2000s, strategy maps, a derivative of the widely implemented Balanced Scorecard methodology, have been somewhat overlooked in the business landscape. It's been dominated by the easier-to-dashboards understand (also somewhat easier to develop and maintain). At best, strategy maps are implemented as a "dead" graph-like visualization of intended cause and effect embedded in a dashboard.

The balanced scorecard, with its simple, long-standing technical feasibility, provides a systematic way to measure performance against strategic goals. In contrast, strategy maps, which are more complex, visualize the relationships and progression between objectives toward these goals.

The Strategy Map is what I feel is the most important of the "Special Structures."

Figure 120 shows a sample of a dashboard with a Strategy Map component towards the lower-right corner.

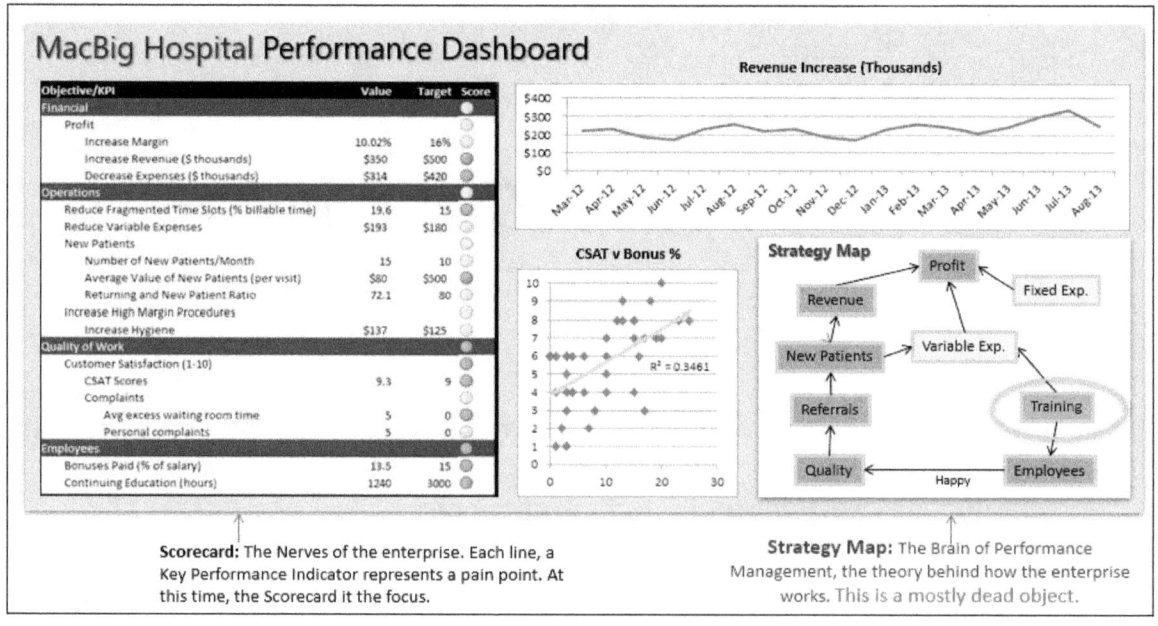

Figure 120: Example of a BI dashboard.

Figure 121 is a more detailed look at a Strategy Map.

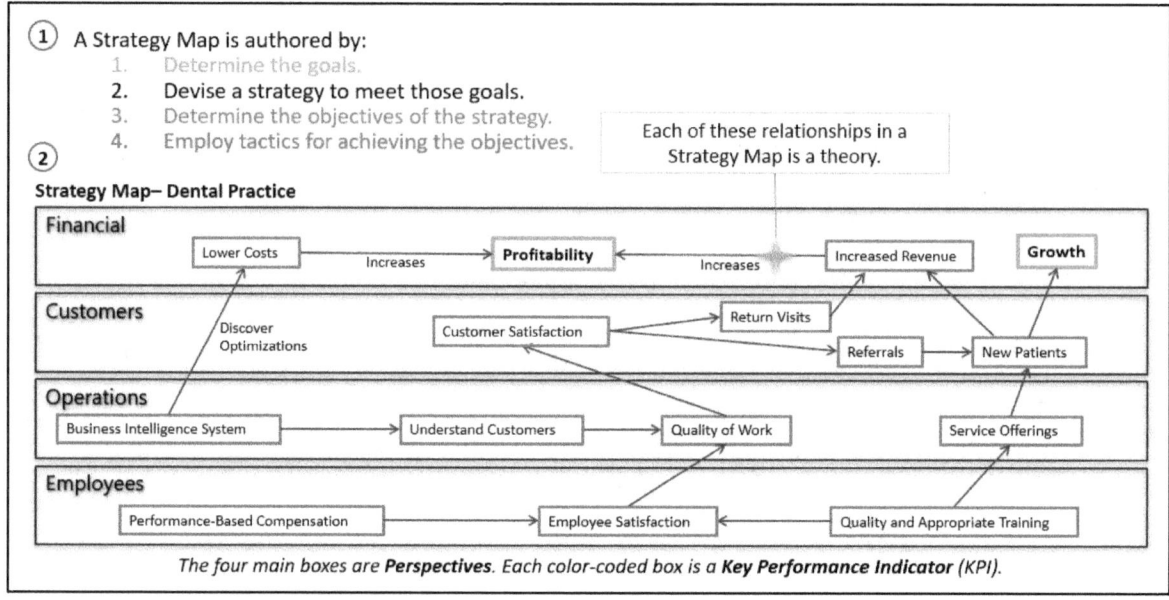

Figure 121: Example of a Strategy Map.

Here is a breakdown of the numbered items:

1. Authoring a Strategy Map.

    a. **Determine the Goals**–Establish the broad, long-term goals that reflect the organization's vision and mission. These are high-level aspirations that provide direction for the business's growth and success.

    b. **Devise a Strategy**–Develop a comprehensive strategy that outlines how the organization intends to achieve these goals. This should include identifying the competitive advantage, market positioning, and allocation of resources. This is the overall "the war".

    c. **Determine the Objectives of the Strategy**–Break down the strategy into specific, measurable, achievable, relevant, and time-bound (SMART) objectives. These objectives should be clear milestones that guide the progress toward the overarching goals. These are "the battles".

    d. **Employ Tactics for Achieving the Objectives**–Plan and implement detailed tactics that will allow the organization to meet its objectives. This includes defining individual actions, assigning responsibilities, setting deadlines, and allocating resources effectively.

2. Perspectives

    a. **Financial**–Looks at financial performance measures that indicate whether the company's strategy, implementation, and execution are contributing to bottom-line improvement. Common metrics include profitability, growth, and shareholder values.

    b. **Customers**–Captures the organization's ability to provide quality goods and services, the effectiveness of their customer relationship management, and overall customer satisfaction and retention.

    c. **Operations**–Focuses on the internal operational goals needed to meet customer objectives. It looks at the critical processes that enable an organization to deliver on the customer proposition and reach financial objectives.

    d. **Employees**–Covers the intangible drivers of future success, such as human resources, systems, company culture, and databases. It's about creating a climate that supports innovation, change, and growth.

When it was introduced, the implementation of strategy maps faced challenges due to technological limitations and a lack of traction in the somewhat early adopter stage of business performance management ("BPfM" as I called it earlier). Being a graph of human knowledge, it faced similar difficulties of authoring and maintenance that faced KGs in general–it is a kind of KG. The notion couldn't take off and mostly faded into oblivion, at least into the background, along with other failed ideas in the buzzword graveyard. Today, the resurgence of KGs, semantic webs, and perhaps even the ISG, serves to remind us of the graph-like strategy map of performance management.

Much has changed since the 2000s! Strategy maps should be revisited, driven by the maturity of graph database and visualization technology, data science, machine learning, and AI. Around the 2010 timeframe I developed a few concepts around integrating Predictive Analytics with BPfM.

The Strategy Map and TCW can be thought of as kindred spirits in that they measure correlations between tuples. We can think of the relationship between the KPI nodes as a strategy map of the effect we believe one has on the other. But the Strategy Map differs from the TCW in that it is purposefully authored by humans–today with AI/ML assistance. The TCW is passively built from BI querying.

Even though Strategy Maps are generally considered part of BPfM (not BI, strictly speaking), the reporting of performance metrics can be considered BI data. KPIs are just a set of calculations, not much different from any other.

This topic will be explored a little more in Chapter 12—"Future Steps," chapters "Investment and Sacrifice" and "Metrics at Scale."

Compact Smarts

One big advantage of the Strategy Map is that it should be much smaller than the TCW or ISG. It's an extremely compressed representation of knowledge. At the large extreme, the TCW and ISG could consist of tens of billions of unique tuples or dataframes (respectively) and possibly relationships numbering in the tens of billions. Even with regular pruning (we'll talk about later), it will still be pretty hefty.

On the other hand, a very large Strategy Map would consist of no more than thousands of KPIs and tens of thousands of relationships between them.

The Theory of our Corporate Strategies

The Strategy Map is part of the Performance Management suite of tools. It's a graph of theoretical cause and effect. But it usually makes a rare appearance as a mostly "dead" graph on dashboards. It might be minimally dynamic, for example, nodes showing up in red/yellow/green, indicating good, OK, or bad status.

In the metaphor of an enterprise as an organism, I facetiously say the KPI Status Map is the emotions, hopes, dreams, fears, and beliefs of the enterprise. We have beliefs about what helps us towards our goals. It maps enterprise activity to the avoidance of bad states (for example, profit loss, noncompliance, employee mutiny) and the attraction of good states (for example, growth and large profit margins).

If we have KPI status values and correlate the values between KPI statuses, we have a rough idea of the level of cause and effect of managerial actions in the enterprise and the validity of the KPI's intent.

Gaming KPIs

For a Strategy Map to effectively guide managerial actions, it's crucial that KPIs are set up in a balanced and holistic manner, with checks in place to prevent and detect gaming behaviors. It underscores the importance of not just setting KPIs but monitoring and interpreting them in the context of overall corporate strategy and ethical considerations.

I don't mean to paint such a pessimistic view of people. But I have frequently witnessed KPI gaming. I should clarify that I believe most KPI gaming isn't done with malicious intent. "It's just a game," as many say about business in general.

The nature of how BPfM is set up makes it unavoidable. A set of KPIs are designed and targets are set for a period of time—usually monthly, quarterly, or annually. Agreements with managers and workers are set at the time of performance reviews. Often the set targets must be achieved—no matter what might change in the interim.

Everyone starts out the period with good intentions. However, things often (usually? always?) don't work out as planned. Quickly enough, the enterprise devolves into a big game of prisoner's dilemma.

Here are some examples of how KPIs are sometimes gamed in a business setting:

- **Short-Term Focus over Long-Term Sustainability**—A sales team might be driven by a KPI focused on the number of products sold. To boost these numbers, the team could resort to aggressive sales techniques or discounts, achieving their short-term target but potentially sacrificing long-term customer loyalty and profitability. Sales' short-term surprises could disrupt an inventory set on forecasts that are no longer relevant, leading to shipping problems, ending with disappointed customers.

- **Sacrificing Quality for Quantity**—If a KPI emphasizes the number of customer service calls handled, representatives might rush through calls without adequately addressing customer concerns—maybe even simply hanging up it the question starts sounding too involved. The KPI would show high performance, but customer satisfaction could suffer.

- **Overemphasis on a Single KPI**—If too much emphasis is placed on one KPI (e.g., growth in new users), teams might neglect lesser-weighted aspects like retaining current users. This can lead to a scenario where there's a high influx of new users but an equally high churn rate, which isn't sustainable.

- **Manipulating Reporting Periods**—Some departments might shift sales or expenditures into different reporting periods to ensure that they meet their KPIs for a specific quarter or year. This doesn't reflect genuine performance and can mislead stakeholders.

KPI Correlation Score

The KPI Strategy Map can be embedded into the EKG as part of the TCW, where each node is a tuple of a KPI and other slices (such as each salesman or store). The KPI tuples are related to each other through a Pearson correlation. I call that correlation between KPI status the KPI Correlation Score (KCS).

The mention of the Pearson correlation means we must store KPI status histories at regular intervals of their statuses. From these histories of statuses, we can calculate correlations between KPIs. This is another fact table of the EKG Analysis component discussed earlier.

Here is an example illustrating the use of the KCS based on a situation I mentioned a few paragraphs ago. Suppose there is a sales manager with a KPI based on sales (more sales, the merrier) and the inventory manager with a KPI based on their just-in-time inventory (the less stuff in the warehouse, the better). If the sales manager found an opportunity to skyrocket sales for the quarter, that sudden surge in sales would lead to a sudden surge in product fulfillment. That could be difficult for the inventory manager. The inability to fulfill sales leads to angry customers.

Each KPI tuple is linked to a node for the tuple and the slice members, which ties that tuple to the DC. For example, the tuple (Sales, Eugene) is linked to a node for the KPI of Sales and a member of the Salesman table—and the Sales KPI node links to the column node for the Salesman table and the sales row of the Metrics table.

Aligning every effort with strategic goals is vital yet challenging in a world that's in constant flux. To aid in this alignment, the KCS measures the actual strength of the relationship between our efforts (KPIs) and their intended outcomes. This tool goes beyond traditional KPI analysis by assessing how changes in and KPI status reflect affect other KPI statuses.

Figure 122 illustrates how BPfM KPIs should be implemented in the TCW. It shows three KPIs as tuples. Each is joined by members that define the elements of the KPI. Let's focus on the left-most KPI:

1. Tuple 1 represents a KPI attribute measuring the KPI status of Employee Satisfaction of Staff Writers. It forms the tuple: (Employee Satisfaction, Staff Writers, Customer Service, Status)—the status of the KPI tracking Employee satisfaction of staff writers in the Customer Service department.

2. Staff Writer is a member of the Roles table.

3. Tuple 1 is denoted as a KPI Status through the Status member of the KPIAttributes table. All three tuples actually point to Status—the extra lines just made things messier.

4. Customer Service is a member of the Organization table—in other words, Customer Service is one of the departments.

5. This is a formula node that acts as a hub for all the measures used to calculate the KPI status. This formula is composed of two measures: Rating and Weight.

6. The three tuples belong to members of the KPI table.

7. This is the KPI correlation score between Tuple 1 and Tuple 2. The 0.75 score shows that there is a fairly strong correlation between the employee satisfaction of staff writers in customer service and the quality of their work.

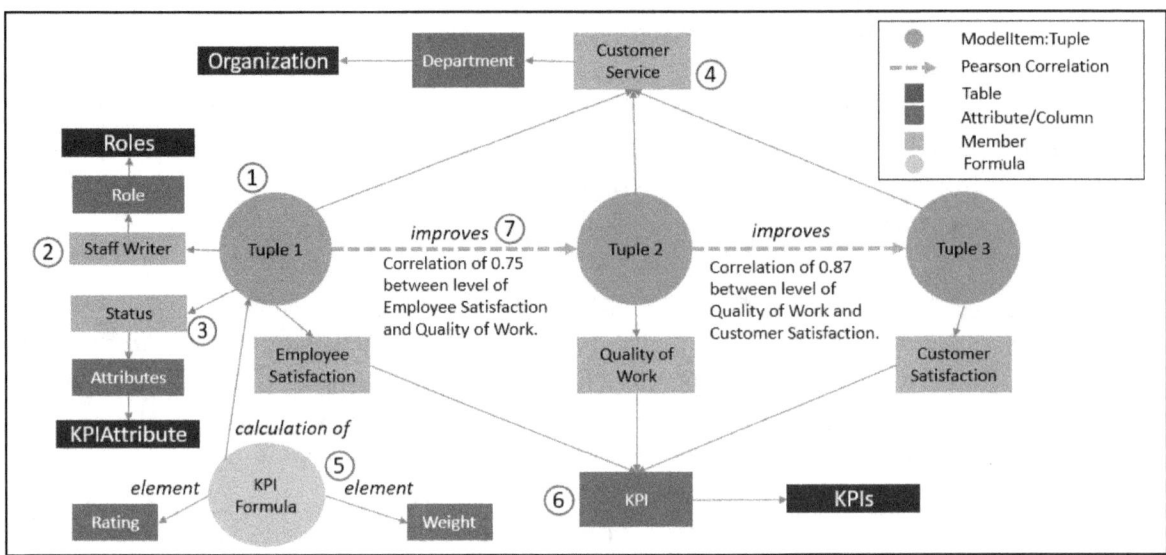

Figure 122: Partial Strategy Map with KPI Correlation Scores.

The KCS is a litmus test for the validity of our strategies, offering a means to navigate the complexities and competitive nature of business. It recognizes that not all strategies endure unchanged in the face of new competitors, market dynamics, or diminishing returns. Thus, the KCS provides a quantitative foundation to support strategic agility, informing businesses to evolve when correlations between efforts and desired results weaken. This concept underscores the need for a dynamic approach to performance management, where strategies are not set in stone but are living entities, subject to review and revision, and tested by actual measurements of success. It's about ensuring that our pursuit of "good" KPIs remains sensible and that our strategies evolve in tandem with the ever-changing business landscape.

Bayesian Belief Networks and Causal Diagrams

As with Strategy Maps, Bayesian Belief Networks (BBN) and Causal Diagrams reveal **how** factors affect other factors. That is, cause and effect (at least as far as SMEs who author BBNs are concerned). This goes beyond correlations of the TCW, which only states there is a correlation between two tuples. It also goes beyond most of the descriptive ontologies loaded into the KG—most ontologies deal with "what," not how and why.

It's very difficult to declare that something causes an effect, even for human intelligence. For example, we "know" the Earth's rotation along an angled axis causes seasons. But that understanding came about only after a great number of very smart people thought about it for centuries.

Nonetheless, we take most actions in our lives on multitudes of cause-and-effect beliefs. Therefore, at least for now, I imagine these two consciously authored structures (meaning, human SMEs need to author these structures), BBN and causal diagrams, are structures that should incorporated into the EKG. Such human-crafted rules asserted in the EKG help to ensure out human intentions continue to play a critical part. Fortunately, AIs can still substantially assist SMEs, along with as data scientists armed with ML algorithms.

Visually and structurally, BBNs and Causal Diagrams can appear very similar, especially in simpler models. For example, in the commonly cited scenario involving a fire alarm system:

- **Bayesian Belief Network-** You might have nodes representing "Fire," "Earthquake," and "Alarm." The edges between these nodes would represent probabilistic dependencies, indicating that the likelihood of the alarm sounding is influenced by the probability of there being a fire or an earthquake.

- **Causal Diagram** - The same nodes could be used, but the edges would represent causal relationships. For instance, an edge from "Fire" to "Alarm" would indicate that a fire causes the alarm to go off. Similarly, an edge from "Earthquake" to "Alarm" signifies that an earthquake can cause the alarm to trigger.

While both networks might use similar nodes and connections, the key difference lies in their interpretation:

- In a BBN, the edges represent conditional probabilities. The focus is on understanding how the probability of one event (like the alarm sounding) is affected by other events (like a fire or earthquake).

- In a Causal Diagram, the edges represent causal effects. The focus is on understanding how changes in one event (like the occurrence of a fire) will causally affect another event (like the triggering of an alarm).

So, even without considering probabilities, these diagrams serve different purposes: Bayesian networks for probabilistic inference and understanding dependencies and causal diagrams for understanding and analyzing cause-and-effect relationships.

Business Process Knowledge

It seems that most discussion of KGs is about the properties of entities and how they relate. But our world is more than things and how they are associated. Our world with its time dimension is made of interacting processes. Processes are chains of events and actions—or cause and effect, or transition and state. Each of these processes has inputs handed off from other processes and it outputs something to yet more processes.

Processes are hierarchical. For example, my respiratory system is a process within the bigger process of my entire body.

Graphs that depict workflows or processes, especially when developed by SMEs, can be referred to by several names depending on their specificity, complexity, and application. Some common terms for such graphs include:

- Process Flow Diagrams (PFDs): These are used primarily in the chemical and process industries to indicate the general flow of plant processes and equipment.

- Workflow Diagrams: A visual way to represent a step-by-step sequence of tasks or activities. These are common in businesses for depicting processes like onboarding a new customer, document approvals, or other sequential tasks.

- Business Process Model (BPM): A more comprehensive diagram that captures the sequence of processes or tasks, decision points, events, and more, to provide an end-to-end view of a business process.

- Flowcharts: A generic term for diagrams that represent a workflow or process, showing the steps as boxes of various kinds and their order by connecting them with arrows.

- Value Stream Maps: Used in lean manufacturing and lean IT, these maps depict the flow of materials and information necessary to bring a product or service to a consumer.

- Functional Flow Block Diagrams (FFBD): Used in systems engineering to represent functions and their interactions.

- System Diagrams: Can be used more broadly to represent how different components (or processes) within a system interact with one another.

- Swimlane Diagrams: A flowchart variation where each lane or "swimlane" represents a different person, role, or department, providing clarity on responsibilities throughout a process.

When developing these diagrams for incorporation into a KG, it's essential to maintain clarity, use standard symbols (if any are associated with that type of diagram), and ensure that the information is kept up-to-date as processes evolve.

Simple AI-Assisted Strategy Map Example

As with other KG components, business processes are designed mostly by people at this time. Again, AI can substantially ameliorate much of the development and maintenance effort. In particular, LLMs, with their broad knowledge, are able to provide a starting point for domain-specific or higher-level strategy maps, offer critique, or offer an analogous situation from which to begin brainstorming.

Figure 123 through Figure 125 demonstrates the surprising ability of ChatGPT to *assist* in the development of a strategy map. The example isn't a "business process" per se, but it is a strategy—a strategy for how to address the clear and present problem of tooth decay. All strategies are about addressing a problem.

Figure 123 is the prompt I submitted to ChatGPT to explain *how* toothpaste with fluoride fights tooth decay. That is a claim I've heard since childhood, but I didn't stop to figure out how that works until high school (centuries before LLMs). Note that I asked for it to output Cypher code so I could upload the process to Neo4j. I also asked ChatGPT to provide enough of a description for each node and relationship so that it could be searched for by a user.

Figure 123: ChatGPT prompt to explain the process of how fluoride reduces cavities.

Its response is a little too high-level, but for a first iteration and the purposes of demonstration, it's good enough. Figure 124 shows the text response. I chose not to show the very codey Cypher code. But you can see the first few relationships with a nice description full of key words.

Figure 124: ChatGPT's explanation.

Figure 125 shows what the process looks like after running the Cypher code and loading it into the KG, which is a Neo4j database:

1. This is the process of defining the problem.

    a. Bacteria produce acids …

    b. Acids attack "remineralization." This really wasn't a great way to phrase this relationship. It really should have said, "Acids exacerbate demineralization." But it's good for a first iteration. The idea is close enough to form the structure of the process.

2. The highlighted node, "Toothpaste," is our subject. Towards the right are details of the highlighted Toothpaste node, including a description, something richer for the purposes of user search.

3. Toothpaste with Fluoride leads to the formation of ...

4. Fluorapatite? I had to look up that word to ensure ChatGPT wasn't hallucinating. It's what forms on teeth brushed with fluoridated toothpaste, helping to fight tooth decay by strengthening tooth enamel and promoting remineralization.

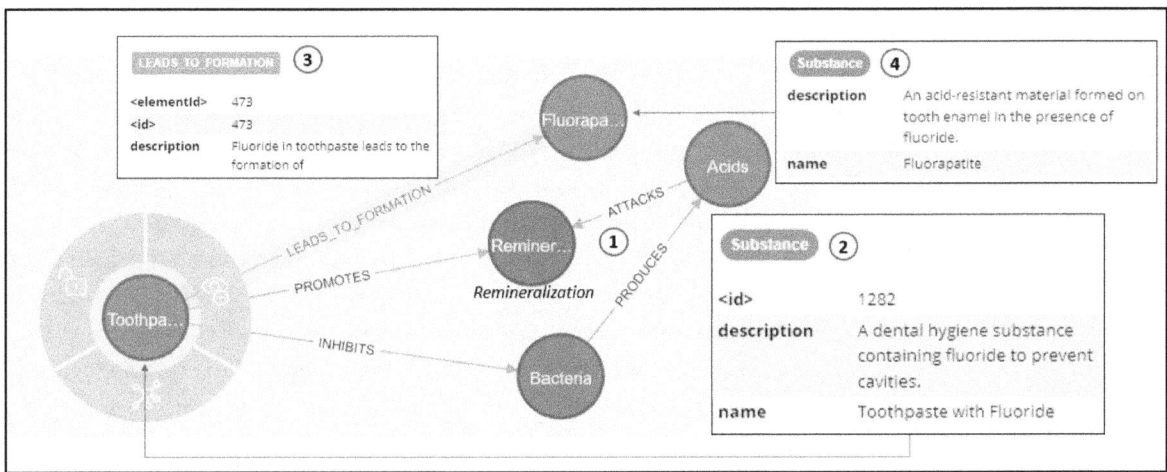

Figure 125: Graphical representation of how fluoride combats cavities.

The reason I chose this simple topic to explain a business process is to highlight that we often don't really know how something works even if we've assumed its truth our entire lives. So when we're asked to encode something that seems so common sense, we might realize that we really don't know. We are mostly taught facts and take them for granted, even if they may no longer be exactly true.

Refining the Workflow

The example above shows how we could add to our KG by relying on ChatGPT's knowledge of an immensely wide range of domains and encode the relationships into Cypher for uploading into our KG.

But building a KG is a highly-iterative and highly-nuanced process. ChatGPT (or another broadly-scoped LLM) is a good way to create a start. However, making subtle modifications indirectly through further prompt engineering and getting ChatGPT to spit out an improved version quickly devolves into a case of "If you want something done right, you need to do it yourself."

Figure 126 and Figure 127 illustrate a little more comprehensive example of a process—this time, an actual *business* process, a simple restaurant. As with the example above, I asked ChatGPT to provide a starting point. This time, instead of creating Cypher code to load directly into Neo4j, I asked ChatGPT to output to a ttl (OWL's Turtle format). I then loaded that ttl file into Protégé.

> **You**
> Can you help me create an RDF ontology in Turtle format for a typical restaurant workflow? I need it to include a hierarchy of classes that represent the essential steps in a restaurant's customer service process, such as greeting, seating, presenting the menu, taking orders, preparing food, serving, and processing payments. Each of these steps should be defined as a class and should be a subclass of a general 'RestaurantWorkflow' class. Also, include object properties to show the sequence of these steps and their interaction with the 'Customer' class. Additionally, I'd like to have each step represented as an individual instance of its respective class, showing the workflow progression. Please use standard RDF, OWL, and RDFS vocabularies, and leave room for potential future expansion like feedback collection and customer service. Include basic prefixes like rdf, owl, and xsd.

Figure 126: Prompt to create a start to a KG of a restaurant.

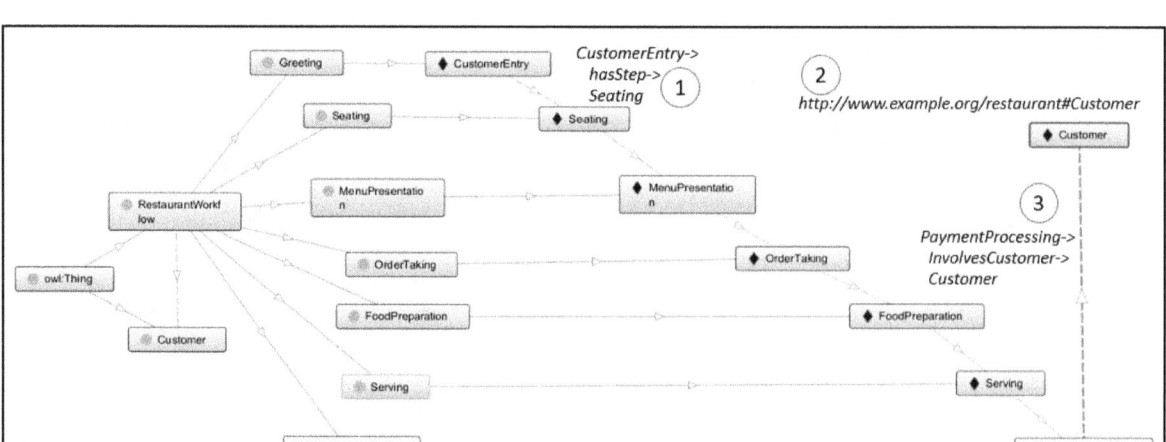

Figure 127: Workflow of a restaurant.

Figure 127 is a snapshot from Protégé after loading the ttl file provided by ChatGPT:

1. These are the steps for a dining experience, starting with the customer entering the restaurant, to Seating, to Menu Presentation, and on.

2. Every node has a unique identifier (URI or IRI). In this case, I'm using the commonly used naming "domain" of http://www.example.org with an appended fragment identifier (restaurant) and a descriptive label (Customer).

3. It's a relationship stating that Payment Processing involves a customer. Further, there could be a relationship stating customers offer a form of payment. Or the payment process requires a form of payment as well as a customer. ChatGPT didn't get that far for this iteration.

For improvements to the ttl, I could proceed in at least a couple of ways:

1. Modify the prompt with more details, getting ChatGPT to create a new ttl. Towards the beginning, this might be a good option. But ChatGPT sometimes does go off on uncontrollable tangents. Once you have something that is a good start, leave well enough alone and move on to #2 ... at least at the time of writing.

2. Make modifications directly in Protégé. ChatGPT would then be demoted to assist with business clarifications or questions on how to do something in Protégé.

Regarding #1, an interesting thought is that the process of iteratively modifying a prompt does help me to articulate what it is that I really want. The end prompt often becomes that elevator pitch that's so hard to write. At that stage, that highly iterated prompt can be given to ChatGPT to refine the prompt into nice text—as a nice side benefit in addition to carrying out a request to create the ttl.

Funny thing to note: Regarding #2, I've fed ChatGPT a fairly complicated ttl I developed to elicit feedback. It's surprisingly good at it. After all, a ttl is well-structured data with no ambiguous language.

Of course, there is much more that goes on in a restaurant than the process of waiting on a customer, but it's a start. In subsequent steps, we could ask ChatGPT to help us with bite-sized chunks. For example, create a start for the processes of preparing orders, dividing tips, shopping for food, cleaning the restaurant, etc. Each of those would be created in its own ttl file and merged into one KG in Protégé. That is similar to the distributed ontology development described in the Art Gallery example back in Chapter 7—Data Mesh.

Limitations of Encoding Knowledge

Encoding how something works in real life as a collection of nodes and relationships in a KG can be very difficult. Human understanding, particularly in nuanced domains, operates on multiple layers of abstraction, context, relationships taken for granted, and prior knowledge. The richness of human understanding contrasts with the more structured and stripped-down nature of database representations like those in Neo4j. Here are some reasons why the Cypher representation might feel less rich compared to human understanding:

- **Dimensionality**—Human understanding captures a wealth of information from multiple perspectives (sensory, emotional, logical, historical, etc.). A graph in Neo4j, on the other hand, represents information in nodes and relationships, which might not fully capture the highly multi-faceted depth of human understanding.

- **Context**—Humans automatically infer a lot of contexts from a given piece of information. For instance, mentioning "toothpaste" might conjure up memories, feelings, and other related knowledge about horrible experiences at the dentist. In a database, "toothpaste" is just a node with properties.

- **Emotion and Sensory Experience**—Human knowledge is intertwined with real-time emotions and the real-time variety of sensory experiences. This adds a layer of richness that's challenging to represent in a database.

- **Flexibility and Adaptability**—Human understanding is highly adaptable. We can understand metaphors, analogies, and abstract concepts, then apply them across different contexts. Databases operate on predefined structures and logic.

- **Implicit Knowledge**— Much human understanding is implicit—we know more than we can easily articulate, largely due to our years of socialization. Databases like Neo4j store explicit knowledge, which is defined and structured. In contrast, large language models (LLMs) capture more implicit knowledge, trained on massive amounts of text that reflect our culture. However, most text (unless you're Mark Twain or Lewis Carroll) falls short of capturing the full richness of what our brains perceive when immersed in the physical world.

- **Semantics–**The semantics of a language, the deeper meanings behind words, and the way concepts interlink are intuitive for humans but are complex to represent in a structured form in databases.

- **Interdisciplinary Integration–**Humans integrate knowledge from multiple disciplines seamlessly. In the toothpaste example, one might factor in chemistry, history of dental care, personal experiences, and societal views. Capturing such an integration in a graph would require a highly complex structure.

While KGs in Neo4j (or any other database) are powerful tools to represent, interlink, and query data, they don't replace the richness of human cognition (ATTOW). Instead, they offer a way to structure and access information in a versatile, machine-readable format, aiding decision-making, data analysis, and other computational tasks.

Trophic Cascades in the TCW

Many of us in the Pacific Northwest are familiar with the term "apex predator" at least in part from the relatively recent re-introduction of wolves into our nearby forests. The intent of the re-introduction of wolves is beyond merely the romantic notion of wolves once again roaming through the birch trees and howling in the distance. More so, the hope is to reinstate the natural regulation of the forest ecosystem that has gone somewhat out of whack due to cascading effects of the populations of the wolves' prey going unchecked, or managed in a "fix one bug, create two more" sort of way.

Apex predators are relatively small in number in comparison to the population of their prey (often solitary, powerful individuals), but their presence or lack of presence results in a disproportionate effect on the environment. That is, not just the obvious effect on the population of its prey, but cascading effects that are often surprising and unintentional.

Figure 128 illustrates something I read long ago about a surprising contributor to the rapid erosion along the California coastline during the early 20th century. The web of cause and effect started with a problem and a collection of somewhat random oddities.

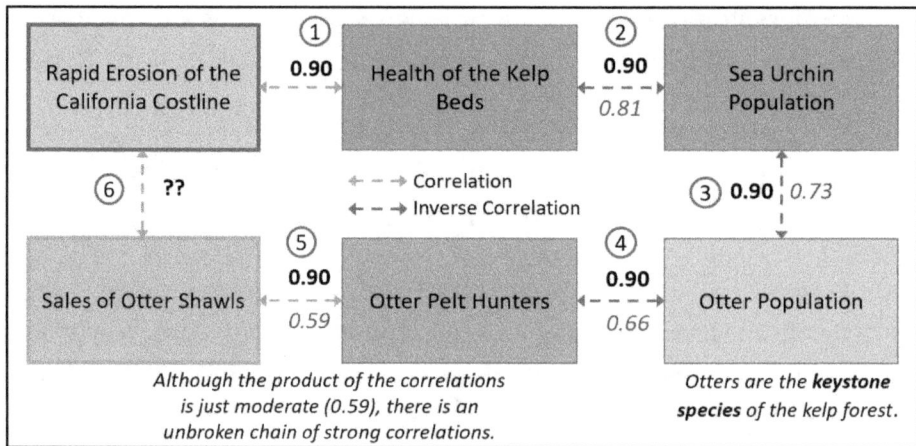

Figure 128: Intriguing and surprising web of cause and effect.

Starting with a collection of clues, we find strong correlations between the set of clues, and construct a chain of strong relationships. That chain of strong relationships is a hypothesis. Between each box in Figure 128, there are two numbers. The darker number is a made-up correlation value (I can't find actual data). The lighter number is a product of the correlations as we traverse the chain:

1. **Coastline Erosion and Kelp Beds** - There is a chronological association where periods of worsening coastline erosion correlate with a declining health of the kelp beds just offshore.

2. **Kelp Beds and Sea Urchin Population** – With the decline in the health of the kelp beds, there tends to be a subsequent rise in the sea urchin population. The light number, 0.81 is the product of 1 and 2 (0.90 x 0.90). That 0.81 is the relationship between Rapid erosion of the CA coastline and Sea Urchin population.

3. **Sea Urchin Population and Otter Population** - An increase in the sea urchin population is often succeeded by a decrease in the otter population. This is directly what's causing the decline in sea urchin population.

4. **Otter Population and Otter Pelt Hunters** - A decrease in the otter population seems correlated with increased activity from otter pelt hunters.

5. **Otter Shawl Sales and Otter Pelt Hunters** - More otter pelt hunters are often seen in times following increased sales of otter shawls.

6. **Otter Shawl Sales and Coastal Erosion** - Did the period of increased otter shawl sales occur concurrently with the period of rapid erosion of the California coastline?

This story of this trophic cascade is indeed the inspiration for the TCW (although very simplified and with made up figures). In Sherlock Holmes-inspired style, a collection of many disparate correlations is the beginning of crafting a novel hypothesis to a novel problem.

The insight into the disproportionate and often surprising effect of apex predators is credited to the pioneering work of Dr. [Robert Paine](). He was a zoologist at the University of Washington, and he had this flash of inspiration for an experiment on biodiversity. The removal of a particular species (in this case, a starfish-Pisaster ochraceus) can result in dramatic effects, whereas the removal of another particular species has little or no effect. He coined the term, "keystone species", to describe the former.

We know of many trophic cascades, such as mice eat grains, cats eat mice, coyotes might eat cats, and cougars might eat a coyote (something like that, anyway). I refer to those as "authored" because smart PhDs go out into the field for a few years to construct such a web of relationships. The concept of a trophic cascade can be creatively applied to business environments to describe how changes at one hierarchical level can lead to cascading effects throughout the organization or even the industry. Following are a few examples:

- **Leadership Changes–**A change in the executive leadership or vision of a company can cascade through all levels of the business. A new CEO may bring a different culture, strategic outlook, or management style, affecting division heads, managers, and eventually every employee. Nodes could represent executives, middle management, and employees. Edges could indicate reporting structures or influence. Properties might include various KPIs, performance metrics, or even employee morale.

- **Product Innovations–**The introduction of a disruptive technology or product can have a trophic-like cascade through an industry. Think of how the iPhone disrupted not just mobile phones but also the camera industry, the GPS industry, and more. Nodes for various products, technologies, and markets can be linked. Edges can represent relationships like "disrupts," "complements," or "competes with."

- **Regulatory Changes**—A change in regulations can have cascading effects throughout a business or industry. For instance, changes in environmental regulations might affect the raw materials a company can use, which in turn affects manufacturing processes, product design, and finally, the retail price. Nodes for laws, regulatory bodies, and affected business units or processes. Edges can represent "impacts," "requires compliance," etc.

- **Market Dynamics**—Changes in consumer preferences can have cascading effects up the supply chain. For example, a shift towards plant-based diets affects not just food producers but also the farmers who supply them. Nodes for consumer preferences, market trends, and products. Edges can indicate "influences," "shifts," or "meets the need."

- **Acquisitions and Mergers**—When a company is acquired or merged, it not only affects that particular organization but also its competitors, suppliers, and the market landscape. Company nodes could be linked to show changes in ownership, partnership agreements, and competitive dynamics. Edges could represent "acquires," "merges with," or "competes with."

- **Employee Turnover**—The departure of a key team member can sometimes have surprisingly large impacts, affecting team morale, productivity, and even the retention of other staff or clients. Nodes for individual employees, their skills, projects they're involved in, and teams they're a part of. Edges can indicate "works on," "leads," "reports to," etc. Nodes can represent the technologies, business processes they affect, and employees trained to use them. Edges can indicate "implements," "requires," or "trains for."

- **Technology Adoption**—The introduction of a new software platform (e.g., an ERP or CRM system) can drastically affect workflows throughout an organization, with implications for efficiency, communication, and even company culture.

- **Customer Feedback Loops**—Sometimes a single customer's feedback (particularly those "influencers") can trigger a series of changes in a product, affecting not only the product team but also marketing, sales, and future iterations of the product. Nodes for customer profiles, products, and individual feedback. Edges could represent "influences," "results in change," or "corresponds to."

In each of these examples, a change at one level triggers a series of consequences that cascade through other levels of the system, much like a trophic cascade in ecology. The crafting of structures illustrating these systems would provide valuable knowledge in a KG. The crazy thing about them is they are rife with unintended consequences and unintended effects—for which we'll someday be grateful we took the time to map.

Time Series ISG Models

Time series are fundamental to the TCW. In the TCW, we define tuple objects with a measure, a date range, then calculate correlations and probabilities between the tuples. However, these time series associated with each tuple can yield models other than correlations with other tuples. The two models discussed here are properties of the time series themselves—as opposed to a correlation measure as a property between two tuples.

Time Series Inflection Points

Time series inflection points signify an event within a time series which can be correlated with other events around that time. They are also properties of the time series dataframes of the ISG. The difference between a time series and a tuple is that a time series involves some value across a period of time. For example, sales of red wine in Brazil is a tuple (red wine, Brazil, sales). A tuple becomes a time series when we select one of the elements as a measure (in this case sales), add a time range, and specify an interval of time (minute, hour, day, month, etc.).

Figure 129 and Figure 130 is created using the "ruptures" Python library which is designed for detecting change points or inflection points in time series data. The penalty value (1) in this context is a critical parameter used to balance the sensitivity of the detection algorithm. A higher penalty value leads to fewer detected change points, enforcing the notion that each identified inflection point must provide a substantial improvement in the fit to override the penalty cost. Conversely, a lower penalty value makes the algorithm more sensitive to changes, potentially resulting in more identified inflection points.

Figure 129 uses a penalty threshold of three that determines how sensitive the algorithm is to changes. Note the list of tuples along the bottom (2), describing the index and actual date of each of the six inflection points (dashed vertical lines).

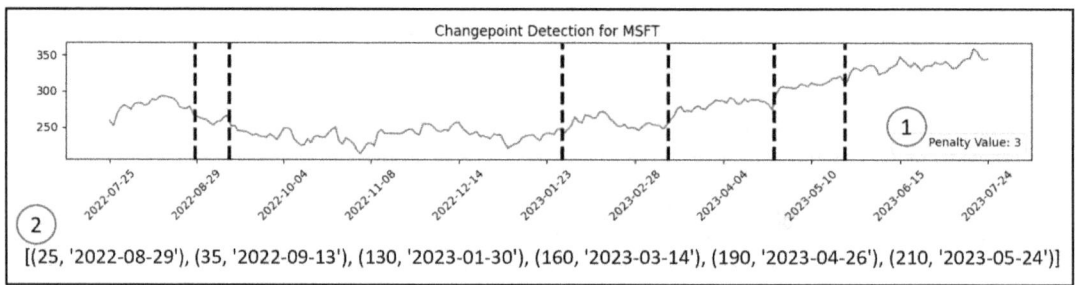

Figure 129: Time series inflection points—insensitive.

For Figure 130, a penalty value of 1 makes the algorithm more sensitive to changes. That results in more inflection points—six versus twelve for Figure 129 and Figure 130, respectively. Note the array of tuples in Figure 130 (1), representing the twelve inflection points.

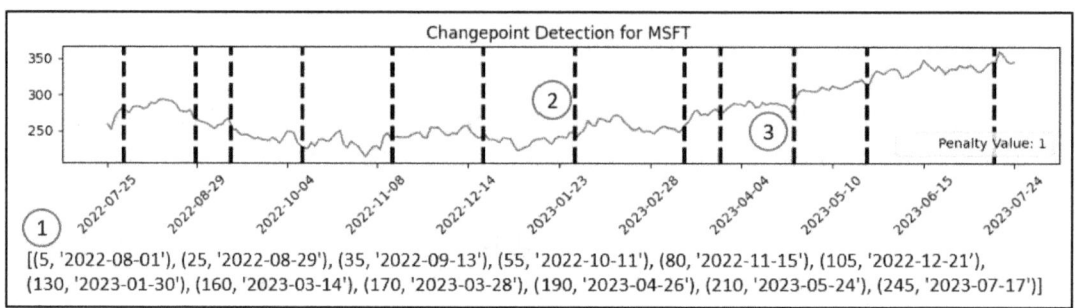

Figure 130: Time series inflection point—sensitive.

Looking at the 2 marker of Figure 130 which is around the 2023-01-23 label, there is an inflection point on 2023-01-30. What happened around that time? According to the blog heading in Figure 131 from the Microsoft site, on January 23, 2023, an event I think most would consider significant happened.

Is this why the Microsoft stock price rose over a relatively sustained period from Jan 23, 2023? I don't know. With Microsoft, there are many significant events. But it gives me a clue about what might be related to events I'm investigating.

Another example is a very favorable press release on April 25, 2023 (near the 3 marker in Figure 130). That is a seemingly very good report a day before one of the inflection points, April 26, 2023.

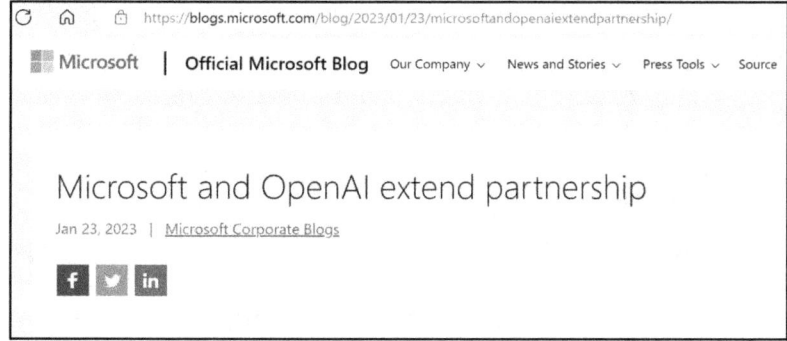

Figure 131: A major event for Microsoft on January 23, 2023.

Earnings Release FY23 Q3

Microsoft Cloud Strength Drives Third Quarter Results

REDMOND, Wash. — April 25, 2023 — Microsoft Corp. today announced the following results for the quarter ended March 31, 2023, as compared to the corresponding period of last fiscal year:

- Revenue was $52.9 billion and increased 7% (up 10% in constant currency)
- Operating income was $22.4 billion and increased 10% (up 15% in constant currency)
- Net income was $18.3 billion and increased 9% (up 14% in constant currency)
- Diluted earnings per share was $2.45 and increased 10% (up 14% in constant currency)

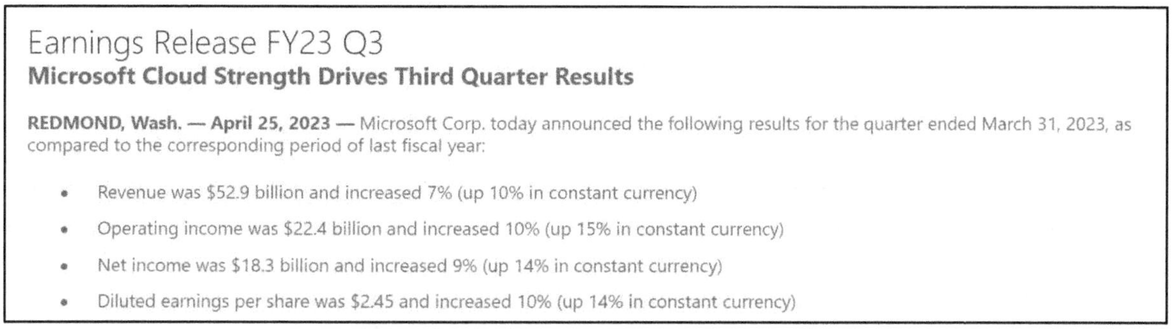

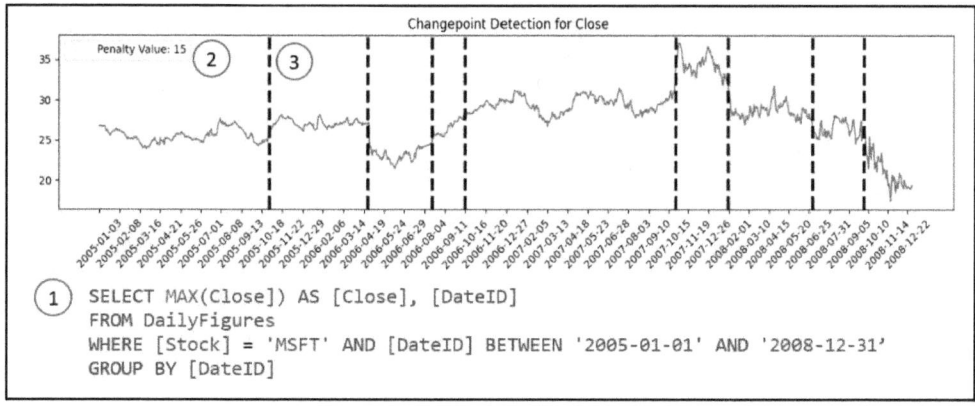

Figure 132: Major event for Microsoft on April 25, 2023.

Figure 133: SQL to the Stocks database and the Inflection Points.

Figure 133 looks at the Microsoft closing stock price over a longer period of time, about four years (2005-01-03 through 2009-12-22), as well as the query and what its inflection points look like in the ISG:

1. The SQL retrieving the time series.

2. Since we're looking over a long four-year period by day, we'll use a very insensitive threshold to detect fewer of the many changes over that longer period. Otherwise, the chart will be covered in black dashed lines.

3. A significant shift upwards in stock price. According to ChatGPT, Microsoft reported a very good fiscal year in September 2005. Whatever the reason, it's a pretty significant change to stand out over the long four-year period.

Figure 134 below shows how this time series and the events look in the KG using the Stocks database:

1. QueryDef - The query's (SQL query) root node.

2. TimeSeries property—This QueryDef is flagged as appropriate for time series analysis.

3. Inflection Point model— The root node for the model of inflection points derived from the query.

4. Penalty_value—The penalty_value of 15 is relatively insensitive. Meaning, the inflection point has to be very noticeable to be detected.

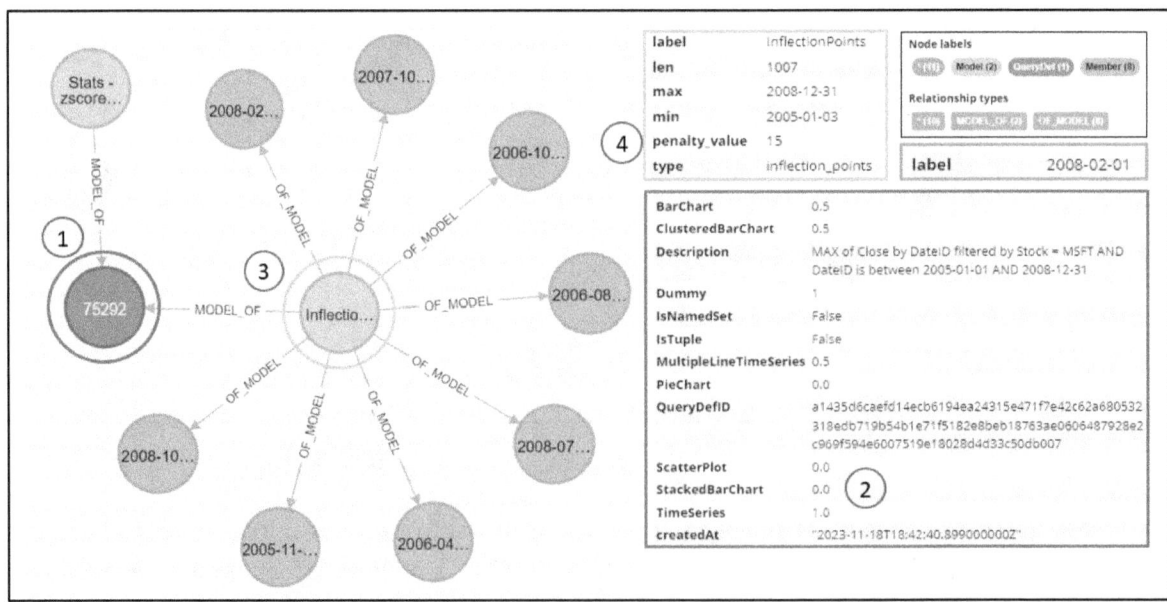

Figure 134: Inflection point model as a model of a QueryDef in the ISG.

Frequency Domain Analysis

I've thought of Fourier Transforms as the closest thing to magic in the statistics bag of tricks. But the ability to decompose a signal (time series) into a set of frequencies makes sense. Waves are fundamental, the most obvious being light and sound. A prism does to light what the Fourier Transform does to a signal. Sound engineers use it to modify recordings, decomposing the sound into individual frequencies. With those component frequencies, they can then add, modify, or remove any of them towards what they desire.

Cycles are the basis for all we experience in life. The fact that there are phenomena that we observe today and things just don't immediately devolve into chaos is due to the cyclical nature of all processes. If life weren't the result of interacting processes, there is nothing to learn because everything would be unpredictably different. Of course, the most well-known and impactful cycles in our normal life world are driven by Earth's 24-hour rotation, its annual trip around the sun, and the moon's roughly month-long orbit of the Earth. Human-implemented cycles, such as semi-monthly pay days and annual taxes influence retail cycles.

Fortunately, the cycles of our life processes aren't perfect. Otherwise, that means they don't change (evolve). If our processes/systems fail to evolve along with other processes, they eventually squeeze out of existence. Even our incredibly highly engineered machines slowly atrophy and require input of energy that won't always be perfectly fed. Cycles slowly morph, blending with other cycles over time. But they live long enough to support the plausibility of making probabilistic predictions of the systems.

As with inflection points, Fourier Transforms in this book mostly relates to the ISG. The decomposed cycles are properties of a time series and can used be to find similarity with other time series. That common ground could be one or more cycles decomposed from those time series with Fourier transforms. For example, the correlation between the sale of cherries in Alaska and the sale of mangoes in Montana may not be strongly correlated. But they may share a frequency that relates to the seasonal characteristics of cherries and mangoes.

Minimum Data Points

To detect annual seasonality using a Fourier transform, you would ideally have at least two full years (cycles) of data. This means a minimum of two years of data to detect a yearly pattern–albeit without much confidence.

However, having more than two years is usually beneficial. With more cycles of data:

1. The seasonality becomes more pronounced and easier to detect.

2. It becomes possible to distinguish between true seasonality and anomalies or one-off events.

3. Noise is better averaged out, making the underlying patterns clearer.

In my experience, having at least 3-5 years of data seems right for a robust analysis of annual seasonality without smashing your cloud storage and compute budget. This is especially so when the time series involves other complexities or when you're trying to differentiate between multiple overlapping seasonality (e.g., daily, weekly, and yearly patterns).

On the other hand, there is a caveat to the duration of data considered: overextended timeframes can encapsulate patterns that are no longer valid, muddying insight into how things work now. For example, the purchasing patterns for a patented drug may shift post-patent expiration, reflecting changes in market behavior. Thus, while historical data is invaluable, it must be contextualized within the dynamic landscape it represents.

Spectral Components

In Fourier analysis, a signal (like closing stock prices over time) is decomposed into a set of tuples with the elements frequency, amplitude, and phase. Each of these tuples are called a spectral component. If you observe a similar spectral component present in other time series, it suggests that each of these series contains a similar periodic component. However, whether the spectral component "means the same thing" in each time series depends on the context and nature of the data. Here are some key points of each tuple element to consider:

- **Frequency**–Represents the rate at which a wave repeats per unit of time. A similar frequency in different time series indicates a wave with the same repeating pattern across these series.

- **Amplitude**–Indicates the strength or intensity of the wave. A similar amplitude means that the wave's strength is comparable across the different time series.

- **Phase**—Refers to the shift or displacement of the wave relative to a reference point in time. A similar phase indicates that the wave's starting point is similarly aligned across the time series.

Component Similarity

If you have two spectral components from Fourier analysis that are very similar in terms of frequency, amplitude, and phase — for example (0.023, 2.66, -1.69) and (0.02301, 2.661, -1.6905) — it is reasonable to hypothesize that the time series from which these tuples were derived might share a common factor or characteristic. Here's why:

- **Frequency Similarity**—The frequencies are almost identical (0.023 versus 0.02301). This suggests that both time series have a periodic component that occurs at nearly the same rate.

- **Amplitude Similarity**—The amplitudes are also very close (2.66 versus 2.661). This means the strength or intensity of the periodic component is almost the same in both time series.

- **Phase Similarity**—The phases are almost the same (-1.69 versus -1.6905), indicating that the timing of the waveforms in both time series is closely aligned.

If we're lucky, a SME or AI might recognize one of the spectral components decomposed from a signal. For instance, a biologist might recognize the component as a recognized biological process, which provides a powerful clue that can link disparate pieces of a puzzle.

Figure 135 illustrates an example of a Fourier Model built from a time series. It is a time series query of the daily closing stock price of MON (Monstanto) from 2005 through 2008:

1. This is the QueryDef object that defines a time series. In this case, it's the daily stock closing prices for 2005 through 2008.

2. A model node acting as a hub for a collection of model items, each representing one of the spectral components extracted from the time series.

3. Two model items, each containing properties of a spectral component— amplitude, frequency, phase.

4. This is an example of another model related to the QueryDef—a model of inflection points of the time series. The other model is the standard statistics (Stats—zscore) with consideration to the removal of lines outside a zscore.

5. A measure node in the DC, the value of the time series.

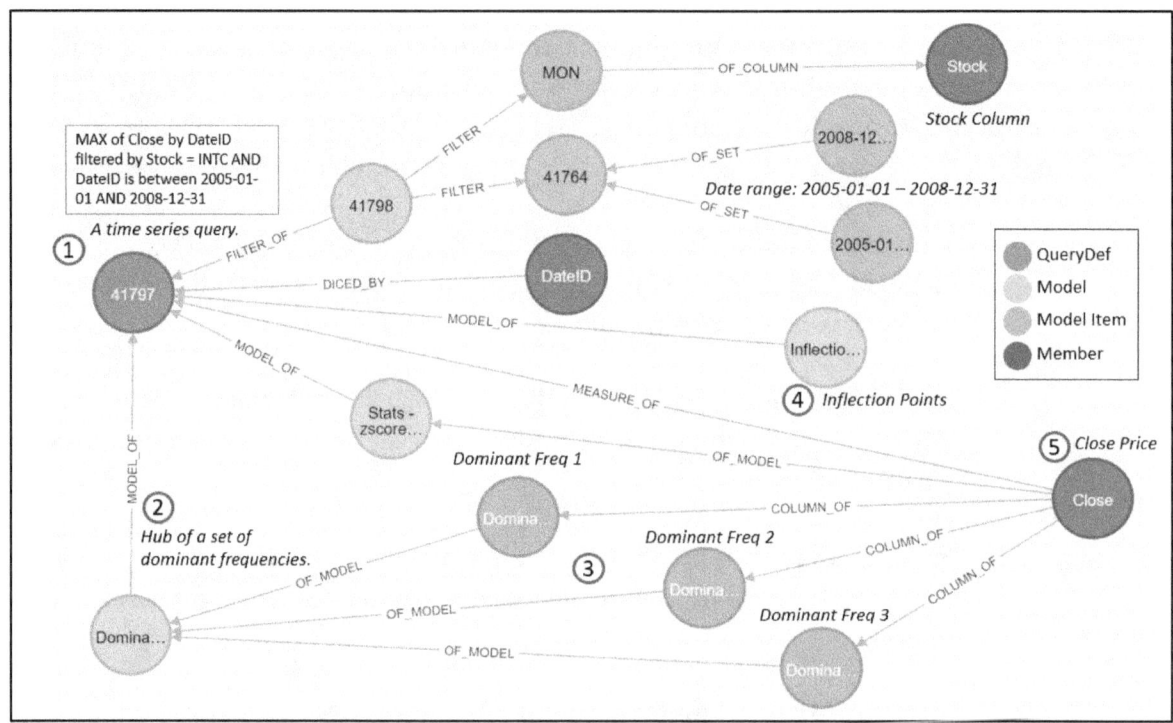

Figure 135: Fourier dominant frequency in ISG.

A signal can be broken down into quite a few spectral components. So we usually focus on the top few, ranked by the largest amplitude (the strongest signal). Confusingly, the set of these top components is referred to as "dominant frequencies"-even though it is really dominant amplitudes.

Figure 136 shows the three dominant frequencies for MON, ordered by amplitude, as depicted by the three Model Item nodes in Figure 135.

The line denoted as 1 (blue line) with its large amplitude is a very dominant frequency, relative to the other two. The line 1 can account up to over a 20 point swing. That's quite a bit for a stock price averaging in the neighborhood of 50-150 during this period, as shown just below in Figure 137, line 1.

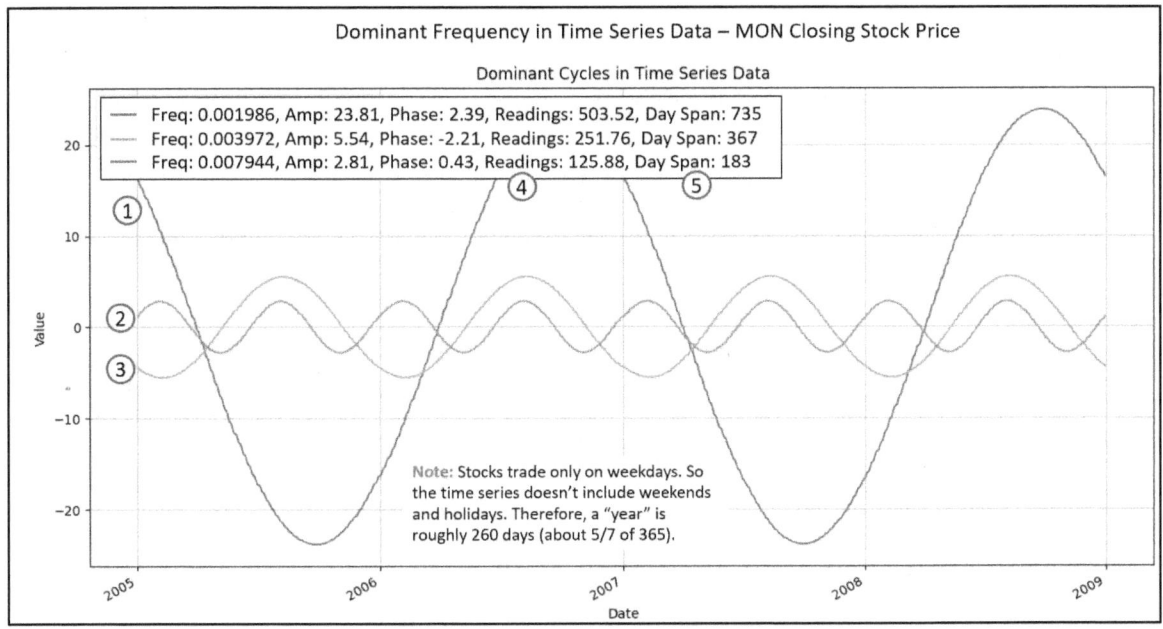

Figure 136: The three dominant frequencies for Monsanto, 2005-2008, shown in Figure 135.

During the period from 2005 through 2008 the three frequencies shown in Figure 136 above represent cycles with 503.52, 251.75, and 125.88 readings (4) per cycle. For the this time series, a reading is the closing stock price of each day. Because they U.S. stock markets are closed on weekends and holidays, I've incorporated those days which changes to day spans (5) of 735, 367, and 183 days per cycle.

These frequencies can sometimes reveal very interesting clues about the makeup of a time series. Sometimes, the identity of the cycle is obvious–for example, seasonality. In this case, line 2 seems to be close enough to a "year" - without the weekends and holidays - 5/7 of a year is 260 days, minus ten holidays—that's about 250 days—close to the 251.75 figure. So MON seems very seasonal since its three dominant frequencies seem to reflect two year, a year, and semi-annual cycles.

However, those frequencies don't account for all the day-to-day stock movement of MON. Figure 137 shows three lines:

1. As mentioned above, this is the actual day-to-day closing stock price of MON.

2. The sum of the three frequencies, shown in Figure 136 above.

3. The amount of the day to day stock price not accounted for by the three dominant frequencies. In other words, the difference between lines 1 and 2.

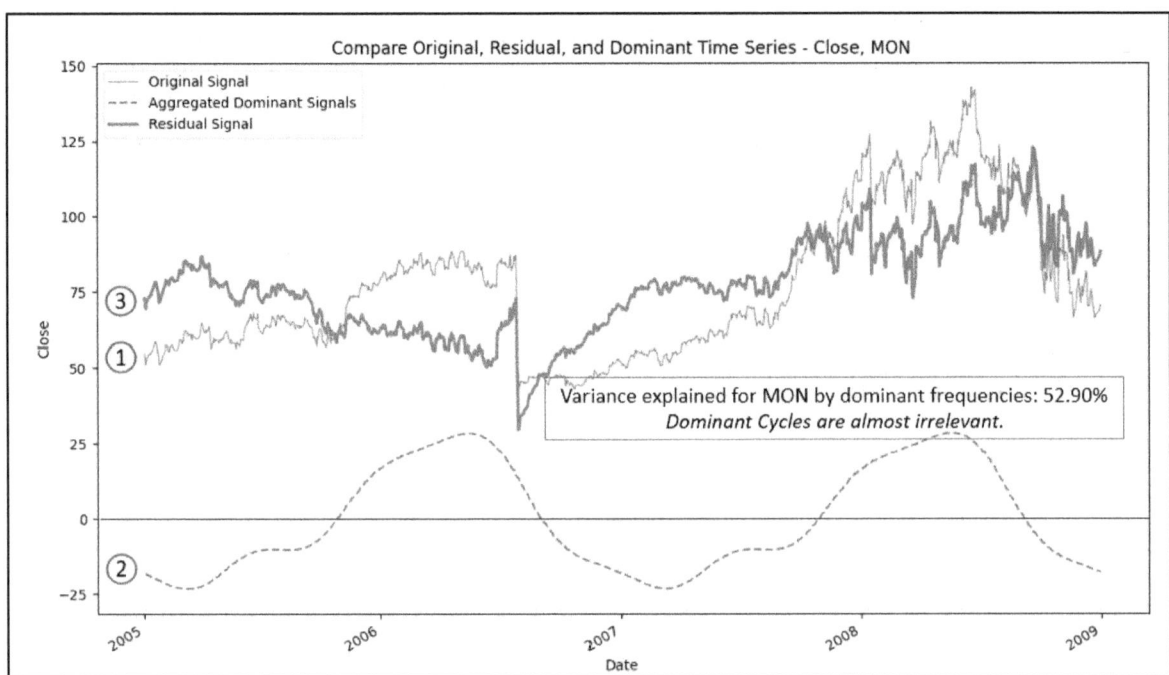

Figure 137: Raw numbers for MON 2005 through 2009.

The residual (line 3) is fairly different from the actual stock price (line 1), indicating there is much more that reflects the MON stock price than seasonality–as would be expected, otherwise we'd all be very rich. However, it is of much value to know objectively that MON is affected in a significant way by seasonality.

Let's look at another stock. Figure 138 shows the dominant cycles for INTC during the same 2005-2009 timeframe.

Notice that Dominant Cycle (1) for INTC is the same, 0.001986. It's the same frequency that coincidently is around two years (without weekends and holidays). Does it imply that a common cycle underlies MON and INTC stock prices? Possibly, but there is one big difference. The phases are different: 2.39 and -2.18, respectively.

And INTC's other two dominant frequencies (2,3) seem to be something other than annual and semi-annual as it is with MON. INTC's stock price is more complicated than MON.

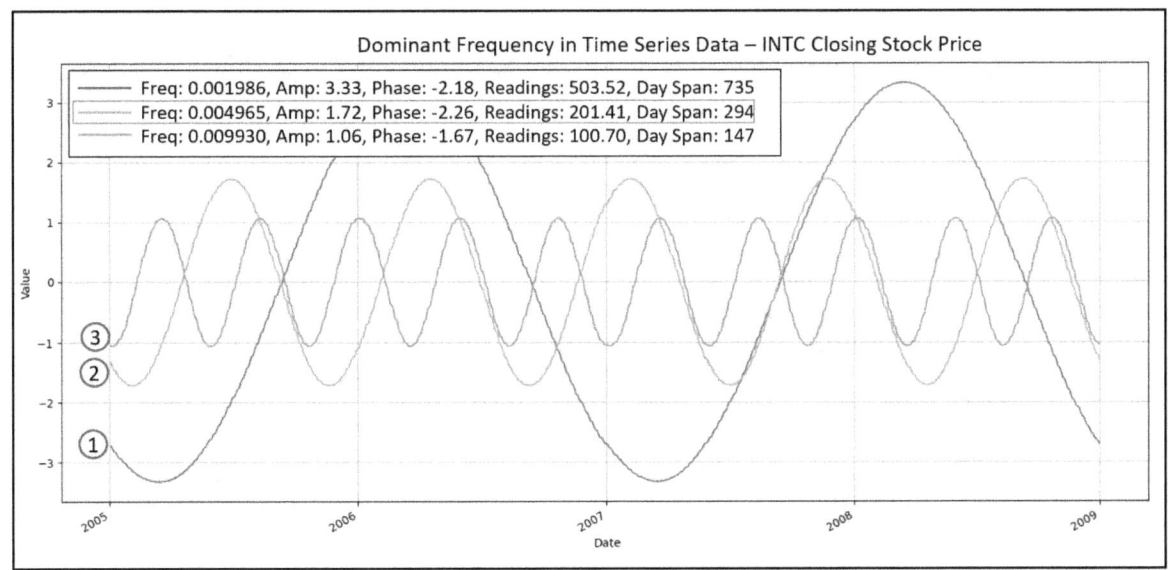

Figure 138: Cycles for INTC daily closing price during the 2005-2008 timeframe.

Figure 139 shows how the three dominant frequencies don't account for enough of the original signal. The difference between the original (light line) and the original signal is quite different.

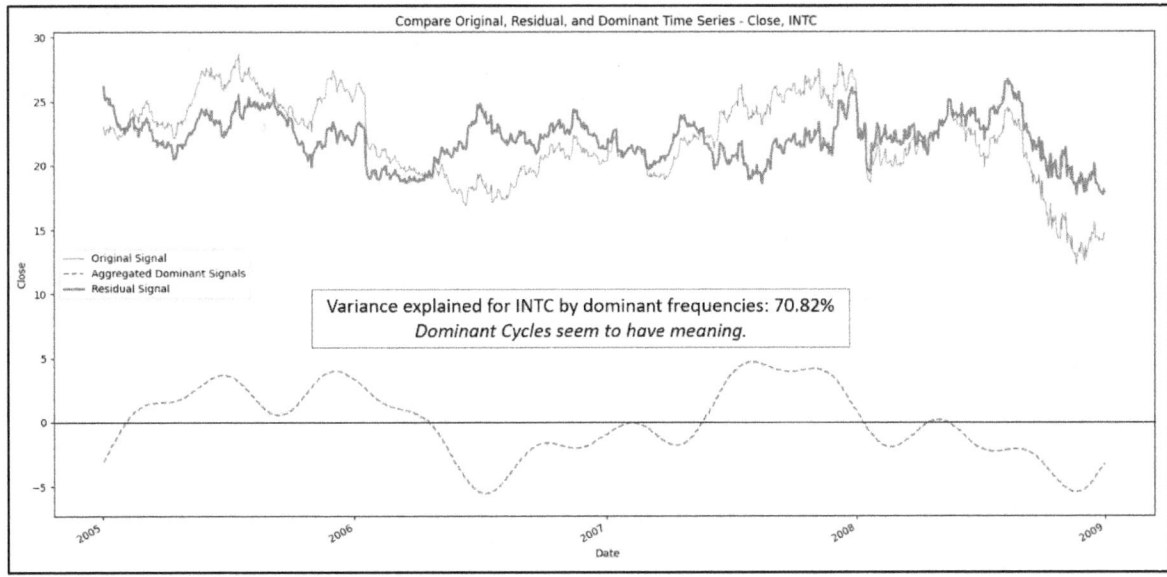

Figure 139: Comparison of residual, original, and aggregated dominant frequencies.

Lastly, Figure 140 shows how one of INTC's dominant frequencies, 0.004965, is shared by other stocks–INTC, BAC, MSFT, GS, and T. That frequency, a cycle of 294 days, doesn't seem to represent seasonality. Is there something to this? I asked ChatGPT and it doesn't know.

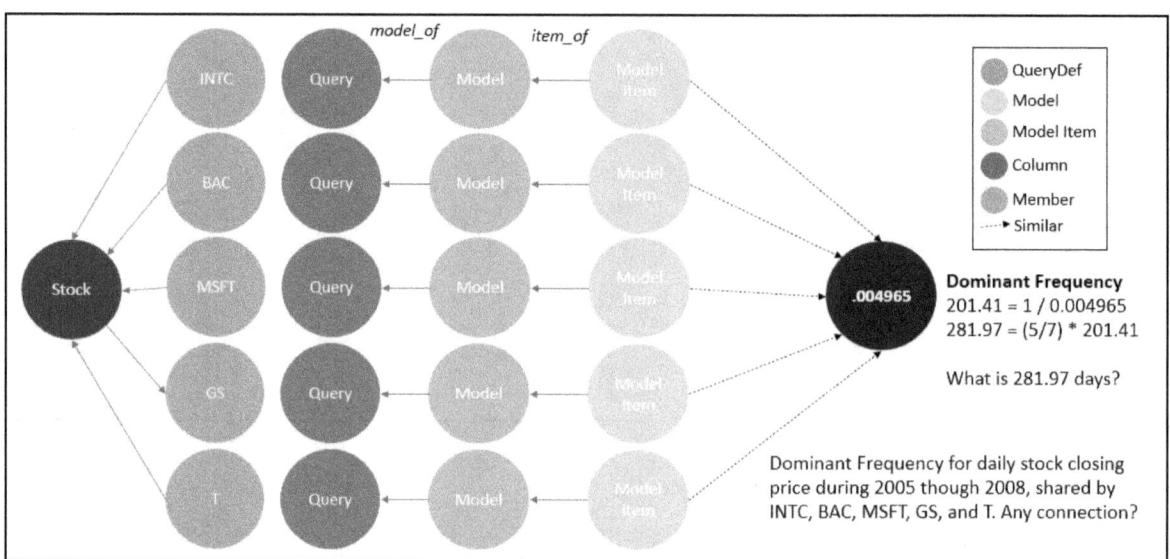

Figure 140: Frequency of 0.004965 is shared by many stocks.

I need to be clear that this is simply about finding what *might* be common factors, in this case, between two time series. It's just a hint, another data point towards the goal of connecting the dots. It's not the job of the EKG itself to explain the correlations. Its job is to record it for either human or AI intelligences to reason through.

CHAPTER ELEVEN

Implementation

At this point, all that has been discussed so far might hopefully sound wonderful. But what does the path to the AEI look like?

This section offers the foundations of how to implement the AEI. However, this is by no means an exhaustive tutorial. The risk of embedding a tutorial directly in this book is that the fields related to analytics (especially AI) are changing so rapidly that lower-level details of a tutorial would quickly become out of date. The intent is to offer a more high-level idea for what the implementation will look like with a set of tools and components. Additionally, this book would be well over a thousand pages with comprehensive tutorials. So I've decoupled any lower-level tutorials related to this book into the GitHub directory. The concepts presented in this book should hold out longer than tutorial code and product features. I'll do my practical best to update the code there. That isn't to say there isn't any code here, but it's almost all easy SQL.

The code and other material I used to create many of the figures in this book are in the GitHub directory as well. Additionally, as I mentioned, future volumes of narrower scope will dive deeper into both conceptual and technical aspects.

Environment

For this sample implementation, I'll refer to the products I've chosen for each niche shown in Figure 141. In the spirit of a "logical model," I had hoped to be as product-agnostic as possible. There are so many options today for each product category.

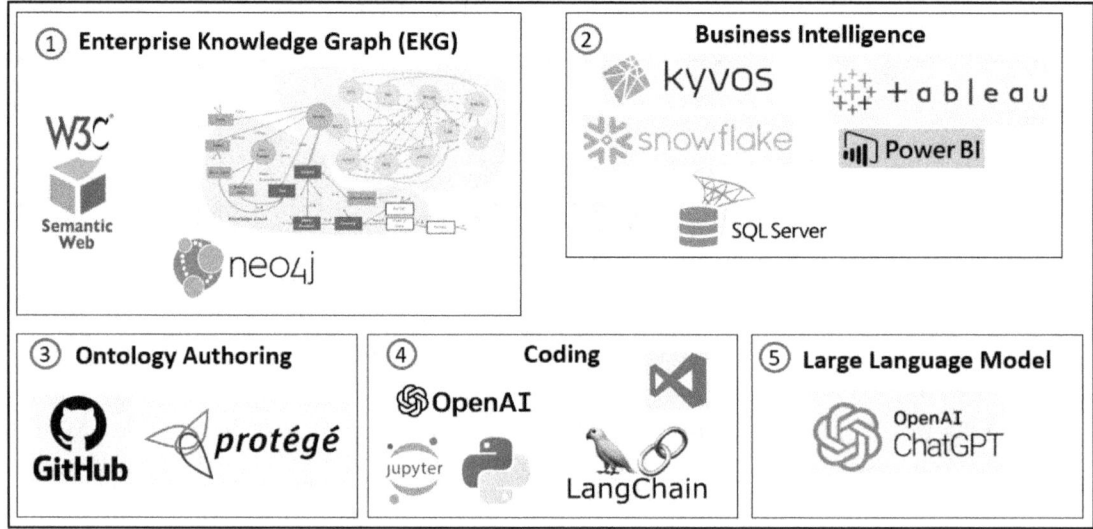

Figure 141: The Selected Development and Infrastructure products.

However, in order to illustrate examples, we need to employ concrete products. I also need to avoid inflating this book by showing examples for multiple products. So I did the next best thing. I chose what I felt were the most popular, "best of breed" when possible, inexpensive, and/or easiest to use components ATTOW. Following are the components I've chosen for the demos:

1. Enterprise Knowledge Graph (EKG)
    a. W3C—semantic web specifications.
    b. Neo4j—The graph database housing the EKG.

2. Business Intelligence
    a. Kyvos—Optimized OLAP cubes.
    b. Snowflake—Data warehouse.
    c. Tableau and PowerBI—BI visualization tools.
    d. SQL Server—A relational database for the Details database. Requires some OLTP type of data updates—which is why Snowflake wouldn't be a good option for the Details database.

3. Ontology Authoring
    a. GitHub—Collaborative development of domain-level ontologies and taxonomies.
    b. Protégé—Development took for domain-level ontologies and taxonomies.

4. Coding
    a. OpenAI API—API to GPT.
    b. Jupyter—Notebooks for DS/ML samples.
    c. Python—The primary language.
    d. Visual Studio Code—Coding tool for Python, SQL, Cypher.
    e. LangChain—RAG API.

5. Large Language Model
    a. Open AI ChatGPT (GPT)—The LLM we've been using.

Regarding ChatGPT, I should point out that ChatGPT is the "chat" version of GPT. GPT is the foundation LLM from which ChatGPT is made. If I were to refer to "GPT via the OpenAI API" throughout the book, the figures depicting prompts to the LLM would have been Python code instead of spoken text - less easy to follow along. But at this point, since this section is about implementation, there is more code involved. And so I need to refer to ChatGPT as well as GPT as appropriate.

The following are notable alternatives to some of the components mentioned above:

- SQL Server (for KG support, including archives, logs, etc.):
    - **MySQL**–A popular open-source relational database management system.
    - **PostgreSQL**–An advanced, enterprise-class, open-source relational database system.

- Neo4j (Graph Database):
    - **Amazon Neptune**–Supports both property graph and RDF graph models.
    - **TigerGraph**–Graph database platform optimized for real-time analytics.

- Kyvos (BI Cube):
    - **Apache Druid**–Known for its real-time data ingestion and querying capabilities, which makes it a good choice for scenarios requiring real-time analytics.
    - **Azure Analysis Services (Microsoft)**–Integrates well with other Microsoft products and offers a robust, enterprise-grade OLAP solution.

- Snowflake (data warehouse):
    - **Amazon Redshift**–AWS's fully managed data warehouse service.
    - **Google BigQuery**– A fully managed, serverless data warehouse that enables super-fast SQL queries.

- ChatGPT/GPT (Large Language Model):
    - LLaMA (Facebook)
    - Gemini (Google)

As the landscape evolves, the GitHub repository should contain material utilizing alternative and/or newly emerged components.

Set Up the KG and DC Environment

This is one of the few exercises embedded in the book. I think we need to get our "feet wet" with a little implementation talk–just the gist of what the AEI looks like. However, it's not an exhaustive step-by-step exercise. This means you still need to access the GitHub repository to *play* along. But with this light setup exercise, you can at least *follow* along to get a better idea of how the EKG is implemented. For this exercise, you will need to install the following components. All of the components have free options. All items are fairly straightforward to install/procure. The full instructions are in install_tutorial_components.docx.

- Obtain a GitHub account in order to access the GitHub repository for this book –https://GitHub.com/MapRock/IntelligenceBusiness

- Install Protégé. This is used to author KGs.

- Procure access to a simple SQL Server or Oracle database with a few databases. Those databases will be used for metadata in the DC. This book involves the famous AdventureWorksDW in the examples. But any database(s) that you have access to will do. SQL Server 2022 Developer Edition is free to download.

- Install Neo4j Desktop (free).

- Obtain an OpenAI (ChatGPT) account.

Additionally, there are a few plugins that must be installed:

- Protégé:
    - OntoGraf—Visualization plugin for viewing the ontology.

- Neo4j:
  - Neosemantics—It is a bridge between Neo4j's property graph world and the W3C semantic web world.

At this point, we don't require Visual Studio Code nor our BI data sources.

For the next three topics, we'll continue with a walkthrough on creating the three major parts of the EKG—the knowledge graph, the data catalog, and the BI-charged components.

Create a Sample Ontology

For a sample ontology, we'll build a simple categorization of stocks. We'll consider three ontologies created in three domains. As samples, we'll use the following ttl files:

1. stocks1.ttl—A basic ontology of a few selected stocks.
2. stocks2.ttl—An ontology of the CEOs of the corporations.
3. stocks3.ttl—A classification (taxonomy) of the stocks.

Towards the goal of viewing the ontologies as a whole, we'll open them one at a time in Protégé. First, we'll load the basic ontology with the selected stocks (stocks1.ttl):

1. Open Protégé.
2. File –> Open –> Select stocks1.ttl.

Following these steps will yield what we see in Figure 142:

1. Click on the OntoGraf tab.
2. Drag the owl:Thing node from the left pane and drop it on the right.
3. Double-click the owl:Thing node in the right pane. It should expand to show the classes Headquarters, Company, and Sector.
4. Double-click all the classes to expand to the individuals. I had to manually arrange the nodes to look like Figure 142.

That represents a very basic ontology of a company stock. In this case, there are companies, companies have a headquarters, are categorized to a company size, and belong to a sector.

366 • ENTERPRISE INTELLIGENCE

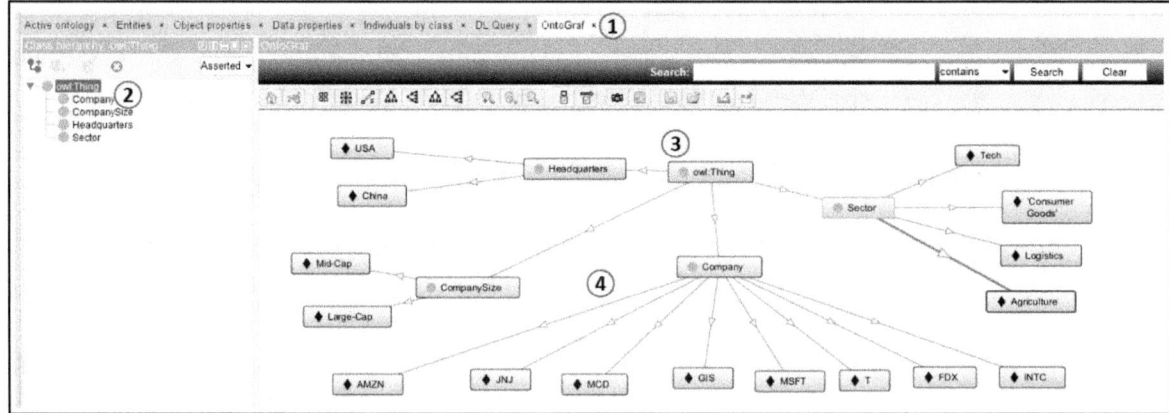

Figure 142: Basic stocks ontology. This is just stocks1.ttl.

If you hover over one of the stocks in the OntoGraf pane, a tip will appear, as shown in Figure 143:

1. This is an ID we've assigned to this stock. The other files (stocks2, stocks3) will match to this URI.
2. These are the relationships of AMZN.

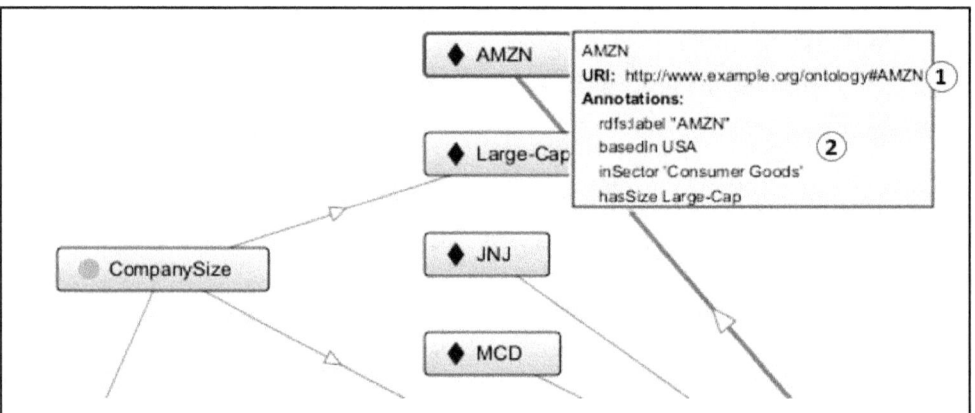

Figure 143: URI (RDF ID) of one of the stocks.

Figure 144 shows how we merge stocks2.ttl into the mix. It contains the CEO as a property of each corporation. Think of the task of maintaining the names of CEOs as a domain function, from which an ontology data product is maintained.

1. Click on the "Active ontology" tab in the main ribbon.
2. Click on the "Ontology imports" tab in the lower pane. Click on the + in the green circle.

3. The "Import ontology wizard" will pop up. Follow the instructions, selecting stocks2.ttl.

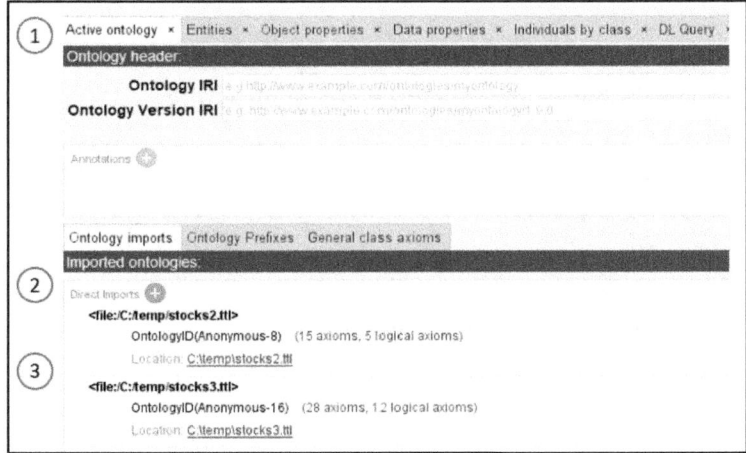

Figure 144: Protege UI for appending ontologies to another ontology.

Repeat the process for stocks3.ttl.

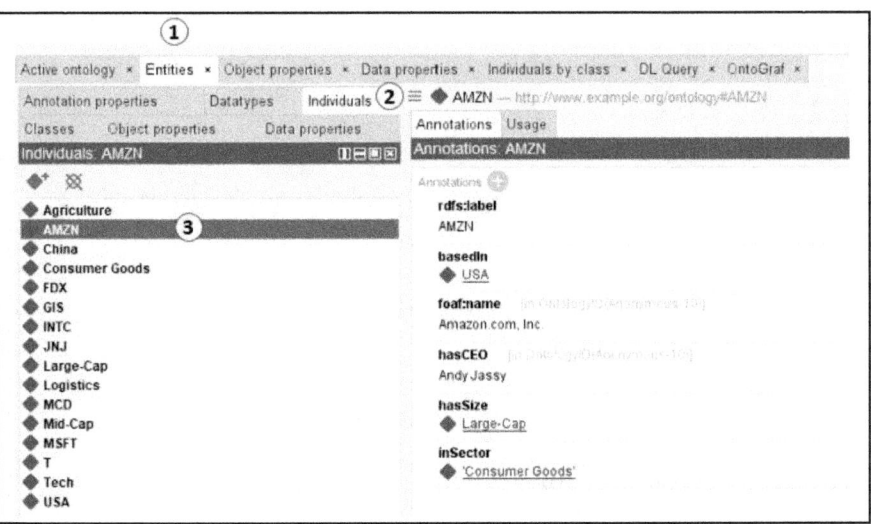

Figure 145: AMZN after adding CEOs (stocks2.ttl) and a corporation taxonomy (stocks3.ttl).

In the end, we can view each company and its relationships through these steps in Figure 145:

1. Select the "Entities" tab.
2. Select the "Individuals" tab from the left pane.
3. Select "AMZN".

Do not save the file. This exercise is meant to demonstrate how we can test what multiple ontology data products would look like when merged before loading it into production (the Neo4j EKG). That is the subject of the next topic.

At this point, the ontology isn't part of the EKG. The EKG lives in Neo4j. Through the Neo4j browser, execute each command, one at a time:

- CALL n10s.rdf.import.fetch('file:///c:/temp/stocks1.ttl', 'Turtle');
- CALL n10s.rdf.import.fetch('file:///c:/temp/stocks2.ttl', 'Turtle');
- CALL n10s.rdf.import.fetch('file:///c:/temp/stocks3.ttl', 'Turtle');

Figure 146 is a snapshot of the simple ontology we built using the Neo4j browser.

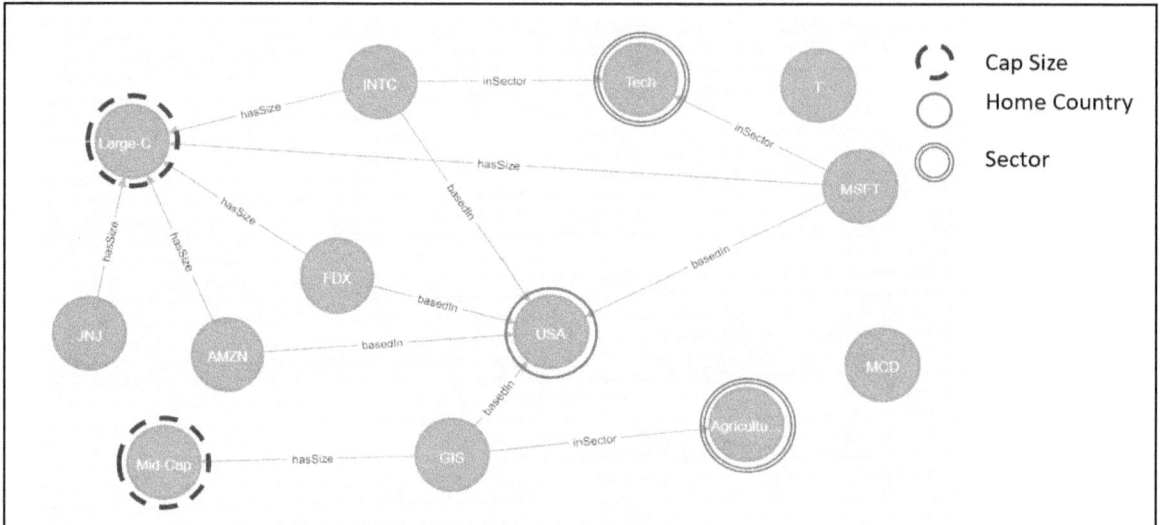

Figure 146: Ontology and taxonomy data are merged into one graph.

In Figure 147, we highlight the MSFT stock node to view its properties.

1. This is the unique URI that identifies the Microsoft stock. Any other ontology that is merged with this ontology can link directly to this node by naming that node with this URI.
2. A property of the node, the CEO of Microsoft, Satya Nadella.
3. This node represents many "is a" properties. It is a company. It is also named individual. It's the addition of individuals where ontologies cross the line into a KG.

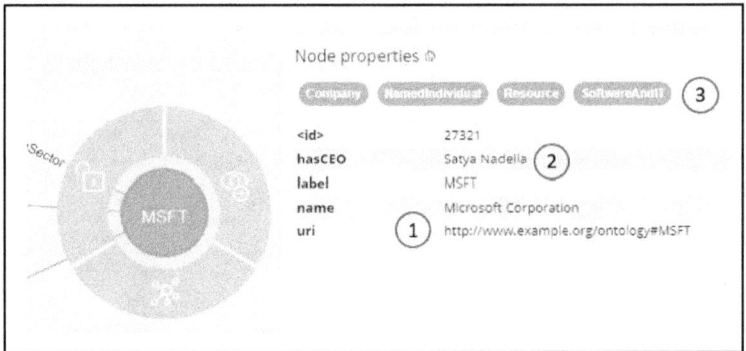

Figure 147: Microsoft entity properties.

Load the Data Catalog

The examples for this book involve three SQL Server (relational) databases:

- Maprocksampledatabase–Custom database I pieced together from free databases.
- adventureworksdw2017–The famous Microsoft sample database of an Internet bike shop.
- Stocks–A custom database I put together from real stock quotes.

Instructions for accessing them are on the GitHub site.

To play along, you'll need a SQL Server installation, at least the SQL Server 2022 Developer Edition. If you don't have access to a SQL Server, instructions for installing SQL Server 2022 Developer Edition are on the GitHub site. Although optimized OLAP cubes are the preferred BI database type for the AEI, for simplicity, the examples involve only the SQL Server databases. For the examples associated with the book, I haven't included OLAP databases. SQL Server is the easiest to deal with. It's almost ubiquitous, especially with the free "Developer Edition" (at least until SQL Server 2022).

Retrieve Data Catalog from SQL Server

Using SQL Server Management Studio (SSMS), run the script, sql_server_entire_server_data_catalog.sql. The end result will be a table of all the databases, tables, and columns in your SQL Server database--the metadata of the SQL Server instance. Figure 148 is a partial result of that metadata.

	ServerName	Catalog	TableSchema	TableName	ColumnName	ColumnType	MaxLength	ObjectType	IsPrimaryKey	ForeignKeyTable	ForeignKeyColumn
28	DESKTOP-N5ISJJF	AdventureWorksDW2017	dbo	DimAccount	Operator	sysname	100	Base Table	NO	NULL	NULL
29	DESKTOP-N5ISJJF	AdventureWorksDW2017	dbo	DimAccount	ParentAccountCodeAlte...	int	4	Base Table	NO	NULL	NULL
30	DESKTOP-N5ISJJF	AdventureWorksDW2017	dbo	DimAccount	ParentAccountKey	int	4	Base Table	NO	DimAccount	AccountKey
31	DESKTOP-N5ISJJF	AdventureWorksDW2017	dbo	DimAccount	ValueType	nvarchar	100	Base Table	NO	NULL	NULL
32	DESKTOP-N5ISJJF	AdventureWorksDW2017	dbo	DimAccount	ValueType	sysname	100	Base Table	NO	NULL	NULL
33	DESKTOP-N5ISJJF	AdventureWorksDW2017	dbo	DimCurrency	CurrencyAlternateKey	nchar	6	Base Table	YES	NULL	NULL
34	DESKTOP-N5ISJJF	AdventureWorksDW2017	dbo	DimCurrency	CurrencyKey	int	4	Base Table	YES	NULL	NULL
35	DESKTOP-N5ISJJF	AdventureWorksDW2017	dbo	DimCurrency	CurrencyName	nvarchar	100	Base Table	NO	NULL	NULL
36	DESKTOP-N5ISJJF	AdventureWorksDW2017	dbo	DimCurrency	CurrencyName	sysname	100	Base Table	NO	NULL	NULL
37	DESKTOP-N5ISJJF	AdventureWorksDW2017	dbo	DimCustomer	AddressLine1	nvarchar	240	Base Table	NO	NULL	NULL
38	DESKTOP-N5ISJJF	AdventureWorksDW2017	dbo	DimCustomer	AddressLine1	sysname	240	Base Table	NO	NULL	NULL
39	DESKTOP-N5ISJJF	AdventureWorksDW2017	dbo	DimCustomer	AddressLine2	nvarchar	240	Base Table	NO	NULL	NULL
40	DESKTOP-N5ISJJF	AdventureWorksDW2017	dbo	DimCustomer	AddressLine2	sysname	240	Base Table	NO	NULL	NULL
41	DESKTOP-N5ISJJF	AdventureWorksDW2017	dbo	DimCustomer	BirthDate	date	3	Base Table	NO	NULL	NULL
42	DESKTOP-N5ISJJF	AdventureWorksDW2017	dbo	DimCustomer	CommuteDistance	nvarchar	30	Base Table	NO	NULL	NULL

Figure 148: Portion of the data catalog from my local SQL Server instance.

Tutorial instructions in the Github directory describe how to save the output to a csv file.

Upload Data Catalog into the EKG

Once the database metadata is retrieved, it's uploaded into the EKG (in Neo4j) through a Cypher script (*load_data_catalog_into_neo4j.cql*) that uses the metadata csv file.

Figure 149 is a partial view of the database metadata loaded into the EKG.

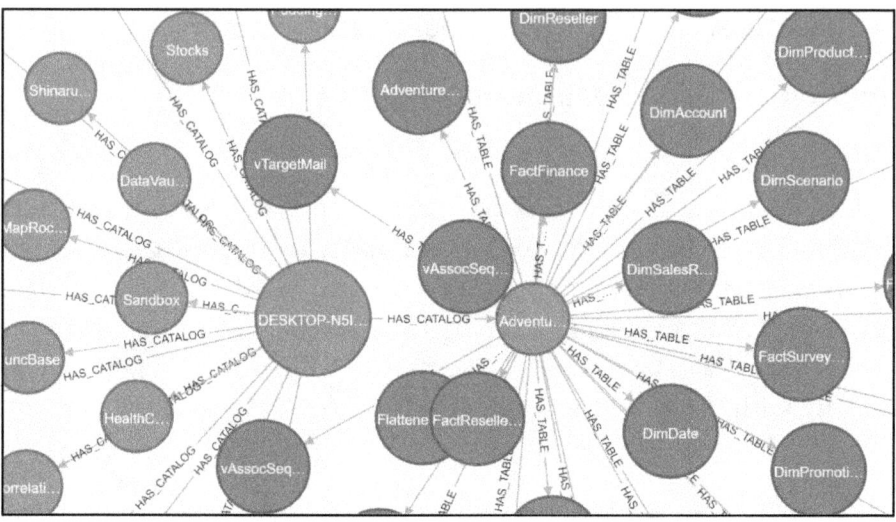

Figure 149: The entire data catalog from my SQL Server instance.

At this point we have two-thirds of the EKG--the KG, and the DC. Now, we'll load the BI-Charged components.

Processing BI Queries into the ISG

This section covers how the BI queries are processed and landed in the ISG. As mentioned, the queries are mostly saved as the actual query text (mostly SQL, MDX, or DAX) submitted from BI visualization tools utilized by human analysts.

As a reminder, the code used to generate the examples is provided in the GitHub directory.

Figure 150 below shows the basic steps of this process, beginning with an analyst building a visualization.

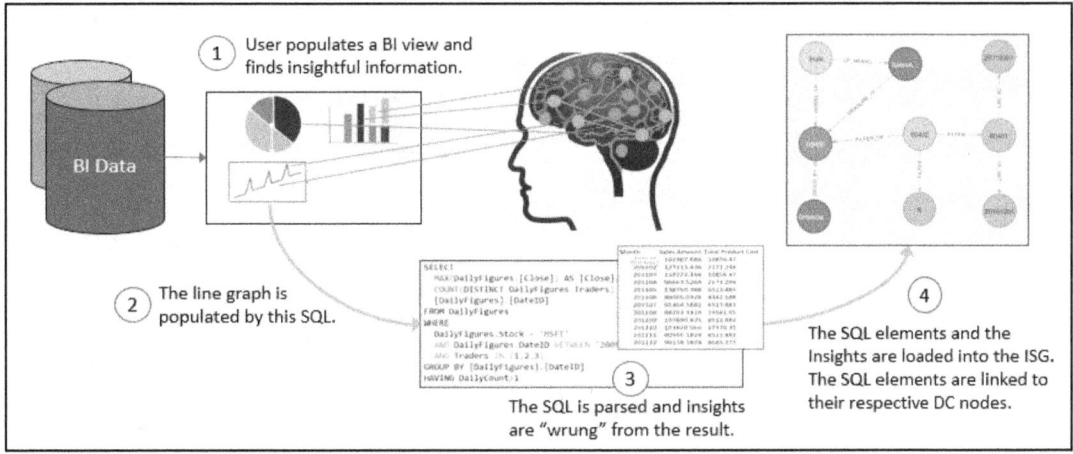

Figure 150: High-level steps from BI data to knowledge graph.

1. This is a typical use case of a BI analyst accessing BI data from a BI visualization tool. The BI visualization typically consists of one or more graphic visualizations. These visualizations convey data in a way that reveals insights to the analyst about data.
2. Focusing on the line graph (a time series) in the BI visualization, the arrow points to the SQL generated to retrieve the data that populates that line graph.
3. The SQL is parsed for all its elements (the SELECT list and parts of the WHERE clause) and the dataframe resulting from the SQL is wrung for whatever nuggets of insights it contains.
4. The SQL and its insights wrung from the resultant dataframe are loaded into the ISG. A QueryDef node is created, representing the SQL, data elements parsed from the SQL are linked to their respective DC nodes, and the insights are linked to the QueryDef node.

However, Steps 2 through 4 happen for all the visualizations the user brought up. In this case, the analyst might only have found the line graph to contain valuable information. But the analyst did bring up the pie and bar chart presumably with a belief that it would contribute towards her insight. Even if not for that analyst, but for another analyst. Keep in mind that those other graphs might be based on data different from that of the line graph.

Query Parsing and Saving

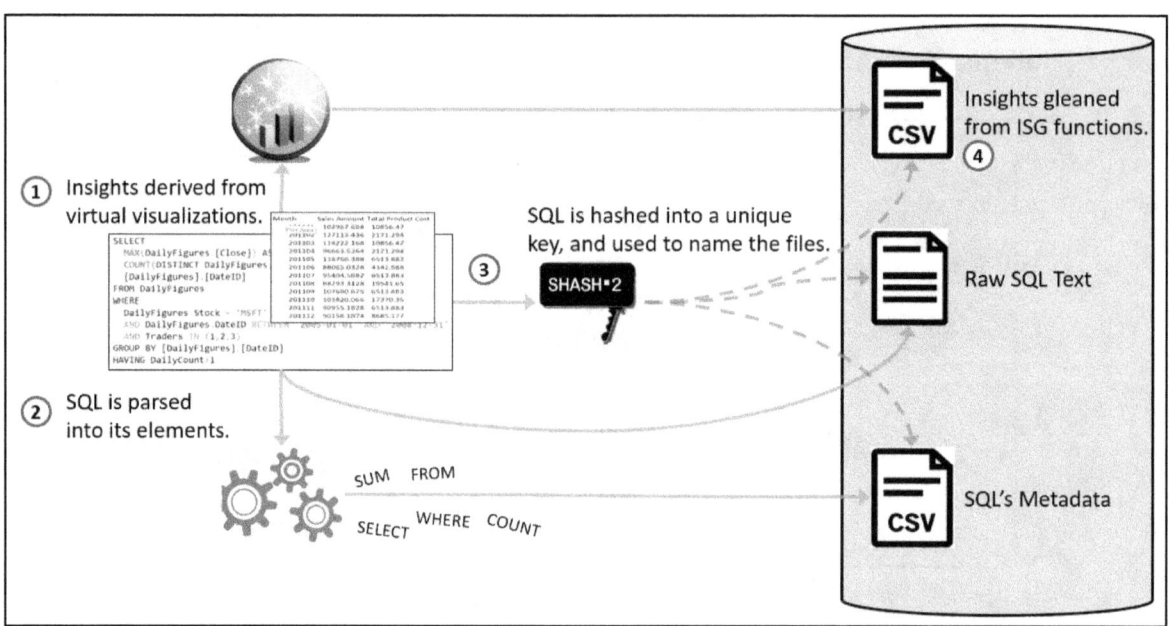

Figure 151: SQL and dataframe are parsed and stored to files as a staging area.

Figure 151 drills into a little more detail about what happens between Steps 2 through 4 in Figure 150 above. The SQL query that populated the line graph and the insights an analyst could mine are ultimately loaded into the EKG. But they are first stored in files as a staging area. This intermediate step enables control over when the EKG is uploaded:

1. The dataframe is wrung for insights that might be gleaned across manifestations in various types of visualizations. The dataframe is first analyzed to see if it can be visualized as a line graph, bar chart, scatter plot, etc. For each of those visualizations, the dataframe is run through an array of insight functions to wring out insights. The results are a csv file of the insights (4).

2. The SQL itself is parsed into tables, columns, functions, and any referenced member (column value). The result is a csv file of the SQL metadata.
3. The SQL query as presented is hashed to form a unique ID. A file containing the SQL is created and named in the format: [sql_hash].sql
4. This is a csv of the captured insights, the actual data that is uploaded into the ISG.

At a chosen ETL time, the "insights gleaned" and SQL metadata files are the source that will be loaded into the ISG (see query.py on GitHub). The files for every SQL will have the same columns, so only one script (Cypher using the LOAD CSV command) is required to load the queries into the ISG.

The QueryDef node created for each SQL will be named with the sql hash (3 in Figure 151). All three of these files are small, therefore, they can be stored in case the ISG must be rebuilt.

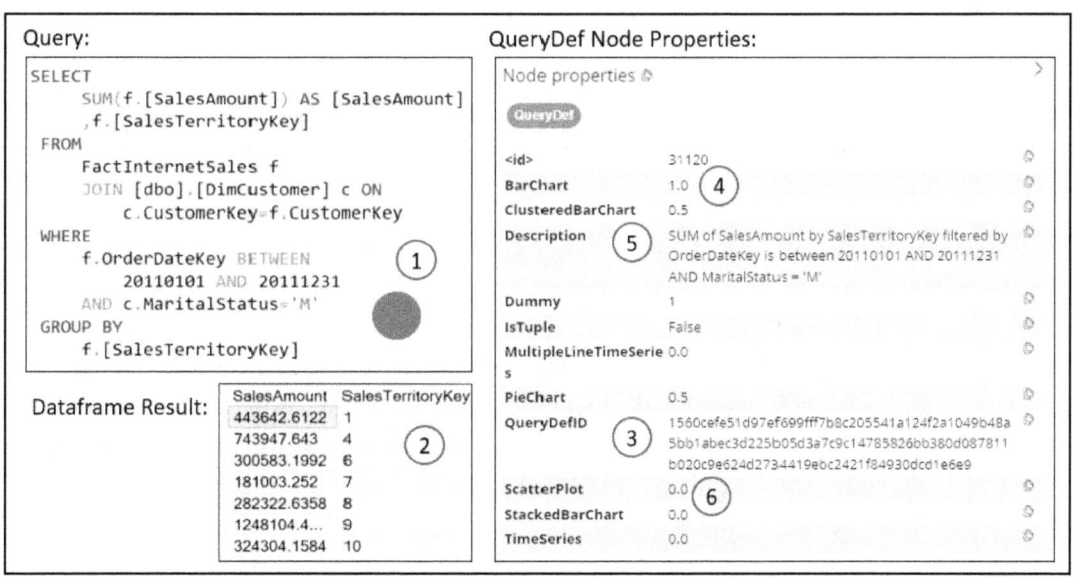

Figure 152: A SQL is converted into a QueryDef node in the EKG.

Figure 152 shows an example of a QueryDef node representing a SQL after it's loaded into the ISG:

1. The SQL statement for the QueryDef.
2. The results of the query.
3. The unique ID for the query, which is a hash of the raw SQL.
4. BarChart of 1.0 indicates that a bar chart is a prime visualization for this query.

5. This is a readily human-readable and machine-readable format. Although humans can understand formats such as JSON, it's not a native language for most people. Also, until the rise of high-quality LLMs, such descriptions were awkward for machine readability.
6. The 0.0 scores for these three visualizations mean they are not appropriate for this dataframe.

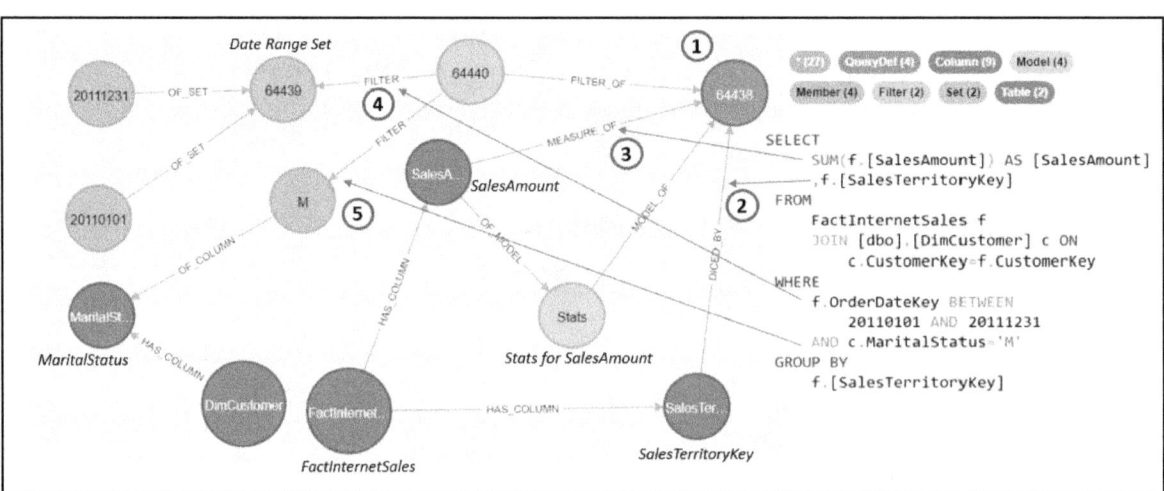

Figure 153: This is the detail of the SQL from Figure 9-12 is uploaded to the EKG.

Figure 153 shows the complete map of all the parts of the SQL shown in Figure 152 as it looks in the ISG.

1. Query Definition (QueryDef): This node represents the overall SQL query definition, encapsulating the entire SELECT statement, including what data to pull (SUM of SalesAmount), from where (FactInternetSales), the conditions for the data to be selected (WHERE clause), and how to group the results (GROUP BY SalesTerritoryKey).
2. SELECT Clause (dice): This node represents granularity of the SQL query, which groups the results by the SalesTerritoryKey to aggregate the measure (3).
3. SELECT Clause (Measure_Of): Represents the SELECT statement in the SQL query, specifically the measure being selected, which in this case is the sum of the sales amount--SUM(f.[SalesAmount]).
4. WHERE Clause (Date Filter): Denotes the date range filter applied in the WHERE clause of the SQL query, specifically using OrderDateKey to filter records within the specified date range.

5. **WHERE Clause (Marital Status Filter):** Symbolizes the filter condition based on marital status within the WHERE clause, filtering the records where the MaritalStatus is 'M'.

Reusable Components

There are a few reusable components in the ISG/TCW—filters, sets, and tuples. They mitigate the number of objects and relationships in the EKG. For example, if two SQLs have the same where clause, we shouldn't create separate nodes and relationships for them. They can be shared.

More importantly, utilizing these three components helps to link QueryDefs and other objects. For example, two reports and/or analysts might filter specifically by Marital_Status='Single' and Education_Level='Masters' (WHERE clause). The fact that two SQL have the same WHERE clause surfaces what might be a valuable relationship or concept.

Figure 154 illustrates examples of three reusable components. This is a brief introduction to the three:

1. **Filters** are components used in querying databases, especially within the context of BI and data analysis. Basically, it's the WHERE clause of a SQL. They apply criteria to data retrieval operations, determining which data points are selected based on specified conditions. Filters often include comparison operations, such as equals, not equals, greater than, or less than, and can be used to refine the scope of a query to target specific data ranges, categories, or metrics, streamlining the data processing workflow.

2. **Sets** in the context of database queries are collections of members or items that a user defines for analysis. Sometimes they are called a cohort. They are often used to group related data points for aggregation or to apply the same filter across multiple items. For instance, a set can include multiple members from the same column or dimension, allowing the user to apply complex filters like range or "IN" clauses, which select data within a certain range or from a specific subset, respectively. In essence, sets allow for the flexible grouping and manipulation of data within a database query.

3. **Tuples** represent specific data points within a multidimensional data space, often in the context of OLAP cubes. Each tuple is a unique combination of

dimension attributes, essentially a single cell within the cube that holds a data value. In an RDBMS context, a tuple can be seen as a row, but in multidimensional databases, it's a specific data point defined by its coordinates across multiple dimensions, such as time, geography, or product categories.

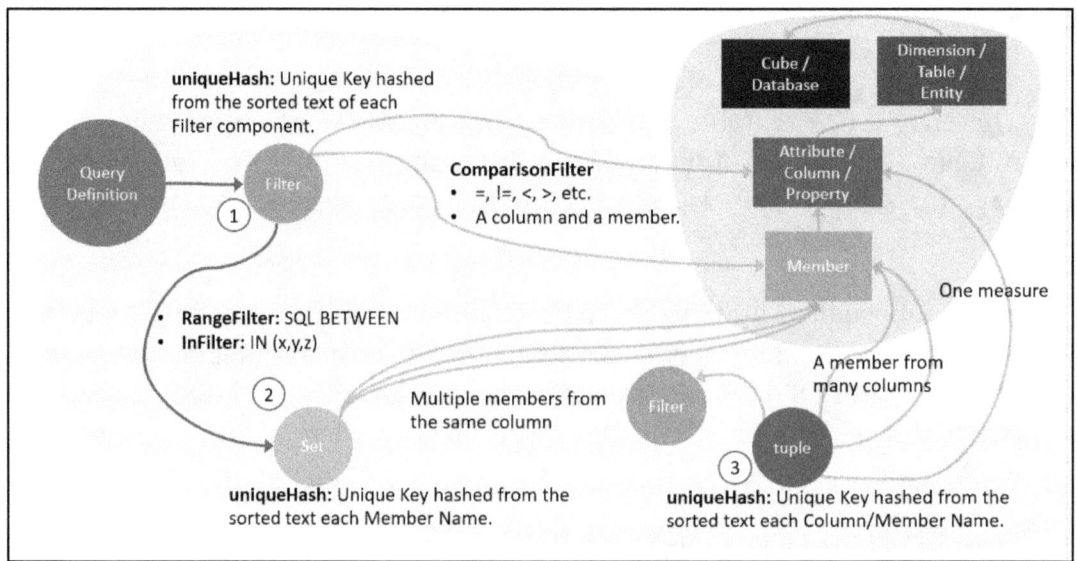

Figure 154: Filter, Set, and Tuple are reusable across many QueryDefs.

Each reusable object has a unique ID that should match no matter the order of the terms. For example, if we look at two SQLs differing in the order of terms in the WHERE clause, they should have the same result:

1. Marital_Status='Single' AND Education_Level='Masters'
2. Education_Level='Masters' AND Marital_Status='Single'

The unique hash ID for that filter is created by sorting the *terms* first, removing whitespace, capitalizing, and retrieving a hash off that formatted string:

HASHBYTES('MD5', 'EDUCATION_LEVEL=MASTERS,MARITAL_STATUS=SINGLE') =

0x6251CD9FB8922C145B3957C6C538BF84

For sets, such as the set of people, {Mari, Luke, Brandi, Kevin}, the *members* will be sorted before calculating a unique hash ID. For example, this set's unique hash ID is:

HASHBYTES('MD5', 'BRANDI,KEVIN,LUKE,MARI)=
0x427DE5FA123F5B3958A283D0DA2B4CCE

For tuples, the elements are not sorted since the position of each member matters:

HASHBYTES('MD5', 'EUGENE,PROGRAMMER,BOISE,1949-02-29') =
0x811BC520705F6F426C526C6800669C4C

Following are deeper discussions of the three reusable components.

Filter Components

A filter is akin to a finely tuned sieve for data. It could be thought of as setting a context. For example, we can set the context of Hawaii by including only data related to Hawaii.

In SQL (MDX, Cypher), the FILTER is embodied in the WHERE clause that determines which records meet specified criteria and should be included in the results. It's the gatekeeper, ensuring that only the relevant pieces of information pass through based on defined conditions, such as specific values, ranges, or patterns. For instance, a filter might narrow down a list of sales records to those occurring within the last quarter or to customers from a particular geographic region.

Considering the SQL shown back in Figure 153, the filter isolates relevant sales from the FactInternetSales table ordered in 2011 by married customers.

Filters are integral to the structure of a QueryDef, serving as the conditional logic that sculpts the data landscape into a meaningful shapes. They are the directives that, when applied, transform a broad query into a source of targeted insights.

Set Components

In the context of this book, a "set" consists of a collection of *like* elements. For example, it could be a set of states comprising the U.S. Pacific Northwest: {WA, OR, ID}. Although sets in the context of math and most programming languages (for example, Python) can be of mixed types, in the OLAP world, a set is a collection of members of an attribute (column).

Figure 155 shows a set of Products isolated from the FactInternetSales table. The result of the SQL is a set of products sold in Sales Territory 6, under marketing promotion 1, ordered in 2011:

1. There is just one column defined. If there are more, it becomes a tuple—more specifically, a set of tuples.

2. The WHERE clause is the filter, which is the context of the set of members resulting from the SQL.
3. The date range is a set of dates.
4. The set of product keys, the result of the SQL.

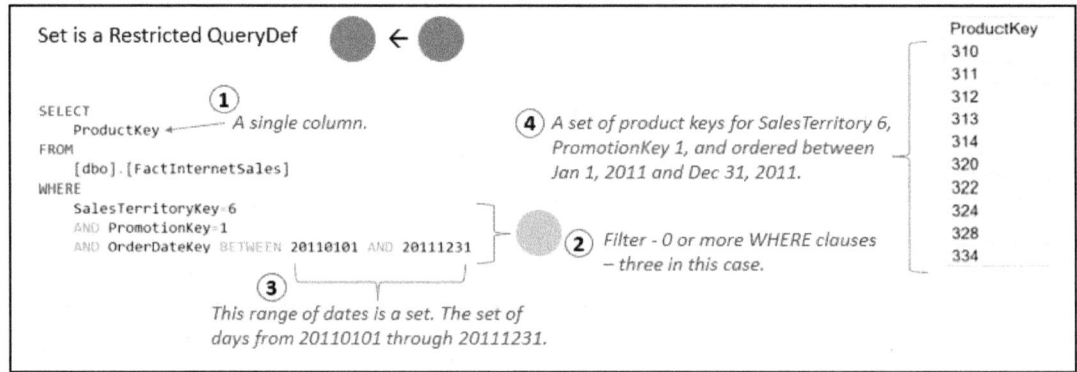

Figure 155: A Set is a subclass of a QueryDef.

Before moving on to tuples, in the world of multidimensional OLAP, a set is a little more complicated. Rather than a set of members—like the members of your family—a set is a set of tuples. A set of tuples is more complicated, but it is more powerful. For example, instead of a simple set of members of your family, such as, *{Eugene, Laurie, Venus, Bodhi}*, a set of tuples might be:

{(Eugene, Human), (Laurie, Human), (Venus, Cat), (Bodhi, Cat)}

The first element is the name of the family member, and the second element is the species. If we added another tuple also named Venus, (Venus, Plant), that's a different entity.

Tuples Components

I covered tuples earlier in the *Cube Space (semantic layer)* sub-topic. Since it is an important concept and one that traditionally is a slippery subject for folks I've introduced to BI, it's worth a bit of review.

Tuple is the name for some coordinate in a multi-dimensional space. The most common tuple in our daily lives might be an appointment to meet someone. For example, Eugene meeting Brad on Friday, December 8, 2023 at 11:30 am at Rib Shack. In tuple notation, this is:

(Eugene, Brad, 2023-12-08, 11:30am, MT, Rib Shack, Eagle, ID)

A similar tuple might be:

(Bill, Steve, 2024-02-25, 11:30am, PT, Taco Palace, Scottsdale, AZ)

The most important thing to notice about the two tuples above is that the order of the elements matter. Each slot represents a specific dimension. In this case, that's organizer, attendee, date, time, time zone, restaurant name, city, and state. For example, adding the following tuple to the set, wouldn't be valid:

(Bill, Steve, Taco Palace, 2024-02-29, 12:30pm, PT, Scottsdale, AZ)

The concept of a tuple most familiar to us is a GPS coordinates. It's a two-element tuple where the first element is latitude and the second element is longitude. For example:

(43.41057923447113, -116.68849012329952)

In the EKG, a tuple is a subclass of a QueryDef. Think of a tuple in the context of the ISG/TCW as a one-row QueryDef. It is really a query with:

- One or more dicing columns in the SELECT.
- Filters that restrict each dicing column to one member.
- One measure value (usually an aggregated sum).

Figure 156 shows a SQL statement used to extract a specific piece of data (SalesAmount) for a defined set of dimension members (the tuple) from a larger dataset. It essentially zooms in on the data cube to find the value at the intersection of the defined dimensions, which in this case is the SalesAmount of $3,578.27. This is useful for detailed analysis within a cube structure, allowing for precise querying and reporting on multidimensional data.

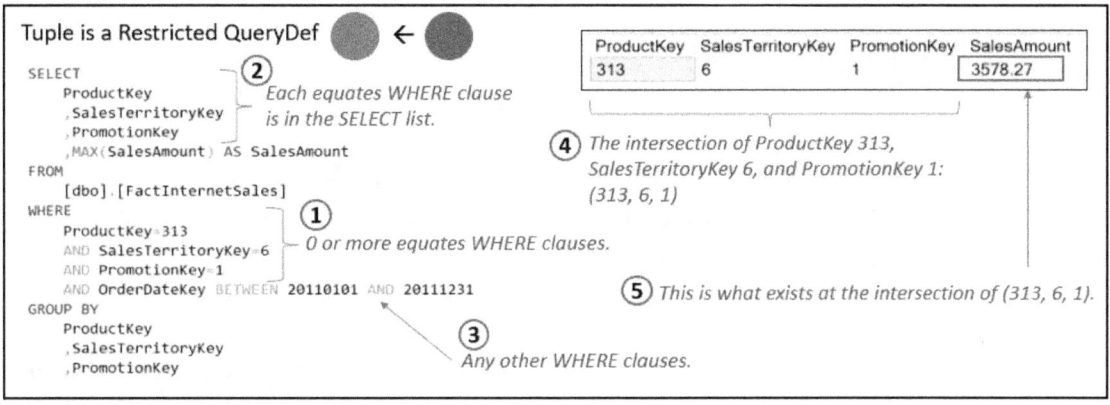

Figure 156: Tuple is a kind of QueryDef—a QueryDef of just one row.

Here are descriptions of the items:

1. **Where Clauses (Tuple Definition)**–The WHERE clause defines the specific members of the tuple. In this query, ProductKey = 313, SalesTerritoryKey = 6, and PromotionKey = 1 are the conditions that pinpoint the exact tuple within the cube.

2. **Select Statement (Tuple Members)**–The SELECT list defines the dimensions of the tuple, which in this case are ProductKey, SalesTerritoryKey, and PromotionKey. Each one of these equates to a WHERE clause, specifying the values that define the slice of data we're interested in.

3. **Contextual Filters**–The range of the OrderDateKey is specifying the context. In other words, the sales amount for the tuple defined as ProductKey = 313, SalesTerritoryKey = 6 and PromotionKey = 1. But only for sales between 20110101 and 20111231, inclusive.

4. **Query Result**–The result set displays the intersection of the dimensions specified by the tuple. For the tuple located at (313, 6, 1), it shows the aggregated SalesAmount that corresponds to this intersection.

5. **Value at Intersection (Tuple Value)**–This is the actual value found at the intersection of the tuple's dimensions. In this case, it shows the SalesAmount that exists where ProductKey is 313, SalesTerritoryKey is 6, and PromotionKey is 1.

Figure 157 below illustrates the main difference between how a QueryDef and Tuple are laid out in the ISG. The difference between a QueryDef (dataframe) and a Tuple is that QueryDef dices are columns and Tuple dices are values of a column. QueryDefs create one or more rows and the Tuples are only one row. In fact, each row of a QueryDef is a tuple. As mentioned, in OLAP cube terminology, what is referred to as a "set" is a "set of tuples."

1. **Query Definition (QueryDef)**–The QueryDef defines columns "Education" and "Marital Sts." It indicates that the query is defined by these columns as dimensions for dicing the data.

2. **Query Result**–The result of the query. It presents the "TotalProdCost" measure across various combinations of "Education" and "MaritalStatus", demonstrating

the multi-dimensional nature of OLAP (Online Analytical Processing) cubes. Each row is actually a tuple.

3. **Tuple**—The Tuple specifying "Education" set to "Graduate Degree" and "Marital Sts" to "M" defines a specific tuple. It represents a single, precise point in the multi-dimensional space: the Total production cost for customers with graduate degrees and are married.

4. **Tuple Query Result**—The result of the tuple. "TotalProdCost" corresponding to the specific tuple defined above (3), which is the result of querying the cube for a particular combination of "Education" and "MaritalStatus."

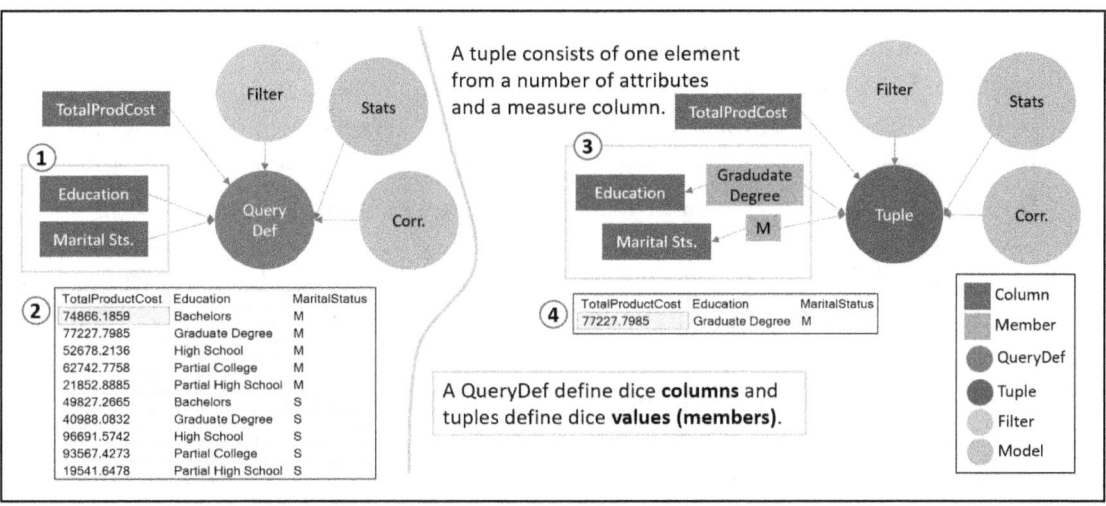

Figure 157: Difference between a QueryDef node and a Tuple node.

The QueryDef is the central object of the ISG, whereas the Tuple (which is a subclass of QueryDef) is the central object of the TCW.

Query Functions

In the BI context of this book, QueryFunctions are usually some sort of calculation. In the context of a SQL statement, that means column values composing a calculation and defining rules, and the result of the calculation aggregated with a function such as SUM, COUNT, or AVG. Figure 158 shows two Queries using such calculations:

1. The left SQL is read: The net sales per (NetPerItem) item by Education.
2. The right SQL is read: Tax per item (TaxPerItem) by Marital Status.

```
SELECT ①                                    SELECT ②
    c.EnglishEducation as Education,            c.MaritalStatus,
    SUM(                                        SUM(f.[TaxAmt] / f.[OrderQuantity]) AS TaxPerItem
        ( f.[SalesAmount]+f.[Freight]+f.[TaxAmt] )   FROM
        / f.[OrderQuantity]                         FactInternetSales f
    )                                               JOIN dbo.DimCustomer c ON
    AS NetPerItem                                       c.CustomerKey=f.CustomerKey
FROM                                            GROUP BY
    FactInternetSales f                             c.MaritalStatus
    JOIN dbo.DimCustomer c ON
        c.CustomerKey=f.CustomerKey
GROUP BY
    c.EnglishEducation,
    f.[Freight] + f.[TaxAmt]
```

- Both SQL include calculations involving common values: TaxAmt and OrderQuantity.
- The valuable information is that both calculations are effected by changes in either value.

Figure 158: Two Queries related through calculations.

The SQL are different. However, the highlighted measures, TaxAmt and OrderQuantity, are common to both SQL. The implication is that changes to either value affect the results of both SQL. For example, if tax rates change, it affects both queries. On the other hand, if freight prices change, it would only directly affect the left query. Figure 159 shows how those connections from the SQL in Figure 158 are laid out in the ISG:

1. NetPerItem is a measure of QueryDef1, but it's a calculation, a function.
2. The NetPerItem function involves SalesAmount, Freight, TaxAmt, and Quantity.
3. TaxPerItem is a measure of QueryDef2. It's a function involving Quantity and TaxAmt.
4. The TaxAmt and Quantity columns are common to both QueryDefs.

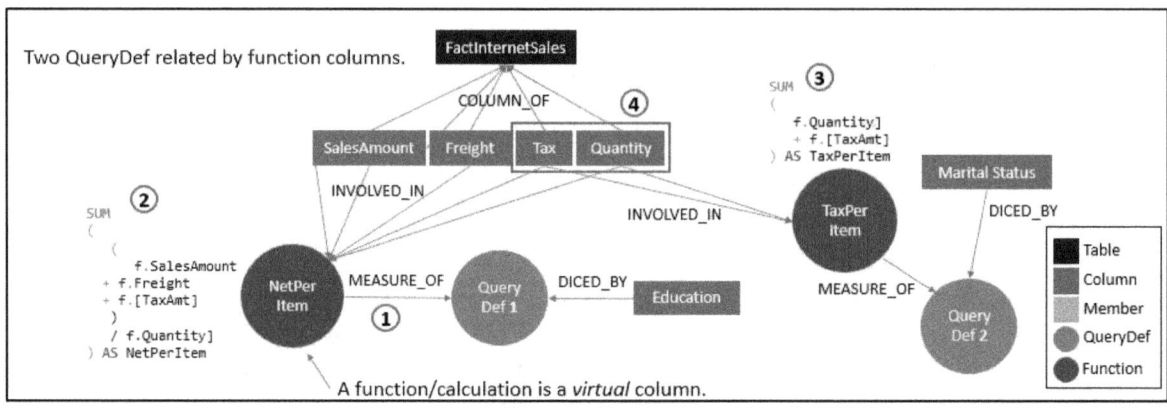

Figure 159: QueryDefs can be related through the parameters of query functions.

Note how the formula elements are linked to table columns (lighter rectangle) defined in the DC. For example, the NetPerItem formula node is linked to the SalesAmount, Freight, TaxAmt, and Quantity columns of the FactInternetSales table.

Uploading to the ISG

The ISG's primary object is the QueryDef. These are queries made by BI analysts going about their normal BI activities using tools, such as Tableau and PowerBI. Or it could be data scientists accessing BI resources for its highly-curated data through Jupyter notebooks. These SQL are captured by the databases' native logging or by data monitoring tools. Depending on criteria, such as the user and the database, the queries are stored in a directory for processing, as described back in Figure 151.

Figure 160 picks up where Figure 151 left off (parsing the SQL and wringing insights from the data). It illustrates the high-level process from SQL query to objects in the ISG.

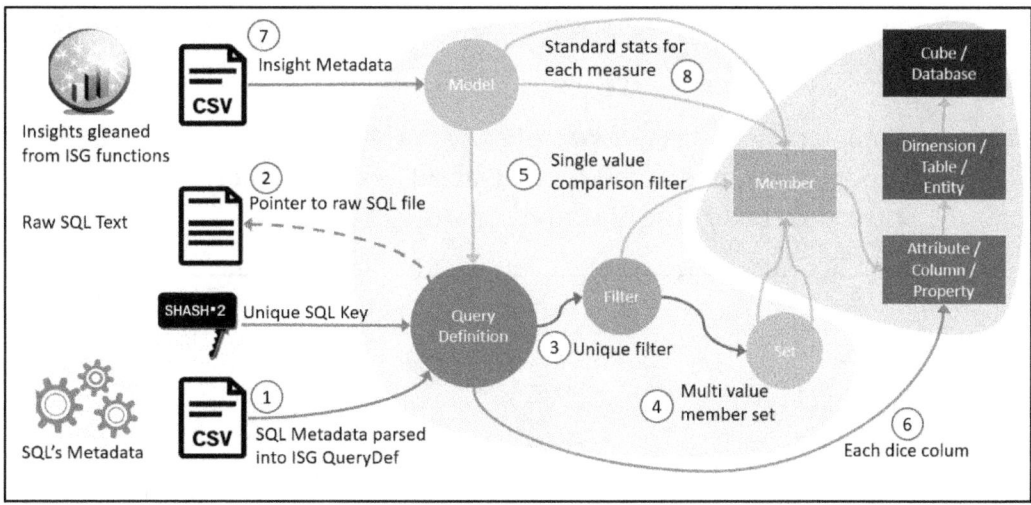

Figure 160: Text files loaded into the KG.

The GitHub repository includes walkthroughs as samples for each of these steps in Figure 160:

1. We start by picking up each SQL statement dropped in a directory. It is parsed using a SQL parser. That includes dice columns, measures, and filters (WHERE clause items). These pieces are loaded into the ISG as an ensemble rooted in the QueryDef node. We'll look at the details of the QueryDef object soon.

2. The parsers may not handle all details of the many SQL dialects exhaustively. Therefore, reconstructing SQL from the QueryDef object might lose some features. So the QueryDef includes a property that is the URI to the raw SQL we just parsed. This way, if we need to re-run the SQL, we can ensure we're executing the same query issued by the user whose activity created the SQL. Note that if the data changed, the result will not be the same.

3. The WHERE clause in its entirety defines the context of the SQL.

4. The WHERE clause might include sets, for example an IN clause. These sets are another way to find commonality between QueryDefs.

5. Any equates clause (for example, Customer = 'Samantha') points to that member in the data catalog.

6. Each measure of the Query points to the measure column in the data catalog.

7. The insights wrung from the results of the SQL are uploaded to the ISG and associated to their respective model. For example, inflection points are in one model.

8. One of the models (set of insights) is a standard set of statistics. This is the only model that is generated for all QueryDefs. The other models must reach a threshold of significance to be saved.

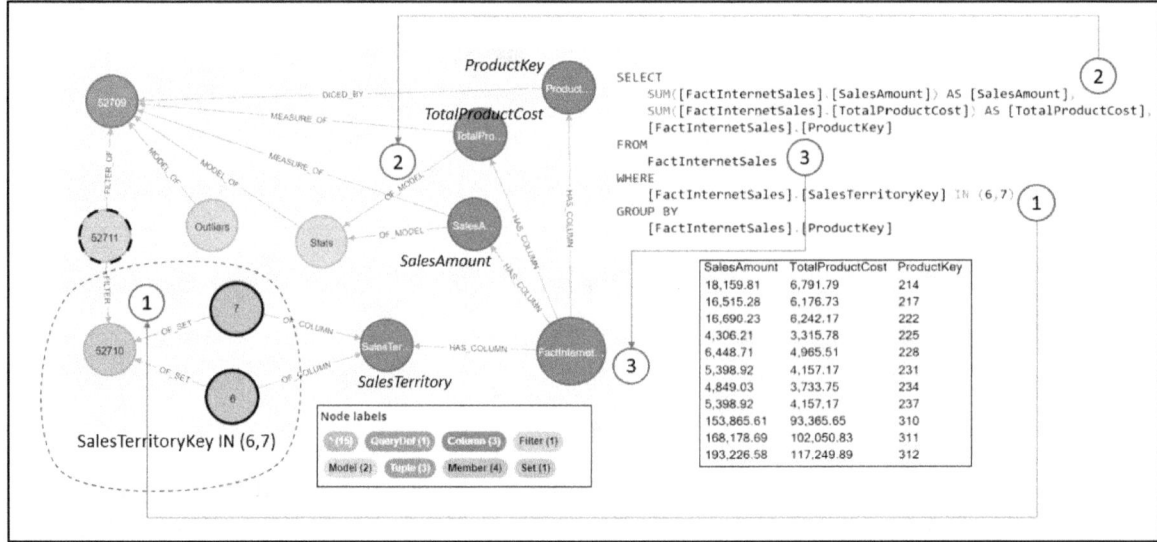

Figure 161: The starting SQL and the detailed end result in the KG.

Figure 161 is a sample of SQL and how it looks once uploaded to the ISG. It shows three categories of elements pointing from the SQL to how they are mapped in the ISG:

1. The WHERE clause is the context of the SQL. In the ISG,
   a. The main object is the filter node (dashed circle).
   b. There is just the IN clause, which references a set of two Sales Territory keys, 6 and 7 (outlined with solid line).
   c. The Sales Territory Keys are members of the Sales Territory column.

2. The SQL consists of two measures, SalesAmount and TotalProductCost, and one dice column, ProductKey. Those three elements are mapped to their respective column objects.

3. This is the table (the raw dataset) referenced in the SQL. Of course, this could include joined tables. All the columns referenced in the SELECT and WHERE parts happen to belong to the table, FactInternetSales.

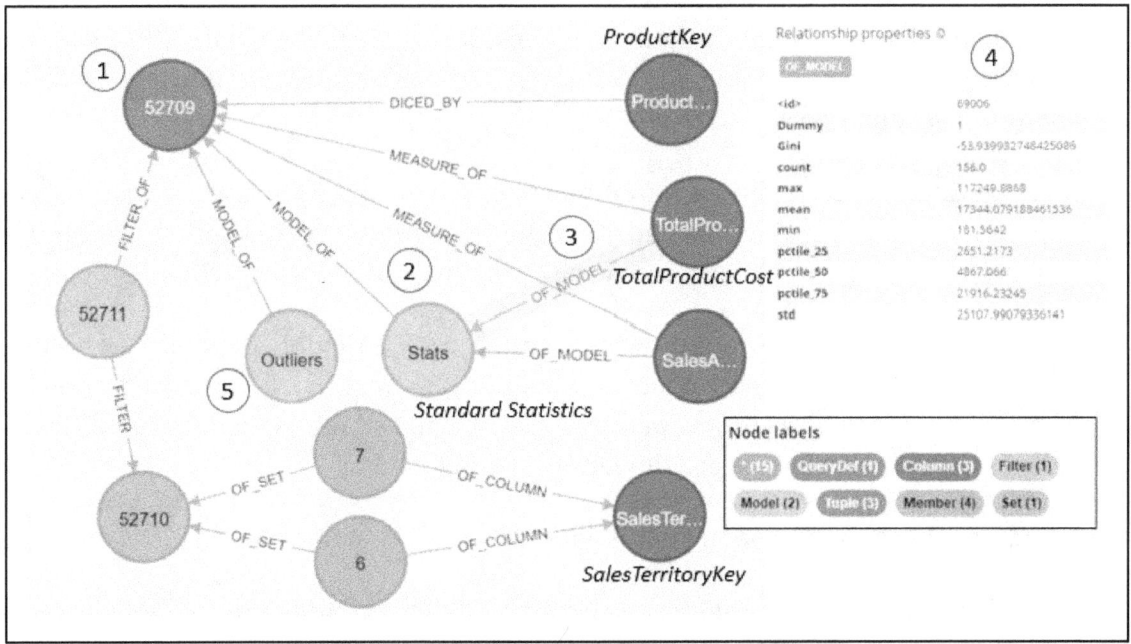

Figure 162: Statistics on TotalProdctCost for SalesTerritory 6 and 7.

Figure 162 continues the example from Figure 161, focusing on the Stats model (standard statistics) of the SQL used in Figure 161.

1. The same QueryDef node.
2. A model root node for the standard statistics of the query's results.

3. The relationship between the Stats model node and the column the measure the stats are based on. In this case, the "Stats" model node is referring to standard statistics of the TotalProductCost measure.
4. The standard statistics are stored as properties of the relationship between the Stats model and the TotalProductCost column.
5. Another model derived from the QueryDef. In this case, a set of outliers. We're covering the Outliers model node soon.

By default, the standard stats model is calculated on all rows of a dataframe (QueryDef result)—the same as shown in Figure 162. However, these statistics would include outliers, which can be problematic for statistics due to their over-sized values which make them outliers. Outliers could be optionally removed to better represent the majority of rows. For example, a BI analyst might remove outliers—any row with a value greater than some multiple of the standard deviation.

That multiple is called a z-score, which indicates how many standard deviations an element is from the mean. A z-score of 3.7 means the data point is 3.7 standard deviations away, which is quite far considering that most data (99.73%) should fall within three standard deviations of the mean in a normal distribution, according to the empirical rule (68–95–99.7 rule).

Removing outliers from an initial query is something BI analysts usually do as a "best practice" when considering statistics. Outliers are rare by definition, so the trade-off of statistics that are more representative of the majority is worthwhile.

However, the cutoff for what defines outlier can be flexible depending on the situation. For example, if we wish to harden a building against Earthquakes, we should be extra careful with a nuclear power plant versus a barn. We might want to build for 4 standard deviations versus 2 standard deviations, respectively.

Figure 163 shows our same query with two models with differing z-scores:

1. Note the two measures of the query–SalesAmount and TotalProductCost. Each has two relationships—one identifying it as a measure of the QueryDef and the other identifying it as the measure of a Model.
2. This is a Standard Stats root model node for TotalProductCost with a z-score threshold of 3.7—about three of 1000. In this case, I manually chose 3.7 as the threshold because I could see for myself that value removed the items I could visually see were outliers on a scatter plot.
3. These are the stats for TotalProductCost within a z-score of 3.7.

4. This is the Standard Stats for SalesAmount with a lower z-score of 2.0. That means two standard deviations—about 1 in 20. I actually set the default in the sample code to 2.0. It seems to be a good balance. That 0.05 value is also the default p-value, so it must be a good default.
5. These are the Stats for SalesAmount within a z-score of 2.0.

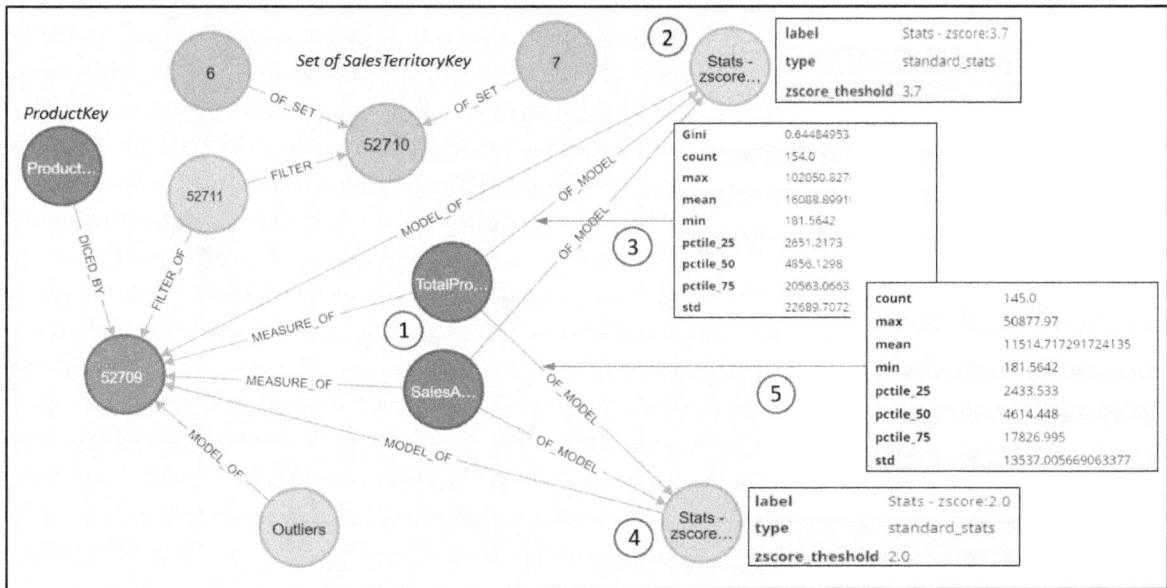

Figure 163: Standard Statistics models for different z-scores.

We just looked at kicking out the outliers. Now we'll look at the outliers themselves. Outliers skew results like a billionaire skewing the average salary of the neighborhood. However, the outliers are usually very interesting, especially in a culture that skews towards favoring "the bigger the better". There's usually much we can learn from them.

So, although we removed the outliers for the standard statistics of the QueryDef, we can build another model for the set of outliers. Figure 164 shows the same QueryDef along with an outlier model:

1. The Outlier model node. The z-score is set at 3.7. With that 3.7 threshold, only three nodes were deemed outliers.
2. One of the outlier nodes is the SalesAmount for ProductKey 312.
3. Node for ProductKey 312 is an outlier for TotalProductCost and SalesAmount.
4. Two other tuple nodes for outliers. The red tuple nodes point to the same measures, TotalProductCost, and their respective ProductKey, 313 and 312.
5. Tuple node 52717 is an outlier linked to the ProductKey 313 member node. It is an outlier for TotalProductCost.

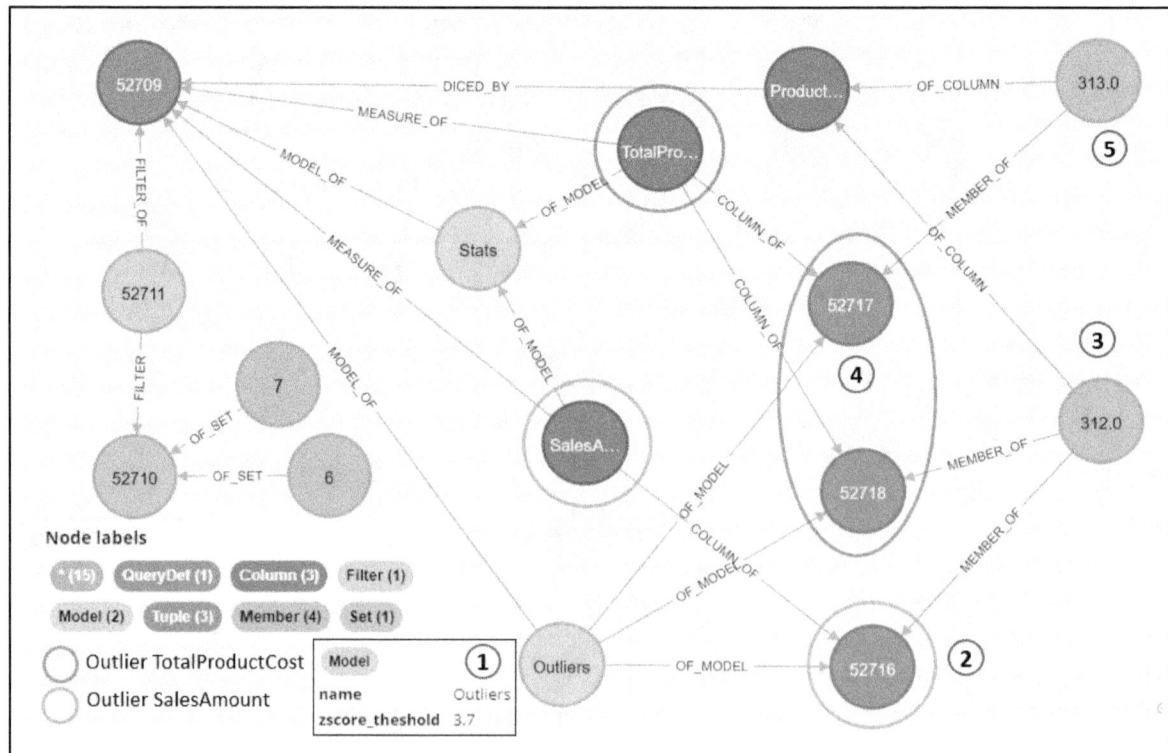

Figure 164: Outliers for TotalProductCost with a zscore_threshold of 3.7.

Lastly, let's look at the dataframe resulting from our Query (Node 52709). Figure 165 is a facsimile of a data analysis tool output for that query. We can see from the grid at the right that ProductKey 312 and 313 have z-scores greater than 3.7:

1. Average "Total Product Cost" of 17344.08.
2. Average "Sales Amount" or 25107.99.
3. A partial table of rows returned by the query.
4. The first row has a TotalProductCost of 117,249.89, very much above the average of 17,344.08.
5. The z-score is 3.98, just above the z-score threshold of 3.97.
6. The calculation for the z-score. This is a standardized score that indicates the number of standard deviations the value is from the mean. A z-score of 3.98 is quite high, suggesting that this product cost is significantly higher than the average product cost for this dataset.

Filters should be thought of as the context of a query result. For example, if I said "Everyone knows about ChatGPT," the context is "most people I work with." If I said,

"Everyone know SQL," again, the context is "most people I work with." The same principle applies to all statements—unless it's a ridiculously descriptive statement.

Similarly, every QueryDef has a context. That context could be spelled out in different places. Common examples are the WHERE clause of a SQL, or in a contents of a particular database, such as a database with data about Idaho versus one about Hawaii.

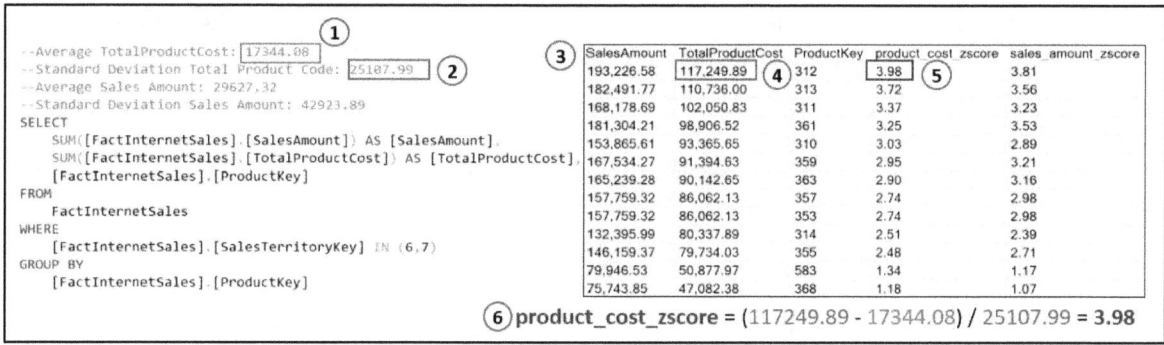

Figure 165: Product 312 is an outlier for TotalProductCost with a z-score of 3.98 (almost 4 x standard deviation).

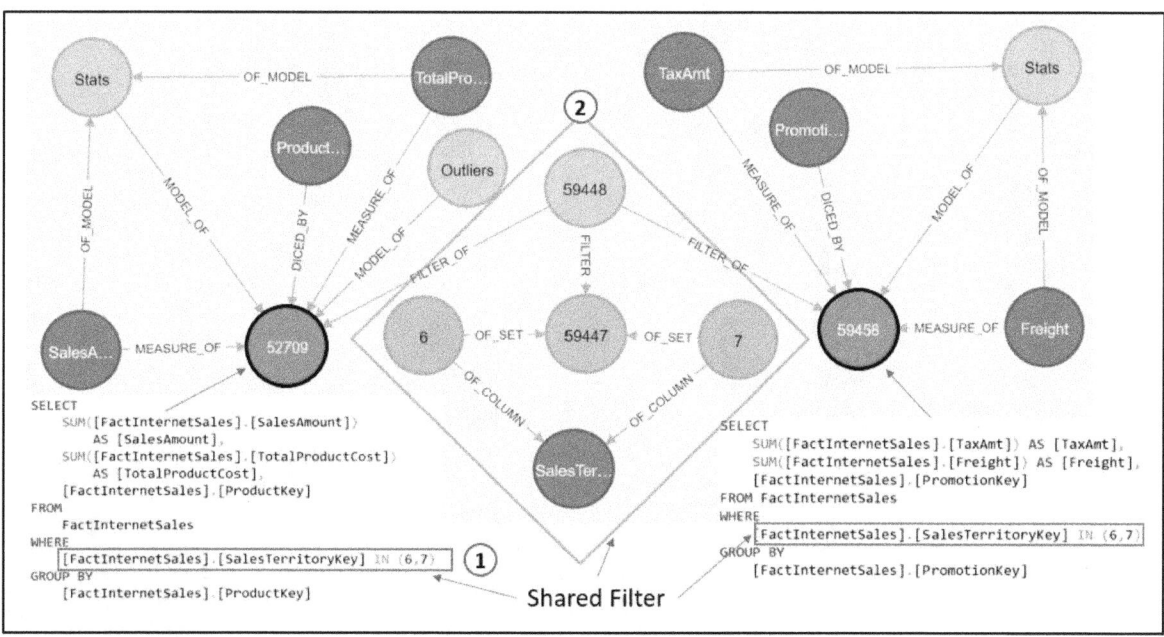

Figure 166: The common Filter used by two different queries is shared.

Figure 166 shows two queries sharing the same filter, the one on the left, our old friend we've been using (node 52709). The one on the right differs in measures and dices, but both have the same WHERE clause:

1. The WHERE clause is the same for both queries. It is about as simple as can be. It states, "In the world of SalesTerritory 6 and 7 combined …"
2. The tan filter node (59448) links to both QueryDef nodes (outlined nodes).

In this simplified case, the WHERE clauses are exactly the same, and so we can create a single filter object they both can reference.

Tuples nodes can be referenced by multiple objects. Their largest role is in the context of the TCW–which is after all, the *Tuple* Correlation Web. But for the ISG, they are used to specify specific rows of a QueryDef.

Figure 167 is a view of a tuple object representing an outlier of an outlier model.

1. First, the tuple we're viewing (3) is associated with this QueryDef. Note the text "QueryDef read as:."
2. The Outlier model of the QueryDef. This node connects to tuples that are deemed outliers.
3. One of the outlier tuples. In this case, It's the Freight Amount for Promotion Key 3, Product 361.

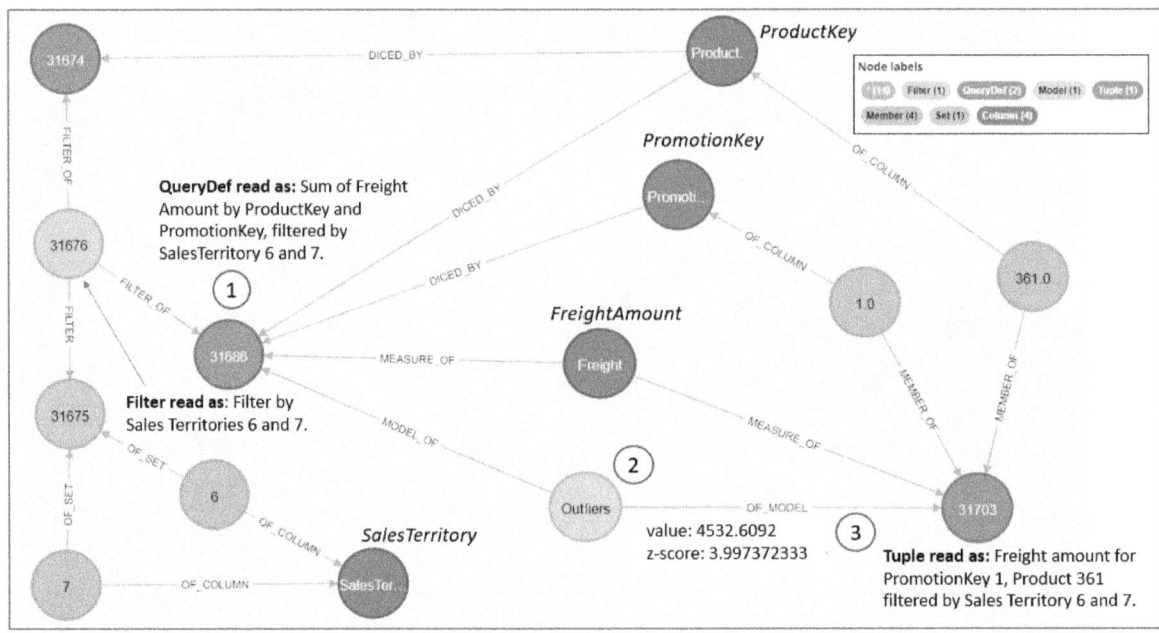

Figure 167: A view of how tuple nodes fit in for outlier models.

Figure 168 focuses more on the tuple definition shown in Figure 167.

1. The same tuple we looked at in Figure 167. But here we see how the member and measure elements of the tuple trace all the way back to the database (AdventureWorksDW).
2. This is the SQL that can be generated from this tuple.
3. A partial result of the SQL (without the WHERE clause), highlighting the row this tuple represents. Note the tuple's high z-score of 3.99737.

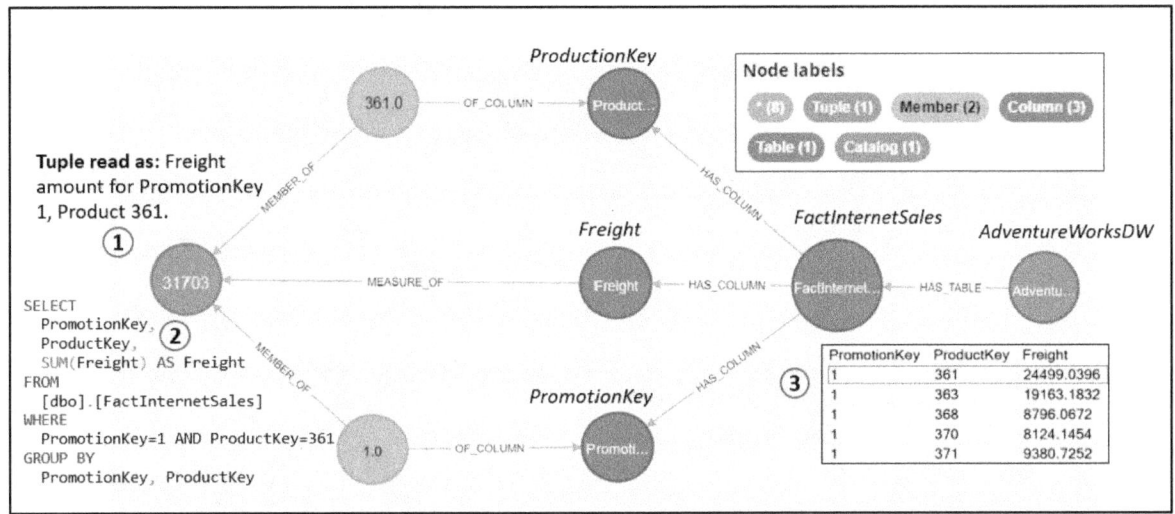

Figure 168: Tuple read as Freight for PromotionKey 1, ProductKey 361, linked to DC objects.

The important thing to note is that the tuple (31703) could be referenced by multiple QueryDefs or other tuples–which we'll cover in "Tuple Correlation Example."

Figure 169 shows examples of two sets as they could appear in the EKG:

1. A range set. The two set members, 2005-01-01 and 2005-12-31, compute to a range of all dates starting from the first member through and including the second member. Other intervals include the usual suspects of date/time intervals, for example, second, minute month, quarter, hour, year, etc. The range sets can also apply to numbers.
2. Itemized set. This means that every member in the set is indicated through a relationship to each member.

As a reminder, members of a set belong to the same table column. Even if members from two tables look the same, they are different members. For example, "Eugene Asahara" in the CRM customer table and in the HR table are different members. However, these members can be linked with a similarity relationship.

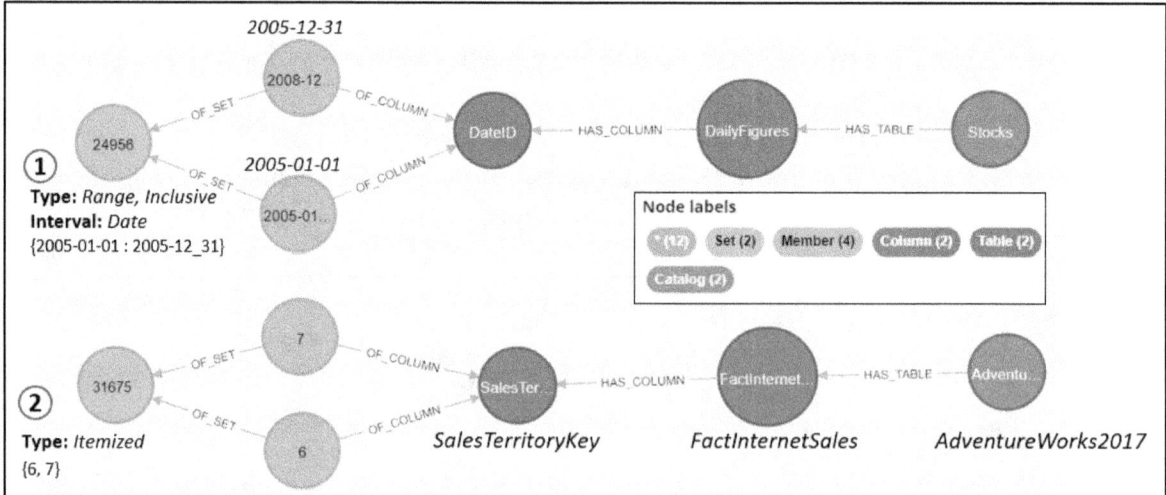

Figure 169: Examples of reusable sets of members.

Tuple Correlation Example

Figure 170 shows two SQL queries and their results. Both are typical BI queries.

1. The left side of the image is a query of sales data by sales territory for married customers ordered by for the year 2011.

2. On the right side, the query is the product cost in sales in Territories 6 and 7 for the year 2011, for each product that list for more than $1000.

3. SalesTerroitoryKey 9 and ProductKey 311 are highlighted. With their respective filters, they form two tuples:

    a. (SalesTerritoryKey=9, MaritalStatus=M, SalesAmount, DateRange=2011)
    b. (ProductKey=311, SalesTerritoryKey={6,7}, ListPrice>1000, TotalProductCost, DateRange=2011)

4. Towards the bottom middle, the question posed is whether there is a correlation between the two tuples.

Before getting to how we answer the question (4), let's look at what the queries look like in the EKG. Figure 171 and Figure 172 show how the left query and right query looks in the EKG, respectively.

IMPLEMENTATION • 393

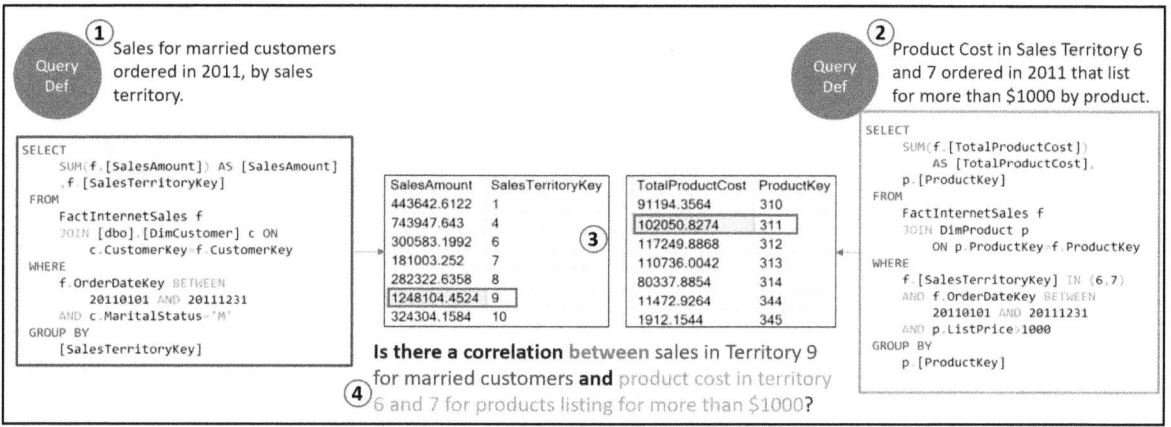

Figure 170: Two queries, select a tuple from both to correlate.

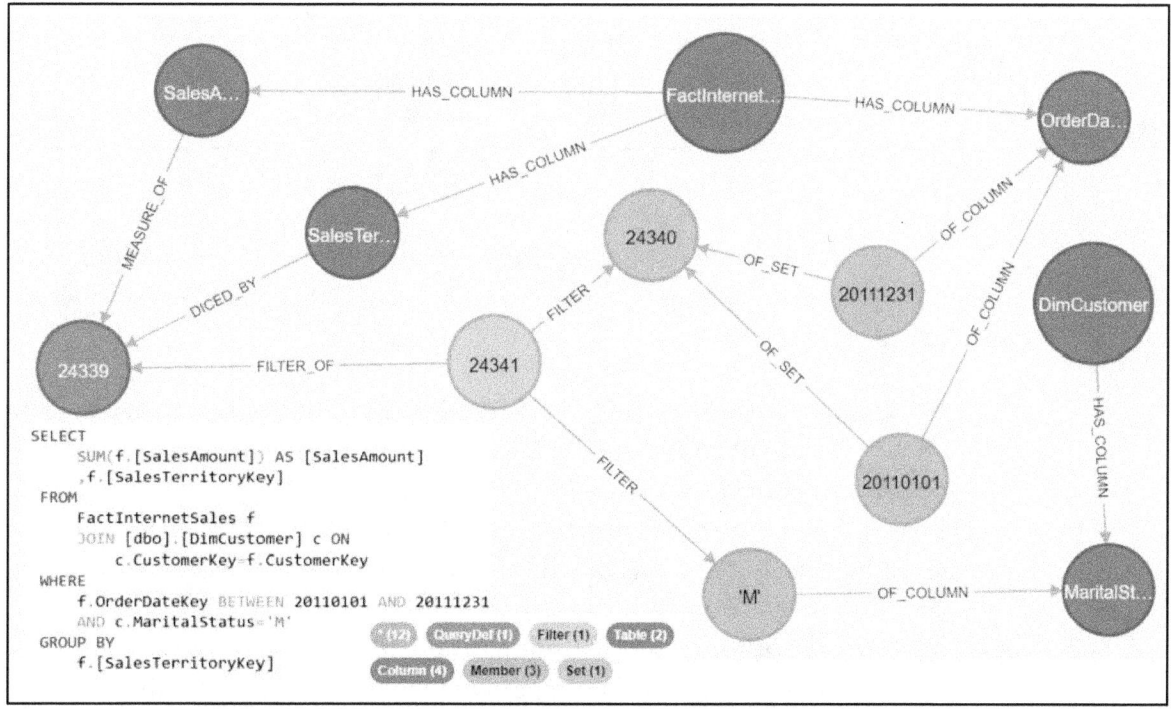

Figure 171: The left SQL it looks in the EKG.

To calculate the correlation between the tuples highlighted in Figure 170, we need to compare values from both tuples across time. The selected tuples are both restricted to the year 2011. So for this example, let's select the twelve months within 2011. Twelve is a fairly good number of data points to notice a correlation. Alternatively, the 52 weeks within 2011 could be better.

394 • ENTERPRISE INTELLIGENCE

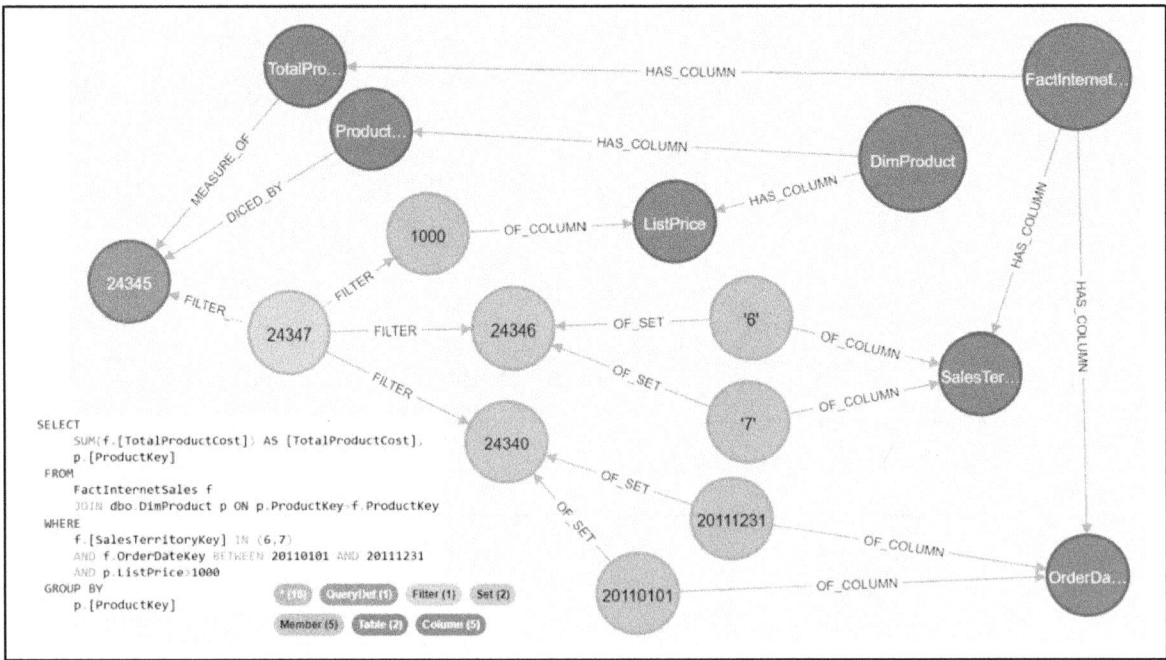

Figure 172: The right-side query as it looks in the EKG.

Figure 173 shows the two SQL queries, each with the WHERE clause modified with the member that was selected back in Figure 170, SalesTerritoryKey=9, and ProductKey=311, respectively:

1. The left query uses the same WHERE clause as the query we met in Figure 170. It is now diced by month of 2011 so a time series is returned and we selected one sales territory: 9.
2. The right query also uses pretty much the same WHERE clause as the query we met in Figure 170. It too is diced by month of 2011, but here, we selected ProductKey 311.
3. This is a table of merged results from the left and right query.
4. A Pearson correlation is calculated over the date range for Value1 and Value2.

Note the descriptions for each tuple towards the top of Figure 173. Additionally, both queries are filtered to a date range within the year 2011.

The correlation calculation shown in the spreadsheet (4) indicates a weak inverse correlation (-0.218089) between the monthly sales amount for married customers in Territory 9 and the monthly total product cost for product 311 in Territories 6 and 7. This suggests that, at least for the year 2011, as sales to married customers in Territory

9 increase, there is a tendency for the total product cost of product 311 in Territories 6 and 7 to decrease, and vice versa.

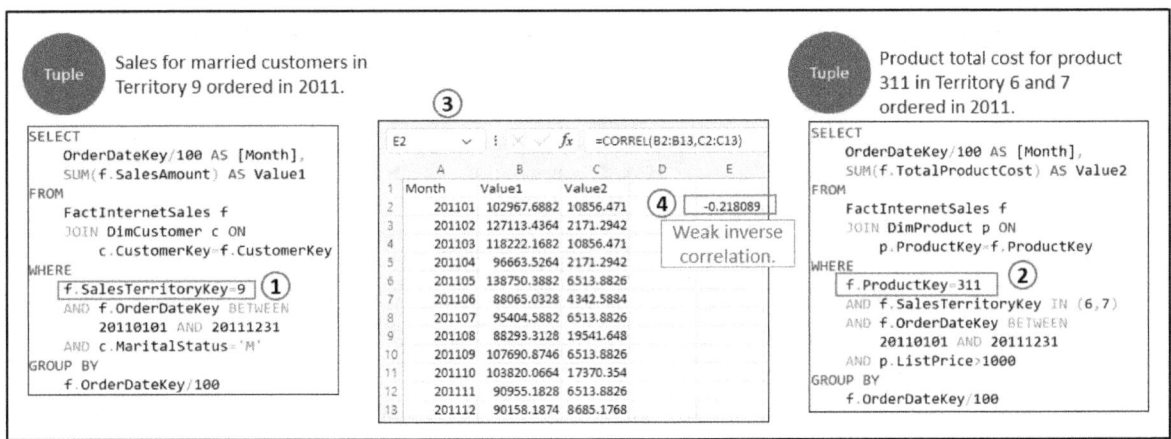

Figure 173: Time series based on both queries. SalesTerritoryKey=9 and ProductKey=311.

The correlation is weak, indicating that the relationship between the two tuples probably isn't worth noticing. However, remember that if we always thought there was a strong relationship between these two tuples, we've now provided data-driven information that it might not be so.

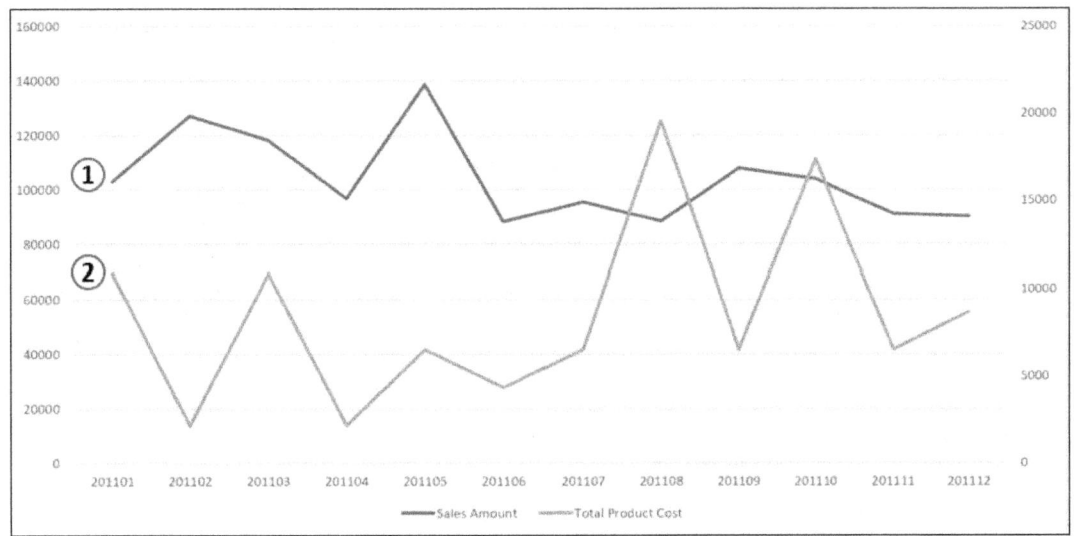

Figure 174: View of the two time series. The inverse correlation is pretty clear.

Figure 174 shows a line graph of two data series: "Sales Amount" and "Total Product Cost" over the months of the year 2011. The "Sales Amount" is represented by blue (line 1), and the "Total Product Cost" is represented by an orange (line 2).

The "Sales Amount" line fluctuates throughout the year with a peak around the middle of the year and another towards the end, while the "Total Product Cost" shows more variability with sharper increases and decreases. The two lines appear different, but if you squint hard enough, you can see the weak inverse correlation.

Figure 175 illustrates how this tuple correlation is saved within the TCW:

1. Both SQL from Figure 173 are represented as Tuple nodes. Tuple nodes are a subclass of a Query. A tuple is composed of one member from different columns, and a measure.
2. The elements of the tuple are specified in the filter.
3. The primary filter items are equates clauses (=). This specifies specific members.
4. A set node storing the date range of 01-01-2011 through 12-31-2011.
5. The correlation relationship. It links correlation models from both tuples and store properties about the correlation.
6. An additional correlation to a third tuple to hit home that correlations form a web between multiple tuples.
7. Another model linked to the right tuple to illustrate that tuples can have multiple kinds of models derived from its data. In this case, it's an Inflections model.

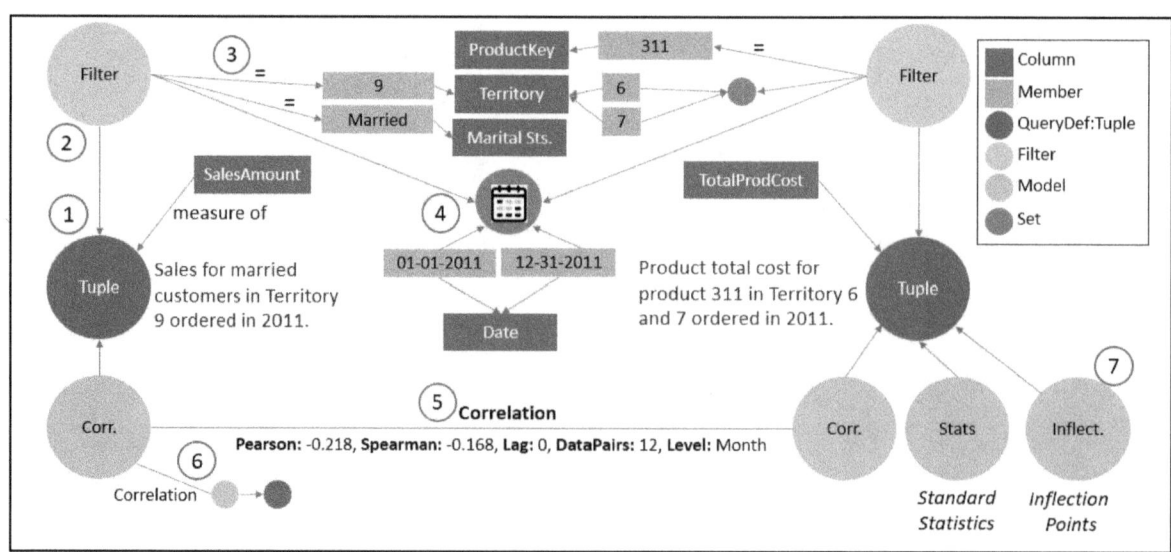

Figure 175: Representation of the correlation between two tuples in the TCW.

Web of Pearson Correlations and Conditional Probabilities

Way back in the topic "Pearson Correlation Example," we looked at the correlations between the closing price of selected stocks. But we only focused on the correlation between one pair of stocks at a time (mostly MSFT and NVDA). Figure 176 shows the results of "casting a wide net" over a selection of stocks. The Pearson correlation is based on the day-to-day percentage changes of the closing price. The darker cells are like the fish we caught in the net—strong correlations. Among those "fish" is the MSFT/NVDA correlation shown in way back in Figure 180—a pretty fair 0.67.

	INTC	GIS	AMD	NVDA	JNJ	AMZN	PFE	MCD	FDX
MSFT	0.53	0.06	0.65	0.67	0.21	0.7	0.28	0.34	0.4
INTC		0.01	0.53	0.43	0.21	0.36	0.34	0.31	0.34
GIS			-0.04	0	0.33	0.01	0.17	0.38	0
AMD				0.79	0.08	0.57	0.17	0.18	0.37
NVDA					0.08	0.52	0.14	0.26	0.34
JNJ						0.16	0.51	0.46	0.14
AMZN							0.19	0.16	0.38
PFE								0.36	0.18
MCD									0.12

Figure 176: Table of Pearson correlations between the day over day % change in the close price of selected stocks from June 25, 2022 through June 24, 2023.

Figure 177 depicts the Pearson chart shown in Figure 176 above as a partial TCW. The circle (reddish) nodes represent tuples. In this case, the tuples are simply the stock and its daily closing price. The square (blue) nodes are DC members representing the elements of the tuples in a database, such as an OLAP cube or data warehouse.

Note the two numbers, 0.93 and 0.67, circled towards the center of Figure 177. They represent the Pearson correlation values for MSFT-NVDA:

1. 0.93—This is the Pearson correlation based on the daily closing price.

2. 0.67—This value reflects the Pearson correlation based on the day-to-day percentage change, as depicted in Figure 176.

I addressed the noticeable difference between the two figures back in "Pearson Correlation Example." This disparity arises because each correlation answers a slightly different question. The first examines the relationship between the absolute price levels, while the second considers the relationship of the returns or daily price fluctuations. Raw stock prices can exhibit greater variability compared to percentage changes, which are effectively "normalized" to smaller values.

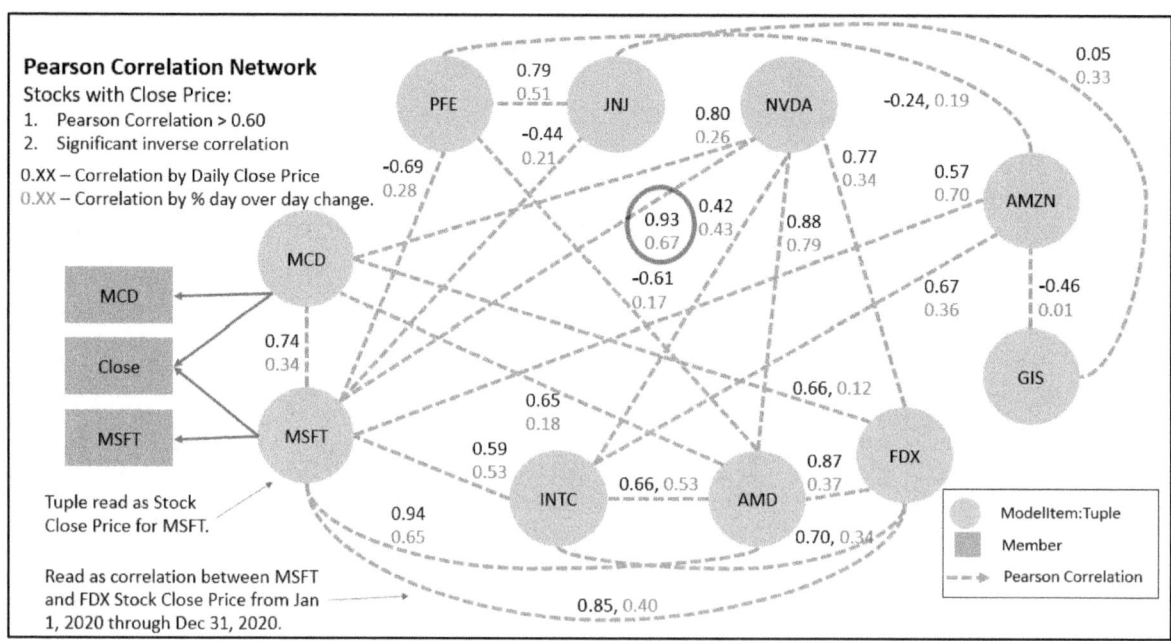

Figure 177: The correlations shown in Figure 176 as a TCW.

Personally, I believe the correlation of the day-to-day percentage change offers a more insightful indication of a relationship between the stocks. It provides insight unfettered by the overarching trend of the market during that time frame.

Conditional Probabilities

Continuing with the same data used in the previous section on Pearson Correlations, Figure 178 is a table of counts and probabilities of the co-occurrence of a few pairs of stocks where the close price changed by more than 1% (a noticeable change) from the previous day, from June 25, 2022, through June 24, 2023. For example, the first row can be read as:

Given Microsoft's stock changed by 1% or more (up or down), there is a 0.71 probability that INTC changed by 1% or more as well. So if I heard that Microsoft's stock was surging, there is a strong chance that INTC is surging as well. So I'd better check my account to ensure I didn't short INTC! Conversely, on the days that INTC changed by 1% or more, there is a 0.59 probability of Microsoft as well.

The difference in probabilities is that the occurrence of Microsoft moving by 1+% happens less often than for INTC. That is, 137 versus 165 days, respectively, from June 2022 through June 2023.

Event B	Event A	A ∩ B	Count B	Count A	P(A|B)	P(B|A)
MSFT	INTC	97	137	165	0.71	0.59
MSFT	GIS	47	137	78	0.34	0.60
MSFT	AMD	117	137	185	0.85	0.63
JNJ	PFE	43	67	107	0.40	0.63
JNJ	AMZN	50	67	163	0.31	0.41
NVDA	AMD	149	184	185	0.81	0.81
NVDA	INTC	130	184	165	0.71	0.79
NVDA	AMZN	121	184	163	0.66	0.74
GIS	JNJ	26	78	67	0.33	0.39
AMZN	PFE	70	163	107	0.43	0.65

Figure 178: Conditional probabilities between a short list of stocks.

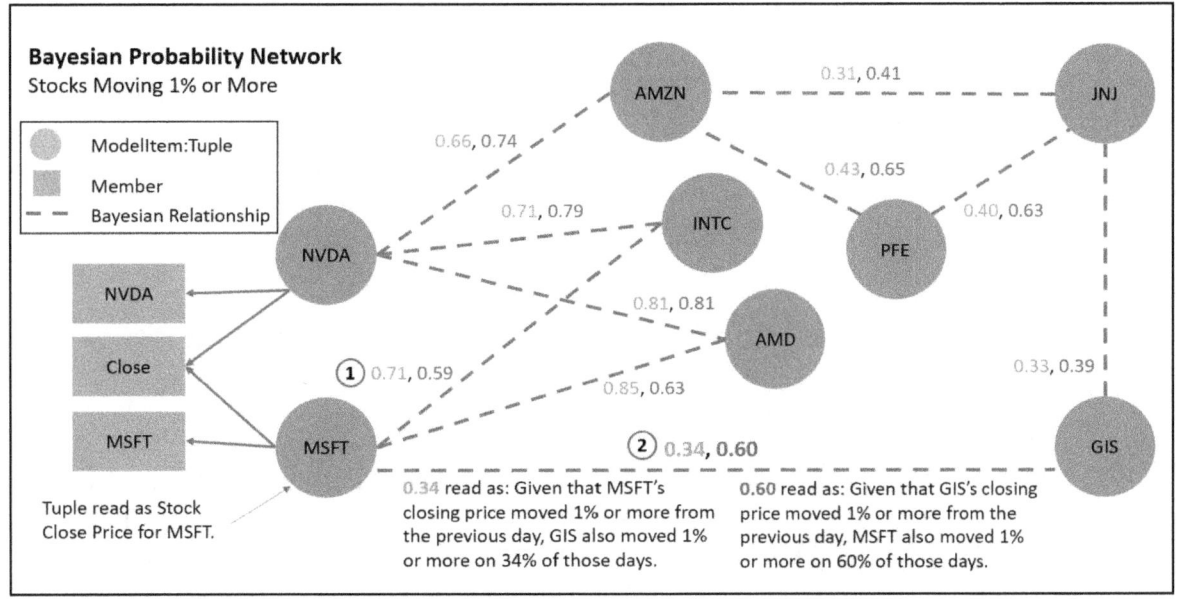

Figure 179: Graphic of the Conditional Probability web-based on the data in Figure 178.

Figure 179 is a graph representation of the table of probabilities from Figure 178 above. Similar to Figure 177 above, the reddish (circle) nodes again represent tuples. The blue (square) nodes are members representing the elements of the tuples in a database:

1. The pair of numbers is the conditional probabilities between MSFT and INTC we just discussed. 0.71 is the probability that given MSFT moved 1% that INTC also did. The other number, 0.59, is the probability that given INTC moved 1% that MSFT did as well.

2. Another example of a conditional probabilities between a pair of stocks, with descriptions.

Figure 180 shows the combined Pearson correlations from Figure 177 (green short-dashed lines) and the conditional probabilities from Figure 179 (blue long-dashed lines). It's also an example of how tuples are leveraged for multiple purposes.

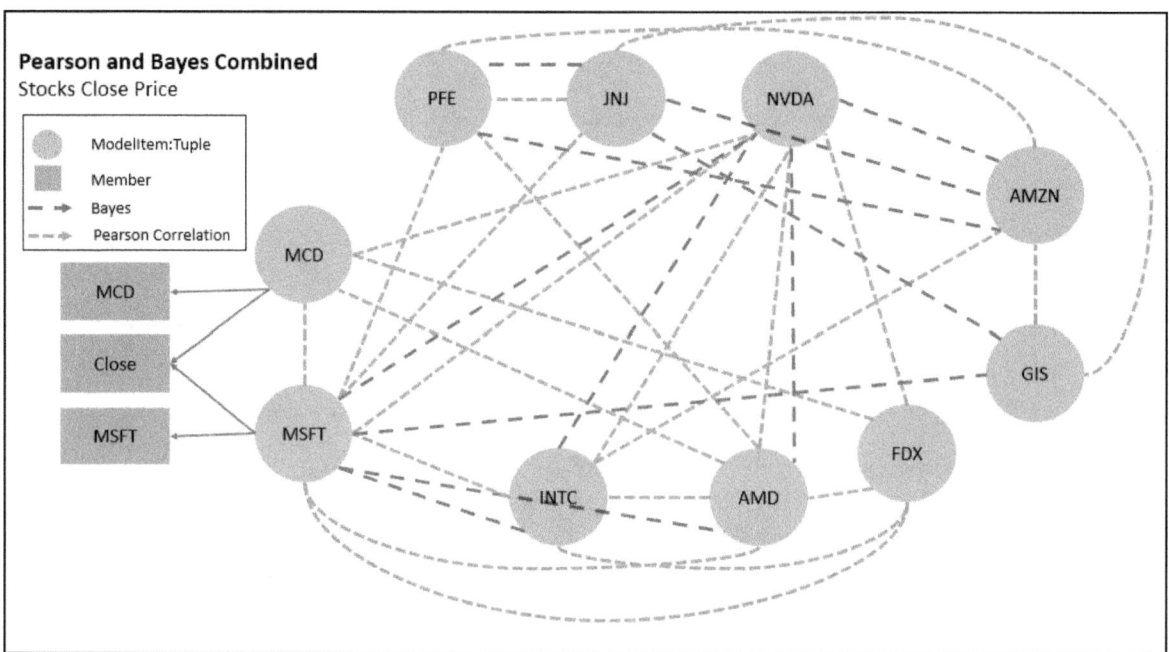

Figure 180: Combined relationships of Pearson (Figure 177) and Bayes (Figure 179).

Both the Pearson correlation and the conditional probability quantify the strength of the relationship between two tuples on a comparable scale, ranging from 0 to 1. Although Pearson's coefficient can exhibit negative values to signify an inverse relationship, when assessing the raw strength of the correlation (how strong of a correlation is it), we can take the absolute value of the coefficient, ABS(r). For example, -0.56 becomes 0.56.

The TCW is a unified and consistent network of measured correlations. That contrasts with an almost ad-hoc mix of varying types of relationships between arbitrary objects as we might see in a rather open KG. The consistent structure (tuples related with a correlative score) of the TCW facilitates streamlined and intuitive traversal of the web of correlations.

Tuple-Level as Opposed to Conditional Probability Table for Conditional Probabilities

Let's now explore two possible implementations of Bayesian representation within the EKG:

1. **Tuple-Level Representation**–Here, individual tuples act as nodes. This approach translates to a densely populated graph since every tuple is represented as a distinct node. This granularity allows for direct path searches, offering insights into direct relationships between specific events.

2. **Attribute-Level Representation with CPTs**–In this approach, nodes represent attributes (or features). Conditional probability tables (CPTs) are employed to link these nodes, capturing the probabilities of inter-relationships. This results in a more concise graph with fewer nodes. However, the trade-off is a shift in query-time computational cost. While the graph is smaller and potentially quicker to traverse, there's additional overhead when querying, as the system must delve into the CPT to determine probabilistic relationships.

Both methods have their advantages and can be employed based on the specific requirements and constraints of a given application. The cardinality of the data can affect implementation choice as well. For example, if tuples are created from a billion customers and 100K products, that would result in a terribly large EKG. In such a case, it's better to offload from the EKG.

Limiting the graph to two primary relationship types, Pearson (or Spearman) and conditional probabilities, further streamlines the process. This restriction prevents the system from being overwhelmed by diverse and potentially arbitrary relationship types and contexts of the calculations (0 through 1 mean roughly the same thing), ensuring more consistent and efficient querying.

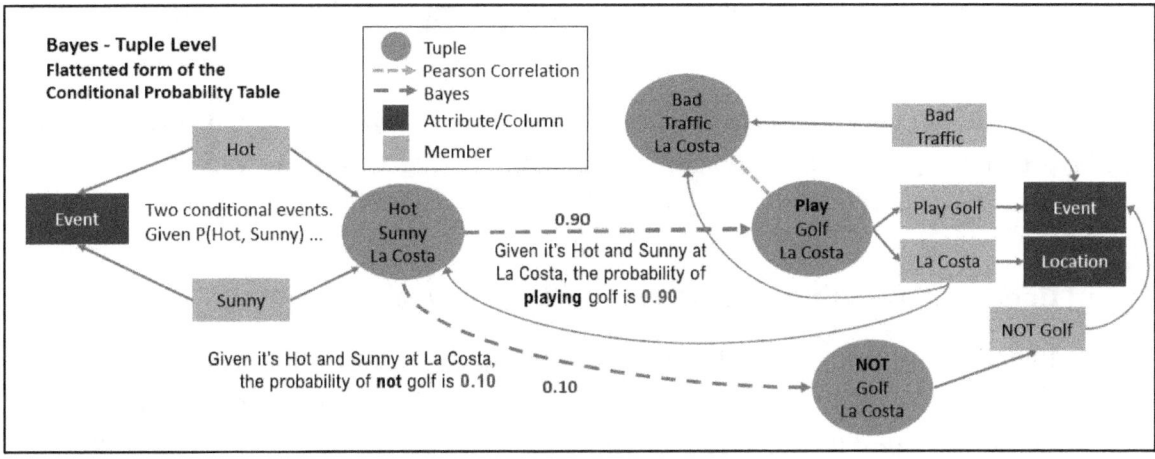

Figure 181: Tuple-Level Conditional probabilities.

Figure 181 and Figure 182 attempt to illustrate the difference. Figure 181 zooms in on a small part of the tuple-level TCW. We see how each tuple node links into the DC and how we leverage the tuples for both Pearson Correlations and conditional probabilities.

Figure 182 illustrates what appears to be a much simpler graph "normalizing" the probabilities into a CPT-based method for encoding conditional probabilities.

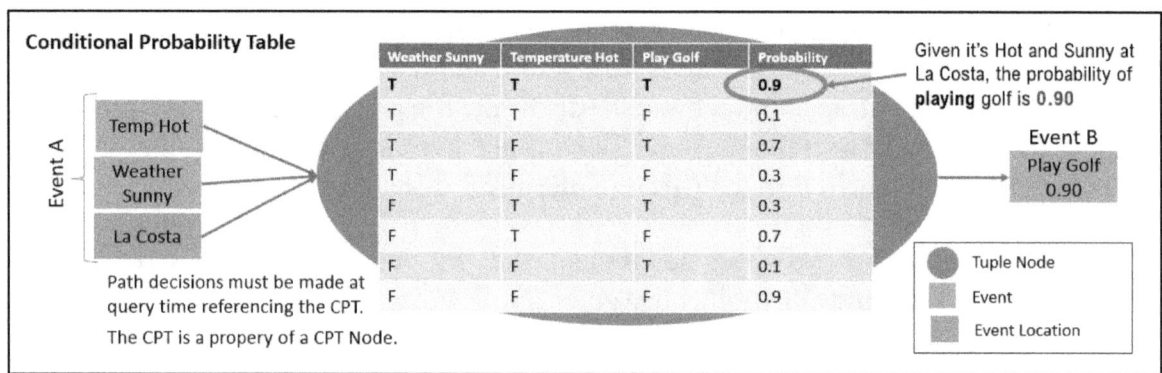

Figure 182: Minimum illustration of encoding conditional probabilities with conditional probability tables.

The CPT is a property of a probability node (the table overlaying the big oval in the middle of Figure 182). If the CPT is small, as it is here, it could be implemented directly into the EKG. However, if it's big (like our billion customers by 100K products), it should be offloaded to another database—for example, a relational database table.

Although the TCW would be much simpler and smaller going the CPT route, query-time searches are no longer purely graph-based computations. We need to query Neo4j and query the CPT at query time.

The tuple level (Figure 181) could be thought of as the CPT (Figure 182) being flattened for query performance reasons. This is kind of analogous to how tables in a relational database might be flattened to avoid query-time joins.

Conditional Probabilities versus Pearson Correlations

I chose conditional probabilities and Pearson Correlations as the relationship functions for the TCW because they are relatively light computations, are mostly time-based (the ubiquitous dimension linking most disparate datasets), and they tell different stories.

Figure 183 illustrates how conditional probabilities and Pearson correlations can provide different insights for the given scenario. We see a table where each row is a day from a seven-day range, along with data and events from that day.

- From Monday, Feb 1, through Friday, Feb 5, the numbers are quite stable. Few people watch sports, and the number of pizza orders is also low.

- Saturday witnesses a huge spike in both match viewers and pizza orders due to the special broadcast of a highly anticipated sports match and a significant discount on pizzas.

- On Sunday, even though there's no special sports broadcast, many people still order pizzas because the discount continues.

Day	People Watching Sports (1000)	Pizza Orders (1000)	Major Sports Event	Pizza Discount	Pizza Sales Spike
Monday (Feb 1)	5	5	x		
Tuesday (Feb 2)	4	3			
Wednesday (Feb 3)	6	4			
Thursday (Feb 4)	7	6	x		x
Friday (Feb 5)	5	5			
Saturday (Feb 6)	100	95	x	x	x
Sunday (Feb 7)	23	90	x	x	x

④ .073

Given a Major Sports Event, the probability of a big spike in pizza sales: ① 0.75 **Probability**
Given a big spike in pizza sales, the probability that a major sports event took place on TV: ② 1.00 **Probability**
Correlation between People watching sports and pizza orders: ③ 0.80 **Pearson**

Figure 183: Difference between Conditional Probabilities and Pearson Correlations.

At the bottom of Figure 183 are three points we can make on our observations of pizza sales, all very different values:

1. If we know there is a Major Sports Event, that translates into big pizza sales 75% of the time (3 out of 4).

2. Conversely, given a spike in pizza sales, there is a 100% chance there is a major sports event (3 out of 3).

3. The Pearson correlation is that there is a pretty strong correlation between televised sports and pizza sales. As sports viewing goes up and down, so do pizza sales.

4. In this example, the Pearson correlation of 0.80 (3) might be a little misleading because, barring a major sports event or big pizza discounts, the correlation between pizza sales and sports is rather weak. If we look at Monday, Feb 1 through Friday, Feb 5 (those drab weekdays), the Pearson correlation is a little weaker at just 0.73.

The following are points to consider when choosing between consideration of Bayes and Pearson:

- Nature of the Data
    - Pearson Correlation—Ideally used for continuous, quantitative data where you want to measure the strength and direction of the linear relationship between two variables.
    - Conditional Probabilities—Best suited for events or occurrences, especially when you want to update the probability of an event as new data becomes available.

- Objective of Analysis
    - Predicting One Variable from Another—Pearson would be the choice since it gives an idea about the linear relationship between two variables.
    - Understanding the Probability of Events Occurring Together—Conditional probabilities would be better, especially if you're interested in the posterior probability after observing new data.

- Interpretability
    - Pearson Correlation—The value (ranging from -1 to 1) directly tells you the strength and direction of the linear relationship. It's easy to understand—values closer to 1 or -1 indicate a stronger correlation.
    - Conditional probabilities—These can provide a direct probability estimate, which might be more intuitive for some questions (e.g., "Given that event A occurred, what's the probability of event B occurring?").

- Complexity and Flexibility
    - Pearson Correlation—Straightforward and assumes a linear relationship, which might not capture complex, non-linear relationships. However, Spearman, which is very similar to Pearson is more sensitive to non-linear relationships.

o Conditional probabilities–More flexible and can incorporate prior knowledge, but might require more complex calculations, especially for large data sets or when integrating multiple sources of evidence.

Conditional Probability Example

The GitHub directory contains a tutorial of what we just covered related to conditional probabilities:

- Load EventEnsemble Events–init_event_ensemble.sql
- Bayesian Stocks Example–bayesian_stocks.sql

It features the EventEnsemble introduced earlier in Chapter 9.

However, in this book, I'd like to cover the gist of that tutorial in order to help drive home the idea of conditional probability.

Figure 184 shows relationships meeting a minimum probability of 0.40 for either P(A|B) or P(B|A)—the probability of A given B or the probability of B given A, respectively. The highlighted line, T (AT&T) and MCD (McDonalds), are the subject of this exercise:

1. The event we're correlating is "big stock price change".

2. "Big stock price change" is defined as any day a stock's closing price changes three percent or more from the prior session. In this case, we set this to 3%.

3. This is the threshold of probabilities we're interested in. In this case, we set it to 0.40, which means to get in this table, the probability of a correlation is at least 0.40 in either direction. In this case, both P(MCD|T) and P(T|MCD) meet that threshold.

Probability **of big stock price change** for A and B. ①			DECLARE @min_change FLOAT = 3.0 ② DECLARE @min_prob FLOAT = 0.40 ③			
ObjectB	ObjectA	A_Intersect_B	CountB	CountA	P_A_given_B	P_B_given_A
JNJ	FDX	576	756	1800	0.7619	0.32
JNJ	GS	684	756	2412	0.9048	0.2836
JNJ	INTC	720	792	1908	0.9091	0.3774
MSFT	JNJ	720	1692	756	0.4255	0.9524
T	JNJ	576	1692	720	0.3404	0.8
T	MCD	756	1800	936	0.42	0.8077

Figure 184: Probabilities of a big stock price change meeting a minimum probability threshold of *0.40*.

Focusing on the highlighted line in Figure 184, the 0.42 figure is read as "given T has a big stock price change, MCD also has a big stock price change 42% of the time." On the other hand, the 0.8077 figure is read as "given MCD has a big stock price change, there is a 0.8077 probability T will change significantly as well."

The high probability of T having a big stock change when MCD has one (0.8077) is interesting. They are both very well-known large companies, but they are in completely different sectors. However, there is a pretty big difference between the two values (0.42 and 0.8077). T is much more sensitive to MCD than the other way around. Why is that?

It could be that people need their phone service in good and bad economic times. On the other hand, eating at McDonald's might be more sensitive to changing economic conditions.

Whatever the case, the discrepancy sheds light on a very intriguing relationship. Of course, it doesn't mean there is a relationship, but it does provide a peculiarity to explore. What we do know is that the values are computed from good data in a rather straightforward and well-understood manner. It's such peculiarities that are beacons to invaluable clues.

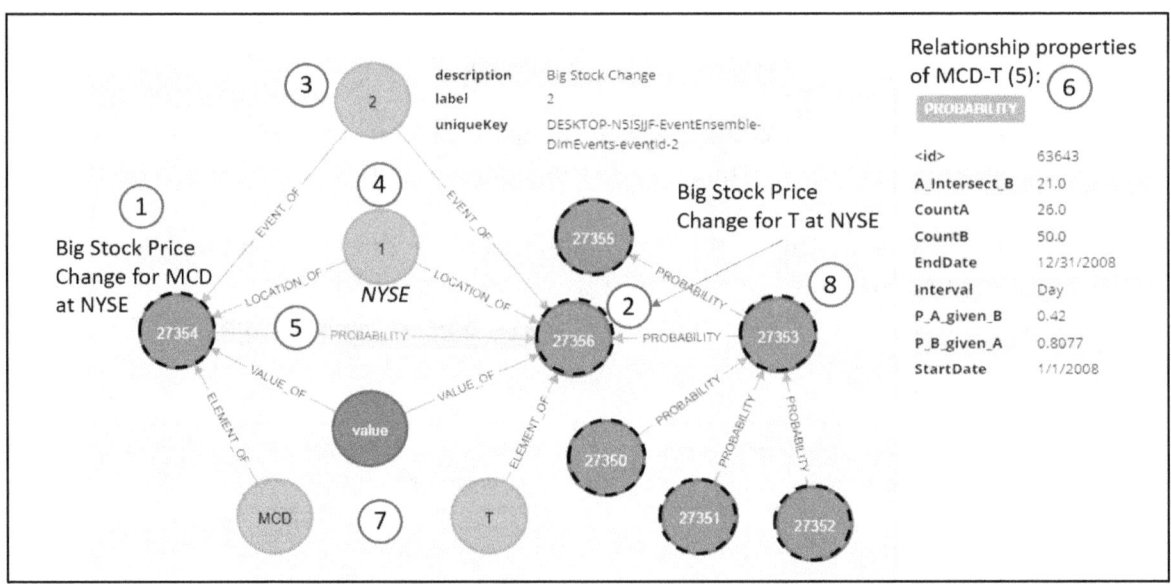

Figure 185: Mini Bayesian Network of probabilities.

Figure 185 shows the nodes for the MCD-T Bayesian relationship as it's laid out in the EKG:

1. The tuple of the big stock movements of MCD at the NYSE.
2. The other tuple, big stock movement of T at NYSE.
3. The event for tuples, "Big Stock Price Change."
4. The location of the "event" for both tuples.
5. This is the probability relationship between MCD and T.
6. The details of the Bayesian probability between MCD and T, the highlighted relationship at 5.
7. The Conditional probabilities are between MCD and T.
8. A third conditional probability forms a "Bayesian Network" between the three tuples. Each relationship between the red tuple nodes is a considerable Bayesian probability.

Casting a Wide Net—Pearson Example

Back in Figure 170, we saw data for two queries, one SalesAmount for each SalesTerritoryKey and TotalProductCost for a selection of ProductKey, both over the period of 2011-10-01 through 2011-12-31. We then explored the correlation between just one selected sales territory and one selected product, sales territory 9 and product 311, respectively. In contrast, Figure 176 introduced the notion of "casting a wide net." Casting a wide net enables us to fetch correlations en masse, resulting in relationships across a grid of members, one from each axis. In that case, it was correlations between a set of stocks.

Now, let's cast a wide net for correlations across the SalesTerritoryKeys and ProductKeys listed back in Figure 170. There is a walkthrough on the GitHub site for this section: *correlation_test_client.py*.

Figure 186 is a crosstab of Pearson correlations for every combination of product keys by sales territories. The stronger, notable correlations are highlighted (encircled). In this case, they are all related to Sales Territory 6.

ProductKey SalesTerritory	310	311	312	313	314	348	350
1	-0.185848	-0.049257	-0.205574	0.441169	0.418569	-0.246534	-0.115097
4	-0.281197	-0.032986	-0.390141	0.445308	0.434664	-0.653393	0.250898
6	0.921339	0.867834	0.710507	0.398051	0.739650	0.381322	-0.103853
7	0.173068	0.338369	0.125105	0.246799	0.275814	-0.338712	0.597850
8	-0.162701	0.231784	0.338487	0.037210	0.454385	0.316886	0.489619
9	-0.204340	-0.218089	-0.454763	-0.557971	-0.487210	-0.329794	0.137154
10	0.155539	-0.023449	0.187340	0.247347	-0.327221	0.521322	-0.190469

Figure 186: Wide Net cast for correlations.

Figure 187 below shows correlations between the four encircled combinations of SalesTerritoryKey and ProductKey (minimum probability threshold of 0.70):

1. This is the correlation that is the focus of this topic. That is the one highlighted with the solid line in Figure 186–ProductKey 312, SalesTerritoryKey 6, correlation of 0.710507.
2. One of the pair of dataframes where each row is a tuple compared to another tuple -the other is the QueryDef mentioned in 6.
3. Filter of the left QueryDef.
4. Model of Correlations for the left QueryDef.
5. One of the tuples from the left QueryDef has found a correlation.
6. The right QueryDef.
7. Model of Correlations for the right QueryDef.
8. The only tuple from the right QueryDef to be in a strong correlation-SalesTerritoryKey=6. It has a correlation of 0.710507 (1) with the ProductKey=311.

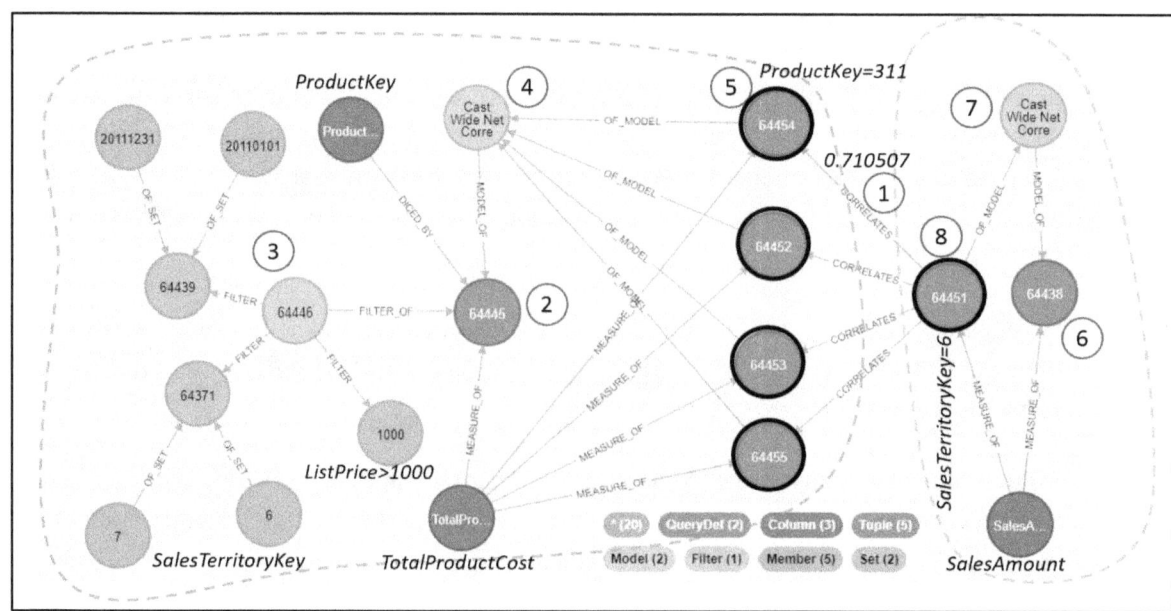

Figure 187: Four strong correlations from Casting of a Wide Net.

Figure 188 drills down into more detail about one of the correlations. It is the correlation between ProductKey 312 and SalesTerritory 6. *Note that the numbers in* Figure 188 *correspond to the numbers in* Figure 187:

- 2 and 6 are the QueryDefs. Note the descriptions of each QueryDef.

- 1 is the correlation between tuples 5 and 8. We see the Pearson and Spearman correlation score. The correlation also notes the date range and the date level (Month).

- 5 and 8 in Figure 9-48 are the tuples represented as 5 and 8 in Figure 187.

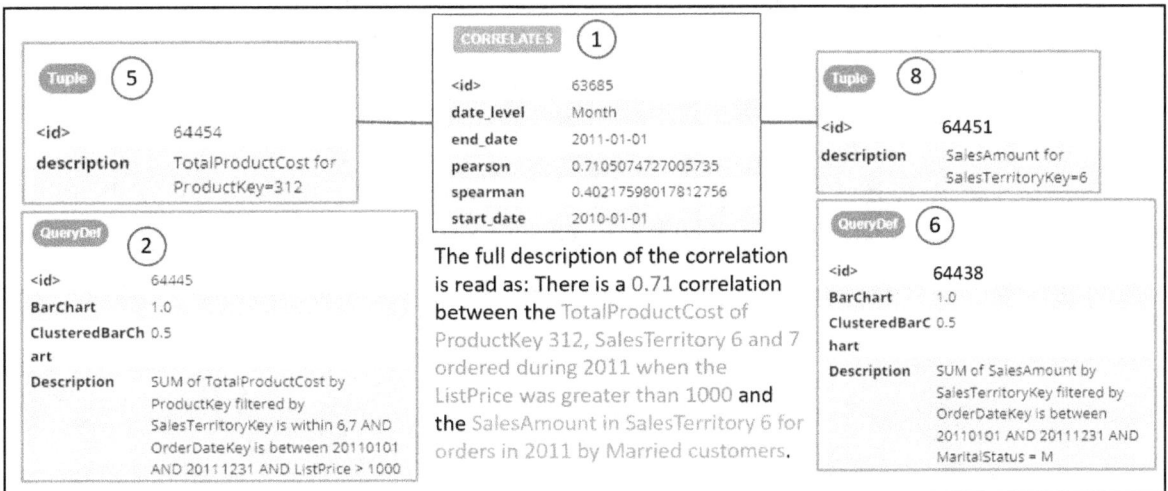

Figure 188: Details of one of the correlations. The numbers reference back to Figure 187.

Figure 189 simply provides more the details of the other relevant nodes, which are not shown in Figure 188. Again, the numbers in Figure 189 correspond to the numbers in Figure 187.

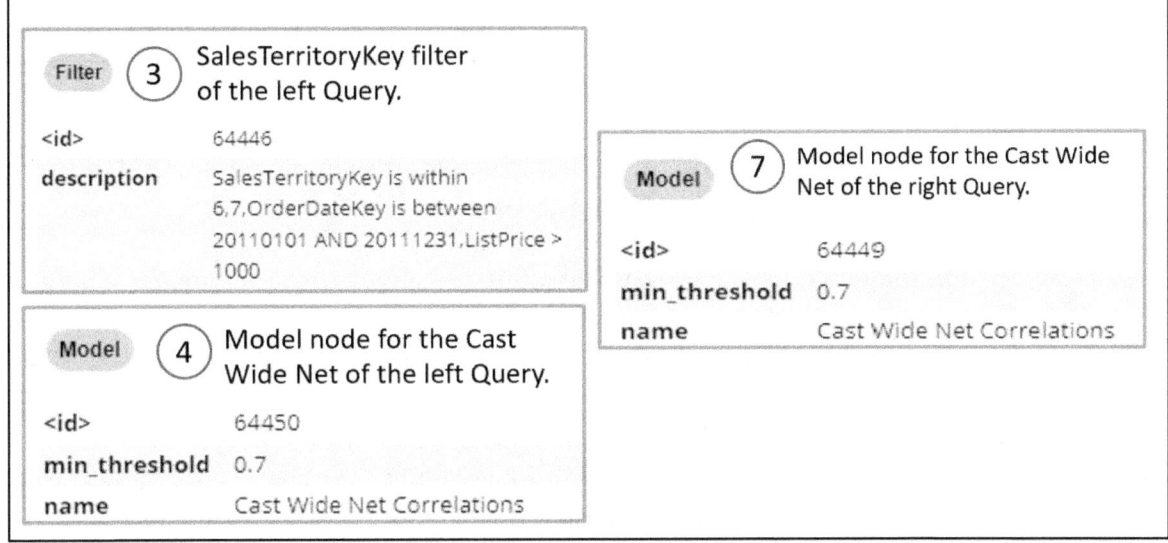

Figure 189: Further details not shown in Figure 188. The numbers reference back to Figure 187.

Casting a Wide Net with Conditional Probabilities

Conditional probabilities are generally between events, not values. They are in the form: "If *this* happens, what is the probability of *that* happening"? For example, if I see Amy the HR gal in the conference room with just one person, how likely is that person being given a promotion? What if Amy the HR gal is in the conference room with just one person and that person's boss? Now what is the probability that person is getting a promotion? For this topic, we're not predicting values such as how much more pay one will receive with the promotion. We're predicting the likelihood of an event.

Let's again explore casting a wide net, but this time with conditional probabilities. There is a walkthrough on the GitHub site, *crosstab_bayes.py*.

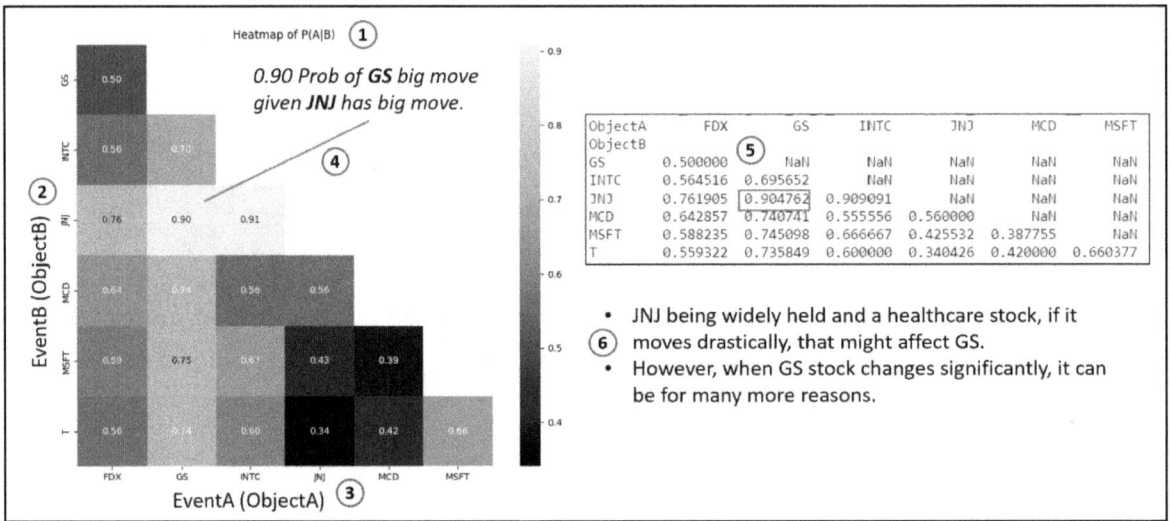

Figure 190: Cast a wide net on the probability of a big stock move based on another stock.

Figure 190 is a diagram on casting a Bayesian net. It's similar to the grid of probabilities in back in Figure 176, but it's a different set of stocks.

1. On the left side is a grid of probabilities - given one stock makes a big move, what is the probability the other goes up.
2. The y-axis (vertical—Event B) contains a list of selected stocks—T, MSFT, MCD, JNJ, INTC, GS.
3. The x-axis (vertical—Event A) is on the same list as the y-axis.
4. We've selected a cell to study in more detail. It is JNJ versus GS in the form of P(A|B) - Given JNJ makes a big move (Event B), what is the probability of GS making a big move (Event A).

5. The right side is the detail of the cell being pointed at in the grid. There is a 0.90 probability that when JNJ makes a big move, GS will as well.
6. A hypothesis of why this might be.

Figure 191 is the same matrix, but Event A and Event B are switched. In fact, the item legend is exactly the same as it is in Figure 190.

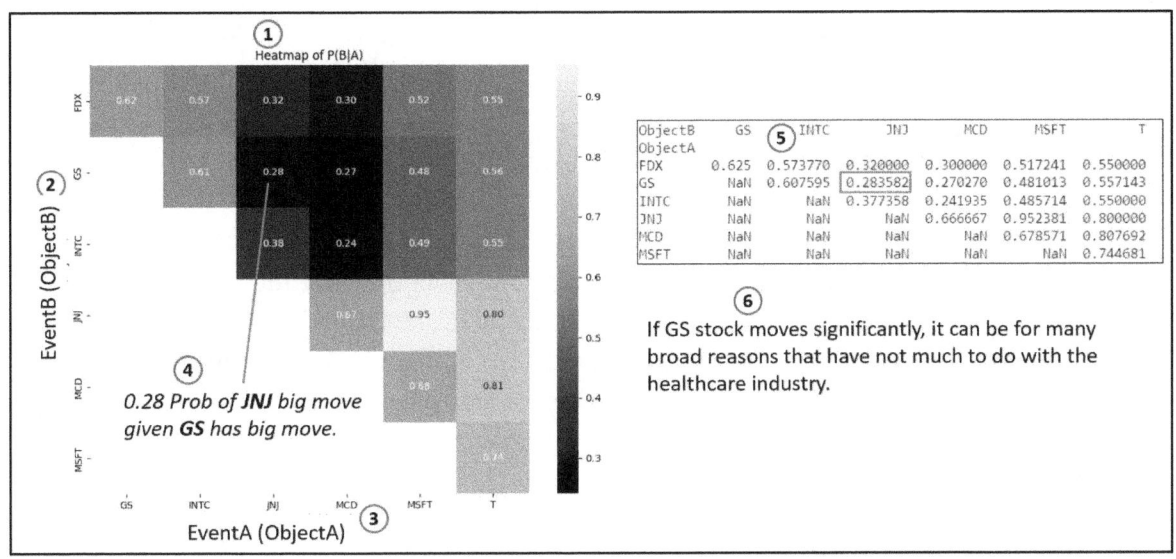

Figure 191: Conditional probabilities are different the other way around.

Whereas Figure 190 above asks:

If JNJ moves big, what is the probability of GS moving big as well?

Figure 191 turns it around and asks:

If GS moves big, what is the probability of JNJ moving big as well?

What difference does it make? The set of reasons for any event happening are different for each kind of event. For example, we all need to shop for food. But we all have different sets of triggers that lead us to shop for food.

In this case, if GS moves big, there is a much smaller probability of JNJ moving big as well.

The higher probability (0.90) of a significant move by Goldman Sachs (GS) following a big move by Johnson & Johnson (JNJ) can suggest that JNJ's stock movements are seen as an indicator of broader economic health. Being a diversified healthcare company,

JNJ's performance might be interpreted as a signal of general consumer and healthcare sector health, which impacts financial services firms like GS. Conversely, a big move by GS might not necessarily impact JNJ in the same way, as financial stocks can be influenced by a variety of factors that don't directly relate to the healthcare sector. Thus, the probability of JNJ moving significantly, given GS's move is lower (0.28), reflecting these sector-specific influences.

Retrieval Augmented Generation

In the symbiotic relationship between today's LLMs and KGs, the concept of Retrieval Augmented Generation (RAG) has emerged as a powerful method by which the EKG is able to aid LLMs in overcoming its inherent limitations. This relationship captures the essence of symbiosis in the digital realm, underscoring a mutual dependency that elevates the capabilities of both systems. Examples of how RAG delivers this powerful value include:

- It engages corroboration from other data sources (such as the EKG) into the LLM query process.

- Information beyond the LLM's training cutoff can supplement its knowledge.

- Information that is private to an enterprise can supplement the LLM (provide the LLM forgets the private information).

This topic on RAG is kind of the "third act" if this book were a movie—where Rocky finally steps in the ring with Apollo Creed. It's through this methodology where everything ties together. That is, the major parts–BI technologies, AI, KG, data mesh, and last but not least, the human workers–meet to form the intelligence of a business.

The value of this book is to augment the fallibility of LLMs, as astoundingly impressive and expansive as they might be. First off, LLMs "hallucinate." Meaning an LLM answer sounds good, but it's valid upon scrutiny or it's a misunderstanding of the data or your question—which is worse than "I don't know." On the other hand, those hallucinations can be highly intriguing, outside of the box thinking—if that's what we're looking for.

As discussed earlier, the symbiotic relationship between KGs and LLMs is that LLMs assist (like an army of interns) in authoring KGs and KGs ground LLMs in reality–through the determinism of KGs primarily authored by (presumably non-hallucinating) human SMEs. And toss in an assist from highly-curated data of BI databases at the disposal of those SMEs.

Another of the significant challenges of LLMs lies in their inherent data latency. The process of training models, like ChatGPT, requires ingesting vast amounts of information from the Web and elsewhere. Given the computational rigor and resource intensity associated with this task, training these models is not only time-consuming (weeks to months ATTOW), but also a mind-bogglingly costly endeavor.

The date of its training is its knowledge cutoff, beyond which the LLM is unaware of subsequent events or information. For example, throughout much of ChatGPT's freshman year, 2023, its knowledge was predominantly frozen, cutoff at September 2021, rendering it oblivious to developments and advances post that date. Therefore, when the subject is on the plethora of things that have happened since September 2021, answers from ChatGPT can be:

- Something along the lines of, "There's no such thing as what you mention and if there is, I don't know anything after September 2021."

- An answer that is valid, but not up to date—This can be dangerous. Even if you receive a seemingly good answer, it might be outdated.

- A "hallucination"–as just mentioned.

For any of the options above, I would need to do my redundant due diligence and double-check all the answers. Or, I could take what it says as truth as long as it's not obviously outrageous. No.

RAG rectifies this problem by stepping in front of the LLM as a coordinator of the answering process. We no longer communicate directly with the LLM. Under a RAG coordinator, the LLM is just one component, albeit a powerful one. Although it doesn't know anything beyond its training date, it still knows a lot of things about a lot of things! That still is very helpful.

But today's LLMs are much more than a glorified encyclopedia. It's an excellent reasoning engine. The Internet is full of examples of ChatGPT coming to hilariously bad or odd conclusions. But in comparison to the bulk of conversations with even the smartest among us, ChatGPT actually does very well. I mean, who else knows at least an intermediate amount of practically everything?

The RAG Coordinator fills the roles of broad encyclopedia, interpreter, planning advisor, and reasoning engine for the LLMs! The RAG Coordinator can also be granted access to any other resources imaginable—as appropriate. Today, that mostly includes *carefully considered* access to up to date, expansive, possibly highly-privileged data sources—BI, OLTP, cloud, the Internet, etc. This integration effectively extends the LLM's knowledge horizon, ensuring that its outputs are not just based on historical data but also encompass more recent and evolving knowledge.

Additionally, the top-billed protagonist of this book, the EKG, is another powerful data source. The EKG captures the semantic knowledge of subject matter experts (KG), a map of enterprise data sources and their anatomies (DC), and a cursory level of "theory of mind" (a sense of what another sentient being is thinking, albeit a high-level sense) across dozens or hundreds of analysts throughout all corners of the enterprise (ISG/TCW).

Given this team of resources, the RAG Coordinator has the tools to orchestrate the generation of responses that are wide-scoped, data-driven, and in the current context.

Even *when* AI reaches the AGI/ASI state, we probably still need some sort of framework for answering questions. As it is for mere mortals, an AGI/ASI will still be vulnerable to making decisions on a variety of forms of imperfect information. It will still need to perform experiments in the physical world (the only legitimately trustworthy model of reality). Answering questions is an iterative process full of sometimes futile exploration.

The world is just too complex for even a super genius AI—unless it can expand outside of our space-time for a higher dimensional view. Otherwise, it's intelligence is fraught with imperfect information, just like it is for the rest of us.

I also don't think there will be one all-knowing AI entity. I think it will be a system of distributed, loosely-coupled entities—the same architecture nature figured out for us. Even our seemingly single brain is a system of components and the entirety of the intelligence of humanity is distributed among all of us. Thus, a systematic, iterative approach would still be relevant.

Figure 192 is a high-level view of one version of a RAG process, suitable for BI, and the one I will be using in this book:

1. An analyst user has a question.
2. The question is submitted in natural language, either by typing or speaking it, to an AI-enabled BI visualization tool.

3. The BI visualization tool is enabled with the ability to accept a natural language query.
4. The BI tool sends the query to a "RAG Coordinator."
5. The RAG Coordinator uses its LLM capability to digest and "unpack" the question and formulates a process to answer the question. It decides how to break down the question into parts, what components available to it can help it. The "Prompt Enrichment" topic explores the details.
6. The RAG Coordinator queries a LLM (for reasoning or broad knowledge) and/or enterprise BI sources (private or up to date information) as needed to fill in the information it needs.
7. The RAG coordinator returns a response. This response can contain data and instructions for the BI tool to render an answer to the BI user.
8. Note that the icon for LLM doesn't include the name "ChatGPT." This is because we're not interfacing with the LLM through the Chat tool. We're now using the OpenAI API to communicate with GPT.

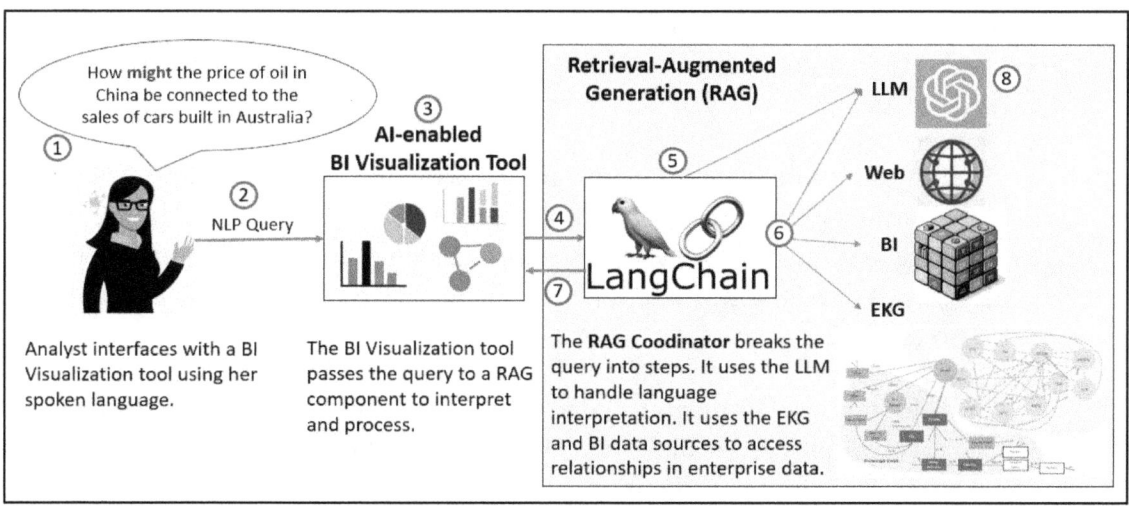

Figure 192: High-level view of where BI and the EKG fit into a RAG process.

The outline of the third-act of this book is as follows:

1. An intuition on the general idea of RAG.
2. An introduction to vector databases. It is the prime way to encode private, updated, or specialized data (mostly unstructured) in a way that is compatible with LLMs.
3. The idea of prompt enrichment.
4. The idea of how the ISG and TCW data come into play.
5. Query templates to help reign in the LLMs, if necessary.

RAG Intuition

Since this book is about tying many disparate pieces into a single framework, I cannot go as deep into individual subjects as I would like. In the case of RAG, it's not only much deeper–it is about each sentient being's biggest super-power after all, inference. Hopefully, since we're sentient beings, the RAG intuition and process should sound somewhat familiar.

Although I'm providing a blurb on something called "self-reflective RAG," I'm not diving deep into it - even though it's one of the most compelling current variations on RAG. That's because RAG is also one of the most rapidly developing aspects of AI at the time of writing. My goal for this sub-topic is to express that rapid evolution by pointing out a couple of the profound ways the state-of-the-art of RAG is expanding. In this volume, I'll provide an intuition for RAG, cover its basics, and introduce the terms "Agentic AI" and "self-reflective RAG."

Towards an intuition of RAG, let's first consider the high-level steps of human problem-solving. This should be somewhat reminiscent of the "Intelligent Query Patterns" covered earlier:

1. **Planning** - Before diving into information gathering, humans often engage in a planning phase. This involves defining the problem, setting objectives, and determining what information is needed and how to go about obtaining it. This step is crucial for efficient problem-solving, ensuring efforts are focused and relevant.

2. **Information Gathering** - Following a plan, humans seek out information from various sources, evaluating its relevance and reliability. This is usually an iterative loop with Planning.

3. **Synthesis and Generation** - With the necessary information at hand, humans synthesize these inputs to generate solutions or answers, integrating new findings with existing knowledge.

4. **Reflection and Adaptation** - After generating solutions, humans reflect on their effectiveness and adapt their approach as necessary, learning from successes and failures.

RAG parallels steps 1, 2, and 3, as I cover it in this section. It doesn't reflect on its answer as suggested in step 4.

Additionally, there should be a reflection on the quality of data at each stage. For example, I wish to value a very old coin found in a box I just inherited. I don't know anything about the coin nor possess numismatic knowledge. But I reason that I need to know what it is, determine if it's real, assess its quality, and assign an appropriate value. At each step, I can engage a number of experts. I may need an archeologist to identify the coin. There may be a need for a chemist to assess its composition. There may be a need for an expert to grade the coin. And finally, a coin dealer to assign a value.

The steps I just listed could have been determined by an LLM engaged by a RAG process. The RAG process would ask: "I've been presented with an old coin I know nothing about. I'd like to value it. What steps should I take? Who or what resources will I need at each step?"

The LLM returns the steps as I suggested above. The RAG process figures out what databases or other services to query–step 2. Lastly, once all the data is collected, those answers are packaged along with a prompt asking: "Given the following information, what is the value of the coin?" That's step 3. However, step 4 is currently a rather advanced aspect of RAG. It doesn't scrutinize the final answer. Indeed, it should scrutinize the answers of all the experts at each step. And the experts should be forthcoming with their confidence in their answer, even providing guidance as to how one might obtain a better answer.

A combination of two terms, Agentic AI and Self-Reflective RAG, address this. Applying these concepts results in a RAG process that is much more "thoughtful" and thorough.

Agentic AI refers to AI systems that exhibit a level of autonomy and the ability to take independent actions to achieve its assigned goals or objectives. These AI agents can make decisions, learn from their environment, and act in ways that are not explicitly programmed. This form of intelligent agency enables these systems to operate with a degree of independence and adaptability, often resembling the role of a subject matter expert (SME).

A common form of AI agents are LLMs fine-tuned with specialized knowledge, for example:

- The knowledge of how to query a particular set of databases and receive its results.
- Knowledge to make decisions, for example, whether more information is needed.
- Enforce regulations and security.

Agentic AI adds "intellectual scalability" to RAG pipelines. By "intellectual scalability" I mean the ability of a system or framework to augment its cognitive capabilities effectively to the complexity of a problem. It's sort of analogous to a good delegator that "scales" a project's intellectual capacity by engaging a number of experts as necessary. A top-level agent orchestrates a number of sub agents, engaging them as needed. In a sense, these specialized AI agents could represent a third way to apply data mesh, since these agents are developed products intended for use in a loosely-coupled system.

Self-Reflective RAG

Self-reflective RAG (self-RAG) is a framework that enhances an LLM's quality and factuality through retrieval of a response to a prompt but followed by a phase its own scrutiny of its response. Unlike straight RAG approaches, self-RAG retrieves on demand, criticizes its own generation, and predicts "reflection tokens" as part of the generation process. It aims to improve the versatility of LLMs without compromising their quality. As I finalize the text for this book, this is a huge and rapidly evolving subject.

The core of self-RAG is an LLM fine-tuned from a foundation LLM with the capability to adaptively retrieve relevant passages, reflect on its accuracy and relevance, and generate critique tokens during the generation process. It contributes to more accurate and reflective language models. This special fine-tuning teaches the foundation LLM to scrutinize its own results before passing it back to the user as the final answer—it's taught to become a self-critic.

Reflection tokens are special markers introduced in self-RAG. When generating responses, the model uses reflection tokens to assess its own output. It reflects on whether the generated content is accurate, relevant, and complete. If the model believes it needs more information, it proposes retrieval by activating reflection tokens. This allows it to retrieve relevant passages and enhance its response. Reflection tokens enable self-RAG to strike a balance between self-generated content and retrieval, resulting in more contextually relevant and factually accurate answers.

The fine-tuning of these self-reflective RAG LLMs is similar in principle to the fine-tuning of LLMs trained as chat bots. A great example is ChatGPT, fine-tuned from GPT to be an expert chat bot. ChatGPT was taught the skills to be a conversationalist. Similarly, a self-reflective RAG LLM is fine-tuned from GPT with the skill and "instinct" to assess the quality of its responses and communicate that assessment.

Back to our scenario of assessing the value of a coin I inherited, the experts we engage will respond with their best answer along with an assessment of the validity. That scrutiny applies mostly at steps 2 and 4, consulting the experts and reviewing our final answer, respectively. For example, the expert may report: "I believe this is a Roman coin from about 50 BCE, but you should check with another expert specializing in Roman coins of that era since there are very many types."

Without self-RAG, we would accept something like, "It's a Roman coin from about 50 BCE," risking a potentially costly error.

Vector Database

The lingua franca that ties the pieces together are vector "embeddings". They transform text into a unique high-dimension vector of numbers. It's kind of like a hash (e.g. MD5, SHA) of text, but these vectors are an encoding of its input text that preserve information about the text. These transformations are performed by an ML model. For this book, GPT has an API call to computes the embeddings for strings of text.

Figure 193 shows a few examples of vector embeddings. However, I only show the first few numbers because the vectors from GPT are 1536 elements in length.

1. The first 100 elements of the vector embedding for "Eugene Asahara." There really isn't a way to look at these numbers and say, "Ah! That's the embedding for Eugene Asahara."

2. The first five elements of the vector embedding for the most popular mispronunciation of my last name, "Ashara" (missing "a" after the "As").

3. A way to spell Eugene in a phonetically equivalent but in an entirely different way.

4. The embeddings for Eugene Asahara (1) and Eugene Ashara (2) has a strong similarity score of 0.883.

5. Interestingly, the phonetically equivalent Youjean Asahara(3) has an even stronger score of 0.935. This is a small demonstration of the power of LLMs. I'm sure none of GPT's training material mentions that Youjean is just a whimsical way of spelling Eugene, but yet, it seems to have picked that up on its own.

① **Vector Embedding of Eugene Asahara** (100 of 1536 elements):
[-0.01373625174164772, -0.0021200592163950205, -0.005329292733222246, -0.007467671297490597, -0.010731862857937813, 0.002161694224923849, -0.008027247153222561, -0.007927322760224342, -0.014895373024046421, -0.009959115646779537, -0.004093562718480825, 0.0012657069601118565, 0.0025580604560673237, 0.0032708533108234406, -0.00671490840613842, -0.010985003784298897, 0.035066746175289154, -0.0008976527024060488, -0.0085335299377267303, -0.010352150537073612, 0.001678727101534605, 0.011744428426027298, -0.006614984478801489, -0.003950337879359722, -0.010871756821870804, 0.00019766262266784906, 0.011391363106667995, -0.025260847061872482, -0.0005974636296741664, -0.02795213833451271, 0.018386058509349823, -0.006764870602637529, 9.050429071066901e-05, -0.015508241020143032, -0.003980315290391445, 0.003117636078968644, -0.0007431865087710321, 0.0025547295808792114, 0.015361685305833817, -0.005918845534324646, 0.012290680781006813, -0.01219075638800859, 0.006531713996082544, -0.015841322019696236, -0.026766370981931686, 0.004243449307978153, -0.013489771634340286, -0.023195745423436165, -0.00999908521771431, 0.033380807760357857, 0.0187191404402256, 0.009006503969430923, -0.016787271946668625, -0.006045415997505188, -0.01545494794845581, -0.0020201350562274456, -0.0031842521857470274, -0.024181663990020752, -0.011917630210518837, -0.009512786753475666, 0.008573499508202076, -0.001306509366258978, -0.03698528930544853, 0.0025963645894040804, 0.004050262272357941, 0.006405143532902002, 0.005872214213013649, 0.010338827036321163, -0.013296584598720074, -0.017546694725751877, 0.019287816295957565, 0.005056166090071201, -0.001785313012078404, -0.02155698835849762, 0.03783797845244408, -0.019771674647927284, -0.015748059377707424, -0.002919452963396907, 0.022462967783212662, -0.01124480739235878, 0.016174402087926865, -0.035386502742767334, 0.01216411031782627, -0.010838449001312256, 0.015907937660813333, 0.001743677887134254, -0.02827189676463604, 0.02173019014298916, 0.002882814276502466, -0.011378039605915546, 0.005922176409512758, 0.005289322696626186, 0.010338827036321163, -6.67722852085717e-05, -0.010825125500559807, -0.001976834377273917, -0.02687295712530613, 0.01406933180987835, -0.009226338006556034, -0.03376106917858124, ...]

② **Vector Embedding of Eugene Ashara** (5 of 1536 elements):
[0.004149786662310362, -0.001955607905983925, -0.018924372270703316, -0.03252626210451126, -0.002229460282251239, ...]

③ **Vector Embedding of Youjean Asahara** (5 of 1536 elements):
[-0.017151400446891785, -0.0051500629633665085, 0.005435256287455559, -0.003916435409337282, -0.004901347681879997, ...]

Similarity between Eugene Asahara and Eugene Ashara: **0.883021088517058** ④
Similarity between Eugene Asahara and Youjean Asahara: **0.9350625330885207** ⑤

Figure 193: Example of vector embeddings.

Embeddings are a key feature of both vector databases and LLMs. However, LLMs are much more complicated, beyond vector databases. That's evident since the function I use to transform text into an embedding is from OpenAI (GPT's creator).

Figure 194 shows examples of a few embeddings of objects an analyst might deal with:

1. A unique key identifying the object. In this case, we have three items. sales_amount and quantity are metrics in a BI cube, and pack_size is an attribute of a cube dimension.

2. Text describing each key. This is what is used to create an embedding.

3. The embedding of the text computed by GPT. It is a 1536 number array.

①	②	③
key	text	embedding
sales_amount	sale amount of products sold to customers, in currency such as dollars and euros. Ex: we sold $500 of paper last	[-0.010877558961510658, -0.008796130307018757, 0.00605096435174346, -0.008209722116589546, -0.0131
quantity	quantity of items sold to customers. For example, we sold 40 units of soda.	[0.007712365128099918, -0.015992669388651848, 0.0028945570811629295, -0.007731726858764887, -0.013
pack_size	gallons or liters or some other unit of volume of products sold to customers	[0.016375085338950157, 0.003610593732446432, -0.01918148621916771, -0.016361847519874573, 0.006198

Figure 194: Example of embeddings.

Information from the EKG can be transformed into vector embeddings through a concatenation of these strings:

- KG nodes and relationships—Entity descriptions and the relationships could be downloaded into a vector database. For example, a triple, "Employee is a Human," could be transformed into a vector and used to compare against text from others such as, "Employees are people."

- QueryDef nodes—Description of the query (or even the SQL itself). I explain more in Figure 195 below.

- Tuple Nodes–Description of the tuple (for example, Consumption of coconut water in Juneau).

- Query Intents and parameters—The descriptions of parameterized queries, which we'll discuss soon.

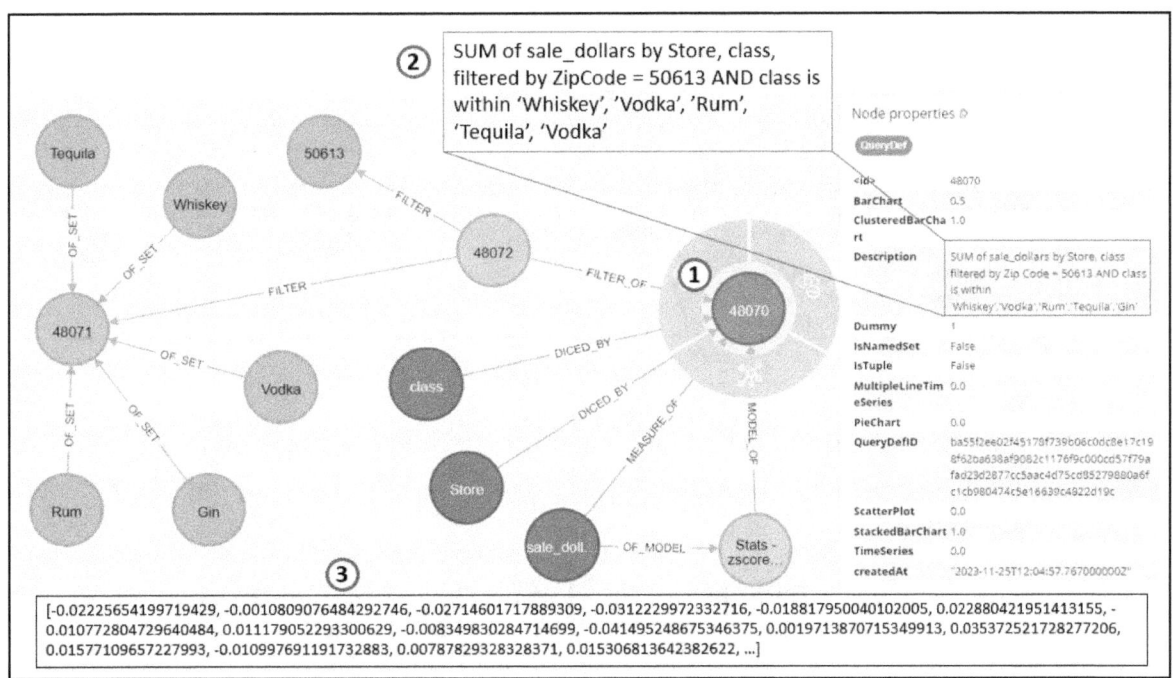

Figure 195: Example of an ISG QueryDef object's vector embedding.

Figure 195 is an example of how an ISG/TCW object is crystalized into a vector embedding and how it has a "description" property we could vectorize.

1. This is a QueryDef object. We saw this object way back in Figure 93.

2. Many node types, such as QueryDef, have a description property that describes the SQL in a language format.

3. This is the vector embedding of the QueryDef's description.

Vectors, in this context, are generated from descriptions of nodes, relationships, and BI-derived insights, using advanced language models like OpenAI's GPT. These vectors effectively capture the nuanced semantic information of your data, enabling more sophisticated and robust similarity searches and analyses.

Figure 196 shows a comparison of three text statements, partial embedding, and their comparison. The three text pieces are shortened and modified versions of the text shown in Figure 195. All three are kind of similar to each other, so their similarity scores will be close.

For s1, s2, and s3, we called a function that creates embeddings. We'll go through that process next. Then, we compared the embeddings against each over, producing a similarity score (0 through 1).

```
s1 = "SUM of sale_dollars by Store, class, filtered by class is within 'Whiskey', 'Vodka'"
s2 = "SUM of sale_dollars by Store, class, filtered by class is within 'Whiskey', 'Rum'"
s3 = "AVG of sale_dollars by class, filtered by ZipCode = 50615 AND class is within 'Whiskey', 'Rum'"

s1 embedding = [-0.016040576621890068, -0.005446721334010363, -0.022624287754297256, -0.024992112070322037, -0.021859074011445045, ...]
s2 embedding = [-0.021926498040556908, 0.0006176214083097875, -0.024344420060515404, -0.017871597781777382, -0.025020236149430275, ...]
s3 embedding = [-0.023648688569664955, -0.0018118831794708967, -0.03444864600896835, -0.02805354818701744, -0.006881680339574814, ...]

s1 vs s2 similarity = 0.9689064384959567
s1 vs s3 similarity = 0.9132881225356722
s2 vs s3 similarity = 0.9176609119341994
```

Figure 196: Similarity between three text statements.

The ability to score similarity between unstructured objects (text in this case) is a critical component of an intelligent system. It's kind of close to our human super-power of abstraction.

Figure 197 dives a little deeper into the process of finding text that closely matches a given text:

1. We want to find the record for a person, but we only remember his first name (Dick) and a bit of the name of his employer ("Strattford" …?). Spoiler alert, we're looking for Dick Loudan, the proprietor of the "Strattfort" Inn in Vermont.

2. In order to search for a vector representing what we're looking for, we need to encode our query, "Dick Strattford," into a vector. Our encoder is GPT. Note that we always use GPT to encode because other encoders might use another algorithm.

3. We receive the vector embedding of "Dick Strattford."

4. We submit our vector to a component that will search the vector database. It will measure the similarity between our vector and vectors in the database. The vector database platform has the ability to search in an efficient manner (not a brute force comparison with every vector).

5. We receive the top few answers. The top answer is what we're looking for. The next closest is the maid of the Strattfort Inn.

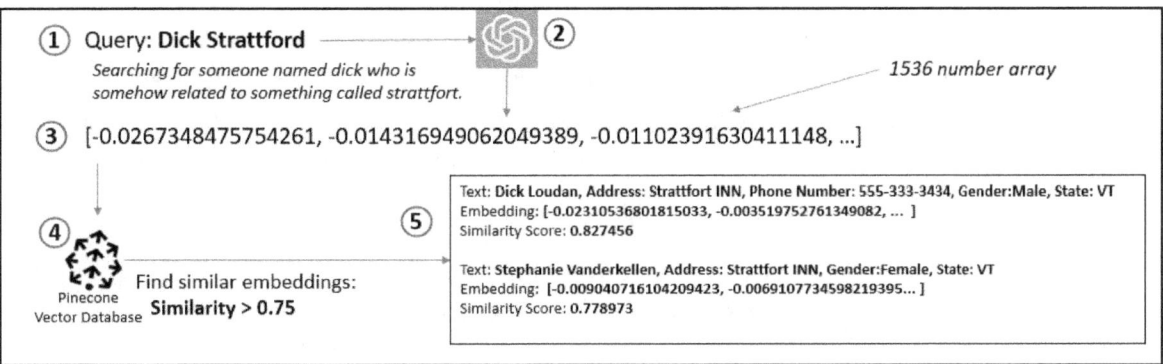

Figure 197: Process for searching the vector database for similarity matches.

Here are two options for handling embeddings:

Leveraging Neo4j GDS for Embedding Management and Similarity Analysis

A key aspect of enhancing the EKG involves the integration of semantic embeddings, which, as we just discussed, are critical for advanced similarity searches and nuanced data interpretations. To achieve this, we turn to the synergy between LLM models (GPT) for generating embeddings and Neo4j's Graph Data Science (GDS) library for embedding storage and similarity calculations. That is, storing the vector embeddings directly in Neo4j bypassing the need for a separate vector database.

1. **Embedding Generation with GPT Models**—The first step in this process involves generating high-dimensional vector embeddings from textual descriptions of nodes or relationships. For this, we utilize state-of-the-art

language models like GPT. These models are adept at capturing the nuanced semantic meanings of text, transforming them into dense vector representations. This transformation allows us to convert qualitative descriptions into quantitative data, suitable for advanced analytical processes.

2. **Storing Embeddings in Neo4j–**Once we have our embeddings, the next step is to store them efficiently. Here, Neo4j's GDS library plays a pivotal role. It allows us to store these high-dimensional vectors as properties of nodes or relationships within our graph. This method of storage maintains the rich, interconnected structure of our EKG while augmenting it with the depth of vector-based information.

3. **Similarity Searches with Neo4j GDS–**The true power of incorporating embeddings into Neo4j is realized in the capability to perform similarity searches. The GDS library provides functions to calculate similarities between vectors, such as cosine similarity. This enables us to query the graph not just based on traditional relational parameters, but also on the basis of semantic similarity. For instance, we can find nodes with descriptions semantically similar to a given query, opening avenues for sophisticated data retrieval and analysis.

By leveraging Neo4j's GDS, we avoid the complexity and overhead of introducing an additional technology like Pinecone for vector management. This approach simplifies our technology stack while still harnessing the benefits of vector-based analyses.

The integration of Neo4j GDS for managing and querying embeddings aligns seamlessly with our objective of building a comprehensive, cognitively-rich EKG. This approach not only capitalizes on the strengths of Neo4j in managing complex data relationships but also extends its capabilities into the realm of AI-driven semantic analysis, making our EKG a more dynamic and insightful tool in the landscape of business intelligence.

Offloading Vector Tasks to a Vector Database

I mentioned earlier that I chose to exclude deeper inclusion of the vector database in this book since it's already packed with many diverse and complex technologies. However, given the potential scale and complexity of vector data in the EKG, especially within the expansive ISG and TCW, a specialized vector database becomes necessary for the efficient handling and querying of this high-dimensional data.

I should clarify the use of "high-dimensional" in terms of a vector database versus a multi-dimensional OLAP cube. Unlike the multi-dimensional structure of OLAP cubes of Kyvos, which are designed for aggregating and analyzing data across various dimensions (like time, geography, and product categories), the "high-dimensional" nature of vector embeddings refers to the vastness of language-space (all the things we could possibly say or write), spanning hundreds to thousands of dimensions, representing intricate features of language in a compressed numerical form.

Fortunately, Pinecone emerges as a highly suitable solution. As a dedicated vector database, Pinecone excels in storing and performing fast, scalable similarity searches on large volumes of vector data. By mapping vectors in Pinecone to unique identifiers in your EKG (like semantic web URIs or hash IDs for ISG/TCW nodes), you create a relatively seamless integration, allowing the rich, graph-structured data of the EKG to be augmented with the powerful similarity search capabilities of Pinecone.

This hybrid approach leverages the strengths of both Neo4j for graph database management and Pinecone for vector-based similarity searches, establishing a robust, scalable infrastructure that significantly enhances the cognitive and analytical functions of your enterprise system.

Although I don't get into the details of Pinecone in the book, the code in the GitHub repository utilizes it.

Prompt Enrichment

Enriching our LLM Prompts with ISG/TCW information

The primary value of the ISG and TCW lies in enhancing our decision-making process with BI data from across dozens to thousands of knowledge workers. Consider an analyst seeking to boost sales of their new fad product, moringa boba matte, at all corners of the world. They might want to identify similar cities where the product is already successful.

Typically, the analyst would use Tableau to compare various cities. The challenge is in determining the factors that drive sales in these cities. These factors encompass a diverse mix of customer demographics, product characteristics, geological climate, political climate, economic conditions, and local features. For instance, local features could include regional economic conditions, cultural preferences, climate, and specific local regulations or policies impacting sales.

Understanding such nuances is essential for crafting strategies that resonate within each potential market. A product popular in a young, tech-savvy urban area may not fare as well in a region with an older, less technology-oriented demographic. Moreover, elements like local marketing trends, the competitive landscape, and city-specific supply chain logistics significantly affect sales dynamics. Integrating these factors into their analysis allows the analyst to uncover deeper insights and develop targeted, effective strategies for each region.

Tracking the interplay of these elements can be complex, especially when relying solely on an analyst's mental mapping while navigating through BI data. Obtaining data that can support making sense of this complexity is where the ISG/TCW comes into play, enabling the storage and linking of significant correlations.

But even with rich data, formulating BI queries in such a detailed, analytical manner can be challenging. It's akin to converting a complex "word problem" into algebraic expressions. The analyst's business challenges need to be translated into actionable steps within the visualization tool.

While human analysts have been performing that task for decades, today that would be unnecessarily daunting. Instead, that energy could be used to increase the scope of the analyst's awareness of the problem space. RAG assists in this translation process, transforming vague concepts into a clear sequence of visualizations to effectively map out the situation.

Let's break down how each part of the process fits into the RAG framework:

1. **Understanding the Query (NLP Component)**–The first step involves the NLP component, where the system interprets the user's query, "Which cities are successfully selling moringa nut coffee that are similar to Boise?" This requires understanding the semantics of the query, including the key terms ("moringa nut coffee," "cities," "similar to Boise") and the intent behind the question.

2. **Identifying the Knowledge Gap (Retrieval Component)**–Given that "moringa nut coffee" might be a new product unknown to the LLM due to its training data cut-off, the system recognizes a knowledge gap. This is where your sales database comes in. The system would formulate a query to retrieve data about the sales of moringa nut coffee, addressing the first problem–"What is moringa nut coffee?"

3. **Interpreting "Similar to Boise" (Retrieval and NLP)**—The next challenge is understanding what "similar to Boise" means in this context. This involves both NLP and retrieval. The system needs to interpret various possible meanings (size, demographics, geography, etc.) and then potentially retrieve data from your KG of cities to identify cities with characteristics similar to Boise.

4. **Generating an Augmented Response (Generation Component)**—Once the system has retrieved the relevant information—sales data for moringa nut coffee and a list of cities similar to Boise in the desired aspect—it then generates a response. This response would ideally list cities that match the criteria (selling moringa nut coffee and similar to Boise in the defined way).

5. **Response to the Augmented Prompt**—The final response is an amalgamation of the retrieved data (sales figures, city characteristics) and the language model's capabilities to synthesize this information into a coherent, informative answer. The facts and data gathered by the RAG Coordinator is composed into a big prompt—similar to a report attorneys might compile and then hand over to the judge for an opinion and resolution. That prompt is submitted to the "know it all" LLM, to which it replies with a very wise response.

In this scenario, our system is effectively utilizing RAG by combining retrieval (from sales databases and KGs) and generation (formulating a coherent response based on retrieved data). This process not only addresses the limitations of the LLM's static knowledge base but also caters to specific, up-to-date, and contextually relevant queries.

As an example, let's continue with the question just discussed: How to sell moringa boba matte elsewhere. With just a LLM tool, the analyst could simply submit that query as is. The LLM might come up with a few valuable suggestions if the question is relatively straightforward. That's useful when a non-expert of a subject is satisfied with a basic, well-known answer.

In my experience with ChatGPT, if I just ask it a question, because LLMs predict the next most likely word, I'll usually get the bottom-support-tier "is it plugged in" responses—the most common things obvious to an analyst. Maybe that is valuable to someone new to analytics or just learning. But for a "production analyst," those answers will be a waste of time.

Remember, all of us are novices or less at *most* things. The LLM knows a good deal about most things, but at least ATTOW, it struggles to keep up with human experts of the thousands of subjects out there. Chances are, the nature of the LLM is such that it will return ideas that are already well-known by experts.

So the analyst should at least rephrase her question with some high-level, broad hints. For example: *Which cities are successfully selling moringa boba matte that are similar to Boise?*

Figure 198 drills a little deeper than Figure 192.

Before moving on, some Steps in Figure 198 might run in parallel with each other or may not be required. In an extreme case, Steps 3 through 7 (which are all sub-queries to various components) could run in parallel with each other, rendezvousing back up at Step 8. And many steps could be run multiple times in order to follow up on questions opened up by previous questions in a manner of conversational refinement.

This process involves adjusting your queries or providing additional context in subsequent interactions to help the LLM better understand your request and provide more accurate or relevant responses. It's a collaborative process where both the user and the model work together to home in on the desired information or outcome. This iterative approach is often crucial in complex or ambiguous situations where the model might need more information to understand the intent or specifics of the query.

Step 1 is the analyst asking that enhanced question.

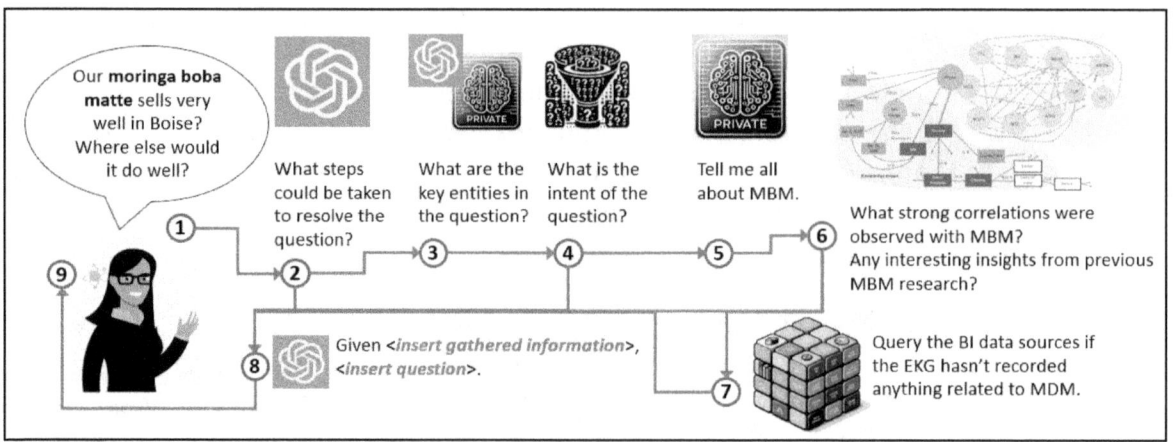

Figure 198: High-level idea of RAG using the EKG and BI.

Step 2 is really the core of agentic RAG. It's here that we ask an AI to break down the problem into a set of steps, where we reason about what we're facing, determine an action, and take that action. It's important to understand that the request to break down the problem into steps must be submitted with careful instructions describing the format of the answer so that the response can be "understood" and properly distributed to other agents (Steps 3—7).

Let's assume a LLM doesn't know anything about moringa boba matte because it has never heard of it. If we're looking to AI for the answer to the question, it needs to craft a plan, breaking down the prompt and analyzing what information it needs. For example, following are sample questions it formulates, along with available resources that could help:

- What is moringa boba matte?
    a. I have a database of sales that could be queried.
    b. I also have documentation on product development and marketing.

- What might "similar to Boise" mean in this context? Is it size, demographics, or geography?

- Once we define "similar," what cities are like Boise with those characteristics?
    a. I have a KG of cities and their characteristics.

Some of these questions could be answered by another AI (a LLM fine-tuned with deep subject data), the EKG, or another data source.

In Step 3, we're parsing out the subjects, verb, and objects of the question. We're mostly interested in the "entities" (subjects and objects), which will probably be a parameter in subsequent queries. For example, "moringa boba matte" and "Boise" would be identified. These answers could be from a private LLM or GPT. The private LLM is most likely to recognize entities that mean something to the enterprise but perhaps not to the world in general. The public LLM would recognize most things that wouldn't normally be of interest to the enterprise.

Step 4 engages a system that maps a question to a database query. This is similar to how Azure Cognitive Language Understanding works. We'll look more closely at this component in "Graph Query Intent Templates."

Step 5 asks our private LLM to tell us more about what isn't yet known to the public LLM, either because it's private to the enterprise or it isn't part of the public LLM's training.

Step 6 queries the EKG for:

1. Information authored by SME in the KG part of the EKG.
2. Correlations captured in the TCW between entities mentioned (mostly from Step 3).
3. Statistical properties captured by the ISG related to entities.

Step 7 might need to query a data source. Hopefully, the EKG (Step 6) holds most if not all of the information required. But if querying the EKG comes up empty, we can explore the BI data sources. It might not be as fast or as versatile as querying the EKG, but if the BI data are OLAP cubes, the query will at least be as consistently fast as possible.

There is also the issue of querying which BI data source. The EKG integrates insights and correlations across BI data sources. If the EKG comes up empty, the DC should be able to provide clues as to which BI data sources might be helpful due to its awareness of the metadata of each BI data source.

At Step 8, we gather all the pieces provided by Steps 3 through 7. We package that data, the original question, some instruction, and submit it to a robust LLM (probably the broad public one) for an answer. Of course, before packaging up, we have a chance to filter out what shouldn't be submitted (security constraints). That kind of sensitive information should be captured by the data sources, but it's worth having the response analyzed for security breaches anyway. We could add to the prompt: "Before answering, please see if there is something that you think might be a security breach."

Step 9 is the response to the analyst taking into consideration all the data gathered by Steps 3 through 7. At the time of writing ChatGPT is capable of not just generating text answers and code but generating BI visualizations. I tested that. I prompted: "If I have you [(CA, 34300), (ID,443), (WA,5005), (OR, 544)] could you generate a pie chart?" It did indeed return a correct pie chart.

Query the TCW like a Social Network

The comparison of the TCW to a social network offers an intuitive way to conceptualize the nature and strength of relationships between tuples, just as a social network showcases the relationships between people.

Bringing this back to the TCW, while we might identify that beach crowds correlate with temperature, and separately, that seagulls correlate with beach crowds, it doesn't necessarily translate to a direct correlation between seagulls and temperature. However, what the TCW does offer, like a social network, is a mapping of relationships. It allows us to make educated conjectures, pulling from the web of interrelated data points—a chain or webs of strong correlations.

This capability to make educated guesses, based on relationships we've learned and observed for ourselves, is a hallmark of human intelligence. While other animals might react based on instinct or relatively simple patterns, and while purely data-driven systems might operate solely on fixed algorithms, humans can assimilate disparate pieces of information, drawing upon them to hypothesize, anticipate, and innovate.

The TCW, by functioning like a social network for data, introduces a nuanced layer of connection-based logic, inching a bit closer to mimicking that quintessential human ability to infer and predict based on connections, albeit within the confines of its data structure.

Following are sample scenarios for querying the TCW. Each of these is an "intent," as described back in Figure 198:

- Identifying Chains of Strong Correlations:
    - Query: What tuples related to oil prices in Beijing have a Pearson Correlation above 0.8?
    - Business Insight: Uncover strong predictors or consequences of rising oil prices in a specific market.

- Uncovering Probabilistic Relationships:
    - Query: What are the Conditional probabilities between water consumption in San Diego and regional agricultural metrics?
    - Business Insight: Determine if agricultural practices significantly impact water consumption.

- Time Series Analysis:
    - Query: For tuples related to a specific product's sales, how do their correlations change over different time intervals?
    - Business Insight: Understand how the interplay of various factors affecting sales evolves over time.

- External Factors Impact:
    - Query: Which tuples, when compared by time series, show increased correlation with local economic indicators during recessionary periods?
    - Business Insight: Identify business areas most sensitive to broader economic shifts.

- Influential Nodes:
  - Query: Which tuple nodes, when analyzed, frequently show up as highly correlated or influential across multiple correlations?
  - Business Insight: Determine key performance drivers or risk factors in the business.

Query the ISG like any Other Ontology

An ontology is a structured representation of knowledge within a specific domain, delineating classes (or concepts), properties (or relationships), and individual entities. Think of a traditional ontology focused on a library. This library ontology would outline classes like Book, Author, and Publisher, and would include relationships, such as writtenBy connecting a Book to an Author, or publishedBy linking a Book to a Publisher. When querying this ontology, one might pose questions like, "Which books were published by Publisher Y?" or "List all authors who have written more than five science-fiction books."

Now, transpose this understanding to the ISG. The ISG can be visualized as a specialized ontology where the primary subject is not entities such as books or authors, but dataframes. In the ISG, the principal class is DataFrame, and we have unique relationships pertinent to this domain, like hasInsight and ColumnsUsed. Each individual entity in this space corresponds to a specific dataframe, encapsulating its unique data and insights. When querying the ISG, it's akin to our traditional ontology. You might ask, "Which dataframes exhibit a downward revenue trend?" or "Identify dataframes that include both CustomerAge and PurchaseHistory columns," or even "Show dataframes created in the last month with any anomaly detected."

In essence, the ISG is fundamentally an ontology, albeit with a specialized focus on dataframes. Its core structure and mechanics mirror that of traditional ontologies, which means the query patterns and methodologies used in conventional ontology queries can be directly applied to the ISG with the same efficacy.

- Identifying Trends:
  - Query: Retrieve all dataframes where the trend is "up" over the last quarter.
  - Business Insight: Allows a business to identify areas that have seen growth or positive momentum.

- Discovering Periodicity:
    - Query: List all dataframes that show "periodicity" and are related to sales metrics.
    - Business Insight: Understand which sales metrics have consistent seasonal or cyclic patterns.

- Pinpointing Anomalies:
    - Query: Fetch dataframes which indicate "spikes" in the last month.
    - Business Insight: Highlight sudden changes in metrics, warranting further investigation.

- Exploring Specific Visualization Insights:
    - Query: Which scatter plots show a positive correlation between advertising spend and sales?
    - Business Insight: Measure the ROI of advertising campaigns.

- Comparative Analysis:
    - Query: Return all bar charts that compare quarterly sales across different regions.
    - Business Insight: Regional performance analysis for targeted marketing strategies.

Graph Query Intent Templates

Back in Figure 198, Step 4, there is a component for determining the intent of an NLP query.

Every "intelligence", including LLMs, are prone to misinterpretation. There are countless questions to ask in countless ways and potentially hundreds of databases consisting of many tens of thousands of columns across the enterprise.

There is a middle ground to submitting an arbitrary question to an AI and leaving it up to the AI to figure out how to answer it. We can provide it with hints and constraints through templates. Although LLMs should know how to query a data source given the database's schema, the idea is to create a fixed set of generalized queries to the TCW and ISG. This isn't much different than providing a cheat sheet to a human to categorize all situations and constraint for how to address questions. However, this "cheat sheet" of templates can span hundreds to thousands of cataloged questions–which is better than exploring an infinity of possible interpretations of a question.

For querying the ISG and TCW, the approach I'm taking is to marshal queries into a robust set of intents. The setup starts out in a manner similar to how Azure Cognitive Services currently sets up:

1. Set up intents, entities, and utterances. Each intent has a template Cypher query, defined parameters, and a collection of utterances.
2. Create embeddings of the sample utterances.

Utterances, much like in other NLP systems, are not designed for exact word-for-word matches but rather to recognize and understand patterns in human language. For instance, the phrases "What are my sales in Idaho?" and "Tell me how much we sold in Idaho" varies significantly in wording, but they share an underlying intent–querying sales data for a specific location. The system uses these utterances to learn the general intent of the user's query, allowing it to respond appropriately to a wide range of similar phrases, even if they are phrased differently. This flexibility enables the service to interact naturally with users, accommodating the variability inherent in human language.

At query time:

1. User asks a question, verbally or in text.
2. An embedding is created for the question and matched to utterances (a catalog of questions asked in various ways).
3. If a close enough utterance is found, the variables are determined and a query (SQL, Cypher, depending on the database) is generated to the EKG or to BI data sources.

Following is a sampling of query intent categories and an example:

- Intuitive Querying:
    - Natural Language Query: "Which sales metrics, when visualized, often show a periodic pattern in Europe?"
    - Business Insight: Identify cyclic sales trends specific to the European market.

- Hypothesis Testing:
    - Natural Language Query: "Based on the insights, does increased advertising in Q4 lead to a spike in sales in Q1?"

- o Business Insight: Measure lagged effects of advertising campaigns.

- Anomaly Explanation:
  - o Natural Language Query: "Can you explain the spike in this particular metric on the graph from last July?"
  - o Business Insight: Using past data and correlations, the LLM could provide possible reasons for anomalies.

Figure 199 shows a high-level view of the process for determining the intent of a question.

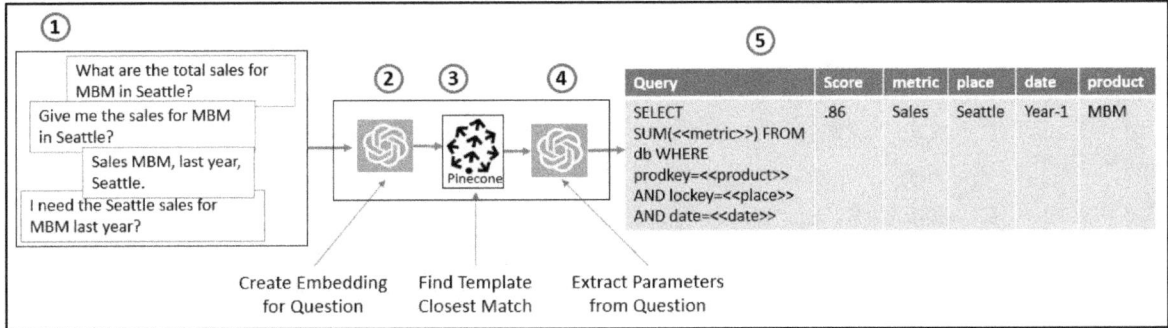

Figure 199: Process for determining the intent of an NLP question.

Here are the steps:

1. **Various NLP Queries**—A variety utterances attempting to communicate an intent.

2. **Create Embedding for Question**—This step involves transforming the queries into a machine-readable format—the embedding we discussed earlier using GPT.

3. **Find Template Closest Match**—The embeddings are then compared to a set of templates to find the best match. Specifically, the embedding of the question is compared to the embeddings of template questions.

4. **Extract Parameters from Question**—After finding the closest template, the system extracts specific parameters from the question, such as the metric, place, and time.

5. **Structured SQL Query**—The final step involves constructing a structured SQL query using the extracted parameters. The example SQL query provided is

designed to calculate the sum of sales for MBM in Seattle from the previous year.

The templates and text files are stored in a directory (referenced by the environment variable CYPHER_TEMPLATES_DIR). Figure 200 shows an example of this directory of query templates.

The files in the directory could reference Cypher, SQL, MDX queries—or even LLM prompts. Figure 201 is an example of one of these query templates. In this case, a Cypher query.

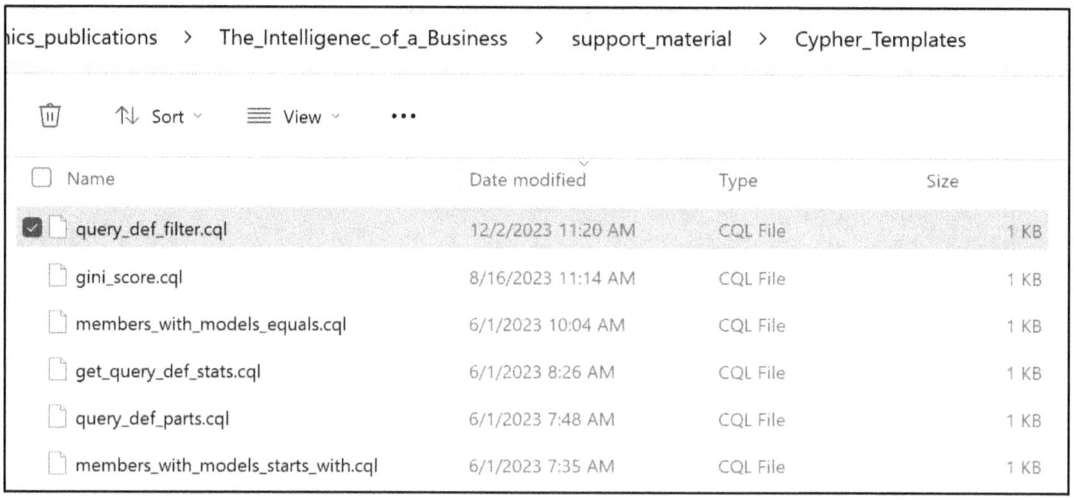
ics_publications > The_Intelligenec_of_a_Business > support_material > Cypher_Templates
Sort
View
Name
Date modified
Type
Size
query_def_filter.cql 12/2/2023 11:20 AM CQL File 1 KB
gini_score.cql 8/16/2023 11:14 AM CQL File 1 KB
members_with_models_equals.cql 6/1/2023 10:04 AM CQL File 1 KB
get_query_def_stats.cql 6/1/2023 8:26 AM CQL File 1 KB
query_def_parts.cql 6/1/2023 7:48 AM CQL File 1 KB
members_with_models_starts_with.cql 6/1/2023 7:35 AM CQL File 1 KB

Figure 200: Sample of a directory of query intent templates.

```
① //Prompt: ["Find queries with a particular <<year>> and <<metric>>.","Query with sales amount for 2010"]

② //Description: This is useful for finding QueryDef objects for a particular measure. Then use the
  OlapQueriesLib to run the query in Kyvos.

③ //{"Variable":"<<year>>", "Prompt":"Year to search is a member of some date dimension. ex: 1998, 2023,
  1997","Direction":"Input"}
  //{"Variable":"<<metric>>","Prompt":"Metric name of a measure of some cube.","Direction":"Input"}
  //{"Variable":"QueryDefHash","Description":"Query objects that match the filter", "Direction":"Output"}

④ MATCH p=(met)-[m1:METRIC]-(n:QueryDef)-[:FILTER]-(m:Member) WHERE m.Name='<<year>>' AND
  met.Name="<<metric>>"
  RETURN n.Hash AS QueryDefHash
```

Figure 201: Sample of a Query template.

Each template consists of metadata and a query template of SQL, Cypher, or MDX.

1. **Prompt–**Each template holds a list of ways a question could be asked. In this case, we see two forms of the question. In many cases, just one form of the

question should be sufficient. But more forms might help provide more context on the real intent of the question.

2. **Description**—This is a longer description of what this template intends to solve. It gives the LLM more context around what this template does.

3. **Variables**—Variables plugged into the query. The AI will try to extract these variables from the user's prompt. Each variable is in its own JSON document.

4. **Query template**—This is a Cypher query to the EKG. Notice the <<year>> and <<metric>> variables.

The sample is: *query_def_filter.cql*.

While this topic may seem very "manual" in the context of an AI book, it's a method for reigning in an AI that ATTOW "thinks" it's smarter than it is, or limiting an AI that might be too smart for our own good.

LLM API

The subject of techniques on how to communicate with LLMs might be changing faster ATTOW than the performance of the LLMs themselves. For this book, I intend only to provide an example of how the pieces I've presented fit into a RAG paradigm. I believe the features I've incorporated will be relevant until the day of AGI/ASI.

For this book (and the accompanying GitHub directory), I've used LangChain and the OpenAI API for retrieval augmented generation. There are very many products coming out every day. This pair of components was the first to be widely popularized within a few months after the launch of ChatGPT 3.5. Together, chain of thought and tree of thought procedures can be run. And, of course, there are other query methodologies out there. But for the purposes of demoing how BI can apply in the AI world, this should suffice.

At the time of writing, AI is far too unreliable to query without some level of constraints. I fully believe this is a temporary situation. Eventually, it will be simple enough to ask an AI anything and it will understand your context to a high enough degree where misunderstanding moves at least another "9" or so towards "5-nines" level of reliability expected in any production environment. Additionally, an AI can potentially take a long time to "think" through some queries. I've had queries take many seconds, which might be OK serving me directly, but is very sub-par for automated use cases "at scale".

Currently, ChatGPT 4 itself performs a RAG by accessing Bing for updated data. To makes things worse, ChatGPT is often down—magnitudes worse than would be tolerable for any production database.

Setting up RAG and using API calls in this manner can seem like a step backwards from the initial "AI can do everything" hype around ChatGPT, towards a glorified NLP setup—and it is, at least in this use case scenario. But that's OK. I've demonstrated using AI in all its inferential glory in other contexts. There's no reason not to assume the long term trend for AI performance is amazing and scary improvement.

The sample code is: *embeddinglib.py*.

Maintenance

This section is much more important than its late mention in the book and relatively small outline would suggest. After all, I've been saying throughout the book that the challenge is beyond just developing KGs. It must also be maintained in an ongoing basis. "Maintain" means to update the KG to reflect the current state of our understanding. KGs are the keystone of the ability to integrate the human intelligence of analysts across many domains and machine intelligence. Therefore, the KG must be up to date just as our skills and understanding must be up to date.

The problem with KGs (until LLMs came along) is the manual labor required to develop a KG and more importantly, how to maintain it. The world is constantly changing, so like a poor editor maintaining an encyclopedia with the most up-to-date knowledge, the work is never done.

There are two major points related to maintenance of the EKG (in order of importance):

1. LLMs provide an adequate level of intellectual capability to automatically map similarities between nodes and even offer validation of the legitimacy of relationships. That's the symbiotic relationship between KGs and LLMs we discussed earlier.

2. Optimized OLAP drastically reduces compute required for calculating/refreshing ISG and TCW values across what is a larger set of users

than the traditionally small set of analysts and managers. Relationships can be updated quickly and in high concurrency.

Regarding #2, we should never underestimate the need to reconstruct major sections or even the entirety of the EKG. Much can happen that can render a KG corrupted or cluttered through age–even with the best of due diligence. Based on the guidance from the Implementation part:

- The KG can be reconstructed through the saved ttl files.

- The DC should be easily reconstructed from Data Fabric functionality.

- The ISG/TCW should be reconstructed from saved queries and executing the query for the insights. With optimized OLAP cubes as the BI data sources, the insights and correlations will be retrieved in the fastest way–better a few seconds per query executed with high concurrency than up to minute per query at lower concurrency.

Deep details pertaining to maintenance are highly intricate. It will be addressed to a deservedly sufficient depth in a follow-up volume. As I mentioned, Chapter 11–Implementation, is like the part of an introductory presentation where the senior technical staff ask their questions—which is followed by subsequent deep-dives. Similarly, deep-dive details will be addressed in a series of targeted follow-up meetings.

Updating the KG

Updating of the TCW and ISG

Ideally, the TCW and ISG are updated (in batch) at low latencies–at least every few minutes up to an hour. For the most part, the EKG itself shouldn't require real-time updates. The EKG is meant for inference, which is different from reporting. If real-time information is required, the RAG query process can supplement real-time information from real-time sources.

Neo4j's throughput, when it comes to updating or inserting nodes and relationships, can vary based on multiple factors, including the complexity of the data model, the nature and number of indexes, constraints, the server hardware, the configuration settings, and the workload mix (reads versus writes). In general, Neo4j can handle thousands to tens of thousands of writes (node and relationship creations or updates) in a matter of seconds on commodity hardware.

Batch Updates for KG Data Products

Without the ISG and TCW components (or other such large components, such as an ontology of billions of all customers), the KG part of the EKG should be comparatively small, so updating of KG data products should not be too much of an issue.

The KG consisting of up to a few million nodes, in contrast to billions, presents a different set of challenges and opportunities. With the scale in the "mere" millions, a single instance of Neo4j is often sufficient, eliminating the need for complex active-passive setups used for larger implementations. The reduced scale means that batch updates can be scheduled with more flexibility, potentially allowing for more frequent updates, even during typical business hours. Real-time updates become more feasible too. They could be directly incorporated into the graph with minimal performance impact.

However, updating a KG consisting of billions of nodes is a monumental task, especially when using Neo4j. This scale introduces a plethora of intricacies that must be navigated to ensure data integrity, consistency, and availability. Here's an architectural approach for tackling updates on such a colossal KG.

Given the scale we've been discussing for the EKG (billions of nodes), the methodology for updating primarily revolves around batch-oriented processes. Batch operations are more efficient and controllable than real-time updates with their unpredictable loads and overhead associated with real-time updating.

Updating the EKG should be approached in a batch-based manner, but in a variety of batch sizes. Batch updates are typically performed during off-peak times to minimize disruption and optimize resource use. Those updates would usually be large and of lower priority. But then there are the smaller batches of higher priority updates. Those could be run in micro-batches at relatively frequent intervals.

Overall, a hybrid approach that leverages both batch updates and "sort of real-time" micro-batches, combined with RAG for immediate data needs, provides a balanced and efficient strategy for maintaining an up-to-date and functional EKG.

The subject of updating is the time to recall and reflect upon the power of the semantic web aspects presented in this book. Applying a URI to elements of the DC and KG (as well as links from the ISG/TCW to the DC) goes a very long way towards mitigating the messiness of updating the EKG. It facilitates updating in a loosely-coupled fashion since updates to the EKG will link to unambiguous nodes.

Additionally, applying data mesh's data product approach towards KG development (the KG is composed of domain-level ontology data products) further mitigates update complexity. By structuring the KG as a collection of domain-specific ontologies, each managed as a separate data product, the update process becomes more modular and manageable. This approach allows for targeted updates to specific domains without disrupting the entire system, enhancing both scalability and maintainability.

Now, let's consider the architecture characteristics to accommodate large-scale graphs:

- Clustered Deployment: A clustered Neo4j setup with multiple replicas can cater to high availability and fault tolerance. While one or more instances handle read requests, another set can be reserved for batch updates, ensuring continuous availability.

- Active-Passive Configuration: To allow uninterrupted querying of the KG, an active-passive setup can be employed. One cluster (active) serves the queries, while the other (passive) undergoes the update. Once the update is complete, roles can switch. This ensures the KG remains available for querying even during massive updates.

- Partitioning and Sharding: Large-scale KGs can benefit from data partitioning and sharding, breaking the graph into more manageable chunks distributed across multiple servers or instances. Updates can then be parallelized across these partitions, speeding up the process.

- Optimized Indexing: As data is updated, re-indexing becomes crucial. Dynamic index management, which adds or updates indexes based on the incoming data, can expedite search operations post-update.

- Monitoring and Alerting: At this scale, real-time monitoring of the update processes is imperative. Monitoring tools can provide insights into bottlenecks, failures, or inefficiencies in the update process. Automated alerts can then be set up to notify administrators of any issues immediately.

- Data Validation and Cleaning: Before integrating updates into the KG, a validation layer should screen the incoming data. This step ensures only clean and relevant data updates the main graph, reducing the need for frequent and intensive maintenance later.

In essence, updating the EKG with billions of nodes necessitates a harmonious blend of batch and real-time update strategies, underpinned by a robust, scalable, and fail-safe architecture. Leveraging the strengths of Neo4j and RAG can ensure that even at this immense scale, results from the EKG remains accurate, up-to-date, and consistently available for querying.

Pruning the ISG and TCW

The high-end enterprise editions of Neo4j can handle the billions of nodes of the EKG, but the bigger the graph, the harder it is to process. And there is a still a significant cost for storing a lot of data that might not be worth the cost of storing.

That concern goes against the idea of holding insights and relationships surfaced through BI activity of analysts that may or may not be of value to other analysts. I hate to say that it's reminiscent of the early data lake sales pitch of throwing everything into the data lake and figuring out if it's useful later—it's better to have it just in case. Fortunately, BI queries are naturally self-selected for high value. A big part of my thesis is that:

1. BI analysts are genuine about solving business problems. So most queries reflect the expertly devised thought of the analyst. Yes, they may go down dead ends, but even those dead ends they chose to explore have some foundation of reason.

2. Enterprise domains don't operate in a vacuum, so there is a good chance that insights by one BI analyst will be useful for other BI analysts on the other side of the fence(s). Most BI analysts look at data through the lens of their specialty. But the same dataframe viewed from the lens of other analysts stands a good chance of filling in a missing piece. In this case, it's like giving a car on the lot a proper chance for the right customer to show up before yanking it off the lot.

Note: As a reminder, I don't intend to store the dataframe (the result of the query) in the graph database, just the metadata of its query. I also don't think the relationships per node will be too bad. Each tuple or dataframe node will be related to the filters and columns that is used to create them—realistically three to ten items per dataframe. Each dataframe and tuple could be related to other dataframes and tuples—say one to 100. Nor do I intend for

Neo4j to perform the calculation of these Bayes, Pearson, or statistical calculations. Query-time calculation would be very cumbersome in Neo4j. Neo4j is just responsible for graph queries.

There could be billions of tuples or dataframes viewed by hundreds to thousands of BI analysts across an enterprise, querying hundreds of data sources. As a reminder, the idea is that each dataframe queried and potentially viewed in a variety of visualizations by an analyst that might contain insights:

- The analyst sees and it is valuable to the analyst–kind of like a True Positive.

- The analyst sees but doesn't find it valuable, at least right now–kind of like a False Positive.

- The analyst misses because it's hidden in a "Where's Waldo" kind of way–kind of like a False Negative.

- The analyst misses because she doesn't know to look for it, kind of like a True Negative.

For all those cases, the insights are saved into the ISG/TCW and are available there for any who could potentially find those insights to be helpful. That can build up a lot of clutter! To mitigate the size of the EKG, we need to engage pruning mechanisms. That is, simply dropping (prune and drop) nodes and relationships that are deemed low value. Or, prune and archive them to a lower-cost storage and format (prune and archive)–for example, serializing the relationships into a JSON format and storing in it in an relatively inexpensive cloud storage location.

Pruning is more than just removing nodes. Like pruning a tree, a talented apple farmer doesn't just hack off branches indiscriminately. This process requires meticulous attention to detail and an understanding of the tree's growth patterns. It must be done not only to maximize the balance of the quality and quantity of the fruit, but also to ensure the overall health and longevity of the tree. There needs to be enough fruit to ensure a sustainable yield, sufficient both to earn a living and to meet the current demand for apples. Yet, the quality has to be such that it is appealing and marketable, satisfying consumer expectations.

Pruning is an art that involves making calculated decisions at specific times of the year, tailored to the tree's life cycle. It's about knowing which branches to trim and which to leave, ensuring the tree maintains a balance that prevents it from splitting or toppling.

This careful balancing act promotes healthy growth, enabling the tree to produce the best possible fruit.

In many ways, pruning can be likened to our sleep patterns. During sleep, our brain doesn't merely remove unused synapses in a haphazard fashion. There is a sophisticated process at play, determining what is important and cleaning out the garbage (byproducts and valueless experiences) that accumulate throughout the day. This is akin to the farmer removing the unnecessary or harmful parts of the tree and removing weeds to promote better health and productivity. Simultaneously, our sleep strengthens other neural connections, much like how a farmer nurtures the growth of healthy branches.

This process is essential for maintaining the brain's efficiency and health, ensuring that it can perform optimally when awake, just as the well-pruned tree yields the best fruit season after season.

Following are a few topics related to pruning or archiving EKG objects.

Re-query with Fast Optimized OLAP

Pruning low-value nodes can be much less painful if recalculating those nodes (should we need them later) is fast and inexpensive. In this book, I strongly suggest the incorporation of optimized OLAP (pre-aggregated OLAP cubes) as the primary query calculation engine for the BI data. Queries will be substantially faster which will make re-query of insights and correlations substantially faster and therefore minimally painful.

As opposed to simply dropping EKG objects, archiving what seems to be low-value ISG/TCW nodes to cheap storage might be an option. However, because it's fast and easier just to recalculate directly from the OLAP databases, it might actually be better to re-query from the OLAP data source instead of from the archive.

If the query is not sourced from an optimized OLAP database, the query could take longer–many seconds to many minutes–so re-query is time-consuming, possibly expensive due to more compute charges.

Related to the topic of pruning and archiving, there is the option of queries never making it into the EKG in the first place. For example, if we were pretty sure that insights from a query would never be useful to anyone, we wouldn't store it. Again, should that information be needed later, it's fast to re-query from the OLAP database. Following are a few ideas for determining not to add a query to the EKG:

- Similar queries have already been saved. It's not exact, but the insights are close enough to fill in a particular niche of knowledge for an analyst. For example, if one analyst looked at sales trends for lemons, it could be that we don't need to additionally save information for limes.

- We could reject tuple or dataframe nodes that include dimensions of high cardinality. For example, we may not want to store tuples at a customer level if that can add millions of customer tuples all by itself. Really, high cardinality dimensions should be categorized by natural (gender, age group, occupation) categories or created clusters, such as through KNN.

- We could have a threshold of correlation or probability between two tuples for the TCW. For the ISG, each insight functions that computes the insights will have a threshold signifying whether to report the insight or not.

- If it's decided not to add the query or tuple correlation to the EKG, we could still add it directly to the archive (cheaper- like a bad movie going "straight to video") as a record of having explored that part of the cube space.

QueryDef Count Settles Down on its Own

For most enterprises, I don't think there will be nodes and relationships in the EKG numbering in the high billions. It would take a lot of activity to come up with many billions of different dataframes and tuples, even by hundreds of analysts. Say a moderately-sized enterprise (which is still a big company) might involve 500 analysts making 500 queries per day. On day 1, that's 250,000 queries if each were unique. At that rate, in 250 working days per year, that's 63 million queries, 630 million over ten years. But as the days go on, a shrinking percentage of queries will be new to the EKG, and thus be saved.

It's reasonable to expect the number of unique dataframes an analyst encounters to stabilize or even decline in subsequent years (assuming the business environment doesn't go through too many revolutions). Here's why:

- Routine Queries: As analysts become more experienced in their roles and with their data sources, they often establish sets of routine queries that they run regularly. These would not contribute to the count of unique dataframes after their initial creation.

- Knowledge Accumulation: Over time, analysts learn which queries are most useful and informative, reducing the need for exploratory querying to some extent.

- Data Source Stability: Unless there are abrupt and significant changes in the data sources or business requirements, the range of useful query types may not expand dramatically.

- Template Utilization: Some BI tools offer templating features, where an analyst can simply plug in new numbers or categories into an existing query template. This improves efficiency but may reduce the number of unique dataframes generated.

- Collaboration: As more analysts work on similar problems, the number of unique queries can decrease because analysts can share queries and insights, reducing duplication of effort.

- Improvement in Tools: BI tools themselves are continually improving in terms of offering better analytics and visualizations out of the box. These enhancements can sometimes reduce the need to create unique dataframes for basic insights. Additionally, the integration of AI assistance (e.g. Microsoft's Copilot) opens the door to new paths of BI tool evolution.

However, that smooth evolution towards discernable query patterns could be disrupted by:

- Business Changes: Mergers, acquisitions, or entry into new markets could require new types of analysis.

- Data Source Changes: Introduction of new data sources can also lead to an increase in unique dataframes.

- Role Changes: If the analyst's role changes, or if they are given new responsibilities, this could also increase the number of unique dataframes encountered.

- Technological Advances: New BI tools or updates to existing tools might offer capabilities that invite new kinds of queries.

Barring such significant changes, it's likely that the number of unique dataframes an analyst creates would stabilize or potentially decrease in subsequent years.

BI Consumers with Widely Diverse Focuses

There are some types of enterprises where vastly diverse areas of the insight-space are concurrently explored. A colleague of mine recently told me of a large bank that fields analysts numbering in the tens of thousands. Each might be working on issues involving different customers and other issues. Such a scale could indeed result in many billions of nodes and relationships rather quickly. In this case, no, the query count will not settle down over time.

The totality of very many knowledge workers exploring different parts of the cube as demonstrated by the bank example above is an extreme—tens of thousands of analysts issuing dozens of queries for tens of thousands of problems. However, I do believe this will not be an extreme case for long.

A major component of the thesis of this book is that the number of BI consumers will substantially expand as more non-analyst knowledge workers (those without "analyst" or "manager" in their titles) become BI consumers. Most of the queries from these knowledge worker BI consumers would be less likely to be of widespread interest. For example, a BI consumer examining shelf space at a specific supermarket probably has less widespread value than queries from an analyst working at a higher-level of detail–for example, by county, as opposed to a single store.

This short discussion isn't itself a tactic for pruning, but just a consideration of what an outlier case might look like. If knowledge workers as BI consumers do grow significantly, this situation will become less and less of an case.

Compelling Statistics Model

We could drop all insights of a QueryDef (keep the QueryDef node itself and its metadata relationships), except for the Standard Statistics model with "interesting" values. Doing this, we remove very many nodes and relationships from the EKG. But we could archive the embedding of the insight node's description to the vector database along with the QueryDef ID as a secondary search of old memories.

But what is "interesting"? Both narrow and wide standard deviations are interesting. A high skew or a classic Gaussian distribution is interesting. Inflection points are interesting, but since inflection points are events, they could be stored in the Event Ensemble.

The rules for what constitutes "interesting" need to be worked out. What will make this an easier task is if we can have the option of inexpensively re-querying what we dropped if we find that our definition of interesting happened to be wrong. Further, in the extreme, even if we drop all models keeping just the QueryDef node, its mere presence means there was something of interest there. And, with optimized OLAP, we have a way to recover that information very quickly.

Time to Live

One commonly used method in data pruning is applying a "Time to Live" (TTL—distinguish the lower-case ttl of semantic web Turtle format) policy. The concept of TTL is akin to asking, "How long should this data remain active?" Or, "When is this data irrelevant?" TTL can be as straightforward as a preset expiration time. For instance, if a QueryDef is added on January 1, 2024, with a TTL of 40 days, it would be scheduled for archiving or deletion around February 9, 2024.

However, a more sophisticated approach to TTL can greatly enhance its effectiveness. Ideally, the TTL should reset each time the same query is issued. During the pruning process, the TTL for each QueryDef set to expire is re-evaluated against the ObjectLog for the last access date. If recent access to this QueryDef is recorded, the TTL is refreshed, extending the data's lifespan.

Moreover, TTL can be dynamic rather than a fixed value. It can be calculated based on certain performance metrics, such as deviation from a norm. For example, consider a scenario where the base TTL is 40 days, and we have established a z-score threshold for outliers at 3.1. If a QueryDef has a z-score of 3.5, it significantly exceeds this threshold, indicating higher noteworthiness–possible importance or relevance.

In such cases, the TTL could be extended proportionally to how much the z-score surpasses the threshold. A possible formula for this could be:

$$TTL = [Base\ TTL] + (Extra\ Days \times ([Outlier\ Z\text{-}Score] - [Threshold\ Z\text{-}Score]))$$

Where:

- Base TTL is the standard duration (e.g., 40 days).

- Extra Days is a constant determining how many additional days are added per unit of z-score above the threshold.

- Threshold Z-Score is the actual z-score of the QueryDef.

- Threshold Z-Score is the z-score threshold for considering a QueryDef an outlier (e.g., 3.1).

This formula allows the TTL to adjust dynamically, reflecting the relative importance of data based on its deviation from typical patterns, thereby ensuring more efficient and relevant data management.

AI Pruning

What if AI determined what's important or helped with the task of determining what "interesting" means? For example, from the strategy map, it can determine or at least score what's important to keep. This is a topic that can become quite big, so it's for another book.

Minimal Relationship Options

Toward the goal of mitigating the size of the EKG, we could simply choose options that require fewer graph objects, even though that might sacrifice query performance or depth of insight.

Turning off Features

While turning off features isn't the same as pruning, turning off features is a way to reduce the size of the EKG. As LLMs grow in intellectual strength and RAG methodologies increase in sophistication, some information in the EKG might become redundant (meaning, the AIs take up more and more of the inference burden). But remember that:

- A strong reason for the EKG is that it can serve not just as way to capture the interests of BI analysts, but for LLMs, it is a cache of updated knowledge and reference beyond the LLMs training data.

- The EKG is like our representatives of the "Human Party" in a Congress where the "AI Party" is gaining more and more seats.

The EKG should prioritize comprehensibility to humans first, not the LLMs. Eventually, LLMs, in one form or another, will figure out how to build something akin to a KG to serve as cache that would best serve a LLM—meaning, it probably will be incomprehensible to humans (as is the neural network that is the LLM). The first topic of "Future Steps" is a discussion of fine-tuning EKG information directly into an LLM.

With varying use cases and the strength of the LLMs, it's possible to exclude some of the features of the BI components of the EKG. For example, we may decide we don't need certain model types, such as Inflection Points and Outliers, which generate many Tuple objects and relationships.

Again, if we later decide we'd like to include things we turned off, we should at least have retained the query text—as discussed in "Cloud File Storage". In a worse-case scenario, we can run the queries and save the information that was previously turned off.

QueryDef Identifiers

Throughout the book, a QueryDef's unique ID is defined by a hash of its unique SQL (and data source), captured character for character, verbatim. This is because it's possible that identical dataframes could be returned by differing SQL. That's possible even if the two SQL are parsed to into graphs we could compare for equivalence. For instance, two queries might produce identical results because one is filtering out a non-existent city.

I chose this method due to the complexities of various SQL dialects, the diverse ways BI tools construct SQL, and the possibility of non-SQL queries. At the moment, I'm afraid that the logic to test the equivalence of SQL query graphs against all others is too compute-intense (at the scale we're discussing).

One solution I thought about was converting the SQL to vector embeddings and finding very close equivalents. But there is still too much room for error. So this is the way it is for this edition of the book (and the samples in the GitHub directory).

Conditional Probability Table

The TCW is a web of a few types of probabilities and correlations. Both serve different purposes, but perhaps we don't require both. For example, conditional probabilities could just be turned off, using just the network of Pearson and/or Spearman correlations. Or vice versa—turn off Pearson correlations and use only conditional probabilities. However, a middle option is using a conditional probability table (CPT). This is akin to "normalizing" a graph. What would be a web of relationships in a graph could be converted into a table and stored as a blob in the EKG or offloaded to storage. We trade off many nodes and relationships in the graph, off-loading some form of Bayesian capability in a more compact form for less straightforward Bayesian queries. This was explained back in Figure 181 and Figure 182.

What would be lost is the ability to query for chains of probabilities directly. With the conditional probabilities in the EKG, we could conceivably issue a single, albeit messy, Cypher query. Instead, we would break up the process into a set of RAG steps at query time performing multi-database queries:

1. The RAG process finds the CPT in cloud storage matching the columns forming "Event A" and the column forming "Event B."
2. We find the row of that CPT matching the columns of Event A and Event B.
3. Return the probability of Event B given the members comprising Event A.

For example, looking back at Figure 182, given the weather is sunny and the temperature is hot, the probability of playing golf is 0.90.

Offloading to a Relational Database

The DC, ISG, and TCW are designed to a schema, shown earlier in Figure 42. That is, for the:

- DC–The Server, database, table, column nodes.
- ISG/TCW - QueryDef, Models, ModelItem, Set, Tuple nodes.

Enforcing such schemas on a graph kind of defeats the "open schema" benefit of graph databases. Graph databases are valued for their flexibility in handling semi-structured or unstructured data, allowing for the dynamic addition of new data types without requiring a rigid schema. This flexibility is a significant advantage, enabling rapid adaptation to changing data needs.

However, there is also an advantage to having an abstract schema such as those applied to the DC and ISG/TCW. An abstract schema provides a level of structure and consistency, which can simplify data integration, querying, and analysis. It allows for a more organized approach to data management while still leveraging the inherent flexibility of graph databases.

The KG part of the EKG is not bound to such a schema, although it is recommended to name resources using public ontologies, such as schema.org. This approach leverages the flexibility of graph databases while maintaining some consistency through widely recognized ontologies.

As for the ISG/TCW, since QueryDefs and Tuples can be recomputed and they have a schema, offloading them to a relational database is very plausible. Relational databases excel at handling structured data and can efficiently manage the schema-defined elements of ISG/TCW, providing a robust environment for recomputation and storage.

Off-Loading to a LLM

Another option for off-loading to a database is to offload ISG/TCW objects to a LLM. I later discuss assimilating the ISG/TCW directly into an LLM as a Future Step ("Fine-Tuning LLMs with BI Data"). There are trade-offs, which I discuss in that section. For the purposes of this topic, that assimilation will drastically reduce the size of the EKG.

Security

The problem with integrating data is that the data must carry over the security requirements from its source at every step. This is tricky and we need to be highly cognizant of those requirements. Fortunately, the variety of databases employed in the AEI have security as a first-class concern.

The top-level method for securing AEI is a benefit of BI as the spearhead of the data. One of the advantages of highly-curated BI is that security concerns are a first-class part of being highly-curated. For example, OLAP cube platforms have sophisticated security mechanisms that dive all the way to "cell-level" access. Therefore, the ISG/TCW depends primarily on the BI data sources for enforcing who gets to add what and who gets to see those nodes. Neo4j would still need to enforce viewing of the nodes, so it would ideally be based on the BI sources.

In BI, PII hardly ever has any analytical value. A Social Security Number or phone number used to hold information on geographical origin, but not anymore. A street address usually doesn't help much unless we're studying the movements of people—but that's usually more of an operational process (tracking down someone for whatever reason might involve visiting past residences). The real names of people today don't hold much analytical value. Of course, names could be good hints of ethnicity, nationality, gender, and sometimes even age. Again, not as much as before. Depending on the scope of the BI, names are eliminated from the BI database.

As for BI's aggregation, it is itself a powerful mechanism for obfuscation. Additionally, it's always been a BI practice to never release information where the fact count is under some threshold—I've always thought of 30 as a good place to start—any count below that isn't adequate for ML training anyway. Of course, users who would drill through to details should only be allowed to with the proper security.

The security features of data warehouses (DWs) implemented on platforms like Snowflake, Redshift, and Synapse (using the familiar dimension model) are likely well-known to readers. This section highlights the security features of less familiar database types.

Securing BI OLAP Cubes

Since I recommend BI as the spearhead of the AEI effort, I'm assuming securing of BI data is well-established. However, because OLAP cubes might not be as familiar, here is a list highlighting the security features of OLAP cubes (Kyvos and SSAS):

- Row-Level Security (RLS): Controls access to data at the row level based on user roles and groups.

- Column-Level Security (CLS): Restricts access to specific columns, with options for data and metadata restrictions.

- Data Masking: Masks sensitive data in columns, preserving original data while ensuring privacy.

- Access Control: Fine-grained access control mechanisms for users and groups.

- Monitoring and Alerts: Real-time monitoring and alerting to detect and respond to security issues promptly.

- Audit Logging: Comprehensive logging of user activities for security audits and compliance.

Securing the Graph Database

Regarding securing at the graph database level, Neo4j's Authorization features control access at granular levels, determining what authenticated users can see and do within the database. Neo4j allows for role-based access control (RBAC), enabling fine-grained permissions for users and roles, including read, write, and schema management capabilities. This is crucial for limiting access to sensitive parts of the EKG, such as the DC, or specific insights within the ISG/TCW.

User-level security:
- **Authentication:** Ensure that only authenticated users can access the Neo4j database. Implement strong authentication mechanisms, such as integrating with LDAP or using Neo4j's native users and roles.

- **Authorization:** Define and enforce user roles and permissions. Neo4j allows for role-based access control, enabling you to specify which roles can read or write to certain parts of the graph.

- **User Management:** Regularly review and manage user accounts. Remove or update access for users who no longer need it or whose role within the organization has changed.

Node-level security:
- **Property-Level Security:** Neo4j Enterprise Edition offers property-level security, allowing you to control access to specific properties within a node. This way, sensitive information can be hidden from users who do not have the necessary permissions.

- **Subgraph Access Control**: Implement access control lists (ACLs) to restrict access to specific subgraphs within your database. This allows for fine-grained control over who can see or modify certain parts of the graph.

- **Encryption:** Use encryption at rest and in transit to protect data. Neo4j supports SSL/TLS for encrypting data as it travels between the server and clients.

Securing the Data Catalog

It's important to remember that KGs should avoid containing fact-level values. KGs are about relationships, not about granular facts. Relationships are usually computations–which could involve much granular, fact-level data. The DC could contain individual members (such as stores and products with row counts in the relatively "small" range, such as thousands), but that dimensional data isn't nearly as voluminous as fact-level data. Holding dimensions numbering in the millions (e.g. customers) should be avoided-even if the customer names are obfuscated.

The values in the ISG and TCW are all highly aggregated/computed values. So, for the most part, it doesn't reveal anything directly about individuals. However, as the infamous NYC Taxi ride dataset showed, very clever folks can figure out a way to match things with other data sets. In the case of taxi rides, they correlated with photos of celebrities taken at the time of the pickup or drop off.

For attribute/column nodes of the DC, we can mark the attribute node with the property, PII, and secure it so that this value is never shown. Or at least the column is flagged as requiring special handling during queries to the EKG–meaning, the column and any information it's linked to in the ISG/TCW could be filtered out of query results. However, as mentioned before, PII (e.g., social security numbers, street addresses, credit card numbers) is typically not very valuable from a BI point of view and likely not even surfaced into the BI databases.

Drill through from the ISG and TCW to the details held in the underlying data sources is an important feature. For this, the underlying data sources from which the values were computed will handle security with their own security configuration. In other words, based on the user of the EKG, the underlying database will enforce its security as it would if it were directly queried by a user.

Securing the ISG/TCW

To further marshal security through fewer paths, the DC plays a large role. As mentioned earlier, columns could be marked as PII, in which case any requests for data through those columns could be filtered. Additionally, tables, columns, and members of the DC could be marked with the property, DoNotLoad–an indicator that any query involving those objects should not be downloaded into the ISG/TCW. So, during the process to upload to the EKG:

1. A list of QueryDefs added since the last upload is collected.
2. A list of Tables, Columns, and Members in the DC marked as DoNotLoad is assembled.
3. The list is checked against the DoNotLoadQueryDef list, and matches are removed.
4. The query elements found on the list of DoNotLoad Tables, Columns, and Members are removed.

Securing the Vector Database

While I didn't involve enterprise-class vector databases (Pinecone) in this book, vector databases do play a big part in the RAG process. Therefore, although I won't cover the details in this book, I must remind the reader that it, too, needs to be secured.

The tricky part is the vector database will include data from many different types of databases. Therefore, security might be tricky since different types of databases secure objects at different levels and angles:

- Documents (unstructured text "chunked" into pieces), each of which could be sensitive. Access to vectors transformed from documents must reflect access levels at the documents' storage.

- Query Templates–Back in the discussion of RAG, there will be vectors used to match a query template to a flexibly-worded prompt. These queries could be sensitive as they could provide hints about the database content and structure.

- Archived objects from the ISG/TCW-- These vectors are based on the node descriptions. It must match the security access of the EKG. Note that EKG objects archived as vectors could be employed in the RAG process as well as simply archived.

Another security aspect is that one of the use cases for the vector database is to funnel an infinite number of flexibly-worded prompts to a fixed list of query intents. For many users, access to the EKG could be through the list of query intents. Because each query intent is a file in file storage, they can be secured through the file storage's security mechanism, and the owners of the template will ensure the intent doesn't return inappropriate data for the user.

Securing Ourselves from the LLM

Last, but probably should have been first, securing (protecting) ourselves from the LLM. C'mon, we've all seen the Terminator movies. "AI safety" refers to the field of research and practices aimed at ensuring that artificial intelligence systems operate reliably, ethically, and without causing unintended harm. This involves designing and implementing safeguards to prevent AI from making harmful decisions, aligning AI behavior with human values, and ensuring that AI systems can be controlled and corrected as necessary. The goal is to maximize the benefits of AI while minimizing risks to individuals and society.

As we've been using a LLM (ChatGPT) in this book, it's in the context of any other Software as a Service (SaaS). We subscribe to it, connect through the Internet, and use it—just like Salesforce, ServiceNow, Microsoft 365, or Zoom.

We know that those SaaS applications collect tons of data on how we use it, down to every key click, scroll, and in some cases every sound we make. The good side is that it helps the vendors to improve the software. But we don't know what else the vendors do with that collected data. I think we're growing accustomed to it, so …

It's different, though, if the SaaS is an AI that operates in our "uncanny valley" most of the time for most of us. "Collecting tons of data on how we use it" has a different meaning for an AI SaaS than those conventional SaaS, especially for the latest generation of LLMs (ATTOW) with their million-plus token context window—which means you can throw entire project plans at it and ask it to evaluate or even improve the quality of them—overlooking something an AI can easily infer that you failed to catch.

I cannot go deep into this subject. That certainly is another book or YouTube channel—of which there are already many. What I will say is to create your private LLMs using open source tools if possible. The cost for building them has gone down by magnitudes since GPT 3 was trained. At the same time, there are also hints that there are diminishing returns for simply increasing the sheer size of the required LLM training material and the "number of parameters" of the LLM.

That means further gains in LLM performance will become more complicated than the 2020's version of simply "throwing more iron at it." Consequently, I believe your ability to create private LLMs that can compete with the best of them is much more feasible than in November 2022. However, further significant AI improvements (not just LLM improvement, but AI that's much more than the commodity product that access to LLMs has become) will involve things beyond simply bigger LLMs and more GPUs.

Chapter Twelve

Future Steps

What I've described in this book is more than a mouthful. However, there are aspects of the intelligence of a business that further make Pinocchio act like a real person. Why is it important for an enterprise to act more like a real person?

Enterprises seem disconnected from we people because their information processing isn't as smoothly-integrated as it is for us. We imbue them with many of the rights of humans as if they are real entities—we've invented the notion of a corporation. Corporations are considered "entities," mostly decoupled from any single person. It can be sued or even executed. Yet corporations cannot really fear pain, remorse, or impending death. Imagine anyone who isn't averse to any of those emotions.

It's my hope that a corporation that is more like a real person is not only a better "member of society", but also a minimally painful place for all us humans who work at them. If work were less painful, as a whole we'd be less focused on minimizing our time and energy spent at work and more time evolving the enterprise (as well as ourselves individually) to a better form. Life will be fuller that way.

As the final chapter of the book, I would like to introduce a few more enticing topics as examples of where we go from here. With the groundwork of the intelligence of a business set in this book, the following topics can be feasibly covered in follow-up books. I've already covered a few simpler topics in "Topics Punted to the Future Books ...." But these topics are deeper reaching.

Fine-Tuning LLMs with BI Data

An option exists to convert the graph-based ISG/TCW directly into text by extracting the descriptions of QueryDefs, Tuples, Correlations, and models, and then assimilating them into the training data of a LLM. This process is fine-tuning, a method where a LLM like GPT is further trained on a specific dataset to tailor its expertise to that context.

The ISG/TCW descriptions, merged with private enterprise data and general text, would be used for this fine-tuning process. This assimilates the BI data fully into a LLM, leveraging the enterprise knowledge encapsulated in the EKG to enrich the LLM's understanding of specific domain relationships and patterns.

This is unlike augmenting LLMs loosely-coupled access to the knowledge of the EKG as described in this book. The advantages of infusing the EKG data directly in a LLM include:

- Reduced need for complex iterative processing, such as Retrieval-Augmented Generation (RAG).

- Utilization of the latest AI-targeted hardware, like GPUs and soon specialized AI chips, as the EKG knowledge becomes an integral part of the LLM.

However, there are benefits to maintaining independent, loosely-coupled components, avoiding the pitfalls of monolithic structures. Maintaining independence between the LLM and the ISG/TCW with a loosely-coupled architecture offers several additional advantages:

- Flexibility in Updates and Maintenance: Keeping the LLM and EKG separate allows for more flexible updates and maintenance. Changes in one system (e.g., updating the TCW with new data or correlations) can be done independently without impacting the other, ensuring minimal downtime and disruption.

- Modularity and Scalability: Independent components offer modularity, allowing for scalable solutions. As the complexity of enterprise data grows, each system can be scaled or modified to suit specific needs without necessitating a complete overhaul of the integrated system.

- Specialization and Optimization: Separation allows each system to be optimized for its specific function. The LLM can be optimized for language processing and generation, while the EKG can be tailored to handle and analyze BI data, ensuring peak performance in both areas.

- Data Security and Privacy: Separation helps maintain better data security and privacy. Sensitive information in the EKG can be protected more effectively without the risk of exposure through the LLM, which might be more publicly accessible or used for a broader range of queries.

- Error Isolation and Risk Mitigation: In a loosely-coupled system, errors in one component are less likely to propagate to the other. This isolation reduces overall system risk and makes troubleshooting more manageable.

- Avoidance of Overfitting: Keeping the LLM separate from the EKG can prevent the LLM from overfitting to the specific patterns and biases in the EKG data, preserving its ability to generalize across diverse datasets and scenarios.

- Facilitating Continuous Learning: By maintaining separate systems, the LLM can continuously learn and evolve from a broader range of data sources beyond the EKG, maintaining its robustness and versatility.

- Compliance and Governance: Independent systems can more easily adhere to specific compliance and governance requirements, as each system can be managed according to its relevant regulatory standards.

While a LLM fully assimilating the EKG has its advantages, maintaining them as independent, loosely-coupled systems offers significant benefits in terms of flexibility, modularity, optimization, and risk management. This decoupled approach aligns with the theme of grounding the LLM in reality to avoid hallucinations–the EKG grounds the predictive LLM with deterministic knowledge.

Inference

This is an intricate topic. Even if we all access the exact same data, we mostly will interpret it differently to varying degrees. There are many reasons, but here are a few:

- Our inference techniques differ, and the "graph of relationships" in our brains, which is used to process the external data we're considering, is different due to our unique experiences and education. Our brains aren't programmed, they are trained.

- Our personalities and biases affect how much we can (or want to) be influenced by other people.

- Many of the rules we've engrained in our heads over the course of our lives are probably obsolete in various ways. Kind of the "can't teach an old dog new tricks."

While there might be some core similarities among us all in how we infer things (culture), fortunately, we all think slightly differently, especially under novel conditions. The Venn diagram of our inference is mostly overlapped, but all the parts that aren't overlapped are a plethora of every permutation of the countless unique thoughts that are the keys to solving any problem we face. None of us overlap with another in exactly the same way. This diversity of thought is one of the most extremely valuable assets of humanity.

Inference on the Semantic Web

The semantic web relies on inference technologies to process and derive meanings from the structured data defined using technologies like RDF, RDFS, and OWL. While SPARQL is the query language for the semantic web and is often compared to SQL in relational databases, it's primarily used for querying and retrieving data, not as much for inferencing. The inference capabilities in the semantic web are more associated with reasoning engines and rule languages. Here's a breakdown:

- **Reasoning Engines**—These are software systems that interpret the ontologies and data written in RDF, RDFS, and OWL, and apply logical rules to infer new knowledge. Some popular reasoning engines for the semantic web include:

    o Apache Jena: A free and open-source Java framework for building semantic web and Linked Data applications. It includes a rule-based inference engine.

    o Pellet: An open-source OWL DL reasoner in Java.

    o Hermit: An OWL reasoner, known for its conformance to OWL 2 standards.

- **Rule Languages**—Besides these reasoning engines, there are rule languages designed for the semantic web. These languages allow you to write more complex and custom rules for inferencing beyond what is possible with just OWL and SPARQL. Examples include:

    o SWRL (Semantic Web Rule Language): A language for expressing rules that can be combined with OWL ontologies. SWRL builds on a combination of OWL DL and RuleML (Rule Markup Language).

    o RIF (Rule Interchange Format): A W3C standard designed for exchanging rules among different systems, which can be used in combination with semantic web technologies.

Back in the Introduction, Version 1—SQL Server Performance Tuning Web, I wrote about a Prolog-based language I wrote named SCL (Soft-Coded Logic). Prolog and LISP were the two popular inference mechanisms many "AI winters" ago, the foundation of "expert systems". Prolog is very similar to SWRL.

Subgraphs and Paths

In the web of data and relationships that form the semantic web, understanding the role of subgraphs becomes crucial for enhanced inference. The concept of subgraphs allows us to narrow our focus, zooming into specific subsets of data for more detailed analysis.

Subgraphs represent a microcosm within the larger data universe, consisting of selected nodes and their interconnections. By isolating these subsets, we can conduct more precise inferencing on specific areas of interest, much like examining a detailed chapter of a vast book. This can be particularly beneficial in complex datasets where the sheer volume of data can muddy critical insights.

In the context of the semantic web, subgraphs can be utilized to:

- Focus on specific domains or subdomains within a larger ontology.

- Analyze relationships and patterns that might be drowned out in the broader context.

- Apply targeted inferencing rules that are more relevant to the specific data subset.

Exploring the dynamics of subgraphs not only complements the broader inferencing techniques discussed earlier, but also enhances our ability to derive meaningful and actionable insights from complex, interrelated data. As we take a high-level swim into subgraphs, we uncover the nuances of data relationships and their impact on inference, providing a richer, more granular understanding of the data landscape.

In graph theory, the concepts of subgraphs, paths, and more complex structures between nodes are well-defined, each with its unique characteristics:

- **Subgraph**–A subgraph is a graph formed from a subset of the vertices (nodes) and edges (relationships) of a larger graph. It retains the connections that existed in the original graph among the selected vertices. A subgraph can include any number of nodes and their relationships as long as they are part of the original graph. There are no restrictions on the number of components, connectivity, or path length within a subgraph.

- **Path**–A path in a graph is a sequence of edges that connects a sequence of distinct vertices. A path is defined between two nodes, but it can traverse through any number of intermediate nodes. The key characteristic of a path is that it does not visit the same node more than once.

- **Walk, Trail, and Circuit**–These are related concepts that extend the idea of a path:
    - Walk: A walk is a sequence of vertices and edges where vertices (and hence edges) can be repeated.
    - Trail: A trail is a walk in which all edges are distinct, but nodes might repeat.
    - Circuit or Cycle: This is a path or trail that starts and ends at the same vertex.

When you talk about "more than two nodes and their connections," this can fit into several categories depending on the specifics:

- If it's a sequence of nodes connected by edges without repetition, it's a path.
- If it includes all nodes and edges of a particular part of the graph, it's a subgraph.
- If it allows for repeating nodes or edges, it might be a walk or a trail.

Each of these structures is defined by the properties of the nodes and edges it includes, rather than by the number of nodes. The difference lies in how these nodes and edges are connected and whether they allow for repetition.

The caveat with thinking about subgraphs is the reality that nothing lives in a vacuum. The great attraction of a KG is that it innately is about holistic knowledge—the ability to create a database of fully-linked information. But principles of divide and conquer and reductionist science definitely does hold valuable wisdom.

Metrics at Scale

One of the big problems in BI and BPfM has been the management of metrics. The population of enterprise metrics is not just what is seemingly relatively few measures derived from fact tables and published in dashboards, internal reports, tax filings, and quarterly earnings reports. There can be many thousands of metrics–maybe tens of thousands counting those practiced by knowledge workers, but not documented anywhere.

Every domain consists of a fairly large number of recommended KPIs. For example, KPI.org and other such organizations point to resources that list hundreds of KPIs across various industries and functional areas. These KPIs cover a wide range of business domains and processes, including finance, HR, IT, marketing, sales, operations, and more, providing a comprehensive resource for organizations seeking to measure and improve their performance.

I've been in situations where current metrics numbered in the tens of thousands across the enterprise. In fairness, it wasn't that there were really that many KPIs. Much of the large number was due to slicing KPIs down to the level of salesperson, district, and line of business. It was something like 200 KPIs by 1000 salespersons, 100 districts, and about 20 lines of business. With existing, relevant combinations, there were about 50,000.

Those were each a tracked KPI, each under the responsibility of someone. But the magnitude of management and maintenance is exacerbated by:

1. Each KPI actually consists of at least four calculations: Value, Trend, Status, and Target.

2. Preserving the history of KPIs. I believe KPIs should evolve along with changes to execution—but we need to preserve the history of the formulas so we have context about the past so we have a better idea of why we made what today might seem like a silly decision. Therefore, we saved a history of the KPI formulas.

3. KPIs could be further broken down in very different ways suitable for the unique needs of unique departments. As a tuple of KPI and entity, each is like a separate metric.

4. I've recommended having multiple status definitions for a KPI to service many points of view of what good, OK, and bad mean. I believe "status" to be a highly subjective value.

Further, as KPIs are set and time moves on, eventually, we forget which are really valuable. Each performance management cycle results in at least a partial replacement of KPIs reflecting new tactics and strategies. Simply applying the same KPIs quarter to quarter is the BPfM version of "That's the way it's always been done"—a terrible reason to do something.

We see that with reports, too. Most enterprises I've worked with count hundreds of reports run on a regular basis. Those hundreds of reports were developed over years or decades by people long gone, for users and purposes also long gone. Many are really almost the same reports with different parameters or slightly different columns. We really don't know who actually uses them and how they are used, so we're afraid to sunset them.

In the vein of "Excel Hell," I tried to think of an equally catchy term for these feral formulas in these zombie reports … hey, that's pretty good. Let's go with "feral formulas" for now!

Adding to the plethora of calculations contributed by the enterprise's performance management KPIs are calculations every analyst is able to create in their BI Visualization tool as a "custom measure."

Typically, these custom measures are private to the BI analyst until the BI workbook (.pbix file for PowerBI, .twbx file for Tableau) is published to a wider audience. From there, the BI workbook could be downloaded by others, who will, in turn, make their own modifications. The variants of the custom measure then propagates throughout like an invasive species, all with unintended consequences.

In fact, one of the benefits of the ISG/TCW is to capture at least a hint of these custom measures from the query submitted to the BI data source from the BI visualization tool. The query is parsed into elements and mapped to a "Formula" node, as discussed in the "Query Functions" topic. However, this isn't helpful if the analyst is merging data from known BI data sources with data not known by IT (meaning, it doesn't appear in the DC, the so-called "shadow IT").

These problems can be addressed with an EKG, which could centralize, rationalize, and provide context to the metrics and calculations used across various business functions—in the versatile manner that is characteristic of a KG. It might be more easily said than done. But the main idea of centralizing information that can be used for inference is the same path nature took when centralized brains began developing in critters.

Where Does Data Science and Machine Learning Fit In?

In the evolving landscape of BI and its interplay with rapidly burgeoning AI, I haven't discussed how DS/ML and MLOps (Machine Learning Operations) fit in extensively enough. How could DS/ML not fit into a book with this title?

While BI focuses on leveraging highly-curated data to inform business decisions and dashboards in a data-driven environment, DS/ML delves wider and deeper, exploring unknown space, and employing complex algorithms and models to unearth insights and predict future trends. This complexity does not overshadow the ultimate objective shared by both fields, which is to enhance business performance, whether through process optimization, new strategies, or the identification of untapped markets.

Given the comprehensive scope of this book, which is dedicated to the intricacies of BI in a rapidly evolving, progressively AI-dominated world, an in-depth exploration of DS/ML and its multifaceted contributions will be reserved for a future volume. For now, I'd like to make a few high-level points on this topic.

BI data, the cornerstone upon which critical business decisions are made, also serves as a vital asset for data scientists. It provides high-quality data sources for the development of predictive models, which in turn are new data products in their own right. Think about it. An ML model is in essence a virtual data table, the "program" that generates a row that maps each combination of input values to an output value. These products, much like any other entity within the data ecosystem, should be governed by the principles of a data mesh, ensuring proper integration within the broader data catalog of the EKG.

Yet, the journey of data science within the enterprise extends beyond the realm of production-ready data. The exploratory datasets, the trial models, and the hypotheses in testing—all of which may not see immediate application—are nonetheless integral to the fabric of the EKG. They represent the burgeoning knowledge and potential insights into the business, akin to an individual's pursuit of education and skill development for future endeavors.

The functional nature of ML models, characterized by their inputs and outputs, reveals a fascinating dynamic within the EKG. Inputs, often tied to specific elements within the data catalog, transform through these models to produce outputs, which in themselves can become inputs for subsequent analytical processes. The output of virtually all ML models is a potential input to another ML model.

This interconnectivity not only exemplifies the complexity inherent in data science but also underscores the potential for these functions to be cataloged and managed within the EKG. Serialized in formats, such as pickle files and stored in cloud infrastructure, these models are poised for seamless integration and reuse across the enterprise.

Moreover, the evolution from BI analyst to data scientist, and potentially to AI engineer, mirrors the progressive deepening of expertise and the broadening of the analytical landscape. Data scientists and those involved in ML operations—or ML operations engineers—embody a crucial nexus in this continuum. Their work, which spans from the creation of predictive models to the deployment and maintenance of AI systems, is indicative of the overlapping skill sets and shared goals that unify BI, data science, and AI engineering.

As we navigate the confluence of these disciplines, it becomes evident that the EKG is not merely a repository of data but a dynamic, living entity that captures the necessarily evolving intelligence of the business. Through the lens of the EKG, the collaborative and iterative endeavors of BI analysts, data scientists, and AI engineers contribute to a holistic understanding of the enterprise, driving innovation and fostering a culture of informed decision-making and strategic foresight.

Investment and Sacrifice

We'll end this book with an overview of a fun topic. The topic is how to emulate in BI systems, our human ability to achieve our goals by taking creative calculated risks and/or doing things we really don't want to do. I believe that ability is at the heart of our ingenuity.

What I think of as ingenuity is beyond the resourcefulness required to craft a meal from random foods in a refrigerator and cupboards. The predictions and categorizations of most ML are like that, mining for things from just the data provided to it by data scientists. ML generally doesn't perform outside-of-the-box thinking.

With our symbolic thinking, we can play limited what-if in our heads, through iterations of leaping from one set of states to another set of states. But for most of us, most of the time, we don't include things that aren't in our refrigerator or cupboard. We're trained to be pragmatic—for example, "Buying IBM".

But some of us are whackos who play real what-if, tossing into the mix things that don't belong. Or we wonder what will happen if we at least temporarily disregard the margin for error or even push something beyond its "known limits".

Ironically, this topic is on some dimensions out of place for this book:

- It doesn't really involve the ISG and TCW. But it is the next step for the KPI Strategy Map, a cousin of the TCW, that I covered earlier.

- It doesn't really incorporate LLMs. But it does incorporate genetic algorithms.

This idea involving the KPI Strategy Map leverages an enterprise's KPI framework and BI data sources to explore combinations of measure values that might lead towards a desired state—without side effects beyond some threshold of tolerance. For example, we don't want to push everyone so hard to meet a target that they all end up with project PTSD ... as I had suffered on a few occasions.

We've all noticed from time to time that we're asked to focus on the clear and present problem at hand. We're asked to focus on the short-term goals that compound the interest of technical debt. Instead, occasionally, we should plan with a sense of delayed gratification, not short-term reward. I addressed this back when discussing "gaming the KPIs."

I spent the entire Holiday season of 2008 working through this idea as an SSAS-based proof of concept, so it's more than I can cover in this mini topic. I only intend to cover enough to get the idea across. This will be a major topic of a future volume.

As it is for the ISG and TCW, a highlight of this topic is that it is a situation where optimized cubes could play a heroic role. However, I need to mention that this technique utilized SSAS's "write-back" capability, which is not currently available in Kyvos. In a future volume, I will present a solution.

That is, it takes advantage of the ability of optimized cubes to service a large number of BI queries, across a wide expanse of cubespace, in a highly-performant and highly-concurrent manner. This situation involves a genetic algorithm, which means there are very many iterations of calculations from many Bi queries.

No Pain, No Gain

Our human ingenuity shoots far beyond simply recognizing the next move based on where we're at. Our responses to problems are much savvier. We know how to invest resources and effort, endure pain, and maybe even tune out warning signals as we strive towards a goal.

We place ourselves in deficits knowing (hoping) the pain will be temporary and we'll come out ahead. This can be as mundane as sacrificing a bite of food using it as bait to catch a big fish. It can be as severe as the many significantly painful side effects from cancer treatment to cure a life-threatening cancer.

Investment and sacrifice are even more complex than logical inference. At each step, we need to assess what we can sacrifice, whether what we're willing to sacrifice will be consumed or wasted, and whether we can bear it. But reaching goals is mostly a multi-step process. Each successful step places us to a state from which it's possible to leap to the next state. Along the way, we need to make one or more investments to get to the next step. This is like paying a toll at each bridge.

The step-wise nature of achieving a goal and the investments of resources (energy) at each step is reminiscent of a KPI Strategy Map. Figure 202 shows a high-level overview of the idea:

1. There is a set of KPIs. The left three are like three KPI statuses. These are part of the Strategy Map.

2. Each of those KPIs has a KPI status formula. The formula computes to a status value from 0 to 1 or -1 to 1.

3. These are data elements involved in the KPI status formulas. We'll play what-if with the value of these elements, in ranges that exceed comfort.

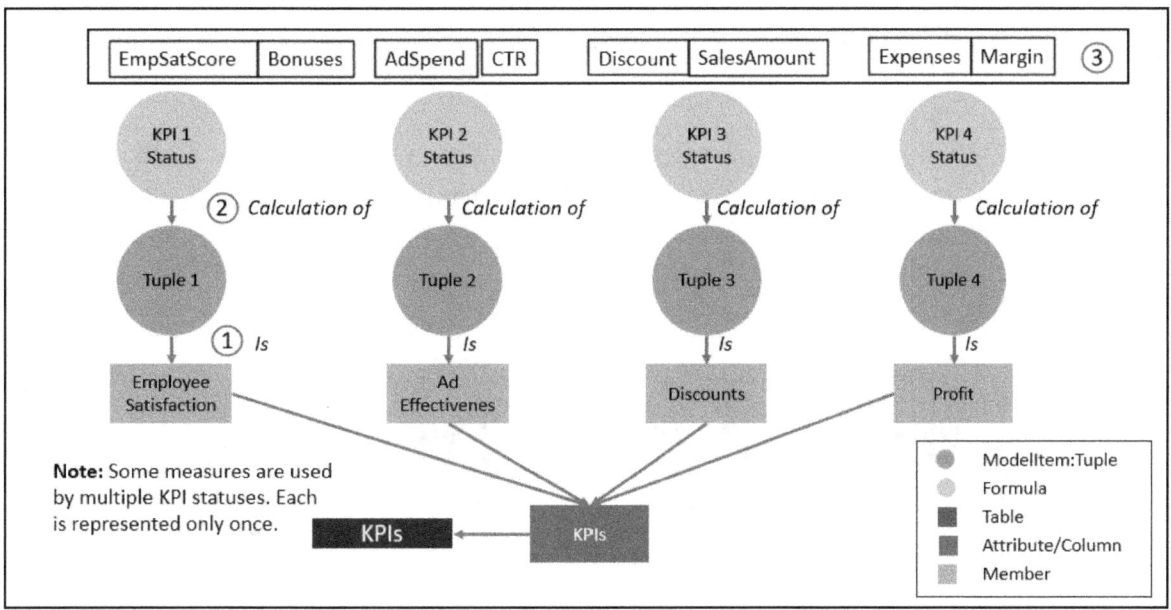

Figure 202: Solutions to Profit as implemented in the EKG.

For this to work well, the elements comprising the KPI status formulas should be shared by multiple formulas. For example, SalesAmount element is probably involved in the Discounts, Profit, and AdEffectiveness KPIs.

Levels of Pain

The notion of sacrifice is reflected in a modification to how KPI statuses are interpreted. For this algorithm, we need to redefine the traditional KPI status value. That value usually ranges from 0 through 1 where 0 is bad and 1 is good. Everything in between are shades of badness or goodness, depending on if you're a half-empty or half-full type of person. However, on BI dashboards, we don't generally see these raw values. Instead, we see a state. For example, instead we might have a red traffic light for bad, a yellow traffic light for warning, and a green traffic light for good.

Another example of a status is the level of physical pain we're experiencing. It isn't a simple continuum of values. Think of the pain scale or pain chart you might have seen at your doctor's office. It's a tool used in medical settings to help patients communicate the intensity of their pain to healthcare providers. The scale typically ranges from 0 to 10, with 0 representing no pain and 10 representing the worst possible pain. But it's not just a dial like the volume knob of your stereo. The scale may include descriptors or facial expressions to help patients quantify their pain levels. For example:

- 0—No pain.
- 1-3—Mild pain, manageable, and doesn't interfere much with daily activities.
- 4-6—Moderate pain, interferes significantly with daily activities.
- 7-9—Severe pain, very debilitating and affecting quality of life.
- 10—Worst possible pain, often incapacitating.

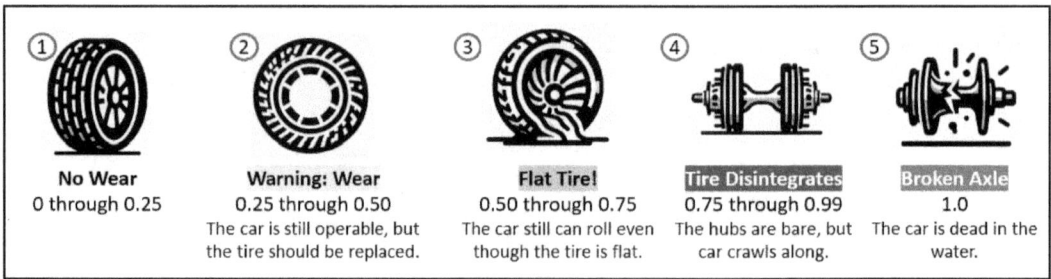

Figure 203: Levels of pain.

Figure 203 is a graphic example of the levels of pain. This example is of tires, but not simply the state of the tire (flat, bald, filled, etc.). Instead, we set the pain levels with consideration to the business function of the tire. The tire facilitates the ability for a car to roll along the road.

1. There is no pain. The tire is fine and the car is rolling along.

2. The tire is showing enough wear such that we should pay attention and proactively install new tires.

3. The tire is flat. But remember, this is about how well the tire serves the car. In reality, the car can still roll. The tire is in need of repair.

4. After rolling down the highly on a flat tire, the tire disintegrates off the hub! But, it can still sort of roll even though sparks are flying! Think about the movie, the Terminator, when he was down to bare metal, just a head and upper torso,

but still relentlessly going after Sarah Conner. At this point, the car needs to be in the car equivalent of ICU.

5. The axle snaps after all that rough riding on bare metal. The car cannot move at all.

Additionally, I believe a KPI should allow for more than one method for determining status. Status, good/OK/bad/terrible is a subjective thing. What is good for a particular department might be terrible for a team or individual. For example, a great response from a marketing campaign means very long days for someone to follow-up with a personal call. So, I'm suggesting that a KPI would have a status for both.

Running the Process

Figure 204 is a high-level diagram of what happens when considering four KPIs (Employee Satisfaction, Ad Effectiveness, Discounts, and Profit):

1. The data elements from the status formulas of the selected KPIs is collected. Min and Max values are, by default, the lowest and highest values in the database. However, the user should set the values beyond what has been seen. Exploring beyond what we've experienced plays a role in thinking outside the box.

2. The max pain level and weights are assigned to KPI statuses. The Max Pain is the maximum level of pain we're willing to endure. For example, we might be OK with a little bit of pain for Profit or willing to accept a lot of pain for AdEffectiveness.

3. The Max Pain for Profit is set at 0, which means we don't want any pain. This signals good Profit to be the state we're looking to achieve.

4. The genetic algorithm spits out various sets of values. It is a Monte Carlo algorithm that starts with random values for each data element, within the specified min/max values.

5. Each vector of element values is passed, in parallel, to a function that runs the KPI statuses. Notice how these vectors resemble genes.

6. This is a function that has loaded the KPI status formulas of the KPIs selected in item 2, and will process the functions with a vector of values as input. As I mentioned earlier, the SSAS solution I wrote back in 2008 utilized its "write-back" feature. That means I took the hypothetical values for each element (items 4 and 5) and updated the OLAP cube with those values. Essentially, I'm telling the OLAP cube to pretend these are the values of the data elements. With these "pretend values" for each data element, we'll see how they affect the KPI statuses.

7. The output will be the vector of calculated status of each KPI.

8. This vector of KPI statuses results in a Profit status of 0.0. This means, this vector of values represents a plausible solution–one with no Profit pain.

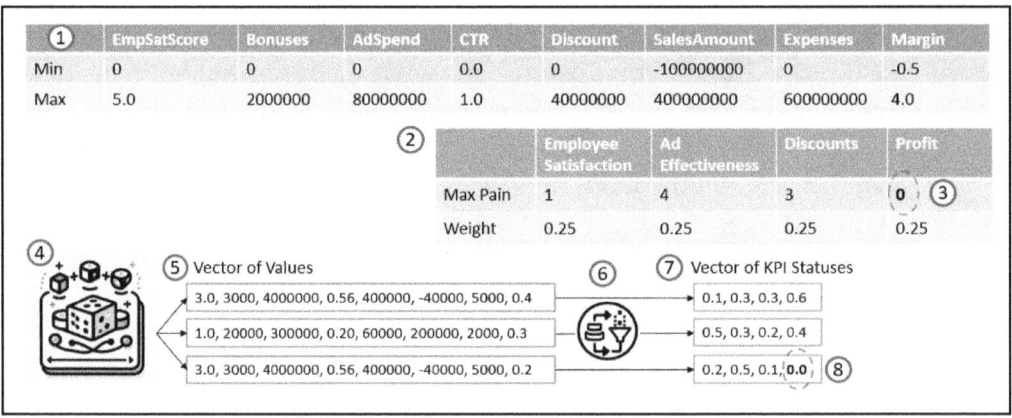

Figure 204: The Monte Carlo process.

The Min and Max values set in item 1 should be less than the least we think we can tolerate and more than in our wildest dreams, respectively. (Remember the adage, "You're stronger than you think.") This enables us to explore options outside of the box. Even if the value might be impractical or thought to be impossible, we might find out that is the solution to a problem that is unsolvable within current parameters–and so we know we need to invent a way to make that possible–like cooling systems in a car to keep the car from overheating.

Although I mentioned earlier that optimized OLAP plays a heroic role, the assessment of the KPI status vectors (item 7 in Figure 204) doesn't involve BI queries. Rather, when good candidate vectors do appear (item 8 in Figure 204), we can query the BI data to validate that this actually might happen. We can run a query to retrieve all measures, find the similarity cosine and see how close it is to the vector of values.

Conclusion to Investment and Sacrifice

The concept of "Investment and Sacrifice" in the realm of BI systems is a key ingredient for the formulation of novel solutions to novel problems—the forte of the human species. It mirrors our human capacity to weigh risks and rewards, encouraging a thoughtful balance between enduring challenges and pursuing success. This approach, especially when integrated with tools like KPI Strategy Maps and genetic algorithms, offers a practical framework for organizations to navigate complex decisions.

By blending traditional BI techniques with insights into human decision-making, we can create systems that are not only more effective but also more attuned to the realities and nuances of business strategy. This method recognizes the importance of every decision's impact, emphasizing the careful consideration of each step towards achieving a goal.

This concept is a step forward in making BI systems more accessible and relatable, bridging the gap between data-driven logic and human intuition. It's an uplifting reminder of how technology, when thoughtfully applied, can enhance our natural abilities and lead to more informed and balanced business decisions.

Conclusion

Well, that's our story. Figure 205 illustrates how all the pieces fit together, coalescing into a framework for Augmented Enterprise Intelligence. We can see the Enterprise Knowledge Graph (EKG) is the capstone of the framework. We see its three primary inputs of:

1. **Data Catalog**—Linking the two hemispheres of OLAP and OLTP.

2. **Business Intelligence**—A light attempt at a "digital twin" (ISG and TCW) of the business problems faced by a growing army of enterprise analysts.

3. **Ontologies**--The domain-level encodings of knowledge authored by the SMEs of the business processes.

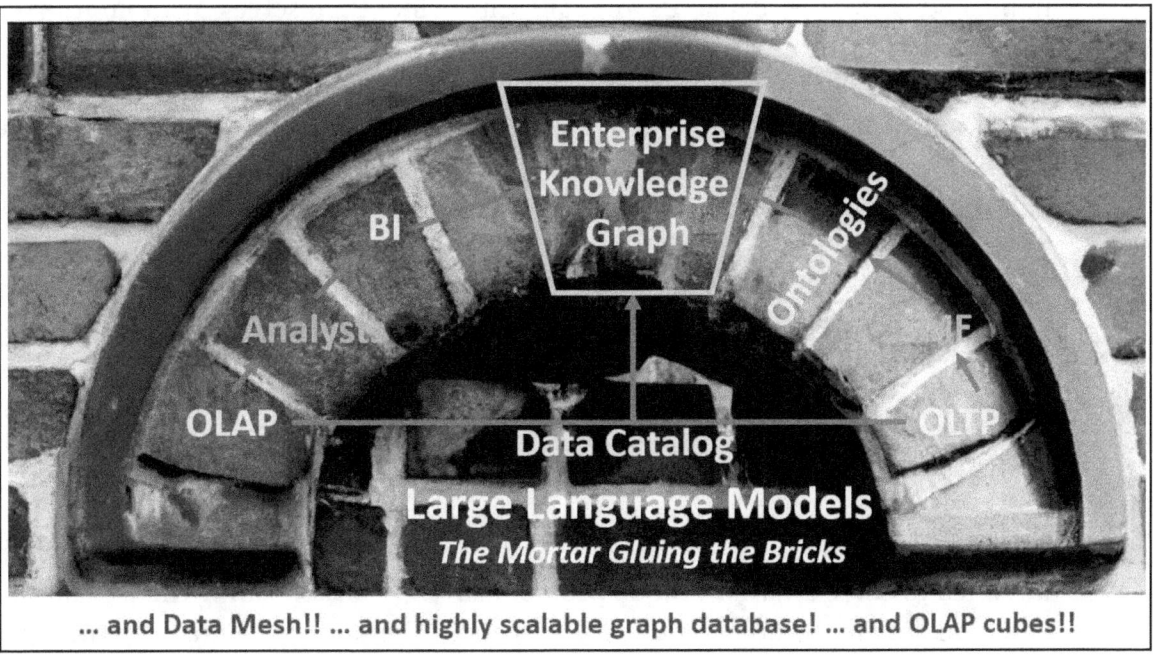

Figure 205 - This is how all of the pieces fit together into an Augmented Enterprise Intelligence.

The framework I presented is a subtle push towards, counter-intuitively, minimizing the application of AI. While many of my customers and colleagues are eager to capitalize on the AI gold rush, a few remain skeptical, waiting to see what pans out after the hype simmers down. There's something about jumping all-in on AI that vaguely reminds me of digging your own grave, while wait-and-see vaguely reminds me being late for the bus and watching your friends go off the summer camp.

The best way to use AI, at least for now, is the middle ground of:

1. Using AI as a precocious junior advisor, junior coder, junior writer, and junior researcher.

2. Remembering the power of information—why data security is so important, why it's good that people can't (yet) read minds, why we're made to sign NDAs, and why Texas hold'em is the most intriguing game.

In today's information age, a paradox has arisen. While people have access to more and more data, our capacity to process it **thoughtfully** remains limited. Many individuals, inundated with the demands of daily life, find themselves without the cognitive bandwidth to critically evaluate and make sense of the deluge of information. To mitigate the information overload, we outsource the mental processing to experts, who are perceived to have superior understanding in some field and assume by default they prioritize your well-being above all others. However, as with everything that involves fallible people, this presumption may not always hold true.

Even if the experts provide valid information, chances are the strategic insights are packaged goods being taught to everyone. There might be some customized work around the fringes, but the meat is mostly the same. There is a difference between eating tomatoes because you've seen others eat them and the art of the eternal battles between predator and prey. Both are about information, but the former is about cooperation, the latter is about competition, the judicious use of information.

The first thing a customer usually asks me after I present a custom-engineered idea intended to solve a rather unique problem is, "Who else is doing this?" Valuing an idea based on how many others are doing it is about the same as telling everyone in town of the gold mine you just found.

We all need consultants. To paraphrase Peter Block ("Flawless Consulting"), in reality we are all consultants. Learn from the experts, but strategize privately—it's more survival of the cleverest than the smartest.

A well-constructed enterprise knowledge graph enables us to think in systems, not just simple cause and effect. For example, the digital realm provides a fertile ground for narratives of all shades fitting whatever the desired outcome. Given the vastness of available data, it is feasible to construct multiple, sometimes contradictory, narratives from the same set of information—generating even more noise, synthetic noise.

This phenomenon is not always driven by an intent to mislead; it often emerges as a side effect of sheer information overload. Information overload can be so intellectually debilitating that in some cases, overwhelming audiences with a barrage of data can be a deliberate strategy, clouding judgment and impeding the formation of coherent conclusions.

Herein lies the value of the AEI, constructed from all those nifty parts shown in Figure 205. Its core strength lies in its ability facilitate the distillation and presentation of data in an objective and multi-faceted manner, cutting through the noise and offering clear insights—BI on steroids.

While the analytics processes presents challenges in data interpretation and decision-making, structures like the EKG, supported by TCW, ISG, and other structures that will be introduced in future volumes, offer promising solutions. They help businesses navigate the intricate labyrinth of information, ensuring decisions are informed, objective, and come with the ability to test whether things still work well when we put the pieces together.

APPENDIX

Ontologies and Taxonomies in OOP Terms

For readers who happen to be proficient with object-oriented programming, I offer a take on understanding ontologies from that point of view.

Ontologies share a conceptual similarity with object-oriented programming (OOP). In OOP, the world is modeled using objects that have attributes (data fields or properties) and behaviors (methods). Similarly, an ontology models a domain by defining a set of concepts or classes, their properties, and the relationships between them.

Classes in an ontology are like classes in OOP—they represent a set of entities with common characteristics. For instance, in an ontology for a dental clinic, the class Dentist might have properties such as Name and Specialization. This is analogous to an OOP class defining objects with attributes. Moreover, the relationships in ontologies, like "has a" or "is a," are akin to associations in OOP, such as composition or inheritance. The "is a" relationship represents a hierarchical link similar to subclassing in OOP, where a subclass inherits attributes and behaviors from a parent class.

Taxonomies within ontologies represent this hierarchical structure explicitly, similar to an inheritance tree in OOP, but they focus on the "is a" relationship exclusively. For example, in a taxonomy, an Orthodontist is a type of Dentist, which parallels how a subclass is a specialized version of its superclass in OOP. Both taxonomies and OOP inheritance hierarchies provide a means to organize knowledge in a way that supports abstraction (generalization) and specificity (specialization).

Just as OOP can create templates (classes) that can be instantiated as objects with specific values for their attributes, ontologies define templates (classes and properties) that can be instantiated as individual entities or nodes in a knowledge graph. These individual entities can have relationships that instantiate the general relationships defined in the ontology, forming a network of interconnected data representing specific instances within the domain.

Glossary

agent—Related to complexity, it's anything with a mind of its own. However, in the world of AI, an agent refers to an autonomous entity which observes through sensors and acts upon an environment using actuators (i.e., it is an AI system that interacts with its environment). In computer science, these AI agents can range from simple, rule-based algorithms to advanced, self-learning systems capable of intelligent decision-making and problem-solving, often designed to perform tasks in a manner similar to how a human agent would.

agentic AI—Refers to artificial intelligence systems designed to autonomously pursue complex goals and workflows with limited direct human supervision. These systems exhibit autonomous decision-making, planning, and adaptive execution to complete multi-step processes. Agentic AI operates independently, learns from its environment, and can make decisions without explicit programming, resembling a form of intelligent agency.

AGI (artificial general intelligence)–The hypothetical ability of an AI system to understand, learn, and apply knowledge across a wide range of tasks at a level comparable to human intelligence.

ASI (artificial superintelligence) – A form of AI that surpasses human intelligence in all aspects, including creativity and problem-solving. ASI represents intelligence far beyond human capabilities, capable of autonomous self-improvement and executing any intellectual task more effectively than humans.

artificial intelligence (AI)—Technology that mimics cognitive functions to perform tasks.

attribute–A property or characteristic of a dimension that can be used to filter or group data, such as 'Month' in the time dimension.

ATTOW—"... at the time of writing ..." A book on LLMs in 2023 when the AI landscape is changing by the day, I find myself saying this a lot in this book.

augmented enterprise intelligence (AEI)–A concept that combines the cognitive and collaborative abilities of human intelligence with the computational power of artificial intelligence (AI) systems and other major components of an enterprise analytics platform. AEI focuses on enhancing the innate understanding and context-awareness that business professionals have by leveraging AI's ability to quickly process and analyze large volumes of data. The goal of AEI is not to replace human creativity or expertise but to amplify it, creating a powerful symbiosis between human and machine for superior decision-making and strategic planning within enterprises. I think of it as the enterprise's version of augmented reality as applied to people.

augmented reality (AR)—A technology that overlays digital information—such as images, videos, 3D models, or data—onto the real world. This enhancement can be experienced through devices, such as smartphones, tablets, AR glasses, and head-mounted displays. AR enriches the user's perception of the real world by adding digital elements in real-time, making it interactive and manipulable.

Azure—Microsoft's cloud computing platform. It offers a suite of cloud services, including computing, storage, and networking capabilities. Azure provides solutions for Infrastructure as a Service (IaaS), Platform as a Service (PaaS), and Software as a Service (SaaS), allowing users to build, deploy, and manage applications in Microsoft's global data centers. The platform supports various programming languages, frameworks, and tools, catering to diverse business and technical needs.

bounded context - In data systems and software design, a bounded context is a set of boundaries within which a particular set of data or functionalities is consistent and meaningful. It defines the limits of applicability for certain data models, ensuring that within these borders, all terms and interactions are uniquely understood and applied. This concept is crucial for managing complexity and ensuring clarity when different parts of a system interact with each other.

business intelligence (BI)—Processes and tools to analyze business data for decision-making.

business performance management (BPfM)—A process that involves the use of various methods and tools to analyze, monitor, and manage the performance of a business. It focuses on setting goals, measuring progress, and implementing strategies to improve efficiency and achieve organizational objectives.

business process management (BPrM)—An organizational approach that aims to improve the efficiency and effectiveness of business processes. It involves identifying, analyzing, and optimizing various business processes to enhance overall performance and meet business goals.

ChatGPT—A variant of the OpenAI GPT model optimized for conversational AI. See GPT.

conditional probability table (CPT)—A table used in probability theory and statistics to illustrate the conditional probabilities of a variable given the values of other variables. CPTs are essential in conditional probability networks and decision-making models, where they help quantify the relationship between a dependent variable and one or more independent variables. They are key in scenarios where the probability of an event or outcome is influenced by other preceding events or states.

core domain (Domain-Driven Design–DDD)—In DDD, the core domain is the central part of a system's domain model, representing the primary area of business expertise and focus. It encapsulates the most fundamental business rules and logic, differentiating the business in its market. The core domain is critical for the business's success and typically receives the majority of development effort and investment, as it provides the most strategic value and competitive advantage.

Cypher—A declarative graph query language used for efficiently querying and manipulating data in graph databases, particularly Neo4j.

data fabric—An integrated set of data services and connectors that provide consistent capabilities across various data assets, locations, and platforms. Data Fabric offers seamless data access, discovery, and governance, enabling a unified and resilient architecture for data management and integration.

dataframe—Term I settled on for a row/column data structure. For example, table (relational database), data set (Spark), dataframe (Python pandas, R).

data lake—A centralized repository designed to store, process, and secure large amounts of structured, semi-structured, and unstructured data. Unlike traditional data sources, such as data warehouses that store data in a structured and processed form, a data lake retains data in its raw format. This approach offers high flexibility and scalability, enabling businesses to easily capture and analyze diverse data types for comprehensive insights.

data mart—A focused subset of a data warehouse designed to provide specific business units or departments with access to relevant data. Data marts contain a segment of the organization's data, often tailored to a specific function or need, such as sales, marketing, or finance. They enable users to perform specialized analysis and reporting, offering a more streamlined and efficient way to access and manipulate data relevant to their specific domain. See Data Warehouse.

data mesh—A decentralized approach to data architecture and organizational structure. Data mesh promotes domain-oriented ownership, self-serve data infrastructure, and product thinking for data. It aims to address the challenges of scaling and integration in monolithic and centralized data platforms.

data product—In the context of a data mesh is a self-contained, domain-specific dataset that is treated as a product. It is owned, managed, and served by a cross-functional team with the goal of providing meaningful and actionable insights to its consumers. Data products are designed to be discoverable, understandable, and trustworthy, with a clear definition, ownership, and accountability for their quality and governance.

data product owner (DPO)—In a data mesh architecture, the data product owner is responsible for managing a domain-oriented data product. They oversee the lifecycle of the data product, ensuring that it is discoverable, trustworthy, self-serve, and effectively meets the needs of consumers within the organization. This role combines aspects of data governance, quality, and analytics to maintain the value and usability of the data product.

data set—A set of related tabular structures (what I refer to as a dataframe in this book). See Dataframe.

data virtualization - A technology approach that allows applications to retrieve and manipulate data without requiring technical details about the data, such as how it's formatted or where it's physically located. This method enables the integration of data from various sources, including databases, big data programs, and cloud services, into a single, unified interface. Through data virtualization, businesses can enhance their agility and decision-making processes by accessing and analyzing data in real-time, without the need for duplicating or moving it, thereby reducing storage costs and data redundancy.

data warehouse—A central repository designed for storing, managing, and analyzing large volumes of structured and processed data from various sources. Data warehouses support business intelligence activities by providing a unified platform for data consolidation, query processing, and reporting. They are optimized for read access, enabling efficient retrieval of historical data for analytical purposes.

dimension—A structure that categorizes data in order to enable users to answer business questions. Commonly used dimensions are time, geography, and product.

domain—A structure within an organization specializing in a particular function or process. It's mostly sufficient to think of them as departments within a business.

drill through (OLAP)—Refers to the ability to navigate from summary-level data to the detailed data underlying it. This feature allows users to click on an aggregated data point within a report or dashboard and access the detailed transactional data that composes that summary, enabling deeper analysis and insights.

enterprise knowledge graph (EKG)—An enhanced Knowledge Graph (KG) customized for enterprise-specific data integration and management. The EKG expands upon the traditional KG, which typically comprises domain-level taxonomies and ontologies curated by data product teams. It includes these elements but also incorporates additional components, such as the enterprise-wide data catalog, Insight Space Graph, and Tuple Correlation Web. It's crucial to differentiate AEI as an overarching concept, of which the EKG is a critical component. The EKG serves as a foundational element within AEI, facilitating the synergy of human expertise and AI capabilities in a corporate setting.

ELT (extract, load, transform)—A data processing technique similar to ETL but with a key difference in the order of operations. Data is first extracted from the original sources and then loaded directly into the target data storage system, which is usually a modern data warehouse capable of handling large-scale transformations. Only after loading is the data transformed as needed for specific analytical tasks. This approach takes advantage of the powerful computational resources of contemporary data warehouses to optimize the transformation process.

ETL (extract, transform, load)–A data integration process that involves extracting data from various sources, transforming the data into a format suitable for analysis, and loading it into a destination system like a data warehouse. The transformation process typically includes cleansing, aggregating, and organizing the data. ETL is used to consolidate disparate data into a cohesive dataset for business intelligence and analytics purposes. Precedes ELT, but is not displaced by it.

fact table–A central table in a star schema of a data warehouse that stores quantitative information for analysis and is surrounded by dimension tables.

facts–Quantifiable data points that can be analyzed and measured, often represented by numerical values, such as sales amount or quantity sold.

fine-tuning–A process of adjusting a pre-trained language model on a specific dataset to enhance its performance or adapt it for a particular task or domain. Fine-tuning tailors the model's knowledge and capabilities to align more closely with the nuances and requirements of the targeted application.

foundation LLM - A base AI model trained on extensive data to mimic human language and reasoning. Despite not always being up-to-date, it encapsulates broad expertise, enabling diverse applications in language processing and decision-making.

generative AI–A category of artificial intelligence that focuses on creating new data samples resembling input data. Techniques include Generative Adversarial Networks (GANs), Variational Autoencoders (VAEs), and certain language models. Used in applications like image synthesis, text generation, and music composition.

GPT–An artificial intelligence language model developed by OpenAI, known for its ability to generate human-like text. It uses deep learning techniques to understand and generate language based on the input it receives. Unlike ChatGPT, GPT is not specifically tuned for conversational contexts and is used in a wider range of applications, including content creation, language translation, and more sophisticated tasks requiring language understanding.

greenfield project-A project that is built from scratch without the need to consider any prior work. It often refers to software development or construction projects where there are no existing constraints or limitations.

HOLAP–A hybrid approach that combines the best features of MOLAP and ROLAP. HOLAP tools can use cube data for summary information and relational databases for detailed data, ensuring high performance of the cube and detailed drill-through capabilities.

IRI (internationalized resource identifier): IRIs extend URIs by allowing a wider range of characters, including those from virtually all languages and scripts around the world. This makes

IRIs more globally accessible and usable, as they can include characters beyond the limited ASCII set, as it is for URIs. IRIs are a critical part of making the web more international and inclusive, as they can represent names and terms in native character sets.

IT (information technology)—A business division focused on the governance and utilization of information and computing resources. It manages hardware, software, networking, and data infrastructure to support organizational operations.

knowledge graph (KG)—A structured graphical representation of knowledge with entities and their relationships.

knowledge worker—Any worker who accesses an enterprise data source in order to help make decisions during their daily activities. With the advent of mobile applications, the number of such workers is much more inclusive. So, in the context of this book, I include not just analysts and managers, but anyone who can carry around some sort of mobile device where data is referenced to help make better decisions. See Non-Analyst Knowledge Worker.

KPI (key performance indicator)—A quantifiable measure used to evaluate the success of an organization, employee, or other entity in achieving key objectives. KPIs are used to gauge performance in terms of meeting strategic and operational goals.

Kyvos Insights—A cloud-based BI platform offering highly scalable OLAP solutions on big data.

lakehouse—A data management architecture that combines the features of data lakes and data warehouses. It provides the expansive storage and big data capabilities of a data lake with the data management and structured query features of a traditional data warehouse. For this book, when referencing "data warehouse," lakehouse is generally interchangeable.

Langchain—A framework that leverages language models to create and orchestrate applications, enabling the integration of language AI capabilities into various software solutions.

large language model (LLM)—A machine learning model trained on vast text data to understand and generate language. ChatGPT, BERT, and Llama are examples of LLMs. See NLP.

loosely-coupled-A term used to describe components of a system that interact with each other, but maintain a high level of independence. This design allows for easier maintenance and scalability because changes to one component generally do not affect others.

machine learning (ML)—A branch of AI that involves the development of algorithms and statistical models enabling computers to perform tasks without explicit instructions, by learning patterns and making inferences from data. Machine learning applications range from simple tasks like email filtering to complex processes, such as image recognition, natural language processing, and predictive analytics. It relies on large datasets to train models which can then make predictions or decisions based on new, unseen data.

master data management (MDM) - A methodical approach that defines and manages an organization's critical data to provide, with data integration, a single point of reference. The goal of MDM is to provide processes for collecting, aggregating, matching, consolidating, quality-assuring, and distributing such data throughout an organization to ensure consistency and control in the ongoing maintenance and usage. Not to be confused with another MDM–Metadata Management.

measure–A specific numeric value of a fact that is stored in the fact table and is used in calculations or aggregations for data analysis, such as sum, average, or total sales.

Mixture of Experts (MoE)—In the context of Agentic AI, refers to a technique that combines multiple specialized models called experts to solve a complex problem. Each expert focuses on different aspects or subsets of the input data.

MOLAP–A data processing method that employs multidimensional cube structures to store data and support the fast retrieval of pre-aggregated, summarized data. MOLAP tools often use proprietary storage, and data is loaded from relational databases into the MOLAP system. See SSAS and Kyvos Insights.

natural language processing (NLP)–NLP is a field of artificial intelligence that focuses on enabling machines to understand, interpret, and respond to human language in a valuable way. In the context of Large Language Models (LLMs) like GPT, NLP involves the analysis and synthesis of language to generate coherent, context-aware responses. It encompasses a range of techniques and algorithms that allow machines to process, analyze, and generate human language in both written and spoken forms.

Neo4j—A popular and highly scalable graph database platform.

non-analyst knowledge worker—Consumers of BI data without "analyst" or "manager" in their titles. This includes what could be many times more users who consume very simple BI data during the course of the day, but are not analysts—for example, lacking deep skill with sophisticated BI visualization tools, the intricacies of OLAP, or even knowledge of SQL.

OLAP (Online Analytical Processing)–Tools and processes for multi-dimensional data analysis.

OLTP (Online Transaction Processing)–Systems focused on managing transaction-based applications.

ontology—A structured framework for representing knowledge, which encompasses a set of concepts, categories, and relationships within a particular domain. Ontologies define the entities within a domain and the ways in which they can relate to one another, enabling a shared understanding and interoperability among diverse systems. They are extensively used in fields, such as artificial intelligence, semantic web, and information science for complex data organization, analysis, and inference.

OpenAI–OpenAI is a research organization committed to ensuring that artificial general intelligence (AGI) benefits all of humanity. Founded in December 2015, OpenAI focuses on conducting cutting-edge AI research and developing technologies that align with its mission of promoting safe and beneficial AI. Known for its contributions to machine learning, natural language processing, and AI ethics, OpenAI has released various influential models and tools, including the GPT (Generative Pre-trained Transformer) series.

optimized cubes/OLAP—What I would normally call Pre-Aggregated OLAP Cubes. These are MOLAP cubes popularized by SQL Server Analysis Services. see MOLAP.

optimized semantic layer–A layer presenting the qualities of BI at its best. As opposed to just a semantic layer, which is at its core a linked schema of analytics data, the optimized semantic layer is highly-performant, highly curated, and user-friendly.

OWL (Web Ontology Language)—A language for defining and instantiating web ontologies.

Pre-Aggregated OLAP cubes—See Optimized Cubes or MOLAP.

prompt (in the context of language models)–A prompt is an input given to a language model like GPT (Generative Pre-trained Transformer) that initiates or guides the model's response. It can be a question, statement, or even a fragment of text, which the model uses as a basis to generate relevant and coherent output. Prompts are crucial in shaping the direction and context of the model's responses.

property graph database–A type of graph database that uses the property graph model, where nodes and relationships are enhanced with properties (key-value pairs), enabling the representation of complex networks and relationships between data points, with Neo4j being a prominent example.

Python—A high-level, general-purpose programming language employed in a wide range of applications.

QueryDef–A node class within the ISG that symbolizes a BI query—generally of the SQL GROUP BY pattern. It acts as a template outlining the structure and elements of a query without holding the resultant data itself.

RDBMS (relational database management system)–A type of database management system that stores data in a structured format, using rows and columns in tables. The relationship between these tables is defined by the data, and the format allows for the efficient retrieval, insertion, updating, and management of data. Has been the dominant database type in enterprises for decades.

reactive AI machines–aka reactive AI systems or reactive machines, are a type of artificial intelligence that relies on predefined rules and programmed algorithms to perform specific tasks. These AI systems do not possess the ability to learn from data or adapt to new situations on their own. Instead, they follow a fixed set of instructions to make decisions and respond to inputs. Until ChatGPT, these models (mostly DS/ML) were what was referred to as AI.

reinforcement learning (RL)–A type of machine learning where an agent learns to make decisions by performing actions in an environment to achieve maximum cumulative reward. This learning process is driven by the feedback the agent receives from its actions in the form of rewards or penalties, which it uses to formulate a strategy or policy that optimizes its long-term objectives.

resource description framework (RDF)—A standard for describing resources on the web.

retrieval augmented generation (RAG)—A technique in natural language processing that enhances the output of generative AI models by incorporating external information retrieved in real time. It combines the strengths of generative models, capable of producing human-like text, with a retrieval system that fetches relevant documents or data snippets to inform and improve the generation process. This approach allows for more accurate, contextually rich, and informed content generation, applicable in tasks, such as question answering, content creation, and conversational AI. RAG bridges the gap between pure generation and information retrieval, leveraging the vast amounts of data available in databases or the internet to produce more nuanced and knowledgeable responses.

ROLAP–A form of online analytical processing (OLAP) that performs dynamic multidimensional analysis of data stored in a relational database. Instead of using a pre-calculated data cube, ROLAP tools create multidimensional views directly from database tables upon user queries.

semantic graph database–A type of database that stores and manages data based on the principles of semantic technology, using standards like RDF (Resource Description Framework), SPARQL (SPARQL Protocol and RDF Query Language), and OWL (Web Ontology Language). It excels at representing complex networks of relationships and supports inferencing, allowing for the discovery of new relationships based on the data's inherent semantics. This database is particularly adept at handling interconnected, context-rich information, making it valuable for applications in knowledge management, data integration, and complex queries that benefit from understanding the meaning of data. Stardog and GraphDB are examples.

semantic web—An extension of the World Wide Web to facilitate machine-readable data and semantics. See W3C.

slice and dice–A term used in BI to describe the process of segmenting and examining data from different viewpoints to uncover patterns and insights. Enables users to "slice" data by isolating specific subsets based on criteria, and "dice" by analyzing these subsets across various dimensions from a data cube structure. Often utilized in BI tools for in-depth analysis, allowing decision makers to drill down into granular data details and perform complex queries.

SME (subject matter expert)—An individual with extensive knowledge and expertise in a specific domain. SMEs provide valuable insights, guidance, and clarity on specialized topics, often aiding in decision-making, training, and problem-solving within their area of proficiency.

snowflake schema—An extension of the star schema where dimension tables are normalized, breaking down into additional tables. This schema resembles a snowflake's structure, with more complex relationships and additional layers of dimension tables, leading to reduced data redundancy but potentially more complex queries. See Star Schema.

SQL (Structured Query Language)—A standardized programming language specifically designed for managing and manipulating relational databases. SQL enables users to perform a wide range of operations, such as querying data, updating records, and managing database structures. It is known for its readability and simplicity, allowing users to write queries that resemble natural language, making it accessible even for those not deeply familiar with programming. SQL is used in various database systems like MySQL, PostgreSQL, and Microsoft SQL Server, and is essential for tasks ranging from simple data retrieval to complex analytical queries and database schema creation.

SPARQL (SPARQL Protocol and RDF Query Language)—A specialized query language used for retrieving and manipulating data stored in RDF (Resource Description Framework) format, which is a standard model for data interchange on the Web. SPARQL enables users to query diverse data sources and extract information in a flexible and efficient manner, making it particularly suited for querying complex datasets with interlinked relationships, such as those found in semantic web applications. It allows for querying not just specific data patterns but also exploring data relationships, aggregating data, and even incorporating logical inferences, making it a powerful tool for working with linked data and knowledge graphs.

SSAS (SQL Server Analysis Services)—A component of Microsoft SQL Server used to create Online Analytical Processing (OLAP) and data mining solutions. SSAS allows for the construction of data cubes, which organize and summarize large volumes of data for fast, efficient analysis. It supports MDX (Multidimensional Expressions) for querying cube data, as well as data mining capabilities through DMX (data mining extensions). In the context of this book, I'm generally referring to the edition known as "Multi-Dimensional." This is the original SSAS creating MOLAP data structures.

star schema—A database schema design that optimizes querying large datasets. It features a central fact table linked to dimension tables, which are directly connected to the fact table and resemble a star's shape. This model facilitates efficient data retrieval by minimizing the number of joins. See Snowflake Schema.

Stardog—An enterprise knowledge graph platform. Stardog differs from Neo4j by focusing more on semantic data models (using RDF, SPARQL), which are well-suited for integrating diverse data sources and ontologies, whereas Neo4j primarily uses a property graph model and Cypher query language, ideal for detailed relationship-driven data analysis.

taxonomy—A systematic arrangement of entities or concepts into a hierarchical structure, where each level represents a category or group based on shared characteristics or attributes. Taxonomies are used to classify and organize complex sets of information into more manageable and understandable formats, often used in various fields, such as biology, information science, and knowledge management.

Theory of Constraints (TOC) -A management paradigm that focuses on identifying and systematically improving the most significant limiting factor (constraint) in achieving a goal. TOC posits that every system has at least one constraint limiting its performance, and improvement efforts should be targeted primarily at this constraint. It is commonly applied in operations, manufacturing, and project management to optimize processes and increase throughput.

tree of thought—A computational approach that models the hierarchical and recursive nature of human thinking, enabling AI to structure and process information in branching sequences akin to decision trees.

triple–The "atom" of the semantic web. It is a subject-verb-object (SVO) term. For example, trout (subject) eat (verb) bugs (object). The verb is sometimes called a predicate.

triple store database–A type of database designed specifically for storing and retrieving triples, a data format used in semantic web technologies. Each triple consists of a subject, predicate, and object, representing a statement about a resource in the form of "subject-predicate-object" (e.g., "Paris - *capital of* - France"). Triple stores facilitate the storage, retrieval, and management of data encoded in Resource Description Framework (RDF) format, and are optimized for querying complex relationships within the data, often using SPARQL, a specialized query language for RDF. See Stardog.

Turtle (ttl)–A syntax for expressing data in the Resource Description Framework (RDF), used in semantic web and linked data applications, known for its compact and readable format for representing relationships among resources. Note that this is different from "Time To Live"–upper-case TTL.

URI (uniform resource identifier): A URI is a string of characters used to identify a resource on the Internet. URIs can be either URLs (Uniform Resource Locators), which provide a means of locating a resource (like a web page address), or URNs (Uniform Resource Names), which name a resource but do not specify how to locate it. URIs are limited to a subset of the ASCII character set and do not support characters from other languages or scripts. See IRI.

vector database—A database designed to store, index, and manage vector embeddings, which are high-dimensional representations of data items, typically derived from complex data types like images, videos, text, and audio through machine learning models. These embeddings capture the semantic similarities between data items, enabling efficient similarity search and retrieval tasks. Vector databases support operations like nearest neighbor search, allowing for applications in recommendation systems, image and voice recognition, and natural language processing. By efficiently handling the complexities of high-dimensional space, vector databases facilitate the rapid querying and analysis of large datasets based on the content's semantic similarity rather than traditional text-based indexing.

virtual graphs–A feature in some semantic graph databases, including Stardog, that enables the integration of external data sources without physically importing data into the database. By defining mappings between the source data schema and the semantic model, virtual graphs allow users to query and federate data across disparate sources as if all data were stored within a single, unified semantic graph. This approach facilitates real-time access to diverse data stores, supports data virtualization, and enables more flexible and scalable data integration strategies.

visualization tool–Software that transforms data into visual formats like charts and graphs for easy analysis. Examples include Excel for basic charts, Tableau for interactive visuals, and Power BI for comprehensive analytics. They help interpret complex data to inform business decisions.

W3C (World Wide Web Consortium)–An international community that develops open standards to ensure the long-term growth of the Web. It is particularly renowned for founding the semantic web, a collaborative movement led by the W3C to facilitate the sharing and reuse of data across various applications and enterprises. The semantic web extends the principles of the Web to data and information, creating an environment where data can be connected and leveraged in innovative ways.

Writeback (SSAS)-- Writeback in SQL Server Analysis Services (SSAS) allows users to modify data in an OLAP cube directly. The changes are usually on a temporary basis. This feature enables real-time data input and adjustments, such as budgeting or forecasting, by writing changes back to the data source. Writeback is typically used in scenarios requiring user-driven data updates and interactive data modeling.

References

1. Knowledge Graph BI Component: Insight Space Graph (https://www.kyvosinsights.com/blog/knowledge-graph-bi-component-insight-space-graph/)

2. Embracing Change with a Wide Breadth of Generalized Events (https://www.kyvosinsights.com/blog/embracing-change-with-a-wide-breadth-of-generalized-events/)

3. Preventing Knowledge Bogs: A Loosely-Coupled Approach to Enterprise Knowledge Graphs (https://www.kyvosinsights.com/blog/revisiting-strategy-maps-bridging-graph-technology-machine-learning-and-ai/)

4. The Tuple Correlation Web: Time Series Correlation of a Knowledge Graph

5. Revisiting Strategy Maps: Bridging Graph Technology, Machine Learning, and AI

6. KPI Status Relationship Graph Revisited with LLMs (https://eugeneasahara.com/2023/06/18/kpi-status-relationship-graph-revisited-with-llms/)

7. Map Rock—10th Anniversary and Some Data Mesh Talk (https://eugeneasahara.com/2021/11/20/map-rock-10th-anniversary/)

8. Data Vault Methodology paired with Domain Driven Design (https://eugeneasahara.com/2021/01/02/data-vault-methodology-and-domain-driven-design/)

9. The Effect of Recent AI Developments on BI Data Volume (https://www.kyvosinsights.com/blog/the-effect-of-recent-ai-developments-on-bi-data-volume/)

The following references are coded so I can renumber them when the book is done.

- Jh1–Memory-prediction framework–Wikipedia (https://en.wikipedia.org/wiki/Memory-prediction_framework)

- atal—Attention is All You Need–Vaswani, A., Shazeer, N., Parmar, N., Uszkoreit, J., Jones, L., Gomez, A. N., ... and Polosukhin, I. (2017). Attention Is All You Need. In Advances in Neural Information Processing Systems (pp. 5998-6008).

Index

800-pound gorilla, 25
ACID. See Atomicity, Consistency, Isolation, Durability
AEI. See augmented enterprise intelligence
agent, 85, 158, 178, 483, 491
AGI. See artificial general intelligence
AI. See artificial intelligence
Amazon S3, 129
AOL, 18, 86, 88
applied AI, 5
ArangoDB, 205
artificial general intelligence, 23, 24, 26, 27, 28, 109, 311, 414, 437, 483, 490
artificial intelligence, 1, 5, 6, 8, 9, 11, 13, 15, 17, 18, 19, 21, 22, 23, 24, 25, 26, 27, 32, 33, 36, 38, 39, 43, 44, 45, 46, 47, 48, 49, 50, 59, 63, 79, 80, 84, 85, 86, 87, 88, 89, 96, 100, 103, 105, 106, 107, 108, 109, 117, 118, 125, 127, 138, 149, 152, 154, 155, 157, 158, 159, 172, 173, 176, 178, 191, 197, 198, 204, 210, 217, 221, 255, 261, 262, 279, 283, 284, 300, 301, 306, 309, 318, 332, 339, 360, 361, 363, 412, 414, 416, 417, 418, 424, 428, 429, 433, 437, 438, 449, 460, 463, 467, 468, 483, 484, 486, 487, 488, 489, 490, 491, 493, 495
artificial superintelligence, 483
ASI. See artificial superintelligence
at the time of writing, 6, 24, 38, 45, 50, 63, 99, 155, 158, 207, 220, 262, 284, 343, 345, 362, 416, 427, 437, 483
Atomicity, Consistency, Isolation, Durability, 181, 223
AtScale, 138
ATTOW. See at the time of writing
attribute, 483
augmented enterprise intelligence, 50, 62, 84, 85, 93, 130, 131, 149, 153, 197, 203, 223, 224, 270, 301, 323, 324, 361, 364, 369, 452, 483, 486
augmented reality, 50, 483, 484
AutoML, 42, 86
Azure, 62, 88, 129, 131, 142, 167, 211, 212, 322, 363, 429, 434, 484
bar chart, 15, 29, 256, 272, 274, 275, 285, 286, 372, 373
Bayesian, 35, 36, 224, 251, 289, 290, 293, 294, 295, 298, 336, 337, 338, 400, 405, 406, 407, 410, 451
Bayesian Belief Networks, 36, 336
Berry, Chuck, 89
BI. See business intelligence
BI analyst, 4, 5, 12, 13, 14, 16, 17, 18, 28, 29, 30, 41, 44, 58, 127, 128, 139, 148, 149, 154, 234, 256, 306, 307, 308, 310, 371, 383, 386, 442, 443, 450, 466, 468
BI professional, 4, 176
BI report, 4
Big Brother, 14, 229
big data, 9, 159
blog, 5, 210, 211, 212, 350
Boise, 234, 276, 290, 304, 426, 427, 428, 429
bounded context, 184, 247, 484
BPfM. See business performance management
BPrM. See business process management
Brown, Doc, 27
business intelligence, 3, 4, 5, 6, 7, 8, 9, 12, 13, 14, 16, 18, 22, 24, 28, 29, 30, 31, 32, 33, 34, 35, 36, 37, 38, 39, 40, 41, 42, 43, 44, 45, 50, 51, 58, 61, 62, 63, 67, 68, 69,

497

74, 75, 76, 77, 78, 79, 80, 82, 83, 85, 86, 87, 90, 91, 94, 101, 104, 123, 125, 126, 127, 128, 130, 133, 134, 137, 138, 139, 141, 144, 146, 147, 148, 149, 150, 151, 152, 153, 154, 155, 156, 157, 158, 159, 160, 161, 162, 163, 164, 165, 166, 167, 168, 171, 174, 176, 177, 178, 179, 182, 183, 184, 186, 187, 197, 199, 200, 203, 204, 209, 210, 214, 215, 218, 220, 221, 224, 225, 226, 229, 230, 232, 234, 235, 244, 254, 255, 256, 258, 260, 265, 266, 267, 268, 270, 272, 279, 280, 284, 285, 286, 287, 288, 289, 295, 304, 305, 306, 307, 308, 309, 310, 316, 326, 330, 332, 362, 363, 365, 370, 371, 378, 381, 383, 386, 392, 412, 413, 414, 415, 420, 422, 424, 425, 426, 428, 430, 434, 437, 439, 442, 443, 444, 446, 447, 450, 452, 453, 455, 460, 461, 465, 466, 467, 468, 469, 470, 471, 474, 475, 484, 486, 487, 488, 489, 490, 491, 492, 494, 495

business knowledge, 9, 10, 11, 310

business performance management, 72, 73, 74, 75, 76, 332, 333, 335, 465, 484

business process management, 72, 484

CEO, 7, 11, 12, 212, 347, 366, 368

chain of thought, 37, 103, 437

ChatGPT, 1, 2, 7, 9, 15, 18, 19, 20, 21, 22, 23, 24, 27, 28, 29, 31, 32, 39, 48, 49, 50, 63, 64, 65, 80, 86, 88, 89, 94, 97, 98, 99, 101, 102, 103, 105, 107, 108, 109, 155, 163, 179, 180, 185, 189, 190, 210, 220, 221, 249, 250, 251, 252, 299, 300, 318, 319, 320, 339, 340, 341, 342, 343, 352, 363, 364, 388, 413, 415, 418, 427, 430, 437, 438, 484, 487, 488, 491

Chesapeake Bay, 102

chess, 17, 173

Cognos, 138

Collibra Data Governance, 136

conditional probability table, 451, 484

Congress, 106

Cooper, Sheldon, 27

copper, 84

core domain, 43, 239, 248, 484

corpus of text, 1, 3, 221

CPT. See conditional probability table

CRM. See Customer Relationship Management

curation, 3, 165, 176, 181

Customer Relationship Management, 110, 119, 125, 233, 239, 240, 348, 391

Cypher, 35, 39, 46, 64, 97, 98, 191, 205, 207, 208, 224, 281, 285, 339, 340, 341, 342, 344, 363, 370, 373, 434, 436, 437, 451, 485, 493

data catalog, 28, 29, 30, 33, 91, 93, 124, 129, 130, 131, 133, 134, 135, 136, 137, 138, 140, 142, 143, 146, 173, 174, 176, 198, 200, 255, 281, 283, 307, 308, 365, 370, 384, 468, 486

data engineering, 10, 11, 156, 181

data fabric, 12, 13, 41, 130, 134, 135, 148, 173, 174, 175, 197, 243, 485

data governance, 131, 133, 137, 168, 169, 176, 485

data integrity, 54, 112, 141, 160, 171, 177, 440

data lake, 60, 63, 70, 96, 136, 150, 151, 162, 181, 183, 485, 488

data landscape, 13, 133, 134, 179, 204, 377, 464

data mart, 60, 129, 156, 167, 172, 179, 204, 485

data mesh, 28, 41, 60, 96, 148, 151, 154, 163, 164, 166, 167, 168, 169, 170, 172, 174, 175, 176, 177, 178, 179, 181, 182, 183, 184, 188, 197, 233, 244, 245, 264, 265, 412, 468, 485

data product, 169, 170, 171, 172, 175, 179, 180, 188, 189, 191, 193, 198, 264, 366, 485, 486

data product owner, 193, 485

data science, 6, 10, 11, 35, 41, 43, 58, 76, 77, 150, 151, 234, 235, 332, 423, 468

data scientist, 2, 42, 58, 85, 133, 151, 156, 199, 337, 383, 467, 468, 469
data services, 13, 173, 176, 485
data set, 76, 78, 153, 271, 485, 486
data source, 3, 4, 41, 90, 140, 142, 147, 160, 174, 188, 228, 265, 295, 414, 429, 430, 433, 444, 467, 488
data storage, 70, 177, 486
data virtualization, 486, 494
data warehouse, 58, 61, 140, 141, 142, 149, 150, 151, 152, 165, 166, 167, 172, 177, 178, 181, 203, 204, 210, 212, 215, 218, 243, 363, 397, 485, 486, 487, 488
database schema, 111, 492
Databricks, 42, 43, 148, 151, 212
dataframe, 485
dataset, 21, 85, 159, 161, 187, 204, 278, 316, 379, 385, 388, 455, 460, 485, 487
DAX, 16, 34, 224, 371
DC. See data catalog
DDD. See Domain-Driven Design
decision makers, 8, 33, 41, 73, 492
digital twin, 38
dimension, 486
dimensional model, 111, 138, 139, 141, 142, 143, 214, 215, 219, 266, 323
domain, 486
domain expert, 10, 11, 246
domain knowledge, 10
Domain-Driven Design, 96, 181, 183, 243, 244, 484
doomsdayer prepper, 26
DPO. See data product owner
DW. See data warehouse
Einstein, 7, 89
EKG. See enterprise knowledge graph
emails, 2, 31, 130, 173
enterprise knowledge, 12, 28, 460, 493
enterprise knowledge graph, 28, 29, 30, 31, 32, 36, 37, 38, 45, 46, 48, 50, 62, 65, 66, 68, 69, 78, 91, 92, 93, 94, 95, 123, 124, 125, 130, 133, 137, 149, 150, 158, 175, 176, 179, 180, 191, 193, 197, 198, 199, 200, 223, 224, 226, 244, 249, 250, 251, 253, 254, 255, 258, 274, 276, 283, 284, 285, 287, 288, 291, 292, 307, 311, 312, 314, 318, 322, 323, 324, 325, 326, 327, 329, 334, 337, 360, 362, 364, 365, 368, 370, 372, 373, 374, 375, 391, 392, 393, 394, 400, 401, 402, 406, 412, 414, 415, 423, 424, 425, 428, 429, 430, 434, 437, 438, 439, 440, 442, 443, 444, 445, 449, 450, 451, 452, 454, 455, 456, 457, 460, 461, 467, 468, 471, 486, 493
enterprise-wide knowledge graph, 146
Essbase, 138
ETL. See extract, transform, load
Excel, 34, 36, 41, 61, 82, 128, 129, 146, 151, 156, 161, 167, 232, 466, 494
expert systems, 19, 46, 48, 463
extract, transform, load, 90, 149, 150, 151, 164, 165, 166, 167, 176, 179, 239, 244, 254, 262, 373, 486, 487
fact table, 231, 234, 237, 238, 240, 242, 243, 323, 324, 487, 489, 492
facts, 487
fine-tuning, 9, 21, 487
foreign key, 111, 140, 191
foundation LLM, 487
framework, 63, 117, 126, 130, 133, 134, 151, 163, 164, 169, 172, 180, 186, 187, 194, 230, 255, 289, 290, 291, 307, 326, 414, 416, 418, 426, 462, 469, 475, 488, 489, 495
French, 18
Friston, Karl, 101
fuzzy, 6
Gemini, 65, 108, 364
generative AI, 487
geographic maps, 161
Geppetto, 7, 8
GitHub, 34, 39, 63, 193, 197, 200, 201, 202, 203, 209, 224, 270, 284, 287, 361, 362, 364, 369, 371, 373, 383, 405, 407, 410, 425, 437
glossary, 31, 39

Google, 18, 52, 80, 81, 88, 108, 214, 284, 290, 311, 363, 364
Google Cloud Storage, 129
GPT, 31, 103, 107, 108, 109, 172, 221, 363, 364, 415, 418, 419, 420, 422, 423, 429, 460, 484, 487, 489, 490
graph database, 46, 57, 59, 63, 127, 128, 137, 205, 206, 207, 208, 219, 223, 322, 451, 485, 494
greenfield project, 244, 245, 487
Grok, 107, 108
hallucinating, 89, 341, 413
Hawaii, 27, 80, 100, 377, 389
Hawkins, Jeff, 2
highly-curated data, 96, 144, 146, 254, 316, 413, 467
histograms, 161
hockey stick curve, 25, 80
HuggingFace, 103
human analysts, 32, 41, 45, 50, 262, 267, 371, 426
human intelligence, 9, 16, 33, 51, 96, 119, 191, 267, 337, 431, 438, 483
human-in-the-loop, 3
humanity, 1, 3
IBM Watson Knowledge Catalog, 136
iCloud, 84
information technology, 488
Inmon, Bill, 172
Insight Space Graph, 28, 29, 33, 79, 91, 104, 105, 123, 124, 130, 131, 147, 149, 155, 161, 199, 200, 215, 223, 224, 226, 227, 228, 229, 230, 234, 254, 255, 256, 259, 260, 263, 265, 266, 267, 268, 274, 284, 285, 286, 307, 311, 312, 314, 315, 323, 325, 329, 332, 349, 351, 352, 353, 356, 371, 373, 374, 375, 379, 380, 381, 382, 383, 385, 390, 414, 415, 421, 424, 425, 426, 430, 432, 433, 434, 438, 439, 440, 443, 444, 445, 451, 452, 454, 455, 456, 460, 467, 469, 470, 479, 486, 490, 495
intelligence gap, 7, 17, 42, 43
internationalized resource identifier, 487

Internet of Things, 85, 154, 177, 178, 210, 218, 231, 232, 233, 234, 235, 243, 261
interpreter, 18, 59, 414
IoT. See Internet of Things
IRI. See internationalized resource identifier
ISG. See Insight Space Graph
IT. See information technology
Japanese, 18
Java, 36, 462
JSON, 87, 129, 136, 171, 189, 224, 374, 437, 443
Kahneman, Daniel, 103
key performance indicator, 488
KG. See knowledge graph
knowledge base, 22, 85, 100, 104, 120, 198, 222, 230, 287, 311, 427
knowledge graph, 7, 9, 19, 28, 29, 30, 31, 33, 38, 44, 46, 47, 48, 49, 51, 56, 62, 63, 67, 69, 82, 91, 92, 93, 94, 95, 96, 97, 98, 99, 100, 101, 102, 103, 104, 105, 106, 107, 108, 112, 116, 118, 119, 120, 121, 123, 124, 125, 126, 130, 131, 132, 133, 135, 137, 158, 164, 170, 171, 179, 180, 181, 182, 183, 184, 185, 186, 187, 188, 189, 191, 193, 194, 195, 196, 197, 204, 205, 207, 220, 224, 225, 244, 253, 257, 281, 282, 283, 284, 285, 291, 318, 332, 337, 339, 340, 341, 342, 343, 344, 349, 352, 363, 368, 370, 383, 384, 400, 412, 414, 421, 427, 429, 430, 438, 439, 440, 441, 442, 450, 455, 479, 486, 488, 492
knowledge space, 83
knowledge worker, 157, 197, 246, 447, 488
KPI. See key performance indicator
Kyvos, 40, 63, 77, 138, 139, 140, 155, 156, 167, 179, 199, 212, 214, 231, 362, 363, 425, 488, 489
lakehouse, 488
Lamborghini, 17
Langchain, 488
LangChain, 103, 363, 437

large language model, 1, 2, 4, 18, 21, 28, 31, 32, 33, 37, 38, 46, 51, 59, 63, 65, 67, 81, 87, 94, 96, 97, 99, 102, 103, 104, 105, 107, 108, 119, 172, 173, 177, 181, 185, 188, 189, 190, 191, 193, 197, 220, 221, 222, 249, 265, 285, 311, 318, 342, 363, 412, 413, 414, 415, 417, 418, 423, 426, 427, 428, 429, 430, 435, 436, 437, 450, 452, 460, 461, 487, 488
Liang, Percy, 172
line graph, 15, 29, 254, 256, 270, 371, 372, 395
LLama, 9
LLM. See large language model
loosely-coupled, 60, 91, 154, 164, 167, 172, 181, 183, 243, 244, 247, 460, 461, 488
machine learning, 2, 6, 37, 41, 63, 167, 176, 199, 204, 232, 257, 279, 300, 332, 488, 490, 491, 494
malachite, 84
Map Rock, 60, 61, 62, 155, 301, 306, 495
master data management, 186, 489
MDM. See master data management
measure, 37, 90, 223, 252, 262, 269, 271, 296, 321, 322, 329, 332, 349, 356, 374, 379, 380, 382, 384, 386, 391, 396, 404, 423, 465, 466, 469, 488, 489
Microsoft, 14, 30, 40, 44, 52, 53, 58, 79, 93, 122, 131, 132, 202, 212, 275, 299, 300, 301, 302, 303, 304, 311, 320, 321, 322, 350, 351, 352, 357, 360, 363, 368, 369, 397, 398, 399, 484, 492
ML. See machine learning
MOLAP, 138, 179, 487, 489, 490, 492
MSFT. See Microsoft
Musk, Elon, 89, 107
natural language processing, 18, 191, 488, 489, 490, 491, 494
Neo4j, 21, 35, 46, 62, 63, 64, 65, 97, 98, 137, 183, 205, 206, 207, 208, 209, 249, 285, 322, 339, 340, 342, 344, 345, 362, 363, 364, 365, 368, 370, 402, 423, 424, 425, 439, 440, 441, 442, 443, 453, 454, 455, 485, 489, 490, 493
Neptune, 206, 363
Netscape, 18, 88
Newton, 7, 89
non-analyst knowledge worker, 489
normalization, 141
NoSQL, 136, 151
OLAP, 6, 34, 44, 76, 78, 90, 128, 129, 136, 138, 139, 140, 141, 142, 143, 146, 147, 149, 150, 151, 152, 155, 156, 157, 167, 171, 174, 175, 176, 178, 179, 183, 184, 199, 200, 204, 209, 210, 211, 212, 213, 214, 215, 216, 217, 218, 219, 220, 231, 232, 258, 262, 263, 264, 266, 269, 279, 284, 285, 288, 295, 325, 363, 369, 375, 377, 378, 380, 381, 397, 425, 430, 438, 439, 444, 448, 474, 488, 489, 490, 491, 492
ontology, 28, 30, 47, 54, 56, 63, 65, 95, 97, 98, 99, 101, 102, 109, 110, 111, 112, 113, 114, 115, 116, 117, 121, 123, 124, 125, 126, 131, 132, 133, 135, 138, 161, 164, 171, 180, 185, 186, 188, 189, 191, 192, 193, 194, 195, 196, 197, 198, 199, 200, 201, 203, 209, 244, 249, 251, 284, 290, 337, 344, 362, 364, 365, 366, 367, 368, 432, 440, 462, 463, 481, 486, 489, 490, 493
Ontotext, 206
OpenAI, 18, 31, 63, 103, 107, 198, 220, 299, 363, 364, 415, 422, 437, 484, 487, 490
optimized cubes, 120, 152, 153, 159, 168, 177, 219, 470, 490
optimized semantic layer, 168, 490
Oracle, 129, 136, 205, 223, 322, 364
organism, 67, 68, 69, 70, 71, 72, 73, 96, 292, 333
OrientDB, 206
OWL, 35, 39, 46, 49, 59, 65, 101, 121, 123, 137, 138, 180, 197, 198, 202, 209, 320, 342, 462, 463, 490, 491
paramecium, 67

Pearson, 29, 35, 37, 60, 90, 251, 291, 296, 297, 298, 300, 301, 302, 303, 305, 306, 307, 316, 318, 321, 322, 334, 394, 397, 398, 400, 401, 402, 403, 404, 407, 409, 431, 443
Pearson Correlation Coefficient, 61
performance management, 8, 13, 332, 336, 466
performance tuning, 52, 53, 55, 56, 59, 64
pidgin, 100
Pinocchio, 7, 8, 459
PowerBI, 29, 81, 82, 151, 154, 157, 161, 167, 199, 200, 215, 306, 307, 362, 383, 466
primary key, 111, 192
Principal Solutions Architect, 155
probabilistic, 46, 81, 90, 99, 100, 101, 104, 199, 237, 254, 290, 309, 337, 338, 353, 401
Prolog, 46, 48, 59, 463
prompt, 19, 21, 28, 29, 31, 64, 65, 75, 97, 217, 249, 251, 318, 339, 340, 342, 343, 415, 417, 427, 430, 456, 490
prompt engineering, 21
property graph database, 490
Protégé, 59, 63, 65, 101, 185, 198, 203, 209, 250, 342, 343, 362, 364, 365
puppet master, 7
putting the 'I' back into BI, 5
Python, 16, 36, 39, 48, 63, 76, 77, 109, 202, 208, 224, 257, 263, 270, 281, 284, 349, 363, 377, 485, 490
QueryDef, 223, 224, 255, 256, 257, 258, 263, 264, 274, 324, 325, 352, 355, 356, 371, 373, 374, 377, 378, 379, 380, 381, 383, 384, 385, 386, 387, 389, 390, 408, 421, 422, 445, 447, 448, 449, 451, 490
RAG. See retrieval augmented generation
RDBMS. See relational database management system
RDF, 35, 39, 46, 49, 65, 101, 121, 122, 123, 135, 137, 138, 179, 180, 186, 188, 189, 198, 202, 206, 209, 282, 319, 320, 363, 366, 462, 491, 492, 493
reactive AI, 491
recommendation engines, 17
Reddit, 18
Reece's Peanut Butter Cups, 4
reinforcement learning, 2, 491
relational database, 57, 87, 96, 97, 111, 127, 132, 136, 142, 151, 191, 205, 207, 219, 223, 462, 487, 489, 492
relational database management system, 363, 490
relational database modeling, 111
retrieval augmented generation, 28, 37, 222, 223, 284, 363, 412, 413, 414, 415, 416, 417, 418, 419, 426, 427, 428, 437, 438, 439, 449, 451, 456, 457, 460, 491
RL. See reinforcement learning, See reinforcement learning
sapient beings, 3
self-driving cars, 17
semantic graph database, 206, 491
semantic layer, 123, 133, 134, 135, 143, 167, 168, 174, 176, 177, 262, 378
semantic web, 9, 63, 121, 180, 206, 490, 491, 492, 493
slice and dice, 148, 162, 255, 324, 491
slicing and dicing, 161, 279
SME. See subject matter expert, See subject matter expert
snowflake, 138, 140, 161, 162, 214, 231, 323, 324, 492
Snowflake, 61, 63, 142, 151, 178, 199, 203, 210, 212, 362, 363, 492
snowflake schema, 138, 140, 214, 231, 323, 324, 492
software developer, 18
spam, 2, 173
Spark, 42, 43, 61, 76, 148, 151, 155, 209, 485
SPARQL, 35, 39, 49, 101, 121, 123, 287, 462, 491, 492, 493

Spearman, 35, 37, 297, 298, 299, 305, 401, 409
SQL, 7, 11, 34, 35, 36, 39, 51, 52, 53, 54, 55, 56, 57, 58, 59, 64, 65, 87, 109, 119, 123, 129, 131, 136, 137, 140, 142, 151, 155, 161, 162, 191, 202, 205, 207, 208, 209, 211, 212, 215, 219, 223, 224, 234, 255, 256, 257, 258, 263, 274, 283, 288, 322, 351, 352, 361, 362, 363, 364, 369, 370, 371, 372, 373, 374, 375, 377, 378, 379, 381, 382, 383, 384, 385, 389, 391, 392, 393, 394, 396, 421, 422, 435, 436, 462, 463, 489, 490, 492
SQL Server 2000, 58
SQL Server Analysis Services, 40, 44, 61, 128, 138, 139, 141, 143, 151, 155, 156, 167, 168, 179, 209, 211, 212, 262, 279, 311, 470, 489, 490, 492
SQLDiag, 58
SSAS. See SQL Server Analysis Services
StackOverflow, 18
Stanford University, 203
star schema, 78, 140, 487, 492
Stardog, 183, 206, 491, 493, 494
statisticians, 36, 42
strategist, 14
subject matter expert, 3, 4, 14, 28, 30, 65, 91, 99, 101, 105, 126, 143, 164, 171, 318, 326, 414, 430, 492
subject-predicate-object, 97, 122, 493
supercomputer, 17
superpower, 26
Swiss Army Knife, 17
synapse network, 2
System 1, 28, 103, 105, 106
System 2, 29, 103, 105, 106, 108
Tableau, 18, 29, 41, 63, 81, 82, 151, 154, 156, 157, 161, 199, 200, 215, 256, 266, 267, 268, 306, 307, 362, 383, 425, 466, 494
tabular, 77, 127, 128, 129, 181, 257, 263, 486
Talend Data Fabric, 136

taxonomy, 95, 101, 113, 121, 138, 164, 171, 180, 244, 284, 362, 481, 486, 493
TCW. See Tuple Correlation Web
the cloud, 42, 62, 149, 150, 151, 152, 209, 210, 211, 212, 261, 275, 301
theoretical physics, 7
Theory of Constraints, 75, 166, 493
Time to Live, 448, 449, 493
TOSN. See trade-off/semantic network
trade-off/semantic network, 54, 56, 58, 60, 61, 62, 63, 64
transformer architecture, 9, 99
translator, 18
tree of thought, 37, 103, 437, 493
treemaps, 161
triple, 493
triple store database, 493
TTL. See Time to Live
tuple, 29, 76, 77, 213, 229, 237, 263, 264, 266, 267, 284, 291, 324, 334, 335, 349, 354, 375, 377, 378, 379, 380, 381, 387, 390, 391, 393, 394, 396, 401, 402, 407, 408, 421, 432, 442, 445, 466
Tuple Correlation Web, 28, 29, 30, 33, 35, 36, 37, 58, 60, 78, 79, 91, 104, 123, 124, 130, 131, 147, 149, 155, 199, 200, 215, 223, 224, 226, 227, 228, 229, 230, 251, 259, 284, 285, 289, 290, 291, 292, 293, 295, 304, 305, 307, 308, 311, 312, 314, 315, 316, 317, 318, 319, 323, 325, 326, 327, 329, 332, 334, 335, 336, 347, 349, 375, 379, 381, 390, 396, 397, 398, 400, 402, 414, 415, 421, 424, 425, 426, 430, 431, 433, 434, 438, 439, 440, 443, 444, 445, 451, 452, 454, 455, 456, 460, 467, 469, 470, 479, 486, 495
turquoise, 84
Turtle, 46, 202, 250, 342, 368, 448, 493
UDM. See unified data model
unified architecture, 13, 134, 175
unified data model, 177
uniform resource identifier, 49, 123, 124, 138, 185, 425, 487, 488, 493

URI. See uniform resource identifiers
user schema, 126
vector database, 222, 223, 423, 424, 425, 456, 457, 494
virtual graphs, 494
Visual Studio Copilot, 22

visualizations, 5, 14, 17, 29, 41, 50, 63, 124, 149, 161, 162, 165, 199, 254, 265, 268, 269, 270, 272, 279, 280, 307, 371, 372, 374, 426, 430, 443, 446
W3C, 62, 122, 137, 206, 362, 365, 463, 491, 494
Yahoo, 88

www.ingramcontent.com/pod-product-compliance
Lightning Source LLC
LaVergne TN
LVHW081526060526
838200LV00045B/2021